The
Soviet
Multinational
State

Titles in the Series

NEW DIRECTIONS IN SOVIET SOCIAL THOUGHT
An Anthology
Murray Yanowitch, ed.

PERESTROIKA AND THE ECONOMY
New Thinking in Soviet Economics
Anthony Jones and William Moskoff, eds.

PARTY, STATE, AND CITIZEN IN THE SOVIET UNION
A Collection of Documents
Mervyn Matthews, ed.

THE SOVIET MULTINATIONAL STATE
Readings and Documents
Martha B. Olcott, ed.

SOVIET HISTORIANS AND PERESTROIKA
The First Phase
Donald J. Raleigh, ed.

The Soviet Multinational State

Readings and Documents

Edited by

Martha B. Olcott

with Lubomyr Hajda
and Anthony Olcott

M. E. Sharpe, Inc.
ARMONK, NEW YORK
LONDON, ENGLAND

Library of Congress Cataloging-in-Publication Data

The Soviet multinational state / edited by Martha Brill Olcott, with
Lubomyr Hajda and Anthony Olcott.
      p.   cm.
  Bibliography: p.
  ISBN 0-87332-389-0
    1. Nationalism—Soviet Union. 2. Soviet Union—Ethnic
relations. 3. Minorities—Soviet Union. 4. Soviet Union—Politics and
government—1982– . I. Olcott, Martha Brill, 1949– . II. Olcott,
Anthony, 1950– . III. Hajda, Lubomyr.
DK33.S668   1989
947.085′4—dc19   88-36747
                                              CIP

Printed in the United States of America

BB   10 9 8 7 6 5 4 3 2 1

To Alison, Andrew, and Hillary

The Soviet Multinational State

Russians

Ukrainians

Belorussians

Balts, Finno-Karelians,
Moldavians, Caucasian peoples
(including Turkic Azerbaijani)

Turkic peoples

Other or sparsely inhabited

Contents

Preface

The Soviet Union is one of the world's most complex multinational societies, home to well over sixty nationalities and ethnic communities. The leadership of the Communist Party of the Soviet Union has always asserted that the relationship among nationalities in the USSR was a harmonious one, with Russians and non-Russians working together to build an internationalist society based upon Lenin's teachings on the national question. In recent years, however, it has become strikingly apparent that the oft-proclaimed friendship among the peoples of the USSR was more an ideal than a reality.

Mikhail S. Gorbachev's policies of *glasnost'* (openness) and *perestroika* (restructuring of the system) have encouraged the minority nationalities of the USSR to give voice to their grievances. The fissures that this has revealed are deep ones. In 1988 Azerbaidzhanis and Armenians rioted in the midst of a struggle over control of disputed territory, while from the three Baltic republics came calls for virtually complete political and economic autonomy. In 1989 interethnic tensions became even more acute. In April, protests in Georgia's capital city of Tbilisi paralyzed the city, but the imposition of martial law led to twenty deaths and aroused nationwide sympathy for the Georgians. In June there was serious rioting in the Fergana Valley region of Uzbekistan, where thousands of unemployed Uzbek youths began attacking Meskhetian Turks, innocently deported from Georgia in the 1940s and resettled in Uzbekistan. Initial efforts to quell the riots failed as the Uzbeks turned their protest into an anti-regime rampage which left more than a hundred dead and a thousand injured.

Although Moscow has continued to assert its ultimate authority to ensure the preservation of the union and the central line of command, these disputes are by no means resolved. Moreover, their resolution is sure to entail some redefinition of the political relationships that have been in place since Stalin's death. Either a great deal more authority will have to devolve to the periphery, or the center will have to make systematic and regular use of force to put down nationalist-inspired unrest. Neither is an attractive option for Gorbachev, who is trying to deal with these problems in an incremental fashion. But such approaches have not worked in the past and they are unlikely to be very effective today.

This anthology of Soviet materials is designed to introduce the Western student of Soviet society to the complexity of the nationality-related problems in the USSR as they developed throughout the 1980s. The focus of the book is on the fifteen major nationalities of the USSR that enjoy republic status. The collection begins with some official statements of nationality policy. We then look at a number of key problem areas—cadre policy, the economy, culture, religion, language policy, political socialization, and the shifting demographic base of the USSR. The concluding part of the book has sections on current problems in the Baltic region and the dispute between Armenia and Azerbaidzhan over the autonomous oblast of Nagorno Kara-bakh. Each section of the book presents materials from the entire decade of the 1980s, and each includes an introductory essay that highlights both the "blank spots" in the Brezhnev-era discussions and the unresolved tensions behind the current, franker discussions.

* * *

While ultimately the editorial responsibility for the preparation of this volume is solely mine, many people made substantive contributions to an earlier, unpublished version of the book—a version that very quickly became outdated when Gorbachev came to power. Their ideas helped me to refine my own understanding of developments during the Brezhnev period. Thus I would like to acknowledge the assistance of Mark Beissinger on party politics, Nancy Lubin on economics, Rosemary Chrisostomo on language policy, Ronald Wixman on demography, Mark Saroyan on religion, Anthony Olcott on literature, William Fierman on patriotic education, and Rasma Karklins on foreign policy. Translations of pre–Gorbachev-era Russian texts were provided by Michel Vale; the more recent materials were translated by Anthony Olcott. Last but not least, I would like to thank Lubomyr Hajda, my co-editor on the initial version of this volume, who helped to select, edit, and annotate some of the Brezhnev-era materials collected here.

MARTHA B. OLCOTT

The
Soviet
Multinational
State

1. Official Soviet Policy and the "National Problem"

Since the time of the Russian Revolution, Soviet leaders have asserted that the national problem in the USSR has been "solved," because a regime that bases its policies on Lenin's theories of nationality relations treats all nationalities justly. Lenin considered national consciousness a false consciousness that developed under the political conditions of capitalism, and he predicted that under communism distinct nationalities would eventually disappear. During the transition period, the Party would permit "progressive" nationalities—those that accepted the primacy of "proletarian-internationalist values"—to participate fully in Soviet life. However, those conservatives who placed the interests of their own national community above those of the country as a whole were labeled "national communists," "national deviationists," or "national chauvinists" and were barred from public life. The definitions of progressive and conservative have varied over time, as official understanding as to how specifically to devise and apply a "Leninist nationality policy" has been modified.

Lenin understood that the multinational makeup of the Russian empire posed special problems for the revolutionary regime, but he suffered a disabling stroke before he could elaborate how relations among nationalities should be worked out in the new Soviet state. For most of his life Lenin held that a federalist system was a threat to a vanguard party trying to launch revolution from above, but shortly before his death he seems to have become convinced that practical politics demanded that Soviet Russia should be a loose federation of semi-autonomous republics. However, it fell to Stalin to devise the Soviet constitutional structure, and he ignored Lenin's final writings on the subject. The constitution which created the USSR established a state that was federalist in form, but highly centralized in practice. The union republics were vested with little more than symbolic authority, as all-union bureaucracies were charged with the direction of the political, economic, and social life of the country. These relationships were reaffirmed in the 1936 and 1977 constitutions, and were not seriously challenged until 1987.

Under Stalin's rule, the rights guaranteed to national minorities under the Soviet constitution were frequently violated. Party politics in the late 1920s and early 1930s made victims of prominent nationalists—including many who had supported as well as those who had opposed the Bolshevik revolution—and Party purges finished off the few credible nationalist figures that remained. On paper Stalin appeared to be committed to the perpetuation of distinct national cultures, advocating the development of cultures that were "national in form, socialist in content." But in practice, he demanded the creation of a homogeneous and ideologically determined cultural life which allowed virtually no leeway for individual, let alone national, self-expression.

When Khrushchev came to power he called for a reconsideration of nationality relations as part of his effort to revitalize official ideology. He was influenced by the more idealistic aspects of Lenin's writings. Khrushchev tried to motivate people to strive for the attainment of communist ideals and thus he stressed the utopian aspects of nationality policy—in particular, the idea that nations should be encouraged to grow closer together (*sblizhenie*) so that in some distant communist future they could fuse (*sliianie*). But Khrushchev's goals gained little support from the nationalities themselves. Having survived Stalin's harsh cultural and social policies, their foremost goal was to develop more independently, with less direct interference from Moscow, and not be consigned to extinction. In fact, Khrushchev did relatively little to enforce his vision, and the relaxation of control during his rule allowed the nationalities greater autonomy in their cultural, and even to some degree in their political, lives. Thus, Khrushchev's policies served to undermine rather than strengthen his ideological goals, and led to a limited cultural renaissance among the national minorities rather than their increased uniformity.

During the Brezhnev years there was a deemphasis on the utopian goals of nationality policy, and little reference was made to the disappearance of nationalities. The rhetoric of official Soviet nationality policy now stressed that while nations were growing closer together as they acquired shared socialist characteristics, their national cultures were simultaneously "flowering" under the conditions of "developed socialism" and the example of socialist Russian culture. While such formulations displeased many national minorities by implicitly downgrading their cultures and languages in favor of Russian, many in the Party criticized the formulation as encouraging the development of nationalism among the non-Russians. Such critics launched an unsuccessful effort to eliminate the national republics during the process of the drafting of the 1977 Constitution. The relevant sections of the Constitution are reproduced below.

Brezhnev firmly maintained that the process of national consolidation could not be artificially induced either to accelerate or to slow down. Nevertheless, criticism of Brezhnev's nationality policy became more intense as he became frailer. As the sixtieth anniversary of the formation of the USSR approached, several senior Party ideologues publicly demanded that the Party, in keeping with Lenin's teachings, advocate a policy that stressed the ultimate fusion of nationalities, and not their development into distinct and stable ethnic and political entities. Critics of Party policy argued that Brezhnev's pronouncements on nationality policy in general, and the vagueness of his statements about the national problem at the Twenty-sixth Party Congress in March 1981 in particular, had allowed national minority cadres to seize authority and use it to foster nationalist rather than internationalist goals.

It fell to Yuri Andropov to deal with both the nationalist critics of Party policy and their opponents. His December 1982 address to mark the anniversary of the USSR, reproduced below, remains the single most important official statement on nationality relations. The policy line developed by Andropov was designed both to condemn nationalist "excesses" and to silence the anti-national sentiments of certain critics within the Party. In his address Andropov pledged the Party to adhere to Lenin's teachings on the national question, and to reaffirm the belief that national differences would eventually be subsumed by a common internationalist consciousness. But he warned that, as Lenin had written, national distinctions will be present into the distant future, and they cannot be artificially curtailed. The goal of the Party is to facilitate the natural integration of the various national communities through policies designed to encourage them to share class interests, cultural values, and ideological goals. Andropov sought to accomplish this by advocating development of a more fully integrated national economy, an improved system of transportation, an expanded communication network made more effective through nationwide fluency in Russian, and the promotion of cultural values that reinforce indebtedness to Russian culture as well as the spread of internationalist values.

Even in the changing conditions of the late 1980s, the ideas expressed in Andropov's speech still inform official thinking on the national question. They were particularly influential for those drafting the new Party Program adopted at the Twenty-seventh Party Congress in 1987. Andropov's themes are also echoed in Gorbachev's report to the congress.

The Party has continued its commitment to federalism as the basis of organization of the Soviet state. The federalist system again came under attack in 1985–86 during public discussions about the new Party Program. Some critics of Soviet federalism argued for a unitary political system, while others urged that the country be divided into economic rather than national regions. Defenders of the national republics—and these included virtually all prominent non-Russian officials—pointed to their importance in preserving the history and cultures of the non-Russian nationalities.

The statement on nationality relations in the new Party Program not only defended the Soviet federal structure but emphasized the responsibility of each union republic to maximize its economic contribution to the development of the Soviet Union as a whole. The statement, reproduced in part below, also spelled out some of the ways in which this was to be accomplished. Each republic was to develop its economy as Moscow saw fit, and not according to its own preference. In practice this meant, for example, that traditional economic pursuits such as subsistence agriculture might have to be abandoned in preference for the farming of cash crops, or that agriculture would be slighted in the interests of industrial development.

The new Party Program reasserted the primacy of the central Party apparatus in the selection of cadres for posts nationwide. It called for an interrepublican exchange of cadres in the appointment of Party officials, so that all-union interests would be defended against more narrow national or local ones. It also endorsed the meeting of economic targets through the deployment of cadres outside of their home republics. Those republics with excess labor were to help out regions that were deficient, and all the republics were expected to contribute workers to develop the new economic regions of the Far East.

The section on nationality relations in the Program stressed that it was inevitable that the nationalities become more interdependent and the national cultures become integrated. The expanded use of Russian as a shared language of communication was described as critical to this process, but unlike the 1961 Party Program, this program gave some limited assurances about the preservation of national cultures, and stated that the right to use the national languages would be protected.

Gorbachev's report to the Twenty-seventh Party Congress focused on the need for political and economic reform in the Soviet Union; the few direct remarks he made on nationality relations (which are reproduced below) were confined to a section on social relations in the USSR more generally. Gorbachev spoke of the development of the economy as the primary responsibility of all nationalities. He stressed the uniqueness of the Soviet people, and their engagement in the process of surmounting national uniqueness with their multinational culture. This, he said, made it possible for people to put the interests of the Soviet Union as a whole ahead of their narrow national interests. The actions of the minority who were nationalistic chauvinists, he warned, would not be tolerated.

In the next three years Gorbachev would learn that "excessive" nationalist demands were not simply confined to a minority of "national chauvinists," but that most non-Russians and many Russians as well were no longer willing to accept platitudes about the friendship of peoples as a substitute for the expansion of their political, economic, and social rights. The freeing-up of public discussion in the Soviet Union has allowed people to voice their objections to, among other things, the way that nationality policy has been applied in the past. In a number of instances—in Kazakhstan, in Armenia, and in Azerbaidzhan—these protests have turned violent, and in the Baltic republics they have led to full-fledged mass movements ("popular fronts") for complete republic autonomy.

As we will see, these events convinced Gorbachev that the Party Program did not go far enough in meeting the demands of the various national communities in the USSR and that, if some of these demands were not met, his economic and political reform program might be endangered. As a result, many of the provisions of the 1986 Party Program have *de facto* become obsolete, although officially they remain as policy.

For example, the Party has had to permit an expanded role for the national languages of the non-Russians, and in the case of Latvia, Lithuania, and Estonia Moscow has acquiesced to the designatation of the national language as the state language. Likewise, legislation has been proposed to make Tadzhik, Uzbek, and Moldavian (that is, Romanian) the official languages of their respective republics.

More serious is the threat to the relationship between center and periphery in the call for the complete financial autonomy of union republics put forward by Latvians, Lithuanians, and Estonians in their draft constitutions and in their program for a proposed economic union. Some of the proposed economic reforms originating in the Baltic republics have been endorsed by Moscow, as they seem to promise increased economic efficiency. Other proposals, such as a call for an internationally negotiable Baltic currency, have been rejected.

Much of the reform program of the Baltic republics has yet to be acted on. Although each of these republics has passed legislation that conflicts with the Constitution of the USSR, Moscow to date has managed to avoid a direct confrontation with their leaderships. But confrontation is inevitable. Despite all the changes that have been permitted, Moscow will not permit any rejection of the primacy of the CPSU, and certainly will refuse even to consider granting independence to the Baltic republics. Indeed, it is Moscow's seemingly unshakeable premise that the historical realities of boundaries must be accepted that has led to the sustained crisis over Nagorno Karabakh, an area claimed by Armenia, but part of Azerbaidzhan since 1922. The insistence on this principle makes the situation in the Baltic region inherently confrontational.

Gorbachev has said that the Leninist foundations of Soviet nationality policy are sound, but that the specific policies through which nationality relations will be governed during the current period of reform and change have yet to be fully worked out. This is to be the task of a special Central Committee plenum called for in February 1988 but repeatedly postponed. As the materials reproduced below show, Gorbachev introduced some "new thinking" on nationality questions at the Nineteenth Party Conference in June 1988. He called for increased economic autonomy for the union republics and he urged that they be able to keep the surplus produced over the economic plan requirements. This is considerably less economic autonomy than many have demanded. Gorbachev tried to hold a middle ground in cultural issues as well. He called for increased attention to the preservation of historical monuments, ecology, and training in the local language for the entire population in union republics, but he did not talk of allowing the republics to develop their own cultural policies. Moreover, he stressed that the governments of the union republics had the responsibility to preserve the rights of all their citizens and not just those of the titular nationality.

All of these points were reiterated in the resolution on nationality relations that was taken at the Nineteenth Party Conference, and is reproduced below. This resolution was designed to introduce Gorbachev's political reforms in the union republics. It described plans for increased political autonomy of local soviets, the supreme soviets of national autonomous regions and union republics, and the Council of Nationalities of the Supreme Soviet of the USSR, which would lead to greater self-regulation of national communities. It described how the authority of the union republics would be better delineated and thus be enhanced, as republics could now exercise more of their constitutional rights, and emphasized how the devolution of authority to localities and enterprises was in the interests of the nationalities.

The resolution made lots of promises to the nationalities, but provided little specific direction as to how the union republics and national regions could exercise additional economic authority or financial independence. Nor did it increase their cultural autonomy, or systematically propose protections for the cultural rights of minority nationalities in union republics. Many of these economic issues were finally addressed in the March 1989 draft legislation on the economic rights and responsibilities of republics, but the implementation of these reforms and the delineation of the cultural rights of nationalities still remain unfinished business. Thus, while greater sensitivity to the needs of national communities was shown in the Gorbachev speech and the conference resolution, little more than that has been done to defuse the pressures created by rising expectations of home rule or local self-goverment in the national regions.

The Constitution of the USSR *

Chapters 8-11

Chapter 8
The USSR—A Federal State

Article 70. The Union of Soviet Socialist Republics is an integral, federal, multi-national state formed on the principle of socialist federalism as a result of the free self-determination of nations and the voluntary association of equal Soviet Socialist Republics.

The USSR embodies the state unity of the Soviet people and draws all its nations and nationalities together for the purpose of jointly building communism.

Article 71. The Union of Soviet Socialist Republics unites:

the Russian Soviet Federative Socialist Republic,

the Ukrainian Soviet Socialist Republic,

the Belorussian Soviet Socialist Republic,

the Uzbek Soviet Socialist Republic,

the Kazakh Soviet Socialist Republic,

the Georgian Soviet Socialist Republic,

the Azerbaidzhan Soviet Socialist Republic,

the Lithuanian Soviet Socialist Republic,

the Moldavian Soviet Socialist Republic,

the Latvian Soviet Socialist Republic,

the Kirghiz Soviet Socialist Republic,

the Tadzhik Soviet Socialist Republic,

the Armenian Soviet Socialist Republic,

the Turkmen Soviet Socialist Republic,

the Estonian Soviet Socialist Republic.

Article 72. Each Union Republic shall retain the right freely to secede from the USSR;

Article 73. The jurisdiction of the Union of Soviet Socialist Republics, as represented by its highest bodies of state authority and administration, shall cover:

1. the admission of new republics to the USSR; endorsement of the formation of new autonomous republics and autonomous regions within Union Republics;

2. determination of the state boundaries of the USSR and approval of changes in the boundaries between Union Republics;

3. establishment of the general principles for the organisation and functioning of republican and local bodies of state authority and administration;

---

*USSR: Sixty Years of the Union, 1922-1982 (Moscow: Progress Publishers, 1982).

4. the ensurance of uniformity of legislative norms throughout the USSR and establishment of the fundamentals of the legislation of the Union of Soviet Socialist Republics and Union Republics;

5. pursuance of a uniform social and economic policy; direction of the country's economy; determination of the main lines of scientific and technological progress and the general measures for rational exploitation and conservation of natural resources; the drafting and approval of state plans for the economic and social development of the USSR, and endorsement of reports on their fulfillment;

6. the drafting and approval of the consolidated Budget of the USSR, and endorsement of the report on its execution; management of a single monetary and credit system; determination of the taxes and revenues forming the Budget of the USSR, and the formulation of prices and wages policy;

7. direction of the sectors of the economy, and of enterprises and amalgamations under Union jurisdiction, and general direction of industries under Union-Republican jurisdiction;

8. issues of war and peace, defence of the sovereignty of the USSR and safeguarding of its frontiers and territory, and organisation of defence; direction of the Armed Forces of the USSR;

9. state security;

10. representation of the USSR in international relations; the USSR's relations with other states and with international organisations; establishment of the general procedure for, and coordination of, the relations of Union Republics with other states and with international organisations; foreign trade and other forms of external economic activity on the basis of state monopoly;

11. control over observance of the Constitution of the USSR, and ensurance of conformity of the Constitutions of Union Republics to the Constitution of the USSR;

12. and settlement of other matters of All-Union importance.

Article 74. The laws of the USSR shall have the same force in all Union Republics. In the event of a discrepancy between a Union Republic law and an All-Union law, the law of the USSR shall prevail.

Article 75. The territory of the Union of Soviet Socialist Republics is a single entity and comprises the territories of the Union Republics.

The sovereignty of the USSR extends throughout its territory.

Chapter 9
The Union Soviet Socialist Republics

Article 76. A Union Republic is a sovereign Soviet socialist state that has united with other Soviet Republics in the Union of Soviet Socialist Republics.

Outside the spheres listed in Article 73 of the Constitution of the USSR, a Union Republic exercises independent authority on its territory.

A Union Republic shall have its own Constitution conforming to the Constitution of the USSR with the specific features of the Republic being taken into account.

Article 77. Union Republics take part in decision-making in the Supreme Soviet of the USSR, the Presidium of the Supreme Soviet of the USSR, the Government of the USSR, and other bodies of the Union of Soviet Socialist Republics in matters that come within the jurisdiction of the Union of Soviet Socialist Republics.

A Union Republic shall ensure comprehensive economic and social development on its territory, facilitate exercise of the powers of the USSR on its territory, and implement the decisions of the highest bodies of state authority and administration of the USSR.

In matters that come within its jurisdiction, a Union Republic shall coordinate and control the activity of enterprises, institutions, and organisations subordinate to the Union.

Article 78. The territory of a Union Republic may not be altered without its consent. The boundaries between Union Republics may be altered by mutual agreement of the Republics concerned, subject to ratification by the Union of Soviet Socialist Republics.

Article 79. A Union Republic shall determine its division into territories, regions, areas, and districts, and decide other matters relating to its administrative and territorial structure.

Article 80. A Union Republic has the right to enter into relations with other states, conclude treaties with them, exchange diplomatic and consular representatives, and take part in the work of international organisations.

Article 81. The sovereign rights of Union Republics shall be safeguarded by the USSR.

Chapter 10
The Autonomous Soviet Socialist Republic

Article 82. An Autonomous Republic is a constituent part of a Union Republic.

In spheres not within the jurisdiction of the Union of Soviet Socialist Republics and the Union Republic, an Autonomous Republic shall deal independently with matters within its jurisdiction.

An Autonomous Republic shall have its own Constitution conforming to the Constitutions of the USSR and the Union Republic with the specific features of the Autonomous Republic being taken into account.

Article 83. An Autonomous Republic takes part in decision-making through the highest bodies of state authority and administration of the USSR and of the Union Republic respectively, in matters that come within the jurisdiction of the USSR and the Union Republic.

An Autonomous Republic shall ensure comprehensive economic and social development on its territory, and implement decisions of the highest bodies of state authority and administration of the USSR and the Union Republic.

In matters within its jurisdiction, an Autonomous Republic shall coordinate and control the activity of enterprises, institutions, and organisations subordinate to the Union or the Union Republic.

Article 84. The territory of an Autonomous Republic may not be altered without its consent.

Article 85. The Russian Soviet Federative Socialist Republic includes the Bashkir, Buriat, Daghestan, Kabardin-Balkar, Kalmyk, Karelian, Komi, Mari, Mordovian, North Ossetian, Tatar, Tuva, Udmurt, Chechen-Ingush, Chuvash, and Yakut Autonomous Soviet Socialist Republics.

The Uzbek Soviet Socialist Republic includes the Kara-Kalpak Autonomous Soviet Socialist Republic.

The Georgian Soviet Socialist Republic includes the Abkhazian and Adzhar Autonomous Soviet Socialist Republics.

The Azerbaidzhan Soviet Socialist Republic includes the Nakhichevan Autonomous Soviet Socialist Republic.

Chapter 11
The Autonomous Region [Oblast] and Autonomous Area [Okrug]

Article 86. An Autonomous Region is a constituent part of a Union Republic or Territory. The Law on an Autonomous Region, upon submission by the Soviet of People's Deputies of the Autonomous Region concerned, shall be adopted by the Supreme Soviet of the Union Republic.

Article 87. The Russian Soviet Federative Socialist Republic includes the Adygei, Gorno-Altai, Jewish, Karachai-Circassian, and Khakas Autonomous Regions.

The Georgian Soviet Socialist Republic includes the South Ossetian Autonomous Region.

The Azerbaidzhan Soviet Socialist Republic includes the Nagorno Karabakh Autonomous Region.

The Tadzhik Soviet Socialist Republic includes the Gorno-Badakhshan Autonomous Region.

Article 88. An Autonomous Area is a constituent part of a Territory or Region. The Law on an Autonomous Area shall be adopted by the Supreme Soviet of the Union Republic concerned.

Sixty Years of the USSR *

Iu. V. ANDROPOV

Dear comrades! Honored guests!

Sixty years ago the peoples of our country liberated by the victorious October Revolution voluntarily united into the Union of Soviet Socialist Republics. (*applause*)

Closing the work of the first combined congress of Soviet republics, which pronounced the formation of the Union of Soviet Socialist Republics, M.I. Kalinin said, "Whole millennia have passed while the best minds of humanity struggle to find forms which would give peoples the possibility, without terrible torment, without mutual struggle, of living in friendship and brotherhood. Only now, today, is the first stone being placed in practical realization of this goal."[1] (*applause*)

The development of capitalism did not lead to the liquidation of national oppression. On the contrary. The oppression of nationalism was augmented and made sharper by the oppression of colonialism. Enslaving hundreds of millions of people, a handful of capitalist powers condemned them to vegetate, closing off their paths to progress. Marxism first revealed the organic connection of the national question with the social and class structure of society, with the predominant type of property ownership. In other words, the roots of national relations descend into a social soil, which is why Marx and Engels drew the fundamental conclusion that destruction of social oppression will serve as a condition and premise of the destruction of national oppression. As Marx said, "the victory of the proletariat over the bourgeoisie is at the same time a signal for the liberation of all oppressed nations."[2] The immortal slogan enunciated by the founders of Marxism, "Proletarians of All Lands, Unite!" became a summons to workers for international struggle against all forms of enslavement, social and national. (*applause*)

Lenin continued the work of K. Marx and F. Engels in new historical conditions. He headed the revolutionary movement when the first flashes of revolution began to glow above Russia. In a country which was properly called "a prison of peoples" the national question naturally moved to one of the first positions in the development of strategies and tactics for the Bolshevik party.

In the center of Lenin's attention was the right of nations to self-determination as the only sure means of insuring their real and reliable rapprochement. Only the right to self-determination could serve as the ideo-political basis of voluntary unification of all nations in the struggle to overthrow tsarism, to create a new society. It was thus

---

*Kommunist, 1983, no. 1 (excerpt). From a report to the festive joint session of the Central Committee of the CPSU, the Supreme Soviet of the USSR, and the Supreme Soviet of the RSFSR, in the Kremlin Palace of Congresses, 21 December 1982.

that Lenin posed the question; it was thus that it became the backbone of national policy for Lenin's party. (*applause*)

The October Revolution transformed political slogans and demands into the stuff of everyday organizational work. Life itself, the most difficult economic and social tasks, tasks of foreign policy and defense, dictated the necessity for all peoples to unify, for the republics which had arisen on the fragments of the Russian Empire to become one.

Today what seems obvious was far from obvious in that stormy time of transition. The search for concrete forms of government, for political institutions, which might contain the general ideas and premises of the national program was one of sharp disagreement. Widely various opinions came into conflict, from a program of fragile, amorphous union of the republics into a confederative framework to the demand simply to bring the republics into the RSFSR as autonomous units. It took the genius and authority of V.I. Lenin to find and insist upon the one true path, the path of socialist federalism.

What is the essence of the path established by Lenin? Briefly, it could be put this way—it is the fully voluntary union of free peoples as the guarantee of maximum durability of the federation of socialist republics. It is the full equality of all nations and national groups, and the concomitant attempt to liquidate inequality among them, not only legally but in fact. It is the free development of every republic, every national group within the framework of their fraternal union. It is the persistent fostering of an internationalist consciousness and an unswerving course for the convergence of all nations and national groups in our country.

It was in that year of the formation of the Soviet Union that V.I. Lenin wrote the words which vividly express the tendency of his reflections on the national question; as he said, "Our experience from trying in five years to resolve the national question in a state which contains such an abundance of nationalities, such as could hardly be found in other countries, wholly convinces us that the only correct attitude to the interests of national groups in such situations is to satisfy them to the maximum and to create conditions such as will exclude any possibility of conflict on this account. Our experience," Lenin continued, "has created in us the unwavering conviction that only an enormous attentiveness to the interests of various national groups will remove grounds for conflicts, will remove mutual distrust, will remove the danger of any intriguing, and will create that trust, especially of workers and peasants who speak different languages, without which both peaceful relations between peoples and any successful development of all that is of value in contemporary civilization are absolutely impossible."[3]

The Leninist heritage, the Leninist principles of national policy are holy for us. Relying on them, systematically affirming them in practice, we have created a mighty state, the Union of Soviet Socialist Republics; its formation was not only a huge step in the development of socialism, but was as well one of the most important watershed moments in the course of world history. (*sustained applause*)

* * *

In sixty years the Soviet Union has travelled an entire epoch. History may well know of no other other such persistent ascent from a condition of backwardness, poverty, and destruction to the might of today's great power, with the highest possible level of culture and the constantly improving living conditions of its people. What then are the most significant conclusions to be drawn from our development?

The historical correctness of Marx and Lenin's teaching that the resolution of the national question may be found only on a class basis is wholly affirmed. Social antagonisms have taken with them into the past national dissension and all forms of racial and national inequality and oppression.

It has been convincingly demonstrated that the Communist Party and its scientifically based policies are the managing, guiding force of the socialist resolution of the national question, and the guarantee of the correctness of this resolution.

Backward national areas where feudal-patriarchal and even clan relations frequently predominated have disappeared.

A unified nation-wide economic complex has formed on a basis of the dynamic economic growth of all republics, guided by a general governmental plan.

The social structure of the republics has qualitatively changed; a modern working class has grown up in each of them, the peasantry is following the new path of the kolkhoz, each has created its own intelligensia, and qualifed cadres have been educated in all spheres of government and public life.

A socialist, multinational culture has blossomed on the basis of progressive traditions and the intensive exchange of spiritual values.

Socialist national groups have formed, to make today a new historical social grouping—the Soviet people. (*prolonged applause*) The interests of the republics intertwine ever more tightly, mutual assistance and mutual relations grow ever more fruitful, channeling the creative efforts of nations and national groups of the Soviet Union into a single stream. The universal development of each of the socialist nations in our country is properly leading to their ever greater rapprochement.

Each of the union republics, the Russian Federation, the Ukraine and Belorussia, Uzbekistan and Kazakhstan, Georgia and Azerbaidzhan, Lithuania and Moldavia, Latvia and Kirghizia, Tadzhikistan and Armenia, Turkmenia and Estonia, each, I repeat, of the union republics makes a unique contribution to the general elevation of the economy and culture of the Soviet Union. And this, comrades, is not the simple addition, but the great multiplicaton of our creative powers. (*applause*)

In this fraternal family all the nations and national groups living in twenty autonomous republics and in eighteen autonomous oblasts and okrugs are successfully developing their opportunities. Millions of Germans, Poles, Koreans, Kurds, and people of other nationalities are also Soviet citizens with full rights, the Soviet Union having become their motherland.

The peoples of our country send particular expressions of indebtedness to the Russian people. Without their disinterested fraternal help the accomplishments of any of the republics would have been impossible. One factor of exceptional importance in the economic, political, and cultural life of the country, in the rapprochement of all of its nations and national groups, in their access to the riches of world civilization, is the service of the Russian language, which has entered naturally into the lives of millions of people of all nationalities. (*applause*) The new Constitution of the USSR is a mighty landmark in the strengthening of the national and governmental underpinnings of Soviet society. This outstanding document not only summarizes the development which we have undergone, but also sets forth firm, lasting, political and legal bases for the further flourishing and rapprochement of all the nations and national groups of the country.

The real, qualitative changes which have taken place in nationality relations in these sixty years bear witness to the fact that the national question, in the form which it was left to us by the exploitative structure of society has been successfully decided, decided definitively and irrefutably. (*prolonged applause*) For the first time in history the multinational nature of a country has been transformed from a source of weakness into the source of its strength and growth. (*applause*)

Speaking in this hall ten years ago Leonid Ilich Brezhnev expressed this very well: "Relationships unique in history have formed in our country, which we may correctly call the Leninist friendship of peoples. This friendship, comrades, is our invaluable achievement, one of the most significant and dearly held by every Soviet man of the conquests of socialism. And we, the Soviet people, will always guard this friendship like the apple of our eye."[4] (*prolonged applause*)

Today, on this festive occasion, we acknowledge the many generations of Soviet people of all nationalities, men and women, workers and peasants, intellectuals, Party and Soviet workers, soldiers of the Armed Forces, Communists and non-Party, everyone who built socialism, who stood behind it in the most difficult possible war, and transformed into reality the millenial dream of equality, friendship, and fraternity of nations. (*prolonged applause*)

Comrades! As we summarize what has been accomplished we naturally pay most attention to that which still needs to be done. Our final goal is clear. In Lenin's words, our goal is "Not simply the rapprochement of nations, but their fusion."[5] The Party well knows that the road to this goal is a long one. Here it is absolutely impossible to dash ahead, just as it is impermissible to impede processes already begun.

Successes in solving the national question in no ways mean that all the problems which can spring from life itself, and from the labor of a multitude of nations and national groups within the framework of a single state, have disappeared. That is scarcely possible, as long as nations exist, as long as there are national differences. And they will exist for a long time, much longer than will the differences of class.

Which is why the perfection of developed socialism—and that is precisely how we may define the main content of the Party and people's activity at the contemporay level—must also include a thoughtful, scientifically-based national policy. I should like to mention certain tasks of such a policy.

It has already been mentioned how great are the benefits and advantages which unificaton into a single union has given the peoples of our country, has given the republics. However the possibilities opened by this unification are still far from exhausted.

Let us take the economy. Modern industrial forces require integration even when separate countries are involved. Even more so these forces demand the close and intelligent joining of efforts by various regions and republics which are within one country. The most intelligent use of natural and labor resources, of the climatic particularities of every republic, the most rational inclusion of this potential into the common national whole is what will bring the greatest benefit to every region, every nation, and national group, just as it will to the state.

This is our principal aim; in order to realize it in life our central and local planning and administrative organs face no little work. It will also be necessary to perfect the distribution of productive forces, regional specialization, and cooperation, the schemata of economic links and shipping. This of course is no simple task, but it is time to solve it, and its solution promises significant benefit.

At present the entire country is at work on the Food Program, which clearly sets out concrete tasks for each union republic, and each of the republics must work fundamentally to make a real contribution—and in the near future at that—to this most important matter of assuring the Soviet people an uninterrupted food supply.

As you know, the program adopted speaks of the first, most pressing tasks, but if we are to think about the long view, then it is impossible not to see that the further development of our agricultural complex—as is true too with the economy of the country as a whole—will demand a more profound and consequential specialization of the agricultural economy on the scale of the entire country.

And there is another question too. In a country as wide-flung as ours, a wholly particular role is played by transportation, a role both economic and political, even, if you wish, psychological. Without a well-run transportation network it is very difficult to insure and accelerate the development of all the republics, or further deepen their economic participation. But transport is important not only for solving purely administrative problems. The development of transportation, of the road network which draws village nearer to city, will in no small measure facilitate, for example, the strengthening of cadre in the villages. It will of course also help the solution of a large social problem, the rational and flexible use of labor resources. In guaranteeing everyday human contact throughout the Soviet Union, live contact between all republics and regions of the country, transportation serves as the means by which people enjoy the achievements of socialist civilization, in the widest possible sense of the term.

Entering into a union became one of the additional sources not only of the material wealth of the Soviet people, but also of its spiritual wealth. However, here too we are far from taking full advantage of all opportunities. It is necessary to search diligently for new methods and forms of work, appropriate to the demands of the day, which will permit the mutual enrichment of cultures to become even more fruitful, which will open for all people even wider access to all that is best in the culture of each of our peoples. Radio and television, as well of course as other media of mass information, must play an ever greater role in this noble task.

Of course in doing this it must be remembered that the spiritual heritage, the traditions, and daily life of every nation contain not only good, but also bad relics. Which gives us another task, not to preserve this bad part, but to free ourselves from all that has aged, all that goes against the norms of Soviet life, socialist morality, and our communist ideals. Life shows that the economic and cultural progress of all nations and national groups is inescapably accompanied by the growth of their national self-consciousness. This is as it should be, an objective process. It is important however that the natural pride of achieved success not become nationalistic arrogance or conceit, that it not give rise to isolationism, to disrespectful attitudes towards other nations and national groups. Negative phenomena of this sort still exist. And it would be incorrect to explain them solely as survivals of the past. They are also fueled at times by our own oversights in work. Here, comrades, there are no trifles. Here everything is important—attitude toward language, toward monuments of the past, and interpretation of historical events and the way in which we transform village and city, for we are acting upon the conditions of people's life and labor.

As a result of natural migration of the population each of our republics is becoming ever more multinational, and so too to some extent or other, each region, each city. Which means that the Party and government organs must increasingly become the conductors and executives of the Party's nationality policy, our on-site cadres. For that reason they are obligated daily to embody the high principles of that policy, insuring the harmonious, fraternal relations of members of all—both the greater and the small in number—of all nations and national groups, in labor and in daily life.

The Party has always paid great attention to the growth of the national ranks of the Soviet working class, the leading force of our society. And the results of this are before us. Today workers are the largest social group in all the union republics. However, in some of them the make up of the working class must be more fully represented by the native nationality. This is the source of the task set by the Twenty-sixth Congress of the CPSU to broaden and improve the preparation of qualified workers from among all the nations and national groups living in the republics. This is necessary for the development of the economy. It is also important politically. Multinational labor collectives, and above all workers' collectives are precisely the environment which best fosters the internationalist spirit, which strengthens the fraternity and friendship of the peoples of the USSR. (*prolonged applause*)

Also extremely important is the question of representation of workers in the Party and governmental organs of the republics and of the Union as a whole. We are not, of course, talking about some sort of formalistic norms of representation. The arithmetical approach to solving such problems is inappropriate. It is necessary though to consistently strive so that all nationalities which live in this republic or that are properly represented in the various links of Party and government organs. Evaluation of work-capabilities and moral-political qualities, attention and concern, great tact in the choice and assignment of cadres, all these are particularly indispensable in conditions of the multinationally constituted union and autonomous republics.

A constant task, unchanging in its significance, is the cultivation in Soviet people of a spirit of mutual respect and friendship of all nations and national groups of the country, of love for our great Soviet Motherland, of internationalism, and of solidarity with workers of other countries. All Party and Komsomol organizations, Soviets and trade unions, our armed forces, which always were a good school of internationalism, all these are challenged to accomplish this task. This must be the daily concern of all the institutions of learning in the country. (*applause*)

In the sphere of internationalist education, as in all ideological and mass political work, large tasks stand before us. Convincing concrete evidence of our achievements, a serious analysis of the new problems to which life constantly gives birth, freshness of thought and word, all this is the way we should perfect our propagandizing, which must always be believable and realistic, as well as interesting, accessible, and thus more effective. (*applause*)

The further development of friendship and cooperation between the peoples of the USSR depends in significant measure on the deepening of socialist democracy. The ever wider participation of workers of all nationalities in the direction of social and governmental affairs is the most concise formulation of the leading tendency of our political life. And the Party will do all it can so that this tendency strengthens and grows.

It follows from what has been said, comrades, that in the conditions of mature socialism the problems of relations between nations are not removed from the agenda. They demand particular concern, and the continual attention of the Communist Party. The Party must penetrate deeply into these problems, point out the way to their solution, creatively enriching the Leninist principles of national policy with the experience of developed socialism. (*applause*)

We speak openly about problems which exist and about unresolved tasks because we know firmly that we are capable of dealing with these problems and tasks, that we can and must resolve them. (*prolonged applause*) An orientation to deeds and not loud words is what we need today to make even stronger the great and powerful Union of Soviet Socialist Republics (*stormy prolonged applause*). I am sure that all of you gathered in this hall, our whole Party, and the entire Soviet people think the same. (*stormy applause*)

* * *

Comrades! Looking back at the road which the Union of Soviet Socialist Republics has travelled in sixty years we see clearly that all our achievements and victories are unbreakably tied to the work of the Leninist party of communists. It is precisely the Party which was and which shall remain that powerful creative mobilizing force which guarantees the uninterrupted forward movement of all sectors of social progress.

In its ideology, in its constituency and structure, our Party is the living embodiment of unity, of the cohesion of all nations and national groups of the Soviet Union. Directing its policies toward the harmonious combination of national and international interests, the Party also creates social conditions in which the flourishing and universal development of every nation serves as the precondition of the progress and flourishing of the whole of our fraternal union.

When we say that "The Party and People are One!" we are affirming that inalterable fact that the goals and tasks which the Party has set itself precisely express the aspirations and needs of all Soviet people. And our people in their many millions are realizing in life with their deeds the policy of the Party. One of the most obvious demonstrations of that is the successes with which all of the republics are greeting today's anniversary. (*applause*)

Permit me, comrades, to express deep indebtedness and thanks to the millions of outstanding workers who fulfilled and overfulfilled their socialist obligations, as sumed in honor of the Sixtieth Anniversary of the USSR. (*sustained applause*)

Allow me, in the name of the Central Committee of the Communist Party of the Soviet Union, the Presidium of the Supreme Soviet and the Soviet of Ministers of the USSR, to extend warm congratulations to all Soviet peoples on the occasion of a great holiday, the birthday of our great Union. (*stormy prolonged applause*)

Long live the friendship of peoples building communism! (*stormy applause*)

Long live proletarian socialist internationalism! (*stormy applause*)

Long live peace throughout the world! (*stormy applause*)

May the Union of Soviet Socialist Republics flourish! (*stormy, prolonged applause. All rise*)

Notes

1. Kalinin, M. I., *Izbrannye proizvedeniia v 4-kh tomakh*, Moscow, 1960, vol. 1, p. 359.
2. Marx, K., Engels, F., *Sochineniia*, vol. 4, p. 371.
3. Lenin, V. I., *Polnoe sobranie sochinenii*, vol. 45, p. 240.
4. Brezhnev, L. I., *Leninskim kursom*, Moscow, 1975, vol. 4, p. 50.
5. Lenin, V. I., *Polnoe sobranie sochinenii*, vol. 27, p. 256.

Political Report
of the CPSU Central Committee
to the Twenty-seventh Party Congress *

M. S. GORBACHEV

**Improvement of social-class relations and
relations among the peoples of the USSR**

Comrades, analyzing problems involved in the *interrelationship of classes and
social groups* is of vital importance for a Marxist-Leninist party. By carefully taking
into account both the community and the specific nature of their interests in its
policy, the Communist Party ensures society's strong unity and successful fulfillment of its most important and complex tasks.

The working class holds a vanguard place in Soviet society. Owing to its position
in the socialist production system, its political experience, high political awareness,
good organization, labor and political activity, the working class unites our society
and plays the leading role in improving socialism, in communist construction. Constant
concern for the consolidation of the alliance of the working class, the peasantry and the
intelligentsia is the cornerstone of the policy pursued by the Communist Party of the
Soviet Union. It is precisely this which enables us to muster forces for the speedy
solution of the economic and social tasks we have set ourselves.

The unity of socialist society by no means implies a levelling of public life.
Socialism encourages diversity of people's interests, requirements and abilities, and
vigorously supports the initiative of social organizations hat express this diversity.
Moreover, socialism needs this diversity, which it regards as an essential condition
for the further promotion of people's creative activity and initiative, and the competition of minds and talents, without which the socialist way of life and the movement
forward would be inconceivable.

Generally speaking, the problem is as follows: unless we elevate competition to a
new, incomparably higher level, in production and in the economy as well as in
science and the arts, we will not be able to cope with the task of accelerating the
country's socioeconomic progress. To improve the socialist way of life is to ensure
the maximum opportunities for fostering collectivism, the cohesion of society, and
individual activity.

The *problems of consolidating the family* are attracting public attention. Our
achievements in cultivating the new, socialist type of family are indisputable. Socialism has emancipated women from economic and social oppression, securing for
them the opportunity to work, obtain an education and participate in public life

---

*English text issued by Novosti Press Agency, 1986 (excerpt).

on an equal footing with men. The socialist family is based on the full equality of men and women and their equal responsibility for the family.

Yet, the formation of the new type of family is no simple matter. It is a complicated process that involves many problems. In particular, although the divorce rate has dropped in the past few years, it is still high. There is still a large number of unhappy families. All this has a negative effect, above all, on the upbringing of children, as well as on the morale of men and women, on their labor and public activity. It stands to reason that society cannot be indifferent to such phenomena. The strong family is one of its principal pillars.

Young families need special care. Young people must be well prepared for family life. More thought should be given to the system of material assistance to newlyweds, above all in solving their housing and everyday problems. It would appear to be a good thing to consider the proposals for improving relevant legislation with a view to heightening the citizens' responsibility for consolidating the family. But that is not all. It is necessary to organize the practical work of state and public organizations to promote in every way a strengthening of the family and its moral foundations. This means the creation of conditions for family participation in public festivities and in cultural and sports events, and for family recreation. Families in which successive generations work in a same profession should be widely honored; good family traditions should be given every support and young people should be brought up on the basis of the experience of older generations. Here a big contribution can be made by the mass information media, television, literature, cinema and the theatre.

Securing living and working conditions for women that would enable them to combine successfully their maternal duties with active involvement in labor and public activity is a prerequisite for solving many family problems. In the 12th five-year period we are planning to extend the practice of letting women work a shorter day or week, or to work at home. Mothers will have paid leaves until their babies are 18 months old. The number of paid days-off granted to mothers to care for sick children will be increased. Lower-income families with children of up to 12 years of age will receive child allowances. We intend to fully satisfy the people's need for preschool children's institutions within the next few years.

Thought should also be given to appropriate organizational forms. Why not reinstitute women's councils within work collectives or residentially, integrating them in a single system with the Soviet Women's Committee at its head? Women's councils could help to resolve a wide range of social problems arising in the life of our society.

Concern for the older generation, for war and labor veterans, should rank as one of the top priorities. The Party and the Soviet Government will do everything possible for the pensioners' well-being to rise with the growth of society's prosperity. In the twelfth five-year period it is planned to increase the minimum old-age, disability, and loss-of-breadwinner pensions paid to factory and office workers, and to raise the previously fixed pensions of collective farmers. But man lives not by bread alone, as the saying goes. According to the information reaching the Central Committee, many retired veterans feel left out of things. Apparently, additional measures should be taken by government and public organizations, centrally and locally, to assist the veterans in becoming more actively involved in production and socio-political life. After all, more than 50 million Soviet people are veterans.

The setting up of a national mass organization of war and labor veterans could be a new step in this direction. It could be instrumental in involving highly experienced people in social and political affairs, and first of all in educating the rising generation. The pensioners' involvement, both on a cooperative and on an individual, family basis, in the services or trade, producing consumer goods or turning out farm produce could be highly useful. The new organization could be helpful in improving everyday and medical services for pensioners and expanding their leisure opportunities. As we see it, it will certainly have a lot of work to do.

Comrades, of tremendous importance for the multinational Soviet state is *development of relations among the peoples of the USSR.* The foundation for solving the nationalities problem in our country was laid by the Great October Socialist Revolution. Relying on Lenin's doctrine and on the gains of socialism the Communist Party has done enormous transformative work in this area. Its results are an outstanding achievement of socialism which has enriched world civilization. National oppression and inequality of all types and forms have been done away with once and for all. The indissoluble friendship among nations and respect for national cultures and for the dignity of all peoples have been established and have taken firm root in the minds of tens of millions of people. The Soviet people is a qualitatively new social and international community, cemented by the same economic interests, ideology and political goals.

However, our achievements must not create the impression that there are no problems in the national processes. Contradictions are inherent in any kind of development, and are unavoidable in this sphere as well. The main thing is to see their emergent aspects and facets, to search for and give prompt and correct answers to questions posed by life. This is all the more important because the tendency towards national isolation, localism, and parasitism still persist and make themselves felt quite painfully at times.

In elaborating guidelines for a long-term nationalities policy, it is especially important to see to it that the republics' contribution to the development of an integrated national economic complex should match their grown economic and spiritual potential. It is in the supreme interests of our multinational state, and each of the republics, to promote cooperation in production, collaboration and mutual assistance among the republics. It is the task of Party organizations and the Soviets to make the fullest possible use of available potentialities in the common interests and to persistently overcome all signs of localism.

We are legitimately proud of the achievements of the multinational Soviet socialist culture. By drawing on the wealth of national forms and characteristics, it is developing into a unique phenomenon in world culture. However, the healthy interest in all that is valuable in each national culture must by no means degenerate into attempts to isolate oneself from the objective process by which national cultures interact and come closer together. This applies, among other things, to certain works of literature and art and scholarly writing in which, under the guise of national originality, attempts are made to depict in idyllic tones reactionary nationalist and religious survivals contrary to our ideology, the socialist way of life, and our scientific world outlook.

Our Party's tradition traceable to Lenin of being particularly circumspect and tactful in all that concerns the nationalities policy and the interests of every nation or nationality, national feelings, calls at the same time for resolute struggle against national narrow-mindedness and arrogance, nationalism and chauvinism, no matter what their guise may be. We Communists must unswervingly follow Lenin's wise teachings, must creatively apply them to the new conditions, and be extremely heedful and principled as regards relations among peoples in the name of the further consolidation of fraternal friendship among all the peoples of the USSR.

The social policy elaborated by the Party has many aspects to it and is quite feasible. However, its success will largely hinge on the social orientation of the cadres, on persistence and initiative in carrying out our plans. Concern for people's needs and interests must be an object of unflagging attention on the part of the Party, government and economic organizations, of trade unions and of each executive. If we succeed in securing a decisive switch to the social sphere, many of the problems that face us today and will face us tomorrow will be solved far more quickly and much more effectively than has so far been the case.

Report of the General Secretary of the Central Committee of the CPSU at the Nineteenth All-Union Conference of the CPSU *

M. S. GORBACHEV

The development of inter-nationality relations

Comrades! One of the greatest achievements of socialism is the union which has formed in our country of equal nations and national groups. Today this permits us to say with great conviction that in the future as well the only healthy basis for development is to systematically follow Leninist nationality policy.

Life has shown the correctness of the idea laid down in the organization of our great union, that the joining, the unification of efforts permitted every nation and society as a whole to sharply accelerate its movement, to advance to new frontiers of historical progress. For all the difficulties which lay in our way, we maintain that this Union has withstood the test of time. It continues to be the decisive precondition of the development of all our peoples.

As you know, there is to be a special plenum of the Central Committee devoted to the question of development of inter-nationality relations. But even now, at our conference, we must treat this extraordinarily important and topical problem. It is important here to see the entire real picture, both the undoubted achievements and the obviously uncompleted jobs, the oversights and difficulties arising from the irresolution of concrete social and economic questions, as well occasional ignorance of how to unite national interests and those common to all peoples.

We must take up in a fundamental way the further development and optimizaton of the existing inter-republic economic, scientific, and technical connectons, more full realize the advantages of the intra-republic division of labor and labor cooperation, and scientifically based regional policy. *Glasnost'* means a great deal here. Workers must be fully in the course of what is developing in their republic and of the place they occupy in the national economic complex. They must know how not just their neighbors are living and developing, but all the republics of the country. This must also be done because sometimes one encounters conversations and judgments about relationships between republics which are based upon insufficient or even one-sided information.

It will be correct if our Party conference will take as reliable compass points for inter-nationality relations in the sphere of economics the principles of justice and fraternal international help for one another, for mutual action, which will guar-

---

*Pravda, 29 June 1988, p. 5 (excerpt).

antee both a general rise and the improvement of economic and social conditions of life for all nations and national groups of the country.

In the contemporary situation the rights of the union republics must be analyzed and brought into accordance with radical economic reform. It clearly has merits that once they have fulfilled their obligations to the all-union fund that they can direct production for their own needs, on the basis of a skilled and enterprising management. This would also meet the demands of social justice in the development of national relations, and would stimulate our common movement ahead.

In recent years the processes of democratization and *glasnost'* have illuminated the sorts of problems whose existence is not always taken sufficiently into account, such as questions connected with language, culture, literature, and art, with historical monuments and the preservation of nature.

The development of our multinational state is naturally accompanied by the growth of national self-consciousness. This is a positive phenomenon, but inasmuch as the new demands which arise in this connection are not always given the necessary attention, certain questions began to grow complicated, in a number of instances acquiring a nationalistic coloration. Although in principle these questions could have been resolved calmly, without giving grounds for any sort of speculation and emotional outbursts.

Recently we have seen with our own eyes how tangled the problems of inter-nationality relations can become. And we must preserve the fraternity and friendship of our peoples like the apple of our eye. There is simply no other path, comrades, no intelligent alternative. (*applause*) He who tries to prove otherwise is deceiving himself and others. Further, to try to incite people of different nationalities against one another, to sow discord and hatred between them is to take upon one's self a heavy responsibility before one's people and before socialist society, to say nothing of before the law. Objectively such actions interfere both with the process of democratization and the business of restructuring.

We must also examine questions of inter-nationality relations in the context of the present developmental stage of the Soviet multinational state. We must generalize our accumulated experience, making use of all that is valuable and at the same time expose what must be avoided. We may say straight out that there is a great deal to think of here. First of all we have to evaluate the many normative acts which regulate the mutual actions of the Union and the republics, how fully they correspond to the present conditions, tasks, and needs of our multinational society, to the level of democracy's development. This clearly also requires clarification of the situation, rights, and obligations of the union and autonomous republics, and of the other national formations.

In the course of this approach it is also necessary to examine this question, that our society is distinguished by great mobility of the population; many people live outside of their own national formations, and there are also national groups which have no territorial autonomy. All this is the reality of our multinational state. There are possible certain collisions here, and there is only one path for their resolution, within the framework of the existing structure of the union republic to guarantee maximum consideration of the interests of every nation and national group and of the entire society of Soviet peoples. Any other approach in our concrete conditions is simply impossible, and any attempt to try another path would be fatal.

Let us take Kazakhstan as an example. It is an enormous republic, with great possibilities for development; it has a true international society, the achievement of which is the result of cooperation by all peoples. This land was conquered by and is now inhabited by Kazakhs, Russians, Ukrainians, Germans, Kirghiz, Tatars, Uz-beks, Turkmen, and representatives of many other nations and national groups. At the same time though no one can doubt the integrity of the Kazakh republic. To some degree or another the same picture may be seen in other republics as well.

We cannot avoid internationalization of the economy and of all social life. And any tendency toward national exclusivity can only lead to economic and spiritual impoverishment. Our socialist approach is different. We strive to make it so that a person of any nationality has full rights in fact in any part of the country, that he might realize his rights and legal interests everywhere.

In speaking for the further strengthening of inter-nationality relations we assume that the development of the state of the Soviet Union, of the international connec-tions and the fraternity of our peoples are all living, dynamic processes. They must be constantly before the eyes of both republic and all-union bodies. The problems connected with them must be solved by relying on the will of the peoples, their mutual consent, with calculation of the interests of all Soviet peoples.

It is very important that within the framework of our political system there should exist, on a permanent basis, government and social institutes which could study the whole complex of inter-nationality relations. I have already said above that this must become one of the primary tasks of the Soviet of Nationalities of the Supreme Soviet of the USSR.

In general, comrades, the Union of Soviet Socialist Republics is our common home. And we, its owners, are obligated ever to care for it, preserving it and improving it, trying to conduct business such that all Soviet people who live in it should feel proud of their socialist Fatherland. (*prolonged applause*)

This plainly must be stressed particularly in the resolution of our conference on improvement of national relations.

The Program of the Communist Party of the Soviet Union *

Further flourishing and drawing closer together of socialist nations and nationalities

The CPSU takes full account in its activities of the multinational composition of Soviet society. The path that has been traversed provides convincing proof that *the nationalities question inherited from the past has been successfully solved in the Soviet Union*. Characteristic of the national relations in our country are both the continued flourishing of the nations and nationalities and the fact that they are steadily and voluntarily drawing closer together on the basis of equality and fraternal cooperation. Neither artificial prodding nor holding back of the objective trends of development is admissible here. In the long-term historical perspective this development will lead to complete unity of the nations.

The CPSU proceeds from the fact that in our socialist multinational state, in which more than one hundred nations and nationalities work and live together, there naturally arise *new tasks of improving national relations*. The Party has carried out, and will continue to carry out such tasks on the basis of the tested principles of the Leninist nationalities policy. It puts forward the following main tasks in this field:

—a buildup of the material and intellectual potential of each republic within the framework of the integral national economic complex. Combining the initiative of the Union and autonomous republics, autonomous regions and autonomous areas with central administration at the countrywide level will make possible the more rational use of the country's resources and of local natural and other features. It is necessary consistently to deepen the division of labor between the republics, even out the conditions of economic management, encourage active participation by the republics in the economic development of new regions, promote inter-republican exchanges of workers and specialists, and broaden and improve the training of qualified personnel from among citizens of all the nations and nationalities inhabiting the republics;

—development of the Soviet people's integral culture, which is socialist in content, diverse in its national forms and internationalist in spirit, on the basis of the greatest achievements and original progressive traditions of the peoples of the USSR. The advancement and drawing together of the national cultures and the consolidation of their interrelationships make mutual enrichment more fruitful and open up the broadest possibilities for the Soviet people to enjoy everything valuable that has been created by the talent of each of the peoples of our country.

The equal right of all citizens of the USSR to use their native languages and the

---

*English text issued by Novosti Press Agency, 1986 (excerpt). The program was approved at the Twenty-seventh Congress of the CPSU on March 1, 1986.

free development of these languages will be ensured in the future as well. At the same time learning the Russian language, which has been voluntarily accepted by the Soviet people as a medium of communication between different nationalities, besides the language of one's nationality, broadens one's access to the achievements of science and technology and of Soviet and world culture.

The Party proceeds from the belief that consistent implementation of the Leninist nationalities policy and a strengthening in every way of the friendship of the peoples are part of the effort to perfect socialism and a way that has been tested in social practice of ensuring the further flourishing of our multinational socialist homeland.

Resolution of the Nineteenth All-Union Conference of the CPSU "On Inter-nationality Relations" *

1. The Soviet socialist state which V. I. Lenin founded embodied the revolutionary will and desires of a multinational family of equal peoples. The community of their historical fate is the basis of international socialist fraternity. As a result of the efforts of many generations of Soviet people there has arisen a unique union of republics. On its banner is enscribed the international unity of the working people of all Soviet nations and nationalities, the right of nations to self-definition, the revival and advancement of national cultures, the accelerated progress for formerly backward national regions, and the elimination of strife between nations. An integral economic complex has emerged, serving as the material foundation of the unity of the peoples of the Soviet Union. The economic, cultural, and manpower potential of all the republics and autonomous regions has risen immeasurably. A new historical community—the Soviet people—has come into being. A natural growth of national self-awareness is taking place.

At the same time the dynamism witnessed during the initial stage of the formation of the multinational Soviet state was substantially undermined by departure from Leninist principles of nationality policy, by breaches of the rule of law during the period of the cult of personality, and by the ideology and psychology of stagnation. The results achieved in solving the nationality question were made absolute. It was claimed that there were no problems in the relations among nationalities. The need for the social, economic, and cultural development of certain republics, autonomous regions, and ethnic groups were not considered sufficiently. Many difficult questions arising from the course of development of nations and national groups were not resolved promptly enough. This led to social dissatisfaction, which at times assumed a character of conflict. Facts of national egoism and arrogance, attitudes of dependence and local chauvinism continue to be in place. Negative phenomena which have accumulated for decades were ignored for a long time, were chased inside and were not given the necessary Party evaluation. Restructuring, democratization, and *glasnost'* have exposed these phenomena and at the same time have created the necessary conditions for their democratic suppression.

2. The Party conference considers it a task of historical importance to affirm insistently and to develop creatively the Leninist norms and principles of nationality policy, decisively cleansing them of artificial additions and deformations. The basis for doing so is the political course elaborated at the Twenty-seventh Congress of the CPSU, which collates satisfaction of the interests of all nations and national groups with the general interests and needs of the country, an internationalist ideology

---

Reprints from the Soviet Press, 15 August 1988, pp. 11–16. Russian text from *Pravda*, 5 July 1988, p. 3.

which is incompatible with any varieties of chauvinism or nationalism.

The Party sees development of the independence of the union republics and autonomous regions as inseparably linked with their responsibility for strengthening and advancing our multinational state. The socialist ideal is not a deadening unification but the full-blooded, dynamic unity of national variety.

3. The Party Conference considers that within the framework of restructuring of the political system it is necessary to create timely measures for the further development and strengthening of the Soviet federation on the basis of democratic principles. Primarily under discussion is broadening of the rights of the union republics and autonomous regions by demarcation of the purviews of the USSR and the Soviet republics, by decentralization and transfer to the localities of a number of administrative functions, by strengthening home rule and responsibility in the spheres of the economy, social and cultural development, and preservation of nature.

One of the central tasks is to create conditions for greater home rule in the regions, to create forms of cooperation in which each republic would have an interest in improving the ultimate results of their economic activity as a basis for their own well-being, increasing the general wealth and power of the Soviet state. Radical economic reform and the process of democratization open broad expanses for the optimal coordination of both national-state formations and of the country as a whole. Business must be so set that that working people know well how much the republic or oblast produces, what contribution it makes to the economy of the country, and how much they receive. The idea of transferring regions and republics to principles of self-financing, with precise calculation of their contribution to completing the all-union program deserves attention.

Internationalization of the economy and of all of social life is a proper process. Any attempt at national exclusivity can lead only to economic and spiritual impoverishment.

A qualitatively new mechanism of drawing up republic and local budgets must be legislated, greatly increasing their role in deciding questions of the social and economic development of the regions. The effective cooperation of territorial administrative bodies with the ministries and offices of the USSR, and with enterprises under all-union control, must be guaranteed, and the responsibility of both republic-level and union-level administrative bodies for the comprehensive development of each region must be strengthened. Questions of development of direct connections between the union republics demand profound legal elaboration and practical decisions.

Those institutes of the political system through which national interests must be revealed and reconciled must be activated. Of primary significance in this connection is increasing the role of the Congress of People's Deputies, especially of the Council of Nationalities of the Supreme Soviet of the USSR, its standing committees, and also the government of the USSR. The creation of standing committees on questions of inter-nationality relations in the Supreme Soviet of the USSR, the Supreme Soviets of the union and autonomous republics, and of the local Soviets where necessary would be useful. It would also be worth considering the question of forming a special government body for nationality affairs and nationality relations.

The conference recommends realizing development and renewal of legislature, taking account of new realities, about the union and autonomous republics, the autonomous oblasts and okrugs, and more fully reflecting their rights and responsibilities, realizing principles of self-government and representation of all national groups in the bodies of power in the center and in the localities. This will require making the corresponding changes in the Constitution of the USSR, and in the constitutions of the union and autonomous republics.

4. It is important that in every national region economic and social progress is accompanied by spiritual progress, based upon the cultural uniqueness of the nations and national groups. Socialist cultural, evolving as it is in a multinational way must also remain in the future a powerful factor in the ideological and moral consolidation of our society.

Care must be taken that nationalities living outside the boundaries of their state and territorial formations, or which do not have them, receive greater opportunities for realization of national and cultural needs, particularly in the sphere of education, communication, native art, as well as of the creation of centers of national culture, of use of the mass media, and satisfaction of religious needs.

A most important principle of our multinational state is the free development and use in equal right by all citizens of the USSR of native languages and mastery of Russian, which Soviet people undertake voluntarily, in its aspect as a means of internationality communication. All conditions must be created to let national language-Russian bilingualism develop harmoniously and naturally, with consideration of the peculiarities of every region, free from formalism. More care should be shown for the active functioning of national languages in various spheres of state, public, and cultural life. Study of the language for whom the republic is named should be encouraged for citizens of other nationalities living in its territory, especially for children and young people. None of this should contradict the democratic principles of free choice in the language of school insturction.

5. Every generation of Soviet people passes through the school of patriotism and internationalism in its own way. It is important that as early as the person's very first social experiences, beginning with the family and school, the Pioneer and Komsomol organizations organically includes these values, that they should emerge as an indivisible whole, excluding both national nihilism and national isolationism. The sources of the friendship of our peoples must be discovered, a culture of internationality communication must be actively formed, and respect for the traditions, language, art, and history of the peoples of the country, and of other peoples of the world must be inculcated. Service in the ranks of the Armed Forces of the USSR must become a true school of internationalism.

The Conference considers that the social and political significance of the all-union holiday on the anniversary of the formation of the USSR must be increased.

Life has shown convincingly that where the practice of Soviet patriotism and socialist internationalism has grown anemic national limitations and chauvinistic arrogance begin to become active. The struggle with this monstrous deviations and elimination of the causes which give rise to them are the civic duty of every Soviet person. Any action which alienates nations and national groups, any attempts to limit the rights of citizens of any nationality must be seen as morally unacceptable and counter to the interests of the Soviet state.

It is necessary to learn to distinguish true national interests from their nationalist distortions. Any pretensions to national exclusivity are impermissible and shameful, including for the people in whose name they are being expressed. In the spirit of the Leninist tradition it is necessary to struggle first of all with the nationalism and chauvinism of one's own nationality, and representatives of the corresponding nationalities must do so first of all.

6. The conference notes that multinationalism in the conditions of our country is a mighty source for the development and mutual spiritual enrichment of peoples. Formation of the socialist, internationalist form of life is the business of the whole Party, and of all Soviet people. For this must be mobilized the political experience, the laboring morale, and moral potential of the working class, the peasants, and the intelligentsia, their deep commitment to the neighborly coexistence of various peoples. A particular role in this work falls to the Soviet intelligentsia. The general climate of nationality relations to an enormous extent depends upon their civic maturity and the depths of their understanding of the fundamental interests of their own peoples and of society as a whole.

All nationality problems require a balanced, comprehensive approach, on the basis of deep analyusis and objective evaluations of every concrete situation. They must be solved calmly, with extraordinary responsibility, within the frameworks of socialist democracy and legality, first of all by means of coming part way to meet one another, taking account of the expanded processes of revolutionary renewal, without harm to the international solidarity of the Soviet people. Matters must tend toward creation of a civic atmosphere in which a person of any nationality would feel himself at home in any part of our socialist Motherland.

7. Contemporary nationality policy needs profound scientific and theoretical reworking. This is a social order of responsibility to the scientific establishments and specialists. For successful completion the corresponding organizational and cadre prerequisites must be created, uniting the efforts of the scientific community. It is worth considering the question of whether to create an all-union level scientific center for the comprehensive study of pressing problems of national relations, and to increase the scientific research and informational work in this area.

8. The Party organizations and Communists of all nationalities are called to be the cementing force, the soul of the socialist union of peoples, active carriers of internationalism. With all their actions they must guarantee the solidarity of working people around the tasks of restructuring, must create healthy public opinion, and must lead the people. It is necessary in the spirit of Leninist demands to adopt a policy to have in Party, state, trade union, Komsomol, and economic bodies, including at the union level, representatives of all nations and national groups, so that the composition of the administrative cadre will more fully reflect the national structure of Soviet society.

The Conference supports the proposal of the Politburo of the Central Committee of the CPSU to hold a Plenum of the Central Committee on questions of nationality relations.

The Conference expresses the firm conviction that the consolidation and unity of all Soviet people is our present and our future. The patriotic and international duty of every citizen, of every communist, is to preserve and multiply everything that serves the unity of Soviet society as the bases of the free development and flourishing of all peoples of the Union of Soviet Socialist Republics, that serves to strengthen the might of our common Fatherland. V. I. Lenin asked us to do this, and by this path the Communist Party will travel.

2. Soviet Scholars and the Study of the "National Problem"

Gorbachev has tried to mobilize Soviet social scientists to help the Party come up with specific solutions to some of the concrete problems that stem from the multinational makeup of the USSR. He has called upon scholars to cease the long-standing practice of offering idealized versions of reality and to replace them with "objective" descriptions of Soviet life. Gorbachev and those around him believe that social science can be scientific and that, through the careful application of social science technique, scholars can help policy makers elaborate "scientific" policies that will cure social ills.

Gorbachev is not the first Soviet leader to look to social scientists with high expectations. Khrushchev recognized that the conditions of scholarship in both the natural sciences and the social sciences had to be modernized if the Soviet Union was to become competitive with the United States. While the reforms he introduced seem quite modest today, they were revolutionary in the context of the Stalinist system to which he was heir. It was Khrushchev who promoted the first international exchanges with foreign scholars, who permitted Soviet libraries to subscribe to Western periodicals and purchase Western books to be placed in limited-access collections, and it was Khrushchev who admitted that there was a place for debate in scholarship as long as the tenets of Marxism-Leninism were upheld.

In the mid-1960s, as Soviet social science began again to expand its intellectual frontiers, one of the goals that Soviet scholars placed on their agendas was to better understand the meaning and functions of nationality in contemporary society. Initially, most scholarship on nationality relations was designed to demonstrate that the ideological goals of the Party were in fact realistic, and that national distinctions were becoming less pronounced.

In 1967, in a symposium on nationality and society held to mark the fiftieth anniversary of the Russian Revolution, a few scholars argued that national differences were no longer politically or economically significant in the USSR, since the process of assimilation of the smaller nationalities by the Russians had gone so far. But even in an environment which claimed that the utopian program of the Communist Party was within reach, there were strong intimations in the works of a number of scholars that national distinctions were not disappearing, that ethnically or religiously inspired cultural practices—"survivals of the past" as they were termed—were being transmitted from generation to generation. Although these scholars offered little or no information as to the percentage of the population that was so "contaminated," they strongly implied that the failures of the regime's social and cultural policies had real economic consequences.

The publication of the 1970 census added new urgency to the study of nationality relations, as it revealed that the non-Slavic nationalities were reproducing at a far more rapid rate than the Slavic ones, and that much of this population lacked the Russian-language skills and technical training necessary for full integration in the Soviet economy. This information, coupled with reports that national communities were retaining their distinctive cultures, led the Party to encourage a further expansion of research on nationality questions. In particular, Soviet scholars were charged with the task of better explaining how social behavior was influenced by national identity. In the early 1970s exposure of Soviet scholars to Western ideas was further expanded, and as long as compatibility with Marxist-Leninist ideas could be preserved, it was now possible to integrate Western theories into Soviet analyses. As time went on, scholarship in this field became more sophisticated, but Soviet scholars had to support the Party's contentions that Soviet nationality relations were harmonious, and thus they downplayed the existence of the deep-rooted nationalist antagonisms that were to erupt in the late 1980s.

The literature on nationality relations written in the early 1980s already provides indications of disagreements among leading scholars as to what types of policies should be introduced to better integrate the non-Russian nationalities into the all-union economy and, more generally, the mainstream of Soviet life. The increasing economic difficulties that the Soviet Union was already experiencing during these years increased the urgency of the debate. As noted above, some claimed that the existence of the union republics was hampering Soviet economic development, and called for a redefinition of the Soviet federal system. Tadevosian's article "The Constitutional Basis of Soviet Statehood," which appeared in a brochure to commemorate the sixtieth anniversary of the USSR, is a defense of the Soviet federal system.

Tadevosian's essay details the various legal statuses provided for national communities, ranging from union republics for the fifteen largest nationalities to autonomous districts (okrugs) for some of the smaller groups. For the most part the article is quite typical of statements from the late Brezhnev period concerning nationality relations, from its stilted prose through its overly optimistic evaluation of the accomplishments of Soviet nationality policy in building an internationalist society.

The article details the various privileges that each constitutional status carries. Tadevosian conforms to the myth that constitutional rights are in fact legal rights, and thus he does not differentiate republic privileges that were intended as symbolic (such as the right of secession) from those that are quite real (such as the responsibility for insuring that the economic plan for the republic or region be fulfilled). Nonetheless, the article clearly shows how a constitutional crisis would occur if two republics were to claim the same territory, as is the case with Nagorno Karabakh. But certainly Tadevosian, at the time of writing this piece, would never have conceived of such a crisis occurring, because until the late 1980s union republics never attempted to exercise their symbolic powers.

Although it seems dated today, Tadevosian's article was considered controversial at the time of its publication on account of its discussion of the rights of minority nationalities. Tadevosian admits that the Party has been less than wholly successful in protecting the rights of the nonindigenous national minorities in a union republic, and his complaints about the underrepresentation of Russians in republic supreme soviets foreshadow Gorbachev's subsequent campaign to end "nationalist" practices in the awarding of Party and state positions in the non-Russian republics.

Moreover, the article helps one understand why Gorbachev sponsored constitutional revisions when he undertook the use of political reforms to transform the Soviet Union from a system run by administrative fiat to one with some legal basis. The 1977 constitution that is described by Tadevosian gave the republics a great deal of authority precisely because they were understood to be in fact totally dependent on Moscow. Once Gorbachev resolved to devolve some real authority to the republics he had to limit their constitutional powers, which he did through constitutional amendment in late 1988, to make clear that the law of the USSR must take precedence over that of its constituent republics. However, the Baltic republics are continuing to maintain that sovereignty rests with the republics themselves, and that if there is a conflict between the laws of the USSR and republic laws, it is the latter that should take precedence. The USSR Supreme Soviet has rejected this premise; but clearly the debate over republic sovereignty is only beginning.

Far more controversial were the pieces included here by Iulian Bromlei, who was director of the Institute of Ethnography of the USSR Academy of Sciences and head of the all-union scientific council for the study of nationality problems. Bromlei was the single most influential academic writing on the national question through the mid-1980s, and he managed to convince the Party leadership that ethnic communities would be an inevitable feature of Soviet life well into the future. Bromlei developed a theory of *ethnos* which postulated the existence of stable ethnic communities that could transcend class distinctions. Each ethnic community had distinct ethnic traits. According to Bromlei these traits would begin to converge over time, as socialist internationalist values became more deeply entrenched, but ethnic self-consciousness as a social-psychological category would continue. Thus Bromlei concluded that talk of the disappearance of national distinctions was premature, and that the Party should concentrate instead on learning to better deal with the political, economic, and social consequences of the unequal historical-development patterns of these national communities. Bromlei's conclusions made him quite unpopular with conservative Party ideologues, but with hindsight his warnings appear understated.

The first of the two selections by Bromlei reproduced here, "Ethnic Processes in the USSR," written in 1983, is characteristic of the interregnum period between Brezhnev and Gorbachev, because while the author implies that there are deficiencies in Soviet nationality policy, he does not elaborate upon what these might be. Nevertheless, the article paints a somber picture of the difficulties to be faced in moving toward an internationalist society. Bromlei states that all national communities, save for the smallest and most dispersed, have been able to perpetuate their ethnic distinctiveness. Moreover, Bromlei states, the cultural distinctions of nationalities are so well established that they affect the ways in which individuals think and behave, and these distinctions will continue to be passed on to subsequent generations even when the Soviet Union has become a wholly classless society. While he states that national differences will become less pronounced as interethnic integration increases, Bromlei implies that the consolidation or assimilation of the major national communities is not a viable option for the foreseeable future.

The second Bromlei article, "Improving National Relations in the USSR," from 1986, is intended to show the ways in which the statement on nationality relations in the new Party Program would lead to the further consolidation of the Soviet people. Bromlei's understanding of what is meant by the term *Soviet people* is somewhat different from Gorbachev's. In the excerpt from Gorbachev's report to the Twenty-seventh Party Congress reproduced in the preceding section of this book, Gorbachev states that "The Soviet people is a qualitatively new social and international community, cemented by the same economic interests, ideology, and political goals." Bromlei states that the Soviet people "is new in its social parameters: common cultural traits have developed that are characteristic of Soviet people of all nationalities." The Bromlei statement is vaguer, and speaks only of common cultural traits and not of the creation of a new community.

The remainder of the Bromlei article is a clearer-cut explanation of the Party Program, and shows how much ideological conformity is maintained even among proponents of "new thinking." Bromlei explains how the development of the union republic economies according to Moscow's guidelines will increase the cultural interdependence of nationalities; this, he claims, will occur through the infusion of technology, the industrialization of predominantly agricultural regions, and the rational utilization of underemployed labor resources both within and between republics. By following this economic agenda, he asserts, national communities will be able to continue the development of the positive features of their national cultures and restrict the negative ones.

However, the tone of Bromlei's statement quickly proved to be unreasonably optimistic. By 1987 the opposition of different national communities to features of the Party Program and Party policy more generally was increasing. As the situation in a number of national regions began to unravel, Gorbachev and other senior officials criticized scholars, such as Bromlei, for their earlier idealized descriptions of nationality relations, and pressed the scholars to explain how ethnicity could be depoliticized and ethnic conflict defused. Finally, in April 1989 Bromlei retired from his post at the Institute of Ethnography.

E. Bagramov's August 1987 *Pravda* essay reflects the new concerns of scholars. His article offers sharp criticism of the academic establishment for failing to provide concrete proposals on how to increase internationalist consciousness in general, as well as how specifically to mobilize citizens to work to accomplish all-union economic goals when these are seen as contrary to local national interests. He is particularly critical of those charged with the development of bilingualism in the union republics, as they have failed both to get non-Russians to master Russian and to get Russians to even begin to learn the language and respect the culture of the titular nationality of the republic in which they reside.

But Bagramov is as guilty as those he criticizes, as he is unable to move from criticism to offering concrete proposals as to how things might be improved. However, given the tremendous failure of nationality policy, as revealed by the rise of interethnic confrontation and the more general politicization of national minorities, it should not be surprising that Soviet scholars are at as great a loss as the policy makers. Social scientists are only as prescient as the analytic models they employ. The success of subsequent Soviet scholarship in predicting and solving social ills is directly linked to the degree to which scholars are compelled to restrict their analyses to the existing Marxist-Leninist framework. But the loosening of ideological restrictions will surely bring conclusions that Moscow will not like, as it is unlikely that the national problem can be ''solved'' without a substantial redefinition of the distribution of authority between Moscow and the periphery.

The Constitutional Basis of Soviet National Statehood *

E. V. TADEVOSIAN

The internationalist essence of the socialist statehood system does not mean that it is nonnational. Under conditions of socialism, international and national elements are not in conflict even in the area of statehood. The internationalism of Soviet socialist statehood necessarily includes consideration for nationally particular and nationally specific features in the organization, functioning, and development of the statehood of the various peoples. Precisely for this reason Soviet national statehood represents an integral unity of national and the international elements, with the international predominating. In a certain sense one may speak of this as a unity that is internationalist in content and national in form.

The national form of Soviet statehood finds the following expression. First of all, Soviet national statehood has been established along the lines of regions distinct in the national composition of the population settled on a given territory. Second, state bodies are composed primarily of members of the indigenous nationality or nationalities, while in cases where such nationalities do not constitute the majority of the population, they are secured by broad representation in such organs. Third, records management and all business in the purview of government and administrative organs in the national regions are conducted, as a rule, in the respective national languages, the languages of the majority of the population in particular regions, or simultaneously in two languages, especially in multinational areas. Fourth, government and administrative organs in various national regions possess certain peculiarities in structure. Fifth, special legislation has been passed defining the particular political and legal status of the respective autonomous state formations and reflecting their national and other specific features (the Law on Autonomous Oblasts, the Law on Autonomous Okrugs). Sixth, general laws (including the All-Union Principles of Legislation) and other governmental acts of the government of the Soviet federal state are applied with due regard for the special features of the national regions. Seventh, the Soviet national republics and the autonomous national state formations possess their special institution for representation in the organs of the integral federal state.

The national statehood of the peoples of the USSR may be defined as the political authority (statehood) exercised by the workers in areas of compact settlement by nations and nationalities of the USSR that is socialist, truly internationalist in content and essence, one in its common political foundation in the soviets, and

*60 let SSSR. Konstitutsiia SSSR—Osnovnoi zakon sovetskogo mnogonatsional'nogo gosudarstva (Moscow, 1982), pp. 42–59. Russian text © 1982 by "Znanie" Publishers.

varied in form. The expressly socialist and internationalist essence of Soviet national statehood is displayed in the fact that each and every form of national statehood in the USSR expresses and protects the will and the interests of workers of all nationalities, not only the titular nationality, of the given republic, oblast, or area. Soviet socialist national statehood serves not to divide workers national attributes, but to unite and consolidate them on a truly internationalist basis. In whatever republic a Soviet man might live, to whatever nation or nationality he might belong, everywhere without exception he is a citizen of the one Union of Soviet Socialist Republics, enjoying equal rights and obligations with everyone on the territory of any national republic or any other national state formation. This is clear proof of the internationalism of socialist democracy.

In the course of the historical development of the Soviet multinational state, the following basic forms of Soviet national statehood have evolved, secured in the Constitution of the USSR: (1) the union republic; (2) the autonomous republic; (3) the autonomous oblast; (4) the autonomous okrug. Let us examine briefly the constitutional status of each of these forms.

A **Union Republic**, as stated in the Constitution of the USSR, is a sovereign Soviet socialist state that has united with other Soviet republics in the Union of Soviet Socialist Republics. Outside the jurisdiction of the USSR, a union republic exercises independent state power on its territory. A union republic has its own Constitution, which conforms to the Constitution of the USSR and takes into account the specific features of the republic (Art. 76). The territory of a union republic may not be altered without its consent. A union republic independently determines its administrative-territorial structure (Art. 79). A union republic has the right to enter into relations with foreign states, conclude treaties with them and exchange diplomatic and consular representatives, and take part in the activities of international organizations (Art. 80). Every union republic retains the right of free secession from the USSR (Art. 72).

The sovereignty of the union republics as component parts of the USSR intrinsically distinguishes a soviet federation, as expressed by the USSR, from another form of a soviet federation, the RSFSR, which includes among its components autonomous Soviet national republics (ASSRs). In the USSR, the sovereignty of the Soviet Union and the sovereignty of its constituent union republics blend harmoniously, as a result, first of all, of the unity of the social order and the political and economic system in Soviet society, as well as of the coincidence of the fundamental interests of all the peoples of the USSR.

In the Soviet multinational state, the concordance between the statehood of the USSR and national statehood is to be observed in the fact that the creation and consolidation of the statehood of the USSR was and remains the paramount condition and the prime guarantee for the successful development and comprehensive enhancement of the national statehood of the republics. All union republics regard the consolidation of the unity and might of the USSR overall as the prime source of their own flourishing and of the strengthening of their own sovereignty. The sovereign rights of the union republics, as stated in Art. 81 of the Constitution of the USSR, are safeguarded by the USSR. In its turn the national Soviet statehood system serves as an important function in the consolidation of the social and internationalist unity of the Soviet people, in the strengthening of the statehood of the USSR and in the development of socialist democracy. A union republic, according to the Constitution of the USSR (Art. 77), facilitates the exercise of the powers of the USSR on its territory, and implements the decisions of the highest organs of state authority and administration of the USSR.

The 1977 Constitution of the USSR not only maintains and ensures the sovereign rights of the union republics, but even expands them and reinforces their guarantees. This is to be seen, first of all, in the fact that the union republics through their supreme organs of state authority have been granted the right of legislative initiative in the Supreme Soviet of the USSR (Art. 113).

Secondly, of great importance is the entrenchment in the Fundamental Law of the USSR of such a new constitutional right of union republics as the right of participation in decision-making by all-union organs in matters that come within the jurisdiction of the USSR. "A union republic," Art. 77 of the Constitution of the USSR states, "takes part in decision making in the Supreme Soviet of the USSR, the Presidium of the Supreme Soviet of the USSR, the Government of the USSR, and other organs of the Union of Soviet Socialist Republics in matters that come within the jurisdiction of the USSR." This right of union republics is guaranteed both by the very structure and by the operation of all-union organs of state authority and administration. Thus, the bicameral structure of the Supreme Soviet of the USSR, which consists of the Soviet of the Union and the Soviet of Nationalities, both sharing equal rights, makes sure that the economic plans, the budget and other laws passed reflect the general interests of all our country's peoples and the specific interests of the union republics. One should not forget to mention that the already established practice of forwarding all of the more important bills to the union republics for review guarantees their broad participation in the drafting of all-union legislation.

Third, for the first time it is set down in the Constitution of the USSR that a union republic ensures integrated economic and social development on its territory.

On matters that come within its jurisdiction, a union republic coordinates and controls the activity of enterprises, institutions and organizations subordinate to the Union (Art. 77). This eliminates certain difficulties in the interrelations between republican organs on the one hand and enterprises, institutions, and organizations subordinated to the union on the other, enhancing the role of union republics in harmonizing the sectoral and territorial aspects of management, and at the same time increases their responsibility for the further systematic and balanced development of our country's economy.

Fourth, in accordance with Art. 114, the union republics have gained the right of submission to the Supreme Soviet of the USSR or the Presidium of the Supreme Soviet of the USSR of proposals for countrywide discussion of bills and other very important matters of state.

Fifth, the extension of the union republics' jurisdiction is also to be seen in the way the jurisdiction of the USSR and its organs, on the one hand, and the jurisdiction of the union republics and their organs on the other are defined in the Constitution of the USSR (articles 73, 76, 121, 131, 137, 142, etc.). By entrusting responsibility for the most important strategic matters as well as direct management of the most crucial areas of public life to Union organs, the Constitution of the USSR allows the republics and local organs to concentrate their work on those problems whose concrete solution is impossible from one center, without proper knowledge of nationality-related and other local conditions and peculiarities. Another case in point that may serve as an example is the division of jurisdiction in the legislative realm.

As was already mentioned, the Constitution of the USSR takes as a point of departure the necessity to ensure the unity of legislative norms throughout the territory of the USSR, reserving this authority to the USSR (Art. 73). But how is this unity to be achieved? The wide-ranging, vigorous legislative activities of the Supreme Soviet of the USSR over the past decade, and in particular the adoption of the Principles of Legislation of the USSR and the Union Republics, not only did not curb, not to say stifle, initiative or vitality of the legislative activities of the union republics' supreme soviets in a variety of areas, but, in fact, stimulated them considerably. In the republics it was precisely during this period that the republican legislation underwent extensive revisions, reflecting the historical, economic-geographical, national, and other features typical of each union republic.

The promulgation of republican legal norms does not contradict the interests of all-union centralized decision making in those problem-areas that require uniform regulation countrywide, for it renders concrete, amplifies and further develops all-union statutes in conformity with local conditions and thus facilitates their implementation. This clearly illustrates the unity and harmonious interrelation between international and national elements in Soviet legislation.

The extensive, genuine rights enjoyed by the union republics within the Soviet federation are further exemplified by the fact that the union republican budgets constitute 42% of the State Budget of the USSR. Through the state budgets of the union republics are financed more than two-fifths of all state expenditures on the economy and about two-thirds of the outlays for sociocultural purposes.[1]

All this is evidence that an enhancement of the national statehood of the republics has been and is proceeding not by way of a mechanical, one-sided, uninterrupted either expansion or constriction of the republics' rights independently of the development of the statehood of the USSR but rather on the basis of a proper blending of the national and the international, and a harmonious unity of national statehood and statehood of the USSR with the latter predominating. As can be seen from experience, an extension of the republics' rights in some spheres may and in fact does take place concurrently with an expansion in the role played by the statehood of the USSR and an extension of the rights of the USSR in other areas, in matters of state or economic life.

The interests of a proper blending of all-union and republican principles, of internationalist and national features in organizing state, economic and sociocultural life are also served by the union-republic form of administration. All-union ministries of the USSR direct the branches of administration entrusted to them throughout the territory of the USSR, directly or through organs created by them. Union-republic ministries of the USSR direct the branches of administration entrusted to them, as a rule, through the respective ministries and other organs of union republics, and directly administer individual enterprises and associations, as well as other organizations and institutions of their branches which are of Union subordination.

The expansion and deepening of the unity and interaction of union statehood and the national statehood of the republics can be observed in the expansion of those spheres exclusively under all-union jurisdiction, as well as in the increase of organs under joint union–republican jurisdiction in matters of state administration. In mid-1978, when the Law "On the Council of Ministers of the USSR" was adopted in our country, there were 38 all-union ministries and state committees of the USSR and 42 union-republican ministries and state committees of the USSR.[3] In subsequent years, a whole series of new ministries and state committees of the USSR were formed, both all-union and union-republic.[4]

An important place within the national-state structure of the USSR belongs to the autonomous forms of Soviet national statehood. In contrast to the 1936 Constitution of the USSR, the new Constitution of the USSR devotes these national-state forms considerably more attention. It provides for the drafting and adoption by the union republican Supreme Soviets of a special Law on Autonomous Regions and a Law on Autonomous Areas, which are intended to define in detail the political-legal status of each of these national-state formations. All this reflects the growing role and importance of Soviet autonomy at the present stage and facilitates the further enhancement of the work of its organs.

Variety and flexibility of forms is a characteristic feature of Soviet national-state development, one that makes it possible to take into account the concrete conditions and distinctive features of various peoples and to ensure the optimal politico-legal conditions for their development. The variety of forms that Soviet national statehood has assumed was historically determined by differences in the levels of socioeconomic, political, and cultural development in the several national regions, differences in population size, the size of territory, and geographical location, the levels of class stratification within the population and formation of a national working class, in the degree of national consolidation and the development of national self-consciousness in the nature and complexity of internationality relations, in the national composition of the population and its settlement patterns, etc. The selection of one or another form of national Soviet statehood was always grounded in the free expression of the will of a nation or nationality, with due consideration for the conditions and interests of development of both the given people and our multinational state as a whole.

An **Autonomous Soviet Socialist Republic** is a national Soviet socialist state that is a constituent part of a union republic, and which, in spheres not within the jurisdiction of the USSR and the union republic, independently decides matters within its jurisdiction. The territory of an autonomous republic may not be altered without its consent (Art. 84). Exclusively within the jurisdiction of the Supreme Soviet of an ASSR are the following: adoption of the Constitution of the ASSR and its amendment; endorsement of state plans for economic and social development, and the autonomous republic's state budget; the formation of organs accountable to it (Art. 143).

The Constitution of the USSR ensures the further expansion of the autonomous republics' rights. Thus, according to Art. 83 of the Fundamental Law of the USSR, an ASSR takes part in decision making in matters that come within the jurisdiction of the USSR and the union republics, through the supreme organs of state authority and administration of the USSR and of the union republic respectively. A number of representatives of the autonomous republics are members of the Presidium of the Supreme Soviet of the USSR. By tradition, the Chairman of the Presidium of the Supreme Soviet of an ASSR is a member of the Presidium of the Supreme Soviet of the union republic in the capacity of Deputy Chairman. The Constitution of the RSFSR—a Soviet federation based on the principles of autonomy—stipulates, for example, that to the Presidium of the Supreme Soviet of the RSFSR are to be elected seventeen Deputy Chairmen, including one from each of the republic's sixteen ASSRs. The Constitution of the Georgian SSR also contains a provision that from each of the two ASSRs within Georgia there be one Deputy Chairman in the Presidium of that union republic's Supreme Soviet.

Exceptionally important is the fact that, according to the new Constitution of the USSR, an ASSR shall ensure integrated economic and social development on its territory, facilitate the exercise of the powers of the USSR and the union republic on its territory, implement the decisions of the highest organs of state authority and administration of the USSR and the union republic. In matters within its jurisdiction an autonomous republic coordinates and controls the activity of enterprises, institutions, and organizations of all-union or republican (union republic) subordination. All this, without any doubt, broadens considerably the legal basis underlying the work conducted by organs of an ASSR and increases their responsibilities for the implementation of the comprehensive and harmonious development of the economy and sociocultural construction.

Of the twenty autonomous republics in our country, sixteen are in the Russian Soviet Federative Socialist Republic (RSFSR), one in the Uzbek, two in the Georgian, and one in the Azerbaidzhani union republics. The population size of the autonomous republics (according to 1979 data) ranges from 237,000 to almost four million, and the territory from 3,000 sq. km to over 3,000,000 sq. km.

An **Autonomous Oblast** is a Soviet socialist national state formation that is part of a union republic or a territory [krai]. In contrast to the ASSRs, autonomous oblasts are not states and enjoy administrative-political but not state political autonomy, with a correspondingly narrower range of rights. At the same time, an autonomous oblast, like an autonomous okrug, differs essentially from an ordinary administrative oblast or raion, for it embodies the sovereign will of a nation or nationality and expresses its self-determination. In accordance with the Constitution of the USSR, the supreme soviets of those union republics that include autonomous oblasts shall adopt, upon the recommendation of the soviets of people's deputies of the autonomous oblasts, a special Law on Autonomous Regions (Art. 86). All this renders the autonomous oblast, as well as the autonomous okrug, a form of national statehood and provides for somewhat broader jurisdiction to be exercised by an autonomous oblast (or autonomous okrug) in comparison with an administrative oblast (or raion). Thus all autonomous oblasts enjoy their separate representation in the Soviet of Nationalities of the Supreme Soviet of the USSR. Autonomous oblasts are also represented in the organs of the union republics and territories of which they are a part. Ratification of the formation of autonomous oblasts is within the jurisdiction of the Supreme Soviet of the USSR. The acts promulgated by state organs of an autonomous oblast possess special legal force and cannot be rescinded by the corresponding higher organs of a territory. An autonomous oblast itself determines the administrative-territorial division of its territory, subject to subsequent confirmation by the Presidium of the Supreme Soviet of the union republic. The organs of state authority and administration of an autonomous oblast are guaranteed the right to treat with the organs of state authority and administration of the union republic either through the territorial [*krai*] organs or directly (see Art. 83 of the 1978 Constitution of the RSFSR.)

In the USSR, autonomous oblasts total eight including five in the RSFSR, and one each in the Georgian, Azerbaidzhani, and Tadzhik union republics. The autonomous oblasts' population size ranges from 100,000 to 500,000, and their territories from 4,000 to 93,000 sq. km.

An **Autonomous Okrug** is a Soviet socialist national-state formation that is a constituent part of a territory or oblast, and represents a form of national statehood for our country's small nationalities. By the end of the 1920s only one national (autonomous) area had been created in the USSR. Most of the national (autonomous) areas were formed in the 1930s on the basis of a resolution passed by the Presidium of the All-Union Central Executive Committee on December 10, 1930, "On the Organization of National Associations in Areas of Settlement by the Small Peoples of the North." In 1937 there were already nine national areas in the country while at the present time there are ten. All are situated on the territory of the RSFSR. The size of their population ranges from 16,000 to 569,000, and their area ranges from 19,000 to 860,000 sq. km. A number of the autonomous okrugs exceed in population many of the autonomous oblasts, and even some autonomous republics, while in area the autonomous okrugs are, as a rule, larger than autonomous oblasts and ASSRs.

In accordance with the new Constitution of the USSR, national areas have been renamed autonomous okrugs. This underscores the growing role of the national-territorial areas within the national-state system of the USSR and an enhancement of the scope of their authority toward closer approximation of other forms of Soviet autonomy. It is quite significant, in this connection, that the new Constitution of the

USSR stipulates the promulgation not of a Regulation on National Districts, but a Law on Autonomous Districts, to be adopted by the Supreme Soviet of a union republic (Art. 88). In the RSFSR this law was adopted in 1980.

At the Seventh (Extraordinary) session of the Supreme Soviet of the USSR, in the course of discussion of the draft Constitution of the USSR, deputy L. G. Tynel', chairman of the Executive Committee of the Chukchi Autonomous District and member of the Presidium of the Supreme Soviet of the USSR, stated:

> The torch of a new life, lit by the great October, was brought to the Far Northeast by emissaries of the party of Lenin in 1919. Every step, every day of the short but ultimately immortal activity of the first Revolutionary Committee of Chukotka became filled with the spirit of October and the spirit of internationalism. From the first days of Soviet power, the small peoples of the North have always been aware of the enormous concern and assistance rendered us by the entire Soviet people. Even now, emissaries from all the fraternal republics of our country are taking part in the transformation of our territory. Allow me to express from this lofty rostrum words of deep appreciation to the great Russian people and to the peoples of all republics of our Fatherland for their enormous contribution to the development of the economy and culture of Chukotka.[5]

Remarkable new prospects for the peoples of the North are envisioned by the resolution adopted in February 1980 by the Central Committee of the CPSU and the Council of Ministers of the USSR, "Measures for the Further Economic and Social Development of the Areas of Settlement by Peoples of the North." After noting that in the wake of the consistent implementation of the Leninist nationality policy dozens of nationalities of the North achieved considerable success in the development of their economies and cultures, the Central Committee of the CPSU and the Council of Ministers of the USSR outlined for the period 1980–1990 a whole series of measures, encompassing the further integrated development of the economy; raising the quality of leadership to oversee economic and cultural development; the development of various branches of industry, national arts and crafts, and reindeer breeding; a comprehensive settlements construction program; and the enlistment of industrial enterprises and organizations for the task of building up rural settlements. The Central Committee of the CPSU and the Council of Ministers of the USSR regard the further development of the economy and culture in areas settled by the peoples of the North as an important state concern.[6]

All this disproves utterly the lies and fabrications concocted by anticommunists trying to misrepresent matters to make it seem that socialism and those forms of Soviet autonomy to which it gave birth ignore the interests of non-Russian nationalities, especially the small peoples, and lead to a "denationalization" of social life. Soviet autonomy has brought about a true rebirth of people, large and small, and their all-embracing and much accelerated progress. It has preserved many peoples from extinction and was successful in finding ways that they could accept a transition from their primitive communal system to socialism, bypassing several intermediate stages. Important to this process were such forms of Soviet state authority specific to the North as clan soviets, which were replaced by national nomadic soviets and in turn, finally, by territorial—rural and village—soviets.

The outstanding achievements realized by Soviet nations and nationalities on the foundations of Soviet autonomy are striking confirmation the vast potential these forms of national state structure represent. Our current task is to make full use of the potential inherent in the various forms of Soviet national statehood, and on that basis to allow all of our nations and nationalities, all the republics, autonomous oblasts and areas, to make their greatest possible contribution toward the further strengthening of the might of our common Motherland—the Union of Soviet Socialist Republics.

Our successful solution of the national question, and our achievement of ever closer unity, comprehensive flourishing and unremitting convergence of Soviet nations and nationalities does not mean, nevertheless, that all problems relating to national relations in our country have been already solved. As was noted at the Twenty-sixth Congress of the CPSU, the dynamics of development in a huge multinational state like ours gives rise to not a few problems requiring the Party's close attention. Among such comparatively new and important problems is how to achieve a fuller reflection of the internationalist essence of socialist statehood in the organizational and functional forms of Soviet national statehood, and to this the Twenty-sixth Congress of the CPSU gave serious consideration.

The significance and relevance of finding a solution to this problem under current conditions stems from the fact that in the course of building communism the internationality and interrepublican mobility of the population naturally intensifies. This is the result of several factors. Major changes are taking place in the location of the country's productive forces. New territories are developed, in the first instance in the East. Vast territorial industrial complexes are being created (such complexes as, for example, the Western Siberian, the Pavlodar-Ekibastuz, the southern Yakutian, the Saian, the Bratsk–Ust'-Ilimsk, the Karatau-Dzhambul, the Mangyshlak, the southern Tadzhikistan, etc.). Major unionwide economic tasks are undertaken by the combined efforts of all the republics (for example, the opening of virgin lands, the construction of the Baikal–Amur railroad, the melioration of the non–black-earth zones of the RSFSR). The socialist division of labor among the republics is deepening and the specialization of their economies increasing. The transportation system is constantly expanding. And there are other factors. It is indicative that in the nine years between the last two all-union censuses of 1970 and 1979, the population of Siberian and Far Eastern territories increased by 11%—and in Tiumen' Oblast 34%, in Magadan and Kamchatka oblasts 32%, and in the Yakut ASSR 25%—while overall the population of the RSFSR during this period grew by 6%. It is also interesting that the population of the ten autonomous okrugs located in the north and east of the RSFSR increased by 38% during this period.[7]

In the report of the Central Committee of the CPSU to the Twenty-sixth Party Congress, L. I. Brezhnev, noting that there is an excess of labor in Central Asia and some areas of the Caucasus, especially in the countryside, called for a "more active recruitment of the population from these areas for the development of our country's new territories."[8]

The populations of our republics are multinational in composition. Suffice it to say that, according to the 1979 all-union population census, in ten of the fifteen union republics members of nonindigenous nationalities constituted more than one-fourth of the republic's total population and in two of these republics, Kazakhstan and Kirghizia, they exceeded half the population. As to the twenty autonomous republics, in most of them the nonindigenous population forms more than half of the total population. Thus, in early 1979 the population of the Kazakh SSR included: Kazakhs—36%, Russians—40.8%, Ukrainians—6.1%, Tatars—2.1%, Uzbeks—1.8%, Belorussians—1.2%, Uighurs—1%, Koreans—0.6%, Azerbaidzhanis—0.5%, Dungans—0.2%, and other nationalities—9.7%. In Kirghizia, the Kirghiz formed 47.9%, Russians—25.9%, Uzbeks—12.1%, Ukrainians—3.1%, Tatars—2%, Uighurs—0.8%, Kazakhs—0.8%, Tadzhiks—0.7%, and other nationalities—6.7%. In Georgia the Georgians constituted 68.8%, Ossetians—3.2%, Abkhaz—1.7%, Armenians—9%, Russians—7.4%, Azerbaidzhanis—5.1%, Greeks—1.9%, Ukrainians—0.9%, and other nationalities—2%. In Latvia the Latvians formed 53.7%, Russians—32.8%, Belorussians—4.5%, Ukrainians—2.7%, Poles—2.5%, Lithuanians—1.5%, Jews—1.1%, and other nationalities—1.2%.[9]

The growth in national heterogeneity among the populations of the Soviet national republics and the considerable increase in the number of citizens belonging to nonindigenous nationalities in a number of republics poses in all its magnitude the problem: how to give fuller and more comprehensive consideration to and how to satisfy their specific interests and needs (including an increase in their representation in Party and state organs of these republics) under conditions of further development of socialist democracy for all the people. In this connection, L. I. Brezhnev said at the Congress: "The population of Soviet republics is multinational in composition. It is natural that all nations have the right to proper representation in their party and state organs—of course, with due consideration of each person's professional and ideological-moral qualities. In recent years there has been a considerable increase in the number of citizens belonging to nonindigenous nationalities in a number of republics. They have their own specific needs in such areas as language, culture, and everyday life. The Central Committees of the communist parties of the union republics, the krai and the oblast committees must delve more deeply into such problems and in due coruse propose ways for solving with them."[10]

The growth of national heterogeneity in the populations of the Soviet republics is naturally leading, and will continue even more, to a broadening of the of nonindigenous nationalities' representation within the organs of authority and administration in these republics and to a further internationalization of their composition. In this is to be seen one of the main tendencies in the internationalization of the very national forms of Soviet statehood of the peoples of the USSR.

It is imperative to point out that even today the national composition of state and party organs in the republics is multinational. Thus, in the tenth Supreme Soviet of the Estonian SSR, elected in 1980, there were among its 285 deputies 209 Estonians, 63 Russians, six Ukrainians, five Belorussians, one Latvian, and one Pole.[11] Among the 440 deputies of the Supreme Soviet of the Georgian SSR there were 351 Georgians, 30 Russians, 17 Armenians, 15 Abkhaz, 10 Azerbaidzhanis, nine Ossetians, and two Ukrainians.[12] The membership of the Central Committee of the Communist Party of Kirghizia included more than 50% Kirghiz, 28% Russian, about 6% Ukrainian, and about 2.5% Uzbek.[13]

As a rule, the national composition of party and state organs in the national republics and oblasts reflects more or less adequately the national composition of their populations. There have been instances, however, where the proper representation of nonindigenous nationalities in the relevant local organs did not receive its due regard; the representation of some nonindigenous nationalities in these organs has been several times less than their proportion in the republic's or region's population. The pertinence and significance of this problem as posed at the Twenty-sixth Congress of the CPSU is evidenced by the fact that Russians, who as a rule, of course, constitute the most substantial share of the nonindigenous population in the fourteen union republics (excluding the RSFSR), and represent 20% of their aggregate population, constitute only 11% of the deputies to the local soviets of people's deputies of these republics.[14]

The Leninist principle of recruitment and promotion of cadres according to their professional, political and ideological-moral qualities is an internationalist one in its basic premises and its very essence. But it would be incorrect to interpret it to imply a rejection of any consideration to national elements in the life of society and the state, including the national structure and national composition of the population included. Lenin viewed the national composition of the population as one of the most important economic factors, although he stressed the need to struggle against a nationalistic absolutizing of this factor and emphasized that it is not the only one, nor the most important among others.[15]

It is clear that a situation which allows for an unjustifiably great overrepresentation of the indigenous nationality at the expense of nonindigenous nationalities (for example, when the indigenous nationality constitutes significantly less than half the population, but significantly more than half, two-thirds, of the deputies) cannot create optimum conditions for the careful consideration and satisfaction of the specific needs of citizens belonging to the nonindigenous nationalities in such areas as language, culture, and everyday life. Therefore the fulfillment of the tasks advanced by the Twenty-sixth Congress of the CPSU in this realm, among others, will play an extremely important role in the further enhancement of scientific management of nationality processes in our country and in the consolidation of the internationalist unity and solidarity of our multinational Soviet society.

> The Party closely follows the new processes and problems which constantly arise in the sphere of nationality relations in the course of development of such a large multinational state as ours to make sure they find full and prompt reflection in the work of Party, soviet, trade-union and Komsomol organizations, and in economic

organs. The correct means to achieve this end lie in the strict observance of scientific principles of leadership, a Leninist style of work, and a Leninist cadres policy.[16]

Closely connected with the growing multinational heterogeneity in the membership of organs of Soviet national statehood is another trend promoting its internationalization—the more extensive use in the work of these organs, alongside the national languages, of Russian as the common language of brotherhood and cooperation among the nationalities and as the second mother tongue of a significant portion of the non-Russian population in the USSR. This is the result, in the first instance, of the ever more extensive and deeper knowledge of by members of the non-Russian nationalities. According to the 1979[a] all-union census data, Russian was declared as their native language by 59% of the country's total population or 153.5 million persons (1970 census: 141.8 million), of them 137.2 million Russians and 16.3 million (1970 census: 13 million) members of other nationalities. Fluency in Russian as either a native or a second language was reported by 77.6 million non-Russians (for 16.3 million as their mother tongue and 61.3 million as a second language), or 62% of the non-Russian population of the USSR (in 1970, 54.8 million or 49%).[17] Today 82% of the country's total population is fluent in Russian.[18] Under these circumstances, it is only natural that the practice of having the organs of Soviet national statehood conduct their business in two or sometimes even three languages should be becoming ever more widespread, as well as a corresponding practice in the publication of official documents, newspapers and literature, in radio and television broadcasting, etc. These, too, are not unimportant factors and indicators of the manifest internationalization that marks the life of the peoples of the USSR, including their statehood.

An important factor promoting the further internationalization of Soviet national statehood is the ever-growing number and proportion of workers serving its organs. Thus, the share of workers among the deputies to the soviets of the autonomous oblasts grew as follows: 1969—35.0%; 1971—37.6%; 1975—40.1%; 1980—47.8%, while the share of workers among the deputies to the soviets of the autonomous districts was, respectively, 37.6%, 41.8%, 46.6% and 47.2%.[18] Among the members of the executive committees of the soviets of peoples' deputies in the five autonomous oblasts of the RSFSR elected in 1980 workers constituted 33.5%, and among members of the executive committees of the soviets of peoples' deputies in the ten autonomous districts—38.2%.[19]

Another most important factor working toward this end is the numerical increase among Communists, the expansion of the leading role of the CPSU and its nationality cohorts, and the growing representation of CPSU members and candidate members on state organs of the national republics and oblasts. Under conditions of developed socialism, the more rapid numerical growth of many national cohorts in the Communist Party of the Soviet Union has continued. Thus with an overall numerical increase in CPSU membership between 1966 and 1981 of 40%, the respective figures for the communist parties of the Ukrainian SSR, Tadzhikistan,

Armenia, Turkmenia, and Azerbaidzhan were 50 to 56%, in Estonia and Latvia—65%, and in Uzbekistan, Belorussia, Moldavia and Lithuania from 70 to 82%.[21] CPSU members and candidate members consistently account for two-thirds of the deputies to the Supreme Soviets in the union and autonomous republics, and over half of the deputies to the soviets in the autonomous oblasts and autonomous districts. On the executive committees of the soviets of people's deputies in the autonomous oblasts and automous districts elected in 1980 CPSU members and candidate members formed 92.7% and 90.3%, respectively.[22] Communists account for 90.3% of all members of the Presidiums of the Supreme Soviets of the union republics, and 85.7% of the members of the Presidiums of the Supreme Soviets of the autonomous republics.[23]

Such, then, are the main trends and operative factors in the ongoing internationalization of Soviet national statehood—one of the most important tendencies which characterize the development of the statehood of the nations and nationalities of the USSR at the stage of developed socialism.

Editors' note

a. The Russian original has 1970, but obviously the census of 1979 is meant.

Notes

1. *Obrazovanie i razvitie Soiuza Sovetskikh Sotsialisticheskikh Respublik. Sbornik dokumentov*, Moscow, 1973, p. 263.
2. Calculated on the basis of the following: V. F. Garbuzov, *O Gosudarstvennom biudzhete SSSR na 1981 god i ob ispolnenii Gosudarstvennogo biudzheta SSSR za 1979 god*, Moscow, 1980, pp. 6, 22, 27.
3. See *Vedomosti Verkhovnogo Soveta SSSR*, 1978, no. 28, p. 436.
4. Created, for example, were: the all-union USSR Ministry of Construction in the Far East and the Transbaikal Regions, and the USSR Ministry of Mineral Fertilizer Production, and the union–republican USSR Ministry of the Fruit and Vegetable Industry, and the USSR State Committee for the Supply of Petroleum Products. In addition, the USSR Ministry of the Timber and Wood Processing Industry and the USSR Ministry of Pulp and Paper Industry were combined into one union–republican USSR Ministry of the Timber, Pulp and Paper, and Wood Processing Industry.
5. *Izvestiia*, 7 October 1977.
6. See *KPSS v rezoliutsiiakh i resheniiakh s"ezdov, konferentsii i plenumov TsK*, 8th ed., vol. 13, Moscow, 1980, pp. 568–577.
7. See *Vestnik statistiki*, 1980, no. 2, pp. 4–5.
8. *Materialy XXVI s"ezda KPSS*, p. 54.
9. See *Naselenie SSSR*, Moscow, 1980, pp. 28–30.
10. *Materialy XXVI s"ezda KPSS*, pp. 56–57.
11. See *Verkhovnyi Sovet Estonskoi SSR. Desiatyi sozyv.* Tallinn, 1981, p. 8.
12. See *Narodnoe khoziaistvo Gruzinskoi SSR za 60 let. Iubileinyi statisticheskii ezhegodnik*, Tbilisi, 1980, p. 31.
13. See T. U. Usubaliev, *Rukovodiashchaia rol' KPSS v ukreplenii edinstva internatsional'nogo i natsional'nogo v sovetskom obraze zhizni*, Frunze, 1981, p. 53.
14. Calculated on the basis of the following: *Naselenie SSSR*, pp. 23, 27; *Itogi vyborov i sostav deputatov mestnykh Sovetov narodnykh deputatov, 1980*, Moscow, 1980, p. 26; *Itogi*

vyborov i sostav deputatov mestykh Sovetov narodnykh deputatov RSFSR, 1980, Moscow, 1980, p. 30.

15. See V. I. Lenin, *Polnoe sobranie sochinenii*, vol. 24, p. 149.

16. *O 60-i godovshchine obrazovaniia Soiuza Sovetskikh Sotsialisticheskikh Respublik*, p. 18.

17. See *Naselenie SSSR*, Moscow, 1980, pp. 26–27; *Vestnik statistiki*, 1980, no. 3, p. 8.

18. See *Pravda*, 21 February 1982.

19. See *Itogi vyborov i sostav deputatov mestnykh Sovetov*, 1969, 1971, 1975, 1980; pp. 78, 79, 88; 76, 77, 88; 78, 79, 89; 80, 81, 91.

20. See *Itogi vyborov i sostav deputatov mestnykh Sovetov narodnykh deputatov RSFSR, 1980g.*, Moscow, 1980, p. 113.

21. Calculated on the basis of the following: *Partiinaia zhizn'*, 1981, no. 14, pp. 13–14.

22. See *Itogi vyborov i sostav deputatov mestnykh Sovetov narodnykh deputatov, 1980g.*, pp. 198–199.

23. See *Itogi vyborov i sostav deputatov Verkhovnykh Sovetov soiuznykh i avtonomnykh respublik 1980 g.*, pp. 64–65, 68–69.

Ethnic Processes in the USSR *

Iu. V. BROMLEI

Ethnic traits are among the features that define nationality. By these we mean all that is specific to particular nationalities, manifested, first of all, in everyday culture, customs, and norms of behavior, but also in distinct mentalities, and particularly value systems. Ethnic features are also necessarily manifested in consciousness.

In focusing on the ethnic aspect of nationality processes one must always keep in mind its organic link with socioeconomic factors. In other words, in viewing national communities and national processes, we may distinguish tentatively two basic aspects—the ethnic and the socioeconomic, although it must be recognized of course, that in ethnosocial processes the socioeconomic base plays the determining role.

A direct focus on the ethnic aspects enables us to probe more deeply into the essence of nationality, in the first instance by providing an unobstructed view of the specific nature of culture and the ways of life of particular peoples which, as is well known, are marked by great stability. But even as we make a distinction between the two aspects of nationality (the socioeconomic and the ethnic proper), we must still study them with reference to their interconnection and interaction. On the whole, under conditions created in the course of building socialism, there takes place a leveling of peoples' social structures—the result of a growing convergence [*sblizhenie*] in the relative weight of the main social groups within their respective populations and the provision of opportunities for more rapid social development of peoples that in the past had a comparatively high share of unskilled workers. Particularly important in this respect was the creation of an indigenous working class in all the republics. Over the years of Soviet rule, there also evolved in the republics an indigenous intelligentsia; while at first this was mainly an artistic and administrative intelligentsia and an intelligentsia of mass professionals (doctors, teachers), in the postwar years there was a rapid growth of an intelligentsia engaged in engineering, scholarship, and most importantly, science and technology. And whereas in the late 1930s white- and blue-collar workers were the numerically dominant group only among the Russians, in 1970 they predominated among all the union-republic titular nationalities except for the Turkmens and Moldavians, and in 1979, among all of them without exception. The growing social homogeneity of nations was also manifested in the increasing convergence of their educational levels.

While in the prewar period all this was manifested primarily in the creation of a uniform class structure among our nations, once such a structure came into being it

Kommunist, 1983, no. 5, pp. 56–64. Russian text © 1983 by "Pravda" Publishers.

53

became increasingly important to enrich it—to boost the role of skilled labor and expand the range of professions to meet the needs of current levels of scientific-technical progress. The rapidity of social change taking place in our own times is clearly evidenced by a comparison of the generations of fathers and sons, on the basis of data obtained in recent years in the course of interrepublican ethnosociological surveys. In this respect, materials relating to Estonia are most revealing. The generation of "grandfathers," who had only an elementary education, was engaged mainly in unskilled labor (63% in rural areas and 56% in the cities). In the younger generation, only 19% in the urban and 30% in the rural areas were engaged in such work, and if we consider only their working children, they (the third generation) have virtually all shifted to skilled labor (only 2% of the urban and 10% of the rural members of this generation are engaged in unskilled labor).

The growing social homogeneity under conditions of developed socialism finds clear expression in the transformation of the Soviet state into a socialist state of all the people—a fact fixed in the Constitution of the USSR. At the present time, the process of convergence of all classes and social groups in Soviet society continues, leading to the formation of its classless structure, which in its main and fundamental features will be achieved within the historical time frame of mature socialism.

But social differences still remain, even on a territorial basis. For example, in 1979 workers in the Kazakh SSR constituted 68% of the total population, while in the Turkmen SSR they constituted 44%. These differences appear even more marked if we consider only the workers belonging to the titular nationalities as a percentage of the populations of their respective union republics. It was for this very reason that Comrade Iu. V. Andropov, in his address "Sixty Years of the USSR," noted particularly that in some union republics "the titular nationality should find fuller representation in the working class."

National features are stably preserved among our country's peoples in the realm of the family. Attitudes, the extent of participation by women and younger family members in deciding important family matters, the division of household responsibilities—all these vary. This gives rise to social problems of no small importance. It has been found that there is an inverse relationship between family size and the number of children on the one hand and the participation of women in skilled labor on the other. According to the 1979 census, the proportion of women in employment is lowest in the Central Asian republics where the families are the largest. In the Baltic region, where the number of children per family is smallest, the rate of employment is highest.

Concentration on the ethnic aspects in current nationality processes has led in recent years to a growing interest in their ethnodemographic parameters, particularly the dynamics of population change among the various nationalities. The relative weight of different peoples in the population has not remained constant. This can be attributed, first of all, to differences in their rates of natural increase. Thus, over the twenty-year period between the 1959 and 1979 censuses, the population of our country's southeastern regions increased by 75–100% or even more, while in the other regions the increase was 10–25% and sometimes even less. The peoples of the

Central Asian republics, many of whom were on the verge of (physical) extinction before the Revolution, today show rates of natural population increase that are among the highest in the world (3–3.5% per year). As a result, the share of Slavic-speaking peoples in the population has decreased from 77.1% in 1959 to 72.8% in 1979, while the share of peoples belonging to the Turkic linguistic group has risen correspondingly from 11.1% to 15.2%.

All this is inextricably linked to ethnodemographic aspects of the reproduction of labor resources—a labor surplus in some regions, a shortage in others. This in turn makes the ethnic aspects of demographic policy especially urgent today. Specifically, raising the allowance benefits for a second and third child may have a certain impact on increasing the birth rate of those peoples among whom it is at present particularly low. At the Twenty-sixth Congress it was especially noted that "provisions will be made for raising allowances for children, especially in connection with the birth of a second and third child." This proposition found confirmation in appropriate legislation. Of course, these are only the first steps.

In connection with studies conducted on the ethnic aspects of the problems involving labor resources, questions have been raised about the role of different traditions of work among the nationalities. If the approach were skillful and flexible, taking these traditions into account could be helpful for the allocation, development and organization of production.

Traditions play a vital role in population migrations, the optimization of which is also important for regulating manpower utilization. In this connection, it has been noted in particular that in Central Asia the mobility of the population, including the rural population, is retarded by traditions of large families and strong ties of kinship—that is, by ethnic factors.

At the same time, population migrations are an important factor in the shifting population balances among nationalities in our country's various regions. Specifically, they are responsible in large measure for the increasingly multinational and polyethnic composition of the republics. The dimensions of this process are enormous. Thus in 1979, the number of inhabitants in the union and autonomous republics who were not members of the respective titular nationalities already reached 55 million, or over 20 percent of all the inhabitants of our country. Thus, as a result, in every union republic there live today representatives of many nonindigenous nationalities, with their particular concerns in the areas of language, culture, and everyday life.

At the same time, we may observe a certain unevenness in the growth of national heterogeneity in the republics. In the period between the 1959 and 1979 censuses the number of Russians living outside the RSFSR grew by 7.6 million, but in some republics (mainly those in the south) they were a diminishing presence in relative terms or even in absolute numbers.

Ethnic processes are vitally affected by ethnic consolidation, ethnic assimilation, and interethnic integration.

By ethnic consolidation what is usually meant is the fusion of several linguistically and culturally kindred ethnic entities, most frequently so-called ethnographic groups (subethnoses) within already existing nations and nationalities. Ethnic assimilation refers to the processes of dissolution of particular groups (or individual members) of one people within another. It is essential to distinguish between forced and natural assimilation. That the former is negative in character is universally accepted. Natural assimilation, however, under conditions prevailing in multinational and polyethnic countries with no barriers to close contacts among peoples, is to a certain extent inevitable. Its progressive character even under the condition of capitalism was especially noted by V. I. Lenin, who stressed that "no one who has not sunk into the mire of nationalist prejudices can fail to perceive that this process of assimilation of nations by capitalism means the greatest historical progress" [*Polnoe Sobranie Sochinenii*, vol. 24, p. 127].

Interethnic integration denotes the appearance of common traits of culture and consciousness among several ethnoses,^a or peoples, but, in contrast to assimilation, without leading to absorption of some ethnic groups by others. At the same time, as evidenced by history, interethnic commonalities usually precede the merger of the main ethnic subdivisions within the bounds of large regions, contributing to the gradual increasing of their depth of cultural integration.

From the first years of Soviet rule, socioeconomic transformations in our country have created conditions conducive to the rapid development of processes leading to ethnic consolidation. In outlying, previously underdeveloped areas of our country, ethnic groups similar in language and culture have coalesced into large nationalities and nations. In this way was completed, for example, the formation of many Central Asian nations, in particular the Turkmens, who were formed from such tribal groups as the Yomuds, Tekinsy, Goklens, and others. As a consequence of this consolidation, many of the peoples of Siberia were formed, among them the Altai, who came to include the Altai-Kizhi, Telengits, Teleuts, and other numerically small tribes and nationalities.

Over the years of Soviet rule, many nations formed long before have become more monolithic. Although in the first years following the October Revolution, the Pomors, the Kerzhaks, some groups of Cossacks, and the Kamchadals sometimes did not consider themselves to be part of the Russian people, since they differed from the majority in their dialects, culture, and habits of daily life, today it would be difficult to single them out as so-called ethnographic groups within the Russian people. The Setu ethnographic group is gradually merging with other Estonians, the Latgalians with the Latvians, and differences between ethnographic groups within the Belorussian, Georgian, Uzbek and other peoples are rapidly vanishing. In such instances the progress of consolidation is manifested in the gradual contraction of territorial dialects and the diffusion of literary standards in the realm of spoken usage,

Over the years of Soviet rule, the ethnic heterogeneity of our country has lessened considerably. This found reflection notably in a reduction in the number of ethnonyms, from 194 in 1926 to 101 in 1979.

At the same time it should be noted that the period of most rapid interethnic consolidation has passed. It is revealing that the list of ethnonyms as it appears in the

1979 census is virtually identical with that of 1970. Among many peoples, ethnic consolidation is still continuing, but not with the same intensity as before.

In our own times changes have been taking place in the territorial concentration of peoples, primarily as a result of migration. Between 1926 and 1979, a decrease in the concentration of population was most apparent among the Russians: in 1926, 95.2% of our country's total Russian population lived in the RSFSR, but in 1979, 82.6%. This is a result of the out migration by Russians from their republic: to Ukraine, Kazakhstan, Uzbekistan, and other republics of our country. The concentration of their populations has also diminished somewhat among the Belorussians and Georgians, although the latter in 1979 were still the most compactly settled of all the union republic nationalities: only some 4% of all the Georgians in our country lived outside Georgia (in 1926—1.8%). Among the Ukrainians, Moldavians, Latvians, and Azerbaidzhanis, the concentration of their populations increased gradually from 1926 through 1970, after which it diminished somewhat. The concentration of Armenians, Lithuanians, and Estonians, grew uninterruptedly, although the Armenians still stand out as the least compactly settled of all union republic nationalities. In the case of autonomous republic nationalities, territorial concentration decreased most markedly since 1926 among the Bashkirs and Tatars.

Some changes in our country's ethnic structure are also linked to processes of assimilation. Such processes take place in all multinational and polyethnic countries. A distinguishing feature of these processes in the USSR is the fact that they occur naturally. This is attested most clearly by the fact that the main path they take is through interethnic marriages, the offspring of which usually choose the ethnic affiliation of one of the parents, thus breaking the ethnic continuity of the other. The development of friendly interethnic relations and the disintegration of religious barriers that occurred over the years of Soviet rule, coupled with the growing territorial intermixture of ethnoses, has led to a considerable increase in such marriages. While in 1925, on a country-wide basis, only one marriage in forty was ethnically mixed, by the end of the 1950s the corresponding figure was one in ten, and in a number of cities even one in every three or four (ethnically mixed marriages are especially frequent in the cities of Moldavia, Ukraine, Belorussia, Latvia, etc.). The percentage of families whose members belong to different ethnic groups continues to grow. While at the time of the 1959 census such families constituted 10.2% of the total number of families countrywide, by 1970 their number had increased to 13.5%. In 1979, such families were almost 15% of the total. The highest proportion of nationally mixed families occurs in the Latvian, Kazakh, and Ukrainian republics (20–21% in 1970 versus 14–16% in 1959).

To a great extent, the direction of assimilation processes depends on the ethnic consequences of nationally mixed marriages. There are substantial regional differences in the determination of ethnic affiliation by adolescents who grew up in mixed families. Thus in the Baltic region, in families in which one of the spouses belongs to the indigenous ethnos (Estonian, Latvian, Lithuanian) while the other is Russian, approximately half of the offspring consider themselves to be Russian, the remainder as belonging to the local nationality. In Chuvashia, on the other hand, the vast majority of adolescents from Chuvash–Russian families call themselves Russian. A different situation prevails in Turkmenia. There, most adolescents from Turkmen–Russian families identify themselves as Turkmens. The outcome in the latter case is to some degree influenced by the fact that among the Turkmens ethnic affiliation is traditionally determined patrilineally; and in nearly all the mixed families in this case the father was a Turkmen. Moreover, the socialization of adolescents takes place in an environment in which Turkmens on the whole predominate. In general, of course, the ethnic structure of the environment in which the socialization of adolescents takes place has a decisive impact on their ethnic self-identification.

Apart from assimilation associated with nationally mixed marriages, changes in ethnic affiliation also occur as a result of, so to speak, "extrafamilial" interaction among members of different ethnoses. To be sure, such "extrafamilial" assimilation—which, of course, also takes place naturally—is mainly a phenomenon of the prewar years and, moreover, predominantly affects ethnically transitional population groups (primarily at the "interfaces" between related peoples). In this connection it has been noted in particular that in 1939 there were approximately one-third fewer Ukrainians outside Ukraine than in 1926. As for the diminishing rates of "extrafamilial" ethnic assimilation on the eve of the war, this was in many respects a particular result of the limitation in choice of nationality, introduced in the late 1930s, exclusively to the nationality of the parents.

As we describe ethnic assimilation overall, it must be stressed especially that in the USSR—while making a rather significant impact on the population size of geographically dispersed peoples (Jews, Mordvinians, Karelians, etc.)—it has affected on the whole a minute segment of the population.

The main trend in ethnic interaction among the peoples of the USSR is represented not by assimilation, but interethnic integration, which becomes manifest, first of all, in the convergence of their cultures, the creation of a layer of culture that is one unified in content though multiple in form, and common traits in way of life. At the root of these processes lie the socioeconomic and ideological-political commonality of the nations and nationalities of the USSR, Marxist-Leninist ideology, and the internationalist solidarity of workers in their support of the CPSU.

The internationalist unity of our people manifested itself with special force in the general patriotic upsurge during the years of the Great Fatherland War[b]. The Soviet multinational people, rising as one in the defense of its Fatherland and the new social order, gave proof of its devotion to its socialist Motherland by heroic exploits at the military fronts and selfless exertions on the home front.

Internationality and interethnic integration is most closely bound up with those processes that led to the emergence and development of a new historic community—the Soviet people. The convergence of nations in the economic, social, and politico-ideological spheres, which formed the basis for this internationalist community, was accompanied by their convergence in the ethnocultural sphere as well, is basically what constitutes interethnic integration. Here, however the trend toward convergence coincides in dialectical fashion with the trend for national cultures to undergo further development. To be sure, these trends are by no means equally apparent in the various components of culture.

Processes of integration are to be observed most typically in the material culture. The most striking feature of changes in this realm is the abandonment of archaic, primitive elements of material culture which had been prevalent before the October Revolution. Obsolete items of the traditional material culture were replaced by articles of modern industrial manufacturing. In the course of urbanization, all Soviet "urban" forms of material culture gained ever broader currency, in response to the heightened requirements of the Soviet people. At the same time, certain elements of traditional culture, developed by one or another people or several peoples in a particular geographic region, gained broad currency throughout the entire Soviet Union (such as Central Asian carpets, Ukrainian men's shirts, Baltic metal and amber ornaments, various foods of the Caucasian, Ukrainian, and Russian cuisines, etc.).

As for ethnic distinctiveness, it clearly persists longer in the interior of the dwelling than in the dwelling itself, in the ornamentation of clothes rather than in the garments themselves, and is very stable in cuisine. This distinctiveness is manifested not so much in the utilitarian properties of things as in their esthetic form. Moreover, there is a link between culture as it is perceived through concrete objects and ethnic consciousness. The latter at times imputes ethnic significance to articles of material culture that earlier had none or very little (that is, their ethnic distinctiveness was not at all clearly realized). In this connection the development of arts and crafts during the Soviet period is quite revealing. Art- and craftwork as a rule preserves its distinctiveness, connected as it is with the transmission of artistic traditions that had evolved within the particular ethnos. Sometimes such articles (for example, the Russian *matrëshka* nesting dolls) even become distinctive ethnic symbols, though admittedly not so much within their own ethnic community as in the eyes of members of other ethnoses. At the same time, as they penetrate the daily life of other peoples they promote its homogenization. Thus, in a modern family of any nationality (especially in the cities), people watch television and listen to radio broadcasts from other republics, read books translated from other languages, and appoint the interior of their homes and apartments in unique combinations of detail— with Ukrainian or Baltic ceramics, Georgian engravings, Uzbek or Turkmenian carpets, Russian embroidery, etc. These may serve either a practical or a merely decoratively function.

In the realm of folk art, our times on the whole have seen the disapppearance or displacement of some elements (mainly those connected with religion) and at the same time the revival of various traditions that had been dying out or confined only to one or another ethnic group. Enormously important in this respect has been the creative readaptation of the traditional components of folk culture and the emergence of its "derivative" forms.

And even under present-day conditions, at a time of growing interest in more international forms of music, people still quite frequently in their leisure turn to folk songs and ethnic music. In general, interest in the most diverse types of folk art can be seen everywhere. Many of them are going through a kind of rebirth.

National distinctiveness in the artistic culture of the peoples of the USSR cannot, however, be reduced only to the legacy of the past and folk art, for to a great extent it is the result of new, professional creative work. During the years of Soviet rule the transformation of literature and art into the common property of the general public has led to an unprecedented expansion of the entire compass of the artistic cultures of the various ethnoses. This means that among all the peoples of the USSR the sum total of works of literature and art increased, while on the other hand the scale of consumption of works of art also grew and the range of workers' spiritual interests expanded. It should be emphasized, moreover, that the dissemination of professional artistic culture among our country's peoples could be achieved only because it developed primarily in national forms. It is also essential to bear in mind that professional artists and writers in every ethnic community in some measure help shape those new features that lend the given culture its original cast and stimulate the appearance within it of new, distinctive traditions. Despite the lively interaction among nationalities, many components of cultures, even as they acquire an international complexion, still do not lose their capacity to preserve their national form or to become embodied in more or less pronounced national variations. At the same time it is precisely in the professional forms of culture that the interpenetration of national elements on the whole occurs most vigorously and assumes great significance for the further development of the artistic culture of the peoples of the USSR. This is especially important to bear in mind, since in the Soviet people's total store of culture it is the professional forms that occupy a central place.

The processes of integration are also clearly to be observed in how people use their leisure time. Data obtained in recent years show, in particular, that approximately the same circles of people among Estonians and Russians, Georgians, Moldavians, and Uzbeks read newspapers in their leisure time (from 70 to 90%, depending on the social group), and that people of different nationalities follow radio and television news broadcasts virtually to the same extent.

An important aspect of current ethnic processes in our country is ethnolinguistic change. A characteristic feature of this change, parallel with the functional expansion of the national languages, is bilingualism, most frequently with Russian as the primary language of internationality communication. Thus, between 1970 and 1979, the percentage of people fluent in Russian in our country's total population increased from 76% to 82%. This general trend shows specific variations among different peoples, according to the latest census. Between 1970 and 1979, the number of people fluent in Russian as a second language grew considerably among some nationalities (from 36.1% to 47.4% among the Moldavians and from 35.9% to 52.1% among the Lithuanians), and only marginally among others (for example, from 21.3% to 26.7% among the Georgians). According to the 1979 census, over 60% of our country's non-Russian population has fluent command of Russian. But at the same time this means that some 40% of this population still lacks proficiency in Russian. One cannot fail to mention that in some cases the increase in the number of students whose instruction is conducted in Russian lags behind the increase in the number of students overall. In some republics it has been noted that young people know Russian less well than people of middle age. Meanwhile, in many national areas, the rate of influx of manpower into industry and their active participation in production is to some extent dependent on the degree to which the rural population has been exposed to urban culture and on their knowledge of the Russian.

Other languages of the peoples of the USSR are, like Russian, rather widely used in our country as second languages, a fact of no little significance for the development of internationality contact in a number of union and autonomous republics in particular. In 1979, 12.3 million persons, or 4.7% of our country's population, declared they were fluent in these languages (in 1970, 6.2 million). Most widely diffused of them are Ukrainian, Belorussian, Uzbek, Tatar, Moldavian, Azerbaidzhani, Tadzhik, Georgian, and other languages. It should also be kept in mind that in our country the broad diffusion of languages of internationality communication is paralleled by a high level of stability in people's declaration of their national language as their mother tongue. Over the years of Soviet rule, the figure has remained virtually unchanged: 94.2% of the country's population in 1926, and 93.1% in 1979.

In the evolution of present-day interethnic processes, as is well known, the diffusion of internationalist norms in interpersonal relations plays an extremely important role. In this connection, it should be noted that the rise in national self-awareness so typical of our times is paralleled among Soviet people by a development of positive attitudes with regard to internationality contact (work in nationally mixed collectives, nationally mixed marriages, etc.). At the same time, in the course of ethnosociological surveys it was determined that a multinational environment in work collectives in and of itself yields necessarily positive results in this respect in cases where there has already been a long experience of favorable contacts. But to achieve the same results in recently established multinational collectives and in regions, including cities, experiencing a rapid influx of people of different nationalities, requires special efforts, large-scale explanatory work, a tactful cadres policy, and special concern to satisfy the cultural needs of people belonging to the nationalities coming in contact there.

Even as we take note of the growing trend toward interethnic integration, we cannot ignore the challenge of overcoming such elements of national narrowness as still prevail among some people. It is important to bear in mind that the more differentiated our methods in the struggle against this phenomenon, the more successful they will be. For the sources of national narrow-mindedness can be discerned in among various strata of our population.

In the light of all these considerations, special importance attaches to investigations of opinions, attitudes, and actions that have a bearing on internationality contacts among people from diverse socio-occupational groups, in urban and in rural environments, in regions with different historical and cultural patterns in the past, and in diverse social situations. Such studies shed light on those social, historical, ethnodemographic, and cultural variables that help promote the strengthening of friendly contacts.

Educational work aiming to mold and strengthen an internationalist world-view among the broad masses of workers remains an extremely important task. This helps promote a more proper understanding of the correlation between national and international factors, thanks to which national narrow-mindedness gives way to an apprehension of the progressive nature of the convergence of nations.

Processes of interethnic integration have also found reflection in social consciousness. Among people in the Soviet Union, as is well known, feelings of love for one's own people and one's own ethnic territory are combined with an ever-growing, broader sense of belonging to the Soviet people—Soviet patriotism, which is based on internationalism and the concept of equality and indissoluble community of our country's peoples.

In a word, interethnic integration is a most important factor in the ever-growing unity of our country's peoples and in our society's further progress on the long march toward the merging [*sliianie*] of nations predicted by Lenin. At the same time, it is essential to keep in mind that national differences, as Comrade Iu. V. Andropov emphasized, "will persist for a long time, much longer than class differences." Meanwhile, under conditions of mature socialism, nations will basically have a classless social structure. Such nations, while preserving to a great extent their ethnocultural distinctiveness, will be not so much ethnosocial as strictly ethnic communities. Accordingly, interethnic integration will become increasingly important for the future merging of nations.

Editor's notes

a. *Ethnos:* Bromlei's term for an elemental ethnic community. Bromlei writes that the most numerous and economically comple ethnoses will form nationalities during the capitalist period of history.

b. Great Fatherland War: Soviet term for World War II.

Annotated by Lubomyr Hajda

Improving National Relations in the USSR *

Iu. V. BROMLEI

The problem of nationalities occupied a substantial place among the wide range of social problems raised at the Twenty-seventh CPSU Congress. The Soviet Union has been a pioneer in addressing the nationality question which, as V. I. Lenin wrote, is a worldwide phenomenon. It is one of the most acute questions in the history of mankind: the engendering of class antagonisms that inevitably entail national oppression, the lack of equality of nationalities before the law, and their inequality. Our country has convincingly demonstrated to the entire world that with the victory of socialism antagonisms in the sphere of nationality relations are being overcome. As noted in the new edition of the CPSU Program, *"the Soviet Union has successfully resolved the national question that was left over from the past."* In the course of socialist construction, the formerly backward national hinterlands have long ago vanished; socialist nations have joined together to form an inter-national community—the Soviet people—that is new in its social parameters; common cultural traits have developed that are characteristic of Soviet people of all nationalities; national discord is a thing of the past; and the fraternal friendship of the peoples, forged in their common creative labor and tested in the most difficult of wars, has become the standard of life.

Consistency and continuity in the Party's implementation of the Leninist principles of nationality policy not only do not exclude, but on the contrary presuppose careful consideration of the changes that have taken place in the life of the USSR's nationalities since the Great October Socialist Revolution, as well as in the quarter-century that has passed since the adoption of the Third Program of the CPSU. As emphasized in the new edition of program, "the consistent implementation of Lenin's policy on nationalities and the all-around strengthening of the friendship of peoples are a component part of the improvement of socialism." A well-conceived nationality policy that has a thorough scientific and socioeconomic foundation must play an important part in the realization of the strategic task of accelerating the nation's socioeconomic progress.

In this regard, it is necessary to concern ourselves first of all with a further increase in the contribution of union and autonomous republics, autonomous oblasts and districts to the development of the integral national economic complex that would accord with their higher economic and spiritual potential. It is the specific character of economic and cultural progress in each republic that permits it to make its own inestimable contribution to the country's general development and that plays

Kommunist, 1986, no. 8. Russian text © 1986 by "Pravda" Publishers.

a large role at the present stage. It is not by chance that the CPSU Program notes the necessity for "consistently intensifying the division of labor among the republics." At the same time, however, we naturally cannot permit any trend toward national isolation or the emergence of feelings of dependency.

The course of socialism's development into communism is being pursued in a multinational country. It is clear that a well-conceived economic strategy, an active social policy, and purposeful ideological and educational work are continuing to strengthen the economic, social, political, and spiritual framework that is the basis for strengthening the unity of the Soviet people as a new social and inter-national community. This is in no small measure promoted by the intensive processes of the scientific-technological revolution, which bring working conditions in different branches and regions closer together, by urbanization, which leads to the qualitative restructuring of the life activity and habitat of nationalities, and by the growth of culture and education, which raise society's creative potential to a new qualitative level.

The deeper and more multifaceted the nature of these integrative processes in economic and cultural construction and in the implementation of large-scale social undertakings such as the Food Program and the Energy Program, the stronger multinational Soviet society becomes. "The development of cooperation in production, collaboration, and mutual aid between republics," the Twenty-seventh CPSU Congress emphasized, "is in the highest interests of our multinational state and of every republic. The task of Party organizations and of the soviets is to make more complete use of existing potential in the common interest, and to steadfastly overcome any manifestations of localistic tendencies." In turn, the growth of integrative trends, which is dominant in the sphere of nationality relations, will expand the possibility for enriching and further developing all aspects of the life of nationalities.

All this is important for the realization of the task repeatedly noted in Party documents: the more concrete and deeper consideration of national specifics, for the subsequent securing of the true equality of peoples and for implementing a policy of social justice.

At the same time, it must be remembered that in no way does equality automatically mean coincidence and identity of levels of economic development of the USSR's peoples, since there are always numerous factors of a historical, socioeconomic, natural, and climatic nature that lead to differences among peoples. Between union and autonomous republics as well as between autonomous oblasts, and, correspondingly, nations and nationalities, there are easily discernible differences in such important indicators as the share of city dwellers, proportions in the development of the national economy, capital and power per worker, the degree of agricultural mechanization, and the average educational level of the population. For a considerable historical period, these indicators have been used to compare the socioeconomic development of different peoples. At the present time, the use of some of these seemingly simple and convincing indicators requires the consideration of additional criteria. Otherwise the picture of the people's life may be incomplete. Even such an indicator as the share of urban population does not always and everywhere reflect the level of development. If agriculture is scientifically and technically advanced and if the city, with its diverse sociocultural infrastructure, is accessible to rural commuters, the fact that a considerable percentage of the people live in the countryside cannot in any way be proof of a lower level of development. The socioeconomic standard of living of nations and nationalities is also attested to by such indicators as aggregate real income of social and occupational groups of the population; the share of persons with higher, secondary specialized, and complete secondary education in various age cohorts; the information potential; the density and time accessibility of transport and personal service networks, etc.

In this connection, science is confronted with the very serious task of forming structural indicators for the needs of managing and planning economic and social development that would really make it possible to see the degree to which vestiges of inequality have been overcome between our peoples. This would serve not to confuse, but to distinguish clearly the *uniqueness* of development from its *level*.

The Guidelines for the Economic and Social Development of the USSR for 1986–1990 and the Period Ending in 2000* call for wholesale qualitative changes in the structure of republic economic complexes.Each republic is implementing a special system of measures aimed at the effective utilization of [its] labor potential. The union-republics of the Transcaucasus are slated to develop machine building on an accelerated basis for a number of branches of the food industry, which must compensate for a drop in the production of winemaking products; in the Central Asian union-republics, in addition to increased specialization in cotton farming, there will be accelerated development of associated branches of production (cotton processing, agricultural machine building, mineral fertilizer production, the textile industry), with the center of gravity shifting to the siting of enterprises in small towns that are closer to rural districts. There is every reason to believe that such a policy will be instrumental in further increasing the share of the working class among the indigenous population.

As M. S. Gorbachev emphasized in his report at the Twenty-seventh CPSU Congress, "Our accomplishments must not create the notion that national processes are problem-free. Contradictions are characteristic of all development and are inevitable in this sphere as well." When examining this question, it is important to remember that the characteristic feature of national processes in our multinational country is the existence of two dialectically interconnected principles within them: the steady economic, social, and cultural development of all nationalities on the one hand, and the further strengthening of their unity based on the growing internationalization of all life with the improvement of socialism on the other. The new edition of CPSU Program states anew that "both the further flowering of nations and nationalities and their progressive convergence are characteristic of national relations in our country."

The existence of these two principles in national processes in the course of our state's development cannot fail to generate problems in the joint life and work of the

---

*The Guidelines are included in part 4 of this collection.

nationalities inhabiting it and new questions in the sphere of nationality relations.

Nor can nationality relations fail to be affected by individual shortcomings in our society's development, in particular by the negative trends of the seventies and early eighties in the economy, which were noted at the Twenty-seventh CPSU Congress. To this group belong, above all, the considerable differences between union-republics in the growth rates of labor productivity in industry. Thus, in the last fifteen years these growth rates were 1.5 times higher in Azerbaidzhan and Belorussia than in Tadzhikistan. At the same time, as noted at the Congress, in Kazakhstan, for example, national income per unit of basic productive capital is one-third less than the national economic average. There has been no growth whatsoever in the productivity of social labor in the last fifteen years in Turkmenia. While differences between republics in the branch structure of industry unquestionably make themselves known here, the specifics of the vocational training of cadres, their lack of the necessary initiative, shortcomings in economic management, and the slow rate at which scientific-technological advances are introduced into production also have an obvious impact.

One serious problem that has grown more acute in recent years is the demographic situation existing in most regions of the nation, especially in the European USSR among Russians, Ukrainians, Belorussians, Balts, and certain other peoples. In both town and country, they have very definitely opted for 1-2–child families. The relatively favorable picture of population reproduction in the USSR as a whole results from the indigenous peoples of Central Asia, the Kazakhs, and the Azerbaidzhanis, whose growth rates are three times higher than the national average.

The unevenness of ethnodemographic processes in combination with different growth rates of labor productivity has in the last fifteen years been accompanied by the differentiation of republics with respect to their development of individual components of the social infrastructure, including housing, personal services, publishing, etc.

Medical care in all union-republics improved considerably in the seventies and early eighties. The number of physicians in the nation rose from 668,000 in 1970 to 1,170,000 in 1985; and the number of hospital beds per 10,000 population rose from 109.4 to 129.7. At the same time, however, the disproportions in these indicators did not decline but, on the contrary, increased between individual republics. While the difference between Georgia and Tadzhikistan in 1970 was 20.5 physicians per 10,000 population, in 1985 this number had grown to 26.9; the gap between the hospital beds-to-population ratios during the same period increased between the extreme cases (Latvia and Armenia) from 33.3 to 53.0 points. While indicators of the development of the system of public dining enterprises is relatively high for all union-republics combined, differences between republics have continued to increase.

The Political Report of the CPSU Central Committee to the Twenty-seventh Party Congress noted that in the process of addressing the problems that arise in this area, "thought should be given to linking the volume of resources allocated for social needs more closely to the effectiveness of regional economies." Nor can we fail to consider the fact that of late the increase in such an indicator of the population's well-being as the volume of trade in state and cooperative networks has been far from uniform in individual republics. Thus, between 1970 and 1985 the gap between the minimum increase in trade (Tadzhik SSR) and the maximum increase (Moldavian SSR) increased 2.2-fold with due regard to change in the size of these republics' populations.

Differences in the ethnodemographic development of individual regions of the country also leave their mark on such a currently important problem for our society as the optimal utilization of labor resources. Where there is a surplus of labor resources in the countryside (in a number of Central Asian republics and in certain other regions of the country), it is important to come up with a series of measures promoting their more rational use locally, in particular at interfarm industrial enterprises and in agro-industrial complexes. It is advisable to develop commuting, in order to encourage the utilization of the countryside's labor resources in nearby cities. This in turn will stimulate the migration of the population to cities, including large cities. On the other hand, in order to promote these processes it is necessary to first analyze and intensify the conditions of agricultural production.

In a word, there arises a complex problem which, dialectically, is full of contradictions. On the one hand, it is necessary to know and consider national and regional (intranational) features of the population's labor behavior when planning investments in the national economy, when siting and developing production. On the other hand, it is necessary to build, and this requires not only taking into account the skills and traditions of the local populace and its stereotypical production behavior, but also altering them purposefully.

As research shows, the problem of interrepublic migration requires a more painstaking approach. This must particularly be borne in mind in implementing the program of expanding the participation of the working people of Central Asia and the Caucasus in transforming the Non–Black-Earth zone and in developing Siberia and the Far East. The forms of this participation may be highly varied and may include the construction of residential housing, social and cultural facilities, and motor roads.

It is also advisable to train specialists for the entire nation at republic institutions of higher learning and, above all, to assign graduates to jobs throughout the Soviet Union as a whole. The interregional mobility of the "labor surplus" rural population and the level of its vocational training can also be raised by training part of the rural youth in agricultural vocational-technical training schools in the Russian Federation.

In recent years, as is known, there has been a substantial reduction in differences between the social and class structures of [Soviet] nations. This process is integrally connected to the increasing size of national detachments of the working class. Their exceptionally rapid growth is obvious. If we compare the data of the last two population censuses—1970 and 1979—we can easily see that the working class is growing at an especially rapid rate in precisely those places where it has arisen only in the relatively recent historical past, for example, among the indigenous nationalities of the Transcaucasian and Central Asian republics. In 1970, when roughly half of the country's population consisted of workers, workers comprised approximately one-third of the Moldavian, Georgian, Turkmen, Tadzhik, and Uzbek populations. In the next population census (1979), differences in the distribution of the working class among the indigenous nationalities of the union republics had been practically eliminated. Workers comprised almost one-half of the population of each nationality with the exception of the Turkmen, i.e., almost equal to the national average. The increase in the number of workers was particularly rapid among Moldavians in the last decade—the share of workers in the population increased from 34% to 54%; the corresponding increase among Tadzhiks was from 36% to 55%.

However, this increase came predominantly in rural areas and was primarily the result of the conversion of collective farms to state farms. Most Tadzhik, Kirghiz, Uzbek, and Moldavian workers, as was the case with Kazakh workers in the past, lived in rural areas (only one-third of Uzbek workers lived in cities; the corresponding figure for Kirghiz and Tadzhik workers was even smaller). As a result, certain differences persist between republics in the share of the working class in their indigenous nationality, particularly in the case of the industrial working class and its skill groups.

Many of the difficulties that our country has experienced in recent years and the difficulties in making the transition to intensive forms of management have been connected with the insufficiency of the general cultural and occupational-skill level of the work force in the national economy. The plans associated with this are grandiose, and their implementation will take a considerable amount of time. This is because we are talking not about years of schooling, but rather about acceptance of the entire urban industrial culture, which can only be accomplished in a number of generations.

The general rise of the educational level is highly important in equalizing the social structure of nationalities. But people's social expectations grow at the same time. Under these conditions, a consistently internationalist personnel policy takes on a special role. Nationality in itself can be neither a source of privilege nor a source of injury.

As E. K. Ligachev noted at the Twenty-seventh CPSU Congress, in the recent past "Here and there, localistic and regional sentiments took the upper hand. They hindered . . . the interregional exchange of cadres, the exchange of experienced personnel between republics and the center, between districts and cities throughout the nation. In a number of cases, this led to self-isolation, to stagnation, and to other negative phenomena." Vestigial forms of former kinship ties have occasionally made themselves known in the process of resolving personnel questions. In some cases, Party committees have not addressed these negative phenomena and scientists have not analyzed their sources.

Party documents of recent years have repeatedly emphasized the need to focus more attention on nonindigenous national groups in union republics; these number approximately 55 million persons. It will be necessary not only to take into account and satisfy the ethnic-specific demands of these groups in the realm of language, culture, and everyday life, but also to ensure their proper representation at all levels of the sociopolitical structure. Naturally, the consistent implementation of the principle of proportional representation is no less a concern in the case of large nationalities (especially nationalities that are different from the titular nationality of the republic).

The state and legal aspects of national processes are acquiring increasing importance under present conditions. The dialectical combination of the two principles is also clearly seen here. As noted in the new edition of the CPSU Program, the Party will continue to strengthen the all-union multinational state and "at the same time will continuously see to it that republics, autonomous oblasts, and autonomous districts continue to play a larger part in the resolution of problems of concern to all the people." In a word, nationality policy must promote the harmonious combination of the development of the activity of each nation and nationality and the further strengthening of a new social and inter-national community—the Soviet people. A considerable role here will be played by the improvement of Soviet democracy, by the consistent implementation of the principles of socialist self-government, by the active participation of working people of all nationalities in the work of organs of power and government. This refers to representation not only on a republic scale, but also in all-union organs of power and in public organizations.

In the concept of the acceleration of the socioeconomic development of socialist society and its attainment of a new qualitative state, a prominent place belongs to the improvement of cultural life. "We are justifiably proud," it was said at the Congress, "of the accomplishments of Soviet multinational socialist culture. Having absorbed the wealth of national forms and colors, it is becoming a unique phenomenon in world culture." The development of a unified culture of the Soviet people that is socialist in content, diverse in national form, and international in spirit on the basis of the best attainments and distinctive progressive traditions of the peoples of the USSR is among the key tasks advanced in the new edition of the CPSU Program of with regard to the improvement of nationality relations.

Naturally, it would be wrong to see only one side—the flowering of national cultures—in this process and to forget about the significance of their convergence and their mutual enrichment. After all, the harmful effect of cultural isolation on a nation is well-known. But it would be no less an oversimplification to construe the principle of internationalism to mean that all peoples must be similar to one's own. Such similarity is impossible and unnecessary. The richness of Soviet and world culture is primarily the result of the diversity of the elements comprising it. The leveling of national features would inevitably impoverish both culture and social life.

As is known, the free development of the languages of the various nationalities of the USSR and the unhindered diffusion of the Russian language as a means of inter-nationality communication among the non-Russian population play an important part in the interaction and reciprocal enrichment of national cultures, in strengthening friendship among peoples, and in consolidating the social and inter-national unity of the Soviet people. Between 1970 and 1979, the proportion of the country's population that was fluent in Russian rose from 76% to 82%. We recall that in the late seventies, one-third of the non-Russian population lacked the fluency in Russian which gives people broader access to the attainments of science, technology, domestic and world culture. At the same time, young people in some republics today do not know Russian as well as people of middle age. Therefore, the further diffusion and qualitative improvement of knowledge of Russian continues to be an important problem, especially in rural areas of Central Asia, the Transcaucasus, and Estonia.

Learning the language of the indigenous populations of the various republics by Russians and other nonindigenous nationalities is an important aspect of the language problem. This improves interpersonal relations and facilitates adaptation to different ethnic environments.

Scholars working in republics must show how the national experience of each people can promote the enrichment of the general atmosphere of spiritual life and thereby promote the acceleration of the country's socioeconomic development. In particular, we must substantially increase the possibility for using the intellectual potential of nations in the interest of energizing society's ideological life. It is useful to recall national folk traditions—particularly their contempt for parasites—to extol these traditions, to propagandize them openly but tactfully (not to the point that they become an annoying cliché) in films, on television, etc. Historians and the mass media should have their say here.

At the same time, it was noted at the Congress that it is important that "a healthy interest in everything of value in every national culture not degenerate into attempts at separation from the objective process of interaction of national cultures and their convergence. This must also be remembered when certain literary, artistic, and scientific works use national distinctiveness in an effort to present an idyllic picture of reactionary nationalistic and religious vestiges that contradict our ideology, the socialist way of life, and the scientific world-view." It was also stated at the Congress that "it is very unfortunate that the past of one or another people is evaluated without regard to class, and that works are published in which the history of one people is idealized while the historical role of another is denigrated." It is alarming that research on the historical past of individual peoples is often carried out essentially in isolation from the history of other, including neighboring, peoples. Under the conditions of increasing national self-awareness there is naturally increased interest in the historical past. This is why we must carefully preserve "everything that is dear to the people's memory." Even though much is being done in this direction, there is still "considerable reason for concern."

As is known, the increased national self-awareness of representatives of all nations and nationalities in our country is harmoniously combined with a feeling of Soviet pride and Soviet self-awareness. And when they speak of the successes of any nation, Soviet people are well aware that these successes stem from the indestructible friendship of [our] fraternal peoples, that they are the result of our common labor and our common Soviet heritage. But naturally it cannot be forgotten that sometimes social awareness and social psychology may not entirely adequately reflect objective social processes, including the flowering of nations and their convergence. The

Party attaches great importance to educating the working people in the spirit of the ideas of socialist patriotism and internationalism. As the new edition of the Party Program emphasizes, the CPSU will strive to see to it that every Soviet person is "intolerant of nationalism and chauvinism, national narrowness and national egotism."

What are the sources of these negative phenomena? The usual reference is to remaining vestiges in people's consciousness and the influence of bourgeois propaganda. While these unquestionably play a considerable role, they do not tell the entire story. Shortcomings in the development of modern society often exert an influence, moreover a considerable influence, in the sphere of social consciousness.

The reasons behind national narrowness among various strata of the population vary. A narrow outlook and insufficient knowledge of the past and present of other peoples are, for example, frequently nurtured by the prejudices of less well-educated circles of society and by people of older age. Broad educative activity and explanatory ideological work by the mass media significantly help to overcome national narrowness.

Perceptions of certain unrealized expectations in specific life situations, most often associated with professional careers, are sometimes expressed in national terms. In such cases, the prevention of undesirable phenomena in inter-nationality communication depends on the regulation of social problems in the current stage of society's development—the correlation between supply and demand for specific types of labor, vocational guidance of youth, the further expansion of housing construction, and the improvement of personal services.

As is known, joint labor and positive social intercourse over an extended period of time generate friendly inter-national contacts. But the task of properly regulating inter-nationality relations is especially important in multinational cities (particularly young cities) and in multinational construction projects. Here people are more aware of the specifics of culture and everyday behavior. It is here that they compare the activities and way of life of their own and other nationalities. Therefore, there is need for a great deal of explanatory work, for a sensitive personnel policy, and concern for satisfying the cultural demands of peoples of all nationalities.

The Political Report of the CPSU Central Committee to the Twenty-seventh Party Congress emphasized in particular the importance of further strengthening the fraternal friendship of peoples of the USSR, of educating the working people in the spirit of Soviet patriotism and socialist internationalism. At the same time, the psychological aspects of national processes, including interpersonal relations, must be studied more attentively. For example, it is necessary to take into account the fact that national self-awareness develops through the prism of "one's own" cultural values. All this requires the exhaustive dissemination of information about characteristic cultural features of different, especially neighboring, peoples in various ways (over television, in literature, in museums, etc.).

The progress of socialist nations and the new conditions of their interaction, when they are equal not only in their rights but also in their actual socioeconomic status, are impossible without the continuous improvement of ideological work. The active propagandization of the successes of republics and peoples that were particularly backward in their development in the past, must be combined with the demonstration of their real practical interest in close contacts and solidarity. There are not nor can there be trivialities in the implementation of the nationality policy of the CPSU and in the realization of its unshakable Leninist principles. It must always be remembered that national phenomena are a very delicate sphere that requires great tact both in its study and especially in the resolution of practical issues.

In light of the decisions of the Twenty-seventh CPSU Congress, of special importance is the in-depth theoretical interpretation of nationality problems, as well as all other problems in our society's development. Unfortunately, there have long been no broad discussions of theoretical aspects of nationality problems in the pages of our leading sociological journals (since the late sixties). Nor are public discussions a very frequent occurrence. Clearly, not enough attention is being devoted to the critical analysis of scholarly literature concerning the sphere of nationality relations. It is important to intensify organizational work substantially in order to overcome all these shortcomings. The Scientific Council on National Problems under the Social Sciences Section of the Presidium of the USSR Academy of Sciences and its regional subdivisions must become more active. It is necessary to raise the role of the council in the coordination of corresponding research and in the critical examination of literature published on nationality problems.

Judging by everything, the time has also come for taking more substantive steps toward providing organizational support for the elaboration and management of national processes and toward creating special subdivisions of the appropriate type. In any case, there is an obvious need for the social sciences to study in greater depth the real content of national processes in all their complexity and contradictoriness. It is specifically this approach that the Party is encouraging us to take.

The National Problem and Social Science *

E. BAGRAMOV

The socialist transformation of national relationships, the affirmation of friendship and fraternity of the peoples are the epochal achievements of socialism, which the Soviet people remark with especial pride on the eve of the Seventieth anniversary of Great October. At the same time a characteristic trait of our time is the sharpness of society's reaction to surviving negative phenomena in the sphere of national relations, the active discussion of brewing questions and unsolved tasks. Rejecting the position that there are no problems in the national process and demonstrating that here too the progressive will find a path through contradictions, the Twenty-seventh Congress of the Communist Party of the Soviet Union unfettered the thinking of social scientists, creating conditions for a theoretical explosion in this branch of science, which suffered from dogmatism almost more than did the other branches.

In conditions of the renewal of socialism, the task of systematically realizing the nationality policy of the CPSU in a way that is grounded in scientific analysis and corresponds to modern requirements has become a pressing one. The resolution of the Central Committee of the CPSU "On the Work of the Kazakh Republic Party Organization in International and Patriotic Education of Workers" says that "Today, when revolutionary processes of renewal embrace all aspects of the life of society, the timely solution of problems arising in the sphere of nationality relations is of the very greatest significance." This supposes a profound assimilation of the Leninist legacy, the skill to evaluate with fresh eyes, free of stereotypic formulae, the dynamic of national relations. The justified criticism of social scientists at the January (1987) plenum of the Central Committee demands closing the gap between scientific investigations and reality.

In the realm of theory this gap is visible in the refusal to analyze the problems that arise realistically and in the preference to study the mechanical selection of numbers and figures about the life of the Soviet republics instead of living reality, in the freezing of scientific thought into certain understandings and definitions (definitions of nationhood, abstract propositions about the future of languages, and so forth), in the endless remastication of common truths, the obviously unsatisfactory processing of questions of nationality policy which correspond to the modern stage of the country's development. Beginning from an oversimplified understanding of the thesis about the resolution of the national question in this country, some social scientists have painted the state of nationality relations only in rosy colors, statistically and metaphysically. Apparently some social scientists lack the philosophical

---

Pravda, 15 August 1987, pp. 2–3. Russian text © 1987 by "Pravda."

culture to characterize what are, in the words of M. S. Gorbachev, very complex and intrinsically contradictory socioeconomic and spiritual processes.

Relations between nations and national groups are a living process of interaction between national and international, where the new is affirmed in a constant battle with the old, not discarding it entirely, but renewing it, retaining what is valuable, positive.

It is also important to understand correctly the substance of the national problem itself, which has never existed anywhere in what might be called a pure form, but instead has always been a complex of economic, social, class, and spiritual relationships which define the mutual connections among peoples. The restructuring of these relationships requires profound changes in the national relationships as well, but because of the relative independence of the national factor, which has its roots in history, the inertia of outlived traditions will long be something that must be dealt with.

The class approach is a reliable one for elucidation of the concrete contents of nationality problems; it excludes any emasculation of their substance, any exaggeration of a national source. It is wrong to try to present the national factor as some sort of rudiment or obstacle on the path of social development.

Internationalization is often discussed as a unification of everything and everybody, as a result of which this multifaceted, most fruitful of processes is depicted as a lifeless abstraction. In this approach, discussion of, for example, the factual equality of peoples is understood statistically, exclusive of the inescapable differences between various regions. There has gradually arisen the illusory idea that society on its own, almost automatically, is moving toward ever greater fraternity of peoples, right up to the fusion of nations into one.

Naturally it is incorrect to go to extremes, to forget that there have also been bold presentations by scientists, writers, journalists, and authoritative works, with well-based recommendations for improvements. Nevertheless in practice the sphere of nationality relations has been put beyond criticism, treated as a zone of general harmony, while anything that doesn't fit into that harmony is tossed aside, branded as a phenomenon of bourgeois nationalism. Many real needs and demands of all-union development, as well as of national development, have in fact been ignored, and social scientists have often not been permitted to pose them as questions.

Thus in the fifties and sixties the correct transition from excessive centralization to the widening of rights of the union republics found no corresponding reworking in the social sciences; there was no clear and precise conception of the relation between the all-union and the local level, the international and the national. There was no reflection in the scientific literature of ways to overcome unhealthy tendencies. The July (1987) Plenum of the Central Committee focused attention on the necessity to take account of a whole complex of interests, of the individual, the collective, the classes, the nations, national groups, social and professional groups. The harmonization of national, republic, and all-national, all-union interests is an important part of restructuring. The Party is evolving new means and forms of addressing the interests of people, educating them and directing them through a new mechanism of administration, democratic institutions, through policy, ideology, and culture.

The Party is working out new paths and forms of influencing the interests of the people, cultivating them and directing them through a new mechanism of management, through democratic institutions, through policy, ideology and culture. Now instead of abstract thoughts about internationalism it will be possible to study the mechanism of how nationality policy is realized. An example is the question of how factual economic equality of peoples should be more closely tied to social justice. The variety of regional and nationality conditions does not exclude the elaboration of a single measure of labor and consumption, in order to introduce it universally on the basis of general criteria of evaluating labor and its results.

In overcoming bureaucratic politics and regional chauvinism the Party is creating possibilities for the concentration of resources in the decisive directions of scientific and technological progress, from which will benefit both the country as a whole and each individual republic. It is important to evaluate fully the specificity of nationality, to support the healthy tendencies of development of local initiative, not permitting such to be overregulated by bureaucratic centralism.

Nationality policy must not be interpreted unilaterally, now stressing the flourishing of nations, now stressing their convergence. Restructuring means the universal affirmation of the Leninist course of the CPSU, meaning attention to the particularities of peoples, to their requirements, in the name of international solidarity, without any opposition from cadres.

In conditions of the growth of democratic beginnings in all spheres of our life, processes of the spiritual life of nations and national groups are under lively discussion, particularly the linguistic ones. Concern for one's native language, for its development alongside that of Russian is wholly natural. Here though we must also consider not only legitimate demands but also the purposeful dramatization, particularly in the writers' environment, of linguistic processes. Language is a most important means of communication, but it is also a part of the spiritual wealth of a nation, binding a person to his native region, his people's creativity, to his national culture. The knowledge of languages is also an element of a worker's qualifications as a worker. It was not chance when filling government posts in a national republic and in other instances that Lenin inquired about the ability of the candidates to make themselves understood in the language of the republic's people. For the intelligentsia, and especially the artistic intelligentsia, language is also a profession, so it is natural that its representatives, workers of the word, show a particular interest in the dissemination of their national language. It is most important that a proper love for one's native language does not become linguistic chauvinism, which could become a barrier in the path to internationalism.

Inattentiveness to the language of the people among whom you live evokes wholly justifed protest. Those who think that being able to choose for themselves the language of instruction removes from them or their children the obligation to show respect for the local language, traditions, and culture of the people are, of course, mistaken. This is a question of tact, of the culture of inter-national living, which is to be found in the masses of Soviet peoples reared in a spirit of internationalism. Parenthetically, practice demonstrates that in a number of instances the worsening of instruction in a national language can as a rule be explained by poor preparation of the instructing cadres, or by a shortage of them. Other authors (for example in Estonia) permit the opposition of the native language and the language of international communication. The good practice of running schools with parallel classes (in the native language and in Russian) which was once promulgated in Latvia deserves wide support.

Bilingualism of Russian and the native language is the main direction of linguistic development in the USSR. This does not change the legal position of the languages, but their equality does not mean an identity of their social functions. Thus Russian as the language of inter-nationality communication is a widely acknowledged means by which the masses may be brought to the culture of the peoples of the USSR and of the whole world. A real concern about the development of one's native language and national culture has nothing in common with any demand to administratively limit the use of Russian. It is also difficult to agree, particularly in conditions of the democratization of our life, with the proposition that the ministries, not the parents, should decide the language and school to which children should be sent.

Thus Marxists are for equality and the free development of languages and are against national privileges. "The Soviet republic unites workers of all nationalities and represents the interests of workers without respect of nationality," Lenin said (volume 36, p. 536). This is the source of the Constitution of the USSR, this is the Leninist way! Soviet citizens respect national feelings. At the same time they are against speculation in these feelings.

Theoretical and methodological clarity in the understandings of "national" and "nationalistic" are vital. The times when social scientists departed from thoughtful analysis of the category "national" (fearing, not without reason, to be taken as petty nationalists) are long past. Still, philosophers have not yet fully elaborated the conditions under which the national, as a phenomenon immanent to socialism, becomes the nationalistic, which is its antipode.

Here is a characteristic situation. In relations between neighboring regions or oblasts of various republics there occasionally arise misunderstandings or even conflicts. People quarrel with one another behind the coulisses, while government and Party workers stay silent, depart from decisions of principle, not striving to head off or dampen these passions. It may be that the questions are too ticklish, too complicated. But why not use some democratic form, such as the study of public opinion, to illuminate the attitudes of the sides on a given question?

Appearances of nationalism are traditionally explained as "the lagging of consciousness behind daily life." But haven't we turned this formula into a kind of passkey, which lets analysis be cut off just where it should be begun? It is important to investigate the full aggregate of objective and subjective factors which influence the tenacity of unhealthy attitudes. This includes both economic irregularities and the violation of Soviet laws, of Leninist principles of cadre policy, as well as poor educational work, acceptance of such attitudes.

It is obvious that national interests, a national consciousness, the feeling of national worth are real attributes of our daily life. And if these manifestations of the spiritual life are not refined by a class consciousness, if international responsibility is not demonstrated, then it is easy to fall into exaggeration or even absolutization of the national. From the viewpoint of social psychology this is ethnocentrism, viewing other peoples through the prism of the values of one's own ethnic group. Nationalism is also to take to the point of exclusivity understandings about one's own people and their mission.

A reliable method exists to avoid falling into nationalism or chauvinism, which is to stand on class positions of the equality of workers of all nations, to think not only of one's nation, but rather to put above it the interests of all. This is what Leninism teaches us, that national interests should not be defended from a position of the particularity of a people's isolation, but rather from that of the international fraternity of workers.

One partial evidence of this is the creation of a commission to examine the problems of the Crimean Tatars. Soviet people understand this as the intention of the Soviet organs to study the question from all sides, taking into account the interests of all peoples, and to reach a decision corresponding to the traditions of friendship of the peoples of the USSR.

Socialism has rejected the myth that antagonism among peoples can not be extirpated. In our country the national factor long ago ceased to separate people. Nevertheless for historical reasons, and because of the multinational character of the country, susceptibility of parts of the population to national problems is still relatively noticeable. Parenthetically, this is what bourgeois ideologues rely on in attempting to exaggerate, to hypertrophy national sentiments, and to oppose national values to international ones.

As the lessons of the incident in Alma-Ata[a] teach us, affirmation of internationalism demands persistent effort, becoming a battle with negative phenomena in Kazakhstan and other republics. It must be said straight out that the theoretical analysis of the social consciousness of the populations of the Central Asian republics and Kazakhstan was clearly unrealistic, that it had permitted the intrusion of idealization. The leap from feudalism to socialism was an enormous achievment of the Soviet system, but in the existng conditions it also had some deficiencies, such as insufficient strata of national cadres in the working class, preservation of remnants of tribal and clan relationships, and so forth. Rapid growth of national self-consciousness without concern for internationalist education conceals the danger of a one-sided orientation to national peculiarities.

In a popular book of the 1970s, *Journey to Zher-Uiuk,* an old *akyn*[b] offers the following characterization of peoples: that the Ukrainian has a jolly disposition, the Georgian is hospitable, the Armenian hardworking, the Russian loves his native land and is courageous, the Estonian is diligent, the Tadzhik strives for education, while the Kazakh has all of these qualities at once. How great, it seems, is the urge to flatter national self-love! And how this contradicts the traditions of the people which gave the world Chokan Valikhanov[c] and Abai Kunanbaev![d] It is no secret that subjective evaluations are most often evident in analysis of national character. Stereotypic judgments about people, many of them far from complimentary, are in wide circulation. Surviving offensive evaluations of the national worth of people are based on these, in significant degree, appearing as everyday nationalism or as chauvinistic superiority, which are often far from combatted in an effective manner.

How are these judgments to be separated from the real particularities of national character? It is necessary to study deeply the history, culture, traditions, and daily life of a people, for it is precisely these that bear the stamp of the true characteristics of the national soul. Socialism is ennobling national sentiments, purifying them of traits of past isolation, egoism, and intolerance.

Today interest is growing in the historic past, in monuments of national culture, folklore, and so on. But why are people who would set the nations against one another because of national differences joining this interest, sacred to Soviet people? And if they call themselves "patriots" then that means we are doing a poor job propagandizing Soviet patriotism as an ideology incompatible with the idea of national exclusivity, whether chauvinism, Zionism, or other manifestations of national arrogance. We should not forget that all peoples are linked by the totality of the historical fates of the peoples of the USSR, the international traditions of the battlers for socialism.

Among peoples living in conditions of one and the same social and economic formation it is difficult to find characteristic properties which are completely alien to other peoples. Clearly the specifics of national character must be sought in the particular mix of qualities common to all people, in the peculiar expression of these traits or those, and not in the the presence of exceptional traits. The task of the scientist, of the artist, is thus not to stress psychological differences one-sidedly, but to expose the variety of forms in which what is common to humanity appears, in that new phenomenon, born of socialism, and the development of a social and international society, the Soviet people.

Fear of diluting national problems in psychology (as though Marxism-Leninism had not elaborated a scientific methodology for studying the psychology of nations and national relations) has for many years made social scientists fail to study these phenomena. Now there are beginning to develop studies of real national processes. I would note though that what is particularly important right now are not uncoordinated studies by historians, philosophers, and so forth, but rather complex interdisciplinary work.

The interests of proletarian solidarity, in Lenin's words, demand that "we never treat the national question formalistically" (vol. 45, p. 360). This must also be understood to mean that there is no final universal answer to what is one of the most complex of humanity's problems, nor can there be. Every new stage brings out new problems. No doubt so shall it be in the future as well, as long as there are nations.

Editors' notes

a. Reference is to the riots in Alma-Ata in December 1986 which followed the appointment of G. Kolbin to replace D. Kunaev as first secretary of the Communist Party of Kazakhstan.

b. *Akyn*: a folk lyric singer.

c. Chokan Valikhanov (1835–1865) was the first Kazakh ethnographer.

d. Abai Kunanbaev (1845–1904) is considered by the Soviets to be the father of Kazakh literature.

3. Party Politics in the National Regions

Since taking over as General Secretary of the Party, Mikhail Gorbachev has repeatedly called for the complete restructuring (*perestroika*) of the CPSU as a necessary precondition for both the country's economic recovery and its restoration to a true Leninist system. Over time the fervor with which Gorbachev has pleaded his case has increased, as too has the magnitude of the changes called for. The demands for the dismissal of corrupt cadres, which seemed controversial when first made in 1985 and 1986, have been overshadowed by the calls for modification of the Party's structure and functions at the Nineteenth Party Conference in the summer of 1988. The proposed reforms call for the democraticization of Party life, with officials to be chosen from their constituencies in multiple-candidate elections, and a shifting of the role of the Party from ruling the country to supervising its economic, social, and political life.

The restructuring of Party life, which has proceeded at different rates in various parts of the country, has created a set of unique and oftentimes contradictory problems in the national republics. The Communist parties of the various union republics have been a special target of the *perestroika* campaign, because Gorbachev has argued that while Party corruption was prevalent throughout the USSR during the Brezhnev years, illegal practices were particularly pervasive in the national regions. It is certainly true that during the Brezhnev years in most union republics Moscow ceded most of the control of day-to-day Party affairs to an elite drawn primarily from the titular nationality. The earlier pattern—which featured a powerful Russian second secretary who would orchestrate events in the name of the locally appointed first secretary—had died out by the early 1970s, when a number of strong national minority leaders rose to prominence first in their home republics and then in the central Party apparatus as well.

At the time of Brezhnev's death four non-Russian republic Party leaders were members of the Politburo: Sh. Rashidov of Uzbekistan and G. Aliev of Azerbaidzhan were candidate members, and D. Kunaev of Kazakhstan and V. Shcherbitsky of the Ukraine were full members of that organization. All four men had succeeded in creating powerful networks of personal control in their home republics, and all four could justly be called corrupt, given the manner in which they rewarded the retinues of followers who helped them keep their republic economies functioning. The four national minority leaders on the Politburo were an example for republic Party leaders throughout the country. At the time of Brezhnev's death, most of the union republics (the Baltic republics excepted) were ruled by local communist overlords. These men distributed goods and services unevenly within their republics, in aid of their friends and supporters in particular but also to the benefit of their co-nationals more generally. The result was that each of these leaders had a stable support base from which to oppose Gorbachev's policies.

The Baltic republics had always been a special case, for even in the relatively lax conditions of Party supervision during Brezhnev's last years, the Latvians, Lithuanians, and Estonians continued to be viewed as suspect politically, and their respective Party organizations were closely overseen by Moscow. Moreover, the Baltic region had continued to experience positive economic growth rates while the economy in most of the rest of the country had begun to stagnate.

Almost immediately after taking over as General Secretary, Iurii Andropov began a campaign to end the abuse of power in the national regions, in furtherance of his goals of economic reform. Unlike Gorbachev, Andropov was careful to respect the reputation of incumbent office-holders, and couched his attack in terms of relatively general claims about abuses of authority. A December 1983 resolution on the failings of the leadership of the Moldavian Party organization laid out the standard of expected behavior for all of the union republics.

Moldavia was chosen for symbolic reasons. The republic was small and its leadership had little stature in Moscow, but it was a place where Brezhnev had served and where he had close personal ties. The Moldavian Party organization was not made the focus of the subsequent drive to cleanse the republic Party organizations of corrupt cadres. While Moldavia has seen its share of dismissals, the incumbent first secretary had yet to be replaced in 1989. Instead, the Central Asian republics in general and Uzbekistan in particular became the target of the anti-corruption drive in the national regions. Central Asia was an area of declining economic performance, but, as a major source of untapped manpower and material resources, it was of increasing importance as well. For Moscow to employ these resources, it had first to place them under more direct control.

In December 1983, the death of Uzbekistan's Party first secretary, Sharif Rashidov, removed a powerful impediment to reform in the most populous of the Central Asian republics. In the months following Rashidov's death, during a time when Konstantin Chernenko was General Secretary but Gorbachev and Ligachev managed most of the day-to-day affairs of the Party, Moscow orchestrated a campaign to rid Uzbekistan's Party organization of its old guard, with Russian cadres from outside the republic being posted to Uzbekistan when efforts to identify honest cadres locally proved disappointing.

Once Gorbachev took over as General Secretary, the campaign against the Central Asian Party organizations intensified, with incumbent Party officials subjected to public attack. As the purge of the republic Party organizations gathered intensity, scandals involving senior Party officials in all five Central Asian republics were revealed. The most publicized of these was in the cotton-growing sector in Uzbekistan, where the republic-wide practice of falsifying statistics for the amount of cotton grown and sold funneled unreported millions of rubles in income into the pockets of the senior leadership of the republic. While the new first secretary held on, more dismissals in Uzbekistan followed these revelations. Shortly before the convening of the Twenty-seventh Party Congress, the first secretaries of the Kirghiz, Turkmen, and Tadzhik parties were all removed in disgrace. The new first secretaries of Kirghizia and Turkmenistan were appointed following a stint of service in the central Party apparatus in Moscow under Ligachev's general direction. These appointments were consistent with the new practice of "exchanging" cadres between republics, which would be ratified at the Twenty-seventh Party Congress as a critical part of nationality policy.

At the congress, Party secretary Egor Ligachev provided the most succinct discussion of Moscow's program for purifying the parties in the national regions, in a speech which is reproduced in part below. The Leninist principles of Party management could only be restored, he argued, if national chauvinism could be controlled. All nationalities must have the right to serve in the Party apparatus and to be appointed without prejudice to their national origin. This would only occur, he maintained, if cadres were rotated nationwide, with officials from the national regions serving part of their careers in Moscow, and Party officials dispatched from Moscow to participate in Party affairs at all levels in the national regions. While Moscow had earlier felt able to assert control through the appointment of Russian second secretaries, now the loyalty of local Russians (who were prey to bribery by regional patronage networks) was also viewed as suspect, and the appointment of individuals who had few ties to the region in which they would serve was made a goal.

The new cadre policy for the national regions received its first major test in Kazakhstan. In December 1986, Kazakhstan's first secretary, D. A. Kunaev, a Politburo member and long-time crony of Brezhnev, was dismissed in disgrace and replaced by a Russian, G. Kolbin, an oblast Party committee first secretary from Ulianovsk. This action sparked several days of rioting by young Kazakhs in the republic's capital city of Alma-Ata.

Subsequently, the tempo of the attack on prominent non-Russian members of the Party leadership was tempered somewhat. Throughout 1987 attacks on corrupt Party practices in the republics where Brezhnev-era appointees remained in control continued (in the Ukraine, Moldavia, Armenia, and Azerbaidzhan), but only lesser figures, such as the Bashkir ASSR's Party first secretary M. Shakirov, were removed. Even the removal of Shakirov did not proceed very smoothly, as the Party plenum at which he was to be dismissed failed to do more than censure him, and a second plenum had to be held a few days later to carry out the actual dismissal. Shakirov was a typical national leader of the Brezhnev style who acquired a strong network of supporters by using his autonomous republic's economic resources to build an extensive patronage system.

The editorial by Shakirov which is reproduced below is typical of the prose with which Brezhnev-era leaders in the national regions announced their support for Moscow's programs. This particular piece was written immediately after the adoption of the food program, still in effect, which was intended to substantially improve the quality and quantity of foodstuffs produced in the USSR. The proud language of praise of Bashkiria's accomplishments and its indebtedness to Moscow is quite typical of the type of effusive tribute paid by loyal Brezhnev stalwarts. The exaggeration of the "friendship" between the Russian and Bashkir peoples is representative of the oversimplification or misrepresentation of history that characterized official statements of Soviet nationality policy during the late Brezhnev years. But while most of the republic Party leaders were effusive about the brilliance of Brezhnev's leadership and their devotion to the great Russian people, they ran their republics with obvious preference to the employment of co-nationals, and to the great personal advantage of their own retinues of relatives and followers.

Gorbachev's campaign to appoint dependable cadres has followed a different course in the Baltic republics, where the population, firmly annexed to the USSR only in 1944, is strongly sympathetic to nationalist aims. Until mid–1988 it was an unchallenged assumption that the Party organizations in these republics would serve Moscow's will and not that of the local population.

The article by K. Vaino, first secretary of the Communist Party of Estonia until June 1988, is characteristic of the types of concerns that preoccupied Party officials in the Baltic region in the early 1980s. Vaino complains of the inefficiency of regional- and enterprise-level Party organizations and their particularly poor work in transmitting Moscow's ideological goals. He expresses particular concern about the growing alienation of youth from the goals of the Communist Party. The organization of mass-supported popular fronts with detailed agendas for social and political change in all three Baltic republics has convincingly demonstrated the widespread dissatisfaction of the population with the preexisting goals and programs of the CPSU and the manner of their implementation in this region.

For the present at least, as is detailed in much greater length in section ten below, Moscow is displaying great sensitivity to many of the demands made by the Latvians, Lithuanians, and Estonians. Rather than continue to pit the republic Party organizations against their local constituencies, Moscow has sought instead to try to gain greater legitimacy for the parties by appointing first secretaries who are seen as having credibility both in Moscow and among local advocates of political reform.

Vaino was removed as republic Party first secretary because Estonians viewed him as being too hard-line. His successor, V. Vialias, the former Soviet ambassador to Nicaragua, has few ties to the local Party leadership, but is expected to be more sympathetic to the nationalist sensibilities of most Estonians. Similarly, the new first secretaries of the Latvian and Lithuanian parties were chosen because of their reputed willingness to work with the reform movements within their republics to further nationalist aims.

Moscow hopes that if the Baltic republics are permitted greater self-rule, their local economies, already more modern and efficient than those of the country generally, will be strengthened as well. However, there are no such hopes when it comes to increasing the local autonomy of other union republics, except perhaps Belorussia. Throughout the rest of the country Gorbachev has continued his policy of appointing as senior union republic figures individuals who have have few direct ties with the local republic Party organization. The individuals chosen in 1988 to head Armenia's, Azerbaidzhan's, and Uzbekistan's communist parties were all members of the respective titular nationality but all had served most of their careers outside their home republic. Thus it could safely be assumed that they owed few favors to the local incumbent Party leaders.

However, even while keeping a tight rein on the appointment of Party leaders, Moscow has found it difficult to transform Party life in many of the national republics. Indeed, the appointments have often provoked ill-will from local Party leaders who felt they had been passed over unfairly, and from the republic Party membership more generally, which tended to feel that their nationality was being slighted or unfairly criticized. This is particularly true of the Uzbeks, who complain that their corruption scandals have been splashed across the country's press, while those of other nationalities have been handled more discreetly.

Yet even with *glasnost'* it is still impolitic to criticize Moscow's appointment policy; local Party leaders are still required to praise those appointed and condemn those dismissed. While Moscow is pushing for greater democraticization of Party life, it is clear that Party self-government is intended to begin at the bottom and not at the elite level. Pleased as many were about the choice of Vialias as Estonian Communist Party first secretary, there was still criticism of the manner of his selection; Vialias was Moscow's choice in a single-candidate election.

Thus, the publication of even a brief note of disgruntlement such as the one that appeared in the Estonian press is extraordinary. Far more typical of discussions of Party politics is the article by former Tashkent oblast first secretary Timur Alimov, reproduced below. Alimov writes of how few Party officials are coming to Uzbekistan from outside the republic and also of the advantages that accrue to all through the exchange of cadres between regions. A year after writing the article Alimov himself was "rotated" from his position.

However, there is little evidence that the rotation of cadres has decisively broken the pattern of corruption. Accounts from Uzbekistan suggest otherwise. In the past two years criminal proceedings have been brought against a former chairman of the Council of Ministers of Uzbekistan, a former deputy chairman of the Supreme Soviet of Uzbekistan, four former secretaries of the Uzbek Party bureau, and six former oblast Party committee secretaries. Both Rashidov and his successor Usmankhodzhaev (living on a pension in Moscow) have been implicated in the cotton scandal, and it appears likely that charges will soon be brought against several oblast Party committee first secretaries dismissed in late 1988. Moreover, there are now rumors that similar scandals will be revealed in other republics, scandals that are allegedly being hushed up by Gorbachev's own appointees.

Thus, while it is clear that Gorbachev is now powerful enough to appoint the individuals of his choice to fill the senior leadership posts throughout the country, control of the appointment process has not afforded him control of day-to-day affairs in many of the union republics. In the Baltic republics concerns of economic efficiency and political stability dictated the appointment of individuals who feel some loyalty to their own population as well as to Moscow. In the Caucasian and Central Asian republics the policy of an inter-republican exhange of cadres has led to the elimination of the anti-reform leadership that had long dominated each of these republics, but it has yet to prove itself to be an effective means of insuring the honesty and efficiency of local Party organizations.

In Friendship Lies our Strength *

M. SHAKIROV

Bashkiria,[a] four times the recipient of decorations of honor, is preparing to celebrate—in company with the whole friendly family of equal Soviet republics jointly
engaged in building communism—a momentous anniversary of our unified multinational state. Born six decades ago, this state has become the great socialist Fatherland of all the nations and nationalities inhabiting the land of the soviets. The
workers of our republic, together with the entire Soviet people—firmly united
behind their beloved Communist Party and its Central Committee, headed by the
faithful continuer of Lenin's work, Comrade L. I. Brezhnev—look forward to this
glorious anniversary in a state of high labor and political enthusiasm, amidst unselfish struggles to implement the historic resolutions of the Twenty-sixth Congress of
the CPSU.

At this moment, the attention of the work collectives of Bashkiria—and of the
entire country—is focused on the resolutions of the May (1982) Plenum of the
Central Committee of the CPSU and on the Food Program of the USSR which it
approved for the period to 1990.

The workers of our republic all welcomed these documents with enormous
enthusiasm and endorsed them wholeheartedly, and they gave their undivided support to the Party's sagacious domestic and foreign policies.

The Plenum materials were the subject of highly vigorous discussions in party
organizations, at sessions of local soviets, and by the collectives on the farms and in
the enterprises. Every worker is conscious of his social responsibility to take part in
the countrywide effort to implement the Food Program.

Agricultural workers are striving to achieve significant results already in this first
year of implementation of the Food Program. They are struggling to increase
production and sales to the state of crops and animal products, laying in fodder at a
rapid pace, and mobilizing in force to bring in the new harvest. Their fine performance in the first half-year holds out realistic prospects for sale of no less than one
million tons of milk to the state in the current year.

For our republic this year is all the more significant for the fact that it ushers in
the 425th anniversary of Bashkiria's voluntary accession to the Russian state.[b]
Bashkiria's incorporation into Russia marked a turning point in the history of the
Bashkir people, for it sealed their friendship and unity with the great Russian people
for all time to come. Close association with this power secured the land from foreign
enslavement and preserved it from fragmentation and internal strife. New economic
ties hastened the break-up of feudal patriarchal relations and paved the way for

---

*Izvestiia, 23 July 1982, p. 3. Russian text © 1982 by "Izvestiia."

Bashkiria's access to advanced material and spiritual culture.

The progressive significance of Bashkiria's inclusion in the Russian state is also manifested in the fact that the working masses of the area rose up in arms, together with the Russian people, to fight against the autocracy. A striking manifestation of the fighting alliance of workers belonging to different nationalities was the peasant war under the leadership of Emelian Pugachev.[c] In this war, the oppressed Bashkirs took an active part, together with Russian working people. We note with pride that at this distant time our people produced from their midst the talented military leader, thinker and poet, one who embodied the best features of our national character—the legendary Salavat Iulaev.[d] However, spontaneous peasant uprisings were unable to bring an end to social and national oppression. It was only when the proletariat of Russia appeared on the political arena that realistic prospects for wiping out exploitation and achieving genuine internationalist solidarity materialized. We are infinitely proud of the fact that the revolutionary movement in our land from its very inception, was guided by Vladimir Il'ich Lenin. In 1900 he visited Bashkiria twice and created there one of the first and strongest bases of support for the newspaper *Iskra*. Vladimir Il'ich and Nadezhda Konstantinova Krupskaia, who were then living in Ufa in exile, nurtured a whole host of staunch revolutionaries, such as A. D. Tsiurupa, I. S. Yakutov, A. I. Sviderskii, N. P. Briukhanov, the Kadomtsev brothers, O. A. Varentsova, T. S. Krivov[e] and many others whose activities left a clear imprint on our heroic history and exerted a strong influence on the formation of class consciousness of the Bashkir people.

Today we note again with profound gratitude, that it was the great Lenin who presided over the creation of Soviet Bashkiria. It was his signature that validated the document proclaiming the formation of the Bashkir Autonomous Soviet Socialist Republic, one of the first state formations that make up the Russian Federation.[f] For the first time in their thousand-year history, a people previously oppressed and deprived of rights acquired their own national state system.

The whole history of the Bashkir ASSR constitutes one impressive chronicle of fraternal friendship among Soviet peoples and clear evidence of the triumph of the Party's wise Leninist nationality policy. The friendship among the Russian, Bashkir and other peoples of our multinational homeland was tempered in the fires of the Civil War and the Great Patriotic War, on the construction sites called into being by the five-year plans, and in the building of a developed socialist society.

Over the years of Soviet power, under the leadership of the Communist Party of the Soviet Union, as part of the fraternal family of peoples of the Russian Federation and the whole country, Bashkiria has been transformed into a flourishing autonomous socialist republic with a powerful industry, highly developed agriculture, and advanced science and culture.

The triumph of the party's Leninist nationality policy is clearly reflected in our republic as it appears today. Its industrial profile is represented by giant oil refineries and petrochemical plants, machine building and power engineering metallurgy and microbiology, light industry and food processing—in all, enterprises covering over 150 branches of the modern economy.

A vast program of capital construction has been carried out in the republic.

Science, education and culture have truly soared. As in the country at large, the transition to universal secondary education has been completed. Every third resident of the republic is studying. Training of highly qualified specialists in some hundred different fields is taking place at ten institutions of higher learning. Fruitful work is conducted at our branch of the Academy of Sciences of the USSR and 50 scientific-research and planning institutes and design offices, engaging 250 doctors and 2,500 candidates of sciences.

Bashkir literature has become an integral part of Soviet multinational culture. The works of our writers have been published in dozens of languages in the USSR and abroad. More than 100 theaters throughout the country have staged the best plays of Bashkir playwrights. All this has been made possible thanks to the Party's unremitting concern for raising the culture of every socialist nation.

Achievements in both the material and spiritual spheres of life have fundamentally transformed the social profile of our land. While at the time of the victorious October Revolution the urban population constituted only six percent of the total, today the corresponding figure is over 50 percent. New cities—Ishimbai, Oktiabr'skii, Salavat, Kumertau, Uchaly, Neftekamsk, Tuimazy, Meleuz—have sprung up. Ufa, Sterlitamak, Beloretsk, Belebei, and Birsk have been modernized beyond recognition.

A child of the Great October and the pride of the republic is our working class—an army more than a million strong. Hundreds of thousands of machine operators and diplomatically qualified specialists form the bulk of the population in the countryside. The large cohort of our splendid illustrious intelligentsia enjoys deserved recognition.

The foundation and material basis for the friendship of peoples of the USSR, which grows stronger by the day, lies in successfully developing our country's unified economic complex. It serves the interests of the entire Soviet people and each socialist nation and nationality.

The economy of each republic occupies an important place in the division of labor in our society and makes an ever greater contribution to national wealth and to the augmentation of our beloved Motherland's might.

The workers of Bashkiria experience fraternal assistance and friendship every day, in the course of their practical affairs. An continuous stream of goods flows our way from all corners of the boundless Soviet land. From Western Siberia comes oil for refining, from Central Asia—natural gas, from the smelters of the Urals, Lipetsk, and the Krivoi Rog region—metals. A true child of our great friendship of peoples is the republic's large chemical industry. The wide variety of equipment for this industry was manufactured by hundreds of production collectives in the many oblasts, krais, and autonomous republics of the RSFSR, Ukraine, Belorussia, the republics of Central Asia, the Transcaucasus, and the Baltic.

And so today, in the year that marks the 60th anniversary of the USSR and commemorates the 425th anniversary of the voluntary accession of Bashkiria to Russia, we express our sincere gratitude to the great Russian people and to all the peoples of our multinational Fatherland for their unselfish friendship and generous assistance.

In its turn, our republic—as an integral part of our country's unified economic complex—makes an appreciable contribution to the all-union and all-Russian division of labor, and participates in its socialist integration. It maintains an important position in the fuel and energy balance. In the past half century, 1.08 billion tons of oil and more than 50 billion cubic meters of natural gas have been extracted from its depths. The greatest oil refining capacity in the country is concentrated here. More than half of the soda ash produced in the RSFSR, and over one-fifth of the caustic soda, some 30 percent of chemical pesticides, and one-third of the oil-extracting equipment is produced in our republic.

We consider our primary duty and sacred obligation to be the effective utilization of the economic potential that has been developed in our republic for the further strengthening of the might of the Motherland.

Socialism has opened up broad vistas for the interchange of spiritual values. In this process the Russian language plays a special role.

"I am not Russian, but I am of Russia.[g] There can be no higher honor—I am a son of the Soviet land." These words of Bashkiria's national poet, Mustai Karim,[h] express an infinite pride and fraternal affection for the great Russian people.

Having forever united their destiny with Russia, the Bashkirs and representatives of other nationalities have come to know the beautiful soul of the Russian people, and its rich and mighty language has become their second native tongue. We can declare with pride: Lenin's behest that every inhabitant of Russia have the opportunity to learn the Russian language has been successfully realized in our republic. More than four-fifths of the non-Russian population have free command of the language of the great Lenin or consider it their native tongue.[i] This is a priceless gift, a fortunate gain.

Comrade L. I. Brezhnev spoke eloquently about our republic: "The Bashkir land is free and, I should add, highly developed. Mighty industries—chemical, energy, machine building, and petroleum—large-scale animal husbandry, considerable expanses of grain fields—all this and much more is to be found in this autonomous republic. Its contribution to the general potential of the Motherland grows from one Five-Year Plan period to the next."

Such extraordinary commendation inspires all the workers of the republic to strive toward new and even higher accomplishments for the glory of our beloved Motherland. And on this solemn day we address words of filial love and infinite gratitude to the heroic party of Lenin, whose revolutionary will brought about the most profound material and spiritual transformations in all corners of our boundless Motherland, and enabled us to overcome centuries of backwardness, attaining the heights of social progress, and participate in the highest forms of political organization of society.

The Communists and all the workers of Bashkiria will become even more firmly united behind the Leninist Central Committee; they will exhibit even greater initiative, creativity, selflessness, and perseverence in their struggle for the shining ideals of communism; they will meet the 60th anniversary of their beloved state with new successes in implementing the historic resolutions of the Twenty-sixth Congress of the CPSU and the May Plenum of the Central Committee; and they will further enhance the prestige of their republic within the fraternal family of peoples of the Union of Soviet Socialist Republics.

Editor's notes

a. One of six neighboring autonomous republics in the ethnically heterogeneous middle Volga–Urals region of the European Russian SFSR, Bashkiria covers an area of 55,450 sq. mi., with a population of 3,876,000 (1982). Originally a steppeland domain of pastoral nomads, the territory, richly endowed with natural resources, now supports well-developed extractive and manufacturing industries. The Bashkirs—a Turkic-speaking, Muslim, traditionally nomadic people, linguistically and culturally close to the more numerous and sedentary Tatars—now constitute a distinct minority in the ASSR—24.3%, outnumbered not only by the Russians (40.3%), but also by the Tatars (24.5%). The capital is Ufa, with a 1982 population of 1,023,000.

b. The annexation of Bashkiria, following the Russian conquest of the Tatar khanate of Kazan' in 1552, is traditionally dated in Soviet historiography from 1557. The pacification of the land, however, was a long process, extending well into the eighteenth century and interspersed with numerous local uprisings. In current Soviet historiography, the territorial expansion of Russia is interpreted as a series of voluntary accessions.

c. The rebellion (1773–1775) led by Emelian Pugachev, an insurrection against the government of Catherine II that was the most serious in eighteenth-century Russia, encompassed at its height huge territories in the Urals and Volga regions. It was joined by diverse social and ethnic groups, each with its own set of grievances, among whom the Bashkirs played an especially prominent role.

d. Salavat Iulaev (b. 1752–d. 1800), revered by the Bashkirs as their great national hero, was the leader of Bashkir contingents in the Pugachev uprising, as well as a bard, whose verse, for long only orally transmitted, is now considered to be the foundation of Bashkir literature.

e. All ethnic Russians, these were among the key figures in the creation of prerevolutionary Marxist cells in the Urals region (primarily in Ufa) or in the Civil War and early years of Bolshevik rule in Bashkiria.

f. The decree establishing the Bashkir ASSR was published on March 23, 1919.

g. In Russian: *ne russkii ia, no rossiianin*. The original does not permit a comprehensible direct translation, for it involves a nuanced distinction between two terms—*russkii* and *rossiianin*—both rendered in English as "Russian" (literally, "I am not Russian, but I am a Russian"). *Russkii* is the ethnic name and national self-designation of Russians—something the Bashkir writer is clearly not. *Rossiianin* has a broader, non-ethnic connotation, derived from *Rossiia*, meaning Russia as a state or territory—the name applied to the former tsarist Empire since the reign of Peter I, or currently to the Russian SFSR. Clearly, the writer intends to convey some affinity or identity with Russia, one that is not ethnically based, but whether it is territorial, historical, cultural, or spiritual is impossible to tell.

h. Mustai Karim: pseudonym of Mustafa Safich Karimov (b. 1919), a much decorated Bashkir poet and a prominent public figure in the Bashkir ASSR.

i. Although the trend is clearly in this direction, the claim is still premature. According to the 1979 census, 73% of the non-Russian population of Bashkiria reported Russian as their first (7.8%) or second (65.2%) language; of the Bashkirs alone, a total of 65.2% reported knowledge of Russian—2.7% as their native, and 62.5% as their second fluent language.

Annotated by Lubomyr Hajda

With a Sound Grasp of the Situation *

K. VAINO

1

Our republican Party organization and the Central Committee of the Communist Party of Estonia keep close and steady watch over all problems connected with ideological work, striving constantly to bring to the practical task of educating workers a more concretely historical approach, one firmly grounded in Marxist-Leninist theory, a sound grasp of the situation, and a well considered plan of action. We organized our work in the realm of workers' ideological-political education with due regard for the conditions peculiar to our republic.

As is well known, the workers of Estonia, together with all the peoples of Russia, fought against the tsarist autocracy and took a most active part in the Great October socialist revolution and the defense of the first workers' and peasants' state in the world. For objective reasons, however, it proved impossible to sustain their revolutionary achievements in Estonia at that time. There ensued a twenty-year period of bourgeois rule.[a] Day after day the ruling circles of the bourgeois republic poisoned the workers' consciousness with the venom of nationalism and fueled hostility toward the Russian people and hatred for the Soviet state. Policy affecting all spheres of life was oriented toward the West.

Soviet power in Estonia was restored only in 1940, but its duration was not long, for shortly afterwards the republic was occupied by fascist Germany.[b] Our ideological adversary nowadays tries to take certain advantage of this, counting on the relative recentness of Soviet power in Estonia and on the fact that one can still find people in our republic whose consciousness was long exposed to the intense influence of bourgeois ideology. The liberation of Estonia from the German fascist invaders prompted the immediate accomplices of Hitlerism, former factory owners, merchants, kulaks, officials of the bourgeois state apparatus, and other such rubbish to emigrate.[c] Among those who left were some people duped by anti-Soviet propaganda. Abroad, mainly in Sweden, there grew up Estonian emigré communities with a leadership engaged in the service of anticommunism and supported by imperialist intelligence agencies. Even now the bourgeois-nationalist, anti-Soviet organizations that were formed there are trying to establish links with citizens of our republic—through correspondence by mail, packages, telephone conversations, personal contacts, etc. Visits to relatives, tourism, and cultural exchanges are also widely used for this purpose. Subversive organizations produce and by various means try to disseminate in our midst publications that are saturated through and through with

---

*Kommunist, 1982, no. 4, pp. 51–61. Russian text © 1983 by "Kommunist."

hatred for our country and full of malicious and mendacious fabrications about Soviet reality. The emigré organizations actively collaborate with hostile radio "voices" in the West.

One also ought to mention our geographical proximity to the major ideological centers of the West. The actions of imperialism directed at Soviet Estonia and the Soviet Union are meant to "correct a historical mistake," as Reagan put it, and bring about the liquidation of socialism and the restoration of capitalism.

Imperialist circles, especially in the United States of America, are turning the ideological struggle against the Soviet Union and the other socialist countries into a kind of "psychological war." The shifting tactics of our increasingly more cunning and insolent ideological adversaries are manifested in novel types of ideological sabotage. One may cite, for example, one such action directed against Soviet Estonia, when letters were sent out to many residents of Tallinn with the call: "Read and pass on."

What did these epistles represent? Vile incitements to engage in strikes similar to those conducted by "Solidarity" in Poland. For example, "If you are for justice and democracy, then take part in a 'half-hour's silence' strike, beginning on December 1. Then do the same every first day of the following months."

The "Voice of America," the "BBC," the "Deutsche Welle," "Radio Sweden," and "Radio Canada" gave broad publicity to this action, contending falsely that a "major strike" would take place in Soviet Estonia on December 1. But the organizers of this hostile campaign suffered a complete fiasco and their scheme fell through ignominiously. And it could not have turned out otherwise.

The ideological saboteurs, who conceived this plan to "sound out the situation" in Estonia, ran into the high degree of organization and unity of our people. The workers of our republic understood perfectly well the nature of the planned provocation, and in so doing demonstrated their political maturity and civic consciousness. Party and economic activists energetically conducted explanatory work among the populace, pointing out the necessity for even greater political vigilance in the future.

V. I. Lenin wrote: "When the bourgeoisie's ideological influence cn the workers declines, is undermined or weakened, the bourgeoisie *everywhere and always* resorts to the most outrageous lies and slander" (*Polnoe Sobranie Sochinenii*, [Collected Works], vol. 25, p. 352). The world situation today could not be better described.

The slightest weakening of communist influence on people's consciousness would objectively help intensify bourgeois influence, for, of course, there never is and cannot be any ideological vacuum. To forget this Marxist-Leninist premise is to court enormous harm.

Not even very long ago, some people in our country reasoned complacently that our modern times bring their own influence to bear, that Soviet reality itself serves to educate people, and so, even if some individuals do not understand everything, there is no special reason for concern. The socialist system does, of course, shape the people's consciousness. But life shows something else as well: a passive, hands-off attitude and inattention to political education undermining the aggressiveness and vigor in the conduct of ideological work.

The Central Committee of the Communist Party of Estonia and the city and raion Party committees managed to appraise the situation in time, take a critical look at the whole of their work, and make the necessary changes. The Fifteenth Plenum of the Central Committee of the Communist Party of Estonia, which convened in July 1979, analyzed the state of ideological work in our republic and drafted concrete measures for its improvement. Such matters, in particular, as heightened militancy and aggressiveness in ideological work and a totally party-spirited, high-principled and uncompromising attitude toward any manifestations of political immaturity or myopia were squarely confronted.

We are trying to make known to every worker the sentiment expressed by the General Secretary of the Central Committee of the CPSU, Comrade Iu. V. Andropov, at the November (1982) Plenum of the Central Committee: "The CPSU opposes turning the battle of ideas into a confrontation between states or peoples, or making weapons and willing to use them as a yardstick of the potentialities of different social systems." Our class adversaries, however, are making every effort to turn the battle of ideas into a confrontation, a "psychological war" against the socialist countries, one that in its scope and intensity would exceed all precedents set during the "Cold War." That is why in the present situation it is especially important to unmask the anti-Soviet, anticommunist campaign and the ideological sabotage conducted by our class enemies.

Our Party activists, and Communists in general, understand full well the challenges we face and the degree of their responsibility for the state of affairs and for the ideological situation in our republic. These problems are always within our Party organization's field of vision. There are, of course, quite a few other matters that still trouble us. Not all Party workers are sufficiently well prepared or possess the necessary knowledge to conduct ideological-educational work with skill and competence, nor do they always come up with correct and timely solutions to problems that arise in the course of life.

One problem area is our small labor collectives, which as a rule have numerically small Party organizations. They account for more than 42% of the total in our republic. Because of their small membership and weakness they do not wield sufficient influence. Meanwhile, it is precisely in the small establishments' various offices, commercial enterprises, and some educational institutions, that the need for stronger ideological influence is most acutely felt, for that is where various rumors and idle gossip circulate and questionable opinions prevail most frequently. For this reason we have undertaken measures to improve the work of the numerically small Party organizations and to strengthen their role.

The city and raion Party committees have now begun to devote significantly more attention to these Party organizations. Matters such as how to energize their activities are discussed at meetings of Party committees and at sessions of their bureaus. The Central Committee of the Communist Party of Estonia has examined the reports of the Kohtla-Järve and Narva City Party Committees on the style of leadership in numerically small Party organizations and the ways of raising the effectiveness of their work.

Attached to the Methodology Council of the Office for Party Organizational Affairs of the Pärnu City Party Committee is a division responsible for numerically small Party organizations. These, experienced Party workers investigate the state of affairs locally, explore the possibilities for creating new Party groups, and conduct seminars. Secretaries of numerically small Party organizations regularly present oral reports to the bureaus of city Party committees. Many Party committees follow appropriately differentiated methods of work with their secretaries. Special emphasis is placed on strengthening the role of Communists as the vanguard of society.

As we proceeded to reorganize our work, we became aware of a critical need to find more effective, broad-based , and, what is most important, competent means of informing workers about the Party's domestic and foreign policies, life in our republic, those difficulties that still exist and problems that remain unsolved. To remedy shortcomings in this area, we introduced, in accordance with the resolution adopted by the Central Committee of the CPSU "On the Further Improvement of Ideological and Politico-educational Work,"a system of uniformly designated "politics days" when republican leaders on a regular basis, at least once a month, address various labor collectives.

Practical experience has also made us aware of other matters, for example, the importance of a comprehensive approach to the planning and coordination of activities conducted by various organizations and establishments. The republican and local Party committees have worked out their long-term comprehensive plans in the area of ideological work and political education with this in mind. These have identified the aims and the practical tasks for Party organizations and those institutions engaged in ideological work, and defined the ways, forms, and methods for solving the challenges they face. In these plans matters dealing with counter-propaganda and the struggle with bourgeois ideology are treated in special sections.

The All-Union Scientific-Practical Conference on "The Intensification of the Ideological Struggle in the World Arena and the Political Education of Workers," held in Tallinn in October 1982, gave fresh stimulus to ideological work in our republic. To implement the recommendations appropriate measures have been designed at the level of the Central Committee of the Communist Party of Estonia, in the city and raion Party committees, and in organizations and institutions engaged in ideological work. Envisaged are improved coordination of measures being implemented in our republic with regard to ideology and more persistent efforts to expose the true nature of imperialist propaganda.

Within the Committee on Ideology of the Central Committee of the Communist Party of Estonia a special section on international information has been set up. Analogous sections or committees are being formed at city and raion Party committees and in other major Party committees. The study of problems connected with the ideological struggle has been significantly expanded, both within the educational system and at the faculties and departments of the university of Marxism-Leninism. Training in the methodology of unmasking bourgeois propaganda is given serious attention. Visiting lecturers engaged by the Party committees and political information specialists who speak publicly on these matters are undergoing specialized training and the level of their training is being improved. Methodological guides and appropriate thematic materials have been developed for amateur performance groups, agitators' brigades, and designers of graphic materials for agitation purposes.

2

Ideological work is multifarious. But I should like to stress here in particular one—in our view, exceptionally important—aspect of this work: the patriotic, internationalist education of the populace and the strengthening of friendship among the Soviet peoples.

At the solemn commemoration of the sixtieth anniversary of the formation of the USSR, Comrade Iu. V. Andropov remarked that: "A constant challenge, of abiding importance, is the education of Soviet people in the spirit of mutual respect and friendship among all the nations and nationalities of our country, love for their great Soviet Motherland, internationalism, and solidarity with the workers of other countries."

Our small republic is multinational. The collectives of industrial workers, scientists, artists, pedagogues that have been formed and carry on their fruitful work here are multinational. Daily collaboration in the workplace helps to entrench such principles of a socialist way of life as collectivism, fellowship, friendship of peoples, and intolerance for deviations from standards of socialist morality.

Patriotism and internationalism—these lofty attributes of the Soviet people— have become a rule of life for the vast majority of the population of our republic's population. Cooperation among our multinational labor collectives and ties that have been formed with many enterprises all over the country, help to ensure the successful fulfillment of our production targets.

At the same time, the enormous scale and growing complexity of the tasks involved in the building of communism, as well as the increasing internationalization of the life of Soviet society on the one hand, and the intensification of the ideological struggle on the other make ever greater demands on the level of Party of the process of development of national relations and the patriotic and internationalist education of the populace.

It is well known that bourgeois ideologues always place their bets on nationalism. Nationalistic conceptions are more and more widely used in their subversive propaganda against the USSR. For example, the objective process of formation of a multinational population in the Estonian SSR, as in every one of our republics, is represented in bourgeois propaganda as "assimilation" or "swallowing up of one nation by another." The natural process of internationalization in the economic, social, cultural, and other spheres of our social life is portrayed as a loss of "national identity," the result of "a policy of forced fusion of nations" and their "Russification."

Though hundreds, even thousands, of facts testify to the robust development of Estonian national culture in the years of Soviet rule, hostile propaganda stubbornly propounds the thesis of some "impending extinction" of the Estonian culture and language. "All sorts of scholars" hammer away on this theme at all possible symposia and meetings. It resounds from bourgeois television screens and from the pages of bourgeois newspapers, and comes up in private conversations. These intrigues by our ideological adversaries are aimed especially at young people, who have not yet been tempered sufficiently by life and class experience, and also at the intelligentsia. And, sad to say, these paltry ideas are sometimes not without interest to other politically naive people.

Recently, the Party organizations in our republic have been devoting more attention to matters of internationalist education. At a series of Central Committee plenums and conferences of Party ideological workers we made a critical assessment of the situation, an exceedingly thorough one both with regard to matters of principle and concrete fact, and directed the local Party organizations to launch a decisive struggle against any manifestations of nationalism. We have begun to speak more frequently and forcefully about these topics with larger contingents of our ideological workers—in courses and seminars, in lectures and discussions, in the course of "politics days," in the press, on television and radio.

Last summer, for example, at the Central Committee of the Communist Party of Estonia there was a detailed discussion of problems dealing with patriotic and internationalist education. Specific measures were approved for further improvements in all aspects of this work—socioeconomic, ideological, scientific, and cultural. Here, the particular features of various population groups were taken into account with special attention to those most susceptible to hostile influences. We have, moreover, taken appropriate steps to satisfy the specific needs—in such areas as culture, language, and everyday life—of citizens belonging to other than the indigenous nationality, and expanded the provision of information on our republican television and radio in the Russian language.

Recognizing the importance of Russian as the language of internationality communication and a factor promoting the sociopolitical and ideological unity of the Soviet people, we are continually striving to improve the quality of Russian language study.

The center of activity with regard to the internationalist education of the workers has shifted to the labor collective, the crucible where all the Party's objectives and all the challenges we face turn into reality and become a living, material force. It is here that we find the most favorable conditions for cultivating a sense of friendship among peoples and the all-national pride of Soviet man.

A matter of constant concern on the part of our republic's Party organizations is the organization of Party studies. Guided by the decree of the Central Committee of the CPSU "On the Further Improvement of Party Studies in Light of the Decisions of the Twenty-Sixth Congress of the CPSU," we have directed our ideological cadres' attention to the need for comprehensive study of matters dealing with the ideological struggle. At present there are in Estonia over 300 study groups looking at these problems. They are given more attention at seminars for propagandists and in courses for the improvement of professional qualifications of Party workers and officials of the soviets. More materials on this topic are in the process of preparation as an aid to lecturers and propagandists.

It is especially important for every Party member to become an active political fighter against hostile propaganda. Unfortunately, some Communists at times lack sufficient boldness, powers of persuasion, and skills to engage in open confrontation with various manifestations of an alien ideology. That is why we consider the problem of improving our Communists' grounding in Marxism-Leninism and their political studies as a fundamental and crucial one. In recent years, the number of Communists in the Party school system who are studying problems of theory, including the Party's nationality policy and the ideological struggle, has almost doubled.

It is would be difficult to overestimate the role that television, radio, and the print media play in the political education of the populace. Under current conditions these are the most important means of influencing people. Radio and television audience surveys confirm the need to provide for more effective interpretation of domestic and international events. This is now taken into account in our republican radio and television programming. For example, various commentaries on international events are broadcast in Estonian up to ten times a day. The scope of music, drama, and sports programming is also being increased.

Quite popular in our republic are thematical broadcasts on political subjects. Estonian television has acquired a great deal of experience in organizing such programs, which have been a steady feature now for over fifteen years. The most successful of these were programs about the Great Fatherland War and about the history of the struggle by the Communist Party of Estonia to win power for the working people and to bring about the victory of socialism. Some additional twenty broadcasts of a literary-journalistic type were also devoted to the Great October socialist revolution. An extensive cycle of programs "In One, United Family" presents a sweeping panorama of life in our republic. Broadly conceived series of broadcasts—"Our Vast Land," "Visiting with Friends," "Sixty Minutes"—describe life in Estonia and all the fraternal republics. As earlier, the republican press, publishing houses, cinema documentaries, and agitation employing visual aids continue to play an important role in the political education of man.

There is a superabundance of facts testifying to the sociopolitical, spiritual, and moral crisis in bourgeois society. But the presentation of this subject in our propaganda is sometimes lacking in the depth of its conclusions and generalizations, apt juxtaposition of facts contrasting the development of the two worlds, power of persuasion and journalistic skill. In this area serious work still remains to be done.

The Central Committee of the CPSU aims to have our ideological cadres demonstrate our achievements, in a convincing, concrete way, analyze seriously those new problems that arise in the course of life itself, and strive for freshness of thought and expression, for in this lies the path to enhancement of all our propaganda, which is called to be ever truthful and realistic, interesting, lucid, and thus—more effective.

It is appropriate to say something here about the place and role of oral propaganda. Views that maintain that the role of the lecturer and the political information specialist is allegedly in connection with the widespread availability of the new media of mass information and propaganda are untenable. Quite the contrary, their role today is growing. Our Party has always gone to the workers with the living word, and this is no less important today than earlier.

Oral communication is first and foremost a trusting, frank communication with people. In our view, these needs are increasingly met by our republic-wide "politics days." On the average about half the workers in our republic take part at the same time in a single, common "politics day." Leading workers appear publicly not only in large but also small labor collectives, on the shop floor, in the brigades, on the farms, at enterprises engaged in retail trade and consumer services, transport and communication, in educational establishments, research institutes and cultural institutions. Other forms of mass political work are also widely practiced: question and answer sessions, and topical discussions which allow us to gain a deeper understanding of public opinion on issues of current interest, to shape this opinion more vigorously, and to unmask slanderous fabrications. In a word, "politics days" are an effective way to conduct political work and to strengthen the ties between the Party and the masses.

We think that leaders should make their appearances not only before organizations under their own jurisdiction. As we have observed, a suitable talk by our republic's Minister of Education about school affairs and problems with, say, construction workers will be of considerable benefit both to the listeners and to the speaker himself. For a leader, be he from the Party or the economic sphere, virtually nothing can take the place of what he learns in direct contact with workers from different cities and districts, enterprises, collective farms, and institutions.

The suggestions we receive in the course of these "politics days" are analyzed and summarized at the Central Committee of the Communist Party of Estonia and at the city and raion Party committees. On the basis of the materials thus obtained, we deal with problems raised by the workers work out and specific measures of propagandistic character. Television and radio, newspapers and magazines carry a regular feature called "A Question Posed During a Politics Day." The introduction of "politics days" has bolstered the Party's influence on people, for the leading workers have become closer and more accessible to the masses. They do not avoid polemics, and have gained experience in answering pointed questions. And people trust them. It is revealing that since these "politics days" have become a regular occurrence, rumors and idle gossip appear much less frequently.

Of course our leaders' direct participation in mass political work in no way obviates the need for presentation by public speakers, lecturers, political information specialists, and agitators.

In recent years the organs of the Party and the soviets in our republic have paid increasing attention to the needs and requirements of city micro-districts. Their population make-up is multinational, and here, in routine daily situations the typical features of the Soviet way of life, internationalist in its very essence, are constantly being strengthened and enriched.

In the cities and the rural districts of Estonia there are over 800 micro-district soviets. They help to carry on mass political and cultural-educational work including the unmasking of bourgeois propaganda, its provocative character and methods. Lecturers and political information specialists meet regularly with the residents of these micro-districts in the reading and recreation rooms at the administrative centers of residential complexes and in houses of culture. Quite active are the youth clubs of international friendship.

Unfortunately, the organization of educational work at the level of residential neighborhoods still lags behind. Lack of facilities and specialists who know how to get things done as well as a certain sluggishness of thought, have impeded its full-scale development. The Ideological Commission of the Central Committee of the Communist Party of Estonia has considered this problem, drawing on the experience of work done in Narva and in the Kalinin district of Tallinn. The materials generated by this discussion provided the basis for methodological recommendations that were prepared and sent out to the various cities and districts.

3

In our single-minded pursuit to unmask the ideology alien to our system, we devote unremitting attention to young people. The falsity, tendentiousness, and misanthropic essence of bourgeois propaganda are bared at Komsomol seminars and study groups, in lecture series for young people, and at topical discussions in youth clubs.

Of great significance are the new rituals and traditions, such as, for example, the "Summer Youth Days," To be sure, the roots of this original ritual go back to the days of bourgeois rule in Estonia. Beginning with the early 1920s, on the initiative of Communists, labor activists, and progressive members of the intelligentsia, there developed a tradition of "Antireligious Days" in the course of which workers, and in the first instance young people, attended lectures on atheistic topics. Often there would be singing of revolutionary songs, reading of poetry devoted to unmasking the reactionary nature of religion, and athletic games. The conclusion of these events was particularly solemn—the presentation of certificates marking the completion of a full course in civic confirmation.

In the late 1950s, as the Party organizations in our republic were becoming more closely involved with problems of strengthening the socialist way of life, among them the propagation of modern rituals, Party veterans remembered this experience from the twenties.

First to revive this tradition, in 1957, were members of the Komsomol in the Paide district. This initiative was approved by the republican Komsomol Congress, and in the very next year "Summer Youth Days" were held in 27 raions, with the participation of 2,260 boys and girls. Festivities celebrating the attainment of majority—age 18—gained growing popularity with each passing year. At present, between 6,000 and 7,000 young people participate in them each summer. Activities are carefully prepared and widely publicized. The Central Committee of the Komsomol Youth of Estonia has overall charge of the "Summer Days," while Party committees lend the necessary practical assistance.

In the course of June, excursions for 18-year-old boys and girls to some of the most beautiful areas of the republic are organized in all the raions and cities. Athletic competitions, concerts by amateur groups, appearances by master artists, and meetings with interesting people, scholars, lawyers, and physicians—this is what fills the "Summer Days." This form of organization successfully combines entertainment with learning, and takes into account young people's predilection for the romantic and for beautiful rituals. The popularity of the "Summer Days" grows year by year. At the same time that they strive to enrich the content of the "Summer Youth Days," the Party and Komsomol organizations are always in search of other forms. "Springtime Children's Days" and "Days of the Newborn" have already become a tradition in Estonia. And only recently such rituals were entirely in possession, so to speak, of the Church.

It is well known that bourgeois propaganda, in its attempt to influence young people in various ways, resorts, among other things, to religious survivals and obsolete traditions and rituals. Thanks to the work conducted in our republic these attempts have proved futile. We might mention, by the way, that for a number of years now young men and women, on reaching their majority, no longer resort to a Church confirmation, preferring the beautiful, emotional, memorable "Youth Days."

Bourgeois propaganda will stoop to anything in its attempts to undermine young people's class consciousness and inculcate them with apolitical views—in a word, to pass off alien views and attitudes under the guise of their being "youthful." To this end, it exploits even fashion, music, and sports, seemingly so remote from politics.

Our enemies are powerless to shake the convictions held by the vast majority of Soviet youth. But we must not ignore the fact that some young men and women are politically naive and immature, and uncritical of attempts by Western ideologues to influence young people by any possible means.

Let us take fashion, for example. Bourgeois propaganda in both pictorial and written form appears extensively on Western products of mass consumption. T-shirts and jerseys with pictures of state symbols or rock music idols, or bags and packs with portraits of popular foreign singers and actors serve a quite definite ideological function and are by no means harmless. Nevertheless, there are teen-agers who become inordinately fascinated by such items. We are instructing the Komsomol not to ignore such "trivia."

Our "Marat" and "Norma" enterprises and the Tartu plastic goods factory have launched the production of our own attractive, modern items. They include, for example, polyethylene shopping bags which today are such a necessary, popular, and convenient part of everyday life. These are now produced with attractive drawings or photos of interesting places in our republic. They also include inexpensive sweatshirts, jerseys and T-shirts with sport symbols, or names of cities and other places.

It might seem that such trivia are not even worth mentioning. But they do represent that very specificity which is at times lacking in our work. An emblem or a polyethylene shopping bag is not merely a detail of everyday life. And it is typical that it was soon after we organized the production of chewing gum in Tallinn that the unhealthy gravitation of adolescents toward Western tourists decreased considerably.

Anticipating changing fashions, responding to them quickly through manufacture of items with an appeal to young people, countering Western products with our own no less popular or fashionable ones, with, if necessary, interesting and attractive symbols, and in this way channeling newly emerging fashions in the proper direction—this we can do, this is in our powers.

Or let us take mass musical culture. It is precisely light music, so popular among the youth, that is used by Western ideologues to prepare the ground for acceptance of the values of the bourgeois world. Once we grasped the extent to which popular and dance tunes influence teenagers, we have become more strict and exacting in our approach to the repertoire of youth ensembles and discotheque programs, or, more precisely, to their ideological orientation. In our republic we have introduced a system of tariffs on ensembles and discothèques, arranged for their regular review, and organized competitions of political songs and festivals of young people's and children's music. This makes it possible to bring some order into a truly mass—and, in many respects, even spontaneous—phenomenon: the emergence of various ensembles and discotheques. (In our republic there is probably not a single school, club, collective farm, or enterprise without its own amateur performing group, not to speak of audio reproduction equipment.)

It follows, then, that all these processes can also be controlled, and here the Komsomol has the opportunity to engaged in a wide range of activities. We have interesting groups which perform Soviet popular and political songs. Even when couched in a modern musical idiom, they are not imitative of Western models or patterned in foreign performers. Such groups are doing good work, and they should be supported.

It would be useful to expand the geographical range and variety of collectives and singers represented at the All-union Political Song Competition in Sochi, by holding preliminary competitions locally. It is high time to introduce competitions among composers and performers for the best Pioneer and Komsomol songs of the year. This would also help to enhance the popularity of Soviet songs, and drive out those "musical imports" which are being so importunately foisted upon us.

In ideological-educational work it is very important to study the ideological situation locally, to study public opinion on the most important aspects of our life, and to analyze the effectiveness of our own work. Especially important is the information that flows in from the factories, collective farms, and institutes. It is bound to shed the light of objectivity on the proposals made by Communists at Party meetings, especially in the course of election campaigns.

In our republic letters from workers to Party organs and offices of the soviets, to the editorial offices of republic-level newspapers, and to television and radio undergo systematic analysis. In the process of classifying this flow of opinion and critical comment we have found that in recent years the relative proportion of questions of an all-Party and all-state significance has considerably increased. Among the letters addressed, for example, to the Central Committee of the Communist Party of Estonia in the first half of 1982, every fourth letter dealt with such problems. These signals emanating from the grass roots help the Party committees to assess more objectively the effectiveness of their work and facilitate the elimination of the root causes of negative phenomena.

An important channel of public opinion that should be studied are the questions posed to speakers and lecturers sponsored by the Party committees. The Central Committee of the Communist Party of Estonia has been engaged in their analysis for many years, it examines them systematically and works out measures to eliminate the shortcomings about which the workers are sending us warning signals. About 10,000 questions reach the Central Committee of the Communist Party of Estonia every year, and their analysis provides us with a clear pictures of what is on people's minds, what their attitudes are to various events and phenomena in social life, how deep is their understanding of Party policies. The results of sociological surveys are also used.

*   *   *

In this article we have touched on only a few aspects of the Estonian Party organization's activities in the area of workers' political education. The work we are doing must, of course, be improved by making more extensive use of the experience we have accumulated and by enriching its forms and methods in a creative way.

Experience has shown—and this is worth repeating—that ideological work demands specificity, convincing arguments, militancy, and aggressiveness. As we expose the inhumane essence of the capitalist system, we must constantly strengthen in people's consciousness the values of socialism, foster ideological firmness, class consciousness, and a capacity to apprehend bourgeois propaganda critically and firmly to resist it.

Editor's notes

a. The domestic upheavals, civil war, and foreign intervention that attended the Russian Revolution found full reflection in Estonia. The independence of Estonia was declared on February 24, 1918. A Soviet republic was proclaimed in November, but by the end of February 1919 Bolshevik forces had been expelled. On February 2, 1920, Soviet Russia by treaty renounced all territorial claims and recognized Estonian independence.

b. Estonia came under the Soviet sphere of influence by terms of the Ribbentrop-Molotov agreement in August 1939. In June 1940, Soviet armed forces entered the country and on August 6, Estonia was formally incorporated in the USSR as a union republic. The Germans occupied Estonia in early July 1941. They were expelled and Soviet rule restored by the end of November 1944.

c. The number of Estonians who fled to the West at the end of World War II is estimated at 70,000. The largest communities are in Sweden, the United States, and Canada.

Annotated by Lubomyr Hajda

Speech to the Twenty-seventh Congress of the CPSU *

E. K. LIGACHEV

Respected comrades! The Twenty-seventh Party Congress will occupy an extremely important place in the political biography of the Party. This is a congress of strategic decisions. The necessity and the possibility of these decisions have been prepared by a little less than seven decades of self-sacrificing, fruitful labor by the Soviet people, by the incomparable achievments of socialism.

These achievements have served as the historical basis and source of inspiration for the elaboration of the April (1985) line of the Plenum of the Central Committee. The strategy of acceleration which the Party elaborated incorporated the extremely rich experience of the CPSU and was a development of Leninist traditions of continuity and innovation. The work done on this basis has in a little less than a year given results, and promises to give more, that can by right be considered among the most important achievments of the Party in the entire inter-congress period.

We have received a mandate from the Party organizations which have sent us their delegates to this congress, to support, strengthen, and develop the line of the April Plenum of the Central Committee. I am convinced that you will support me if I say that our congress is taking place in precisely that spirit, demonstrating the Party's maturity, and the strength of its Party ranks (*applause*). As a member of the Central Committee I would like to report to the congress delegates that the ideas of the April Plenum have become the defining ones for the actions of the Party Central Committee, the Politburo, and the Secretariat, under the leadership of Mikhail Sergeevich Gorbachev (*applause*).

As you know, in the recent past most of the time matters never went beyond discussion of this question or that. The wise and simple legacy left for political leaders by great Lenin was forgotten, that "Discussion is discussion, but it is necessary to live and act."[1] The Politburo broke the practice of foot-dragging and red-tape. It became the rule that concrete steps were not to be avoided, that ripe problems should not be filed away in a long drawer.

The Politburo's daring, unusual actions in the area of internal policy paved the way for improvement of control of the economy and science, the economic mechanism, and the strengthening of public morale. The Politburo took an innovative approach to international problems. The entire world acknowledges the far-reaching Soviet foreign-policy initiatives, stimulated by concern about the safety of all nations and peoples, and which give the world community reliable orientation points

XVII S"ezd Kommunisticheskoi partii Sovetskogo soiuza, Stenograficheskii otchet, vol. 1 (Moscow: Izd. polit. lit., 1986), pp. 232–240.

for moving into the twenty-first century, and faith in the future.

It is important to stress that in all instances, whether internal or external policies, immediate problems or strategic tasks, the Politburo and the Secretariat of the Central Committee of the CPSU act in a collegial manner, in an atmosphere of extreme scrupulousness and the frank exchange of opinions. The members of the Politburo, the candidate members, and the secretaries of the Central Committee of the Party, as you well know, are constantly travelling to the localities, to Party organizations and labor collectives. The live contact of Party and government leaders with the working masses is not a tribute to form; rather this is the very essence of the Leninist style of working. We all understand that only by knowing the life of the people well, the real interests of people, is it possible to count on success in the elaboration and realization of the Party's course. (*applause*)

I think that the delegates of the congress will express their approval of this style of work by the leading organs of our Party. (*applause*)

Comrades! There is good sense in having our congress accept the new edition of the Party Program, the Party Rules with its proposed changes, and the Primary Directives at the same time, to stress that at this turning point the CPSU is strictly following our unchanging demand for the unity of the Party's ideological, theoretical, organizational, and all practical activities.

The success of our undertakings to a decisive degree depends upon on an involved and responsible attitude to work, on the knowledge and skill, on the personal qualities of every worker. Precisely every worker, and particularly those who are entrusted with leadership.

Before the congress the process of deployment of fresh forces has strengthened, increasing the body of the Party's experienced cadres with new people, who understand better than others what has to be done in contemporary conditions. (*applause*) This is a natural and proper process, the most important part of the restructuring which is taking place in the country, which joins accumulated experience with new demands, new knowledge, and new decisions. Communists and workers in their letters and speeches are saying with complete frankness that precisely for the successful realization of the tasks of our program it is necessary to rethink some things in our cadre policy, to learn the lessons of the past. And let us say openly that there are such lessons. It is well known that our necessary faith in the cadre was often replaced with unsupervised trust, which in fact meant lack of control. Complacency and indulgence often took cover beneath the correct words about a caring attitude toward cadres. The line for the stability of cadre staff was widely turned into immobility.

Who cannot see, comrades, that in the conditions of our multinational country untiring care for the growth of local cadres, their education in the spirit of nationalism, is a necessity. In some places though parochial, old-boy attitudes came to the surface, interfered with the movement of representatives of all the nationalities to leadership positions, interfered with the inter-regional exchange of cadres, the exchange of experienced workers between the republics and the center, between the regions and the cities of the country. This led in a number of instances to self-isolation, inertia, and other negative phenomena.

Practice demonstrates convincingly that recruitment and deployment of administrators must be conducted in two ways, from among local comrades, and by moving workers from the center and other regions of the country. In this way experience is more quickly conveyed, and the general level of the cadres grows more rapidly. Yesterday comrade Usmankhodzhaev[a] spoke about this from this tribune, the tribune of the congress.

There are also a number of instances when searching, actively thinking people have not received support. Our people cannot have their patriotism, determination and talents denied, but at times the creative purposefulness of the people, which is the most valuable of the people's achievments, is expended in vain. We all know how much harm is done by the innumerable limitations and instructions. This is "production" by people who, like a certain literary personage, go every morning "to the post," understanding acceleration as the mechanical acceleration of paper-shuffling. Overcoming these obstacles innovators and enthusiasts as a rule ultimately achieve what they want to, as did, for example, Doctor Gavriil Abramovich Ilizarov, of Kurgan, or the machine-tool operator Vladimir Pavlovich Kabaidze, who, by the way, are both delegates at our congress. They achieve their ends because they care for their work, because they are supported and actively helped by the Communist Party. We need to do all we can to encourage creative, to enable people to act independently, people with their own opinion who will dare to take large responsibilities upon themselves. (*applause*)

Taking account of all these lessons the Party is decisively correcting shortcomings and squabbles in cadre work. This is warmly supported and approved of by the people.

The political qualities of the worker are among the crucial criteria for selecting cadres. After all, a communist in a leadership position is a political entity, whose duty is to express the will of the Party, the will of the working masses.

However, let us say straight out that evaluation of the political qualities of cadres is sometimes one-sided. A leader must have whole-hearted committment to our communist task. And the worker's service record must be known, and known very well. But it is absolutely vital as well to imagine precisely whether this person is able to evaluate his actions from the heights of Party-wide and government interests, and to forsee the political consequences of his decisions and acts.

Some leaders, it seems, plan to acquire their political authority largely through broadcasting loud slogans, like "Make this a model establishment!" and "Make this a communist city!" Challenges, though, must be set out intelligently, and in a modern way, and must be strengthened by colossal organizational efforts, which people sometimes fail to worry about. Let us recall Lenin more often, comrades: "Big words must be regarded circumspectly. The difficulties of turning them into big deeds are enormous."[2]

Undervaluing the political side of things also results in an incorrect attitude toward the development of the material basis of the social and cultural sphere of the country. As is noted in the Political Report of the Central Committee, a situation has developed in this regard which must not be considered normal. The construction of housing, schools, hospitals, and the creation of a healthy routine for production are often excluded from the circle of primary concerns. For many leaders it has become customary to fail at these tasks. Sometimes you ask about someone, what kind of worker is he? They answer that he is ideologically sound and politically literate. In fact, this is obvious political failure. Because we are speaking, without exaggeration, precisely about big politics, since everything that is done or not done in the social and cultural sphere does not escape attention in the workers' answering evaluation.

Something truly well organized in this sphere, even if sometimes not overly noticeable, will yield great results. Take for example the experience of the instrument makers of Riga, the metallurgists of Lipetsk, and the Belorussian chemists in creating modern social-support facilities at their places of work, which the Central Committee has approved. This shows the social, economic, and moral effect that can be achieved by a leadership's attitude of concern about the daily necessities of working collectives.

It must be kept in mind that the political stability of Soviet society, the progress of our nation, is in many ways defined precisely by the correct social policy of the Party. Thus the development of the material and technical basis of the social and cultural complex, its attaining of the very highest level, is the most important task of Party and government organs. Here we need initiative and the faithful political thought of all our cadres.

In the Party education of the leading cadres, and in all our activities, the role of constructive criticism and self-criticism is very great. Criticism is a means of resolving contradictions, which means society's movement forward. An irreplaceable role is played here by the press, television, and radio. The level of critical materials in, let's say, a regional or special-interest newspaper, permits us to judge accurately, and I should like to stress that, judge accurately the general condition of criticism in a given region or field. It is also necessary to examine facts from this angle, such as those recently under consideration by the Party's Central Committee. The difficulties suffered by the editors of a city newspaper and two departmental ones which had published critical remarks were under discussion. And who proved to play the role of persecutor of the critics? The Nizhnevartov City Party Committee, the Ministry of Civil Aviation, and the Ministry of the Civil Fleet. However, something else must also be said, comrades. In the period before the congress the press, television, and the radio have activated the struggle against all that is unacceptable, and for the affirmation of the Soviet way of life. This is, as they say, the positive balance. However, unfortunately certain newspapers have permitted errors, something which not even the editors of the newspaper *Pravda* have avoided. Criticism must be directed at rooting out that which has outlived its utility, and to strengthening the development of socialist democracy and our social structure in all ways possible. (*applause*)

Yesterday's speakers here, at this tribune, put the question to the congress, what must be done to avoid such negative phenomena in our society as inertness in leadership, abuse of one's post, and bureaucratism?

It seems to me, comrades, that an exhaustive answer to this question is given by the Political Report of the Central Committee of the Party. (*applause*)

The Central Committee's Political Report stresses the Party's principal position, that no Party organization, no Party worker may be beyond control, beyond criticism. Speaking of this, as you know, this position is also included in the new edition of the Party Program and in the Party Rules.

In this connection I would like to say the following. It is true that I have been led to say this in a small circle, but today I would like to say it in front of all the delegates. All of the ministries and institutions, including the Ministries of Internal Affairs and of Foreign Trade, and any other and all organizations, whether in Moscow, Leningrad, Ukraine, Kazakhstan, Stavropol', Tomsk, or Sverdlovsk, all of them must be within the zone of criticism and accessible to Party criticism. (*applause*) Free, comradely criticism must enter organically into our work and our daily life, as part of the natural working condition of society, of every collective. In the past comrades, as you know, we had "frosts" and "thaws" in this connection, when what we really need is persistent good weather. We need a constant atmosphere of frankness, honesty, Party principles, and truth. I am wholly certain that only in such an atmosphere is real movement forward possible. (*applause*)

Comrades! During the solution of problems of accelerating the social and economic development of the country it is necessary to take full advantage of the transformational power of Marxist-Leninist ideology. After all the birth and strengthening of Bolshevism was connected with the Leninist fundamental idea that the success of revolutionary practice is impossible without revolutionary theory. Such is our conviction today, too, when the theoretical arsenal of the Party has been enriched by a range of powerful new documents which contain important theoretical and political conclusions. The materials of the April Plenum of the Central Committee will long be significant for the organizational, ideological, and educational activity of the Party, as will the conferences on questions of scientific and technical progress and the all-union scientific and practical conference on problems of ideological work, as well as the reports made at them by comrade Mikhail Sergeevich Gorbachev.

The greatest achievement of contemporary Marxist-Leninist thought is the new edition of the Party Program and the Political Report of the Central Committee to the Twenty-seventh Party Congress. They open broad new possibilities and perspectives before our social sciences, challenge us and obligate us to develop the propagation of the ideas of Marxist-Leninism, and permit no inertia in social thought. They include an enormous potential for improving the ideological activity of the Party for the period to come.

I would like here to bring up certain questions. First of all, as it seems to me, we must make more active use of the extremely rich experience of the CPSU for the education of communists, for the solution of new tasks. We must learn how to draw lessons for today and tomorrow from the past. This obligates us to make a much more fundamental study of the history of the Communist Party of the Soviet Union than we have so far done, and do it in such a way, comrades, that there is no hint of scholasticism, so that people can have it penetrate their consciousness that the history of the Leninist Party is not a glorious past which has sounded its last. This is an inseparable part of the living modern political work and intelligence of all communists.

The Party values highly and supports the rise of patriotic feelings which we all feel, the growing interest of society in the history of the Fatherland, the riches of our age-old, multinational culture. I would like to stress with satisfaction that in many places we are genuinely concerned about the preservation of all that is dear to the people's memory. In general a lot is being done, but you will also agree that there are also grounds enough for worry.

Take for example the danger hanging over Yasnaya Polyana,[a] this pearl of our Fatherland's culture. All the decisions made earlier were not carried out. This refers first of all to the Ministry of Mineral Fertilizer Production. Things have come to such a state that we must take radical measures. The people who raise their voices in alarm about the architectural visage of our famous old cities are correct. The Party's demands in cases of carelessness with national treasures must be strict. History, the revolution, and their monuments are a mighty source for education of the people. And people of our day must be educated in a way which will make them jealous guardians of the spirit of the people, the spirit which lives in the monuments of history and culture, in stone and bronze, in the very sound of the unique names of our towns, villages, and streets. (applause)

There is a great deal which must be done in the near future in the sphere of education, comrades, as Mikhail Sergeevich Gorbachev said in the Political Report. Here there are at least two fairly complex tasks, first, to guarantee the forward-moving development of the secondary schools and institutions of higher education—and I repeat, forward-moving, even in comparison with the technical reconstruction of the economy. And second, to repair, or even better, to restructure the state system of retraining and the constant professional growth of cadres. Socialism cannot permit and will not permit scientific and technical progress to mean that significant groups of workers, and their numbers could go into the millions, should become superfluous people in society, who are not prepared for work in new conditions.

After the general school reform [of 1984], which the country has begun to realize, there must be the elaboration of propositions for the restructuring of higher education.[b] The point of this work is to strengthen the general scientific and professional preparation of specialists, and to make higher education respond to the demands of the development of the country.

It is already possible to say that the basis for this work will be the integration of education, production, and science. To this end it is proposed to undertake the preparation of specialists to order from the branches of the economy, to build relations between them and the higher educational establishments on the basis of contracts, to more widely attract leading scientists and organizers of production to the preparation and elevation of the qualifications of specialists. The teachers at higher educational institutions will not be left dependent on the student "chaff," but rather will raise their responsibility for the education and teaching of student youth. The opinion is being expressed that the administration of the higher educational establishments should be concentrated into a single government organ.[c]

Comrades, the higher education is an important part of the entire system of the Party's cadre policy. Naturally restructuring of institutions of higher education must be undertaken in close conjunction with the solution of economic, social, and organizational-administrative problems.

One more thing. In conditions of scientific and technical progress the equipment of ideological organizations has a particular significance, or I would even say that of society's entire spiritual sphere, which should have all modern means of information and electronics. Measures for the creation of high-volume production of video technology have been set, plans have been made to develop scientific instrument making, domestic printing, and to modernize the technical basis of television. A special role has been assigned to the ministries of electronics, instrument-making, and communication in this. The Party has before it a major task of creating a genuinely modern, powerful technological basis for ideology, science, and culture in our country.

Comrades! It has already been said of these days, with justice, that this is a time of hope. Yes, this is true. For you and me though, for communists, this is first and foremost a time for real action.

The restructuring, the transformation of life sets the tempos which embrace all spheres of society. Our country approaches the beginning of the third millenium with an impressive program of perfecting established socialism and of moving toward communism, with large-scale plans for peace and disarmament, for the peaceful exploitation of space by the efforts of all mankind. These tasks are of exceptional innovation and a truly historical scope. And we are equal to them. (*applause*) We will prove equal to them even if in some instances the extreme concentration of all our powers may be required. We will prove equal to them because we are faithful to the Leninist legacy that ''Admitting our mistakes should never be feared, nor should oft repeated efforts to correct them, and we shall reach the very heights.''[3]

The Party has the whole-hearted support of the people on its side, and the limitless possibilities of the socialist order. We have the truth of life and the power of scientific conclusions behind us. We have the truth and majesty of our communist task behind us! (*applause*)

Editor's notes

a. I. B. Usmankodzhaev: first secretary of the Communist Party of Uzbekistan from 1983 to 1987.

b. Yasnaya Polyana: the site of Leo Tolstoy's house and estate, now a museum.

c. Reference is to the consolidation of the higher educational establishment under a single state committee which was implemented in 1988.

Notes

1. Lenin, V.I., *Polnoe Sobranie sochinenii*, vol. 15, pp. 183–184.
2. Lenin, V.I., *Polnoe Sobranie sochinenii*, vol. 11, p. 366.
3. Lenin, V.I., *Polnoe Sobranie sochinenii*, vol. 44, p. 423.

The Constructive Power of Brotherhood *

Interrepublican Exchange of Cadres Accelerates the Socioeconomic Development of the Country

TIMUR ALIMOV

Lidiia Kazantseva came to Tashkent from the Moscow area as a young girl, accompanying her mother, a weaver, and during the war they stood side by side at their work stations. Maria Kovaleva, a tractor driver from Voronezh, and Pavel Saulkin were sent to Uzbekistan from Penza on Komsomol assignments in the 1950s, which also was not a time of easy bread. Maria was sent to the Virgin Lands,[a] and Pavel to a backward kolkhoz.

Over the years the new and unknown land became their native land, the concerns of this land, their concerns. All of these people are Heroes of Socialist Labor[b] today, their accomplishments for the republic widely known. It was Lidiia Kazantseva who is known for the multi-loom movement in weaving, while Maria Aleksandrovna, a brigade leader and mechanic for the "Kremlin" sovkhoz, is known for introducing intensive technology to cotton production. The "Sixty Years of October" kolkhoz which Pavel Fedorovich heads has proven that in cotton-based farming it is possible and necessary to have high-volume livestock breeding, which assists the republic get by with fewer subsidies of milk and meat. When you talk with any of them, you see how much they have adopted from the good habits and practices of their new region, but at the same time you see how much good they have brought from the font of Russian traditions, how many good people they have produced, how many they have taught their professions. A few names: U. Bukurova, from Kovaleva's brigade, is now a brigade leader herself, and a bureau member of the regional committee of the Party; a student of Saulkin, the kolkhoz economist M. Abdulkarimov, is president of the regional executive committee; and Kazantseva's student K. Iakubaeva is a famous textile worker, as well as a deputy of the Supreme Soviet of the USSR.

Three typical biographies of people of labor, but how brightly their fates express the movement of our time, its inner essence.

It is noteworthy that even in the years of the first five-year plans weavers and spinners from the Moscow area and Ivanov came to help their friends in Tashkent and Fergana, while hundreds of Uzbek lads went to Orekhovo-Zuevo and Shuia. These veterans of labor flourish even today, former craftsmen and electricians who got their Party cards in the factories of Russia.

Exchange of cadres of different nationalities has now become a part of government planning. Today this broad and multifaceted process is becoming an important

*Pravda vostoka, 3 January 1987, p. 2. Russian text © 1987 by "Pravda vostoka."

factor of economic and social progress, showing new and unique traits evoked by the particularities of the present day. Time, however, also names new problems. First and foremost are those connected with the demographic situation characteristic for the Central Asian republics.

It is paradoxical but true that in conditions of a high natural growth rate of the population and a surplus of idle working hands, many institutions and building sites here experience intense labor shortages. This causes incomplete shifts at institutions and affects the labor co-efficient of power usage. At the same time it is clear that we cannot continue endlessly to fill out the work force by importing workers into the republic. The question of how to accelerate preparation of our own qualified workers is growing acute.

Let us say directly that we knew about this problem in Uzbekistan before, but had not come fully up against it. The low percentage of workers from the local nationality is one of the reasons for the republic's poor showing in a number of the most important indicators; this also is one of the causes of the persistence of religious and private-ownership survivals.

Today the state of affairs is beginning to change. Certain institutions in Tashkent and a metallurgical factory in Bekabad have undertaken seriously the preparation of a native working shift. However, even now, for example, the proportion of Uzbek workers in our tractor factory (*Tashselmash*) is two times smaller than the representative weight of the Uzbek population of the capital. How are we going to repair this situation?

There is one way that strikes us as fruitful. In the current five-year plan about a million youths will complete trade schools (PTUs) here. The Party oblast committee and the executive committee of the regional soviet are decisively correcting the leaders of those institutions that are not getting on with widening the network of special trade schools (SPTUs). Three thousand of our young men and women were accepted this year to educational institutions in the RSFSR, the Ukraine, and Belorussia, including 600 Tashkent youths who are studying at SPTUs in Ivanovsk and Volgograd oblasts. We hope in this way, over the five-year plan, to prepare three thousand young people for the oblast, and no fewer than 15 thousand young workers for the republic as a whole.

The RSFSR, the Ukraine, and Belorussia will assist Uzbekistan in the rearing of professionally literate, cultured, and socially active young people. All of these measures ought to evoke an answering wave.

There is also another facet of this problem. It used to be the normal thing that workers and specialists came to us, to building sites, to institutions, to the Virgin Lands. Now the situation is changing. Today the Russian Federation has its own shortage of workers. The time has come for us to help our friends, and with highly qualified cadres as well.

Large detachments of workers and specialists from Uzbekistan today are helping to cultivate the non–black-earth lands, are irrigating the steppe lands beyond the Volga, are building roads and dwellings in the north of Tiumen, are repairing the oil wells in Samotlor, and are working on the Baikal–Amur magistral (BAM).[c] By the end of the five-year plan the number of representatives of our republic employed in the exploitation of new economic regions will surpass thirty thousand, while their annual work volume will surpass a half billion rubles. And this must be seen as but our first steps.

In addition, eight oblasts of Uzbekistan which have labor surpluses have established direct links with areas and oblasts of the RSFSR which do not have sufficient cadres of their own, so that, for example, Khorezm oblast is linked with Chitinsk oblast, Bukhara with Tomsk, Tashkent with Ivanovsk. In this way we are strengthening our ties with the people of Ivanovsk, ties which already exist for many decades. We are also considering the voluntary resettlement of families from our zone to areas of the RSFSR. We will also send large detachments of seasonal workers there, including workers for construction of large agricultural complexes.

This beginning was born not on paper, but was evoked by the demands of life. For example in addition to the special train "Uzbekistan-Ivanovo" that we sent to Ivanovsk oblast with more than 130 families—546 people—from our valleys to resettle along the Volga, we also sent large detachments of seasonal workers for roadwork and to the animal breeding farms of their region.

It must be said though that there have already arisen complex problems with these new connections. These settlers from the south are not always finding the housing they have been promised, nor normal conditions for living and working. The expenses of moving people based on these agreements of direct contact have not yet been put into the planning and financial columns. And we ourselves here at home must radically improve the quality of the voluntary resettlers and seasonal workers for the new economic regions.

Even further, I think, the time has come for an entire system of organizational and social measures to "raise" the mobility of the population of Central Asia, especially its youth, to turn the inertia of its attachment to "the land of our forefathers," to cultivate here a desire for change.. This will have to be aided by the serious restructuring we have already begun of the system of teaching the language of internationality communication, Russian.

In our opinion, no less important is the inter-republican exchange of experienced political, administrative, and economic organizers. As is well known, three years ago a battle began in Uzbekistan with negative phenomena. Among these was the flourishing practice in the republic of promoting people to supervisory responsibilities not on their qualities of work, political undertanding, or morals, but because of relationships of blood or place of birth, because of old-boy networks and sycophancy. The disintegration of the apparat significantly affected workers at the raion, oblast, and republic level. Many people had to be replaced.

In doing so we made use of the resources of strength inherent in the multi-national make-up of the Party organization itself, and the selection organs of the oblast. Thus the first secretary of Bostanlyk [regional Party committee], A. Aidarkulov, a Kazakh, was selected as secretary of the obkom [oblast Party committee], while the raiispolkom [regional executive committee] president Kh. Pirnapasov, a Turkmen, was made first secretary of the Party raikom. Recommended from the reserves as presidents of raiispolkoms were R. Khikmatulloev, a Tadzhik, and S. Shermatov, a Kirghiz.

The Chinaz raion flamed with passions of regionalism. When the decision was made as to whom to recommend there for the first secretaryship of the raikom no two opinions were possible—it was V. G. Grishchuk. More than 30 years ago, a mere lad who had just finished the technicuum, he came to us from the Ukraine, became the animal technician of a backward kolkhoz, helped raise its production, and learned the local languages. Studying at night he got a higher education, and also was involved in Komsomol and Party work. Squabbles disappeared in a wink, and the raion became one of the best.

How many such comrades have we prepared among us for responsible posts! In the past year 82 percent of the replacement gorkom and raikom Party secretaries, presidents and vice-presidents of ispolkoms of city and regional soviets have been promoted from out of the reserves. Thanks to this the oblast has strengthened the speed of development in almost all indicators of industrial and agricultural production.

Still, when the republic began to be put in order, which required the energetic replacement of poor cadres, it became immediately obvious that we couldn't get by on our manpower reserves alone. So once again with new force we felt the assistance of the Central Committee of the CPSU. Following the request of the Central Committee of the Communist Party of Uzbekistan, experienced Party men are being assigned to the republic to work, as well as workers of the Soviet organs, experienced economic supervisors from Moscow, Leningrad, from the krais and oblasts of the RSFSR and other republics.

Some among us, to say nothing of course of the West, are prepared to see these measures to strengthen the managing links in the republic as virtually an antinational campaign. The positive changes which have taken place in Uzbekistan over the past few years show the full futility of such attempts. We are ever more strongly convincing ourselves of the urgent necessity to strengthen and develop the bases of all our daily practices of internationalism.

It is clear to all today that the help given Uzbekistan by cadres of Party, government, and administrative organizers is mandated by the Party's concern to turn the republic as swiftly as possible into the broad flow, broad as the Greater Fergana Canal, of full-blooded political and economic life, and to increase its future contribution to the economic complex of the ntion.

A great deal links these people with those the Party sent to Turkestan in the first years of Soviet power. Coming to work for us today is for these commnists not just a duty, but a movement of the spirit as well. Families are moving from the banks of the Neva to the Kzyl Kum, from abundant Belgorod they are resettling in Karshin steppe, from frozen Cheliabinsk to torrid Tashkent. It is no easy thing to enter a new life, to take upon one's self the responsibility for work of incomparable complexity and scope, to come against the need for extraordinary measures, which makes the desire of these people to share our difficulties all the more valuable. Their energy and skills, their readiness to plunge into work, to share their knowledge and experience with others, in a word, all this is what our comrades have brought to our life.

I. Ovsiuk has worked at the Uzbek metallurgical factory less than a year, and not everything that he wants to do has been accomplished, but the Urals tempering of this new director is already making itself felt, and progress has been made. Captain N. Tymkiv came from the Ukraine to the metallurgical city of Almalyk to head the local division of militia, and a great deal has changed in the militia work of the town today.

What is characteristic is that Uzbekistan is also teaching these people a great deal. As a rule, they usually have much more responsibility here, their work being greater in scope and significance. E. Rizaev, a local man who is returning here after Party work in Murmansk, was made the first vice-president of the Tashkent city executive committee. A. Klepikov, from Voronezh, after two years of work in the Tashkent oblast executive committee was chosen first secretary of the Syr-Dar'ia obkom of the Party, in an oblast which is one of our most multinational.

On the other hand, it is very important now that our youth get experience in the large industrial centers of the country. We are sending a large group of promising workers, mostly of the local nationalities, to the central organs, so as later to have them as a reserve of administrative cadre both for Uzbekistan and for other republics.

There is also another outflow from Uzbekistan to the large industrial and cultural centers of the country, for eighteen month or two-year periods as Party and government workers. Directors and specialists of large combines and factories, administrators of large construction projects will undergo retraining courses there. The contingent of students sent from Uzbekistan to the Social Sciences Academy of the Central Committee of the CPSU and the Economic Academy of the USSR has been enlarged; a large number of our young workers are also studying in the Party schools of Leningrad, Novosibirsk, Rostov, Saratov, and Sverdlovsk.

In this way the inter-republican exchange of cadres is growing and widening. Today this exchange is one of the vivid phenomena of Leninist national politics, based on mutual aid, equality, and the indissoluble friendship among all peoples of our Soviet nation.

Editor's notes

a. The Virgin Lands: lands opened for cultivation by Khrushchev.

b. A Hero of Socialist Labor—the highest civilian honor in the USSR—is awarded a gold star.

c. The Baikal-Amur magistral (BAM) is a new railroad line across Siberia.

4. Economic Development and the National Regions

One of the prime concerns of the Soviet leadership always has been to assure that economic development proceeds smoothly throughout the Soviet Union. The economic goals of each of the union republics are spelled out in detail in the five-year plans, and the responsibility for supervising these plans falls on the Party leadership of each republic, as well as on the all-union and union republic ministries charged with the management of the economy.

One of Gorbachev's major goals is to preside over the reconstruction and modernization of the Soviet economy. The mandated "rational" development of the union republics has clear implications for nationality relations. As outlined in the 1986 Party Program, this means that each republic will be expected to develop economic specializations according to Moscow's guidelines—specializations that inevitably will further disrupt the traditional, largely subsistence-based economy of many republics. They will also be expected to meet their plan quotas, on time, and with standard quality goods. In addition they will have to meet their all-union responsibilities and, for example, to send men and materials as needed to contribute to the opening of new economic regions, especially in the Far East. While recently proposed legislation promises to greatly increase the discretionary authority of the republics over their economies, Moscow remains the hub of economic decision making.

Throughout his years in office Gorbachev has been continually rethinking the problem of how to go about reforming the Soviet economy. Initially Gorbachev was reluctant to tamper with the division of authority between the center and the republics. Few of the ideas about the regulation of economic relations between union republics that are spelled out in the new Party Program and the resolutions of the Twenty-seventh Party Congress were new. The 1982 article below by the Novosibirsk-based economist Granberg gives a description of interrepublican links that is mirrored in these documents. However, Gorbachev, unlike his recent predecessors, is holding cadres responsible for the fulfillment of their economic tasks. It is no longer tolerable for economic performance figures for entire republics to be forged, as was the case for Uzbekistan and Turkmenistan for a number of years, or for entire industries to report fraudulent statistics, as did the oil industry of Tiumen' and the tea-growing industry of Georgia. While fraudulent practices are certainly continuing, corruption has been localized, as the entire economy has been subjected to more rigorous monitoring and cost-accounting procedures.

Since the Twenty-seventh Party Congress the CPSU has endorsed a number of additional economic reforms that have direct implications for the economic development of the union republics. The first reforms, passed during the period March 1986–March 1989, were designed to provide for greater economic self-management both by enterprise managers and by workers. They are also designed to provide for greater financial autonomy of individual enterprises and, eventually, of whole sectors of the economy. Nonetheless these reforms left the basic division of authority between the central planners and economic administrative authorities largely untouched.

However, in March 1989 the CPSU endorsed legislation (which was still under discussion in June 1989) that was designed to shift much of the burden of economic management to the republics. While Moscow remained the center of economic planning for the country as a whole, it was proposed that the republics be given greater authority to determine their direction of economic development. Many industries were slated to move from central to republic administration. Over all, the shift would be on the order of from 5 percent to approximately 36 percent republic control; and in the Baltic region, from an average of 8 percent to an average of 65 percent. As we will see in greater detail in part 10 of this volume, the "popular front" movements in the three Baltic republics are pushing for complete economic independence, with each of the republics to have its own convertible currency and the ability to enter into trade agreements with foreign powers.

Pressures for further decentralization of the economy can be expected to continue, and so too can resistance from Moscow. The thesis of the Granberg article included here is that the Soviet Union is a unitary economic complex, with the economic development of one region definitionally linked to the development of all others. While Granberg's article paints an overly optimistic picture of the level of economic integration and the general level of economic production (a tendency characteristic of work published in the late Brezhnev years), it nonetheless clearly documents how the pattern of industrial and agricultural development pursued over the past fifty years has created a situation of dependency among the republics. Thus, when workers went on strike in Nagorno Karabakh, Ukrainians were forced to postpone the opening of new apartment buildings (as Ukrainian Party First Secretary V. Shcherbitsky angrily pointed out) because the elevators, produced in Stepanakert, were not delivered. This inability to regulate the supply of goods to a region or to an enterprise has serious consequences for the self-financing of enterprises, let alone economic regions; very little has been done to provide for regional self-sufficiency in industrial production.

Moreover, should one part of the country become self-sufficient, especially if it is a more developed economic region such as the Baltic, and should that area be given the right to sell its goods directly abroad, then the economy of the rest of the country is sure to suffer. The difficulties in regulating the supply side of the economy must also have a negative effect on efforts to reform the price and wage structure, making it more difficult for prices to reflect the real cost of a good, and enterprises to show the profits necessary to raise wages.

The main thrust of Gorbachev's entire economic program has been to increase the accountability of economic enterprises (and those who supervise them) for fulfilling their responsibilities in the economic plan. The specific economic responsibilities of each of the union republics are spelled out in the Basic Guidelines reproduced below, and subsequent economic reforms have not reversed the trend. This economic plan provides ambitious goals for all of the union republics, but it requires the economies of a number of republics to grow faster than that of the USSR as a whole, where an industrial growth rate of 21–24 percent and an agricultural growth rate of 14–16 percent are planned. In Moldavia both industry and agriculture are slated to grow at faster than all-union rates. In Lithuania, where there is an especially severe problem of rural depopulation, agriculture is projected to grow at the most rapid rate in the USSR.

In Armenia, Azerbaidzhan, Georgia, Kazakhstan, and Uzbekistan, industrial development is to proceed at higher than the USSR rate. These are all republics where there is excess labor; and this labor is slated to be deployed in industrial development within each republic and in the development of the new economic regions of the Far East. There are a number of ways in which this surplus labor is to be directed to Siberia.

All of the Central Asian and Caucasian republics are involved in Komsomol-sponsored shock-labor projects in Siberia, such as the one described in the article on Kogalym. In addition there are efforts made to recruit laborers to move permanently to Siberia, usually to live in settlements with their co-nationals. Komsomol brigades are formed by that organization in schools and in enterprise cells. Most of the recruitment of permanent settlers is done through advertisements in the local press such as those that are reproduced at the end of this section, following the Kogalym article.

But while the press, in pieces such as "Kogalym," tries to paint life in the new regions in positive terms, word of the harsh conditions spreads quickly, and the inducements to move offered by the regime are really quite minimal. Thus it is highly unlikely that the targeted goals for the resettlement of Central Asians or Caucasians in either Siberia or the non-black earth zone of the RSFSR will be met. As is clear in the interview with T. S. Saidbaev reproduced below, it is difficult enough to get Central Asians and Caucasians to train for and accept industrial jobs within their home republics, let alone get them to relocate.

The text of the Guidelines also provides a lot of useful information about the economic strengths and weaknesses of the various republics. It documents how much more modern the economies of the three Baltic republics are, and makes clear why they feel hampered by the lower growth rates of the rest of the economy. It also explains why many in the Central Asia (Kazakhstan, Kirghizia, Tadzhikistan, Turkmenistan and Uzbekistan) and the Caucasusian republics (Armenia, Azerbaidzhan, and Georgia) have expressed deep concern about their ability to fulfill the tasks that they have been assigned.

The Baltic republics are the site of a substantial portion of the Soviet computer, electronics, and communications industries, and most of the high quality goods produced in these industries come from this region. In addition the Baltic area is successful agriculturally and has the capacity to produce more than enough meat and milk to meet local needs. Thus the Baltic republics are capable of being self-sufficient financially and of earning hard currency through the export of their industrial products.

The situation in Central Asia and the Caucasus is the opposite. These republics are still completely dependent upon the "import" of technology and trained cadres for the expansion of industrial development. The most severe economic problems are in Central Asia. The types of industries being developed in Central Asia— energy, chemicals, and some consumer durables—are largely designed for local use and are of limited exportability. Moreover, there is real controversy over agricultural development. Many in these republics are opposed to the continued promotion of cash crops, such as cotton, over the cultivation of food crops. Everyone agrees that Central Asia could better feed itself, but Moscow and the regional authorities disagree over how this can be accomplished. Moscow sees the problem as being soluble through the elimination of corrupt and inefficient practices; Central Asian leaders demand massive investment in their republics.

This tension is seen most clearly in the series of battles fought over the Siberian River diversion project, a proposal to divert water from the Ob and the Irtysh rivers in Siberia to the Aral Sea basin in Central Asia. The plans for this were ratified, in an experimental form, at the Twenty-fifth and Twenty-sixth Party Congresses (1976 and 1981). However, they were the subject of great controversy from the onset. The articles reproduced below from *Literaturnaia gazeta* (published in Moscow) and *Pravda Vostoka* (published in Tashkent, capital of the Uzbek SSR) outline the positions of those favoring and opposing the plan in the early 1980s.

By the mid-1980s economists and planners who criticized the water diversion scheme as overly costly, based on unsound engineering, and unlikely to produce more usable water in Central Asia than could be gained by repairing existing irrigation canals and supplementing them with drip-irrigation and the development of underground water supplies, were joined by a powerful new lobbying group. Some leading Russian intellectuals began to campaign publicly for the preservation of the Russian north, whose ancient churches and other architectural treasures, they claimed, would be drowned by the diverted flood waters. The critics of the scheme won. In August 1986 the Central Committee of the CPSU announced the cancellation of plans to divert the Siberian rivers for the foreseeable future.

Central Asians have continued to fight for the restitution of these plans. The excerpt from *Zvezda vostoka* is typical of the arguments that they make, arguing that existing means of irrigation, even supplemented with better use of drip-irrigation and underground water, cannot save the Aral Sea from evaporation or supply Central Asia enough water to feed its population. An all-union campaign to save the Aral Sea is being mounted, with environmentalists using newly published evidence about the spread of typhoid and other water-borne diseases to demonstrate the dangers inherent in the deteriorating water supply in Central Asia. In October 1988 the Politburo announced a plan to save the Aral sea which relied heavily on improving irrigation and land reclamation projects. Whether or not this will be successful remains to be seen.

The water shortage in Central Asia is a critical problem for economic planners.

But the debate over the water diversion scheme also illustrates the growing role of environmentalists in the USSR. Since the mid–1980s growing numbers of nationalists and conservationists have joined together in an effort to halt economic programs that they believe are destructive of their national territories. Since the fire at the Chernobyl reactor in 1986, the construction of atomic energy stations has provoked public protest throughout the country, with protests being most severe in Lithuania. Similarly, the Estonians have begun pushing for a sharp cutback in the extraction of phosphates in their republic, and throughout the Baltic republics there is a growing concern over the contamination of the Baltic Sea itself.

Public protests over economic decisions that are seen as antithetical to the interests of a specific national community are likely to increase in intensity and to spread throughout the Soviet Union. As we will see in part 10, the protests in the Baltic republics and in the Caucasus have dealt in part with the allocation of economic resources. As Moscow has conceded the legitimacy of some of these claims, other nationalities will certainly feel it in their own interest to push their demands as well. Thus the rise in nationalist sentiments throughout the USSR further complicates the calculus of decision making as Gorbachev tries to find new approaches to solving the Soviet Union's economic problems.

Economic Relations among the Republics *

Forms and Essential Features

A. G. GRANBERG

The formation of the USSR gave rise to new economic relations, among which the *economic relations* among the soviet socialist republics occupy an important place.

In the economic organization of the USSR, socialist federalism is combined with democratic centralism. One of the principal functions of the Union, as embodied in the highest bodies of state power and government, is to "conduct a unified socioeconomic policy, and to manage the economy of the country" (the Constitution of the USSR, art. 73). But the union republics have a broad economic independence as well, and are invested with tangible means for coping with those tasks specific to them. Each union republic constitutes a complex economic entity, with characteristic processes of reproduction of the population and the labor force and utilizing the natural conditions and those previously created elements of national wealth. Pursuant to the Constitution of the USSR (art. 77), a union republic "is responsible for the all-round economic and social development throughout its territory." However, the all-round development of republics has nothing in common with economic autarky. The complex economic system of no union republic can function effectively without broad and diversified relations with other republics.

Since the late 1960s, the concept of "the integral national economic complex of the USSR" has become a permanent part of the political and economic vocabulary. It is defined essentially in the materials of the Twenty-fourth, Twenty-fifth, and Twenty-sixth Party Congresses, and in art. 16 of the Constitution of the USSR.

The economic integration of the Soviet republics into an integral national economic complex has been made possible by the development of economic ties among the republics and the evolution of union-wide infrastructural and economic organizational systems.

Transportation, communications, energy supplies, material and technical equipment, and trade are the most important infrastructural systems of nationwide significance; the rudiments of an interrepublic water supply are currently taking shape. The economic organizational foundation of the integral national economic complex of the USSR is state control and a union-wide economic mechanism, the elements of which are the circulation of money, the generation and distribution of incomes, price setting, finances, and credit, etc.

Economic ties among republics evolve in diverse forms. These include, specifically, the exchange of the products of material production and scientific and techni-

EKO, no. 12, 1982, pp. 2–37. Russian text © 1982 by "Nauka" Publishers.

cal information, the migration of the population and the training of skilled personnel, providing commercial, everyday, and cultural facilities to the migrating population, and industrial services. Under commodity and monetary relations, the material, human, and information flows are mediated in part by financial flows among republics.

The interrepublic exchange of the products of the various sectors of industry and agriculture are a necessary condition and the most important consequence of the territorial distribution of labor in the nation's economy.

All the varied resources of our country, fuel and energy, minerals and raw materials, forests, the soil, and our waters, are distributed very unevenly throughout its vast territory; the different republics and regions differ widely in their climatic conditions, geographic position, the concentration and composition of the population, and basic stocks. Hence it is practically impossible for all the basic industries necessary to meet local needs to be developed in each republic, and the range and scale of economically effective industries narrow considerably. Latvia, Lithuania, Moldavia, for example, do not have any known industrial deposits of coal and oil, or ferrous and nonferrous ores. Uzbekistan and Turkmenia have water shortages and no forest resources of economic significance. The climatic conditions of northern Siberia and the Far East make human life difficult, and the development of traditional agriculture impossible.

Modern technological processes, production, and resources are so varied that every republic inevitably has some advantages in certain aspects of economic activity, and moreover on a scale that exceeds its own needs. Thus, the northern regions of Siberia have oil and gas deposits and deposits of nonferrous and precious metals. Turkmenia and Tadzhikistan have favorable conditions for raising cotton and other crops thriving in warm climates. In Uzbekistan and Azerbaidzhan all the conditions exist for the development of labor-intensive production processes in the processing industry. The high technical level and skill composition of workers in Latvia and Estonia facilitate the development of the construction of precision machinery and instruments. Because of its climate, and location near the sea, Georgia is able to develop Union-wide bases for health and recreation.

The economic specialization of each of the republics stimulates bilateral exchange of goods between republics; moreover, ties among republics are closely intertwined with ties among the different sectors and branches of industry. Interrepublic turnover (the sum of exports or imports in terms of value) is one-fifth the total output of industry and agriculture and has a tendency to grow faster than the material production of each of the union republics.

The material ties among republics are in commodity form; however, this does not entail the financial commitments characteristic of relations between states. A discrepancy between total exports and total imports (at existing prices) means a redistribution of the national income (net output) created on the territory of each of the republics. If total exports exceeds total imports, this means that part of the national income created in a particular republic is shifted to other republics, and vice versa. Usually, the national income is redistributed to the benefit of those republics producing less of the national income per capita of the population.[2]

The material ties among republics are also reflected in the interrelationship between Union and republic budgets. Funds are redistributed through the budgets both directly, and by means of a turnover tax and budgetary regulation of the difference between distribution prices and calculated prices (mainly, in agricultural raw materials). The budgets of the republics of Central Asia, Kazakhstan, and others were for many years covered by subsidies from the national budget. For example, in 1924–25, the share of internal income in Turkmenia's budget was slightly higher than 10%, while in the Tadzhik SSR in 1927 it was 8%.

In a modern economy, exchange of the fruits of research, designing, and experimental construction developments plays a special role. Earlier, science and designing was concentrated in Moscow and Leningrad, and a few other centers, while scientific and technical relations among republics was mainly unilateral. The accelerated development of science in new centers, and its closer contact with production substantially changed the geography of scientific and technical ties. Moscow, Leningrad and Kiev still maintain their leading positions in scientific and technical progress (one third of the country's scientific personnel work in Moscow). But the output of scientific and designing organizations of all the republics is more and more extending beyond the confines of the individual republics. The union-wide territorial distribution of labor is extending more and more deeply into intellectual activity as well.

The large centers for economic activity, culture, and leisure meet the needs of the population of many of the union republics in commerce, culture and medical facilities. The migration of consumer demand among the republics has become an important element in commerce and money circulation in the USSR.

At first glance *the interrepublic migration of the population and the labor force* with changes in domicile seems relatively small: approximately 2% annually of the total population of the country. However, this is twice as high as the natural increment of the population and five times higher than the increment in the labor force.

The migration of the population among the republics mediates the training of specialists for the needs of the different republics. This form of interrepublic cooperation has played a key role in the development of local cadres of skilled workers, engineers and technical workers in the republics of Central Asia, the Transcaucasus, Kazakhstan, and Moldavia. However, its possibilities are still not being fully utilized. One of the reasons for the disproportionalities in satisfying the country's needs for specialists of various profiles, as Brezhnev pointed out, has been "the manifestations of provincialism, the endeavor to place specialists in jobs necessarily in their own republics, and indeed even in areas for which they are not trained, although other regions have a shortage in workers of that particular profile." Seasonal migration of the population, related mainly with the development of Union-wide bases for tourism and recreation and, to a lesser extent, on the movement of the workforce among the republics (expeditionary development of natural resources, seasonal construction and agricultural work) is growing quite rapidly in the country.

The contemporary demographic situation in the USSR and its evolution require an activation of processes of interrepublic movement of the population and of the labor force. The territorial differentiation of the population growth rate has intensified in the past twenty and thirty years. Whereas in the RSFSR the annual increment in the population is now 0.5–0.6%, in the republics of Central Asia it is 2.5–3%. By the end of the century, three-fourths in the national increment in the employable population will be provided by Central Asia, Kazakhstan, and Azerbaidzhan, i.e., republics that already have surplus labor reserves. At the same time the shortage of labor in most of the western and central districts of the country, and especially in Siberia and the Far East, is growing more acute.

Even a partial utilization of the excess demographic potential of the southern republics to replenish the labor resources of, first, the eastern regions of the RSFSR, would have a considerable economic and social effect. This task was outlined in the Annual Report of the Central Committee of the CPSU to the Twenty-sixth Congress of the Party: "the implementation of programs for developing western Siberia and the area around the new Siberian rail line, and other localities in the Asian parts of the country, has augmented the flow of the population to these areas. Still, people often prefer to move from north to south and from east to west, although a rational deployment of productive forces requires movements in the opposite directions. . . . In Central Asia, in a number of areas of the Caucasus, on the other hand, there is a surplus labor force, especially in the countryside. This means that it is necessary more actively to recruit the population of these places into the development of the country's new territories." Brezhnev went on to substantiate this task in a speech given in Tashkent: "It is no secret that there is still a surplus of labor force in the republic. . . . The shortage of labor is felt especially acutely in those areas of western Siberia and the Far East where the main fuel and energy base of the country is formed, and huge industrial centers are being created. . . . Hence we must provide comprehensive support to the efforts of the youth of our republic to take a personal part in the major construction projects of our century. . . . This, comrades, is a remarkable school for an internationalist education of our citizenry."

Cooperation among Soviet republics is clearly manifested in the way that the major national economic problems requiring a concentration of resources are dealt with. These problems include the development of the virgin lands in Kazakhstan, the development of the Russian non–black-earth region, the construction of the Baikal–Amur rail line, and the construction of territorial industrial complexes in Siberia and the Far East. In addition to the regular forms of interrepublic ties, large groups of industrial personnel are routinely recruited to these areas from many republics.

Thus more than 30,000 drillers and craftsmen from the Ukraine, Belorussia, the northern Caucasus, the Volga region, and other areas of the RSFSR are participating in the development of oil and gas deposits in Western Siberia, flown here as members of temporary brigades. Construction organizations from Moscow, Leningrad, Ukraine, Belorussia, Lithuania, Latvia, Estonia, and a number of cities of the RSFSR are participating in the construction of the western Siberian oil and gas complex. They are building over 0.5 million square meters of living space every year as well as many industrial projects. Organizations from Kazakhstan, Latvia, and Uzbekistan are building highways. This form of economic cooperation among the republics will be used in the future as well in large-scale regional programs of nationwide importance.

Thus diverse forms of interrepublic economic ties are growing vigorously in the USSR. But can these forms be integrated, is their impact on the economies of the individual republics and on the economy of the nation as a whole commensurate?

The concept of "interrepublic economic interaction" (the interaction of the complex economic systems of the various republics) corresponds to a higher systemic level of analysis of the interdependency and mutual determination of the different republics in their development and growth. Essentially the approach involves a study not only of individual relations (in their specific form) between individual regions (the supply of specific types of products or the migrational flows between two republics) and their direct influence, but also the totality of relations (however broad they may be) and their joint impact on all the essential characteristics of all the complex economic systems of the various republics. Of course this task can be resolved only with the aid of structural mathematical models for the economy, reflecting the conditions of development of the different republics and the economic ties between them.

The role of interrepublican material ties
in their economies

Every union republic participates in interrepublic exchange of the products of many of the sectors of industry and agriculture. However, the dependence of the economy of a particular republic on its external links is by no means identical in all cases. There is a close correlation between the intensity of external ties of a republic and its area. It is quite understandable that the economy of the RSFSR, which covers 76% of the territory of the country, and features the most varied natural and economic conditions, will be more self-sufficient than the economies of the small republics (Moldavian, Armenian, Estonian) which have no objective means for effectively developing many of the sectors of industry.[3]

In all of the union republics with the exception of the RSFSR, the Ukraine and Kazakhstan, the share of exports in industrial and agricultural output is more than 25%, while the share of imports exceeds 30% of the total volume of industrial and agricultural goods consumed on a republic's territory (see Table 1).

The creation of a modern multisectoral economy in every republic and the evening out of the levels of economic development of the different republics is not accompanied by the unifying of their economic structures. On the contrary, the predominant tendency is toward a deepening of specialization.

In the past decade, interrepublic trade grew on the whole more rapidly than production. Its share (separately for exports and imports) increased by 1%. The share of exports increased in nine republics and the share of imports in ten. The share of interrepublic trade in the total social product increased especially notably in

Table 1

Export and Import of Industrial and Agricultural Products by Union Republics, in %

Republic	Ratio of exports to production	Ratio of imports to intra-republic consumption
Ukraine	17	17
Belorussia	32	32
Uzbekistan	25	30
Kazakhstan	14	24
Georgia	33	36
Azerbaidzhan	37	35
Lithuania	28	32
Moldavia	29	31
Tadzhik	30	35
Turkmen	37	38
Estonia	30	31

Note: Here and in the following, exports include foreign exports, and imports include foreign imports. All measurements are in the end consumer prices, i.e., taking into account turnover tax, trade and transport fees, etc.

Turkmenia (from 24% to 34% for exports and from 30% to 35% for imports), in Belorussia (from 25% to 33% and from 25% to 32%) and in Azerbaidzhan and Georgia. The relative importance of interrepublic exchange decreased somewhat in Uzbekistan, Kazakhstan, Tadzhikistan, and the Kirghiz republic. In these republics, the extension of the fuel base, the creation of industries for processing local raw materials, intrarepublic cooperation in machine construction and metal processing had a substantial impact.

The contemporary material structure of interrepublic ties is extremely varied; this is characteristic of all Union republics without exception. The one-sided division of the republics into producers of agricultural goods and raw materials on the one hand and industrial republics on the other hand has been eliminated as a result of fundamental transformations in the economies of the former national areas; the growing complexity of industrial structures demands broad and multifaceted interrepublic links.

Let us take the Georgian SSR as an example. Today it transports to other republics and exports abroad manganese ores, ferrous alloys, steel pipes, rolled steel, technological equipment for the food industry, electric trains and trucks, metal cutting machines, welding apparatus, electrotechnical goods and instruments, mineral raw materials, synthetic materials, essential oils, the products of light industry, canned goods, wines and tobacco products, tea, citrus products, etc.

According to the data of republic intersectoral balance sheets, products from 96 sectors of other republics are used in the Kazakh SSR. In turn Kazakhstan ships its products from 74 economic sectors to other republics. The Moldavian SSR obtains products from 93 sectors and ships the output of 70 sectors to other republics. Georgia receives products from 100 sectors in all the Union republics, while 82 sectors of the other republics of the USSR receive products from Georgia.

The data in Table 2 show the broad participation of the different republics in the national division of labor and their close interdependence. The volumes of goods produced and consumed on the territories of the different republics also differ substantially along the profile of large sectors of industry. The consumption of the output of ferrous metallurgy, for example, exceeds internal production by 4.5 times in Belorussia, by four times in Latvia, and by nine times in Kirghizia; consumption exceeds production in the fuel industry by 3.2 times in Lithuania, and 7.7 times in Latvia. On the other hand, the production of machinery in Belorussia is 26% greater than consumption in that republic, while in Armenia this figure is 28%. It is fundamentally important that each Union republic has a positive balance in interrepublic exchange (net exports) in some aggregate sectors of industry and agriculture.

It should be borne in mind that the data on aggregate sectors level out considerably the real correlations in regional volumes of production and consumption. Intrasectoral exchange, which is especially important in machinery construction, the chemical industry and light industry, falls from view. An analysis by sector, and even more so by individual types of products, discloses much greater differences in production and consumption.

A comparison of Tables 2 and 3 shows that in aggregate sectors exports and imports cancel out one another to a large extent, creating the illusion that the republic production and consumption balance sheets represent relatively closed circles. In reality this is not the case: usually different types of products within sectoral groups participate in mutual exchange. For example, in the Kazakh SSR production and consumption of the products of the fuel industry differ by only 3%, but Kazakhstan exports 40% of the products of its fuel industry and imports 37% (basically petroleum processing products). In the Kirghiz SSR, the "net" import of machinery and the products of metal processing industry is 5% of the volume of consumption, but Kirghizia exports 53% of the output of this sector, and imports 58% of the volume of production. With the exception of Kazakhstan, all the republics export more than 50% of their machinery output; the various republics import more than one-third of the consumed output of light industry, independently of the scale of their own production. A considerable share of imported products are not interchangeable, i.e., they cannot be replaced by products produced by internal industry (this is referred to as "noncomplementary" import). The quite modest position of agriculture in the system of interrepublic links is striking. Imbalances in production and consumption of agricultural output are only 3–7% in seven republics (see Tables 2, 3). The share of exported output is also relatively small. How may this be explained? A considerable share of agricultural raw material produced is processed within the republic (fodder, live cattle, milk, industrial crops) and exported in the form of the products of light industry and the food industry. Fresh vegetables and potatoes are provided mainly from sources within the republic; the output of private plots is also mainly consumed within the republic. But such subsidiary sectors as the

Table 2

Ratio of Internal Production to Consumption on the Territory of the Republic, in %

Sector	Belorussia	Kazakhstan	Georgia	Lithuania	Latvia	Kirghizia	Armenia
Ferrous metallurgy	22	75	105	25	34	11	16
Fuel	87	103	75	31	13	37	15
Machinery construction and metal processing	126	64	76	103	116	95	128
Chemical	108	77	59	103	88	19	124
Forestry	99	67	70	60	105	56	52
Light industry	105	77	102	107	112	104	114
Food industry	100	90	125	107	113	99	97
Agriculture	95	107	97	96	90	97	96

Table 3

Ratio of Exports and Imports of Republic Output to Volumes of Production, in %

Republic Sector	Belorussia		Kazakhstan		Latvia		Kirghizia		Armenia	
	E	I	E	I	E	I	E	I	E	I
Ferrous metallurgy	36	389	6	39	67	257	54	902	14	551
Fuel	57	72	40	37	26	675	55	222	1	566
Machine construction and metal processing	62	41	5	63	66	53	53	58	59	37
Chemical	77	69	28	57	72	86	29	452	60	41
Forestry	30	31	4	54	32	26	5	82	3	95
Food industry	20	20	9	20	29	18	22	21	23	26
Light industry	39	34	16	45	41	30	41	37	46	33
Agriculture	3	8	9	2	2	13	3	5	3	7

commercial production of fresh fruits, grapes, and warm climate vegetables have not yet acquired a notable position in the structure of the total agricultural output of the USSR.

In most of the republics, machinery construction and metal processing play a leading role in interrepublic turnover. It accounts for more than 30% of goods shipped out of the RSFSR, the Ukraine, Belorussia, Lithuania, Kirghizia, and Armenia (its share in goods imported from other republics is 20–30% for all the republics). In international trade practice, such a high proportion of machinery construction in exports is considered a sign of a high level of industrial development. The fact that formerly some of the most backward regions of Tsarist Russia have become suppliers of products from advanced sectors of the machinery construction industry is one of the firmest achievements of the economic and political union of Soviet republics. For instances, in Kirghizia, the export of machinery has reached 35% of the total exports; Uzbekistan exports goods from 26 subsectors of the machinery industry of the 33 listed in the intersectoral balance classification, including eleven items totalling up more than 10 billion rubles (lifting and transport equipment, electrotechnical products, chemical and petroleum equipment, tractors and farm machinery, radio electronics, etc.).

Usually 65–80% of a republic's turnover is accounted for by three sectors: machinery, light industry and the food industry. Exceptions are Kazakhstan (high proportions of exports of fuel and agricultural products), the Ukraine (exports of ferrous metallurgy products), the RSFSR and Azerbaidzhan (export of fuel). The export of unprocessed industrial and agricultural raw material does not occupy a leading position in any of the republics. The Ukraine has the highest portion of the products of ferrous metallurgy (18%), Azerbaidzhan the highest proportion of the fuel industry (20%), Belorussia the highest percentage of the machinery construction and chemical industry (38% and 15% respectively), Tadzhikistan the highest percentage of the products of light industry (59%), Georgia the highest percentage of the food industry (33%), and Kazakhstan the highest percentage of agricultural products (16%).

The dynamics of interrepublic commerce is influenced by a variety of factors. Some of them promote a deepening of specialization (utilization of favorable natural factors, and the advantages of a concentration of production) and consequently an accelerated growth in interrepublic commerce. Others, on the other hand, are conducive to a diversification of the regional economies, and the development of industries oriented to the local market (saving on transport costs, reliable supplies, agglomeration effects, the utilization of local resources where they are in general in short supply, etc.).

The growing differentiation of the extent to which the various republics are provided with fuel and energy, minerals and raw materials, and forest resources has led to a growth in the flows of products from the extracting branches of industry, especially from the RSFSR. Interrepublic trade is continuing to grow faster than production in the machinery construction and in certain sectors of Group B as well (owing to the increase in the scale of production and specialization and to the demands for a variety of goods). With regard to the processing of natural raw materials, a number of qualitatively diverse factors are operative here, and it is much more difficult reliably to predict the dynamics of the interrepublic division of labor. The food program adopted by the May (1982) Plenum of the CPSU provides for the development of national bases for the production of high quality grains, groats, meat, fruits and vegetables, grapes, and consequently an increase in interrepublic deliveries of these food products. But the population's need for potatoes, late vegetables, dairy products, and eggs will principally be covered by regional production.

Export and import data compared with the volumes of production and consumption by the different branches of production reflect only the direct influence of external ties on the formation and distribution of republic resources in certain types of product, and consequently only the direct participation of republic sectors in the nationwide division of labor. The limitation of an analysis of these data alone is that it ignores intersectoral interrelations that are shaped as a result of interrepublic trade in the different sectors.

Let us assume that a republic has a shortage of electric power and has no possibilities for substantially increasing its internal production in the near future. One of the ways to overcome or alleviate the shortage in electric power is to rationalize the external economic links of the republic. The simplest way out is to increase the import of electric power or to reduce its transmission to other republics. However, this solution is not necessarily the best; moreover, it may be totally unrealistic, for example, owing to the limited capacities of the power lines from other republics. A broader approach is required to the problem, based on an analysis of the structure of interrepublic exchange to reduce the indirect export of electric power by limiting the export of areas of production that require a considerable consumption of power or, on the other hand, to increase its indirect import by importing products of industries using a lot of power. Then the indirect interrepublic exchange of electric power will exceed by dozens and even hundreds of times its direct transmission, which makes it possible to maneuver the electric balances of the republics within quite broad limits.

A step toward a systemic analysis of interrepublic interactions is the calculation of indices of "total export" and "total import." These indices make it possible to study the impact of the totality of external material links on all the most important characteristics of the complex economic system of a republic.

The total export of a particular product (let us say, metal) is equal to the volume of its production within the republic, necessary to cover the direct export of the products of all sectors directly or indirectly using this product (in the particular example this would be machinery construction, building, etc.). On the other hand, total import described the potential reduction in the production of a particular product in the republic as a result of the direct import of products in all its sectors. Calculations of total export (import) are done with an intersectoral balance model.

Total export and import in the individual republics considerably exceeds the corresponding values for direct export and import. For example, the total export of

Table 4

Shares of Total Exports and Imports of Republic Output in Total Social Product (TSP), in %

Republics	Ratio of total exports to production TSP	Total import to consumption TSP
Ukraine	36	36
Belorussia	64	64
Kazakhstan	25	47
Georgia	64	67
Azerbaidzhan	72	73
Lithuania	61	66
Latvia	77	74
Kirghizia	52	64
Tadzhikistan	53	65

fuel from Latvia was 23 times greater than the direct export, the total export of the products of the chemical industry from Georgia was 3.2 times greater, total export of the products of the forestry industry from Armenia exceeded direct exports by 25 times. A considerable excess of total export over direct export is characteristic for agricultural output: in Latvia by a factor of 21, in Lithuania a factor of 40, and in Kirghizia a factor of 13, which confirms the view that agriculture participates mainly indirectly in interrepublic exchange (mainly through provision of products from the food and light industries manufactured from agricultural raw material).

The ratio of total exports (imports) to direct export (import) for the entire output of material production varies between 2.2 and 2.5 for the different republics. This ratio is greater the greater the share of products from the final stages of social production (machinery construction, light and food industries) in interrepublic trade. If a republic traded only primary resources, the ratio of total export (import) to direct export (import) would approach unity.

To save transport costs, it is clearly preferable to exchange products that have been intensely processed (with a higher cost per unit weight) and not to transport unconcentrated coal and ore, round timber, chemical raw materials, etc. Hence the coefficient showing the excess of total export (import) over direct export (import) and their patterns of change serve as indicators of a sort of the rationality of the material structure of interrepublic trade. According to calculations, most of the union republics show a characteristic rational shift in the structure of trade from the standpoint of the correlation between the extracting and processing sectors as compared with the structure of products produced and traded within a republic.

Total export in the union republics (with the exception of the RSFSR, the Ukraine and Kazakhstan) is greater than half of the total social product, while in Latvia it is 77% (see Table 4). These proportions have increased in the last decade for eleven republics, which is one of the principal signs of an intensification of economic relations between the Soviet republics. The share of total import is more than half of the consumed total social product in twelve republics, and in most of them it is more than two-thirds. Moreover, if the output of the construction industry, not entering either directly or indirectly in interrepublic exchange, is subtracted from the total social product (in accordance with the method of constructing intersectoral balances), the share of total exports and imports in the produced and consumed product increases by another 5–8 percentage points.

In a number of sectors (ferrous and nonferrous metallurgy, fuel, the chemical industry, etc.) total exports in most republics exceed the volume of production, owing, in the first place, to the indirect exports of the products of the consuming sectors. For example, the indirect export of ferrous metals is a consequence of the direct export of the products of machinery construction industry. But the total imports in many republics in these sectors considerably exceeds the intrarepublic consumption.

Calculations of total exports and imports thus show a much greater interrepublic intermeshing of production and consumption of the output of the various sectors than meets the eye from an examination of the data of direct interrepublic turnover. The development of interrepublic exchange will continue to be based on a deepening of the sectoral distribution of labor and a growing complexity of intersectoral interrelations.

Hence more complete instruments of analysis and planning of interrepublic relations, enhancing the effectiveness of the country's complex economic system, are required.

Economic interaction between the RSFSR and the union republics

The Resolution of the Central Committee of the CPSU on the 60th Anniversary of the Formation of the USSR states that "the RSFSR has played a decisive role in the construction of a single Union State and all the other Soviet republics have freely joined ranks around it."

The Russian Federation is a republic, first among equals; it plays a leading role in the single complex national economy. In the RSFSR are concentrated approximately 60% of the nation's economic potential, and in a number of sectors of prime importance, especially in heavy industry, it makes a crucial contribution to union-wide production. Thus in 1980, 62% of the country's electric power, 91% of its oil, 55% of its coal, 58% of its rolled ferrous metals, 53% of its chemical fibers, 86% of its automobiles, 54% of its farm machinery, 92% of its industrial wood, 67% of its cloth, 53% of its televisions, and 61% of its whole milk products were produced in the RSFSR in 1980.

Because of its territorial dimensions, the economy of the RSFSR meets a larger portion of its own needs with its own production than do other union republics. In the late '70s, the export of its output (including foreign exports) constituted about

9% of its gross produced social product, while import (including foreign imports) exceeded 11% of the total social product consumed on the territory of the RSFSR.

The products of heavy industry, machinery construction and metal processing, fuels, the chemical industry, and the forestry industry occupy a key place in the sectoral structure of exports from the Russian Federation to the other union republics: up to one-fifth of the output of these sectors is exported. More than half of the imports to the RSFSR (expressed in value terms) is accounted for by the output of three sectors: light industry, the food industry, and agriculture. According to calculations on the basis of intersectoral balances for 1972, capital goods accounted for 70% of the goods exported from the RSFSR, while consumer goods accounted for 30%; approximately 60% of imports were capital goods, and 40% were consumer goods. Thus, a characteristic feature of the interaction of the RSFSR with the economies of the other republics is the export of capital goods in exchange for consumer goods.

We should stress that even the relatively small portion of exports from the RSFSR has a very important economic role for the other Union republics. Six percent of the exports from the RSFSR go to Uzbekistan, but for Uzbekistan this makes up 5% of its imports. Classified by territory, the RSFSR accounts for 63% of Uzbekistan's imports in petroleum products, 96% of its imports in synthetic resins and plastics, more than 80% of its imports of automobiles, 66% of its tractors and farm machinery, almost 100% of its imports in timber, and 60% of its imports in fish and fish products, etc.

According to the calculations, at the end of the '70s, the total exports of goods from the RSFSR was 2.3 times higher than the volume of direct imports (in end consumer prices) and reached (including foreign exports) 20–22% of the produced total social product of the RSFSR. Total import of goods into the republic exceeded direct imports by 2.4 times and amounted to (including foreign imports) 27–29% of the total social product consumed on the territory of the Russian Federation.

Taking into account both direct and indirect links, the RSFSR has a positive balance for interrepublic exchange in the output of the fuel industry, electric power, ferrous metallurgy, the forest industry, the construction materials industry, etc. In particular, the total balance for exports and imports of fuel was about 15%, while for forest products it was 20% of the volumes of production. Total imports exceeded exports in ferrous metallurgy and especially in light industry and the foodstuffs industry and agriculture.

The greatest share of operating productive capital and labor resources do not participate directly in republic exchange. However, these resources are expended in the production of exported products (or are economised on as a consequence of the import of such products since the republic "is relieved" from producing it). Thus the union republics may indirectly "exchange" basic productive capital and labor power.

An intersectoral analysis carried out at the Institute of Economics and Organization of Industrial Production of the Siberian Division of the Academy of Sciences of the USSR showed an important and stable trend in economic relations between the

Table 5

Redistribution of Resources between the RSFSR and Other Union Republics for Final Utilization of Republic Output (in % of volume of resources in the supplier zone)

	Total expenditures on the utilized final product	Including	
		nonproductive consumption fund	accumulation fund
RSFSR for other union republics			
total product	12.0	7.2	2.5
labor reserves	10.2	6.2	3.0
capital goods	13.1	6.9	3.0
Other union republics for the RSFSR			
total product	19.1	14.4	2.7
labor resources	16.7	13.6	1.9
capital goods	20.1	13.7	3.3

union republics: the Russian Federation indirectly "exports" capital goods and indirectly attracts labor resources. Thus in 1972, 0.3 billion rubles of basic capital was exported indirectly from the RSFSR, while 0.8 million annual workers were indirectly drawn upon. In the following years, because of the growth in the dimensions and change in the structure of interrepublic exchange, the indirect export of capital goods from the RSFSR increased considerably, and in our estimates exceeded 3 billion rubles. In most areas of Russia, the tension in the balances of the workforce is increasing because of demographic shifts. Hence such a structural reorganization of economic relations of the RSFSR which would help to bring about a relative decrease in the demand for labor power assumes particular significance. In this sphere of interrepublic relations there are many unutilized reserves.

For an analysis of the growth of the RSFSR within the overall complex national economy, the Institute of Economics and the Organization of Industrial Production of the Siberian Division of the Academy of Sciences of the USSR has made a few modifications in intersectoral models of the national economy. The territory of the country was divided into two areas: the RSFSR and other union republics. Calculations in two-zone models provide a much more profound idea of the mechanisms of interrepublic and intersectoral interactions. Table 5 shows the results of calculations using one model of a two-zone intersectoral balance for the USSR for 1972. These figures show the mutual participation of the republics in the final utilization of output for consumption and accumulation.

A unique functional division of labor was developed and is growing stronger in the national economy of the USSR: the Russian Federation has a significant responsibility for forming the accumulation fund in all the other union republics, while the other republics channel considerable resources into the consumption fund of the

RSFSR. The territorial division of labor helps to save on labor resources on the territory of the RSFSR, but increases the republic's need for capital goods. Analysis indicates that specialization of the two economic zones of the country is deepening progressively, direct and indirect interzonal relations are intensifying, the interdependence and mutual complementarity of the economies of the RSFSR and the other Union republics are growing.

The Soviet system, i.e., a single state of Soviet republics enjoying equal rights, based on social ownership of the means of production, has fundamental advantages over other forms of economic cooperation among nations and regions. As Comrade L. I. Brezhnev said in his report on the 50th Anniversary of the USSR, "The fusion of economic means and resources of all the republics accelerates the development of each of them, from the smallest to the largest. Union-wide economic management and planning has made it possible rationally to approach the distribution of productive forces, has created more freedom to maneuver economically, and has deepened cooperation and specialization, wherein the general advantage is much greater than a simple arithmetic sum of the components, i.e., the efforts of each republic, district and region."

The economic effect of interaction between the Soviet republics creates a universal economic interest in close cooperation, and a fundamental basis for bringing Union and republic socioeconomic interests in line with one another.

Because of the Leninist national policy, the Soviet Union has been able within a short historical period to eliminate the backwardness of former national regions of Tsarist Russia, and to bring nations and nationalities socialist forms of economy on a contemporary scientific technical foundation. Every Soviet republic is today a developed complex economic system with a multi-sectoral production structure, service sector, and a unique culture.

In the present stage, it is especially important to make fuller use of the advantages of the union-wide division of labor and interrepublic cooperation to increase the strength and effectiveness of the nation's overall economy. As the resolution of the Central Committee of the CPSU on the 60th anniversary of the USSR states: "To accomplish all economic and social tasks, first and foremost from a general perspective for the country as a whole, and to struggle with all manifestations of local provincialism and bureaucratic narrowness is an unfailing requirement of a truly Party-minded and internationalist approach to the matter."

Notes

1. The correlations between produced and consumed national income for the Union republics is determined in many respects by the prices of imported and exported output. But price formation in the USSR is not directly pegged to interrepublic "economic self-sufficiency." Hence quantitative estimates of the redistribution of the national income among the republics are quite provisional.

2. The coefficient of rank correlation between territories of a republic and the proportion of exports in the total volume of production is about 0.8 (maximum value for the coefficient is 1).

3. See P. Guzhvin and V. Luk'ianov, "Balans proizvodstva i raspredeleniia produktsii RSFSR," *Vestnik statistiki*, 1976, No. 5.

The Basic Guidelines for Economic and Social Development *

The following basic guidelines for the union republics' economic and social development are to be laid down.

In the RSFSR, production of industrial output is to increase 20–23%. Machine building and the gas, chemical, and microbiological industries are to be developed at an accelerated pace. In 1990 electricity generation is to be increased to 1,120–1,160 billion kilowatt-hours, oil and gas condensate production is to be increased to 560–575 million metric tons, gas production to 640–650 billion cubic meters, and coal production to 440–445 million metric tons.

The average annual volume of gross agricultural output is to be increase 13–15%. Grain production is to be increased in 1990 to 140–142 million metric tons, sugar beet production to 31–32 million metric tons, potato production to 45–47 million metric tons, vegetable production to 14.5–15 million metric tons, meat production (slaughter weight) to 10–10.2 million metric tons, milk production to 54–55 million metric tons, and egg production to 45–46 billion eggs. During the five-year period, 1,485,000 hectares of irrigated land are to be commissioned and 1.63 million hectares of marshy and waterlogged land are to be drained. Amelioration work is to be carried out on land which does not require draining over an area of up to 6 million hectares.

The energy base of the European part of the RSFSR is to be strengthened. The construction of the Kalinin AES [Atomic Energy Station] and the second stage of the Smolensk AES is to be completed, capacities are to be commissioned at the Kursk, Balakovo, Tatar, and Rostov AES's and the Gorkii and Voronezh nuclear heat supply stations, and construction of the Kostroma AES and the Volgograd Nuclear TETS is to be developed. Construction of the Krasnodar AES and the third stage of the Kola AES is to be started. Construction of the Irganai GES is to be accelerated, the Zagorsk GAES [pumped storage electric power station] is to be commissioned, and construction of the Leningrad GAES is to be developed.

The further development and improvement of the efficiency of the agro-industrial complex of the RSFSR's non–black-earth zone are to be ensured. The construction of housing, roads, and services sphere projects is to be continued on a large scale and the working and living conditions of the rural population are to be improved.

In the cities of Moscow and Leningrad and in Moscow and Leningrad oblasts better use is to be made of the existing scientific and production potential to accelerate scientific and technical progress and enhance the efficiency of the country's national economy. Production is to be increased only by means of the retooling

---

Pravda, 9 March 1986. The Guidelines were adopted at the Twenty-seventh Party Congress.

and reconstruction of existing enterprises, the broad application of modern technologies, flexible automated systems, and robot technology, the deepening of specialization, the development of intersectoral production facilities, and the improvement of labor productivity, ensuring a reduction in the number of work places. The elimination of production facilities and enterprises in the cities of Moscow and Leningrad whose further development in these locations is economically inexpedient is to be accelerated. The territory of Moscow city and its forest and park zone is to be utilized rationally, with regard to demands concerning the protection of the environment. The interconnected comprehensive development of Moscow city and Oblast and of Leningrad city and Oblast is to be ensured. The construction of structures to protect Leningrad city from flooding is to be continued.

The further development of the Timano-Pechora territorial production complex is to be ensured; the construction of coal mines and the start of development work in new oil fields is to be accelerated; and preparatory work linked with the extraction of bauxite and titanium ores is to begin. More comprehensive use is to be made of the Kola Peninsula's minerals.

New capacities are to be created in the Kursk magnetic anomaly territorial production complex for the extraction and enrichment of iron ore and the production of electric steel and rolled metal; fuller use is to be made of overburden rock and waste from mining and enriching enterprises. Shops are to be constructed for the production of cold-rolled strip at the Orel steel rolling mill. The development of heavy industry and the agro-industrial complex of the Central Black-Earth economic region is to be rationally combined.

The construction of the main projects of an industrial complex for the production of technological equipment for the food industry, trade, and public catering in the city of Volzhsk in the Mari ASSR, as well as a shop for the production of oil-grade, corrosion-resistant pipes at the Volga pipe plant, is to be carried out. Capacities for the extraction and processing of gas and condensate and the production of sulfur are to be commissioned at the industrial center being formed on the basis of the Astrakhan gas condensate deposit. The lands of the Volga Akhtuba floodplain are to be opened up more efficiently.

In the Urals, capacities at the Bashkir, South Urals, and Beloiarsk AES's, the Perm GRES, and the Cheliabinsk TETS are to be commissioned. The first stage of the Magnitogorsk metallurgical combine's steel smelting facility and low-capacity metallurgical plants are to be reconstructed.

The accelerated development of Siberia's economy is to be ensured. Work to build up fuel and energy base capacities in this region is to be accelerated. Measures are to implemented which aim to ensure the comprehensive processing of mineral, raw material, and timber resources, the enhancement of the region's share in all-union output by the energy-intensive sectors of industry, and the proportional development of processing sectors and machine building in particular. The local food base is to be consolidated. The construction industry, construction materials industry, and transportation are to develop at preferential rates.

The formation of the West Siberia territorial production complex is to continue.

The prospecting for, construction and equipping, and development of petroleum and gas deposits are to be increased. Main gas pipelines are to be built in the European part of the country and in Siberia's southern regions. The construction of Surgut's GRES-2 is to be completed, and capacities at the Nizhnevartovsk and Urengoi GRES's are to be commissioned.

The building and reconstruction of coal enterprises in the Kuzbass are to be accelerated. The building of the Katunskaia GES, the Altai nitrogen fertilizers plans, and the Tiumen' chemical plant is to be developed. The reconstruction of the Kuznetsk metallurgical combine is to be implemented. Land reclamation work is to continue in West Siberia's southern regions, the construction of the Aleisk irrigation system in Altai Krai is to be completed, and the construction of Altai Krai's Bulinskaia irrigation system is to be continued.

Power units at the Berezovskaia No. 1 GRES and coal extraction capacities are the Berezovskii No. 1 open pit are to be commissioned, the building of the "Borodinskii" No. 2 open coal pit is to be undertaken, the construction of Berezovskaia No. 2 GRES is to be developed, and other work is to be carried out in the formation of the Kansk-Achinsk territorial production complex.

The commissioning of capacities at enterprises under construction in the Saianskii territorial production complex is to be ensured and the construction of the Saianskii aluminum plant is to be accelerated. The opening up of resources in the lower Angara region is to be developed and construction of the Boguchanskaia GES is to continue; preparatory work is to begin on the construction of the Sredneeniseiskaia GES and the opening up of the Gorevskoe lead and zinc deposit. The opening up of the Ozernoe polymetallic deposit is to be undertaken, the building of the Tugnuyskii open coal pit is to be developed, and the capacity of the Kharanorskii open cut coal pit is to be increased. Capacities at the second stage of the Gusinoozerskaia GRES and at the Ulan-Ude TETS-2 are to be commissioned.

The entire length of the Baikal-Amur Main Railroad is to be brought into permanent use and the large-scale economic development of the zone incorporating this railroad is to be undertaken. The formation of the South Yakut territorial production complex is to continue. Capacities at the second stage of the Neryungri GRES are to be commissioned, construction of the Seligdarskii apatite plant is to begin, and preparatory work is to be carried out on the creation of a metallurgical base in the Far East using local coking coal and iron ore. The construction of the Berakit-Tommot-Yakutsk railroad is to be developed.

The extraction of nonferrous and rare metals in the Far East is to be increased. The preferential development of the fuel industry and electric power generation is to be ensured. The Okha-Komsomolsk-na-Amure gas pipeline and the first units of the Viliuisk GES-3 and the Bureia GES, the Komsomolskaia TETS-3, and the Ussuri TETS are to be commissioned, and construction of the UST-Srednekanskaia GES and the Yakutsk GRES-2 is to be undertaken. Construction of the Deputatskii mining and enriching combine in the Yakut ASSR is to be completed. Fish catches, the extraction of sea products, and the output of high-quality edible fish products are to be increased. The production of soybean, rice, and other agricultural products is to be stepped up.

In order to retain cadres in northern, Siberian, and Far Eastern regions, the preferential rise in the living standards for the population of these regions is to be ensured.

The traditional forms of economic activity by the north's ethnic groups are to be improved on a new technological base.

In the Ukrainian SSR, industrial production is to increase 18–21%. By 1990, electricity generation is to increase to 320 billion kilowatt-hours. The construction of the Chernobyl and Zaporozhe AES's is to be completed, capacities at the Khmelnitskii, Rovno, South Ukrainian, and Crimean EAS's and the Odessa nuclear TETS are to be commissioned, and construction is to begin on the Kharkov nuclear TETS and the Dnester and Kanev GAES's.

The reconstruction and retooling of coal industry and ferrous metallurgy enterprises are to continue, primarily in the Donbass. Capacities for the processing of oxidized iron ore at the Krivoi Rog mining and enriching combine and for the extraction and processing of manganese ores at the Tavricheskii mining and enriching combine are to be commissioned. The production of chemical industry and machine-building output is to increase approximately 30%. There is to be a considerable expansion of light industry output, particularly of linen fabrics and knitwear.

The average annual volume of gross agricultural output is to increase 13–15%. By 1990 production figures are to be as follows; 52–54 million metric tons of grain, 53–55 million metric tons of sugar beets, 2.9 million metric tons of sunflowers, 8.6 million metric tons of vegetables, 4.5 million metric tons of fruit and berries, 4.9–5 million metric tons of meat (slaughter weight), 24.5–25 million metric tons of milk, and 16–17 billion eggs. Guaranteed production of corn for grain is to be established on lands under irrigation. Some 500,000 hectares of irrigated land and 640,000 hectares of drained land are to be commissioned during the five-year period.

In the Belorussian SSR, industrial production is to increase 22–25%. The preferential development of machine tool building, instrument building, the radio engineering, electronic, and electrical equipment industries, and machine building for stockraising and feed production is to be ensured.

The first power unit of the Minsk nuclear TETS, capacities for the production of petroleum products and chemical raw materials at the "Novopolotsknefterogintez" Association and the Mozyr petroleum refinery, and for the production of metal cord at the Belorussian metallurgical plan in Zhlobin are to be commissioned. The reconstruction and expansion of enterprises under the jurisdiction of the "V.I. Lenin Minsk Tractor Plant" association are to continue.

The average annual volume of gross agricultural output is to increase 12–14%. By 1990 production figures are to be as follows: 8–8.2 million metric tons of grain, no less than 13 million metric tons of potatoes, 27–28 million metric tons of feed (in feed units), 1.2–1.3 million metric tons of meat (slaughter weight), 7.1–7.3 million metric tons of milk, and 3.4–3.5 billion eggs.

Some 520,000 hectares of waterlogged and swampland are to be drained during the five-year period, including 420,000 hectares by the closed drainage method. The construction of priority flood protection projects for agricultural land in the Polesskaia depression is to be completed.

In the Uzbek SSR, industrial production is to increase 24–27%. The chemical, electrical equipment, and light industries, instrument building, and the processing of agricultural products are to be developed at higher rates. Electricity generation is to increase 25–27% and sulfuric acid production by 34–36%. Capacities at the Angren open coal pit, the Novoangrenskaia and Talimardzhan GRES's, and the Uzbek metallurgical plant are to be commissioned. Construction of an agricultural machinery plant is to begin.

The average annual volume of gross agricultural output is to increase 14–16%. By 1990 production figures are to be as follows: 1.8–1.93 million metric tons of cotton fiber, including at least 154,000 metric tons of fine-fiber varieties of raw cotton, 3.2–3.5 milion metric tons of grain, 20 million metric tons of feed (in feed units), 540,000–560,000 metric tons of meat (slaughter weight), 3.3–3.5 million metric tons of milk, and 2.7–3 billion eggs. The accelerated development of the production of fruit and vegetable and melon crops is to be provided for.

The reconstruction and improved utilization of existing irrigation systems is to be ensured, 360,000 hectares of irrigated land are to be commissioned during the five-year period, 1.1 million hectares of pastureland are to be supplied with water, and the water supply system for some 4.8 million hectares of pastureland is to be reconstructed. The comprehensive opening of the Karshi and Dzhizak steppes to be continued.

In the Kazakh SSR, industrial production is to increase 23–26%. Provision is to be made for further development of the fuel and energy complex, ferrous and nonferrous metallurgy, machine building, and the chemical and petrochemical industries.

The formation of the Pavlodar-Ekibastuz territorial production complex is to continue. Coal extraction in the Ekibastuz field is to be increase considerably, the opening up of the Maikiubenskii coalfield is to begin, capacities at Ekibastuz GRES–2 are to be commissioned, and construction of the Ekibastuz GRES–3 and the South Kazakhstan GRES is to be developed. The construction of Shulbinskaia GES is to be completed.

The opening up of the Tengizskoe petroleum field and the Karachaganak gas condensate deposit is to be accelerated. Capacities for the extraction and processing of ores at the Zhairem mining and enriching combine and the Dzezkazgan mining and metallurgical combine are to be expanded; the Shalkiia deposit is to be opened up. The building of the Bakyrchikskii mining and metallurgical combine, the Kairakty tungsten mining and enriching combine, the Koktenkolskii molybdenum mining and enriching combine, and the Bushchekulskii copper mining and enriching combines is to begin.

The average annual volume of gross agricultural output is to increase 13–15%. By 1990 production figures are to be as follows: 30–31 million metric tons of grain, 1.4–1.5 million metric tons of meat (in slaughter weight), 5.4–5.5 million metric tons of mil, 4.2–4.3 billion eggs, no less than 120,000 metric tons of wool, and 55–

58 million metric tons of feeds (in feed units). The commodity production of high quality hard and strong what varieties, and of millet and buckwheat is to be considerably expanded. The development of cattle breeding for meat and of fine- and semi-fine-fleeced sheep breeding is to be continued. Work is to be done on the quality improvement of irrigated land and the technical improvement of existing irrigation systems on an area of 670,000 hectares. Some 410,000 hectares of irrigated land are to be commissioned during the five-year period.

In the Georgian SSR, industrial production is to increase 22–25%. Preferential growth is to be ensured for the electrical equipment, electronic, and radio industries and for instrument building. The first units of the Khudonskaia GES are to be commissioned, the building of the Georgian AES and of the Marbeuli nonstandard equipment plant and component casting plant is to begin, as is also the reconstruction of the Rustavi metallurgical plant and the expansion of Tibilisi GRES. A plant for the production of tractors and machinery for mountain crop farming and the second stage of the Kutaisi motor vehicle plan are to be built. The Marabda-Akhalkalaki railroad is to be commissioned. The building of the Caucasus mountain railroad is to begin.

The average annual volume of gross agricultural output is to increase 14–16%. By 1990, production figures are to be as follows: 650,000 metric tons of high quality tea, 1.1–1.4 million metric tons of fruit, berries, and citrus fruit, 230,000 metric tons of meat (in slaughter weight), 850,000–900,000 metric tons of milk, and 1.2 billion eggs. Some 60,000 hectares of irrigated land are to be commissioned during the five-year period and 35,000 hectares of waterlogged and swamp land are to be drained. Work on the reclamation and development of land in the Kolkhida depression is to be continued, existing irrigation systems are to be reconstructed, and the further development of resort and tourist facilities is to be ensured.

In the Azerbaidzhan SSR, industrial production is to increase 22–25%. The preferential development of the electronic and radio equipment industries and of instrument building and the further growth of the power, petrochemical, and food industries is envisaged. Petroleum prospecting and development drilling in the Caspian Sea and in the republic's western and central regions is to be expanded. Some 14–15 million metric tons of petroleum are to be extracted in 1990.

Capacities at Azerbaidzhan GRES are to be commissioned and the construction of an AEA, the Novobakinskaia TETS, and the Kirovabad trucks plant is to get under way. Installations for the production and processing of ethylene and propylene are to be commissioned.

The average annual volume of gross agricultural output is to be increased 14–16%. By 1990, production figures are to be as follows: 1.6 million metric tons of grain, 238,000 metric tons of cotton fiber, 1.2 million metric tons of vegetable and melon crops, 7.2–7.4 million metric tons of feed units, 229,00–225,000 metric tons of meat (in slaughter weight), 1.2–1.3 million metric tons of milk, and 1.3 billion eggs. Work on the improvement of the technical state of irrigation systems on an area of 600,000 hectares of irrigated lands is to be carried out during the five-year period and 75,000 hectares of irrigated land are to be commissioned.

Work on the creation of a resort zone of all-union importance along the Caspian Sea coast is to be launched.

In the Lithuanian SSR, industrial production is to increase 13–16%. The production of computer equipment, instruments and means of automation, and goods for cultural, consumer, and household purposes is to be developed at a preferential pace. The output of chemical products, canned meat and dairy products, furniture, linen fabrics, and leather footwear is to be expanded. Ignalina AES and Kayshyadoris GAES, complexes for the production of sulfuric acid at the Kedaynyay chemical plant and for the intensive processing of petroleum at the Mazheykyay petroleum refinery, and the USSR-GDR railroad ferry crossing are to be commissioned.

The average annual volume of gross agricultural output is to increase 14–16%. By 1990 production figures are to be as follows: 4 million metric tons of grain, 2.5 million metric tons of potatoes, at least 11 million metric tons of feed (in feed units), 600,000–620,000 metric tons of meat (in slaughter weight), and 3.2–3.3 million metric tons of milk. A pedigree stockbreeding base for supplying other republics with cattle is to be expanded. Some 450,000 hectares of drained land are to be commissioned during the five-year period.

In the Moldavian SSR, industrial production is to be increased 22–25%. Development of the agro-industrial complex is to continue and its efficiency increased. The construction of the "Plodselkhozmash" and "Moldsekhozmash" plants and the reconstruction of the Bendery silk combine are to be completed and plants producing well-drilling geophysical equipment and computer equipment are to be built. The output of fabrics, knitwear, and canned goods is to be boosted.

The average annual gross output of agricultural products is to be increased by 15–17%. By 1990 the gross harvest of vegetables is to be increased to 1.5 million metric tons and fruit and berries to 1.7 million metric tons, production of milk to 1.4–1.5 million metric tons, and meat (slaughter weight) to 350,000–360,000 metric tons, and sales of hybrid corn seeds to 70,000 metric tons and sunflower seeds to 10,000 metric tons. Some 150,000 hectares of irrigated lands are to be brought into use during the five-year period.

In the Latvian SSR, industrial production is to be increased by 13–16% with preferential growth in the electronics, electrical equipment, chemicals, and communications industries. The production of high-quality consumer goods is to be developed and the range of fish products expanded. The retooling and reconstruction of light industry and construction industry enterprises are to be continued. Power units at the Daugavpils GES and the first phase of the industrial robot plant in the city of Riga are to be commissioned. The reconstruction of the "Sarkanays Metallurges" plant is to begin. The provision of gas to the republic's economy is to be accelerated.

The average annual gross output of agriculture is to be increased by 12–14%. By 1990, grain production is to be increased to 2.3 million metric tons, potatoes to 1.8 million metric tons, meat (slaughter weight) to 360,000–370,000 metric tons, and milk to 2–2.2 million metric tons. At least 260,000 hectares of waterlogged lands are to be drained during the five-year period.

The development of maritime transport and the fishing fleet is to continue and port facilities are to be consolidated. The construction of sanatoriums, health establishments, and facilities forming part of the Yurmala health resort's infrastructure is to be accelerated.

In the Kirghiz SSR, industrial production is to be increased by 21–24% with accelerated development of electric power, nonferrous metallurgy, electronics, and light industry. The Tash-Kumyr and Shamaldy-Sai GES's and thermal power capacities at the Frunze TETS-2 and Tash-Kumyr semiconductor materials plant are to be commissioned. Construction of the Kambaratinskii GES and the Sary-Dzhaz mining and enriching combine is to be started. The construction of the Kirghiz gold ore combine is to be completed. The belovodskoe fruit-glucose syrup combine is to be built.

The average annual gross output of agriculture is to be increased by 13–15%. The livestock feed base is to be consolidated by reclaiming pasture land. By 1990, meat production (slaughter weight) is to be increased to 220,000–230,000 metric tons, milk to 850,000–860,000 metric tons, the number of eggs to 640 million, and wool to 40,000 metric tons and the supply of sugar beet seed to the all-union pool is to increase to 15,000 metric tons and that of alfalfa seed to 6,500–7,000 metric tons. Some 45,000 hectares of irrigated land is to be brought into use during the five-year period. Work to comprehensively exploit the water and energy resources of the Sary-Dzhaz river to begin.

In the Tadzhik SSR, industrial production is to be increased by 23–26% with preferential development of electric power, chemicals, the light and food industries, and machine building. The South Tadzhik territorial production complex is to be further developed. Capacities at the Rogun GES are to be commissioned, construction of the Sangtuda GES is to begin, construction of the Yavanskii electrochemical plant is to be continued, and construction of the Tadzhik aluminum plant is to be completed. Construction of the Tadzhik gold ore combine and a plant producing storage cells in the city of Kulyab is to start. Spinning and weaving factories are to be constructed in the cities of Kanibadam and Kulyab and in the Faizabadskii raion. Construction of the Pamir GES and the Kurgan-Tyube-Kulyab railroad is to begin.

The average annual gross output of agriculture is to be increased by 12–14%. By 1990, the production of cotton fiber is to be increased to 290,000 metric tons (of which fine-fibered strains will be increased to 88,000 metric tons), meat (slaughter weight) to 140,000–143,000 metric tons, milk to 630,000–640,000 metric tons, and the number of eggs to 710–720 million. Planting of orchards and vineyards is to be expanded and the formation of vegetable growing and dairy zones close to cities is to be completed for the most part. A stable base for the production of potatoes for use as food is to be created in mountainous and foothill regions. Some 65,000 hectares are to be irrigated during the five-year period and the development of land in the Dangarinskii steppe and in the Beshkentskaia Dolina is to continue.

In the Armenian SSR, industrial production is to be increased by 24–26%. Reconstruction, retooling, and expansion of a number of existing enterprises in machine building, chemicals, light industry, nonferrous metallurgy, and the construction materials industry is to be carried out.

The construction of the second phase of the Armenian AES and the Bardenis-Dzhermuk railroad is to begin and plants producing programmable control units, hydraulic equipment for automatic manipulators, and specialized technical equipment, and a knitted fabric factory in the city of Kafan are to be built. Capacities for producing knitwear and leather footwear are to be expanded.

The average annual gross output of agriculture is to be increased by 12–14%. By 1990, grain production is to be increased to 330,000 metric tons, vegetables to 500,000 metric tons, fruit and berries to 240,000 metric tons, meat (slaughter weight) to 130,000 metric tons, milk to 625,000 metric tons, and the number of eggs to 680 million. Irrigation systems are to be reconstructed and 35,000 hectares of irrigated land are to be commissioned during the five-year period.

In the Turkmen SSR, industrial production is to be expanded by 20–23%. The production of mineral fertilizers is to be increased 2.6 times and gas extraction is to be increased to 86 billion cubic meters. Geological prospecting work for petroleum and gas is to be increased. Electric power, the light and food industries, and machine building are to be developed at a faster rate. The construction of the Mary GRES is to be completed, the commissioning of the Chardzhouskii petroleum refining plant is to be accelerated, the construction of the first phase of the graphitized electrodes plant in the city of Tashauz and the Turkmen hard alloy products plant is to be started. Construction of the Central Asian potassium fertilizers plant is to begin. Research and planning work on establishing the East Turkmen territorial production complex is to continue.

The average annual gross output of agriculture is to be increased 12–14%. By 1990, cotton fiber production is to be increased to 398,000 metric tons, of which fine-fiber strains will increase to 108,000 metric tons, vegetables and cucurbits to 900,000 metric tons, meat (slaughter weight) to 120,000 metric tons, milk to 380,000 metric tons, the number of eggs to 390 million, wool to 14–15,000 metric tons, and feed to 5.3 million metric tons of feed units.

Some 100,000 hectares of irrigated land are to be brought into use during the five-year period. Water supply construction and the comprehensive opening up of lands in the Karakum Canal zone are to be continued.

In the Estonian SSR, industrial production is to be increased by 13–16% with preferential growth rates occurring in the shale processing and electronics industries and instrument marking. The output of cultural, consumer-domestic, and household goods is to be increased. Construction of the Kuremyae shale mine is to begin. The construction of the new Tallin seaport is to be completed. The Bireshi-Tallin gas pipeline is to be built.

The average annual gross output of agriculture is to be increased by 12–14%. By 1990, feed production is to be increased to 4.4 million metric tons of feed units, meat (slaughter weight) to 245,000–250,000 metric tons, and milk to 1.4 million metric tons. Hog raising for bacon is to be developed. Some 85,000 hectares of waterlogged agricultural land is to be drained.

The Siberian River Diversion Debate

The "Project of the Century" from Several Viewpoints *

Academician E. Fedorov's article "Nothing Comes Free!" (LG, no. 47, 1981), a considerable part of which the author devoted to the problem of diverting part of the flow of northern and Siberian rivers to the southern regions of the country, evoked an interested response from readers. This is evidently not fortuitous: the problem of diversion is complex and multifaceted and affects a very extensive list of social, economic, and ecological issues.

It is now important for the public to hear the opinion of specialists and have a full grasp of the meaning of the considerable transformation of natural processes. We give the floor to I. Gerardi, chief engineer of the plan to divert part of the flow of Siberian rivers to Kazakhstan and Central Asia, and V. Perevedentsev, candidate of economics.

The Calculations Are Convincing (An Interview with I. Gerardi)

Q Igor Andreevich, it is now 15 years since experts embarked on a study of the question of diverting part of the flow of northern and Siberian rivers to our country's southern regions. The idea has stirred the public's very interested attention. Many arguments have arisen. You are the chief engineer of the plan to divert part of the flow of Siberian rivers to Central Asia which is being developed by the "Soiuzgiprovodkhoz" Institute. What is your attitude toward the criticism which has been leveled at the planning organizations and the numerous observations of the participants in various discussions of the plan?

A Such an interested and lively reaction is natural: the history of mankind has many instances of the unsuccessful invasion of natural processes, and people of course ask: has everything been sufficiently thought out? This is an undesirable concern, and one cannot take offense here.

What is bad is something else: the questions connected with the use of, I stress, only a small part of the tremendous flow of water of the Siberian rivers for guaranteed grain production are sometimes discussed without a serious preliminary study of the food problem. Without investigating all its economic and social significance for the country, certain people express their thoughts merely on the basis of emotions or superficial impressions of various discussions.

Literaturnaia gazeta, 1982, no. 10 (10 March). Russian text © 1982 by the USSR Union of Writers.

The slight removal of water from the Siberian rivers is sometimes portrayed as an intention to reverse the Siberian rivers and an attempt to limit the development of irrigable farming in the south of West Siberia. There is also the following "horror scenario": the designers intend to add on reservoirs to the Ob and Lower Irtysh and thereby inundate or swamp hundreds of thousands of hectares of valuable river bottom land and so forth.

The plan contains nothing of the kind: of the 1,350 cubic kilometers of the average multiyear water flow of the rivers of West Siberia being discharged into the Sea of Karsk basin, it is planned to take for the first stage of the diversion only 25 cubic kilometers and for the second stage 60. It is planned neither to build reservoirs nor inundate the bottom land of the Ob in its lower and central courses and in the lower course of the Irtysh.

The demand is often heard that the project be thoroughly substantiated ecologically, down to trifling matters. I have the feeling that we are belittling knowledge that has already been accumulated, confusing the problem and burying its tremendous socioeconomic essence under an excess of detail.

And the essence is such: the harvests of cereals cultivated under conditions of their natural causes, and the sole rational method of ridding ourselves of such sharp fluctuations is the organization of guaranteed grain production in the Central Asian republics and the southern oblasts of Kazakhstan on new irrigated land. On the basis of the use of a very small part of the water resources of Siberian rivers we can additionally produce annually first 25–30 million tons and subsequently 50–60 million tons of corn grain.

Furthermore, the grain program, of which the diversion is the basis, is not counterposed to the further development of cotton growing in the Central Asian republics, vegetable growing, viticulture and so forth but is being tackled in a single complex with them.

The intelligent comprehensive use of the tremendous water potential of the rivers of Siberia, Kazakhstan and Central Asia and the vacant land of the arid steppe, semidesert and desert parts of the country could feed over 200 million people. Can there be endlesss discussion of the problem of diverting Siberian water south in disregard of this most important social factor!

Q Various versions of the diversion project have surfaced in the discussion process. Which has proved the more promising?

A Yes, we are sometimes told: "You will dehydrate the Arctic." This is said of an ocean which obtains annually from USSR territory alone an average of over 2,800 cubic kilometers of water: in addition to this the Atlantic brings it 350,000–450,000 cubic kilometers of its own water. As you can see, the magnitude of the influx of water into the Arctic and the planned diversion of water from the Siberian rivers are incommensurable.

Nor will the ocean's temperature and ice conditions be disturbed—this has been specified by calculations of the USSR State Committee for Hydrometeorology and Environmental Control Arctic and Antarctic Institute.

If the removal of the water will be reflected in anything, it will be in the fish. According to calculations of the "Gidroroibproekt" Institute, we will lose approximately 7,000 tons of fish per year, including only 320 tons of valuable species. However, the same calculations show that there will be an addition in the south of the country: 27,000 tons of fish of valuable herbivorous species which will be produced by the renewed lakes along the path of the canal and also the Syr Daria and Amu Daria deltas.

Q Will the Aral Sea be helped?

A The Aral will get nothing from the first stage. Only the second stage may give the shrinking sea some support. Certain measures are now being formulated to maintain the level of the sea and prevent the desert encroachment of the territory surrounding the sea—they need to be described separately. I will give only my personal opinion here: I believe that after the year 2000 part of the Siberian water will need to be channeled into the Aral Sea in order to preserve it.

Q Will not the canal be too costly? Might it not be more economical to channel resources into the modernization of irrigation systems? Specialists express the opinion that before transferring water from far afield we need to bring order to bear in irrigation and not use water in vain.

A The one cannot be counterposed to the other. We do not intend using Siberian water in technically backward systems. The USSR Ministry of Land Reclamation and Water Resources is working continuously on the modernization and technical improvement of old irrigation systems, and much has been done in this direction. The final completion of this work is scheduled exactly for the time of the arrival of Siberian water in Central Asia, and an irrigation system efficiency of 0.79–0.80 is accepted in all the water-balance calculations of this region, which is rougly equal to that of the Moscow water main.

Q Many specialists emphasize the need for the development of economical methods of irrigation like overhead irrigation, drip irrigation and others.

A Yes, these are important progressive methods. But not a panacea. But this is exactly how they sound in the claims of certain specialists. Overhead irrigation is provided for in the diversion plan 100% where it may be applied, in accordance with meliorative conditions. But a transition to drip irrigation on the loamy saline and salinization-prone irrigable land of the Central Asian republics is simply impermissible: this form of irrigation will be applied where it is profitable—in the foothill regions and on sandy soil.

You speak of the canal's expense. But outlays should be recouped in 10 years. In addition, it will be navigable—with a depth of 10–15 meters and a breadth of 200 meters. This is a very important circumstance. The second stage of the canal will be joined with the Caspian: there you have a direct, without tansshipment, waterway from Siberia to Europe. And the significance of such a water-transport artery for the country does not, I would assume, need special explanation.

For this reason the Twenty-fifth and -sixth Party Congresses pointed to the need for the continuation of scientific and planning work.

Q Is your ministry—the Ministry of Land Reclamation and Water Resources—ready to begin construction?

A   We could begin construction at the end of the current 5-year plan. The amount of earth work for the first stage is only 5.5 billion cubic meters, and the USSR Ministry of Land Reclamation and Water Resources currently performs earth work of the order 7.5 billion cubic meters a year. The USSR Ministry of Land Reclamation and Water Resources has strong construction organizations in the Central Asian republics and Kazakhstan.

Q   Consequently, no longer any doubts?

A   We have worked on the technical-economic substantiation of the transfer for more than 25 years. Over 250 scientific research and planning organizations have participated together with us at different stages of the development of this problem.

Delay in the construction will prevent us, owing to the water insufficiency, making proper use of the industrial and agricultural potential of the Central Asian republics, the southern, central and western oblasts of Kazkhstan and also Orenburg, Cheliabinsk, Kurgan, and Tiumen oblasts. Essentially we are losing over 20 billion rubles annually. Every cubic kilometer of water supplied from Siberia for the agrarian-industrial complexes of Uzbekistan alone (calculations of the Uzbek SSR Council for the Study of Production Forces) ensures the production of output in these complexes totaling 500 million rubles annually. The figures speak for themselves. Such is the price of the doubts being expressed with respect to a huge national economic problem!

V. Perevedentsev: The Idea Is Intriguing, But . . .

The idea of linking Siberian waters with Central Asia's land and sun emerged more than 100 years ago. An alluring idea, undoubtedly, but from the idea to embodiment is a tremendous distance, and this distance needs to be traveled in very well-considered fashion. The Twenty-fifth CPSU Congress recorded in its decisions: "To carry out scientific research and on this basis draw up planning studies connected with the problem of diverting part of the flow of northern and Siberian rivers to Central Asia, Kazakhstan, and the Volga River basin." Perfectly clearly put: the planning studies should be based on scientific research.

I have participated on many occasions in recent years in scientific conferences on questions of the diversion of part of the flow of Siberian rivers to Central Asia. The most common feature of these conferences has been the "confrontation" between the planners of the Giprovodkhoz and workers of the Ministry of Land Reclamation and Water Resources on the one hand and scientific workers of other departments on the other. The planners have accused science of complicating the problem, throwing wrenches in the works and impeding the construction and charged them with the fact that the country is incurring tremendous losses because the canal is not being built, that every year the postponement of the construction costs the state tens of billions of rubles in unobtained products and so forth. The scientific workers, for their part, claim that the plans for the canal (there have been many variants) lack a truly scientific foundation, that many questions of fundamental importance are vague, that serious hydrological, ecological and other problems arise and that the "project of the century" lacks economic substantiation.

Research specialists ask the planners serious questions.

Primarily, what proportion of the water taken from the Ob will reach the areas where it will be used? To what extent will this water be mineralized at the end of a trunk canal more than 2,000 kilometers long—in the lower reaches of the Syr Daria and Amu Daria? How will the flora and fauna of the cold Siberian water behave in the hot desert climate? What will be the consequences for Siberia of the transfer of the water? What will the final cost of the canal be and when will it be recouped? And so on and so forth.

We sometimes hear the following answers: there will be virtually no loss of water en route ("well, some 5%, 10% at the most"); virtually as much water will arrive as is diverted from the Ob; expenditure on the canal will be recouped very quickly; and so forth. And the answers are given, furthermore, in the most general form, as a rule. But it is not laymen who are putting the questions. Hydrologists and hydrogeologists are inquiring about the water losses, hydrochemists about the water mineralization and economists about the canal's recoupability. And it is specialists who are not satisfied with the answers they obtain.

This is because, I believe, "the cart was put before the horse": planning was embarked upon before the essential scientific data for this were obtained. For many individual reasons we now inevitably come across general questions for which there are either no answers at all or which are very approximate. It is becoming more apparent than ever that the decision concerning the transfer must be shorn of any smack of "departmentalism."

I can entirely understand the perplexity of the hydrologists and hydrochemists. Why, say, in canal more than 2,000 kilometers long will the losses of water constitute a lesser proportion than in the comparatively short canals of Central Asia? The geologists say that hundreds of kilometers of the canal's path lie over places with very severe water absorption, where it will be necessary, as a consequence of this, to concretize the bed. Yet an earth canal is proposed for the entire length. And evaporation will be great.

But let us turn to economics. I hear constantly from the planners that the canal will be very profitable economically and that it will recoup expenditure rapidly. But why, I repeat, have I never heard any serious economic evidence?

Following an all-union conference in Moscow, the planners invited a group of its participants to the "Soiuzgiprovodkhoz" Institute, promising to convince everyone conclusively and irreversibly of the canal's great economic advantageousness. A big table with data on corn and soybean production in the USSR and the United States was hung on the wall. And it was said that much corn could be obtained in Central Asia, but that it could not be cultivated in Siberia; much meat and milk could be obtained on the basis of corn. Those were all the arguments there were. No data on the correlation of expenditure and results—and this alone can be evidence of the economic efficiency of any given project—were provided.

At a meeting in Novosibirsk in the fall of 1979 Academician A. G. Aganbegian said plainly that the canal had no economic substantiation. As far as I can judge, it still has none.

"Prove the canal's inefficiency," the planners sometimes say to doubters. I would mention that the burden of proof should lie with those who propose, and not the other way about. But inasmuch as they decline this, we must tackle some simple economic computations.

The recoupability on irrigation systems is 5–6 years in the Central Asian republics (at best). Indeed, at best. Considerably longer in other cases. In the planned canal from the Ob to the Amu Daria we must add to the outlays which are usual in these cases capital and current expenditure on the trunk canal. How much will this cost? There are various figures. The Giprovodkhoz suggested some time ago 10 billion rubles; Siberian economists no less than 20 billion rubles (inasmuch as, inter alia, the canal bed will, nonetheless, have to be concretized over a large distance); and an expert commission of the USSR Gosplan determined capital investment in the canal of the order of 14 billion rubles. We will dwell on this middle figure.

How much water will reach the fields?

After the regulating Tegiz Reservoir the trunk canal is designed for a discharge of 17 cubic kilometers of water a year. In the technically accomplished irrigation systems of Central Asia 75–80% of the water taken from the source reaches the field. Let us suppose, for simplicity's sake, that the irrigable fields obtain 14 billion cubic meters of water a year. Then for the canal alone it will be necessary to spend 1 ruble per cubic meter of water.

I have heard many times that expenditure on the diversion of Siberian waters to Central Asia will be recouped in 10 years. Is this possible?

Let us suppose that only 10,000 cubic meters of water will be used per hectare of sown area (it is now considerably more). In other words, with the capital investments in the canal being recouped in 10 years it would be necessary to discharge per hectare of sown area annually water at a cost of 1,000 rubles, that is, to obtain, as a minimum, 1,000 rubles of net product per hectare. From 1,000 cubic meters of water, 100 rubles of net product. Yet the cotton sovkhozes of Andizhan Oblast (and cotton is more profitable than fodder crops) obtain only 8–50 rubles of net income per 1,000 cubic meters of water. Even with an income of 50 rubles per 1,000 cubic meters of irrigation water (which is unlikely) expenditure on the canal (only on the canal!) would only be recouped in 20 years. And we are not yet taking into consideration considerable current expenditure on operation of the canal.

Obviously, a minimum of 5 years to be added to the recovery of expenditure on a local irrigation system and the preparation of the land for irrigation. And, in addition, we need to take into consideration the long freezing of the capital investments of the first years of the canal's construction.

Given the inadequacy of the data, it is impossible to say precisely how long it would take for the diversion of water to Central Asia to pay for itself.

However, it may be accurately asserted that it would not pay for itself in 10 years. It is highly doubtful that it would pay for itself in 30 years even.

I have heard of the great economic advantageousness of the canal on many occasions from Igor Andreevich Gerardi, chief engineer of the project. I hope that the project has a chief economist also. And it is his observations concerning the economic aspect of this project that I would like to hear.

Construction of Ob–Amu Daria canal with the indicators available today and at the present level of production would lead to an appreciable decline in the efficiency of capital investments in agriculture and cause the country huge economic losses.

None of this, of course, by any means indicates that such a canal will never be built. The progress of excavating equipment, increased labor productivity in irrigation, the increased value of water, the growth of harvests, the possible discovery of better versions of the canal and so forth—all these could, in time, considerably change the economic indicators of the transfer of Siberian waters to Central Asia.

I believe that this project should be regarded not as something in itself but as part of a goal-oriented comprehensive food program and as a hypothetical version of the accomplishment of certain tasks. I believe that this version is uncompetitive for the present: there are more profitable ways of achieving the same results. I heard of some of them also during discussion of the canal project. Thus a sharp increase in grain production is perfectly possible with the help of the irrigation of vast areas in West Siberia and North Kazakhstan, where the harvests are now small and unstable. Irrigation here should be supplementary to atmospheric irrigation and, for this reason, inexpensive. The soil in Siberia and Kazakhstan is severly lacking in phosphorus. Fertilization of the fields and irrigation could provide for very high and stable cereals' harvests here. Other variants are possible also.

However, can Central Asia develop without the waters of the Ob?

It is said that all sources of water will have been used up there by 1990 and that the further extension of irrigable land is impossible without long-range assistance.

Yes, if water is used as it has been hitherto. It will soon be exhausted. But can we irrigate in this way in our day?

In many of the old irrigation systems less than half of the water taken from a river or reservoir reaches the field. Frequently some 1.5 times more water is discharged onto the field than is necessary. There is no interyear regulation of the flow in the rivers. Virtually no use is made of ground waters. And so on and so forth. Some specialists claim that the rational use of local Central Asian waters would make it possible to no less than double the irrigated areas.

In the summer of 1980 I visited an experimental area of new irrigation methods of the Tadzhik branch of the All-Union Scientific Research Institute of Hydroreclamation south of Dushanbe. I was shown many remarkable methods by which land can be irrigated on plains, on steep inclines, on heavy clay soil and on light sandy soil and how it is possible to greatly economize on water, furthermore, and increase harvests and labor productivity. But where have these methods been introduced? On one kolkhoz, it turned out, over an area of 10 hectares. And this is all.

Nor is the Ministry of Land Reclamation and Water Resources displaying much interest in the modernization of the old irrigation systems, in which water is used extremely wastefully. It is evidently more profitable to irrigate new land than to undertake modernization. Yes, this modernization really is very costly. Nonetheless, it will provide water at approximately half the cost of that transferred from Siberia.

A huge reserve of Central Asia is interyear regulation of the flow. It will be possible in the Amu Daria basin after the construction of the Rogunskaia GES. But the preceding Nurek GES was under construction for two decades, and, to judge by the start, the Rogunskaia will take just as long. There is sense in accelerating hydropower construction on the rivers of Central Asia. Interyear regulation of the flow will enable us to increase it by 20-25 cubic kilometers in dry years, that is, provide the fields with far more moisture than could be brought by the first stage of a canal from the Ob.

And, of course, significant results would be produced by such an economical method as the introduction of a charge for the water. It is currently free for the kolkhozes and sovkhozes. But this is what they have done in Kirgizia: the state has begun to allocate day-to-day resources for irrigation not to the Ministry of Land Reclamation and Water Resources but to the kolkhozes and sovkhozes, and these have transferred this money to establishments of the Ministry of Land Reclamation and Water Resources as they are supplied with water. But if the farm fails to keep within the set limits, it then pays with its own money. The amounts are small, but this measure also has produced a perceptible saving of irrigation water.

It is striking, but a fact that the biggest cotton harvests are obtained in years with a water shortage. And a survey of many Barren Steppe sovkhozes showed this. On sovkhozes where the water supply was within the limits of 0.9-1 of the norm the cotton yield constituted 22.5 quintals per hectare, the gross product per hectare of sown area was assessed at 843 rubles, income per 1,000 cubic meters of water was 94 rubles, and 3,900 cubic meters of water were used per ton of raw cotton. But on sovkhozes where the water supply was in excess of 1.1 of the norm the corresponding figures were 18.1 quintals per hectare, 757 rubles and 69 rubles, and 6,000 cubic meters of water.

Overwatering often causes soil salinization, and this requires its leaching. As we can see, the possibilities of the further development of the economy of Central Asia on the basis of its own water are still considerable. And, in any event, they should be used before the Siberian rivers get here.

I do not see sufficient grounds for rushing the diversion of Siberian waters to Central Asia. As is known, the Twenty-sixth CPSU Congress planned "to continue scientific and planning studies on the diversion of part of the water of Siberian rivers to Central Asia and Kazakhstan." To continue!

One-sided pressure is dangerous for the cause. What is needed is not the confrontation of the scientists and planners but their amicable, joint work, which will enable us to find the optimum solutions.

The "Project of the Century" Does Not Brook Dilettantism *

S. ZIADULLAEV, A. BOSTANZHOGLO, and A. PUGACHEV

We read with tremendous interest the page devoted to "The 'Project of the Century' from Different Viewpoints" in issue no. 10 of *Literaturnaia gazeta* for 1982. It was not an idle interest—each of us has devoted his whole life to the development of the production forces and hydroeconomic construction. And we can only rejoice that a very authoritative and popular newspaper has focused the attention of millions of readers on an exceptionally important problem—the plan to divert part of the flow of the Siberian rivers to Central Asia and Kazakhstan.

Under the conditions of irrigated farming, on the basis of which the entire economy of our region, primarily, cotton growing, is developing with giant strides, water resources are of vital importance. The tremendous amount of work on hydroeconomic construction and the development of new virgin land (100,000 hectares are developed annually in Uzbekistan alone) and the conversion of the land of the Barren, Karshi, Dzhizak and other steppe, which had remained barren for millennia, into flourishing oases have led to the water resources of the Syr Daria and Amu Daria diminishing with every passing years, the level of the Aral Sea falling and an ever increasing water shortage. This development of new land is the basis of the unswerving increase in the production of agricultural products with the expansion of irrigated land, it is for this reason that the UzSSR occupies one of the first places in the country in agricultural product growth rate.

The republic's party organization, which at the ceremonial meeting in Tashkent for the presentation to Uzbekistan of the third Order of Lenin Leonid Il 'ich Brezhnev termed a combat detachment of the CPSU, is directing the working people's efforts toward an increase in the rate and scale of growth and the achievement of new heights in agricutural production in order to increase yet further Uzbekistan's contribution to the accomplishment of the country's food program.

However, scientists and specialists have calculated that the water resources of our rivers will be exhausted in the near future. In the twelfth and, particularly, the thirteenth five-year plans there will be a sharp decline in the growth of irrigated land with all the negative consequences ensuing therefrom. For the purpose of removing the discrepancies between growing requirements and the production of agricultural products in the long term the Twenty-fifth and -sixth CPSU congresses focused attention in their decisions on the need for scientific research and planning studies on the diversion of part of the flow of Siberian rivers to the Central Asia region. This problem had been raised in a number of decisions of the CPSU Central Committee and USSR Council of Ministers even earlier. At the behest of the USSR State Committee for Science and Technology approximately 150 of the country's scientific

Pravda vostoka, 3 April 1982, p. 3. Russian text 1982 by "Pravda vostoka." Ziadullaev is a member of the Uzbek SSR Academy of Sciences; Bostanzhoglo and Pugachev are irrigators emeritus of the Uzbek SSR.

research and planning organizations have been engaged in this work over the last fifteen years. The "Soiuzgiprovodkhoz" completed the development of the technical-economic substantiation (TEO) of the diversion in 1980 on the basis of these studies. Having studied the TEO attentively, our scientists and specialists approved it. And we are in full agreement with the basic propositions of Chief Engineer I. Gerardi's article in *Literaturnaia gazeta*. The question is clear, it might have seemed.

But in an article carried on the same page in *Literaturnaia gazeta*, Candidate of Economics V. Perevedentsev expresses doubts and not simply doubts but also a negative attitude toward the project, which is evoking astonishment and concern in and categorical objections from scientists and specialists both with respect to the tendentious nature of the judgements and the distortion of the actual situation in the region's water supply.

First, the author informs the reader of some conflict situation that has been created between planners and scientists and even writes that "there is no authentic scientific basis," "many questions of fundamental importance are vague," "serious hydrological, ecological and other problems arise," "there is no economic substantiation of the 'project of the century'" and so forth. The author rejects the TEO compiled by the "Soiuzgiprovodkhoz" and submitted for examination to the USSR Gosplan's State Examination Commission as lacking, he personally believes, the necessary scientific data. The disregard for the 150 scientific research (which include 23 scientific research institutes of the USSR Academy of Sciences) and planning organizations of the country in the preparation of the "Basic Propositions" and TEO, the results of whose research and recommendations were taken into consideration by the "Soiuzgiprovodkhoz," is a matter for this economist's conscience.

Deliberately selecting the opinions of certain organizations whose recommendations were at variance with those adopted in the TEO [Technical-Economic Study], the author draws the conclusion on a manifestly groundless basis of disagreements between the planners and "all of science."

The absurdity of such juggling of the facts is hardly commonsense, we believe.

Second, the author sharply criticized the current use of water in the Central Asian republics: "overwatering by a factor of 1.5 of the norm, water losses of over 50% from the diversion and primitive watering methods" and "a lack of interest in the modernization of old irrigation systems," which, the author believes, could provide water at approximately half the cost of the diversion from Siberia.

If he knew just a little of the history of irrigation and the measures adopted by the CPSU Central Committee and Vladimir Il'ich Lenin in the solution of problems of irrigation in our region, the author would not express such baseless judgments.

Hydroeconomic construction has been performed on an extensive scale in Central Asia in the years of Soviet power; trunk canals of great length have been laid, reservoirs and dams have been installed, the water-supply network has been equipped with modern hydraulic works and engineering structures and huge resources are being invested to raise the technical level of the irrigation systems and land reclamation. Plan-based work is being performed on increasing the efficiency of the irrigation systems, which by 1980 had reached 0.6 and higher in places. The quality of the irrigations has improved appreciably, the skill of the irrigators has increased and mechnization in irrigation is increasinly constantly. And Perevedentsev reduces all this to nothing—all the achievements of the Central Asian republics in the sphere of irrigation and irrigable farming and the selfless labor of millions of people, kolkhoz members, workers, water and agricultural specialists and scientists.

Attempting to prove the opposite, the author makes use of someone's (the names are not given) opinion that the rational use of local Central Asian waters will make it possible to no less than double the opinion of "unknown specialists" sufficient for making it. But behind this facility of the pen is a manifest lack of understanding of the many years' experience of hydroeconomic scientists and practitioners, findings and studies with respect to the diversion problems and the opinions of many authoritative commissions on the inevitability of the exhaustion of the water resources of the Aral basin, which may be resisted only by the diversion of part of the flow of the Siberian rivers to Central Asia.

Calculations and many years of experience show that given the complete modernization of all the irrigation systems in Uzbekistan it is possible to obtain a saving of water resources of no more than 3–4 cubic kilometers. A detailed study of planning and scientific research material shows that to complete the modernization of the irrigation systems in full and obtain this saving it will be necessary to employ huge capital investments (more than R10 billion for Uzbekistan alone) and unimaginable material resources, and this will take no less than 30 years, moreover. But even then there could be no question of large reserves of water calculated in tens of billions of cubic meters. This colossal expenditure would not provide for a cardinal solution of the question concerning the region's water supply. And the author should have familiarized himself in more detail with the actual state of affairs before expressing unfounded doubts.

Third, how much water diverted from the Ob will reach the areas where it is to be used? According to the detailed calculations of the country's planning and scientific research institutes, in the year the work is started 2.5 cubic kilometers and in the twentieth year 1.5 cubic kilometers, that is, from 6 to 10% will be consumed by evaporation, in accordance with the known climatic elements of the route, and seepage (considering the filtering properties of the soil, the depth of the occurrence of ground waters, the length of the canal, the dimensions and forms of its cross and lengthwise sections, the speeds of the passage of water and so forth). From 22.5 to 25.5 cubic kilometers will remain for use. And having read a textbook on irrigation a little, it would have been worth taking a look at the TEO, and Perevedentsev would have learned that the losses depend not only on the soil (about which he speaks incompetently, incidentally) but on both the level of the ground waters and the flow rate of the canal. If the ground waters are near the water line in the canal, there will be practically no losses from filtration; there will be losses when they are somewhat deeper, but not big losses. And this applies particularly to canals with great flow rates, in which comparative losses are less than in small canals.

How mineralized will this water be at the end of the trunk canal? Two specialized scientific research institutes—the VNIIVO and the Central Asian Scientific Research Institute of Irrigation—have made forecasts on this score. Account was taken in the forecasting of filtration and evaporation from the canal, the influx of mineralized ground waters, surface runoff, aeolian pollution, return water from irrigation, effluent from centers of population and the waste from a small fleet and so forth, that is, everything necessary in accordance with the standards and procedure of the All-Union Scientific Research Institute of Water Supply, Sewer Systems, Hydraulic Engineering Structures and Engineering Hydrogeology. They constitute 485 milligrams per liter, that is, below the permissible norm.

Nor is there any doubt as to the unsbustantiated nature of the author's arguments concerning the time that will be taken for the canal to pay for itself. According to the scientists' and planners' calculations, this will take 8–10 years. And these are entirely correct calculations.

Thus on these questions also Perevendentsev's doubts reflect rhetorical skill more than relevance to the matter at hand.

Fourth, what will be the consequences for Siberia of the diversion of the waters? This question was answered precisely and clearly by Academician Ye. Fedorov in the article "Nothing Comes Free," which was published in the same *Literaturnaia gazeta* (no. 47, 1981). He clearly observed that "the studies of many years standing of dozens of research institutes and thousands of specialthe article "Nothing Comes Free," which was published in the same *Literaturnaia gazeta* (no. 47, 1981). He clearly observed that "the studies of many years standing of dozens of research institutes and thousands of specialists have determined that the removal of a small part of the flow of the Ob . . . will entail no changes in climate and will not disturb natural features on a global or regional scale."

Furthermore, for those who raise the question of the consequences for Siberia of the removal of part of the flow of its rivers the conclusions reached by the executant of this subject as per the plan of the USSR State Committee for Science and Technology—the USSR Academy of Sciences' Institute of Geography—are not without interest. Its summary report points out that removal of part of the flow of the rivers of West Siberia to Central Asia and Kazakhstan will serve as a factor of the reclamative improvement of this vast, uniquely swamply territory of the USSR and that "under the conditions of removal of part of the flow and the increased anthropogenic impact there will be a sharp improvement in the control of the water conditions of the river bottom land (the most valuable land in West Siberia's agriculture), its artificial watering, irrigation and so forth."

The USSR Academy of Sciences' Institute of Geography finds that the supply of part of the flow of Siberian rivers to Central Asia and Kazakhstan would serve as a powerful factor of the increased productiveness of the natural environment of the Siberian regions themselves. Would it not seem to those interested in ecological problems that the main one is tackled most propitiously by the diversion and that this fact, if the proper demands are made of the economic computations, must appropriately be taken into consideration in the revenue part of the project.

Fifth, a few words about Perevedentsev's personal opinion that in the elaboration of the question "the cart was put before the horse," that is, the planning outdistanced the science. This is not borne out by the information adduced above on the number of workers engaged in the science (approximately 150 institutions, of which 23 are academic). It is rather a matter of certain people evidently not reading what has been written in the scientific reports or in the TEO itself even. And there is something to be read. In addition to the ample basic material the TEO alone adduces 10 volumes of appendices containing 40 books (not counting albums and illustrations) based on the reports of the corresponding scientific research institutes.

To resort, like Perevedentsev, to allegory: his article prompts one to the belief not that "the cart was put before the horse" but rather that there are still passengers who have missed the cart. And in such a situation it is easier to put questions than to answer them.

We do not deny in such a big matter shortcomings and loose ends in a number of the TEO standpoints, which are entirely removable with the help of scientists and specialists. But the main thing is that we must no lose precious time in superfluous and unsubstantiated arguments.

We hope that a most important problem of the century—diversion of part of the flow of Siberian rivers to Central Asia and Kazkhstan—will soon be settled positively and that millions of hectares of the area's now barren virgin land will become a flourishing region and will produce cotton, grain, vegetables, fruit, grapes and animal husbandry products—everything necessary for the solution of the country's food problem.

The Desert—A Strategy for Development *

A. BABAIEV

Many people believe that the desert is a lifeless, sun-scorched expanse of land. Indeed, when one views it from an airplane or train window, one sees only a yellow ocean of sand. But its interior contains nonferrous metals, oil, gas and coal. Cities and industrial enterprises have grown of "dead" land at the service of the national economy. And they are such that the desert today should be considered a viable and even rich sphere with high economic potential.

The experience of the Central Asian republics and Kazkhstan also shows that deserts can be zones of stable agricultural production. Cotton, wheat, vegetables, grapes, fruit and other crops are now being cultivated on millions of hectares of previously infertile sand. The development of such areas is not always a straightforward and inexpensive business. But one very important quality has to be borne in

*Pravda vostoka, 3 April 1982. Russian text © 1982 by "Pravda vostoka." A. Babaiev is president of the Turkmen SSR Academy of Sciences and corresponding member of the USSR Academy of Sciences.

mind: like no other, this land is supplied with heat. And the imperceptible vegetation of the desert has always been a source for the keep of millions of head of sheep and camels. Economists have calculated that the animal husbandry product in a desert zone costs half as much as in an average belt of the country. And the possibilities of its development in this region are still far from exhausted. The scientific task of the enrichment of the natural fodder resources of desert pasture was found and verified and are being introduced in production extensively. They do not require big capital investments and make it possible to increase the yield of the fodder land several times over.

A great deal of experience has also been accumulated in the development of desert territory. Scientists have passed on to the production workers a number of tested recommendations. But they are as yet being used insufficiently. Yet the benefits from their introduction are obvious: invested capital is recouped quite rapidly.

The main thing necessary for the development of the desert is water. It is said in Central Asia: "It is not the earth which gives birth but water." With the help of irrigation it is in this region that it is possible to reduce agriculture's dependence on the elements to a minimum, obtaining big harvests of the most varied crops.

However, the desert is extremely poor in fresh water. According to scientists' calculations, in the next ten to fifteen years the entire flow of the main rivers of Central Asia—the Amu Daria and Syr Daria—will be channeled fully into irrigation and other hydroeconomic needs of the Aral basin. But even given this condition it is impossible to solve the age-old problem of the shortage of water over vast territories which are promising for industry and agriculture. And it is with good reason that the possibilities of diverting part of the flow of Siberian rivers to Central Asia and southern Kazkhstan are being studied.

But the scientists are confronted with a difficult question: what will the consequences be and how will this influence the ecological and socioeconomic conditions of the regions? And while the debate and search for the best version of the project are under way it is necessary to look for opportunities to improve the water balance of the desert itself.

There are two methods here: using fresh ground waters and collecting atmospheric precipitation. The first is already being employed to a certain extent. For example, the industrial complex of West Turkmenistan consumes water found by hydrogeologists in the Karakumy. The second method is being employed on a limited scale and, frankly speaking, has yet to emerge from the crude stage. Since time immemorial cattle breeders have collected rainwater by the simplest means from cayey areas, giving it a chance to accumulate in underground wells. Thus a certian store of moisture is formed: 1 hectare can provide enough for a year's watering of 1,000 sheep. The scientists have perfected this ancient fold method and developed engineering installations. It is possible by applying these to obtain even more cheap fresh water. Unfortunately, the innovations are not being introduced quickly enough.

The brackish drainage water which is run off from the fields annually and in hugh quantities should also be an important resource. Not only is it as yet not being used but it is causing damage. It is simply discharged into the desert, destroying certain components of the ecological system. Yet such water could water livestock, for example. Furthermore, it is easier to freshen than sea water and, given this, could be an important source of the desert's water supply.

Energy and resources have to be spent for this, of course. But developing and working the natural resources of the desert are altogether inconceivable without electric power. But there are as yet no power facilities in the Karakumy and Kyzyl-Kumy in practice. But the possibilities for their organization exist   power stations in comparatively densely populated areas could be built on the basis of oil and gas deposits.

Things are a little bit more complex when it comes to the stockbreeders. The pasture land is scattered, and every point of operation needs a little power. It is most profitable to obtain electricity here by forcing the wind and sun to "work." There are already test generators converting solar energy into electric power. Specialists believe that they are still imperfect, it is true: they are of low performance efficiency and are quite costly. But these shortcomings are secondary in small power plants. Thus it is time to begin broad experiments on the practical use of solar installations for the desert's small centers of population.

Wind-driven power generators were a problem that was solved long ago. But it is amazing that people who have spent their whole life working in the desert rarely see these most simple mechanism anywhere. Yet in many areas of the Central Asian desert a steady wind is guaranteed almost daily. Wind-driven power stations of 1–39-kilowatt capacity could provide the power minimum in small centers of population. It is good to use them on pasture land for hoisting water from the wells, irrigating the attached plots and freshening the water. In a word, it is possible to switch to the mass electrification of desert animal husbandry. This would be a big contribution to the development of sheep breeding on desert pasture.

In the complex, many-sided task of development of the desert it is necessary to look far ahead otherwise fascination with the solution of one problem engenders another. For example, the usc of a large part of the flow of the Amu Daria and Syr Daria for irrigation has led to a sharp decline in the water reaching the Aral Sea. Specialists this will be difficult, given the present acute shortage of fresh water. It is therefore essential to have an accurate forecast of the possible changes in natural conditions in order to adopt precautionary measures in good time.

Man is confronted with the need to transform natural conditions. But he is obliged here to learn to foresee the possible consequences of his actions. Scientists, engineers and other specialists are currently performing painstaking work on the redistribution and rational use of the water resources of Central Asia and Kazkhstan. I would like to be sure that the task will be tackled competently and that we will not go beyond the limits of permissible changes in the natural environment.

In logical connection witht he future of the Aral Sea a further ecological problem is troubling us currently. Two years ago a solid dam spanned the strait linking the Caspian with the Kara-Bogaz Gulf. The path for 6–7 cubic kilometers of water annually reaching Kara-Bogaz from the Caspian and evaporating from its surface was cut off. Without speeding the fall in the level of the Caspian, this measure made it possible to take from the rivers running into it approximately the same quantity of water for irrigation. But, naturally, the gulf itself has begun to gradually dry up. Its bottom is becoming increasingly exposed, and the wind is spreading the salt which is appearing on the earth's surface. The gulf's unique chemical wealth is disappearing. We now have to ponder how to combat this extremely unpleasant phenomenon.

The above example shows for the umpteenth time how carefully we have to study the possible consequences of "surgical intervention" in nature in order that the gain in one place not lead to a loss in another. No transformation is effected for the sake of the transformation itself but to strengthen the economic might of our country as a whole. It is necessary here to attach particular significance to the long-term forecasting of natural processes in places of man's active impact on the environment. It must always be remembered that the desert is not an every whom man has to defeat but his good partner, to whom he should adopt a kindly attitude.

When one thinks about the desert and about what it could provide for man, anxiety also commingless with the feeling of joy. After all, every department is operating independently here, failing to take many things into account. And this sometimes leads to unnecessary outlays which do not produce tangible results. It is finally time to have a single scientifically substantiated strategy of desert development. It is hardly possible to hope for further appreciable successes without a comprehensive plan.

Not enough canals for irrigation and watering holes are being built, and the sand is being stabilized insufficiently. It is essential to plan the development of farming as a whole, in a harmonious correlation, and then outlays will be considerably less and economic efficiency will increase many times over.

More has been done to develop the desert in our country than has been done anywhere else in the world. But if we compare what has been done with what is possible and with the tremendous results which could be obtained from the desert (it occupies 250 million hectares in our country—more than the country's entire arable land), we will have to recognize what has been done merely as successful exploration. Our deserts are essentially still further virgin lands awaiting their intelligent developers.

An Editorial: Does Central Asia Need Siberian Water? *

The most vivid sight of our region is irrigated agriculture. It has been shaped for centuries, for centuries accumulating experience in the intelligent union of land and water into the symbol of the region, the cotton boll, the wheat stalk, and the corn ear, in the heavy bunch of grapes, in the fruit of the pomegranate, blood-red as the setting sun. Generation passes to generation the habit of treating water like an unchanging, unique thing of value. Water is water; it is primal, like earth, like mother and father.

Zvezda vostoka, 1987, no. 6 (June). Russian text © 1987 by "Zvezda vostoka."

It is the source of life. In a land which is large part desert no other attitude toward water is even possible. The conditions of life, the environment existence dictate behavior, customs, and traditions. Their essence is clear—water means bountiful fields, good harvests, plenty, and a shining tomorrow. So it was, so it is, and so everything about us tells us that it shall be in the future.

Soviet power has increased the irrigated acreage of Uzbekistan almost three times. Approximately the same speed of development of irrigation occurred in southern Kazakhstan, Kirghizia, Tadzhikistan, and Turkmenia. Even before the war, independence in cotton was won. An enormous contribution to this historic achievement of socialism was made by the peoples of the Central Asian republics and by the Russians, who gave our region invaluable internationalist assistance in the restructuring of water resources on a modern basis. Up to the present the region has seen the creation of hydrotechnical plants, irrigation and reclamation systems which evoke the respect and healthy envy of reclamationists from all over the world. These are such things as the Great Fergana Canal and the Kattakurgan Reservoir, which astonished the world with the pathos of construction by the people, a socialist *khashar*; the Nurek Hydroelectrical Station on the Vaksh River, which has a dam three hundred meters high, high than which none has yet been built; the Toktogul water network, with a 225 meter concrete dam which fully regulates the flow of the river Naryn; the Andizhan Reservoir on the Kara Daria River, which has a dam the size of the one at the Bratsk Hydroelectric Station; the Tuiamuiun Reservoir in the lower reaches of the Amu Daria; the Southern Hungry Steppe Canal, the Karshin Railroad Canal, the Amu-Bukhara Canal, the Dzhizak Canal, and others, which often have unique pumping stations which guaranteed water for the virgin lands for hundreds of thousands of hectares. Finally, there is the complex of methods for reclaiming arid land which has received the acknowledgement of the entire nation.

And here the general aridity of the region, its general lack of water, has its weighty word. The limits are clearly marked, that only this much more land can be reclaimed, and then we must stop. After all, every further hectare will be irrigated from the same source, the reserves of which are already assigned and distributed down to the last cubic meter of water. In fact, water in our region is increasingly regarded as one of the strictly limited basic materials, just like steel, fuel, cement, and wood. Quantitatively it looks like this: in a year of average moisture the rivers of Aral Sea Basin can supply about 100 cubic kilometers of precious fluid, eighty percent of which is already used for the irrrigation of seven million hectares of cultivated land. The remaining reserves will be fully deployed by 1995. This is the basin of the Amu Daria; the Syr Daria is already fully used for irrigation. The rivers of the Aral Sea Basin have long failed to reach the Aral itself, which is silting up catastrophically. The deficit of water has been revealed and defined, quantitatively and territorially, and it is high time to put the question on the agenda of how the deficit is to be made up. How are things to be; where is the missing water to come from?

Here life does not present us with many options. She doesn't even give us two options. Just one. The water that Central Asia needs is in the rivers of Siberia, in the

Ob and the Enisei. There isn't anywhere else; all the other water is beyond the possibilities of man's present capabilities, beyond the realm of the possible. Is there a lot of water in these rivers? The aggregate flow of the Ob and the Enisei is about a thousand cubic kilometers, which is precisely a factor of ten higher than the flow of the rivers of the Aral Basin. It is natural and proper that a part of this enormous water, which now falls into the Arctic Ocean without any apparent benefit to man, should be directed to the south, to our arid lands.

The republics of Central Asia have been encountering for several years a range of unfavorable tendencies, which constitute a progressive deficit of water resources. And this is not just our problem in Uzbekistan. It also affects the interests of all the Central Asian republics and Kazakhstan. Guaranteeing the water needs of irrigated agriculture is the first and most important condition of fulfilling the plans for the social and economic development of the republics of our region. This is also a guarantee of work for those who just today are gladdening their young parents with their arrival in the world. As is known, our region has the highest growth of population in the country, and in Uzbekistan alone every year hundreds of thousands of young men and women enter into independent life. This is the guarantee of future enlargement of the contribution made by Uzbekistan, Kazakhstan, Turkmenia, Tadzhikistan, and Kirgizia to the all-union food fund, the guarantee of meeting the needs of our country and of the brother nations of socialist friendship in cotton fiber, silk, kenaf, Persian lamb, the needs of the Ural and Siberia for vegetables and fruit, especially spring ones. For the normal development of the productive powers of Uzbekistan and the entire Central Asian region, including the oblasts of southern Kazakhstan, in order to forestall deep inequalities and disruptions of the economy we are very shortly going to need additional water.

The idea of moving part of the flow of the Siberian rivers into the Aral Sea basin is not a new one; it has been around for more than 100 years. The possibility of doing so however has only now materialized. And just as soon as we glimpsed and understood these possibilities, just as soon as we began to speak of real capital application, then the voices of opponenets of such a diversion immediately were raised. At first the experts did not take them seriously, as it was emotion instead of arguments. What are the main objections of the opponents of diversion? Their main argument is extremely weak, that since reclamation did not prove to be highly efficient in the Chernozem and other regions of the RSFSR, then reclamation is inefficient everywhere. In effect this is the same as saying that if I can't make something stick, nobody can! To conduct a scientific argument on that level is at the very least illogical. During planning, construction, and use of reclamation systems experience is of enormous significance, the ability to find mistakes, to correct them and not repeat them again. In the black-earth zone there is in effect little such experience, but our arid zone has accumulated a great deal. Why then apply their modest experience to our region?

The results of practice also do not permit us to agree with the assertion that the Ministry of Water Conservation of the USSR gives a great deal more water volume to irrigation than it in fact needs. In Central Asia there is no such waste in water conservation. Our plans for the water use of kolkhozes and sovkhozes are drawn up taking account of all factors which affect the ultimate production of crops on the irrigated field. There simply is no extra water here that might be squandered. In addition to everything else, the millenia of agricultural experience here tell of the enormous dangers of excessive watering. Too much water sent to a field in the conditions of Central Asia causes swamping and salination of the soil, and an overload of the drainage system.

One of the most common criticisms levelled at us is that we use our own water poorly. Is it true? Take the basin of the Syr Daria River, the resources of which are essentially exhausted. We have not even once filled the Toktogul Reservoir to the planned height, even though its holding area permits the collection of more than half the annual flow of the Naryn River. The Fergana Valley, which annually produces more than 1.5 million tons of cotton, has very productive irrigated lands; here a hectare produces nearly two thousand rubles, or as much as seven unirrigated hectares. However the irrigation systems are old here, with a coefficient of utility close to 0.6. Does this mean though that we lose almost half of the irrigation water in this depression between the mountains? Far from it. The natural conditions of the valley are such that all the ground water returns to the Syr Daria, though further downstream, and from the Kara-Kum Reservoir are used on the fields of Leninabad Oblast, while the waters from the Farkhad Reservoir are used on the Hungry and Dzhizak steppes. In total the coefficient of use of the Syr Daria water approaches 1.0. This is a very high index. However, along with raising it, the quality of the water in the lower reaches of the river grows increasingly poor. Of course there are sufficient examples of the irrational use of Syr Daria water, leading to swamping and salination. However the poor administration of some administrators in no way defines the nature of our water conservation policies. Parenthetically, the increased efficiency of water use is also attested by the collective data. Thus in the past twenty years the water allocation for the needs of agriculture in the region rose 40%, while the productivity of the irrigated portion increased 91%, while water allocation per one billion rubles of agricultural production during this period was cut in half.

For the workers of Central Asia the coming of Siberian water is the most pressing problem of the day. The problem was not invented by specialists, but rather brought out by life, by the pace of the region's economic development, by the tasks of the future. Thus it is absolutely incorrect to speak of any lack of support among the people of our region for the diversion of Siberian water to the Aral Sea Basin. The opposite is true; tens of thousands of people from all social levels have extremely convincing arguments in favor of the most rapid possible completion of this project. Nor is this just local patriotism, a local desire to take greater capital investment from the government; it is our internationalist desire, as we have been educated by the Party, to give as much as we can to our native land. The opinion is about that it is possible to conserve 10 cubic kilometers of water in Central Asia for irrigation that now are wasted annually on flushing salinated soil. Let's take a simple example. If the vegetation on an irrigated hectare gets 10,000 cubic meters of water, and if each liter contains one gram of salt, which is the average, then every year the hectare is going to get an additional ten tons of salt. If it is not flushed, then the soil very quickly loses fertility. Since the mineralization of the water in the irrigation sources is going to grow along with the growth of the water shortage, the expenditure of water for flushing the soil is not going to be successful.

The complete reconstruction of the irrigation system on lands under the old systems also cannot be worth of attention as an alternative to diversion, since this would cost 29 billion rubles, while saving only 4.5 billion cubic meters of water. According to the Central Asian Scientific and Research Institute for Irrigation, every ruble invested in irrigation and reclamation in Central Asia is repaid in about six years. This index is the highest in the nation. In fact, the natural and socio-economic conditions for the development of irrigation in Central Asia are extremely favorable. The human resources of the region very soon will permit the working of about 15 million hectares of irrigated land. The power of the construction organizations however is not as great, but they are still in a condition to bring the area under irrigation in the region to 10 million hectares, in two or three five-year plans. Our own water resources permit discussion of only 8.3 million hectares under irrigation, while the present-day fund of our irrigated land is almost 7 million hectares. The tempo of claiming new land is already somewhat lower than in 1970–1980. In this connection the Uzbek SSR will suffer a loss every year. The gross loss to the year 2000 will be significantly larger than the capital investment for construction of the facilities for the first stage of diversion, including reclamation of the land. The water conservation, economic, and demographic situations in the region are such as to demand additional water resources without delay.

Diversion of part of the flow of the Siberian rivers will at the same time solve a number of other problems which if solved separately would increase their cost many times. A Siberia–Central Asia canal would guarantee jobs for one million people in agriculture and branches of the agricultural industrial complex. The resettlement of the same number of people out of Central Asia, providing them with jobs in other regions of the country, would cost 16–28 billion rubles. The Siberian water would reduce the mineralization of water in the lower Syr Daria and Amu Daria to an acceptable level. It is apropos here to mention that water purification for domestic supplies will cost 4–5 billion rubles. The total cost for separate solution of these problems is more than 60 billion rubles, and might reach as much as 60 billion rubles. The economic and social significance of each of these problems is such that they can not remain unresolved.

What are the development trends of world agriculture? What does world experience suggest to us? Right now 16% of agricultural land is irrigated in the world, but that land gives precisely half the food products. It is wholly possible that by the year 2000 there will be another 150 million hectares under irrigation, meaning that the total area of irrigated land will reach 400 million hectares. That means that our plans are also counted in the world current, answering the world tendency to stress reclamation and intensive technological cultivation of food and technical crops.

And if the country once again gives our region this truly priceless assistance, sharing the Siberian waters with us at the enormous material costs necessary to make the project work, then this will be a factor of extraordinary importance in the further unification of our peoples, in the strengthening of friendship and brotherhood of the Soviet peoples on the international basis elaborated by Vladimir Il'ich Lenin.

Without the Siberian waters we cannot guarantee the fast-growing population of the region will have food stuffs of their own production. There is a persistent qualitative and quantitative depletion of water resources in Central Asia. The scale of man's economic activity gives the process an irreversible character. Evidence for this is the ever-greater shortfall in production in dry years, the falling quality of water in the lower Syr Daria and Amu Daria, and the progressive evaporation of the Aral Sea. We are speaking of the health of hundreds of thousands of people who live in the lower reaches of these rivers, but this is not a problem of a local nature. When one of our people fall into trouble, he is extended helping hands by tens or hundreds of people. In order to divert disaster from hundreds of thousands of people in the lower Central Asian rivers we must have the efforts of the entire country; we must have the very clean Siberian water with its almost non-existent solid sediment. In this sense the problem of water supply in Central Asia has long since acquired an all-governmental character, and its resolution demands that the problem be approached precisely on that basis, on the basis of the further increase of the region's contribution to the economic potential of the country. The beneficial results of building a Siberia–Central Asia canal are countless. Siberian water will define the future of the region for decades, if not for the entire age, giving a mighty impulse to the development of productive capacity, leading to the creation of an agricultural complex comparable in potential to the granaries of the Ukraine, the Northern Caucasus, and the Volga region, but far more stable in its indices because of its independence from weather conditions. That is why the scientists and workers of Uzbekistan, Kazakhstan, Kirghizia, Tadzhikistan, and Turkmenia are ready to sign open letters to the writer S. P. Zalygin in defense of the project diverting part of the Siberian river flow into Central Asia, for the beneficial effect of the proposed changes for the future of the region are obvious to them. In publishing these letters [not translated here—Ed.], the editors of the journal *Zvezda vostoka* wish to stress that the country has not just opponents of the Siberia–Central Asia canal, but ardent supporters as well, whose arguments are far from insubstantial.

Labor Recruitment

A Shortage ... Despite the Availability?
(A Conversation with Professor T. S. Saidbaev) *

Q Talib Sarymsakovich, the task that has been posed by the [Twenty-sixth] Party Congress—the task of improving the training of national cadres of workers—is one of the vitally important political tasks . . .

A . . . and it is the objective reflection of the natural laws underlying our social development. During the years of Soviet power, a large-scale, diversified industry has been created in all the union republics, and there has been a steady increase in the number of industrial workers who are representatives of the local population. In the society of mature socialism, the working class has become not simply the largest class, but also the majority of the working population. It is not by accident that sociologists begin specifically from this point when they characterize the social composition of the new historic community—the Soviet people.

And what do we mean by "the majority of the working population"? This includes two-thirds of the people employed in production, the tremendous mass of the workers who are united into labor collective. And, at the present-day stage, we are dealing with that category of workers, four-fifths of whom are people with complete or incomplete secondary or higher education. And this largely determines what is now the different role played by the working man. His labor takes on greater and greater intellectual content, and is combined more and more harmoniously with the conditions and requirements of the scientific-technical revolution and with the growing level of socialist culture. I think also that the interest of this newspaper in the topic of our discussion has been predetermined by this: writers cannot fail to be excited by the social processes that are occurring so intensively.

Q I would like to note that the problems we are considering have much more to do with literature than might appear at first glance. I'm not speaking about sociopolitical journalism: its participation in the raising and the resolution of any socially significant task is not only natural, but also mandatory . . . I will emphasize something else—the necessity of studying more boldly and more frequently the processes of the formation of the national working class in novels and short stories. The topic is an acute and vitally important one . . . What should one do, then, sit the situation out in the literary trench?

A Sit it out? By no means. Of course you are right: studying the processes of the formation of national working cadres is a task of primary importance for writers. I have mentioned the fact the much was said about this, in particular, in the "topical interviews" that were conducted by the newspaper just before the sixtieth anniver-

---

*The interview was conducted by Special Correspondent Iurii Zarechkin. *Literaturnaia gazeta*, 1983, no. 24 (16 June). Russian text © 1983 by the USSR Union of Writers.

sary of the USSR. One of the discussions in the series—the discussion with the first secretary of the Tadzhik Communist Party Central Committee—was, I recall, entirely devoted to problems of the republic's working class.

This interest in the topic is logical. And we are proceeding here primarily from the Party and state tasks, from the specifics of that period which our society is living through. The Party has always devoted a tremendous amount of attention to the growth of the national detachments of the Soviet working class, Yuri Vladimirovich Andropov said in his report "Sixty Years of the USSR," and the results of that are completely apparent to everyone. Currently the workers constitute the largest social group in all the union republics. At the same time the general secretary of the Party's Central Committee noted that in some of them the indigenous nationality should be more completely represented in the makeup of the working class, and for that reason it is necessary to expend the training of the local cadres. He also mentioned the political importance of the task that was posed, because the multinational, and primarily the workers, the collectives are precisely that environment in which one can best nurture an internationalistic spirit and in which the fraternity and friendship of the nations of the USSR are reinforced.

I assume that when it is a matter of studying the processes in the environment of the national working class—and that is specifically the way the question is posed, the *studying* of them—then the direction taken by the search must also be tied in with the political, ideological aspects . . .

Q Do you have in mind a literary process, the writer's search?

A Primarily, yes. In my opinion, literature has moved ahead very little here during recent years, especially in those republics where the local working class needs its final consolidation as the leading social force. How many books, for example, during the past five years have been published on the topic we are discussing in Central Asia? To the best of my recollection, there have not been too many of them: Mirmukhsin's *Syn liteishchika* [Foundryman's Son] and Abdullankhanov's *Uragan* [Hurricane], by the Uzbeks . . . , *Vzryv* [The Explosion] by the Kazakh Sarsekeev and *Nurek* by the Tadzhik Akobirov . . .

Q I think that you're being somewhat subjective. The number of books published on work topics is a bit larger than that, but it is not only by quantity of what has been produced that one evaluates literature's contribution.

A I agree, that it is not just a matter of quantity. . . Incidentally, the same thing pertains to scientific developments. And I must state outright: they do not always have sufficient content. As a rule, they present the situation in a particular region, and formulate and pose the problem of training national worker cadres . . . But the number of ways for resolving that problem which are proposed is very small. Moreover, the substantiation of the problem frequently is, to a considerable degree, a reflection of the past, rather than the present.

Q But how in this instance does one evaluate the appearance of a number of books with very promising titles? One book that was published, for example, was Timofeev's monograph *The Formation of National Cadres of the Working Class in the USSR*. Another was Boiko and Vasil'ev's *The Social and Occupational Mobility of the Evenkin and Eveny of Yakutiia*. And still another was the work produced by a group of authors, *The Youth of Siberia: Education and Choice of Occupation*.

A Timofeev's book, in essence, is a historical one. It deals with the rise of the working class in our country, but it does not touch upon modern problems. Rather, it states facts, basically through the use of figures, rather than explaining the nature of the processes that are occurring. But, most importantly, the formation of the national cadres is mentioned without a consideration of the national peculiarities of the population of the republic or specific region.

As for the two other books that you mentioned, I would like to mention, without however denying their indisputable value, the obvious disproportion in the scientific interest: it is good, of course, to have a detailed analysis of the life of small nationalities . . . but are we really to believe that there is less acute need for such research studies for the peoples of Uzbekistan or Turkmenia?

But, disregarding these books now, I shall say that in analyzing a situation what is important for us is not the existence of various figures, but, rather, a realistic explanation of the situation and the substantiation of the future prospects. In Tadzhikistan, for example, practically every person in production represents the first generation of the working class. Is that important? Of course it is. Or, should one forget that many of the peoples of the East, having bypassed the capitalist stage of development, prior to the October Revolution did not have their own working class and continue to the present day to be primarily agrarian? (Among the Turkmens, in particular, workers constitute 39% of the total size of the republic's population, and peasants and kolkhoz members constitute 45%.) And, naturally, one should not fail to consider the fact, when attempting to determine the assumed dynamics of the growth of the national worker cadres, that in Uzbekistan, for example, there is a large percentage of rural inhabitants who have been, since time immemorial, in an environment of a single nationality and who therefore have a particularly difficult time in adjusting to another life style, to other working and everyday conditions.

Q Do you mean that this is how you are illustrating the need for taking into consideration the national peculiarities when forming the local working class?

A Yes, that is exactly what I'm talking about. Any complications in the sphere of indoctrinating young national cadres are explained by one thing: the Central Asian peoples do not have any profound working traditions in the system of their life values or psychological principles.

What is typical in this sense is the microclimate in the Uzbek or Tadzhik family. Large family clans consisting of representatives of two or three generations, extensive ties of kinship, have a tangible influence upon the formation of the views and ideas of the young people when choosing an occupation and their life paths. The older people act as guardians of the traditions, which are at time obviously archaic and which do not help the young people to acquire an independent, meaningful life.

The leap across an entire socioeconomic formation cannot be made without leaving a trace. And if today the Central Asian peoples continue to be the least urbanized, and the rural areas in the East are distinguished by their low rate of mobility and are not always eager to provide working hands to the city, then the determining factor here is the roots that go far back into history.

Q The low mobility of the Central Asian rural areas has led to a situation in which a surplus of manpower has developed there. And at the Twenty-sixth CPSU Congress mention was made of the acute need to use those reserves. You will agree that that situation is far from a common one to observe. To a definite degree it is even unique for our conditions.

A Not only unique, but also paradoxical. Despite the availability of many of thousands of people in reserve, dozens of enterprises at the same time are experiencing a great shortage of working hands and are frequently forced to hold back their growth rates. And, even worse, the administrators of factories, plants, and construction organizations expend a tremendous amount of effort every year, using any truth or falsehood, to lure hundreds of skilled workers from other parts of the country that have just as great a need for labor resources.

Q In Ashkhabad Oblast I happened to become acquainted with a practice of that nature. One of the plants in the construction industry there employs people who have been called in from Tataria, Bashkiria, the central zone of Russia, and even from Siberian cities.

A It is a measure that has been forced on the administrators of those enterprises. . . . It is obvious that one of the tasks is the creation of conditions for the resolution of personnel problems by drawing on the local labor resources. I think that it is no simple matter to state unequivocally what should be done.

It would be naive to assume that the rural population of Central Asia does not have any idea of city life, or is afraid of it. According to data provided by sociologists, the intensity of the contacts between rural and urban inhabitants here is no lower than it is in the more mobile RSFSR. But, the share of the people who want to move from, say, Kalinin Oblast is 16%, while those who want to move from the villages of Uzbekistan represent only 5.5%. In Tadzhikistan the research shows that among school graduates—and we are discussing not only rural schools—the share of those who want to work in industry is still very small. The preference is given to the branches that are traditional for the region—textiles, pottery, footwear, handicrafts, trade, public nutrition . . .

What should be done?—that was the question I asked. It is necessary, indisputably, to improve the system of occupational training for young people. It is necessary to use the means of local enterprises for the construction of new vocational-technical schools, and to fill up many of the half-empty vocational technical schools in the central part of Russia with young men and women from the parts of Central Asia in which there are surplus labor resources. In those "surplus" areas, as many people already realize, it is advantageous to create branches of urban enterprises. Not only do they make a rather large profit, but, in addition, the people in the rural areas become adjusted to work that is new to them and to a new way of life. . . . What is needed, of course, are scientifically substantiated recommendations on how to train and indoctrinate workers from the local national milieu.

Incidentally, I must note that specific, well-substantiated recommendations are extremely important to everyone. Once, I recall, a group of scientists that was studying the working, training, and everyday conditions of young workers at enterprises in Russia and the Ukraine departed for Samarkand with precisely the same program. It is easy to guess what happened . . .

Q What you have mentioned, it seems to me, fails to take into consideration yet another important factor.

A The ideological one? But the system of indoctrinating young worker cadres also presupposes the ideological support of the process—in the school, and primarily in the vocational-technical school.

Q I have in mind not only the ideological factor, but also the sociological support of the indoctrinational process. In the school or vocational-technical institute there must be not only an occupational orientation, but also a social one . . .

A It is possible and necessary to change the social landmarks for the schoolchildren, and to reinforce in the young people in the Central Asian or Transcaucasian republics a steady interest in the worker occupations. Something that must become an especially powerful lever is international indoctrination, which provides the opportunity to make broad use of the social experience of the most diverse regions of the country. However, is our propaganda arsenal ready for this task? I assume that that it is not always ready, or, at least, not in all respects.

Take, for instance, the book-publishing policy, or the number of books that are being published on work topics. The decree of the CPSU Central Committee concerning literary and artistic magazines and their relationship with life, I recall, mentioned in very specific terms the shortage of such works both for the USSR as a whole and in individual republics. But even though one can still find a few things in Russian, where can one find this literature—or more serious literature on social and political topics—in the national languages of the East? That literature is practically nonexistent. Or try finding a single magazine in Tashkent, Dushanbe, Ashkhabad, or Frunze of the type of the Moscow or nationwide *Smena*, or popular-science magazines like *Tekhnika–Molodezhi* or *Modelist–Konstruktor*. They too are nonexistent.

And how do we work with the newcomers—Tadzhik or Uzbek—who have arrived in production? Undoubtedly, the workload and the burdens of their indoctrinators, their mentors, are great. And much is indeed being done for young people—who would deny that? But at the same time the number of lectures provided for them in their native language—and they are people who are not yet acquainted with the work atmosphere—is still small. They are not offered books from the local nationality publishing houses that could help them to understand the essentials of production life . . . What happens is that we sometimes forget to give our propaganda or mass political work the proper orientation, with a proper consideration of national peculiarities. Now that really is a paradox!

In my opinion, it's high time to make this proposal. The Twenty-sixth CPSU Congress, as we have noted, isolated as a special, self-contained task the resolution of the questions linked with the formation of national detachments of the working class in Central Asia and the Caucasus. Why not, in development of this, create special-topic regional programs for these two parts of our country? In the comprehensive programs one could stipulate all the basic trends for scientific research, the economic and ideological support of the process of training and indoctrinating the generation of the national working class.

Q   Talib Sarimsakovich, I would not like to prejudge the fate of your proposals. In the final analysis, what has been stated is good food for thought and, let us hope, will lead to the making of decisions . . .

A   In any case, the job ahead is no simple one, and its overall trends, I feel, are well known. Nevertheless, I would like once again to emphasize the correctness and immediacy of the task: the working class today must become the majority of every major Soviet nation that constitutes the basic population of a union republic. The overall tendency confirms the natural regularity of precisely this development. Whereas in 1959 workers with families were the largest group of the population in six of the union republics and in 1970 in 13, since 1975 they constitute the largest group in all the republics without exception. Sociologists note that these dynamics have coincided with the advent of mature socialism—a period when a qualitatively new phase in the working class's fulfillment of its historic mission is beginning.

Properly speaking, this is what today, I think, should determine the political role both of science and of literature in the process of the formation of national detachments of the working class.

We justifiably expect literature to provide us with a profound study of these questions. We have a right to expect a more consistent and more complete elaboration of the topic, in order to keep us from rushing off to some extreme or flying into a rage, after striking the "golden vein." It is important to preserve the variety of the research field. To cultivate that field ceaselessly, painstakingly, on every plot of land. And then the time will come to bring in the harvest.

The Baku Floors of Kogalym:
A Report from the Videotheque of Azeri TV *

A production group from the republic television network has prepared a new program, "Addresses of Friendship," about the sponsored assistance of envoys from Azerbaidzhan for the city of Kogalym, now being built in western Siberia.

An enormous bobbin turns smoothly. The TV recorder shows frames taken at the end of February 1986. The place of action is a construction site. The location of the film is western Siberia, the town of Kogalym. The film records the founding of a new microraion, an Azerbaidzhani one, with modern houses and various structures for functions of everyday life.

Kogalym . . . just a few years ago this word was little known even in the Surgut Raion of Tiumen' Oblast, to say nothing of the rest of the country. Today, however, Kogalym is connected to a decisive new step in exploitation of the region's oil deposits. This little dot on the map has become a focus for application of the creative

---

Molodezh' Azerbaidzhana, 4 November 1986, p. 4. The report is by F. Zorin, senior editor, State Television and Radio, Azerbaidzhan SSR.

powers of youth, who have transformed this region of tundra into an intensive Komsomol building site.

The first labor assault troops arrived here from the Soviet Baltic. They, along with temporary workers, laid the foundations for the future city of oil workers, raising the first basic buildings. Then our republic took over sponsorship for the future construction of Kogalym.

The Siberians rejoiced at the arrival of the first Komsomols sent from Azerbaidzhan. Soon the people of Kogalym were convinced that the newcomers were not narrow specialists. Each of them had equal mastery of cement work, carpentry, crane operation. First, however, the labor front had to be prepared, equipped to receive the technical and construction materials being sent from Azerbaidzhan. The first arrivals always find things hard. It was also difficult for the southerners to get used to the harsh climatic conditions of western Siberia . . .

. . . On the screen, a panorama of a construction site. Then close-ups and pans of young workers, ruddy, as if each had been made up, with silver hoar frost on their mustaches and beards . . .

The meters of video tape pile up, recording the great amount of significant work that has been done in Kogalym in just a few years. But how do matters stand there today, and what is the outlook for the future? On the screen is the regular announcer of the program cycle "Friendship" from the main editorial board of Azeri TV, candidate of technical sciences Shakhriiar Kiiasbeili, speaking with the chief engineer of DSK–1 of *Glavbakstroi* [the main construction firm in Azerbaidzhan's capital city of Baku], Adil Abbasov. I should explain that this institution developed the technology of preparing reinforced concrete structures for housing in Kogalym.

A. Abbasov: "We were in Kogalym and saw clearly that in this case our typical production could only be used for interior ceilings. Buildings in Kogalym have to have a warm attic, thicker walls, and triple-glazed windows. After studying the question with specialists from the Azgosproekt [Azerbaidzhan state project] Institute, we chose to use walls made of three panels. Their production was set up very quickly, lowering the plan for basic production with existing technology. We have already sent the builders of Kogalym more than four thousand such panels. Special pyramid-shaped metal structures are used in shipping them. With their help the panels are securely fastened to the rail cars. . ."

Moderator: "How are things today in Kogalym?"

A. Abbasov: "Specialists from the Glavbakstroi administration attached to the Azerbaidzhani Tiumen' construction firm are building the Azerbaidzhani microraion. In the first year of the twelfth Five Year Plan the the collective has committed itself to producing not the five thousand square meters of living space that is in the plan, but seven thousand. This is a substantial contribution to the solution of one of the most important problems in Kogalym, that of living space. . ."

A model of an apartment building appears on the screen, projected for the Azerbaidzhani microraion in Kogalym. The blueprints were creatively worked out by young specialists from the No. 7 workshop of Azgosproekt, architect Azimkhan

Gasanov, engineer Naira Alieva, and many others. They took care not only to provide people with comfortable conditions but also were particularly careful in treating the external details of the building's profile and interior.

The film shows that by 1990 there must be 60 thousand square meters of living space built in Kogalym, including five kindergartens.

"We understand that helping the people of Kogalym is not a one-time thing. This is meant for many years," A. Abbasov says from the screen. "Considering this, we decided to create a new basis to guarantee our Siberian workers reinforced concrete buildings. The plans for this were worked out by workers of the PKTB of Glavbakstroi. We planned a special section for the preparation of triple wall-panels. The new production point will begin to function in January 1987."

. . . The time of tent colonies has passed in Kogalym. The floors of Kogalym are thrusting upwards, and the gas and oil production complex is developing. There still is no end of work, including in the town itself. So far there is no movie theater, public library, hotel, restaurant, or cafe. At the same time there is a good possibility for youth to prove itself, to test its character. And from the screen comes an appeal by the first assistant of the general director of the Bashneft [oil] production combine for western Siberia, Vakhid Iusufovich Alekperov, to the young men and women of the republic: "I advise my fellow countrymen to come to western Siberia, come for a long time and live and work, and those who already are registered to live in Kogalym will never forget that their work is valued as the work of a representative, an emissary of Azerbaidzhan."

. . . The television pictures change. Many of the episodes are really chronicles, but in time they might acquire the character of a historical document. Watching the film you feel a sense of pride in our contemporaries, who for a time are exchanging comforts to build a modern city in the tundra. And it is joyous that the international detachments of builders of Kogalym and those who are supplying the intensive building site with the technical means and necessary materials are our countrymen, products of the Komsomol of Azerbaidzhan.

THE UZBEK SSR STATE COMMITTEE ON LABOR
IS CARRYING OUT AN ORGANIZED RESETTLEMENT OF FAMILIES
to a permanent place of residence on the collective farms and state farms of the Primorskii Krai and the Ivanovskaia Oblast.

The registration of citizens declaring their desire to be resettled will take place in the Primorskii Krai up to April 10 and in the Ivanovskaia Oblast up to March 20.

Families registered for resettlement will be given free of charge their journey and the transport of their belongings. They will be paid a lump sum money subsidy, and will be offered houses or apartments, and household plots without buildings.

For two years the new settlers will live rent free and for eight years they will be exempted from taxes.

For all information on registration, inquire: In cities, at the Labor Sections of the Regional Executive Committees and in the Employment Offices, and in the City of Nukus at the Labor Administration of the Council of Ministers of the Karakalpak ASSR; In the oblasts, at the official representatives of the Administration of Labor of the Council of Ministers of the Karakalpak ASSR and the Labor Sections of the Regional Executive Committee; in the City of Tashkent Proletarskaia Street No. 4, third floor, room 6, Privokzalnaia Street No. 30, and in District Job Placement Centers.

(From: *Pravda Vostoka*, 15 March 1984)

AMUR OBLAST AWAITS YOU
In order to give brotherly assistance to the Russian Federation in exploiting the natural riches of Siberia and the Far East, the labor organs of the republic are undertaking the resettlement of families to kolkhozes and sovkhozes of the Amur Oblast.

Resettlers are paid a nonreturnable grant, are given houses with outbuildings, allotted garden plots, livestock and fowl at government cost, cafeteria food and other benefits, for which they are eligible for eight years.

Resettlers and their property are taken at government expense to the place of resettlement in special trains.

The departure of the first resettlement echelon is set for 18 March.

For information and registration contact the labor divisions of the oblast executive committees or the authorities in the place of residence.

Dear comrades! Take active part in the settlement of the fruitful lands of the Amur Oblast!   STATE LABOR COMMITTEE, TURKMEN SSR

(From: *Komsomolets Turkmenistana*, 27 January 1987)

ANNOUNCEMENT

DEAR COMRADES! The State Labor Committee of the Azerbaidzhan SSR and its local organs are choosing families who have expressed the desire to resettle in kolkhozes and sovkhozes of the **Amur oblast of the RSFSR**.

Families will be accepted for resettlement if they have not less than two working members, fit for physical labor in agriculture or single soldiers transferred to the reserves or released after the expiration of their year of reserve status.

All agricultural professions are needed: tractor drivers, combine drivers, milkers, pig breeders, cattlemen, and calf handlers, as well as carpenters, joiners, and others.

Families accepted for resettlement will receive free train transportation and moving of their property, as well as one-time payments of 200 rubles to the family head, plus 75 rubles per family member.

The kolkhozes and sovkhozes of the Amur oblast agree to guarantee every family at the time of arrival an apartment or house with yard buildings, and garden plot, as well as to assist in obtaining piglets and poultry. Gosbank [state bank] credits will be extended to obtain cows. They will also offer all advantages available for resettlers.

Pay for workers of the sovkhozes of the area is job rate plus bonuses. To the base rate of pay is added **a Far Eastern factor**. Registration of families wishing to resettle will continue until 10 February 1987.

To register or get information refer to a responsible labor official or the bureau of labor of the populace, in the executive committee of the Soviet of Workers' Deputies in the place of residence.

For additional information contact the administration of the relocation of labor forces committee of the State Labor Committee of the Azerbaidzhan SSR at Baku, Administrative Building, 10th floor, room 1003. Telephone 93-13-00, 93-10-04, 93-29-63.

(From: *Molodezh' Azerbaidzhana*, 24 December 1986)

5. Ethnodemographic Trends

During the post–World War II period the birth rates of the Slavic and Baltic nationalities of the USSR have been declining, while those of most of the Central Asian and Caucasian nationalities have grown so fast that these populations have doubled in size over the past quarter-century. The shifting demographic makeup of the USSR poses a number of concrete problems for Soviet policy makers. The most serious and immediate of these problems are those that affect Soviet economic development, as Moscow must simultaneously contend with shortages of trained labor in the Western parts of the country and underutilized sources of manpower in the Caucasus and Central Asia. Official efforts to deploy manpower as needed are hampered by the pervasiveness of traditional cultural values among the various Central Asian and Caucasian nationalities; these values have made them reluctant to train for certain occupations or to move from their national regions.

Soviet scholars writing during the Khrushchev and Brezhnev eras predicted the gradual assimilation of the non-Russian nationalities by the sovietized Russians, as the unique national traits and values of the non-Russian peoples became overshadowed by common Soviet ones. The centrally controlled education system was seen as playing the key role in promoting these changes. It was assumed that a uniform internationalist curriculum, conducted in Russian wherever possible, would promote the acquisition of common cultural traits, which in turn would encourage a high level of intermarriage between national communities and lead to a further diminution of national consciousness. The realities of the situation proved quite different; only the smallest and most isolated nationalities have begun to be assimilated by their neighbors. The reverse of the predicted pattern has been observed for the major nationalities. Even where there is a significant incidence of ethnic intermarriage, as there is for some of the Baltic nationalities, identification with the national community has remained strong and even increased over time. Today many Soviet groups, especially intellectuals, frame their political, social, and economic demands in terms of the interests of their national community, bringing more visibilty to nationality issues than ever before.

The articles in this section describe the shift in the ethnic balance in the USSR that has occurred in the past two decades, and some of the specific problems created by recent demographic trends. They also highlight the ways in which the vocabulary and mindset of the Brezhnev period worked to conceal them and thus hampered their resolution, and show how the approach to these problems is now beginning to change.

Viktor Kozlov is a prominent Soviet demographer. His *Nationalities of the USSR* is the standard introduction to demographic problems related to nationality issues. In the section excerpted below Kozlov examines the differential growth rates of Soviet nationalities over time in a way that illustrates both the strengths and the weaknesses of Soviet demography during the Brezhnev years. While Kozlov discusses some of the difficulties of using Soviet statistics for measuring population change, such as the redefinition of the Soviet borders in the western republics, he ignores a number of others. For example, he makes no mention of the unreliability of the 1939 census, which replaced the suppressed 1936 census and was designed to conceal the significant population losses attributable to collectivization and the subsequent famines. Similarly, there is no mention of the suppression of much of the data by nationality in the 1979 census in order to hide the existence of differential economic and social development patterns, nor of the problems of reliability with some of the nationality-related data published from that census.

In general Kozlov accepts the conventional "blank pages" of history that were not discussed during the Brezhnev era. Thus he posits a thesis of "natural" changes in the national communities to explain the decline of the Ukrainian and Kazakh populations during the intercensal period of 1926–1939, whereas in fact these were the two groups most devastated by the policies of collectivization—a far from "natural" cause of demographic decline. Problematic too is his discussion of the Koreans, whom he depicts as choosing to live in Central Asia in order to cultivate rice. In fact, almost all the Koreans living in Central Asia were forced to settle there after they were deported from the Soviet Far East at the time of the Japanese conquest of Manchuria.

Kozlov also never mentions the demographic impact of the involuntary movement of peoples. He makes no reference of the deportation of Russian and Ukrainian "kulaks" in the 1920s, nor of the deportation of the Crimean Tatars and several North Caucasian national groups during World War II, nor of the exile of hundreds of thousands of people from each of the three Baltic republics in 1940–1941 and 1944–1948. The reliability of his data for the three Baltic republics is particularly suspect, as the Lithuanians have recently published statistics indicating that their population did not reach prewar levels until 1959, whereas Kozlov reports that the number of Lithuanians increased 14.1 percent between 1939 and 1959.

However, Kozlov's article does provide very useful information about demographic trends in the USSR for the period 1959–1979. This information will not become outdated until after the completion and publication of the 1989 census. Kozlov shows how the Uzbeks, Tadzhiks, and Turkmens all doubled in number between 1959 and 1979, while the Kazakhs, Kirghiz, and Azerbaidzhanis came close to doubling in population. The census data that he reproduces also shows that the birthrate of the Russian and Ukrainian populations dropped below the national average for the first time, and the Baltic nationalities (the Estonians and Latvians in particular) registered virtually no population increases.

Typically cautious politically, Kozlov drew few conclusions from this data, although he noted that demographic potential (the future size of the population based on the numbers of people who have not yet reached their child-bearing years) of the Uzbeks now outstrips that of the Belorussians, and by 2000 will outstrip the Ukrainians as well. However, his data help explain a number of Soviet policies of the past decade, such as the efforts to encourage larger families in Slavic regions, but population control in the Caucasus and Central Asia. They explain official concern over manpower issues, the heightening of official attention to problems of Russian language training of non-Slavs, and the difficulties of cultural assimilation more generally. They also help explain some of the behaviors of the national minorities themselves, such as the Central Asians' calls for greater investment in their republics, the Baltic peoples' concern over the dwindling of their national communities, and increasing expressions of xenophobia by the Russians themselves.

L. Drobizheva's piece on "The Role of Education and Cultural Perspective in Interpersonal Relations," from a book called *The Spiritual Community of the Soviet Peoples*, is another example of the type of research on nationality-related demographic problems that was conducted during the Brezhnev years. It provides a good introduction to Soviet survey research as it relates to the national question, both in terms of the type of questions asked and the simplicity of statistical measures used. The data in this and the following article by Drobizheva reproduced below are drawn from a five-republic (RSFSR, Estonia, Georgia, Moldavia, and Uzbekistan) survey that was conducted over the years 1971–1982. This study was the most sophisticated large-scale project on nationality relations carried out during this period, yet the conclusions published from the study give no evidence of the scale and seriousness of ethnic tensions soon to be revealed. In fact, the impression gained from reading Drobizheva's article is exactly the opposite: that ethnic toleration is increasing in the USSR. While Drobizheva admits that intermarriage has not ensured cultural assimilation, and that most non-European groups in the USSR tenaciously defend the integrity of their communities, she argues that the spread of internationalist values through Russian language education is gradually breaking down social patterns of national exclusivity.

Time has shown Drobizheva's optimism to be misplaced. As we will see in the next section, the performance of the Soviet educational system in the non-European regions of the country has been sharply deficient in general and particularly deficient with regard to Russian language training. Moreover, knowledge of Russian language and Russian culture has not always led to more "internationalist" attitudes. A seemingly russified intelligentsia can become articulate proponents of their own national interests, as Drobizheva herself implies in her 1985 article, "National Self-Awareness."

Although Drobizheva's 1985 article is based on the same body of data as the earlier article, in the second, in keeping with the changing agendas of research for Soviet scholars, her focus is on the persistence of national self-awareness. The thesis of her article is that national self-awareness remains an important factor in explaining individual behavior, even though generally there has been a diminution of ethnically specific traits.

The second article reflects some major conceptual shifts that have occurred in Soviet scholarship on nationality relations during the 1980s, including most prominently a public recognition of the importance of understanding the social psychology of individuals in order to study their group behavior. Drobizheva clearly states the problem which Soviet scholars on nationality relations must now confront: that ties to national communities remain strong even as particularistic customs begin to die out or become transformed, and that the rise of nationalist feelings leads to a renewal of particularistic ethnic practices. With the caution characteristic of Soviet scholars, Drobizheva offers few explanations for this problem, or its implications for Soviet policies. Instead she concludes by observing that the Party recognizes that national loyalties will inevitably be expressed under present conditions, and that the perpetuation of national identity is acceptable as long as it does not impede the general goals of the state.

However, as is clearly stated in the article by Ostapenko and Susokolov, the pervasiveness of ethnic loyalties does *impede* the economic development of the country along the lines decided by Moscow, because of the unwillingness of various national communities to accept technical training or to relocate outside of their national regions. Both of these problems have received a great deal of attention from Soviet scholars and policy makers in the last few years. All-union reforms of the general education system in 1984, and of the system of specialized secondary and higher education in 1986, were designed to improve the quality of technical education. While these reforms themselves have come under attack for not doing enough to remedy shortages of equipment and to raise the level of instruction (problems which are particularly severe in the labor rich areas of Central Asia and the Caucasus), no amount of reform will produce the necessary technicians if Central Asian and Caucasian youths refuse to enroll in technical schools, or take up jobs in heavy industry if assigned.

In the last several years the press nationwide has been full of articles about the lengths to which young people will go to try and train for "prestige" professions in education, culture and health-care, while PTUs (specialized technical high schools and post–high-school programs) and technical institutes remain unfilled. Programs designed to increase the numbers of Central Asians and Caucasians receiving technical education, such as the establishment of "sister institutions" in the RSFSR and the Ukraine SSR which will receive groups of young people from a paired school or region, have met with disappointing results. So too, as Ostapenko and Susokolov report, have efforts to resettle large numbers of Central Asians and Caucasians permanently outside of their republics.

Recent reforms, which stress the rights of access of minority nationalities to education, publications, and media in their national languages, may make leaving their republics more attractive to some, but these measures are unlikely to make the majority of Caucasians and Central Asians willing to leave their home territories. Moreover, as Ostapenko and Susokolov note, efforts to place trained specialists in the labor-short regions of European Russia or in the Far East leave Central Asia and the Caucasus with even greater shortages of trained technicians.

In the past, Soviet leaders have grudgingly accepted the cultural impediments to the development of the Central Asian and Transcaucasian republics. While official policy statements routinely call for the elimination of national differences in the distribution of occupations, and educational reforms continue to state this as an important goal, nonetheless, only limited financial resources have been put aside for programs designed to transform traditional occupational patterns. In recent years the leadership in Moscow has expressed serious concern over the low economic growth rates in the Central Asian and Caucasian republics, and has cited this as one of the main reasons for purging the local party apparatuses in these regions.

But until very recently no one would blame these economic shortcomings on the national character of the nationalities themselves. Now some people are beginning to make precisely this argument. This is the premise of Drobizheva's 1988 letter to the editors of the journal *Political Education*, in which she argues that differential rates of economic performance between republics are in part a product of the different cultural orientations toward labor of various national communities. Then she goes one step further and raises the possibility of Moscow deciding to make differential investments in republics based on their levels of economic productivity. Others have put it more crudely, and have argued that if some nationalities want lots of children and would rather not work very hard, then they don't need to eat well.

Gorbachev's economic reforms and the move toward financial autonomy of enterprises and whole regions seems to signal the end of the era of family and regional subsidies, as well as the demise of an official commitment to maintaining a uniformly high level of development across republics. While this would probably reduce the pressure on the Central Asian and Caucasian republics to meet the high economic growth rates that were projected in the Twelfth Five-Year Plan, it would also signal a drop in investment, which would mean a sharp drop in the standard of living as well. Talk of ending the subsidized development of union republics is popular among certain nationalities, but it poses the threat of increasing political and social unrest among others.

Processes of Ethnic Change and Population Dynamics among the Peoples of the USSR *

V. I. KOZLOV

The proper next step after examining ethnic processes, in the first instance the process of ethnic change, is to analyze their effect on the population dynamics of the peoples of the USSR. Changes in these peoples' population size have been determined primarily by natural increase (the correlation between their birth and death rates) and ethnic processes. Another important factor—migration (in this case, out-migration), or changes in state borders which produce essentially the same results—has had a significant impact on the population of only some of the peoples of the USSR.

To assess properly the role of ethnic processes in these dynamics, it is essential to take into account the impact of demographic factors, but for the lack of necessary data this is, unfortunately, by no means always possible. It becomes necessary to resort to various indirect calculations and estimates. To illustrate the methodology of some such calculations, and also the extent of the possible influence of ethnic processes on the population dynamics of peoples of the USSR, let us consider somewhat more closely the example of the Mordvinians.[a] On the basis of available data on the birth and death rates among the peoples of the Volga region in 1927 and population figures for the autonomous republics of the Volga region in 1940, the natural increase of the Mordvinians between 1926 and 1939 was roughly the same as that of the Chuvash,[b] or even somewhat higher. The Chuvash population during this period increased by 22.6% (see Table), despite ongoing processes of ethnic assimilation, which, admittedly, were negligible in those years. One might assume, then, that by 1939 the number of Mordvinians should also have grown by no less than 24% and reached approximately 1,650,000. The difference of about 200,000 between this latter figure and the recorded number of Mordvinians in 1939 was probably entirely the result of natural assimilation.

If we juxtapose the population growth of the Mordvinians with that of their neighbors, the Chuvash and the Mari,[c] who were more slowly drawn into ethnic processes in the ensuing years (1939–1959), the number of Mordvinians recorded in the 1959 census should have reached about 1,600,000, but was in fact 1,285,000; the difference between these figures—more than 300,000—may again be explained by the ethnic fusion of some groups of Mordvinians primarily with the Russians. From 1959 to 1970, the number of Mordvinians decreased by 1.7%, and by 1979 by another 5.6%, while in the corresponding periods the Mari population increased by

*Natsional'nosti SSSR, 2nd edition (Moscow, 1982), pp. 282–295. Russian text © 1982 by "Finansy i statistika" Publishers.

18.7% and 3.9%, respectively. The comparatively small increase in the Mari population between 1970 and 1979, as well as other indicators, in the first instance a quickening in their linguistic assimilation, suggest that they, too, have begun to be affected by ethnic assimilation. If this were not the case, their increase over the period 1959 to 1979 should have amounted to about 30%, and not 23.4% as the census showed. If we assume for the Mordvinians an even lower hypothetical growth index than for the Mari—25%—their number should still have exceeded 1,600,000 in 1979, rather than stand at 1,192,000 as the census showed. Thus, their overall decrease as a result of assimilation over the previous twenty years has exceeded 400,000.

The key factor promoting this ethnic change has been mixed marriages between Mordvinians and Russians, which have become more frequent as a result of the growing migration of Mordvinians to the cities, especially outside the Mordvinian ASSR. Within their own republic, the Mordvinians, like other peoples of union republic and autonomous republic status, maintain a rather stable national identity.

When in the course of our examination of population dynamics among the peoples of the USSR, data from Soviet population censuses conducted in 1926, 1939, 1959, 1970 and 1979 (Table), it must be remembered that between 1939 and 1959 significant territorial changes had taken place in connection with the reunification of Western Ukraine with the Ukrainian SSR and Western Belorussia with the Belorussian SSR, as well as the accession to the USSR of the Baltic republics and other territories, with a total population of about 20 million. Thus, in analyzing changes in population patterns among different peoples during this period, we must rely on such population estimates as are available for Russians and the indigenous nationalities of the western republics as of 1939 within the country's new frontiers.

The Soviet census data reveal the multinational structure of the USSR's population and show great dissimilarities in size among the various peoples. The Russians and Ukrainians stand out in strength of numbers, constituting over two-thirds of the country's population in 1979. Apart from them, only eleven other peoples numbered over two million, and another nine peoples—more than one million (in 1926 only thirteen peoples numbered over one million each). The vast majority of peoples however, number considerably, of them fifty nationalities under 100,000 each, and some (the Iganasan, Yukaghirs, Negidals)[d] even less than 1,000. Indeed, for the smaller ethnic groups of the USSR (those numbering less than 10,000), it is difficult to establish definite regularities in their patterns of population change, and for that reason they are excluded from the Table.[1] Now let us examine the main developments as they are reflected in the table, concentrating on the more significant deviations, in both directions, from the average rate of increase countrywide.

According to the 1939 census, over the previous thirteen years, while the population of the country as a whole (within the 1926 borders) grew by 15.7%, the number of Ukrainians decreased by almost 10%. A decline in the rate of natural increase (especially in Ukraine in the early 1930s) could have accounted for slower growth among the Ukrainians, but not for a decrease in their number. The latter phenomenon was evidently due to the fact that significantly large population groups in the

Population Dynamics of Nationalities of the USSR (according to census data for given years)

Nationality	Population (in thousands)					Increase (in percent)				
	1926	1939	1959	1970	1979	1926-1939	1939-1959	1959-1970	1970-1979	1959-1979
Total population	147,027.9	170,557.1	208,826.7	241,720.1	262,084.7	15.7	9.5*	15.3	8.4	25.5
Russians	77,791.1	99,591.5	114,113.6	129,015.1	137,397.1	28.0	13.7*	13.0	6.5	20.4
Ukrainians	31,195.0	28,111.0	37,252.9	40,753.2	42,347.4	-9.9	4.6*	9.4	3.9	13.7
Belorussians	4,738.9	5,275.4	7,913.5	9,051.8	9,462.7	11.3	-4.4*	14.4	4.5	19.5
Lithuanians	41.5	32.6	2,326.1	2,664.9	2,850.9	-21.4	14.4*	14.6	7.0	22.6
Latvians	141.6	128.0	1,399.5	1,429.8	1,439.0	-9.6	-14.1*	2.2	0.6	2.8
Estonians	154.7	143.6	988.6	1,007.4	1,019.9	-7.2	-13.6*	1.9	1.2	3.2
Moldavians	278.9	260.4	2,214.1	2,698.0	2,968.2	-6.6	7.5*	21.8	10.0	34.0
Georgians	1,821.2	2,249.6	2,692.0	3,245.3	3,570.5	23.5	19.7	20.5	10.0	32.7
Armenians	1,567.6	2,152.9	2,786.9	3,559.2	4,151.2	37.3	29.4	27.7	16.6	48.9
Azerbaidzhanis	1,706.6	2,275.7	2,939.7	4,379.9	5,477.3	33.3	29.2	49.0	25.0	86.3
Kazakhs	3,968.3	3,100.9	3,621.6	5,298.6	6,556.4	-21.9	16.8	46.3	23.7	81.0
Uzbeks	3,904.6	4,845.1	6,015.4	9,195.1	12,456.0	24.1	24.2	52.8	35.5	107.1
Turkmen	763.9	812.4	1,001.6	1,525.3	2,027.9	6.3	23.3	52.2	33.0	102.5
Tadzhiks	978.7	1,229.2	1,396.9	2,135.9	2,897.7	25.6	13.6	52.9	35.7	107.4
Kirghiz	762.7	884.6	968.7	1,452.2	1,906.3	16.0	9.5	49.9	31.2	96.8
Karelians	248.1	252.7	167.3	146.1	138.4	1.8	-33.8	-12.7	-5.3	-17.3
Komi, Komi-Permiaks	375.9	422.3	430.9	475.3	477.5	12.0	2.0	10.2	0.6	10.9
Mordvinians	1,340.4	1,456.3	1,285.1	1,262.7	1,191.8	8.4	-11.8	-1.7	-5.6	-7.2
Mari	428.2	481.6	504.2	598.6	622.0	12.5	4.7	18.7	3.9	23.4
Udmurt	504.2	606.3	624.8	704.3	713.7	20.2	3.1	12.7	1.0	13.8
Chuvash	1,117.4	1,369.6	1,469.8	1,694.4	1,751.4	22.6	7.3	15.2	3.3	19.1
Tatars	2,916.3	4,313.5	4,967.7	5,930.7	6,317.5	47.9	15.7	19.4	6.5	27.2

Nationality	Population (in thousands)					Increase (in percent)				
	1926	1939	1959	1970	1979	1926-1939	1939-1959	1959-1970	1970-1979	1959-1979
Bashkirs	713.7	843.6	989.0	1,239.2	1,371.5	18.2	17.2	25.4	10.6	38.6
Kalmyks	132.0	134.4	106.1	137.2	146.6	1.8	−21.1	29.1	6.9	38.2
Kabardinians	139.9	164.2	203.6	279.9	321.7	17.4	24.0	37.5	14.9	58.0
Karachai	55.1	75.8	81.4	112.7	131.1	37.6	7.4	38.4	16.3	61.0
Cherkess	65.3	—	30.5	39.8	46.5	—	—	30.5	16.8	52.5
Balkars	33.3	42.7	42.4	59.5	66.4	28.2	−0.7	40.3	11.6	56.6
Ossetians	272.2	354.8	412.6	488.0	541.9	30.3	16.3	18.3	11.1	31.4
Chechens	318.5	408.0	418.8	612.7	755.8	28.1	2.6	46.3	23.3	80.5
Ingush	74.1	92.1	106.0	157.6	186.2	24.3	15.1	48.7	18.1	75.7
Avars	158.8	252.8	270.4	396.3	482.8	59.2	7.0	46.6	21.2	78.6
Lezghins	134.5	221.0	223.1	323.8	382.6	64.3	1.0	45.1	18.2	71.5
Darghins	109.0	153.8	158.1	230.9	287.3	41.1	2.8	46.1	24.4	81.7
Kumyks	94.6	112.6	135.0	188.8	228.4	19.0	19.9	39.8	21.0	69.2
Laks	40.4	56.1	63.5	85.8	100.1	38.9	13.2	35.1	16.7	57.6
Nogais	36.3	36.6	38.6	61.8	59.5	0.8	5.5	34.2	14.9	54.1
Tabasarans	32.0	33.6	34.7	55.2	75.2	5.0	3.3	59.1	36.2	116.7
Rutulians	10.5	—	6.7	12.1	15.0	—	—	80.6	24.0	124.0
Tsakhurs	19.1	—	7.3	11.0	13.5	—	—	50.7	22.7	85.0
Aguls	7.7	—	6.7	8.8	12.1	—	—	31.3	37.5	80.5
Abkhaz	57.0	59.0	65.4	83.2	90.9	3.5	10.8	27.2	9.3	39.0
Abaza	13.8	15.3	19.6	25.4	29.5	10.9	28.1	29.6	16.1	50.5
Adygei	65.3	88.1	79.6	99.9	108.7	39.8	−9.6	25.5	8.8	36.6
Tats	28.7	—	11.5	17.1	22.4	—	—	48.7	31.0	94.8
Karakalpaks	146.3	185.8	172.6	236.0	303.3	27.0	−7.1	36.8	28.5	75.7
Tuvinians	—	0.8	100.1	139.4	166.1	—	—	39.3	19.2	65.9

Buriats	237.5	224.7	253.0	314.7	352.6	−5.4	12.6	24.4	12.2	39.5
Yakuts	240.7	242.1	236.7	296.2	328.0	0.6	−2.2	25.1	10.7	38.6
Altai	37.6	47.9	45.3	55.8	60.0	27.4	−5.4	23.2	7.5	32.5
Khakass	45.6	52.8	56.8	66.7	70.8	15.8	7.6	17.4	6.1	24.6
Shor	12.6	16.3	15.3	16.5	16.0	29.4	−6.1	7.8	−3.0	4.6
Evenki	32.8	29.7	24.7	25.1	27.5	−9.5	−16.8	1.6	9.6	11.3
Nenets	18.8	24.8	23.0	28.7	29.9	31.9	−7.3	24.5	4.1	30.0
Khanty	17.7	18.5	19.4	21.1	20.9	4.3	4.9	8.8	−0.9	7.7
Chukchi	13.1	13.9	11.7	13.6	14.0	6.1	−15.8	16.2	3.0	20.0
Nanais	5.3	8.5	8.0	10.0	10.5	16.0	−6.0	25.0	5.0	31.3
Eveny	—	9.7	9.1	12.0	12.3	—	−16.2	31.9	2.5	35.2
Jews	2,600.9	3,028.5	2,267.8	2,150.7	1,810.9	16.4	—	−5.2	−15.8	−20.1
Germans	1,238.5	1,427.2	1,619.7	1,846.3	1,936.2	15.2	—	14.0	10.5	19.5
Poles	782.3	630.1	1,380.3	1,167.5	1,151.0	−19.5	—	−15.5	−1.5	−16.6
Bulgarians	111.2	113.5	324.2	351.2	361.1	2.1	—	8.3	2.8	11.4
Greeks	213.8	286.4	309.3	336.9	343.8	34.0	8.0	9.0	2.1	11.2
Hungarians	5.5	—	154.7	166.5	170.6	—	—	7.6	2.5	10.3
Romanians	4.6	—	106.4	119.3	128.8	—	—	12.2	8.0	21.1
Gypsies	61.2	88.2	132.0	175.3	209.2	44.1	49.6	32.5	19.3	58.5
Gagauz	0.8	—	123.8	156.6	173.2	—	—	26.5	10.6	39.8
Finns	19.5	—	92.7	84.8	77.1	—	—	−8.5	−9.1	−16.8
Koreans	87.0	182.3	313.7	357.5	388.5	109.5	72.1	14.0	8.8	24.0
Uighurs	42.6	—	95.2	173.3	210.65	—	—	82.0	21.5	112.2
Kurds	55.6	—	58.8	88.9	115.9	—	—	51.4	30.4	97.2
Dungans	14.6	—	21.9	38.6	51.7	—	—	76.3	33.9	36.1
Turks	8.6	—	35.3	—	92.7	—	—	—	—	162.6

*The increase is calculated on the basis of population figures after September 17, 1939 (including the western territories that became part of the USSR), which, according to estimates by the Central Statistical Administration, were: Russians—100,392,000, Ukrainians—35,611,000, Belorussians—8,275,000, Lithuanians—2,033,000, Latvians—1,628,000, Estonians—1,144,000, Moldavians—2,060,000 (see: *Narody SSSR. Kratkii spravochnik.* Moscow, 1958). For lack of similar estimates as of 1939 for Jews, Germans, Poles and some other peoples, their increase for the period 1939–1959 was not computed.

Note: The table includes indigenous nationalities of the USSR with a population in excess of 10,000 in 1979 and nationalities whose majority resides outside our country but with a population in excess of 50,000.

southern and other regions of the European RSFSR, who at the time of the 1926 census identified themselves as Ukrainians, were actually in an ethnically transitional phase, and by the 1939 census already considered themselves to be Russian; this ethnic reidentification is probably due, to some extent, to a modification of the relevant question on the census form (in 1926 the question concerned ethnicity [narodnost'], while in the 1939 and subsequent censuses the reference was to nationality [natsional'nost']). In 1926 there were 3,107,000 Ukrainians on the territory of the Northern Caucasus region, while in 1959 on the roughly equivalent territory of the Northern Caucasus economic region there were only 170,000 Ukrainians; in 1926, there were in the aggregate 1,633,000 Ukrainians in the Voronezh and Kursk gubernias, while in 1959 in the territorially roughly equivalent Belgorod, Voronezh, and Kursk oblasts there were only 261,000 Ukrainians—and the vast majority of these reported Russian as their native language. As a result of this fusion with the Russians of large ethnically transitional groups of Ukrainians, as well as some groups of Belorussians and other nationalities, the overall increase of the Russians between 1926 and 1939 was much higher than the average for the population of the country as a whole.

The decrease in the number of Poles by almost 20% can be attributed to assimilation of some numbers of them by the Belorussians and Ukrainians, but principally by the Russians, since within the RSFSR the settlement of Poles was characterized by the greatest dispersion. The population size of Latvians, Lithuanians and Estonians, small groups of whom lived at the time mainly within the RSFSR, diminished for the same reason; especially revealing in this respect is the case of the Latvians, whose number diminished despite the fact that included in their total in the 1939 census were the Latgalians,[e] who in the 1926 census had been listed separately (then about 10,000).

The lower than average growth of the Mordvinians, Karelians,[f] and Bulgarians, can also be attributed to assimilation of some numbers of them by surrounding peoples (the Mordvinians and Karelians by the Russians, the Bulgarians primarily by the Ukrainians); in the case of these and a number of other peoples of the country the quickening of assimilation processes was reflected in the growing percentage of those claiming as their native tongue the language of another nationality. The number of Kazakhs between 1926 and 1939 fell considerably, which can be explained in part by a decrease in their natural rate of growth in the early 1930s, and in part by to the nomadic migrations of some Kazakh groups to their kinsmen in Xinjiang. Critically important in explaining this phenomenon as well is the fact that the number of Kazakhs in the 1926 census had been exaggerated at the cost of some improperly registered Kirghiz and possibly other Turkic-speaking groups. Some cases of lower than average growth rates (Turkmen, Kalmyks, Buryats, Yakuts,[g] and others) require further study.

Very high rates of growth between 1926 and 1939 were exhibited by the Tatars,[h] the major peoples of Daghestan[i] (Avars, Lezghins, Darghins), and particularly the Koreans, who more than doubled in number. In this last case the increase was apparently due to an influx to the USSR of new groups of Korean settlers, attracted by the prospects of introducing rice cultivation in suitable areas of Central Asia (mainly in Uzbekistan) and southern Kazakhstan.

In analyzing the pattern of population change among the Tatars two circumstances must be taken into account. First of all, the reduction of their death rate, in the first instance child mortality, proceeded more rapidly than, for example, among peoples of Central Asia close to them in some elements of culture and way of life (linked, in part, with the Muslim religion), and this, given their continuing high birth rates resulted in a rapid natural increase. Secondly, processes of ethnic consolidation among the Tatars led to the amalgamation with the Tatars proper of several Turkic-speaking groups in the Volga and Ural regions, which had been listed separately in the 1926 census as distinct ethnic groups in their own right: the Mishars—242,600, the Kriashens—101,400, the Teptiars—27,400 (some of the Teptiars, apparently, coalesced with the Bashkirs[j]), the Nagaibaks—11,200, et al. This consolidation alone would have raised the number of Tatars by more than 13% in comparison with their figure in 1926.

The Georgians came to include the Adzhars (71,000 in 1926) whose main difference lay in religion (Adzhar believers being Muslims). The considerable increase in the number of Avars can be explained in large measure by the fact that by the 1939 census they had absorbed the Andi, Akhvakh, Botlikh, and some other small ethnic groups of Daghestan, while the Kubachi coalesced with the Darghins. It should also be noted that in the 1939 census aggregated with the Uzbeks were some Turkic-speaking groups which had consolidated with them (the Kipchaks, who numbered 33,500 in 1926, and the Kurams—50,200, et al.); the Udmurts[k] came to include the Besermians (10,000); a part of the Cherkess had merged with the Adygei,[l] and so forth. As a result of all these and other amalgamations, the list of Soviet nationalities as it emerged in the course of processing the 1939 census data was reduced by almost half in comparison with the 1926 population census.

An analysis of changes in the ethnic structure of the population between 1939 and 1959 proves to be very difficult. The difficulty stems, first of all, from the accession to the USSR—already after the completion of the 1939 census—of Western Ukraine, Western Belorussia, the Baltic, and other regions for which sufficiently accurate information on the national composition of the population was lacking (the number of Belorussians in the western territories, for example, was only tentatively estimated at 3 million, the number of Ukrainians at 7.5 million, etc.). The inevitable inexactness in the estimated figures for Russians, Ukrainians, Belorussians, Lithuanians, Latvians, Estonians, Moldavians, and some other nationalities for 1939 in terms of present-day borders of the USSR may have significant bearing on our calculations in percentage terms of the gains (or losses) among these nationalities in the period 1939 to 1959. This difficulty in analysis is compounded by the paucity of statistical materials for this period on the natural movement of people with reference to nationality, the absence of data on absolute or relative losses suffered by particular peoples of our country in the years of the Great Patriotic War, and on the outmigration of some nationalities.[2]

We may state with some confidence that the increase in the number of Russians, higher than the countrywide average, despite their enormous war losses, resulted in part from ethnic assimilation of some groups of Ukrainians, Belorussians and Jews, mainly those residing in the RSFSR, as well as of Karelians, Mordvinians, Udmurts, Komi,[m] and some other nationalities; this also explains to some extent the reduced population growth (or actual loss) among these nationalities.

Particularly dramatic was the decrease (almost by half) over this period in the number of the Veps, a small Finnic-speaking people living to the south of Lake Onega,[n] interspersed among the Russians and long under their strong linguistic and cultural influence; in the 1959 census, more than half of the Vepsy named Russian as their native language. The above-average growth rate of the Armenians is partly explained by the resettlement in Armenia of some numbers of Armenians from abroad, and that of the Azerbaidzhanis by their absorption of the Talysh,[o] who in 1939 had been listed as a separate nationality (88,000 in number). The ethnic assimilation of the Talysh was evidently not yet complete as of 1959, since 10,500 of them still declared Talysh as their native language.

Easiest to analyze for patterns of population change among the peoples of the USSR is the period since 1959. During this time no shifts in the country's borders took place; out-migration was negligible (one need only mention the emigration of a relatively small number of Jews); and processes of national consolidation were completed in all regions of the country even before 1959, so that the list of nationalities as it emerged in the course of processing the 1970 and 1979 census data was virtually identical with that of 1959. Changes in the numerical strength of the peoples of our country were the result of only two factors—the specific patterns of their natural reproduction, and, in part, continuing processes of ethnic assimilation.

A comparison of the 1970 and 1959 census data reveals substantial differences in the patterns of change among the peoples of our country over eleven years: some of them grew by more than half, others showed a negligible increase, and some even fell in number. The number of Uzbeks, Tadzhiks and Turkmen grew especially sharply, and at roughly the same rates (52–53%). Only slightly lower were the rates of increase among Kazakhs, Kirghiz, Azerbaidzhanis, as well as Chechens,[p] Avars, Lezghins, and some other peoples. Typical for all of them were, on the one hand, very high rates of birth and natural increase, and on the other, a relatively weak development of interethnic contacts (primarily the result of lower than average urbanization levels), low levels of ethnically mixed marriages, and low rates of linguistic change—and, in consequence, a weak development of processes of ethnic change.

High rates of growth (20–30%) were to be observed among Armenians, Georgians, Moldavians, Bashkirs, Kalmyks, Buriats, and some other peoples with high birth rates and relatively small losses (or even a net gain) from ethnic assimilation. In contrast low rates of growth (less than 10%, compared to the 15.3% countrywide average) were exhibited by peoples with low birth rates or a significant negative balance resulting from ethnic assimilation: the Ukrainians, Latvians, Estonians, etc. The number of Poles showed a substantial drop since 1959, the result primarily of their decrease in Belorussia (from 538,800 to 382,600). Quite probably, substantial groups of Poles in this republic (for the most part in the western oblasts) were already at a transitional ethnic stage at the time of the 1959 census and hence did not possess a well-defined national conciousness; some of them, apparently, descended from Belorussians who had adopted Catholicism in the past. It should be noted also that were it not for their assimilation of the Poles, the rate of increase among Belorussians by 1970 would have approximated that of the Ukrainians. The number of Jews, Mordvinians, and Karelians declined, primarily as a result of their continuing ethnic assimilation.

For the first time the Russian rate of growth was lower than the countrywide average. Absorption by the Russians of some groups belonging to other nationalities (primarily from among Ukrainians, Belorussians, and others living in the RSFSR) was insufficient to compensate for the sharp drop in the birth rate of the Russians themselves.

Some changes in the size of particular nationalities are not completely clear. Difficult to explain, for example, is the very high increase (over 80%) of the Rutulians, one of the small ethnic groups in Daghestan. One may surmise that this reflects some kind of undercount of the Rutulians in the 1959 census (when their reported number was considerably lower than in 1926). The rapid growth of Uighurs[q] (82%) may be explained, apparently, by a new influx to the USSR of groups from Xinjiang, where by decision of Beijing authorities, the Xinjiang-Uighur Autonomous District implimented a policy of oppression of national minorities.

Almost all the main features of population dynamics among the Soviet nationalities that we observed for 1959–1970 continued during the intercensal period 1970—1979, with only a few atypical new phenomena. Hence, to avoid redundancy and a simple recapitulation of the tabulated data, it seems more useful to examine the already well-established trends in terms of broader groupings of nationalities and to venture some forecasts for the coming decades.[3]

Between 1959 and 1970, the number of East Slavs (Russians, Ukrainians and Belorussians) grew by 18.8%, i.e., their rates of increase were lower (by almost half, in the case of the Ukrainians) than the USSR average. There is reason to expect that these peoples' rates of natural increase in the near future will diminish even further, and that this diminished growth will not be compensated by their (primarily the Russians') absorption of other nationality groups through ethnic assimilation. If their rate of growth remains at its previous level, by the year 2000 the aggregate numbers of this group will constitute about two-thirds of the country's population (in 1959 it was slightly more than three-fourths); Russians alone will account for about one-half of all the inhabitants of the USSR (compared with 55% in 1959).

The diminution in the proportion of East Slavic peoples, including Russians, is mainly the result of rapid growth among the peoples of the Turkic group and neighboring peoples of Central Asia and the Caucasus, similar to them in culture, way of life, and demographic behavior. The population of Turkic peoples grew since 1959 by almost 72%; if these rates hold up, by the year 2000 they will account for more than one-fifth of the country's inhabitants (compared with 11% in 1959). The largest people of this group—the Uzbeks—in 1939 were outnumbered by the Belorussians (within present-day borders of the USSR) by a factor of 1.7, but by 1970 already surpassed them in numbers. By the year 2000, the number of Uzbeks may reach 25 million, exceeding the Belorussians almost 2.5 times; in their demographic potential (the number of children born) the Uzbeks by that time may have surpassed the Ukrainians. Within this group, a significant deceleration in the rate of growth has been observed only among the Tatars and the Chuvash, resulting from decreasing birth rates (connected with urbanization and other factors) and, partly assimilation.

Very high rates of growth have been maintained by peoples of the Iranian (especially Tadzhiks) and the Nakh-Daghestan groups. The numerical growth of Moldavians in the last decades has slowed appreciably, primarily because of a declining rate of natural increase, which apparently will be higher than the countrywide average through the year 2000.

The long established pattern of low growth rates among the Baltic peoples will, apparently, continue in the future; it is quite possible that the numerical growth of Latvians and Estonians will cease altogether. While in 1959 these peoples, together with the Lithuanians, were 1.6 times as numerous as the Azerbaidzhanis, by the year 2000 the Azerbaidzhanis will outnumber them approximately two-fold. Estonians belong to the Finnic group, other large peoples of which (Mordvinians, Udmurts, etc.) possess autonomous republics in the European part of the RSFSR. The numerical strength of the Mordvinians and Karelians, which has been declining since 1939, will probably continue to decrease up to the year 2000; it is not impossible that the number of Komis and Udmurts will begin to decrease on account of ethnic assimilation, so that the relative proportion of peoples of this group among the inhabitants of the USSR will decrease. A further decrease in the number of Jews and Poles may also be expected; the number of other relatively large nationalities (Germans, Bulgarians, Greeks, Koreans, etc.) will increase, although in most cases at very low rates. The increment of peoples of the Mongolian group (the Kalmyks and Buriats) and the Gypsies will continue to be higher than the national average.

Patterns of change in the number of some of the smaller nations in southern Siberia who are part of the Turkish group (the Altais, Khakasy, and Shors) as well as peoples of the north (Evenki, Nentsy, etc.) are strikingly stable. However, the number of the vast majority of these peoples will increase. Predictions found in pre-revolutionary literature of the rapid disappearance (and even the "dying out") of these people have been refuted during the course of implementation of a Leninist national policy, thanks to special measures taken to preserve these peoples.

Whereas no changes are expected in the list of nationalities in the USSR before the end of this century, substantial changes have already begun to take place in the national composition of the population of the country in the relative proportions of large peoples, as should be clear from the foregoing, and these trends should continue even more distinctly in the future. The theory and practice of communist construction should take these changes into account.

The activation of a demographic policy as outlined by the Twenty-sixth Congress of the CPSU will produce substantial results only after some time has passed, since demographic behavior is rather inert, and the mothers of children born twenty years from now have already been born and it is hardly possible to increase their number. Hence demographic policy should clearly be rounded out by a number of measures aimed, for example, at increasing the territorial and social and occupational mobility of the population, and especially of those nationalities that have a considerable natural increment in their number. In particular, greater fluency in the Russian language, the dissemination of an all-Soviet culture, etc.

Editor's notes

a. Mordvinians: a Finnic people of the middle Volga region in the RSFSR. Officially recognized as one nationality and endowed with one autonomous republic (ASSR), they speak a number of sometimes mutually unintelligible dialects and possess two literary languages that are both used in primary education and some publishing. They are the most widely dispersed of the Volga peoples, with less than one-third residing in their titular ASSR.

b. Chuvash: an ASSR-level nationality of the middle Volga region. They speak a radically divergent form of Turkic and are further differentiated from other neighboring Turkic peoples by their traditional Christian (Russian Orthodox) religion.

c. Mari: an ASSR-level nationality of the middle Volga region. Hiostorically and culturally closely associated with the Chuvash, they are, however, linguistically Finnic.

d. These are three of the approximately thirty small peoples of the Soviet Far North and Siberia.

e. The Latgalians are a subgroup of the Latvians, distinguished by some dialectal and ethnographic features, but mainly by their Catholic religion, most Latvians being Lutheran.

f. Karelians: the Finnic-speaking inhabitants of Soviet territories adjoining Finland (whose standard literary Finnish language they actually use). Their administrative unit possessed union-republic status (as the Karelo-Finnish SSR) from 1940 to 1956, when it was reduced to ASSR level.

g. The Kalmyks are a Mongolian-speaking, Buddhist people who migrated in the 17th century to the north-western shores of the Caspian Sea, where they now have an ASSR. The Buriats and Yakuts are, respectively, a Mongol- and a Turkic-speaking people; they are two largest nationalities of Siberia, where both have their own ASSRs.

h. The ethnonym Tatar, once widely applied to diverse Turkic peoples, is now limited to two—the Crimean Tatars (resettled from Crimea to Central Asia toward the end of World War II) and the more numerous Tatars of the Volga, who are presumably meant here.

i. Daghestan: an area and ASSR on the north-western shores of the Caspian Sea in the North Caucasus. It is inhabited by an exceedingly great variety and intermixture of peoples, none of whom has a preponderance in the ASSR's population, which is called simply "peoples of Daghestan."

j. Bashkirs: a Turkic, Muslim nationality of the Volga-Urals region, closely related in many features to the Volga Tatars, the two nationalities having adjoining ASSRs.

k. Udmurts: a Finnic, ASSR-level nationality of the middle Volga region.

l. The Cherkess and Adygei, together with the Kabardinians, are three closely related peoples of the North Caucasus. The Cherkess and Kabardinians share a single literary language (Adygei have their own variant), and all three use the same ethnonym as a self-designation.

m. Komi: a Finnic people of ASSR status (the closely related Komi-Permiaks have an autonomous oblast) in northern European RSFSR.

n. That is, to the northeast of Leningrad.

o. Talysh: an Iranian-speaking ethnic group in Azerbaidzhan.

p. Chechens: one of the larger nationalities of the North Caucasus, sharing an ASSR with the closely related Ingush.

q. Uighurs: a Turkic, Muslim nationality living in the Sino-Soviet border region, primarily in the Kazakh SSR, but also in the Uzbek SSR and Kirghiz SSR. The majority of Uighurs live in the People's Republic of China, in the Xinjiang-Uighur Autonomous Region situated in the adjacent areas east of Soviet Central Asia.

Annotated by Lubomyr Hajda

Notes

1. In 1979 these numbered (in thousands): Veps—8.1; Koriaks—7.9; Mansi—7.6; Udin—6.9; Dolgans—5.1; Nivkhi—4.4; Selkup—3.6; Karaims—3.3; Ulchi—2.6; Saami—1.9; Udegei—1.6; Eskimos—1.5; Itelmen—1.4; Orochi—1.2; Ket—1.1; Nganasan—0.9; Yukaghir—0.8; Tofalar—0.8; Izhora—0.7; Aleuts—0.5; and Negidals—0.5.

2. These include, in particular, the Ukrainians, Latvians, Estonians and representatives of other nationalities driven into forced labor in Germany during the war years and after the war numbered among the so-called refugees and displaced persons.

3. The forecasts are based on data in: G. A. Bondarskaia, *Rozhdaemost' v SSSR*, pp. 93–96.

The Role of Education and Cultural Perspective in Interpersonal Relations among Nationalities *

L. M. DROBIZHEVA

Education is a primary means by which a world view and a society's prevailing moral standards are formed. It is not only a fund of knowledge, which substantially broadens one's understanding of the world, one's own and other peoples, and their place in the historical process, but also a purposeful training which can be used to fortify in men's consciousness friendly attitudes toward other peoples.

The role of education in overcoming narrowly national predilections and prejudices is not exhausted by the fact that it expands a man's consciousness and thus makes him less prone to prejudice.[1] A systematic education in the humanities conveys to people that ideology which prevails in their society. Therefore the link between education and attitudes toward other peoples in societies with differing social psychologies is not identical.[2] In Soviet society, education is entirely in the hands of the state and its aim is to foster in people a feeling of internationalism. Furthermore, the expansion of education overall tends to promote similar perceptions, identical responses to events and phenomena, and, finally, a common way of life—in effect, it forms the basis for mutual understanding in inter-nationality communication.

And although education in and of itself is not a guarantee against inter-nationality tensions, national prejudices are often associated, not only in social science literature but also in ordinary people's minds, with a certain degree of cultural backwardness.

It is natural to assume, then, that raising their level of learning is particularly significant for overcoming prejudices among the less-educated segments of the population. The results of the earliest ethnosociological surveys have borne out this hypothesis.[3] Now that such surveys are conducted in various regions of our country, it is possible to say that this conclusion holds for all these regions.

At the same time it has become quite apparent that the positive effects of education on inter-nationality relations have been more noticeable among peoples that had experienced a particularly rapid upsurge in education during the 1960s and 1970s, which raised the overall cultural level of the whole population and was accompanied by a high degree of social mobility (especially intergenerational, i.e., from parents to children). Among the peoples we studied, this was most typical of Moldavians and Uzbeks. Among the urban Moldavians and Uzbeks with a 7–10th grade education,

*Dukhovnaia obshchnost' narodov SSSR (Moscow, 1981), pp. 172–83. Russian text © 1981 by "Mysl'" Publishers.

the number of people favorably disposed to working in nationally mixed collectives was higher practically by a third than among the semiliterate and illiterate (to be sure, these groups included more people of the older generation).[4]

About 60% of the Moldavians (rural and urban) with up to a 4th-grade education considered the nationality of prospective marriage partners for their daughters, sons, sisters, or brothers not to be significant, while among those who completed grades 7 through 10, between 70% and 82% held this view. In Uzbekistan education had a positive effect on attitudes toward inter-nationality relations at the work place, where they depend more on the concrete present-day situation (and most viewed this situation favorably). On the other hand, it had no noticeable impact on attitudes toward mixed marriages. Endogamous marriages are solidly rooted in the overall system of traditional culture among Central Asian peoples. Attitudes toward inter-ethnic marriages have been deeply conditioned by traditions. These traditions are still strong among the older generation, which is, moreover, less well educated. And under conditions of deep-rooted, unfailing respect toward one's elders, for the younger and middle generations to "break" this tradition in the family is not easy.

A similar situation prevails in Georgia. Here education has had a positive effect primarily on attitudes toward social relations in the work place. Among urban Georgians with more than a 7th-grade education those who do not attach significance to nationality in social relations at work were about one-third more numerous than among people with seven years of schooling or less (in rural areas the tendency was the same).

But with regard to mixed marriages, in the Caucasus and Transcaucasia, just as in Central Asia, traditional attitudes are still quite strong, and they show little variation by levels of education.

The situation in Estonia is different. There the entire population has already possessed a certain minimum amount of education for a comparatively long historical period, while traditions had not erected as rigid a taboo on nationally mixed marriages as exists, say, among the Muslim peoples. Under conditions of Soviet rule, the entrenchment of the Marxist ideology of internationalism and the growth of education among workers occurred simultaneously, and this was conducive to overcoming prejudices, but changes, for reasons of history and cultural traditions, have not been as striking as in regions that in the past had lagged significantly behind in terms of cultural development. At present, differences in levels of education are not a significant factor in determining attitudes toward inter-nationality relations, either among Estonians or Russians, or other nationalities represented in Estonia. Among rural Estonians attitudes toward mixed marriages differ not at all by levels of education. In the cities, better-educated people (those with an incomplete secondary, secondary, and higher education) object categorically to mixed marriages more rarely than the less educated strata of the population (those with an education through the 7th grade) (19% versus 30%).

Among the Russians residing in other regions of the country, as also among the Ukrainians (insofar as we may judge on the basis of those who live in Moldavia), education has an effect on overcoming prejudices, but as was the case among

Estonians, differences in attitudes toward inter-nationality communication between groups with different levels of education are slight, especially in the cities.

Thus, among the Russians (in Georgia and Moldavia) and Ukrainians (in Moldavia), attitudes toward interethnic relations at work are not markedly influenced by education. They are somewhat less favorable only in the group of semi-literates (and these do not exceed 4–5% of the population). As for attitudes toward informal inter-nationality contacts, they show improvement as the educational level among these nationalities rises (about 70% or more of the Ukrainians with a secondary or higher education do not consider nationality a significant factor in the decision to marry, and some 55% of those with an education through the 7th grade; for the Russians the comparable figures are about 80% for those with a higher or secondary education, and about 70% for those with a 7th-grade education or less. In Georgia, among the urban Russians some 10% of the total have a totally negative view of mixed marriages, but 18% of the semi-literates).

In the rural areas of Saratov Oblast, of Russians with an education of more than four years, 90% attach no significance to nationality in relations in the workplace and 65–73% in marriage; of those with four years of education or less, the figures are 73%—at work and 60%—within the family.[5]

These sociocultural situations show a distinctive cast in the light of variations in attitudes toward inter-nationality contact by age groups. There is a general tendency among the nationalities for favorable attitudes and real inter-nationality contacts to increase among the youth and people of middle age in comparison with the older generation.

These age-specific differences are related to differences in levels of education and type of socio-occupational activity. Among nationalities that in the past had especially low educational levels, the older age groups, those that grew up in the prerevolutionary period or in the first two decades of Soviet rule, still show the effects of former cultural backwardness. In these groups there are more people with low levels of education and occupational skills and with a limited experience of intercultural contact, and this cannot help but find reflection in some measure of conservatism in their attitudes toward inter-nationality relations. That is why the differences in attitudes toward inter-nationality relations between the middle and younger generations on the one hand and the older generation on the other are more pronounced in those cases when the peoples coming into contact are those whose cultures in the past were fundamentally dissimilar but whose relations expanded markedly in recent decades (in the case of Uzbeks for example, those favorable disposed toward such contacts are one-third again as many among those under 50 as those over 60).

At the same time, in regions where the overall situation with regard to inter-nationality relations over the last 15–20 years has been more stable, and a certain minimum of education had long prevailed among the nationalities—as, for example, in Estonia—intergenerational differences in interethnic attitudes and contacts are less pronounced. Among the Estonians there are not such differences in levels of culture between the middle and older generations on the one hand and the young generation on the other that are encountered in the two abovementioned republics, which in the past had lagged behind in the levels of education of their inhabitants.

In other urbanized regions, in Tataria, for example, we also observed smaller intergenerational variations in attitudes toward interethnic relations among the urban population. In the villages of the Tatar ASSR, however, where the cultural backwardness of the past still made itself felt, an increase in favorable attitudes toward inter-nationality relations in the younger age groups was quite apparent.[6]

Among rural Estonians as well, there is a tendency for attitudes toward interethnic contact to improve in the younger and middle-aged cohorts, in comparison with their elders. Thus, among Estonians sixty years of age or older 64% would not object to having close relatives enter into nationally mixed marriages, while for those aged 40–49 the figure was 68%, and for young people aged 20–24 it was 78.4%. The coefficient of correlation between indicators of reciprocal information attests to a link between interethnic attitudes and differences in age.

Among the rural inhabitants of Estonia variations in attitudes toward inter-nationality relations at work also correlate with age.[7]

It is a fundamentally important fact that all these nuanced differences exist against a background of overwhelmingly friendly, favorable interpersonal relations. This is revealed in the virtual absence of nationality-based conflicts in multinational (work) collectives, in mutual assistance rendered by people of various nationalities—so often mentioned by the respondents during our interviews—and in the widespread ties of friendship and even kinship.

Education is only one of the most obvious indices of people's level of culture, and it is not, of course, the only factor that helps expand one's cultural horizons and overcome prejudices. Also important is the totality of sociopolitical and cultural information which provides an objective basis for comparisons between various national features, and a broader historical view of the experience of neighboring peoples—namely, which wards off a narrowly national approach to understanding various events and phenomena. The spread of bilingualism and the acquisition of Russian as the language of inter-nationality communication also serve this end.

In regions with a rapidly changing and more dynamic cultural environment, the spread of total cultural information, as well as education, has had a more pronounced impact on overcoming national prejudices among people.

Thus among Uzbeks who read literature of a more serious psychological content, watch television, either selectively or regularly, and know Russian in addition to their native language, the number who have friends belonging to other nationalities and exhibit a positive attitude toward inter-nationality relations (including informal relations) is one and a half to two times higher (both in urban and rural areas) than among those who do not have such cultural habits.

In the case of Moldavians—among whom 80–90% of the urban workers attach no significance to the nationality of their co-workers—the breadth of cultural perspective on inter-nationality relations is, generally speaking, more difficult to detect.[8]

Among the Estonians as well, the breadth of cultural perspective has a more pronounced impact on the everyday sphere of social relations. The most significant indicator of the Estonians' cultural perspective is the extent to which they read literature (virtually everyone here watches television to the same extent, the intelligentsia sometimes even to a lesser degree, being more discriminating in programs they find interesting). Among regular readers of literature, the number of those who attach no significance to the nationality of their co-workers is one-fifth higher and of those who are absolutely opposed to mixed marriages one-third lower than among the non-reading public.

In Transcaucasia and Central Asia attitudes toward nationally mixed marriages are most often dictated not by the degree of friendly feelings toward other nationalities, but by deeply rooted traditions of marrying within the national group. Among the peoples of these regions, therefore, greater exposure to cultural information, as also rising levels of education, do not affect attitudes toward mixed marriages more than they do attitudes toward relations at the workplace, although relations within the family are, on the whole, more closely linked to culture. Thus among Georgians, the share of those favorably disposed to inter-nationality contacts within the family and at work is respectively 17% and 15% higher among people with an active interest in cultural information than among the culturally passive part of the population.

As for the effect of cultural information on interethnic relations in various occupational groups, the survey results have shown that in the case of Moldavians, Georgians and (urban) Estonians it exerts a more markedly positive impact on workers engaged primarily in physical labor. This confirms the conclusion drawn earlier from the findings of the ethnosociological survey conducted in the Tatar ASSR, to the effect that series of cultural measures attenuates narrow-minded attitudes toward inter-nationality relations primarily among the less skilled (and less educated) strata of the population and a significant portion of the rural inhabitants.[9]

It now becomes clear that for those strata of the population for whom rather high levels of culture have already become a common, ordinary fact—for example, for the majority of urban Estonians and Russians living in the cities of Moldavia and Uzbekistan—an increase in the scope of general cultural knowledge alone does not play a noticeable role in the formation of attitudes toward interethnic relations, as shown by our statistical calculations.[10]

In multinational regions, a special role attaches to fluency in the language of inter-nationality communication as an element of general culture. For the non-Russian nationalities it serves not only as a medium of inter-nationality communication, but also as an important means by which to assimilate the store of knowledge and attainments built up by other peoples of the USSR and, to a great extent, by world civilization. That the spread of Russian, especially its acquisition by children of school age, has a positive effect on the reinforcement of internationalist views was established already in the course of the earliest ethnosociological studies conducted in the Tatar ASSR.[11] Public opinion surveys in other republics have confirmed this conclusion. The positive role of national-language–Russian bilingualism becomes especially apparent in areas where it is less prevalent. In the case of the Moldavians, no fewer than 70% of whom in the cities of the Moldavian SSR speak Russian fluently, attitudes toward inter-nationality relations are practically indistinguishable between different groups with varying degress of proficiency in Russian: 80.1% of those fluent only in their own language and 85% of those fluent both in Moldavian and Russian attach no significance to nationality in relations at work. Of urban Estonians and Georgians, 40–50% speak Russian fluently, and among them the number of those for whom the nationality of their comrades has no significance is somewhat larger (by 12–13%). Among rural inhabitants of these nationalities the differences are even more pronounced: over 80% of bilingual Georgians and Estonians are favorably disposed toward working in multinational collectives, while among those who speak Russian poorly or not at all the figure is lower by one fourth. According to the 1970 census, among most of the nations who have their own Soviet republics, the highest percentage of speakers of Russian as a second language occurs in the age groups 20–29 or 30–39. Among Moldavians aged 20–29 some 70% have command of fluent Russian, among Estonians aged 30–39—almost 60%, and among Georgians and Uzbeks—35%.[12] Of course, many more people may speak Russian than simply those who consider their knowledge of Russian to be fluent. Nevertheless, the potential for the dissemination of Russian as a medium of inter-nationality communication has by no means been yet exhausted.

A lack of knowledge, or even insufficient knowledge of the common language of communication constitutes both a real and a psychological barrier that constrains contact among people. Let us recall a situation familiar to almost everyone: when we receive people of another nationality, for all our possible good will, we ask someone who knows their language better than we to carry on the conversation. As a result those who already know the language best improve their knowledge even further, while all the rest remain in an "awkward" situation. That is why language training is most effective in childhood, inasmuch as children not only remember things more easily and imitate more freely, but usually are also not embarrassed to speak with mistakes, and often are more likely to show off what they know.

The extent of Russian language knowledge among individuals of non-Russian nationality varies, of course, in different socio-occupational groups. This is associated with education and the different ethnic environments in which people work. The more skilled population groups usually know Russian not only as a result of formal training, but also because both at the institutions where they were educated and at their place of work the collectives are usually multinational. For example, over 80% of the Moldavian intelligentsia in Kishinev not only speak fluently, but also think in Russian, while among unskilled workers engaged in physical labor only 53% have this degree of mastery. Such differences are even more pronounced among nationalities with fewer speakers of Russian. It follows that, for the less highly skilled population groups, in whose case other forms of "cultural prophylaxis" against prejudices (education and breadth of cultural interests) are less operative, the acquisition of the Russian language serves as a particularly important means to help attenuate a narrowly national perspective in attitudes and behavior. As relevant studies have shown, the most effective means for the diffusion of the Russian language in this case may be, and actually are, the school and the army.[13]

Concrete investigations of linguistic processes taking place in our country, including those conducted with the help of population surveys, evidence a general trend everywhere toward national-language–Russian bilingualism—that is, the continued functioning of native languages and the concurrent use of Russian as the language of inter-nationality communication.[14]

In this process, the extent of gravitation toward Russian varies among the republics. In most autonomous republics, as researchers have observed, the desire to have one's children taught through the medium of Russian exceeds the capacity of the school system to satisfy the demand.[15] In the union republics the "linguistic" predilections reflect more closely the actual proportions of pupils in schools with either the national language or Russian as the language of instruction, as well as in so-called dual schools. But even in the republics with a prevailing gravitation to the national language for purposes of instruction (e.g., in Georgia), there are more parents who wish to provide their children with an education in Russian or to send them to schools in which some classes are held in the national language and others in Russian, than such schools can actually accommodate (over 35% versus 20%).

As is well known, in recent years the governments of several union republics have adopted special measures to improve the study of the Russian language. In particular, special decrees were passed by the governments of the Kirghiz and Georgian SSRs.

Judging from the results of our surveys, a gravitation toward instruction through the medium of Russian correlates with an overall predisposition toward inter-nationality relations. Thus, among Georgians who consider it better for their children to be taught in some classes in the national language and in others in Russian, or simply entirely in Russian, the number of those who do not attach any importance to nationality in relations at work is one-third higher than among those who prefer to have their children's schools conducted in Georgian.

Thus, orientation toward instruction through the medium of Russian can serve as a kind of tentative index of attitudes toward other nationalities, although, of course, the need for one or another language is dictated primarily by objective circumstances—the ethnic environment, opportunities for further study, etc.

The ethnic environment also determines in large measure the extent to which Russians and members of other nationalities know the language of the titular nationality of the republics in which they live. This is evidenced by the fact that according to the 1970 all-union census, in the Armenian and Lithuanian SSRs, where the proportion of Russians is lower than in the other union republics, the percentage of urban Russians who declared the language of the titular nationality to be their mother tongue was greater than the percentage of members of the titular nationality declaring Russian as their mother tongue.[16]

It must be emphasized that for the Russian residents of the various republics as well, knowledge of a second language, which in such cases means the language of the numerically dominant nationality, is very important—important not only for inter-nationality linguistic contact but also for sociopsychological adaptation overall. The Russian population of Estonia represents a case in point: among Russians who know Estonian the share of those who attach no significance to nationality in daily practical relations is not less than one-third higher than among those who do not.

The results of our interviews with the Russians of Georgia also show that, among Russians who know Georgian, and especially "old residents," a widespread preference for life in Georgia, and their attitudes toward inter-nationality relations and toward the traditions of the local population are notably favorable.

Promotion of bilingualism and education, and more intense inculcation of cultural habits—these are all measures that, while undoubtedly laborious to implement, are sufficiently amenable to state and social regulation. And in fact these ways of influencing people's beliefs and behavior have always been utilized, but it is perfectly clear that their potential is far from exhausted. It is only a question, therefore, of a more careful attention to regional peculiarities which are bound up with the ethnic structure of the given population, historico-cultural conditions and the concrete social context of social relations, and also to the need for differentiated measures in the realm of culture to enhance their effectivenss among various socio-occupational groups, in urban and in rural areas. A more complicated and even less well studied problem is the relationship between the content of cultural information which so to speak "goes out" to the workers and their attitudes toward inter-nationality relations. We will try to examine this problem in more detail.

Notes

1. I. S. Kon, in his critique of foreign studies of interethnic relations, has correctly noted that education "makes man's thinking more flexible and thus less stereotyped." I. S. Kon, "Psikhologiia predrassudkov," *Novyi mir*, 1966, no. 9, p. 197.

2. J. Harding and his colleagues note that many Western sociologists have established a generally negative correlation between levels of education and prejudice among most people. At the same time they cite examples of positive results achieved through "special education programs," which are designed to eliminate discrimination (we should note that these were implemented in the presence of other conditions conducive to interethnic contacts). (J. Harding, H. Proshansky, B. Kutner, and I. Shane, "Prejudice and Ethnic Relations," in: *The Handbook of Social Psychology*, vol. 5, 2nd ed., 1969, pp. 29, 60.

3. Iu. V. Arutiunian, "Konkretno-sotsiologicheskoe issledovanie natsional'nykh otnoshenii," *Voprosy filosofii*, 1969, no. 12; L. M. Drobizheva, "Sotsial'no-kul'turnye osobennosti lichnosti i natsional'nye ustanovki," *Sovetskaia etnografiia*, 1971, no. 3; and others.

4. That such differences in inter-nationality attitudes are linked to education and not only age is evidenced by the fact that age-specific differences in the share of individuals with a positive attitude toward inter-nationality relations (even at opposite poles) are considerably smaller (e.g., among Moldavians aged 60 and older it is 7% lower).

5. We noted the same tendencies in Tataria. See *Sotsial'noe i natsional'noe*. Opyt etnosotsiologicheskikh issledovanii po materialam Tatarskoi ASSR, Moscow, 1973, pp. 288–289.

6. See *Sotsial'noe i natsional'noe*, pp. 285–287.

7. The share of those who thought that the national composition of their work collective was unimportant was 10% higher in the group under 30 years of age than in the age group 60 and older.

8. The correlation coefficient for these indicators of "level of culture" and attitudes toward interethnic contacts was statistically significant here only for attitudes toward mixed marriages. The correlation of the indicators was calculated on the basis of Joule coefficients. Two indicators of cultural interests and exposure to cultural information were selected: the reading of literature as the most significant indicator of the level of cultural interest, and television viewing as the most popular form of cultural recreation.

9. See Iu. V. Arutiunian, "Konkretno-sotsiologicheskoe issledovanie natsional'nykh otnoshenii," *Voprosy filosofii*, 1969, no. 12; L. M. Drobizheva, "Sotsial'no-kul'turnye osobennosti lichnosti i natsional'nye ustanovki," *Sovetskaia etnografiia*, 1971, no. 3.

10. The calculations were done using Student's *t*-variable criterion.

11. Iu. V. Arutiunian, "Konkretno-sotsiologicheskoe issledovanie natsional'nykh otnoshenii," *Voprosy filosofii*, 1969, no. 12, p. 133; *Sotsial'noe i natsional'noe*, pp. 268, 290.

12. *Itogi Vsesoiuznoi perepisi naseleniia 1970 g.*, vol. 4, p. 360.

13. See I. Bruk and M. N. Guboglo, "Faktory rasprostraneniia dvuiazychiia u narodov SSSR," *Sovetskaia etnografiia*, 1975, no. 5.

14. On this subject there is already a considerable literature. Some works have taken into account the most recent tendencies and attempted some projections. See, for example, S. I. Bruk and M. N. Guboglo, "Dvuiazychie i sblizhenie natsii v SSSR," *Sovetskaia etnografiia*, 1975, no. 4; *Sovremennye etnicheskie protsessy v SSSR*, 2d ed., Moscow, 1977; M. N. Guboglo, *Razvitie dvuiazychiia v Moldavskoi SSR*, Kishinev, 1979; and others.

15. M. I. Kulichenko, "Natsii i natsional'nye otnosheniia v SSSR na sovremennom etape," *Voprosy istorii*, 1971, no. 9, p. 23; *Sotsial'noe i natsional'noe*, pp. 240–241.

16. *Itogi Vsesoiuznoi perepisi naseleniia 1970 g.*, vol. 4, pp. 12–15.

National Self-awareness

The Basis on Which It Is Formed and the Sociocultural Factors Stimulating Its Development *

L. M. DROBIZHEVA

Anthropologists, sociologists, historians, and philosophers have all recently been interested in the study of national self-awareness.[1]

The scientific and practical significance of the study of this phenomenon in our multinational country is evident. As noted in the documents of the Communist Party, the growth of national self-awareness among the people of the USSR is an objective, lawful process. But society has an interest in not permitting it to become exaggerated.[2] For this to be achieved it is important to know the basis and the mechanism of its formation, potential factors stimulating its growth, and those real situations that, while promoting the natural development of national self-awareness, do not impede amicable relations between national groups, or, conversely, those situations that disrupt this harmony.

It is of course not possible to examine all these questions within a single essay. Our purpose is only to combine a theoretical treatment of problems with empirical findings from ethnosociological studies, and in the process attempt to determine why, as ethnically specific traits tend to diminish in a culture, national self-awareness does not lose the soil in which it grows,[3] as well as to form an idea of how the base of formation of national self-awareness changes, and what sociocultural factors may stimulate its development under present-day conditions.

It has been stated in the literature that national self-awareness has two aspects, ideological and psychological, and functions both at the level of the community at large and at the level of the individual.[4] Of course one cannot completely separate the study of these two levels of national self-awareness, as investigators have indeed justly pointed out. The self-awareness of a national community as "a functioning reality is manifested only if it is given effective form in the thought of individual people. In a word, it would be incorrect both to equate the self-awareness of an national community with the national self-awareness of an individual, but also to give the differences between them an absolute status."[5] A concrete study of national self-awareness at the level of the individual person has man as its object, i.e., man as the representative of a national community or, more accurately, the individual person in a group.

The national self-awareness of the individual is an awareness by the subject of the totality of his national (ethnic) ties and his relation to them.[6] It is a component part of the structure of the self-awareness of the individual as a whole. Psychologists

*Sovetskaia etnografiia, 1985, no. 5. Russian text © by "Nauka" Publishers.

distinguish three components in self-awareness: cognitive (knowing oneself), emotional and normative (relation to oneself) and regulatory (the individual's self-regulation of his own behavior).[7] But studies that take into account all these components on the basis of samples that are sufficiently representative for inter-ethnic comparisons have not, as far as we know, been carried out in Soviet social psychology.

To address the problems put forth in this essay, it is important to have a substantive description of national self-awareness, and to know the substantive structure of the ideas and knowledge people regard as reflecting their bonds to the national group, and their attitude to those bonds. Hence in defining the structural elements of national self-awareness we use definitions from the anthropological and historical literature.

These elements have been singled out in the context of an understanding of national self-awareness in the narrow sense as national self-determination or identification, or also in the broad sense to which scholars who have uttered views on this question are now inclined.[8] Even in the latter case the set of elements varies in composition: some authors see them in more general terms, others in more concrete terms. Of course the latter is more appropriate for an empirical study. Iu. V. Bromlei in his "Essays on a Theory of an Ethnos" has provided the fullest notion of national self-awareness such as would be suitable for the search for an operational definition and for indicators reflecting the elements of its structure. The structure of national self-awareness also contains elements such as national identification,[9] "an idea of the typical features of one's own community, its properties as as whole, and about the common historical past of a people. As regards ethnosocial formations (nations are such formations), these have a territory in common, and the idea of 'one's native land' is also a part of self-awareness. The same may be said about belonging to the same state. Awareness of being part of a common state may be a part of national self-awareness, or interact with it, depending on the specific historical political situation in which the people of a particular national identity live. Ideas about one's own ethnic group are not simply the sum of certain features; they also determine a 'normative relation to them. . .'"[10] Hence one can speak of a conscious relation to the material and spiritual values of an ethnic groups,[11] its achievements, and how it is guided by them as if these things were an independent element. Finally, an awareness of national interest is an important element in national self-awareness.[12] As I. S. Kon observed, "self-awareness entails a de facto unity, a continuity, and a consistency in attitudes and value orientations, consciously perceived as personal interests and inclinations."[13] Practically all the elements are linked in some measure to feelings, moods, perception, attitudes, and orientations. We shall attempt to examine all these elements on the basis of findings of ethnosociological studies and in the light of the principal aspects of the theory of self-awareness:[14] people's conscious perception of their national identity, their idea about the traits characteristic of their ethnic group, and finally the normative value, the ideological substance of national self-awareness.

A concrete study of national self-awareness is complicated above all because it is difficult to find indicators that are appropriate to each of its elements. Even among one people, it may show up as pride in historical figures and war heroes, it may accumulate around the anniversary of a major historical event, or it may concentrate on the celebration of a song or the name of an athlete who had won world acclaim. It focuses on different symbols for different peoples during the same period—for example, on language among the French Canadians, on religion among the northern Irish, on establishing one's own state among peoples who have struggled against colonial dependence, etc. At the individual level, national self-awareness will vary not only depending on age, but also on the particular situations in which a person may find himself. All these nuances must be taken into account in both studying and interpreting the phenomenon of national self-awareness. Still, investigators have attempted to find some more or less stable manifestations of this phenomenon. For instance they have assumed that as the phenomena of the external world are reflected in consciousness, their meaning for the individual, and his attitude to them are also defined.[15] This is reflected in the formation of the corresponding attitudes, value orientations, interest, ambitions, and feelings. Consequently, delimiting these phenomena and the actions in which they are expressed can be useful for the study of the self-awareness of the individual, including national self-awareness. While fully aware that the accuracy of attempts to pinpoint national self-awareness can only be relative (because of the limited number of indicators used in the study, as well as the rather narrow field of investigations), let us nevertheless attempt to generalize data on how each of the elements in national self-awareness functions, as well as data on the objective basis on which it grows.

We possess representative data on the nations and the main groups of non-indigenous nationalities in the union republics of the RSFSR, Uzbek SSR, Georgian SSR, Moldavian SSR, and Estonian SSR, which were studied in the course of the All-Union Ethnosociological Investigation carried out in 1971–82 by the Sector on Concrete Sociological Research of the Institute of Ethnography of the USSR Academy of Sciences.[16] Ethnic identification was studied among the Udmurts[17] as well as the Karelians and Veps in the Karelian ASSR.[18] Although the groups in which we studied the particular elements of national self-awareness were not completely compatible (the elements of national self-awareness were more fully presented in their interrelationships during the second set of studies by the Sector of Sociological Research of the Institute of Ethnography of the USSR Academy of Sciences in 1979–82 in the capitals of the union republics), nonetheless the material accumulated does permit certain conclusions to be drawn.

Even before all the elements in national self-awareness had been delimited theoretically, investigators had concentrated on national identification, which they used as a reference in judging the development of self-awareness of people of a particular national group. Conscious perception of one's national identity is truly one of the most obvious manifestations of national self-awareness. However, to evaluate the importance of this indicator, the following important circumstance must be methodologically borne in mind. As a person develops in interaction with his environment, he acquires a notion of the reality around him, or, as psychologists say, an "image of the world," and an image of his "self," as a part of the image of the world takes form.[19] Hence one's idea of one's national identity is only part of one's self-image. The importance of this part for the individual is relative to other aspects of an individual's identity: his perceived membership in a class, a professional stratum, a local community, etc. The national group does not always fulfill critically important social functions, as the real social group, class, socio-professional stratum, etc. may do. If social and national divisions do not coincide, if there are no rival social groups that differ ethnically, if there are no interethnic conflicts and tensions, membership in a national community becomes for the individual, if not a formal criterion, in any case an incomparably less important attribute than his membership in a sociopolitical group or collective. The distinctive feature of the sociopolitical situation in which a national community finds itself determines how clearly people perceive their national identity.

In normal conditions, or more precisely, where there are no tensions and "external pressure" toward national identification, cultural differences of which people become aware in the process of inter-national comparisons and contrasts become more important. This is of particular interest for anthropologists so far as it will shed light on the interaction between the nationally specific features currently operating in a culture and their reflection in national self-awareness. In analyzing the data from specific studies, let us first dwell on the distinctness of national identification, since this indicator is most often used in assessing the basis of national self-awareness in general, as well as for evaluating the stability of the ethnic characteristics of an ethnic group.

First of all, the degree of national identification will differ appreciably from one people to another; this is related to the conservation of specific ethnocultural traits, which by no means tend to change at a uniform rate, as is sometimes imagined. This conclusion is quite obvious if we compare materials on Georgians in Tbilisi (i.e., that part of the Georgian population which, it may be forecasted, will tend to maintain intact ethnic traits), the urban Udmurts (representatives of a nation with respect to which, according to specialists, while it is suffering a gradual decline in ethnic sensibility, in the near future we can scarcely expect a sharp decline in the ethnicity of the people as a whole),[20] the Karelians and Veps in the Karelian Autonomous SSR (where the integrational processes in the culture are most pronounced, according to anthropologists). Among the Karelians, the Veps, and to a certain extent the Udmurts, the importance of those attributes with regard to which persons of these nationalities identify themselves with their people is relatively minor (32–35% responded that it was the native language that kept them close to their people, 9–12% said that it was customs and rituals, and 6–18% said it was psychological characteristics[21]); 80% of those interviewed in Karelia had never given a thought to what linked them to their people.[22] Among the Georgians, however, the picture was completely different: over 80% of them said that it was language that bound them to their people, over 70% named customs and rituals, and over 50% said that they were bound by intellectual culture, character traits, and place of residence. No more than 10% of Georgians had any difficulty answering such questions. Of course one must take into account who the respondents were. More educated people, who more often come into contact with peoples of other nationalities, of course give a fuller and more aware set of attributes defining their identification. But clearly, in the present case the differences are by no means solely attributable to the social characteristics of the respondents. Only a third of Udmurts find it important to observe traditional wedding customs and prefer folk dances and songs; about 40% expressed an interest in Udmurt professional music and 30% read books of Udmurt authors; 69.5% of the urban population considered the Udmurt language their native language, but 5.3% spoke the language on the job, and 15% spoke it at home.[23] The Georgians had another basis for identification. According to the findings of ethnosociological studies, no less than half of all Georgians, even those living in the cities, prefer to keep to ethnic wedding customs, 73% observe tradition in the relations between husband and wife and the family, 61% do so in the norms of social intercourse between parents and children,[24] 99% of Georgians consider the Georgian language their native language,[25] over 90% speak it at home, and over 80% speak it at work. Although there is a trend toward democratization in relations between family members, and bilingualism is widespread among the younger population and in the more highly educated groups of the population, nevertheless the native language and the ethnic culture, even at the everyday level, function quite stably. Thus, although there is a tendency for the specific ethnocultural traits to play a decreasing role as a basis for ethnic identification, it would be unwarranted to exaggerate the importance of this process. Among all peoples, however, language remains a stable basis for national identification.

As we have said, we have assumed that national self-awareness was broader than awareness of membership in a specific ethnic group. It also includes elements and attributes with regard to which a person associates himself with a specific ethnic community. These include conceptions about the character traits of a particular people—so-called autostereotypes—schematized, simplified notions, characteristic of the common consciousness, and ascribed to all members of a community without sufficient awareness of potential differences between them. These take shape in the process of contrast and comparison with notions about other peoples (ethnic stereotypes or heterostereotypes). Ideas about one's native land and a common historical destiny are also attributes with regard to which a person associates himself with his ethnic group.

A conception of typical traits of one's ethnic group is a basis for association with it. Of course, such notions change and depend first of all on functional, typical features inherent not only to the ethnic group, but also to the social type of personality characteristic for the society and for each stage in its historical development. The individual person, the individual bearer of social qualities, is a complex unity of the individual, the private and the social. In studying mass phenomena and processes we must abstract from the individual, but the specific (in the particular case the ethnically specific) must be at the center of our attention. The content and intensity of everyday notions concerning the traits of one's own and other ethnic groups, i.e., the characteristics and sources of behavior ascribed to the group (in social psychology this phenomenon is described as causal attribution in the process of interpersonal perception)[26] depend in an essential way on the social and political situation in a society, and to some extent on historical traditions. This was persuasively demonstrated by I. S. Kon in his article "Ethnic Character: Myth or Reality?"[27] The formation of autostereotypes and ethnic stereotypes is based on an everyday psychological interpretation of intercultural differences in people's behavior.

Under present-day conditions, given the broad variety of individual distinctive features, social characteristics[28] shared by all citizens, rather than national characteristics, have assumed prime importance among the Soviet people. This phenomenon is also reflected in people's conceptions of the traits of their own ethnic group (autostereotypes). For instance, in Moldavia, when persons of non-indigenous nationalities were interviewed in 1976, 20% of those interviewed did not even answer the question of what qualities they thought were inherent to people of their nationality (the question was formulated as follows: "All peoples have features that are common to them specifically, but there are also characteristics that are related to the historical past, and to the distinctive features of culture and character. What features do you think are characteristic of people of your nationality?"). About 50% of those interviewed experienced difficulties in answering inasmuch as they gave stereotyped responses, naming qualities included in a leading question, i.e., a question with a prompting. (The question was formulated as follows: "Below are a list of qualities inherent in people of all nationalities. Please select those that in your opinion are especially characteristic for people of your own nationality.") Then a set of the most frequently mentioned characteristics and traits was given, e.g., goodness, hospitality, tidiness, industriousness, etc. Only one or two features characteristic for their ethnic group were cited by 20% of the respondents. Even in the case of Tbilisi Georgians, who had an autostereotype with a broader range of traits than other indigenous nationalities in the capitals of union republics, half of the respondents mentioned only three or four traits. We will not dwell here on the content of autostereotypes and ethnic stereotypes (i.e., conceptions of other people) since this must be a subject of a special analysis. The important point for now is that the conception of those specific features presumed to be typical of representatives of an ethnic group is relatively weak in national self-awareness. This phenomenon is also a result of the internationalization of people's style of life, and of behavioral norms and values, and a reflection of favorable inter-ethnic relations in the country.

Psychological methods help to bring to light fuller and richer autostereotypes and national stereotypes held by representatives of ethnic groups that are in direct contact with one another.[29] However, these methods are not sufficiently compact and are hardly suitable for large-scale studies. In addition, it is difficult in using them to take into account all the ethnocultural characteristics of every ethnic group, and this often reduces the possibility of conducting reliable comparative studies. But the instruments used in mass interviews provided, as we have said, a basis for drawing comparable conclusions concerning conceptions, on the whole not very vivid, of the specific psychological features of an ethnic group. This may of course indicate that these features have faded and have become less important for people than other personal characteristics. The "fading" of ethnic autostereotypes does not mean that the ideas a particular people have about man, his objective world, and his system of values have also undergone a corresponding blurring. The study of such conceptions could be fruitful, but this is already another way of looking at the specific properties of an ethnic group with a view toward arriving at a scientific understanding of them.

As regards those elements of national self-awareness such as a conception of common territory, common state, and a consciousness of a bond with preceding generations of one's people (which in the sociopsychological literature is defined as an element of the psychological time of the individual person[30]), these of course are also subject to change, but each of these elements undoubtedly has more stability in its objective foundations than do "ethnic stereotypes." Even persons living outside the main territory of settlement of their people usually preserve a conception of that territory as something with which they can identify. Thus practically a third of Russians living in Tbilisi considered the RSFSR to be their homeland [rodina] (according to results of surveys in the early 1980s). Of course a conception of one's homeland is considerably broader than a conception of the territory where one's people live. Hence most Russians in Tbilisi (over 55%) considered the Soviet Union as a whole to be their homeland. Still, the majority (30% of 45%) of those for whom this conception was more concretely and locally defined called the republic where their people mainly lived their homeland.

Among nations for whom ethnically specific traits were relatively more firmly entrenched in their culture, e.g., the Georgians, a common territory was not among the most important attributes of identification (as pointed out, in Tbilisi only 50% of Georgians questioned named place of residence as a basis for identification). But among those nationalities experiencing inter-ethnic integrational processes especially intensely and for whom ethnocultural attributes were losing their consolidating role (e.g., among the Karelians and Veps, especially those engaged in intellectual work) the attribute "homeland" was among the identifiers of primary importance.[31] In principle, the importance of attributes—i.e., common territory, common state— may vary, but in the USSR the base for a conception about them remains.

As regards concepts of a common historical past, the base on which they rest is naturally retained. Roughly two-thirds of Georgians in Tbilisi answering the question "What identifies you with your people?" named a common historical past. An interest in literature about the past of one's own people may to a certain extent serve as an indicator of this element of national self-awareness. This indicator was quite high, according to results of ethnosociological surveys in the 1970s. Among books grouped according to seven topics (society and politics, some area of specialization, the psychology of human relations, love and friendship, adventures and fantasy, war, and literature on the past of one's people), Georgians showed the most interest in literature about the past of their people. This type of literature ranked second among the Uzbeks, third among the Estonians, and fourth among the Russians (although literature about war, which is also a part of history, was ranked in first place by the Russians).[32]

The desire to listen to or watch radio or television programs on this topic also testifies to interest shown in the history of one's own people. For example, among Moldavians, 70% showed this desire.

Of course the past is most often revived when people try to understand the present. The psychologists E. I. Golovakha and A. A. Kronik have cited M. Shaginian's statement: "How many times in my life has the past come up today and even tomorrow!"[33]

In interpreting ethnosociological data on a lively interest in the past, we of course must bear in mind the special circumstances in which this element of ethnic self-awareness functions. Ethnic autostereotypes and heterostereotypes are scientifically defined as the ascription of specific characteristics to all members of an ethnic group without sufficient awareness of potential differences; it is understood that the danger exists that they may be used politically to set people against one another. Propaganda therefore deliberately downplays these stereotypes. But society's attitude to the historical past is different. Historical events are assessed from class positions, thus serving as a basis for instilling patriotism, and are widely used in propaganda. This element of national self-awareness, then, is continually broadening its basis, giving the latter a more pronounced ideological aspect; but the same is true about the attitude to the cultural values and achievements of one's people. As noted in the literature,[34] ethnosociological studies have found quite a marked diversity in attitudes to ethnic intellectual culture. Among the nations studied in the project, "Optimization of sociocultural conditions of development and the convergence of nations in the USSR," a little more than a third of Estonians, as many as 60–70% of Georgians and Moldavians, and over 80% of Uzbeks expressed a preference for national music and dances (the data are for the urban population, for whom internationalization processes are more active). Of course attitudes to ethnic music and dances, as well as to customs and rituals, do not fully correspond to their actual popularity. This attitude rather reflects an orientation to the ethnically specific elements in the intellectual culture of a particular ethnic group. Comparative findings on rural and urban populations, age groups, and nations differing in the extent to which they have been caught up in urbanization processes indicate that the basis for this element of ethnic self-awareness is narrowing in terms of parameters of traditional culture (although it is still quite important, especially among indigenous populations of Central Asia, the Transcausasus, and Moldavia), but with regard to the parameters of professional culture it is expanding.

Of course we are fully aware that a preference for national and especially folk music or dances is a rather arbitrary indicator of national self-awareness. One can love national music and dances and perform them, without perceiving them as important values for oneself, and, on the other hand, one may be interested in conserving them without listening to this music or performing the dances. To single out groups having this interest one can try to include in their definition those people who are similarly oriented toward the ethnic factor in the different spheres (intellectual, material) and forms (e.g., music, dances, literature, socionormative culture) of culture. The number of people with such pronounced ethnic cultural orientations decreases considerably even if indicators of material importance for national self-

awareness are included among the set of parameters. The temptation to encompass
the largest number of indicators is very great. We have visually observed how even
some elements of the material culture (skull caps, etc.) acquire a symbolic ethnic
value. But as soon as we begin to study this phenomenon using a large material
sample, we find that the group of people who, say, wear elements of ethnic clothing
(with the exception of the Central Asian peoples) is very small, and adding only this
indicator immediately reduces the proportion of people with a full set of orientations
to ethnic forms of culture (8–10% among Georgians and Moldavians, and even less
among Estonians and Russians). It is therefore necessary to select those attributes of
the relation to ethnic culture that are capable of close association with an expression
of national self-awareness among the broad masses of the population. One such
attribute used in ethnosociological studies was, in our view, the respondents' choice
of their favorite outstanding cultural figures. Of course in their choices respondents
in all republics named writers, scientists, composers, and artists not only of their
own nationality, but also some who had made contributions to Soviet and world
culture. But if defining the group of persons with preference predominantly for
personages of the ethnic culture (which may serve as a more weighty indicator of the
extent of ethnic self-awareness), we find that this group comprises 65–70% of
Estonians, Russians, Georgians, and Uzbeks, but only 22% of Moldavians. An
orientation to professional ethnic culture, and the attitude toward it, are obviously
connected with the level of development of that culture among each people, as well
as with the overall range of cultural interest of individuals. There is no evidence that
the base for relating to folk achievements is decreasing; on the contrary, not only are
outstanding artistic works of the past becoming the possession of ever-broader
masses, but even contemporary ethnic artistic culture is acquiring universal recognition and becoming an object of pride. These folk values and achievements are by no
means limited to artistic culture; economic accomplishments, the exploitation of
valuable national resources, scientific discoveries, etc. also rank with them.

The base for another, socially the most significant element in the structure of
national self-awareness, i.e., national interests, is closely linked to economic and
cultural progress. The areas of possible concentration of national interests expand
with the development of the objective world of which people of different national
communities are a part. A historical approach is, of course, necessary in analyzing
the emergence and development of self-awareness as a whole, but it is especially
fruitful with respect to national interests.

National interests are one of the most complex sociopsychological elements in
national self-awareness. Collective forms of activity, of which the individual is a
part, play a crucial role in the formation of these conscious interests and in transforming needs into interests. National interests are based on a range of different
interests—social, political, economic, intellectual, etc. It was no accident that the
Twenty-sixth Congress of the CPSU discussed giving heed to the interests of the
populations of the multi-ethnic Soviet republics, while at the same time the CPSU
Central Committee called attention to the fact that "all nations have the right to due
representation in their party and state bodies," and to the necessity to "probe more

deeply'' into the specific demands of citizens of nonindigenous nationalities in language, culture, and everyday life.[36] National interests may of course be manifested in the most varied areas of life, i.e., they are by no means confined to ethnocultural phenomena—their range is immeasurably broader, and though the nationally specific traits in cultural and everyday life may be diminishing, this range is not narrowing. It is another question that the areas of revival of national interests are mobile and can vary relatively rapidly in historical terms, for they are always dependent on social interests. Even for one and the same people, yesterday this may have been a struggle for state independence, but today it means buttressing economic interests, involvement in the development of culture, language, etc. In our view, national interests are linked to a phenomenon which S. A. Artiunov, M. V. Kriukov, and K. V. Chistov described as the capacity for ethnic self-awareness to revive the ethnic factor, especially in the intellectual life of a people.[37] Of course, it is primarily cultural figures who are involved in folk music ensembles created to revive and spread popular dances and songs, in disseminating artifacts of the material culture— whether that be a headdress or old areas of a city restored in the traditional style— and in the preservation of former geographic names as ethnic symbols. But we do not think that the popularity of these things can be explained solely in terms of people's need for a variety of impressions, or a tendency away from the standardization of modern life. All these phenomena, if they really undergo mass dissemination, exercise a consolidating function, and behind them are ethnic interests based on social needs of one type or another. It is no accident that in some places cafes decorated in an ethnic style become simply a place of leisure and eating, embroidered shirts are stocked in shops for tourists, while in other places, areas in a restored old city become the site for mass holidays, like Tbilisoba. Indeed, national interests have been very little studied with regard to nations and peoples, whether on the basis of historical or concrete sociological material, although this is an extremely timely political as well as sociopsychological theme.

The expansion and enrichment of the spheres of people's vital activity in today's society creates a basis for the potential expression of national interests. Of course this does not mean that national interests, which the broad masses of the population perceive as needs, are being manifested or will be making themselves felt more and more frequently in real life; everything depends on the social situation in the broad sense of the term. However, in the USSR national interests often coincide with the interests of the republics and the entire Soviet society in general.

Thus the objective basis of national self-awareness has been transformed (as the reader will be aware, we regarded this base not in itself but as far as possible in interrelation with the way it is reflected in people's consciousness). In fact, a number of objective reasons for subjectively perceived ethnicity will disappear, and above all conceptions concerning the traits and attributes of one's ethnic community. Autostereotypes, as we have seen, caused our respondents major difficulties and were most often limited to a small set of characteristics, indicating the predominance of general rather than particular (ethnic, socially significant) characteristics in the minds of Soviet people. Ethnically specific traits are becoming increasingly indistinct in a number of areas of the cultural and everyday life of peoples (this is one of the reasons for the ethnic paradox: as objective ethnicity disappears, subjective ethnicity grows). But let us take a closer look: the diminution in the role of that which is ethnically specific in everyday life is reflected for the most part in but one of the elements of national self-awareness, namely national identification. It has no essential importance even for such an element as the attitude to the material and intellectual values and achievements of one's people. In the orientation of individuals, the place of an ethnically colored traditional culture is replaced by their professional culture, even in secondary forms symbolizing traditional culture.

As we have seen, there is no evidence that the objective factors behind such elements of national self-awareness as the conception of a common historical past or living on a common territory, or even more so the national interests on which the entire public life of a people is based, are disappearing.

We are also quite aware that a very broad range of phenomena from economics to politics and ideology—and not only those of their components capable of assuming ethnic forms—rank among the changing conditions that influence self-awareness and determine people's life activities. These have been singled out inasmuch as national self-awareness is born and shaped as a "psychological mechanism" that incorporates individual existence into the life of society with its ethnic forms. As we concentrate our attention on the personal level of the functioning of national self-awareness we should continually bear in mind that a person's consciousness is formed and developed in an unbroken connection with public consciousness.[38] As B. F. Lomov says: "Different types (forms) of public consciousness are in some way or other incorporated into the system of factors determining the mental development of the individual, exerting a considerable influence on shaping that individual's world view, on his social orientations, on his subjective personal attitudes, and on his consciousness as a whole, thereby regulating the individual's behavior in society. . . ."[39] Consciousness and self-awareness, including national self-awareness, are directly dependent not only on the changing conditions of an individual's life activities, but also on his own social activism.

If the objective reality reflected in national self-awareness, or its base, conventionally speaking, may be compared with the soil out of which this "plant sprouts," the phenomena attendant on an increased individual social activism will be the "moisture" stimulating its growth. Hence, an increase in people's level of education, skills, and knowledge, their penetration into more and more new spheres of activity, and their cultural activism—all these characteristics of the present stage of the life of peoples will lead to a growth in national self-awareness.

At the individual level, the relationship between an individual's social activism and the development of the individual components of his national self-awareness have not been subjected to a special study. But we can get some idea of the influence of people's engagement in social and cultural progress on the growth in their national self-awareness on the basis of the mass findings of concrete sociological studies. This influence is manifested, in particular, in the fact that the set of attributes in terms of which people identify themselves with their ethnic group is much fuller and varied in more educated and highly skilled groups. According to M. N. Guboglo, who made a special study of the importance of ethnic attributes for a national identification on a small sample of Moldavians, intellectual workers had a broader set of attributes of intellectual culture with regard to which they associated themselves with their ethnic group.[40] According to the data of A. A. Kozhanov, intellectual workers among the Karelians and Veps identify themselves ethnically in terms of these attributes twice as frequently as persons engaged in physical labor.[41]

V. V. Pimenov analyzed the results of studies made among the Udmurts and concluded that ethnic links were not only more pronounced among intellectuals, but that there was also an occupationally oriented combination of ethnic factors.[42]

People with a relatively low level of education replaced a definition of individual personal positions ("I am a Moldavian, hence . . .") with an attempt to explain group characteristics ("We Moldavians are, for example," followed by a list of traits), indicating the importance of education and knowledge in general for ethnic identification. People with a higher level of education did not have such definitions (our observations in this regard coincided with the results of Kozhanov's studies).[43] Ethnic self-awareness is also stimulated by such factors as education, which gives people an idea of the history of their own and other people, their language and their culture; by an attachment to literature, and the information provided by the mass media, which helps the individual to assimilate social experience; and finally by expanding direct contacts of individuals of different nationalities, facilitating inter-ethnic comparisons.

Knowledge as a product of the reflection of sociohistorical practice, and accepted norms, values, and judgments determine not only the national self-identification aspect of national self-awareness, as we discussed earlier, but also other elements in this self-awareness: conceptions of a common origin, a common historical fate, or a common territory, which also become richer as the level of education and individual activism increases. It is no accident that a common historical destiny is more often mentioned as an attribute that links a person to his people, and in particular, people from among the more educated strata of the population. Finally, national interests consciously perceived by the individual (in our view one of the most important elements characterizing the extent of national self-awareness) are also stimulated by an increase in people's social engagement and an expansion of the spheres of their activity. It is no accident that the ethnosociological studies carried out under the direction of Iu. V. Arutiunian showed that the most highly skilled people, the urban intelligentsia, and in particular, representatives of the scientific and humanistic intelligentsia, named the development of a national culture, the economic progress of nations, and the struggle against chauvinism and nationalism most frequently among the problems of prime social importance. Whereas only 2% of rural Molda-vians listed these problems, 13% of urban dwellers, including more than 20% of the intelligentsia, and 30% of the scientific and humanistic intelligentsia did so. These evaluations made in the Moldavian SSR were practically the same among both the Moldavian and the Russian intelligentsia. The same pattern was found in other republics. The more educated and highly skilled groups in a people, the more frequently such choices were found. None of these factors precluded that on the whole interests common to all peoples predominated, e.g., a strengthening of peace, the country's defense, strengthening of discipline, the ideological upbringing of youth, etc. A general Soviet self-awareness and Soviet interests are combined with their ethnic counterparts.

Thus, the gradual disappearance of specific ethnic traits from cultural and everyday life and the emergence in people of common human and common Soviet features is reflected in the set of national identification symbols and in the weak content of national and group autostereotypes. In actuality, the "grounds" for national identification change, but people continue nevertheless to identify themselves with some national group, and as their general competence and knowledge grows, they do so even more freely. For national self-awareness as a whole, moreover, "grounds" in the form of specific national traits in the cultural and everyday life of a people and in the form of its particular psychological characteristics in no way disappear. As we have seen, this base is much wider. The historic past of a people cannot disappear. The professional culture of nations, being national in form, develops dynamically. Nations' achievements in production, science, and culture multiply, and this forms the basis on which concepts of national values are preserved. The data show that the express orientation is toward national values mixed with orientation toward common Soviet and common human achievements; this is evidence that the process of intermixing of orientations is at work. The base of national interests is all the spheres of social life, and we cannot speak here of any sort of disappearance of "grounds." On the contrary, they are capable of growing stronger. This does not ignore the fact that national interests more often than not coincide with common Soviet interests.

Thus, the objective base of national self-awareness does not disappear, it simply changes. Indeed, the foundations for its continued growth expand. As noted in Communist Party documents: "The economic and cultural progress of all nations and nationalities is inevitably accompanied by the growth of national self-awareness. This is a natural, objective process. It is important, however, that the natural pride in acclaimed achievements does not degenerate into national arrogance or conceit and does not give rise to self-isolation and a disrespectful attitude toward other nations and nationalities."[44] The data from solid research, as we have seen, points to the expansion of factors that stimulate the growth of national self-awareness.

This article of course cannot claim to be a full explication of all factors capable of stimulating the development of national self-awareness. It is only an attempt to examine the existing findings of ethnosociological studies in a first approximation. The genesis and development of national self-awareness must be examined more thoroughly and concretely within the contexts of sociological, anthropological, and psychological conceptions. In particular, while acknowledging the importance of the ethnopsychological approach to the study of this phenomenon, we must nonetheless say that there do not yet exist the necessary conceptions for studying the mechanisms of its functioning, nor sufficient empirical data. But the ethnosociological and ethnographic data that have been accumulated already require a sociopsychological explanation.

As regards the relationship between the growth in national self-awareness and the development of inter-ethnic relations, this is a special question, which we have already touched upon.[45] Our conclusion was that with the favorable sociopolitical conditions in our country, national self-awareness does not hinder the development of amicable inter-ethnic relations. It can serve as a basis for strengthening both national and general Soviet patriotism. The task of society is to see to it that unfavorable social situations do not arise that could cause a hyperbolization of national self-awareness and split our peoples. The task of future research is to study ways to prevent such situations, as well as to explore ideological factors and the psychological mechanisms of development of national and general Soviet consciousness and their channeling into a positive interethnic interaction.

Notes

1. There is a very detailed historiographic review of studies on this problem in the book by K. N. Khabibulin, *Samosoznanie i internatsional'naia otvetstvennost'sotsialisticheskikh natsii. Uchebnoe posobie*, Perm, 1974; M. I. Kulichenko, *Rastsvet i sblizhenie natsii v SSSR. Problemy teorii i metodologii*, Moscow: "Mysl'" Publishers, 1981, pp. 86–101; Iu. V. Bromlei, *Ocherki teorii etnosa*, Moscow: "Nauka" Publishers, 1983, pp. 173–179.

2. *XXVI s"ezd Komunisticheskoi partii Sovetskogo Soiuza. Stenograficheskii otchet*, vol. 1, Moscow: Politizdat, 1981, pp. 74–75; Iu. V. Andropov, "Shest'-desiat let obrazovaniia SSSR," *Izbrannye rechi i stat'i*, Moscow: Politizdat, 1983, p. 11; *Materialy plenuma Tsentral'nogo komiteta KPSS 14–15 iiunia 1983 g*, Moscow: Politizdat, 1983, pp. 17, 18, 72.

3. We use the term "national self-awareness" not only because empirical studies have been carried out among the nations of the Soviet Union, but also because, as has been noted in the literature, the adjective "national" may be regarded as a derivative from both the word "nation"(in the broad sense) and the word "nationality"(the narrow sense, of the same status as the ethnic) (see Bromlei, p. 175).

4. A. F. Dashdamirov, *Natsiia i lichnost'*, Baku: Elm, 1976, pp. 137ff; Bromlei, p. 176; G. O. Zimanas, "Proletarskii internatsionalizm i mirovoi revoliutsionnyi protsess," *Kommunist* (Vilnius), 1970, no. 8, pp. 26–27.

5. Bromlei, p. 177.

6. Dashdamirov, *Natsional'nye momenty individual'nogo samosoznaniia*, dissertation for Candidate in Philosophy degree, Moscow: Institut Filosofii, AN SSSR, 1968, pp. 17–18; B. D. Parygin, *Osnovy sotsial'no-psikhologicheskoi teorii*, Moscow: "Mysl'" Publishers, 1971, pp. 128–29; A. A. Kozhanov, *Metodika issledovaniia natsional'nogo samosoznaniia*, dissertation for Candidate in History degree, Moscow: Institut Etnografii, AN SSSR, 1978, pp. 11–12.

7. I. I. Chesnokova, *Problema samosoznaniia v psikhologii*, Moscow: "Nauka" Publishers, 1977, pp. 30, 142; I. S. Kon, *V poiskakh sebia*, Moscow: Politizdat, 1984, pp. 29–30; V. V. Stolin, *Samosoznanie lichnosti*, Moscow, "MGU" Publishers, 1983, pp. 104–105.

8. Bromlei, *Etnos i etnografiia*, Moscow: "Nauka" Publishers, 1973, p. 97; idem, *Ocherki teorii etnosa*, p. 76; Dashdamirov, p. 137ff.; S. T. Kaltakhchian, *Leninism o sushchnosti natsii i puti obrazovaniia internatsional'noi obshchnosti liudei*, Moscow, 1969; Kulichenko, p. 94; V. V. Pimenov, *Udmurti. Opyt komponentnogo analisa etnosa*, Lenigrad: "Nauka" Publishers, 1977, pp. 202ff.

9. V. I. Kozlov sees membership in a national group not only as the principal attribute of national self-awareness, but as practically an all-embracing attribute. See Kozlov, "Problema etnicheskogo samosoznaniia i ee mesto v teorii etnosa," *Sov. etnografiia*, 1974, no. 2.

10. See Bromlei, *Ocherki teorii etnosa*, pp. 176, 182, 183, 189.

11. M. I. Kulichenko includes this element in the structure of national consciousness. But he also believes that national self-awareness is an awareness of the commonality of people "of themselves" (Kulichenko, p. 85), hence this element enters in the structure of "national self-awareness."

12. Kulichenko mentions as a component of the conscious perception of nations the necessity of achieving a self-awareness for defending national interests; see Kulichenko, p. 92.

13. I. S. Kon, *Sotsiologiia lichnosti*, Moscow: Politizdat, 1967, p. 56.

14. Studies by I. S. Kon played a major role in developing this theory. See Kon, "K probleme natsional'nogo kharaktera" in *Istoriia i psikhologiia*, Moscow: "Nauka" Publishers, 1971; idem, *Otkrytie "Ia"*, Moscow: Politizdat, 1978; idem, *V poiskakh sebia*; see also I. I. Chesnokova.

15. See S. L. Rubinshtein, *Bytie i soznanie*, Moscow: USSR Academy of Sciences, 1957, p. 244.

16. The director of the study and the author of the program "Optimization of sociocultural conditions of the development and convergence of nations in the USSR" was Iu. V. Arutiunian. In the broadest mass studies, problems of national self-awareness were not the cornerstone of investigation. The following works were devoted especially to it: A. A. Kozhanova; E. I. Klement'ev, *Sotsial'naia struktura i natsional'noe samosoznanie*, dissertation for Candidate in History degree, Moscow: Institut Etnografii, AN SSSR, 1975; I. A. Snezhkova, "K probleme izucheniia etnicheskogo samosoznaniie u detei i iunoshestva, "*Sov. etnografiia*, 1982, no. 1.

17. Pimenov.

18. Klement'ev; Kozhanova.

19. Kon, *Otkrytie "Ia."*; Rauste von Vyskht, M. L. "Obraz 'Ia' kak podstruktura lichnosti," in *Problemy psikhologii lichnosti*, Moscow: "Nauka" Publishers, 1982, p. 104.

20. Pimenov, p. 220.

21. Kozhanov, p. 89; Pimenov, p. 99.

22. Kozhanov, p. 88.

23. Pimenov, pp. 96, 97, 124, 174, 180, 191, 198.

24. Arutiunian, "O nekotorykh tendentsiiakh kul'turnogo sblizheniia narodov SSSR na etape razvitogo sotsializma," *Istoriia SSSR*, 1978, no. 4, p. 102.

25. *Chislennost'i sostav naseleniia SSSR*, Moscow: Statistika, 1984, p. 124.

26. See G. M. Andreeva, "Mezhlichnostnoe vospriiatie v usloviiakh sovmestnoi deiatelnosti," in *Problemy psikhologii lichnosti*, pp. 68, 71, 72.

27. *Inostrannaia literatura*, 1968, no. 9.

28. On the characteristic traits of the socialist type of personality, see G. Smirnov, "K. Marks o lichnosti, usloviiakh ee osvobozhdeniia i razvitiia," *Kommunist*, 1984, no. 13, p. 38.

29. An interesting study of autostereotypes and heterostereotypes was made on the basis of findings from an ethnically mixed group in the Checheno-Ingush ASSR by graduate student G. U. Ktsoeva at the Institute of Psychology of the USSR Academy of Sciences. See Ktsoeva, "Metody izucheniia etnicheskikh stereotipov," in *Sotsial'naia psikhologiia i obshchestvennaia praktika*, Moscow: "Nauka" Publishers, 1985.

30. See E. I Golovakha, and A. A. Kronik, "Psikhologicheskoe vremia lichnosti," *Znanie–Sila*, 1983, no. 9, pp. 25–27.

31. Khozhanov, p. 83.

32. S. S. Savoskul made an analysis of data from surveys on this attrubite.

33. Golovakha and Kronik, p. 26.

34. Arutiunian; L. M. Drobizheva, *Dukhovnaia obshchnost' narodov SSSR. Istorikosotsiologicheskii ocherk mezhnatsional'nykh otnoshenii*, Moscow: "Mysl'" Publishers, 1981; and others.

35. See: *Ob istoricheskom razvitii poznavatel'nykh protsessov*, Moscow, 1974; A. G.

Spirkin, *Proiskhozhdenie soznaniia*, Moscow: Gospolitizdat, 1960; and others.

36. *XXVI s"ezd Kommunisticheskoi partii Sovetskogo Soiuza. Stenograf. otchet*, vol. 1, Moscow, 1981, p. 75.

37. See Chistov, K. V. "Etnicheskaia obshchnost', etnicheskoe soznanie i nekotorye problemy dukhovnoi kul'tury," *Sov. etnografiia*, 1972, no. 3, p. 78; S. A. Arutiunov, "Ethnograficheskaia nauka i izuchenie kul'turnoi dinamiki," in *Issledovaniia po obshchei etnografii*, Moscow: "Nauka" Publishers, 1979, pp. 39, 46, 50; M. V. Kriukov, "Evoliutsiia etnicheskogo samosoznaniia i problema etnogeneza," *Rasy i narodi*, 1976, p. 58; idem, "Kitaiskie uchenye o problemakh teorii etnosa," *Sov. etnografiia*, 1984, no. 6, p. 148.

38. K. A. Abul'khanova, *O sub"ekte psikicheskoi deiatel'nosti*, Moscow: "Nauka" Publishers, 1973, p. 288; K. A. Abul'khanova-Slavskaia, *Deiatel'nost' i psikhologiia lichnosti*, Moscow: "Nauka" Publishers, 1980.

39. B. F. Lomov, *Metodologicheskie i teoreticheskie problemy psikhologii*, Moscow: "Nauka" Publishers, 1984, p. 180.

40. M. N. Guboglo, "Integriruiushchaia funktsiia iazyka," in *Sotsiolingvisticheskie problemy razvivaiushchikhsia stran*, Moscow: "Nauka" Publishers, 1975.

41. Kozhanov, p. 96.

42. Pimenov, pp. 102, 205.

43. Kozhanov, p. 85.

44. Andropov, Iu. V., p. 11.

45. See Arutiunian, Drobizheva, V. V. Kondrat'ev, and A. A. Susokolov, *Etnosotsiologiia: tseli, metody i nekotorye resul'taty issledovaniia*, Moscow, "Nauka" Publishers, 1984, pp. 217–19.

The Interregional Mixing and National Composition of Labor Resources *

L. V. OSTAPENKO and A. A. SUSOKOLOV

The Soviet Union might be compared to a multinational labor collective. This comparison is not simply a metaphor.[1] In every republic work people of many nationalities. Such collectives are particularly numerous in cities. In rural locales there are fewer multinational collectives, but here too the percentage is constantly growing.

At the same time definite international differences persist in spheres of labor application. They are connected with significant differences in the natural conditions of regions and in the specifics of historical development of the peoples. The particularities of level of occupation among certain peoples of our country were more noticeable 10–20 years ago than they are today. However, it is only in the recent past that this circle of phenomena has attracted the attention of sociologists, demographers, and of society. The major reason for the increased attention to this problem is the increasingly complex situation in deployment of labor resources.

According to the 1979 census 51.5% of the nation's population was occupied in the national economy.[2] This is the highest degree of occupation in social production in the world. At the same time, because of falling birth rates in the industrially more developed regions of the nation, the growth of labor resources in the Twelfth Five-year Plan will be significantly less than in the previous decades. The major growth will come in republics with high birth rates (Central Asia, Kazakhstan, and the North Caucasus).[3] At the same time the development of a socialist economy demands a constant flow of new labor resources, in manufacturing above all, and the rational exploitation of existing labor cadres, taking account of their ethnic particularities.

Of course the major direction for solving problems of labor reserves in our country lies in the necessity of future intensification of production, in raising the productivity of the nation's laborers. It is these tasks which the Party is setting forth as key in solving all basic questions of economic development. At the same time the improvement of territorial and branch deployment of the working population, to bring it into correspondence with new tendencies in the development of the demographic and economic situation is an objective necessity.

One of the central questions is, what sources, interregional or intraregional, can become basic for the solution of the problems of labors reserves in each region and branch of industry? Regional differences in natural growth at first glance suggest the

---

Sto natsii i narodnostei: etnodemograficheskoe razvitie SSSR (Moscow, 1985), pp. 40–56. Russian text © 1985 by "Mysl'" Publishers.

utility of the interregional approach. However, a deeper analysis of the concrete processes, in our opinion, frequently indicates an entire range of difficulties which affect prospects for massive interregional movement of labor resources. Many of them are one way or another connected with the national composition of the working population, and first of all with the fact that people of the indigenous population in union republics rarely wish to move permanently to other regions of the country.

This article, without pretending to exhaustive analysis, will attempt to examine certain of the questions which arise in this connection, on the basis of three concrete problematic situations which concern possibilities of interregional resettlement of labor resources. These three are prospects for guaranteeing an agricultural work force in the Non–Black-Earth zone, the assurance of a work force for certain branches of the urban economy, and the problems of sending young specialists, graduates of institutes of higher education, into other regions.

Agriculture usually served as one of the most important sources of labor reserves for ''urban'' occupations. The high level of natural population growth in the southern and southeastern regions of our country occurs primarily because of the rural population. Thus when speaking of possible increases in the interregional mobility of labor reserves, what is primarily meant is moving rural residents of these republics. For example, in Tadzhikistan and the Kirghiz SSR rural inhabitants constitute more than 60% of the population. In the Uzbek, Georgian, Azerbaidzhani, and Tadzhik SSRs in the past 10–15 years the percentage of people working in the rural sector grew within the total working population.

The diametrically opposite situation holds in agriculture of the Non–Black-Earth area of the RSFSR, which includes 29 oblasts, with a population of 62 million people. The percentage of rural residents is significantly lower than the percentage of urban ones, while the percentage of rural workers, among the entire working population, is even lower. Given the low fertility of the soil and the still insufficient productivity of the agricultural work force, this size rural populace can scarcely work the soil properly. Despite the constantly increasing volume of capital investment in agriculture in the Non–Black-Earth zone, the number of workers has continued to fall for many years. However, in the last few years the number has stabilized in certain oblasts, and in some instances the number of machine-operating cadres has even risen. The deficit continues, however (see Table 1).

As we see, the number of agricultural implements grows faster than the number of operators. The deficit of qualified cadres sometimes also affects the quality of the work force, because tractors or combines are sometimes driven by poorly prepared people, which affects labor productivity most of all, when the machinery must be used.

One approach to solution of the problem of labor reserves in the Non–Black-Earth zone sometimes considered is the possibility of attracting part of the rural population from republics with a high birthrate, sometimes called labor-surplus areas. Since this involves contacts not just between regions, but also between peoples, the consideration of ethnic factors in such recruitment is very important, from a practical point of view.

Table 1

Number of Agricultural Machines vs. Machine Operators in Ivanov Oblast

	1971	1976	1981
Tractors, combines, heavy trucks in agriculture (thousands)	3.2	17.5	24.0
Machine operators (thousands)	10.8	13.7	16.0

Source: Ivanovskaia oblast' v desiatoi piatiletke, Iaroslavl', 1981, p. 44, 81.

The Non–Black-Earth zone receives fraternal aid primarily in the work of a series of organizations which attempt to cultivate new lands, restore abandoned lands, build farms, hot houses, and dwellings. The workers in these organizations are specialists, builders and irrigators from Central Asia and other southern republics. However, they are primarily temporary, and after completion of their work they return to their native areas. The question arises how purposeful is the participation of natives of Central Asia and other regions with a high percentage of rural population in this process? First, there is at present not only an outflow of population from the villages of the Non–Black-Earth zone, about which a great deal has been written in the scientific and popular-science literature, but there is also an increasing number who are moving to live in the villages. They are moving primarily from the cities of the RSFSR, primarily from the oblasts of the Non–Black-Earth zone. The percentage of such among the arrivals is from half to two-thirds. A significant percentage is also migrants from rural areas of other regions of the RSFSR. Migrants are attracted by the possibility of improving their living conditions, higher wages, rural life, the possibility of private agriculture, the climate, and other circumstances.

A number of oblasts continue to have an exodus of local rural population, including at times young people who have agricultural or industrial professions. In the same oblasts where there is active agricultural construction (such as Ivanovsk), because of high migration, there is little net population growth.

The opinion is sometimes expressed that migration from the cities to the villages of the Non–Black-Earth zone must be made even more intensive. It seems unlikely though that the problem may be solved in this way. The number of people coming to rural areas is large already, and besides, people are also very much needed in cities, and there is no certainty that a growth of inmigration will not cause a proportional growth in the out-migration of population. Of course it makes sense constantly to strengthen the arriving population. Calculations indicate that if it were possible to reduce the out-migration from the villages to the cities in a number of the oblasts of the Non–Black-Earth zone by even 5%–7% then the problem of agricultural cadres in these oblasts (such as in Ivanovsk, whose statistics form Table 1) could be solved in a few years. Reducing the outflow and improving the likelihood of remaining would also help make the rural population younger, which in turn would raise the birth rate of the region.

Let us return to the question of the possibilities and purposes of using the labor reserves of Central Asia. The percentage of Central Asians among all immigrants to the villages of the Non–Black-Earth zone is small. The balance of migration is extremely insignificant. It hardly seems possible to count on any noticeable portion of the Central Asians who are now doing reclamation and construction in the sovkhozes and construction sites settling in the area.

Of course a certain number of people move from the labor-surplus areas to rural locales of the Non–Black-Earth zone to settle and work here. There is both organized and unorganized migration. However, it can scarcely be expected that a strengthening of this flow will permit any significant resolution of the problem of labor resources in the near future. Thus for example beginning in 1983 more than a 100 families annually were sent in organized fashion from Uzbekistan to the villages of Ivanovsk oblast, and even more to rural locales of Tomsk Oblast and Primorskii Krai. Residents of Kirghizia and Kazakhstan settle independently in new sovkhozes of the Novgorod and several other oblasts.

However, the role of these sources must not be overestimated, for it is defined not only by the quantity of immigrants, but also by their quality. First, the settlers from Central Asia are primarily urban, that is, people who are not given to agriculture. According to a study done by the Institute of Ethnography, of the settlers in rural Ivanovsk from Uzbekistan only about 20% had worked more than a year in agriculture before coming, another 19%–20% had worked sporadically or for several months, and almost two thirds of the settlers were wholly unacquainted with agriculture. It is clear that the results for the economy of the labor of the majority of such settlers for the first years can hardly be profitable, and that the settlers themselves will often not be satisifed with their own work.

Rural residents of labor-surplus areas, primarily from Kirghizia and Kazakhstan, also move to the Non–Black-Earth zone. The majority of them are qualified machine operators, animal herders, and agricultural specialists. However, as a rule these specialists are also needed in the regions they have left. It should also be noted that about two thirds of the immigrants are ethnic Russian families, while another 10%–20% are ethnically mixed, and about the same number again are ethnically uniform families of Ukrainian, Tatar, or German nationality.

Thus the out-flow from labor surplus areas to the villages of the Non–Black-Earth zone which has been noted in the past few years can hardly attest to an increase in interregional labor mobility of the indigenous populations of Central Asia and Kazakhstan, that is, of the very population whose high natural growth rates allow the regions to be considered as ones of labor surplus. It seems to us that in order to be able to use the rural populations of labor-surplus areas it is necessary first of all to bring the qualification level of the indigenous rural population of the labor-surplus regions themselves into correspondence with the economic needs of these regions.

The question of why the migration mobility of a number of indigenous populations of the Central Asian and Caucasian republics is so low is widely considered in the scientific literature, with various opinions expressed. However, this important aspect unquestionably deserves special examination, which goes beyond the scope of the present work. A number of economists and demographers consider that most effective both in the economic and social sense is more active participation of the indigenous rural population of labor-surplus republics in the development of the economy of their own regions, first of all in a whole range of branches of industrial production. Many of these branches are inseparably associated with cities and urban populations. However, the labor shortage is felt precisely in the entire range of *"urban" branches*, including in those regions which are considered to have labor surpluses. The problem of this deficit has also long been solved in large degree by interregional relocation of the labor resources.

As materials of ethnosociological studies indicate, there are now noticeable changes in the labor orientation of youth among the indigenous populations of Central Asia, Kazakhstan, and several other regions. Increasingly these young people prefer nonagricultural professions. However, their orientation towards living in rural areas remains strong. Familiar social and natural surroundings, the moral and economic support of relatives and friends, a reduced likelihood of psychological stresses (a common companion for rural migrants to large cities) all slow resettlement to the city, even within one's own republic. A certain portion of the rural population of these regions, continuing to live in the village, is brought into nonagricultural spheres of production, which (to some degree) promotes migration into the republican cities from rural areas. In certain republics a "breakthrough" in the migrational mobility of the rural indigenous population has already begun.

Thus not long ago among the republics with a high concentration of indigenous population engaged in agriculture and low mobility were Moldavia, Kazakhstan, and Kirghizia. However, in the last 10–15 years the situation there has changed substantially. At the present time the intrarepublican territorial mobility of the indigenous populations of these republics is one of the highest among all the indigenous populations of the union republics. Migration is proceeding primarily from villages to the towns and from smaller cities to larger ones.

However, an increase in labor and territorial mobility still does not mean the problem of labor reserves has been solved. It is important not only to relocate population into "urban" branches, but also into exactly the branches to which these populations are primarily attracted, because in labor-surplus areas often the same branches of industry are labor deficient as are labor deficient in labor-short areas. For example, in republics like Georgia and Uzbekistan, where about a quarter of the work force works in the industrial sector, about half of the empty work slots in the second half of the 1970s and the beginning of the 1980s came precisely in manufacturing. It would seem that labor resources must first of all be made to correspond to the production needs of their own republics. The achievement of this sort of equilibrium should assure the optimal path by which the indigenous population can adapt to the conditions of industrial production and the urban environment, and at the same time increase the possibilities for fraternal assistance to other republics.

The shortage of cadres in industry and a range of other branches of the economy arises, as a rule, because of insufficiently intense recruitment into the given branches of the indigenous populations of a series of union republics. This situation demands

Table 2

The "Index of Participation" of Indigenous and Russian Nationalities in Some Branches of the Economy in the Capitals of Four Union Republics (data from a survey at the end of the 1970s–beginning of the 1980s)

City	Nationality	Branch of Industry				
		Manufacturing construction, transport, and communications	Trade and services	Health care	Education and culture	Science
Tashkent	Uzbek	0.9	1.5	1.1	1.3	0.9
	Russian	1.1	0.7	0.9	0.8	1.1
Tbilisi	Georgian	0.9	0.9	1.2	1.2	1.2
	Russian	1.1	0.7	0.7	0.7	0.8
Kishinev	Moldavian	1.1	1.0	0.9	0.9	1.1
	Russian	1.0	0.9	1.0	1.1	1.3
Tallin	Estonian	0.9	1.2	1.2	1.4	1.4
	Russian	1.1	0.8	0.8	0.7	0.7

now that other nationalities be recruited for these branches from other regions, which leads to the development of differences in the national composition of the work force in different branches in a city. Table 2 permits a more visible examination of the character and scope of *variations among branches of industry* in the national composition of *the urban work force*. The table shows the "index of participation"[4] of indigenous and Russian populations in some of the most important branches of industry in the capitals of four union republics in which studies were conducted in the program "Optimization of social and cultural conditions for the development and convergence of nationalities in the USSR."

As may be seen from the table data, common to three cities (Tashkent, Tbilisi, and Tallin) is a smaller percentage of indigenous population in spheres of industrial production. Only in Kishinev does the percentage of Moldavians in industry correspond to their percentage in the population. Within industry itself the attraction of various branches for the indigenous populations of the union republics is far from uniform. The most attractive are branches of industry which produce goods for consumer usage, such as the food industry, clothes factories, and printing plants. At the same time the percentage of people of the indigenous populations among workers in machine building and metallurgy is not great.[5] This rule is characteristic of the Caucasus and Central Asia, but it may also be seen in a number of other union republics. Thus in Estonia, which has an old tradition of industrial development, the number of Estonian workers among the urban population is approximately one fifth higher than the number of Russian workers, but in the spheres of machine building and metallurgy these proportions are reversed.

A completely different situation obtains in trade and service, where all four capitals show a higher percentage of people of the indigenous population.

The relationship of nationalities in such branches of the economy as culture, health care, and science are also dissimilar for various cities. Where the capital of Moldavia shows a proportional representation of the most numerous populations in these branches, Tallin and Tbilisi show that the percentage of natives in these branches is significantly higher than their representation in the population.

It is important to know what historical and social factors influenced the particularity of the national composition of the population of various branches of industry in a city. If data about the national composition of branches of industry at the beginning of the century (using data from the 1897 census) are compared with the contemporary situation, then the following general rule may be observed: The higher the percentage was of the basic indigenous population in the cities, and particularly in the branches most important for the city's economy (industry and craft, trade, some service), the higher will be their "degree of participation" in such branches as science, culture, and health care in the modern city. By these indicators Tashkent, Tallin, and Tbilisi are noticeably distinct from Kishinev.

In the first three cities the basic indigenous populations were at the end of the last century concentrated to a significant degree in the "main" urban branches of industry. The population of Tashkent at the end of the 19th century consisted almost entirely of representatives of the indigenous Central Asian peoples who in Soviet times became the nucleus for formation of a unified Uzbek people. Just as in Tashkent, the leading role in the ethnic composition of the industrial structure of Revel (now Tallin) at the end of the 19th century was taken by the indigenous population, the Estonians.

In Tbilisi at that time Georgians were about a third of the population. The basic development tendency in the ethnic environment of this city was the rapid "indigenization" of the populace, and a raised percentage of Georgians among the urban population.

Russians and members of other nationalities in all three cities were concentrated primarily in the army and administration, in such branches as culture, health care, education, as well as among the private servants. However, the specific gravity of these branches among the entire working population was relatively small. Kishinev presented a different picture in the distribution of nationalities; its ethnic makeup significantly differed from that of the surrounding rural population, which was primarily Moldavian. In the cities Russians and Jews dominated numerically, occupying the key positions in all basic branches of industry. The Moldavians had their greatest representation among workers in agriculture, service, as well as among those living on proceeds from capital or living on government or private means.

In the spheres of culture, science, and health care the basic indigenous populations did not occupy a leading position in any of the cities. However, in those cities where there was a significant native contingent adapted to conditions of city life (even in a "traditional" city, like Tashkent), the future attraction of this population into new, socially prestigious, and rapidly developing spheres of activity proceeded more quickly than in, for example, Kishinev. In a number of places the national composition of the work force was also affected by other factors.

Thus the more than twenty years that western Bessarabia was occupied significantly slowed not only the growth of Kishinev, but also the attraction of the native
population into urban spheres of activity. Nationalities were sharply differentiated
by levels of education, which also affected the tempos of social mobility.

Traditions of working in one branch or another have a direct effect on the
contemporary picture of the nationality composition by branch. The sharpest outline
of this influence of traditions may be seen in the examples of branches of industry
which produce consumer goods. Thus the traditional "attraction" of Estonians for
the woodworking industry, of Uzbeks for the textile and leather industries; the
percentage of Georgians in the food industry is relatively high, as is that of Moldavians in construction and the production of construction materials, and in the leather
industry.

A whole range of branches "typical" for the indigenous populations formed
comparatively recently. Thus, for example, before the war in Tallin and Kishinev,
which were temporarily not part of the USSR, primarily light industry and the food
industry were developed, as well as certain specific branches such as printing. This
also left a mark on the contemporary distribution of nationalities by branch. Thus
the percentage of Estonians and Moldavians in the leather industry and shoe industry,
as well as in printing, is higher than their percentage in the population. However, the
leather industry in Tallin was poorly developed at the end of the nineteenth century
and did not attract Estonians, while the percentage of Estonians and Moldavians
among printers was lower than the composition of the entire population. Here the
border between tradition and modernity becomes very flexible and conditional. Life
changes, new factors arise to affect orientation by branch of industry.

However, traditions are not sufficient to explain a number of particularities of the
national composition of workers by branch of industry. Most of all this is true for the
more numerous groups of industrial workers, machine-builders and metal workers.
At present the percentage of workers of the basic indigenous population in these
branches is lower in all four of these cities than its percentage of the population.
However, this disproportion was "traditional" only in Tashkent and Tbilisi. In
Tallin at the turn of the century metal-working could have been called a typical
industry, for the percentage of Estonians was higher in it than average, and yet in the
last 10–15 years there is even a drop in the percentage of Estonians in this sphere of
labor. Thus even the preservation of most traditions in the sphere of urban labor may
be explained first of all by social interests and by particularities of the contemporary
social situation in the republic. As in the rural setting, the improvement of the
working situation in the multinational cities of the Soviet Union must to a decisive
degree be defined by the intrarepublic distribution of labor resources. In this the
most important tendency is the improvement of labor conditions in the most promising branches of industry, improving their attractiveness for members of the basic
indigenous populations, both in labor-surplus and labor-deficit republics, to bring
them into correspondence with the work traditions of each nation and with the social
interests of various levels of the republic's population.

What are the perspectives for the future convergence of the composition by branch of various nationalities of our country in the union republics? To a certain degree this question is answered by the statistics for specialized education.

Referring to the national composition of students in trade schools, technicums, and institutes of higher education, it may be seen that differences in professional specialization by branch are less noticeable than among the working population, though certain particularities continue to be preserved. It is extremely important that in the trade schools of Central Asia and the Caucasus which prepare new cadres for industry and transport that the percentage of indigenous youth be increased. Thus for example among trade school graduates sent into machine-building and metallurgy in Uzbekistan in the second half of the 1970s, the relative number of Uzbeks was significantly higher than their representation among workers of those branches, but was nevertheless lower than their representation in the population of the republic. To some degree this is connected with still insufficient development of the network of trade schools in some union republics, most of all in rural areas, and with poor propaganda for trade school study among local youth, as well as to the relatively low attractiveness of trade schools for girls from some indigenous populations. In Uzbekistan for example among the native students there are currently 5–6 times fewer girls than boys. At the same time, as recently as the 1940s it was exceptional to have Uzbek girls studying in a trade school.

Preparation of qualified worker cadres of the indigenous nationalities of the union and autonomous republics is one of the most important components of the economic and national policy of our Party. However, the attractiveness of the working professions, despite the high tempo of equalization, is not uniform. Thus in Uzbekistan the percentage of Uzbeks studying in trade schools is still lower than the percentage of Uzbeks in the population, while the percentage of Russians is 1.5 times higher. However, in Georgia, where the disproportion of representation by branch was even recently quite noticeable, the percentage of Georgians among students at trade schools is now 1.1 times higher than their representation in the population, while the representation of Russians is lower than their representation in the population.

A significant role in the convergence of the professional and branch distribution of national composition is played by *higher education*. Soviet power brought a radical break to the system of preparation of cadres in the national regions of our country. It is enough to recall that of the 105 higher educational institutions in prerevolutionary Russia (1914), 72 were in cities of the present-day RSFSR, 27 were in the Ukraine, and 5 were in the Baltic region.[6] At present there are virtually no differences among the republics in level of access to higher education.

Development of a system of higher schools has a primary significance for preparation of specialists from among the youth of the basic indigenous populations of the republics. By the 1980s the percentage of young men and women of the basic indigenous populations of the union republics among the student body of the corresponding republics was either significantly close to their representation in the population or was even higher than it. The average significance of the "index of participation'' of the basic indigenous populations among students for the 1980–1981 academic year was 105%.[7]

This indicator may be explained by the fact that in the last few years in a number of union republics (Kazakhstan, Lithuania, Kirghizia, Armenia, Estonia) preparation of the native populace for higher education and middle specialized education proceeded more quickly than for the Russian population.

We will note that even now certain differences in the composition by branch of the intelligenstia are preserved among the republics. This may be explained by the fact that the level of development of the intelligentsia of various peoples of our country varied significantly before the Revolution. The first task which higher education undertook in the years of Soviet power was the preparation of an intelligentsia for the mass professions, primarily teachers. Thus in a number of republics among the technical and scientific workers, and often among the doctors, there was a large number of imported specialists, primarily Russians, Ukrainians, and other urban residents of the European part of the USSR.

Particularities of distribution of specialists of various nationalities by branch of industry to some degree are still preserved. However, in the distribution among students the data of difference are significantly lower. The process of convergence of the professional specialization composition of the student body of particular nationalities was particularly intensive in the past two decades. Thus the technical schools of a number of union republics raised the percentage representation of students of the indigenous population. For example in the mid-1970s the percentage of Georgian students in technical schools surpassed the percentage of the Georgian population in the republic. The percentage of Moldavians among students of technical schools is at present equal to their representation in the population. The rate of growth of the percentage of students in the given direction among all students of Uzbek nationality has in Uzbekistan in the last two decades exceeded all other groups of students, save those in university.

Such tendencies are particularly important if we consider that in recent years in most republics (except Georgia, Estonia, Armenia, Lithuania, and the RSFSR) the percentage of people of the indigenous population in the composition of the engineering and technical workforce is lower than their weight in the population. At the same time in almost all republics the percentage of Russians in the engineering and technical workforce is higher than their representation in the population of the given republic. The representation of Russian students remains sufficiently high in the trade schools and technicums of the various republics. This shows particularly clearly in the Central Asian regions, where the percentage of rural population, less oriented to technical professions, is high. At the same time in Estonia in the past 20 years the percentage of Estonians in higher technical education has dropped somewhat, and the percentage of Russians has grown.

Compared to other sorts of higher education institutions the percentage of youth of the indigenous population has grown particularly quickly among the student body of the republican universities which prepare the greatest part of the scientific workers and teachers. At present in many republics the percentage of native youth in the universities is equal to or higher than their representation in the population of the republics. In republics like Estonia and Georgia, where the educational level of the indigenous population is especially high and native specialists are represented relatively numerously in various branches of the economy, the percentage of nonindigenous students has dropped in recent years.

The percentage of native students in agricultural higher schools and technicums has in all republics in recent years exceeded the representation of the nationalities in the population.

Specialists of the indigenous population are numerically very well represented in the population of the union republics among workers of the mass professions, such as teachers and medics. At present in most republics the percentage of natives among students of higher educational institutes and students of pedagogic and medical technicums corresponds to their representation in the population or even exceeds it.

The change in national composition among the intelligentsia and student body affects perspectives for the labor potential of these republics in other regions of the country. A resolution of the Central Committee of the CPSU, "On the Sixtieth Anniversary of the Formation of the USSR" notes that "It is also important in the future to improve the system of planning and the quality of preparation of specialists, to consider more accurately the real needs of the republics and of the USSR as a whole, given their present distribution, to make fuller use of their creative potential in the interests of communist construction."[8]

Despite the fact that in all the republics the tempos of producing new workers with higher and middle specialized education, particularly from among the indigenous population, are reasonably high, in some regions the demands of the economy for specialists is still not being entirely satisfied. In such conditions the question arises of possible means of attracting specialists from other republics to participate in solving a given specialized task, especially from those areas were the concentration of specialists in the economy is especially high.

However, not all specialists from the indigenous populations, including graduates of higher and middle specialized institutes are oriented toward a move to other regions of the country. According to the findings of our study, in the middle of the 1970s only 6–7% of Georgian specialists with a higher education wanted to move to a new place, and of those the great majority wanted to move only to another city in the republic. In Moldavia about 19% of the Moldavian specialists with higher education were oriented to moving, and a part of them wished to move to another republic.

These numbers give reason to suppose that the tempos of producing specialists of the indigenous population can scarcely influence in any significant way the situation for migration. In both republics mentioned above the percentage of potential emigrants was higher among the nonindigenous population, including Russians. Thus among specialists in Georgian cities more than 40% of the Russians answered that in principle they would be willing to change their place of residence, and primarily, to leave the republic.

It seems that in a number of labor-surplus regions the numerical growth of the republic's intelligentsia, accompanied by a growth of the percentage of natives among it, will probably not lead to an increased role for the interrepublic distribution of specialists. Thus it seems that the higher education institutes of the republics must so set their work as first of all to guarantee the economic needs of their own republics. It is vital to consider here that the percentage of natives is highest among teachers and agricultural specialists, and lowest among specialists of the technical and natural science specialities.

Thus in our view one of the most important tasks of economic and social planning at present is to improve the balance of labor resources in every union republic, whether or not it is considered a labor-surplus or labor-deficient area. This does not mean, of course, that migration of labor resources from one republic to another is unimportant, but the perspectives for such migration must be defined not only by indicators of the natural movement of the population, but also by the particularities of population distribution, by the professional, qualificational, and ethnic composition of the population. If a surplus of specialists arises in a republic in some branches of industry, then getting rid of this disproportion requires first and foremost the improvement of the system of preparing cadres in the republic. In planning interrepublic labor migration a number of factors must be considered, including the national composition of the "potential" emigrants. At the same time account must also be taken of, on the one hand, the form of movement (interrepublic or all-union) and, on the other, the problems of adaptation in a new and different ethnic milieu.

In other words, at the country's present stage of social and economic development, when conditions and possibilities have been created for the more rational economic use of labor resources from labor-surplus regions, it is apparent that account must be taken not only of the technical preparedness of cadres, but of their national particularities as well.

Notes

1. The present study makes use of material from an ethnosociological questionnaire from the study "Optimization of the social and cultural conditions for the convergence of nationalities," conducted in the 1970s in five republics by the Institute of Ethnography of the Academy of Sciences of the USSR. See I. V. Arutiunian, V. S. Drobizheva, A. A. Susokolov, *Etnosotsiologiia: tseli, metodiy, i nekotorye rezul'taty issledovaniia*, Moscow, 1984.

2. See *Naselenie SSSR*, Moscow, 1983, p. 153.

3. See L. Chizhova, "Kharakteristika zaniatogo naseleniia po raionam strany" in *Naselenie SSSR segodnia*, Moscow, 1982, p. 20.

4. The "index of participation" is the fraction of the nationality work force in a branch of industry, divided by the percentage representation of the nationality in the entire work force. For example, if nationality "A" is 25% of the work force in industry and 20% among the entire work force, then the index of that nationality's participation will equal $25\%/20\% = 1.25$.

5. A higher percentage of indigenous population among the work force of one branch or another does not mean that problems of labor reserves are resolved in that branch. As special studies have shown, despite the fact that the percentage of Uzbek women in the textile industry

of the republic is higher than their percentage in the population, in recent years this branch has experienced a shortage of workers.

6. *Narodnoe obrazovanie, nauka, i kul'tura v SSSR. Statisticheskii sbornik*, Moscow, 1971, p. 166.

7. See L. V. Ostapenko and A. A. Suskolov, "Etnosotsial'nye osobennosti vosproiz-vodstva intelligentsii" in *Sotsiologicheskie issledovaniia*, 1983, N. 1.

8. *O 60-oi godovshchine obrazovaniia Soiuza Sovetskikh Sotsialisticheskikh Respublik*, Moscow, 1982, p. 11.

More Democracy *

L. DROBIZHEVA

I shall pause briefly on only two of what seem to me the main questions in the national sphere connected with the further democratization of our society and our economic life, and which have not received sufficient reflection in the dialogue.

The first is the scale and effectiveness of economic investments in the national regions that took place in the 1960s and 1970s. The second is why in conditions of democratization we have eruptions of nationalism and how this is to be explained, by the growth of national self-consciousness or by some other phenomena.

In considering the first question it seems very important to imagine the real situation which came to exist in our country in the course of a long historical period. In the 1970s and beginning of the 1980s there were no particular changes in nationality policy from the point of view of financial investment in the economies of the national republics. This was a continuation of the policy set out in the Tenth and Twelfth Party Congresses[a] (see *Desiatyi s"ezd RKP(B). Stenograficheskii otchet.* Moscow, 1963, p. 604; *Dvenadtsatyi s"ezd RKP(B). Stenograficheskii otchet,* Moscow, 1968, p. 694), which was directed toward insuring in fact the cultural and economic equality of peoples.

Even before the war we had achieved substantial successes in this regard. Differences of a formational nature had disappeared among the Soviet peoples, and the country's backwardness as a whole had been overcome, although in relation to the peoples who had bypassed the stage of capitalist development, the necessary tasks in some aspects were also resolved in the years afterward. However, the task of the further equalization of the levels of economic and cultural development of the peoples was never fully achieved. At least as much as this was frequently written about in the literature.

No one can deny what the peoples of our country have acheived. The workers, and primarily workers in industry, have become a weighty social force in the majority of national groups. Many Soviet national groups have formed their own productive and scientific, including technical-scientific intelligentsia. After all in the postwar years not only the Central Asian peoples, the Kazakhs, and the Moldavians, but also the Belorussians and the Lithuanians had as their intelligentsia primarily by government service personnel, teachers and other educational workers, doctors, and only a small portion was creative intelligentsia.

The new social structure reflected the economic and cultural development of the peoples. The successes of education are not to be doubted. With all its evident shortcomings, secondary education of youth truly became universal. This created

Politicheskoe obrazovanie, 1988, no. 3, pp. 49–51. Russian text © 1988 by "Pravda" Publishers.

the basis for the real possibilities for people of all national groups to have equal social movement, and an equal contribution to the economy and culture of the country. At the same time it was precisely against this background of great achievements in the realization of nationality policy that we began to feel differences in the effectivity of labor in the republics.

I will offer just a few examples. The rate of growth of productive labor in industry in the 1970s and early 1980s was 1.5 times higher than in Tadzhikistan, for example. In Turkmenia these indices essentially did not rise, while in Kazakhstan the national profit "took" a third less from the units of the basic productive funds than the average for the country as a whole. Georgia was one of the republics with the very highest indices for education level of the populace, but in labor productivity for 1975 it lagged behind the average all-union level. In the end of the 1970s and beginning of the 1980s the rates of growth in productive labor grew here, but for the same period Belorussia, where the educational level of workers is lower than in Georgia, continued to be more productive. By the indices of education of the working population, the populations of Uzbekistan, Kazakhstan, and Turkmenia are higher than the all-union average, but in the growth of productive labor they lagged behind the average for the country, behind the RSFSR, Belorussia, and the Baltic republics (see *Narodnoe khoziaistvo SSSR v 1984 godu*, Moscow, 1985, p. 31, 148, 323).

The new social situation in international relations, in which the peoples work together, their former inequalities overcome, also revealed those problems of the national sphere which are directly connected to restructuring of the economic life and the democratization of our country. These problems are to a significant degree connected with the national variety of the human factor, which makes itself felt in the sphere of economics, just as it does in politics.

In the conditions of the scientific and technical revolution differences in orientation to labor activities showed up clearly. I will refer to one example, which speaks to the significance of the human factor, which expresses both the influence of the historical past and of cultural tradition. According to data from representative ethnosociological studies, about 80% of the Russian city dwellers considered interesting work a necessary condition for a happy life (that is, a recognized personal value), as did two-thirds of the Estonians. Among Uzbeks this opinion was supported by about half the urban respondents (see *Sotsial'no-kul'turnyi oblik sovetskikh natsii*, Moscow, 1986, p. 251). In the middle of the 1970s there were more Estonians who linked improvement of the conditions of work activity with expansion of initiative than there were, for example, Georgians. Among Uzbeks and Moldavians expectations in this regard were primarily linked to raising the discipline of labor.

The specifics of ethnocultural traditions which appear in the human factor will also have significance in the years to come. It is not only in informal meetings among urbanized peoples but also in scientific circles that the question of whether to invest in regions which don't give rapid and complete returns is being discussed. It must be said that such questions arise not only in our country, but in other developed, multinational countries as well. In the United States, for example, the so-called special economic programs for ethnic minorities have often evoked protests from the majority of the population.

A group of Estonian scientists published a proposal to raise the principal of unaided viability to the republic level. This is also a reaction to the problem revealed, which had already come up in the 1970s and beginning of the 1980s. After all there was then already talk of increasing the contribution of all the republics to the all-union fund. Now, however, with the transition to new economic methods of management, this problem will become even sharper.

Can we now renounce policies of the directed stimulation of development of peoples who in the past lagged behind? In my view, we can not wholly do so. And not solely because of the humanity of our nationality policy. Our multinational Union is a single organism, and if one part or another functions below its possibilities, all the parts will lose, slowing movement in general. And if we wish for general movement forward, it is important to find methods and forms which take account of the national peculiarities in the life of the peoples. And this is true not only for the economic sphere, but also for the political.

Now about the other problem, which grew sharper in the 1970s and which is extraordinarily important for the future, the democratization of life in our society and national relations. This is a multi-leveled problem which can not be examined in all its facets and nuances in a short manner. I will dwell on just two aspects. In bringing democratization into being it is important to take account of the preparedness for it among various groups of the population. This means national groups as well. That this is true is demonstrated at least by this fact, that in ethnosociological surveys in the middle of the 1970s and beginning of the 1980s (that is, before restructuring), in listing the most important problem for the country, about one-fifth of the population named the further democratization of society. At the same time, there were more Estonians who considered this a necessity than there were Uzbeks or Moldavians. That means that it is important to find and make use of those forms of democracy which correspond to the traditions of the peoples. It is known, for example, that among the Russian people there were traditions of the *obshchina*,[b] while for the Uzbeks the *mahale*[c] plays a big role even now. But in order to have the possibility of using nationally-specific forms of democratization, the republics must have the right and be oriented to the democratic realization of democratization itself. In other words, I am saying that democratization must be realized on all levels, including at the level of the republics.

And a second moment, connected to the processes of democratization. Sometimes the idea is expressed that we have collided with phenomena of nationalism because of democratization. People say that if there had not been possibilities for free demonstrations and free speech, then there would also be no nationalistic attitudes. This of course is not true. These attitudes came to be in significant part because of the insufficient democratization of the past.

As a consequence of the rapid social growth of the nationalities who in the past had been backward a national intelligentsia has appeared everywhere, as each has its specialists. Competition to occupy scarce places appeared in the labor sphere. Psychological restructuring was necessary. People of the basic native nationality in each republic must of course consider that their national identity in and of itself does not give any special rights to advancement, while Russians, Ukrainians, and people of other nationalities who have assisted the development of the peoples must always remember that they are working with people of equal status. Restructuring is of course not easy. In other countries too, when there are changes in the social status of peoples in contact with one another (as for example in Belgium and Canada in the 1960s and 1970s) there are tensions. Our situation is favorable in that the government laws prohibit nationalism and chauvinism.

In carrying out social policy, or more precisely, cadre policy, it is important at the level of a specific city, town, or collective to put forward workers for the scarce and socially prestigious posts according to their qualities for the work, not excluding, of course, ideological, moral, and political qualities. Party documents are oriented towards this.

However, the absence of the necessary democratization, that is, of widespread *glasnost'* and elective choice has slowed realization of this orientation. Now in the conditions of the development of democratization, there is the opportunity to better resolve the national problems in the social and psychological spheres. Deepening democratization must be accompanied by improvements in the culture of international communication. *Glasnost'* and openness in the sphere of international relations will be effective only when maximum tact is observed and the national feelings of people considered. In the process of democratization it is possible to remove dissatisfaction with those sides of everyday cultural and ordinary life which are sufficiently easily controllable in the localities. Let us take, for example, the question of schools which teach in this language or that. Let's say in Belorussia, with instruction in Belorussian, in the Russian cities, for Tatars living outside the Tatar ASSR, for the Azerbaidzhanis in Georgia, and so forth. I think that the most intelligent path to resolving these questions is to have a preliminary sounding of public opinion and broad discussion of the point of opening such schools in the localities.

No one would lose if in those regions of the RSFSR and other republics where there are significant groups of non-native population the local newspapers were printed in bigger press runs and, if this is necessary, that in the spirit of national traditions, holidays be noted. People of other nationalities could come to the celebrations, to watch the dances, to hear the songs, to try the dishes of another people. Unfortunately, in the recent past the celebration of such holidays has not been encouraged among us, while their spontaneous appearance has even caused alarm. At the same time these holidays were not only an expression of people's national self-consciousness, but also a manifestation of people's need for closer human solidarity, wholly understandable in conditions of intensifying individualization of human life, especially in the cities. This process is developing, incidentally, throughout the world, and it is far from always a social protest. Ethnic groups show solidarity, meeting on a national cultural basis, in schools, cafes, clubs, and churches, and quickly adapt in the environment of the majority, of which Armenians in US cities are an example.

It is precisely democratization which will help us to find new, non-formal, effective forms of battling phenomena of nationalism and chauvinism. It is noteworthy, for example, that after appearances by the extremist parts of the informal organization *Pamiat* [d] an entire range of "interclubs" and "interbrigades" [international organizations] appeared (also on an informal basis, because of people's wishes). In a number of instances they switched over to activities directed primarily toward international solidarity, to the fight to strengthen internationalism in our country. At a meeting of representatives of informal organizations in August 1987 they all adopted the "three no's": no to extremism, no to racism, and no to nationalism.

I would like to remind people that the area of national relations is not an isolated sphere of society's life. In a multi-national environment the resolution of all social, cultural, and daily problems has a "national projection." Thus not just election of administrative cadre and *glasnost'* in recommendations of workers will beneficially influence inter-nationality relations, but also wide discussion of other questions, such as the principles of receiving housing, providing the children of workers at organizations with kindergartens, creches, and Pioneer camps, and so forth.

Editor's notes

a. The Tenth Party Congress was held in March 1921; the Twelfth Party Congress was held in August 1922.

b. *Obshchina*: the old Russian peasant commune.

c. *Mahale*: the traditional walled Muslim city.

d. *Pamiat'*: a contemporary Russian nationalist organization of extremist bent.

6. Language Training and Nationality Relations

National language is probably the single most important component of national identity. It helps define national uniqueness, and its preservation is generally perceived as being critical to the preservation of the distinctiveness of the nation itself. Some of the most heated disputes in Soviet nationality relations have focused on Soviet language policy. These policies have varied over time, and thus so too have the disputes; but what is constant is that throughout Soviet history Party officials have sought to use language policy as an instrument for the control of national minorities.

In the 1920s and 1930s Soviet policy makers devoted considerable attention to alphabet reform of the non-Slavic languages in general and the Turkic and Persian languages in particular (those written in the Arabic script). The effort was made to differentiate ethnic communities from one another and to cut all of them off from their co-nationals or co-religionists outside of the Soviet Union. First, in the 1920s, the government introduced distinct written national languages in the five Central Asian republics and in Azerbaidzhan, all of which were written in the Latin alphabet as were the written languages of the Volga and Crimean Tatars. Then, in the late 1930s, there was a decision to make the Cyrillic alphabet used for Russian the alphabet of the Soviet peoples. Of all the titular republic nationalities only the Armenians and Georgians, with their centuries of tradition of written language, were exempted from this. Later the Baltic peoples, following their annexation in the 1940s, were permitted to preserve their Latin alphabet.

On the whole the efforts at alphabet reform were unpopular, but successful. The introduction of the new orthographies and the accompanying "standardization" of grammar and vocabulary helped differentiate the various national communities, particularly within Central Asia and North Caucasia, and reduced the potential for pan-national opposition to Moscow's policies.

Under Khrushchev, nationality policy became more assimilationist in orientation. Russian-language education was seen as a means to attain cultural uniformity, and so became a greater priority. Sociological studies done in the 1950s and 1960s reported that schools were successfully socializing young people through the teaching of Russian, and that instruction in Russian helped transmit a common Soviet culture in the place of nationally specific traits and customs.

However, the publication of the 1970 census showed that among many non-Russian nationalities a majority of the population was still not fluent in Russian. Similarly, sociological research revealed that some of the cultural "survivals of the past" were undeniably being transmitted to the younger generation. Moreover, the shifting ethnic balance of the Soviet population gave new immediacy to the problem of Russian-language education, as the non-Slavic population would increasingly have to serve as a source of manpower for technical jobs in the Soviet economy and in the armed forces—tasks that required Russian-language skills.

From the mid-1970s on Soviet officials began to express concern over the deficiencies of Russian-language education in the non-Russian regions, particularly in the Caucasian and Central Asian republics. In 1979 an all-union conference on Russian-language education, held in Tashkent, called for a revamping of the curriculum for teaching the Russian language to non-Russians. In the early 1980s new programs and texts were introduced and the facilities for training teachers of Russian language were greatly expanded in non-Russian regions. The 1984 General Education Reform, which mandated that beginning in 1990 fluency in Russian would be a high-school graduation requirement, drew even greater attention to the deficiencies of Russian-language education. Problems of Russian-language education have been further spotlighted in the years since Gorbachev came to power.

While the focus of Russian-language education has been on the need to improve technical skills, developing Russian-language fluency for the non-Russian population is considered important for ideological reasons as well. Soviet scholars have managed to convince policy makers that the acquisition of Russian-language skills brings with it a Russian way of thinking, and eventually Russian cultural values.

While the regime has gone to great lengths to stress that Russian-language bilingualism for non-Russians does not dictate their Russification, many non-Russians continue to complain of the degradation of their national languages and express fears about their ultimate cultural assimilation. In the Baltic and Caucasian republics in particular, there has been widespread concern over the loss of status of the national languages. At the time of the drafting of the new Georgian constitution in the mid–1970s there were demonstrations demanding constitutional guarantees that Georgian would remain an official language within the republic. Similar concessions were then granted in Armenia and Azerbaidzhan. Party officials in the other republics were also sensitive to the concerns of their national constituencies; even while they offered florid endorsements of Russian-language bilingualism, they promoted the policy in a half-hearted fashion.

The protests against language policy were concealed, and there were few public signs of discord concerning the encouragement of Russian-language bilingualism for the non-Russian population. This was particularly true in scholarly writings. Typically authors emphasized the importance of the policy designed to produce Russian-language bilingualism, ignoring or minimizing the difficulties that the Party was having in achieving this goal. The article by Khanazarov, reproduced below, is typical of how authors writing during the Brezhnev period substituted rhetorical flourishes for a discussion of problems in an effort to conceal the inconsistencies of the policies themselves. Khanazarov's article offers a lengthy discussion of the various potential meanings of the concept of bilingualism, but it ignores the practical difficulties of achieving a bilingual population.

Khanazarov displays some of the ''blind spots'' that were characteristic of the Brezhnev period. He writes of the mutual enrichment of languages through the development of a bilingual population, but he makes no mention of Russians learning non-Russian languages or of how the Russian language is enriched by its contact with other Soviet languages. He also describes as voluntary many processes of language acquisition that have occurred because the peoples concerned have little choice. Thus he describes the Lithuanian-language skills of Poles and Kazakh bilingualism among Uighurs as successes of Soviet language policy, neglecting to mention the near total absence of Polish and Uighur language education or publications in the republics of Lithuania and Kazakhstan respectively. While there is now some attention to the linguistic rights of minority nationalities in the union republics, during the Brezhnev period there was none, nor were such rights considered to be legitimate.

Guboglo's article "The General and the Particular in the Development of the Linguistic Life of Soviet Society" was also written in the early 1980s and it suffers from some of the same defects as the Khanazarov piece. Guboglo, a noted scholar of problems of ethnicity and language who has done extensive survey research on linguistic problems in his native Moldavia, is himself a member of an ethnic minority (Gagauz, a Turkic people), and has first-hand knowledge both of the problems of minority nationalities and of bilingualism more generally. But as a successful academic of the Brezhnev period he too accepted the conventions of scholarly discourse of the day, and for this some of his colleagues have begun to criticize him. After Brezhnev's death Guboglo would write that the Uzbek and the Estonian census data on language from 1979 were incorrect; he claimed that the Uzbeks had deliberately overrepresented the number of people fluent in Russian while the Estonians had chosen to underrepresent the size of their bilingual population. But despite these convictions, in this article Guboglo offers conclusions that imply the accuracy of the 1979 census data. More than that, he offers an elaborate analysis of the role of schools in producing a wholly bilingual generation of young people in Uzbekistan, although he knew that the increase in the size of the bilingual Uzbek population between 1970 and 1979 exceeded the number of young people newly enrolled in schools.

Nonetheless, in this article, and even more so in his 1987 piece "Factors and Tendencies of Development of Bilingualism in the Russian Population Living in the Union Republics," Guboglo offers some useful analytic distinctions for studying the acquisition of bilingualism. He argues that the way in which a second language is learned is important, that the nature of the learning experience can affect the socialization that accompanies the acquisition of a language. He states that there is a differential impact of bilingualism acquired through social exchange in a common environment as opposed to bilingualism acquired through education. Whereas the Soviet schools emphasize education for the development of a bilingual population, Guboglo implies that language skills acquired more informally are more likely to result in an increase in ethnic tolerance.

Guboglo introduces the distinction between private and public exchange, and raises issue with the validity of the measures of bilingualism that are being officially employed. He distinguishes between the level of proficiency necessary for technical communication and the degree of proficiency necessary to create an atmosphere of ethnic toleration. While the former level of proficiency is necessary for non-Russians to fulfill technical tasks successfully, he states that Russians who acquire local language skills may be satisfied with a lower level of proficiency. The data Guboglo presents (now nearly a decade old) imply that a large number of Russians living in union republics may have some ability to communicate in the local language. According to Guboglo, the number of Russians with some proficiency in the local language varies greatly from republic to republic, with the Russians' bilingual skills being most prevalent in Ukraine and Belorussia and least prevalent in Central Asia.

But the proficiency figures reproduced by Guboglo ignore the whole question of when and where people will use their language skills. Recent complaints from all of the union republics suggest that Russians expect their language to be the language of official discourse in every part of the country. Thus there are reports that doctors, lawyers, and even store clerks will assert control and possibly greatly inconvenience those that they are serving by speaking only in Russian, rather than conduct business in the local language. While official policy has always spoken of the reciprocity of the development of bilingual skills, discussions of ethnic toleration have always been about non-Russians developing Russian-language skills. It was not until after the Alma-Ata riots in December 1986 that Party officials nationwide began to call for universal training in the national language of a republic as well as in Russian. Kazakhstan was the first republic to develop such a program, as part of an effort to persuade the people that the removal of Kazakh Party leader Kunaev was not intended as a national insult, but would further the legitimate interests of the Kazakh people.

However, during 1987 committees on nationality and inter-nationality relations were formed in every republic to promote toleration and to make sure that the goals of Soviet nationality policies were being met. One of the tasks of these committees was to help insure that local educational officials were adequately supervising the development of Russian-language skills among the indigenous population. They were also given responsibility for promoting national language training among the Russian population.

The report from Latvia's Committee for Nationality and Inter-nationality Relations that is reproduced below details the types of measures that were initially proposed to promote bilingualism. Proponents of Latvian-language education were the first to gain substantial concessions (such as the introduction of a proficiency exam in Latvian as a high school graduation requirement), but this document makes clear that Russian-language education must take precedence over national language education.

However, by October 1988 the primacy of Russian-language instruction had been challenged in various regions of the country, as nationalist activists in a number of republics called for their national language to be instituted as their republic's state language. In October 1988 the Supreme Soviet of the Latvian SSR endorsed Latvian as the state language of the republic and elaborated a number of additional measures for improved Latvian-language education. Lithuania and Estonia soon followed suit. The legislation which has been introduced in these three republics has been opposed by many of the resident Russians, who maintain that the requirement that the local language become the sole language of official discourse in administration and in local economic enterprises is intended to drive out the nonindigenous population.

In Moldavia, legislation has been proposed to make Moldavian the official language of the republic, and also to restore use of the Latin alphabet. In some variants of this proposal the Moldavian language is identified as being the same as Romanian. Thus, the laws being drafted in Moldavia would create precedents both for alphabet reform and for linguistic consolidation (e.g., of the various Turkic dialects). However, the draft legislation proposed in the Central Asian republics has been comparatively modest. While national-language education has been mandated for the entire population, only a gradual transition to use of the national language in official life is planned. In Kazakhstan, the national language has been made one of two official languages in the republic—the other, of course, being Russian.

The legislation on language that has been passed in the Baltic republics and is pending elsewhere is certain to create myriad problems. The goal of introducing national-language proficiency among the nonindigenous populations of the various republics puts an enormous additional strain on the educational system, already struggling with the longstanding official commitment to achieve Russian-language proficiency in the indigenous population. In many republics this goal is still a distant one. Between one-third and one-half of the young people drafted into the Red Army from the Caucasian and Central Asian republics are deficient in Russian. In these republics, as well as in Moldavia and Estonia, Russian-language training remains deficient, and programs to develop Russian-language proficiency among the older generation are virtually nonexistent. Recent educational reforms have been undermined by the same problems that have always made Russian-language education a limited success. Russian-language teachers are poorly trained; qualified applicants are difficult to attract to teacher-training programs and difficult to retain as teachers. Texts are poorly written and in short supply. Classrooms are overcrowded. Adequate time may be allotted for Russian-language education, but in reality a number of other tasks, including sending students out into the fields at harvest time, often take precedence, substantially reducing the amount of instruction provided.

The situation relating to national language instruction is even worse. An area of longstanding official neglect, as the notice from Turkmenistan reproduced here suggests, the necessary curricular materials are nonexistent and qualified teachers are in extremely short supply. Moreover, with the possible exception of the Baltic republics, republic-level and local officials generally consider the problem of national language education as symbolic and hence not worthy of major investment. Finally, there is the problem of getting Russians to learn and use the local national languages. In each of the Baltic republics, Russian opponents to the national fronts have formed their own "inter-national" organizations whose goals include the preservation of Russian as the official language of each republic. A recent spate of letters in the Russian-language press in these republics suggests real hostility on the part of many Russians toward giving the local national languages status as official or co-official republic languages—guaranteeing the further politicization of the language question and a further heightening of competition over scarce educational resources in the various union republics.

Bilingualism *

A Characteristic Feature of Nations and Nationalities under Developed Socialism

K. Kh. KHANAZAROV

Every historical period, insofar as it manifests certain unique features, leaves a distinct imprint on a nation's or nationality's language and linguistic life. In language, the imprint of a given period is to be seen, first of all, in changes in its vocabulary, especially its enrichment with words that reflect the new levels of economic and sociopolitical development, culture and spiritual life as a whole. A nation's or nationality's linguistic life also undergoes change. *A people's linguistic life is defined by all the languages it uses, taking into account their total number and actual function, all the languages a people draws on to achieve the maximum degree of social intercourse and exchange of ideas at the given stage of their development.* Advancement in a nation's or nationality's linguistic life, it follows, is a more complex and variegated process than the development of their language, for it includes not only the alteration of the particular language as a system, but also the expansion and acceleration in the use of second, third, or even further languages— and one must keep in mind their total number and mutual interaction—by the various nations and nationalities.

Substantial changes in the linguistic life of all nations and nationalities are taking place under developed socialism. Among the different nations and nationalities the incidence of use and relative importance of languages other than their own national languages is growing with each year. This is reflected especially in the increasing role of Russian language as a medium of inter-nationality communication. It is a matter of common knowledge that at the present time there are, in fact, no territories in our country that are inhabited exclusively by a single nationality. With every passing year the multinational character of our republics increases, while both the economic interdependence and the territorial and spiritual-cultural interpenetration among nations and nationalities intensifies.

Under developed socialism the economies and cultures of the republics are being raised to new and ever higher levels. There is a growing exchange of cadres, large numbers of specialists in diverse branches of the economy are constantly moving among the republics, and mutual enrichment in the realm of culture is growing in importance with each year. The intensity of social intercourse among various nations and nationalities has multiplied many times over. These objective and historically

*Reshenie natsional'no-iazykovoi problemy v SSSR, 2nd ed. (Moscow, 1982), pp. 153–165. Russian text © 1982 by "Politizdat."

progressive changes in society cannot but leave a substantial imprint on the nature of the medium of social intercourse among nations and nationalities. As economic specialization and cultural exchange intensify, people of every nation and nationality in ever growing numbers are entering into direct relations with representatives of other nations and nationalities, both within their own republic and also with those who live beyond its borders. This means that with every passing year people in ever larger numbers are using, along with the language of their own nation, languages of other nations and nationalities.

The linguistic life of one nation or nationality can never replicate the linguistic life of another nation or nationality, since this linguistic life in each concrete case has its own nuances, peculiarities, and unique features. But at the same time, under conditions of developed socialism nations and nationalities have that in common in their linguistic life that all of them require for purposes of social intercourse, besides their own national language, a knowledge of other languages and first of all a language of inter-nationality communication.

Developed socialism opens broad vistas for people's reciprocal study of each other's languages, their voluntary mastery and use in everyday social contact. According to the 1970 census, 62.8 million of the 112.7 million non-Russians in our country (i.e., 55.7%), and in 1979 already 72.9 million of the 124.7 million non-Russians (i.e., 58.3%), were either fluent in a second language of the peoples of the USSR or considered as their mother tongue the language of a different nationality.[1]

The creation of ever more democratic conditions and full freedom for the study and use of any and all languages has hastened many times over the resolution of language problems in general and the problem of a language of inter-nationality communication in particular. This had the practical effect of letting Soviet people of all nationalities discover for themselves that the study and mastery of all languages is impossible and, more importantly, unjustified, and that it is more advantageous to concentrate one's attention on the study of a language that is the most suitable for communication among the nations and nationalities. This language turns out to be Russian, the mother tongue of almost three-fifths of our country's population, the carrier of the greatest quantity of scientific-technical information and an inexhaustible spiritual treasure-house.

Human capacities for studying languages are limited by historical conditions. In view of the fact that the study and complete mastery of every new language is a labor requiring many years of intensive effort, the Communist Party supports the aspirations of citizens of all nationalities to attain fluency in primarily two languages— Russian in its capacity as the language of inter-national communication, and the national native tongue. *Bilingualism based on the voluntary mastery of the language of inter-nationality communication and the national mother tongue is the fundamental, leading, and determinant type of bilingualism in the USSR.*

As was observed earlier, in the USSR there are as many as 130 languages, the great majority of whose speakers have lived on the territory of our country from time immemorial. If in addition we take into account the languages of the Germans, Slovaks, Hungarians, Koreans, Poles, Greeks, Rumanians, Finns, and Iranians, all of whom are represented in the USSR by national groups numbering in the many thousands, the number of languages spoken by the population of our country rises to 160 or more. The various combinations of these languages yield such diverse forms and types of bilingualism as practically to exceed imagination. Poles living on the territory of the Lithuanian SSR are bilingual—in Polish and Lithuanian; the Gagauz, who live in the Moldavian and Ukrainian republics, are also bilingual—in Gagauz and Ukrainian or Moldavian; the Uzbeks and Tadzhiks who inhabit the border regions of Uzbekistan and Tadzhikistan are bilingual and, as a rule, fluent in each other's language.

The bilingualism of the Uighurs in Kazakhstan, considerable numbers of whom are fluent in Kazakh, promotes cooperation and team work between Uighurs and the Kazakhs on the job, and helps the Uighurs and Kazakhs to gain access to each other's cultural achievements as well as to learn from each other's industrial experience and economic skills. With their fluency in Georgian, considerable numbers of Ossetians in the South Ossetian Autonomous Oblast are able to study the rich Georgian socialist culture and to expedite mutual understanding and coordination in joint efforts with other speakers of Georgian. Millions of Soviet people of different nationalities with a fluent reading knowledge of English, French, German, Spanish, and other languages gain broad familiarity with the life and struggles of workers abroad, and thus benefit from additional sources of information on the sociopolitical life, economics, and culture of a considerable number of capitalist and socialist countries. Dozens of such examples could be cited.

Thus bilingualism—the knowledge and use of two languages—is a widespread phenomenon in Soviet society. Not only individuals whose profession requires knowledge of some language besides their mother tongue are bilingual, but so are entire peoples or large segments of them.

Bilingualism is a profoundly progressive phenomenon in the development of Soviet society. The words and combinations of each people constitute the repository and material expression of the end product of that people's thought processes and cognition over the entire course of its history. A person who apart from his own mother tongue knows the language of another people can communicate with a larger number of people, gain access to the spiritual riches created by the speakers of the second language he has learned, and acquire a closer and deeper familiarity with their material culture. In light of the enormously positive influence bilingualism brings to bear on the accelerated building of communism, developed socialism considers it an important social phenomenon in the life of all the nationalities of the USSR.

Socialist society manages the development of the linguistic life of nations and nationalities scientifically. The scientific management of linguistic life involves, first of all, a determination of which from the whole variety of forms and types of language skills are most suitable for the practical demands required by the building of communism, those that form the primary link in the chain of linguistic processes and phenomena.

Study of the patterns of linguistic life of socialist nations and nationalities under developed socialism shows that for its advancement a historically essential step is the identification of the primary form and primary type of bilingualism, with the utmost possible encouragement for its accelerated dissemination. The type and the form of bilingualism are organically related and inseparable. The forms of bilingualism are the outward manifestations of their internal functional organization in people's speech and consciousness, depending on the extent of their mastery of these languages. There may, of course, be many forms, depending on the number of languages that may be combined, for any given individual or given nation or nationality may concurrently use one, two, three, or even more languages. The leading form of bilingualism under conditions of developed socialism is the use in everyday oral and written communication of two primary languages—the language of inter-national communication and the national language. Form directs our attention to the languages on whose basis bilingualism develops. Type refers to the extent and quality of command of the two languages. Type signifies a model, which should be emulated and toward which one should aspire. Types of language mastery or usage may also vary, depending on what is considered as a model. The primary type of language mastery under conditions of developed socialism is a good knowledge by citizens of their own national language and a fluency in the language of inter-nationality communication.

It is no coincidence that the writer and commentator Chingiz Aitmatov compares the two languages—the national language and the language of inter-nationality communication—with his two hands, so necessary and irreplaceable is each of them.[2] The two languages are two levers for the development of thought, for the articulation and solution of urgent tasks connected with the development of mature socialism and the building of communism.

Fluency of all citizens of the USSR in their national (mother) tongue and in Russian as the medium of inter-nationality communication—this is the ideal toward which developed socialist society strives. Such is the prime task in the advancement of linguistic life which faces all Soviet nations and nationalities. "Our principal task in language policy," write the authors of the book *The Russian Language as the Medium of Inter-nationality Communication*, "is to facilitate by all means possible the flourishing of national literary languages and at the same time to strive for full mastery of Russian on the part of all citizens of the USSR."[3]

If the problem of bilingualism is put forward as problem number one under developed socialism, then obviously it is essential to define what bilingualism is. *We can say that bilingualism exists where people have a command of a second language to an extent sufficient for intercourse and the exchange of ideas in the process of production of material and spiritual goods.* It should be noted that the mastery of the two languages on the part of the interlocutors may differ in depth, richness, and refinement, but nevertheless for the main and fundamental reason that language exists—for the exchange of ideas—it still meets the requirements of the interlocutors. At the same time we will not raise the question whether an individual thinks in the second language or formulates his thoughts in his first, native, tongue and translates them for purpose of communication into the second language. What is important is not in which language a person thinks, but whether he can communicate and exchange ideas with the help of the second language.

Bilingualism is a dynamic, evolving and changing category.[4] This is due above all to the essential nature of developed socialism, which is typified by rapid rates of economic and cultural development and an unprecedented intensification in inter-course, cooperation, and mutual assistance among our nations and nationalities, with a resulting widespread and accelerating dissemination of bilingualism. Hence, under conditions of mature socialism there is a constant process of improvement and modification of bilingualism. This, as is well known, *begins* when an individual has mastered a second language to a sufficient extent to enable the reciprocal exchange of opinions and for communication with a speaker of the second language. This initial stage of bilingualism gradually evolves into fluency in the two languages, a point when the individual uses the second language as freely and naturally as the first. The *culminating* form of bilingualism is perfect command of both languages, which requires special preparation and work in each of the two languages.

The needs of mature socialism are best met not by the initial but by the second stage of bilingualism: fluency of all citizens in two languages—Russian as the inter-national medium and the national language. A good knowledge of the inter-national medium means the securing of a common linguistic basis for cooperation among all our nations and nationalities. The more people of a given nation or nationality gain fluency in Russian as the inter-nationality medium, the easier and more versatile becomes their intercourse with other nations and nationalities of our country, the more extensive their exchange of opinions, the more effective their cooperation and the process of adoption of each other's best features.

Fluency in the national language binds each Soviet man more closely to his nation or nationality and enables him better to appreciate and utilize more fully the whole spectrum of his nation's long-evolving perception of the environment and reflection of man's inner world.

A nation's language forms and develops in the context of its history and character, the nature of its productive forces and productive relations, its forms of settlement, the dialectical peculiarities of its language, its national oral literary culture, the specifically national features of its way of life, the family, etc. Reflecting in the first instance that which is intrinsic to the given nation, it manifests its own particular qualities and richness and is able to convey the specific nuances of national life. With reference to intrinsically national realities it is capacious and expressive. But at the same time a national language has limited capacities to serve the general public on a national territory since the latter, as a rule, comprises representatives of several nationalities.

The national and inter-national languages, which constitute a single unity on the lips of the Soviet people, provide the optimal medium for exchanging ideas and information. Hence the interaction and complementariness of the inter-national and national languages more fully correspond to the interests of building communism. The national and international languages form a dialectical unity. It is this unity, complementariness, and cooperation between the national and international languages that provide the fullness of communication and information necessary for the strengthening and development of socialist society and the Soviet people. Without an inter-national language it will be impossible to achieve a level of mutual understanding among the dozens of nations and nationalities all speaking different languages sufficient to ensure not simple elementary communication, but a multifaceted and profound unity in our advance toward communism.

The language of inter-nationality communication ushers into the all-union and international arenas everything of significance that may be communicated with the help of national languages, infuses the latter with new vigor and ideas, a new stimulus for development and enrichment, and increases their expressive capacities and their role as an effective medium for mobilizing Soviet people for the great tasks involved in building communism.

Thus, while it fully welcomes the study of languages of the peoples of the USSR and foreign countries by Soviet people, developed socialism regards as of paramount importance the problem of fluency in the international Russian language and one's own national (native) tongue.

To be successful, the building of communism imposes ever new tasks with regard to advancing the linguistic life of Soviet nations and nationalities. A good deal still remains to be done. As the data of the 1979 census show, over one-third of the non-Russian population had a poor or no command of Russian as the medium of inter-nationality communication.

The international Russian language is the most important element in the linguistic life of the nations and nationalities of our country under conditions of developed socialism. It serves the noble cause of economic cooperation and mutual cultural enrichment of all nations and nationalities, as well as their sociopolitical solidarity and unity. The building of communism involves such quickening in communication among the entire multinational population of the USSR and such intensification in the exchange of material and spiritual values, that without a common international language they would be inconceivable; in the life of every nation and nationality under developed socialism the language of internationality communication is just as essential as the national language. The international Russian language has become an inseparable part of the Soviet socialist way of life and one of its essential features. It is "a powerful catalyst in the process of convergence of nations."[5] The Soviet socialist system, the de facto equality of nations, and the Communist Party's consistent implementation of the Leninist nationality policy all have created fundamentally new conditions in our country owing to which bilingualism in the USSR has been transformed into a historically new type of bilingualism.

The propagation of the international Russian language and its significance and functions in the life and destiny of the first land of socialism as well as in the continued strengthening of the internationalist unity of Soviet society in the building of communism is one of the most important components of ideological work and political education under present-day conditions. The point is that while all citizens of the USSR understand the importance of the language of inter-nationality communication, this understanding must be transformed into a profound conviction. Books, pamphlets, and articles filled with interesting facts and written in a colorful and lucid language, explaining in a thoroughly scientific way the essence and role of bilingualism in the USSR,[6] will help the Soviet people to become passionate and staunch propagators of Russian as the language of inter-nationality communication and as a prerequisite for continued successes in the building of communism.[7]

Reliance of every nation and nationality on two languages—the language of internationality communication and the national language—is a characteristic feature of developed socialism, one that promotes their continued flourishing and convergence in the process of building communism.

Notes

1. Calculated from: *Itogi Vsesoiuznoi perepisi naseleniia 1970 goda*, vol. 4, p. 20; *Naselenie SSSR*, p. 23; these do not include data on individuals who have less than fluent knowledge of a second language, that is, those unable to "converse fluently in this language" (cf. *Vsesoiuznaia perepis' naseleniia—vsenarodnoe delo*, Moscow, 1969, p. 46), but apparently still able to read and understand the spoken language. Such, it may be surmised, are considerably more numerous than those who are fluent in a second language. It should be noted that the census instructions state: ". . . if the respondent is fluent in two or more languages of the peoples of the USSR in addition to his mother tongue, only that language in which he is more fluent should be recorded" (*ibid.*). Consequently, the census does not take into account persons who may be fluent in two, three, or more languages of the peoples of the USSR or foreign countries. Such people in our country number in the many millions (for example, Karakalpaks who are fluent in R⋅⋅ssian, Uzbek, and Kazakh; Kirghiz fluent in Russian, Kazakh, and Uzbek; Tadzhiks—in Russian and Uzbek; Uzbeks—in Russian and Tadzhik; Armenians—in Azerbaidzhani and Russian, and so on).

2. See *Voprosy literatury*, 1976, no. 8, pp. 162–163.

3. *Russkii iazyk kak sredstvo mezhnatsional'nogo obshcheniia*, p. 3.

4. See Iu. D. Desheriev and I. F. Protchenko, "Osnovnye aspekty issledovaniia dvuiazychiia i mnogoiazychiia," in *Problemy dvuiazychiia i mnogoiazychiia*, p. 34.

5. Sh. R. Rashidov, "Moguchee sredstvo internatsional'nogo vospitaniia," *Kommunist Uzbekistana*, 1972, no. 6, p. 5.

6. See ibid. and, by the same author: "Iazyk bratstva i druzhby narodov," *Kommunist*, 1976, No. 3, pp. 15–26; *Iazyk druzhby i bratstva*, Tashkent, 1978; *Iazyk nashego edinstva i sotrudnichestva*, Moscow, 1979; and *Iazyk druzhby, bratstva i sotrudnichestva*, Tashkent, 1979; I. K. Beloded, *Russkii iazyk—iazyk mezhnatsional'nogo obshcheniia narodov SSSR*, Kiev, 1962; V. G. Kostomarov, *Programma KPSS o russkom iazyke*, Moscow, 1963; M. Musin, *Bratstvo narodov, sodruzhestvo iazykov*, Kazan, 1964; *Russkii iazyk v sovremennom mire*, Moscow, 1974; N. G. Samsonov, *Im razgovarival Lenin*, Yakutsk, 1974; V. G. Kostomarov, *Russkii iazyk sredi drugikh iazykov mira*, Moscow, 1975; Iu. Desheriev and B. Khasanov, *Iazyk mezhnatsional'nogo obshcheniia*, Alma Ata, 1976; A. K. Kanimetov, *Iazyk bratskogo edinstva*, Frunze, 1976; *Russkii iazyk—iazyk mezhnatsional'nogo obshcheniia narodov SSSR*, Moscow, 1976; *Russkii iazyk—iazyk mezhnatsional'nogo obshcheniia i edineniia narodov SSSR*, Kiev, 1976; *Russkii iazyk—iazyk druzhby i sotrudnichestva narodov SSSR*, Moscow, 1980; S. Sh. Shermakhamedov, *Russkii iazyk—velikoe i moguchee sredstvo obshcheniia sovetskogo naroda*, Moscow, 1980; and others.

7. See M. S. Dzhunusov, "Sotsial'nye aspekty dvuiazychiia v SSSR," in *Sotsiologiia i ideologiia*, Moscow, 1969, pp. 433–44; M. M. Mikhailov, *Dvuiazychie*, Cheboksary, 1969; F. P. Filin, "Istoriia obshchestva i razvitie dvuiazychiia," *Izvestiia AN SSSR OLIa*, 1970, no. 3; *Problemy dvuiazychiia i mnogoiazychiia*, Moscow, 1972; N. S. Motrich, "Svobodnoe razvitie iazykov narodov SSSR na osnove ravnopraviia i vzaimoobogashcheniia kak neobkhodimoe uslovie dvuiazychiia," in *Ideologicheskaia bor'ba i aktual'nye voprosy filologii*, Dnepropetrovsk, 1974; S. I. Bruk and M. N. Guboglo, "Dvuiazychie i sblizhenie natsii SSSR," *Sovetskaia etnografiia*, 1975, no. 4; D. I. Marinesku, *Dvuiazychie—faktor sblizheniia sotsialisticheskikh natsii i narodnostei*, Kishinev, 1975; K. Kh. Khanazarov, "Dvuiazychie," *Kommunist Latvii*, 1976, no. 4; A. D. Shveitser, *Sovremennaia sotsiolingvistika: Teoriia, problemy, metody*, Moscow, 1976; and others.

The General and the Particular in the Development of the Linguistic Life of Soviet Society *

M. N. GUBOGLO

The dialectical unity of national and international elements in all spheres of social life draws the ever growing interest of social scientists. It has quite rightly become one of the main topics in the study of current nationality problems. Its relevance stems from the fact that the consistent implementation of the Leninist nationalities policy has created favorable conditions for the fruitful development and convergence of the ways of life, science, culture, and customs of all the nationalities of the USSR. A most important role in this belongs to ethnolinguistic processes—those processes that encompass the functional development, interaction, and mutual enrichment of the languages of the nations and nationalities of the USSR in the course of interaction among their speakers. Under present-day conditions—with the development of our country's economy as a unified economic complex and the further consolidation of internationalist unity within the new historical community that is the Soviet people—an objectively expanding role attaches to such processes as the rise and development of bilingualism in our country. This includes the growing role of Russian as the language of inter-nationality communication in such tasks as the building of communism, the further refinement of nationality-related aspects in the processes of social change, the consolidation of internal unity of the nations and nationalities of the USSR, the education of the new man, and gaining access to the treasures of world culture.

Nationality problems, including the linguistic dimensions of national life and inter-nationality relations, occupy a prominent place in V. I. Lenin's theoretical legacy. They are still pertinent today, as the scientific-technological revolution necessarily helps strengthen ties among the nationalities, promoting the growth and consolidation of friendship and brotherhood among the peoples of the USSR. The linguistic aspects of nationality relations are also a factor of no small importance in the present-day ideological struggle, especially vis-à-vis the numerous attacks by anticommunists on the Soviet approach to solving language problems within the context of the overall solution of the national question in our country.

The development of linguistic life in the multinational Soviet society is a dynamically evolving reality which gives rise to ever new problems and challenges. In parallel with the development of the mother tongues of the nations and nationalities

---

*Sotsial'nye aspekty istorii sovetskogo naroda kak novoi sotsial'no-internatsional'noi obshchnosti liudei (Moscow, 1982), pp. 218–30. Russian text © 1982 by Moscow University Press.

of the USSR, there is taking place a continuing diffusion of Russian, an intensification of its influence on all aspects of the population's economic and spiritual life, and the development on this basis of bilingualism in the national language and Russian—a milestone in the historical development of the linguistic life of our country as it heads toward communism. The expanding role of Russian in the unflagging development and convergence of the nations and nationalities of the Soviet Union meets the fundamental needs of all our peoples and represents an objective, historically determined process, a dialectical unity between the general and the particular in our country's linguistic life. This process, as has been noted in a series of Party documents, should be neither forcibly hastened nor, even more, artificially held back, since this would be counter to the main tendency that characterizes the linguistic life of a mature socialist society. In his message of greeting to the participants at the All-Union Scientific-Theoretical Conference on "The Russian Language as the Language of Friendship and Cooperation among the Peoples of the USSR," held in Tashkent in May 1979, the General Secretary of the Central Committee of the CPSU and Chairman of the Presidium of the Supreme Soviet of the USSR, L. I. Brezhnev, wrote: "Under conditions of developed socialism, with our country's economy already transformed into a unified economic complex, there has emerged a new historical community, the Soviet people, and there is taking place an objective expansion in the role of Russian as the language of inter-nationality communication in the building of communism and the education of the new man."[1] Already in the prerevolutionary period Lenin noted that reasons of economic necessity "will always cause nationalities living within the confines of a single state (so long as they desire to live together) to learn the language of the majority. The more democratic the order in Russia will be, the more inexorably will the demands of economic interaction impel the various nationalities to learn the language most suitable for general commercial intercourse."[2] And Lenin had no doubt that in our country it was Russian that was predestined by history itself to fulfill a crucial mission—to become naturally and without compulsion, the language of inter-nationality communication. "People whose conditions of life and work require knowledge of the Russian language will learn it without the rod," he emphasized in the article "Is a Compulsory Official Language Necessary?" "Coercion (the rod) will lead to only one thing: it will hinder the great and mighty Russian language from spreading to other national groups and, most importantly, it will sharpen antagonism, create friction in a million new forms, increase resentment, mutual misunderstanding, and so on."[3]

The correlation between the general and the particular in the panorama of linguistic life of the nations and nationalities of the USSR is revealed most strikingly in the 1979 census data. These returns show that over the historically speaking relatively short nine-year span between censuses, under conditions of developed socialism the total number of persons fluent in Russian (including Russians themselves) increased from 183.7 to 214.8 million, i.e., from 76% to 82% of the population. In other words, while in 1970 three out of every four persons were fluent in Russian, in 1979 four out of five of residents of the USSR were fluent in the language.[4] Over the same period, the number of persons of non-Russian nationality claiming fluency in Russian as a second language increased by almost 20 million, from 41.9 to 61.3 million. At the same time the segment of non-Russian population claiming Russian as their mother tongue grew from 13.0 to 16.3 million. Thus, while in 1970 about half (48.7%) of the total non-Russian population had fluent command of Russian, by 1979 almost two-thirds (62.2%) did. This, without question, corroborates the fact that the main trend characterizing the development of various types of bilingualism in our country today is the spread of national-Russian bilingualism.

Concurrently, the position of international factors is also becoming stronger. This process does not occur spontaneously, or at the expense of the role played by the national languages, but through the comprehensive functional development of national factors, the incorporation of the national in the international, and the consolidation of the international within the national. While the share of our country's population that was fluent in some non-Russian language as a second language grew by one-half percentage point in the intercensal period, the share that was fluent in Russian grew by 6.1 percentage points. It is an interesting fact, first of all, that the continuing diffusion of Russian as a medium of inter-nationality communication in no way inhibits the development of other types of bilingualism and multilingualism in which some non-Russian language figures as the second language. Again, as of 1979, the proportion of the Russian population that was fluent in a non-Russian language as a second language had increased by 0.5 percentage point. In other words, the total number of bilinguals among the Russians represented 4.8 million persons. Secondly, the widespread diffusion of various types of bilingualism, including national-language–Russian bilingualism, has not led to linguistic assimilation. The relative share of the total population of the USSR (including Russians) who consider the language of their own nationality as their mother tongue remained essentially unchanged, decreasing only from 93.9% in 1970 to 93.1% in 1979.

As we turn to an analysis of the data in Table 1, we should mention that in the course of our description of the main trends in our country's linguistic life as it is connected with the spread of national-language–Russian bilingualism, some questions may arise with regard to the other nationalities. For this reason, it may be well to present (as is done in Table 1) all the titular nationalities of the union republics, with the exception of the Russians, in the order of increasing relative proportion of national-language–Russian bilingualism within each nationality as of 1970. Thus, it may be clearly seen that the differential between Uzbeks and Belorussians, who at that time were at the opposite extremes in terms of this index (14.5% and 49.0 %), was 34.5 percentage points. By 1979 a shift had occurred in the variations among the nationalities: first of all, the extremes were now occupied by Belorussians and Estonians (57.0% and 24.2%) and, secondly, the differential had decreased to under 32.8 percentage points. In other words, the general line of development in our country's linguistic life has been tending toward equalization among the union-republic nationalities with regard to the share of their members who are fluent in the language of inter-nationality communication. Among most of the union-republic

Table 1

Changes in the Size of the Bilingual Population in the Union Republics

	Changes in the size of the population fluent in a second language of the peoples of the USSR (in %)					
	Russian			Other		
	Year			Year		
Nationality	1970	1979	Change 1970–1979	1970	1979	Change 1970–1979
Total population of the USSR	17.3	23.4	+ 6.1	4.2	4.7	+ 0.5
including:						
Russians	—	—	—	3.0	3.5	+ 0.5
Uzbeks	14.5	49.3	+ 34.8	3.3	2.8	− 0.5
Tadzhiks	15.4	29.6	+ 14.2	12.0	10.6	− 1.4
Turkmens	15.4	25.4	+ 10.0	1.3	1.6	+ 0.3
Azerbaidzhanis	16.6	29.5	+ 12.9	2.5	2.0	− 0.5
Kirghiz	19.1	29.4	+ 10.3	3.3	4.1	+ 0.8
Georgians	21.3	26.7	+ 5.4	1.0	0.9	− 0.1
Estonians	29.0	24.2	− 4.8	2.0	1.9	− 0.1
Armenians	30.1	38.6	+ 8.5	6.0	5.7	− 0.3
Lithuanians	35.9	52.1	+ 16.2	1.9	1.5	− 0.4
Moldavians	36.1	47.4	+ 11.3	3.6	3.9	+ 0.3
Ukrainians	36.3	49.8	+ 13.5	6.0	7.1	+ 1.1
Kazakhs	41.8	52.3	+ 10.5	1.8	2.1	+ 0.3
Latvians	45.2	56.7	+ 11.5	2.4	2.2	− 0.2
Belorussians	49.0	57.0	+ 8.0	7.3	11.7	+ 4.4

Sources: Itogi Vsesoiuznoi perepisi naseleniia 1970 g., vol. 4; *Naselenie SSSR. Po dannym Vsesoiuznoi perepisi naseleniia 1979 g.*
Note: The plus and minus signs indicate the percentage point change (increased +, or decreased −) in the share of bilinguals (covering all varieties of bilingualism: national-language–Russian, Russian–national-language, and national–national) among the union republic nationalities in 1979 in comparison with 1970.

nationalities the spread of national-language–Russian bilingualism has proceeded at a relatively uniform rate. Thus, for example, among the Kazakhs, Turkmen, Kirghiz, Moldavians, Latvians, Azerbaidzhanis, Ukrainians, Tadzhiks, and Lithuanians, the share of those fluent in Russian grew by 10.0 to 16.2 percentage points. Somewhat lower—between 5.4 and 8.5 percentage points—was the increase in the share of Georgians, Belorussians, and Armenians who were bilingual in their national tongue and in Russian. As far as the Belorussians are concerned, the small increase in the percentage of bilinguals is easily explained by the fact that already by 1970 about half the Belorussians were fluent in Russian and a further 19.0% claimed it as their mother tongue. Consequently, the possibilities for a substantial increase in

Belorussian–Russian bilingualism were relatively limited, since elderly people have relatively fewer opportunities to master the language of another nationality in comparison with young people. And indeed, the further increase in the share of bilinguals is occurring mainly among the younger generations.

The relatively low incidence of knowledge of Russian among Georgians and Armenians may be explained by the fact that some young people, especially in rural localities, do not manage to achieve sufficient mastery of Russian in their school years. This has been pointed out in the literature. Accordingly, in the late 1970s a whole series of measures were undertaken in the Georgian and Armenian SSRs to facilitate the acquisition of Russian by young people and to improve the quality of instruction in Russian in the national schools.

In his address on "The Sixtieth Anniversary of the Victory of Soviet Power in Georgia and the Formation of the Communist Party of Georgia," First Secretary of the Central Committee of the Communist Party of the Georgian SSR, E. A. Shevardnadze, paid special attention to the linguistic aspects of nationality relations. "Considerable attention is devoted [in the republic—M.G.] to the Russian language, the language of inter-nationality communication," it was particularly stressed. "The matter stands as follows: Alongside his mother tongue, every inhabitant of our republic should acquire a perfect knowledge of Russian—the language of brotherhood for all peoples of the USSR, the language of October, the language of Lenin."[5]

Judging from the 1979 census data, the ethnolinguistic experience of the Uzbeks and Estonians will most certainly elicit the greatest interest among researchers and practical workers. Indeed, how can one explain the fast-growing increase in national-language–Russian bilingualism among Uzbeks and the decrease in the share of bilingual Estonians? Clearly, a comparative analysis of these two examples has not only scholarly but also quite significant practical importance.

Let us turn to the basic variables in the development of current ethnolinguistic processes and examine in particular how they are manifested in the linguistic life of the Uzbeks and the Estonians. As our source material for an analysis of this kind we can take the results of representative ethnosociological surveys carried out by the Institute of Ethnography of the USSR Academy of Sciences in a number of union and autonomous republics, including Uzbekistan and Estonia.[6]

As ethnosociological studies have shown, in the acquisition of Russian by Uzbeks the general education school plays the most important role. It is not by chance that in response to the question where they learned Russian, 41.5% of urban Uzbeks answered that it was in school. By way of contrast, all other responses, such as military service, the parental home, contacts with friends, study at institutions of higher learning, accounted for only 21.8% in the aggregate. (For the countryside the corresponding figures were 29.8% and 18.2%.) Consequently, the outcome of ethnolinguistic processes as a whole, and the direction and scope of Uzbek–Russian bilingualism in particular, are determined mainly at school. Such a conclusion is in complete accord with the 1970 census data, according to which the general education school played the decisive role in the spread of bilingualism among the non-Russian population of our country. We might recall that, on the average, the proportion of bilinguals in the age group 11-19 was more than five times higher than in the next younger age group (0-10 years), and, although it did not reach its potential maximum, it still accounted for almost half of the youth of the non-Russian union-republic nationalities.

Consequently, we may assume that the higher the share that school-age children and youth constitute within the population of a particular nationality, the higher, comparatively speaking, will be the indices for the prevalence of bilingualism, thanks to the influence of the school factor. A comparison of the age structures of Uzbeks and Estonians as of 1970 confirms this hypothesis. And in fact, among the Uzbeks children under the age of ten constitute 38.6% of the total, while for Estonians this figure is 14.7%. This means that a highly significant, objective variable that accounts for the difference between Uzbeks and Estonians in their acquisition of Russian appears to be difference in their demographic structure. We should expect no significant changes to take place in the panorama of ethnolinguistic life of the Uzbek and Estonian populations in the near future, since between 1970 and 1979 the total number of Uzbeks grew by 35.5% while that of Estonians grew by 1.3%.

Age structure, of course, is by no means the only objective variable that accounts for the faster spread of Russian among the Uzbek population. Clearly, a number of other factors have made their influence felt, such as the specific ethnic mix of work collectives at a number of enterprises, especially in the republic's cities. Subjective factors, certainly, were also significant, in the first instance the enormous efforts made by Party and soviet organizations in the Uzbek SSR to create the most favorable conditions possible for Uzbeks to master Russian. A feature of general nature in the management of current ethnolinguistic processes is to be seen in the fact that Party and soviet organizations in the union and autonomous republics view the language factor as an inseparable component of the nationality factor. In this sense what is common to all the republics and regions of our country is the fact that the improvement of relations among the nationalities represents an aggregate of tasks whose purpose is to guarantee the following: first, the unflagging development of the nations and nationalities of the USSR; second, the further gradual convergence of nations and the consolidation of friendship among peoples as an important factor in the comprehensive development of Soviet society; third, an optimal balance between the general and the particular, the national and the international, a balance that corresponds to the particular historical stage in the development of Soviet society; fourth, the strengthening of the USSR as a type of state that has stood the test of history, one that harmoniously reflects all-union and national-autonomous interests; fifth, the education of the new man, the builder of communism, as a confirmed internationalist, free from every manifestation of nationalism and chauvinism, national egoism, or national nihilism.[8] In attributing such importance to the refinement of the entire system of nationality relations and all possible forms and methods for the internationalist education of workers, the CPSU is aware of the enormous role to be played by the spread of bilingualism, especially of the national-language-Russian kind. In recent years, as is well known, a series of important measures have been undertaken in Uzbekistan whose goal is the further improvement in the teaching of Russian throughout the entire system of preschool, general, and higher education. Particularly important was the introduction of Russian-language teaching in the national school starting with the first grade. Considerable efforts have also been made in the republic to increase the numbers and to raise the professional qualifications of Russian-language teachers who are trained at fourteen pedagogical institutes, three universities, and a number of special secondary educational institutions. In addition, hundreds of graduates from Uzbek schools have acquired a specialization in the teaching of Russian at thirty pedagogical institutes in the RSFSR and the Ukrainian SSR.[9]

In addition to these measures, the republic has also devoted serious attention to such matters as strengthening the pedagogical and material base for the teaching of Russian language and literature, equipping Russian language laboratories with audio-visual aids, and improving the work of the mass media—radio and television, the press; the preparation in accordance with scientific principles of textbooks and teaching aids for Russian, dictionaries, and guides to methodology; and the translation into Uzbek of the best works of world belle-lettres and social-science literature, first and foremost the forty-five volumes of V. I. Lenin's *Polnoe sobranie sochinenii* [Complete Collected Works] and the works of L. I. Brezhnev, *Leninskim kursom* [On a Leninist Course].

Measures undertaken in the Uzbek republic to stimulate knowledge of Russian and to reinforce the non-Russian population's desire to master it more fully have not been negligible. Thus, in particular, more than five hundred dual-language schools have been established in the Uzbek SSR with Russian as one of the languages of instruction. Since 1973 annual republic-wide school competitions have been held to test knowledge of the Russian language and Russian literature. Many of the participants and champions in these contests have gained entry to the language departments of our country's pedagogical institutes and universities. Much success derives from work in preschool education and extracurricular activities. For example, in school clubs and Pioneer palaces so-called "five-minute periods" during which poems, fairy-tales, and stories are read in Russian have become quite widespread. An all-republic boarding school has been successfully established in Tashkent, and more than fifteen others in which Russian is studied according to an intensive curriculum have been set up throughout the rest of the republic.

Especially significant in this regard are the All-Union Scientific-Practical Conferences on Current Problems in Teaching Russian and the Spread of National-Language–Russian Bilingualism, held in Tashkent, that have already become something of a tradition. A valuable contribution toward the propagation of Russian as the language of friendship and fraternity among the peoples of the USSR has been made by Sh. R. Rashidov, the First Secretary of the Central Committee of the Communist Party of Uzbekistan, both through his scholarly and organizational activities and through his own writings.

Thus, through a combination of objective and subjective factors, but first and

Table 2

Changes in the Size of Populations of the Autonomous Republics of the RSFSR with Fluency in a Second Language of the Peoples of the USSR (in %, according to 1979 census data)

	Fluent in					
	Russian			Other		
	Year			Year		
Nationality	1970	1979	Change 1970–1979	1970	1979	Change 1970–1979
Tuvinians	38.9	59.2	+ 20.3	0.4	0.2	− 0.2
Daghestanis	41.7	60.3	+ 18.6	8.9	8.3	− 0.6
Yakuts	41.7	55.6	+ 13.9	1.1	1.1	+ − 0
Bashkirs	53.3	64.9	+ 11.6	2.6	2.8	+ 0.2
Chuvash	58.4	64.8	+ 6.4	5.5	5.5	+ − 0
Ossetians	58.6	64.9	+ 6.3	10.7	12.2	+ 1.5
Mari	62.4	69.9	+ 7.5	6.2	5.5	− 0.7
Tatars	6.25	68.9	+ 6.4	5.3	4.9	− 0.4
Udmurts	63.3	64.4	+ 1.1	6.9	6.4	− 0.5
Komi	64.8	64.4	− 0.4	5.2	5.8	+ 0.6
Mordvinians	65.7	65.5	− 0.2	8.1	7.7	− 0.4
Chechens	66.7	76.0	+ 9.3	1.0	0.7	− 0.3
Buriats	66.7	71.9	+ 5.2	2.7	2.5	− 0.2
Karachai	67.6	75.5	+ 7.9	1.2	0.9	− 0.3
Ingush	71.2	79.6	+ 8.4	0.9	0.6	− 0.3
Kabardinians	71.4	76.7	+ 5.2	0.8	0.6	− 0.2
Balkars	71.5	77.4	+ 5.9	2.5	1.4	− 1.1
Kalmyks	81.1	84.1	+ 3.0	1.5	1.0	− 0.5
Karelians	59.1	51.3	− 7.8	15.1	13.2	− 1.9

Sources: Itogi Vsesoiuznoi perepisi naseleniia, 1970 g. vol. 4; *Naselenie SSSR. Po dannym Vsesoiuznoi perepisi naseleniia 1979 g.*

foremost through the purposeful language policy conducted in the Uzbek SSSR, significant achievements in the diffusion of the Russian language and the formation of Uzbek–Russian bilingualism have been made during the 1970s. Naturally, in this process the desire of Uzbeks themselves to master more fully the language of inter-nationality communication played a role of no small importance. It is no coincidence that above-mentioned ethnosociological studies revealed a widespread desire among Uzbeks to have school instruction of their children conducted in the Russian lan-guage. In favor of this, to be precise, were 28.6% of urban Uzbeks and one-fifth of the rural inhabitants. Furthermore, this tendency proved to be stronger as one moved from older to younger age groups and from socio-occupational groups engaged in physical labor to groups engaged in mental labor. It follows, then, that with the growing urbanization and intellectualization of our society, and the levelling of differences between the city and the countryside and between mental and physical labor, the demand for Russian will increase. The ethnolinguistic experience of Uzbekistan discussed here is a vivid example of its successful realization.

If we turn now to peoples organized in autonomous republics and oblasts, where national-language–Russian bilingualism began to develop earlier and somewhat more widely than in the union republics, we will easily discern a considerable proportion of bilingual individuals not only among youth but also among older people (Table 2).

Thus, the formation and development of the new historical community—the Soviet people—quite obviously has stimulated a tendency toward further diffusion of Russian as the main medium of social discourse and a most important factor promoting extensive communication among all the nations and nationalities of the USSR and the acceleration of processes of their development and convergence.

V. I. Lenin's fervent dream was "that the closest possible intercourse and fraternal unity should be established among the oppressed classes of all the nations that inhabit Russia, without distinction," and that every resident of our country "should have the opportunity to learn the great Russian language."[10] Today this dream of Lenin's, as L. I. Brezhnev stressed in his letter of greeting to the participants at the Tashkent conference, "is truly becoming a reality."[11]

The dialectical unity of the national and the international, the general and the specific, in our linguistic life finds clear reflection not only in columns of figures from census statistics. It appears everywhere, in every sphere of social life, including in belle-lettres.

In the Report of the Central Committee of the CPSU to the Twenty-sixth Congress, much attention was devoted to the development and convergence of the nations and nationalities of the USSR and a profound analysis given to the social function of nationality-related issues in the overall course of the building of communism. And although its linguistic aspects were not discussed in the materials of the Congress, their relevance is perfectly clear. It follows both from the resolutions of the Twenty-fourth and Twenty-fifth Party congresses and from a whole series of other Party documents. Enormously important in this regard, in both sociopolitical and scientific-theoretical terms, were the above-mentioned conference in Tashkent and L. I. Brezhnev's letter of greeting to its participants. In its very essence this is a most important political document, with a powerful ideological message. It provides an impressive overview of the "consistent implementation" of the Leninist nationality policy and of the "fruitful process of cultural, scientific, and educational development in all the union and autonomous republics and the autonomous districts of our country." As L. I .Brezhnev emphasized, "in this, the languages of all the nations and nationalities of the USSR play a most important role. As they develop, freely and on an equal basis, and mutually enrich one another, they contribute to the progress of the national cultures, which are united by the inviolable commonality of their socialist content."[12]

As well as ascertaining the general lines of development of our country's linguistic life, especially trends in bilingualism, it is also necessary to know its sociocultural function, sociopolitical effect, and ideological impact. Let us examine in this connection some examples of national-language–Russian bilingualism as it affects the development and interaction of the cultures of the peoples of the USSR.

Culture, let us remind ourselves, in the broad sociological sense of the word, refers to the production of cultural values, the objectified products of creative activity, their dissemination, and finally, their assimilation by the popular masses—that is, it is understood as the creation and consumption of cultural goods.

The dialectical unity of the general and the particular, the international and national, is clearly to be seen in what people read, the reading habits of people belonging to different social groups and nationalities. The Soviet people are the most avid readers in the world. This is now a well-known fact. But in every nation and nationality, national and ethnic group in our country there are active and passive readers, young and old, highly educated and barely literate—all with an interest in writers of their own nationality and those of other nationalities. In the final analysis these differences are not particularly important. The main point is that with each passing year books and reading habits are becoming a more deeply ingrained part of our lives. If we take into account that language is a book's most important formal attribute, then our analysis of reading tastes according to the language of the works of literature being read will show none other than the functional interaction of national languages and national cultures of the peoples of the USSR.

In reference to reading habits, the national and the international consists in the fact that the non-Russian peoples of our country have the opportunity to read both in their own language and in the language of some other nationality. The Russians in their turn become familiar with the national cultures of the peoples of the USSR through translations of national works into their own language. In fact, all the non-Russian peoples[a] eagerly take advantage of the opportunity to read literature in two languages—their mother tongue and in the language of inter-nationality communication. However, the relative proportion of reading done in one language or another differs, of course, among various peoples. The speakers of languages with only a recent history of literary use, who have not yet created their own extensive multi-genre national literature, in order not to fall behind the mainstream of development of general Soviet culture frequently turn to literatures written in languages with a long-established literary tradition, especially Russian, and with the aid of Russian, they also gain access to the literary heritage of all other peoples of the USSR. But even among the union-republic nationalities there are significant variations in incidence of reading in two languages. Ethnosociological studies, in particular, have shown that among the Moldavian urban and rural population the proportion of persons who read literature in two languages (Moldavian and Russian) is over five times greater than among the Estonians. Especially impressive is the extent of "bilingual" reading among peoples of autonomous-republic status, though even here one may observe wide fluctuations. The relative weight of persons who read in two languages among Karelian rural residents is almost five times higher than the proportion of bilingual readers among rural Tatars.

Investigations of our population's reading habits have shown that in the postwar

period the younger generations of Moldavians, Uzbeks, and Estonians read literature in the language of their own nationality more than their older countrymen do.

But in the late 1960s and early 1970s many representatives of the non-Russian
peoples began to sense a deeper need for a good knowledge of Russian and for its use
in various spheres of life.

Especially revealing in this respect is the experience of youth aged 18–19 who
began to participate in cultural life at the stage of developed socialism, and that of
people of the middle generation (30–39 years old) whose period of socialization
coincided with the years of the Great Fatherland War and the first postwar years. In
both of these age groups, the habit of reading literature in Russian or alternately in
two languages (Russian and the national language) has become more deeply ingrained than among older people.

In other words, in the postwar period the population's growing need to develop their
particular national cultures led to an accelerated growth of original national literature.
The existence of the latter then extended the potential for developing reading habits in
one's mother tongue. In its turn, the overall rise in the spiritual wealth and intellectual
potential of our nations led to a gradual extension, from one generation to the next, in
the scope of literary bilingualism in the sphere of acculturation.

On the whole the development of bilingualism of the national-language–Russian
type, like its development in other forms, provides the bilingual population with
much broader possibilities by comparison with the monolingual population.

But as experience has shown, it is not merely a matter of cultural consumption.
The interrelationship between ethnolinguistic and ethnocultural processes goes
much deeper. Academician P. N. Fedoseev has argued persuasively that at the
current stage of development of nationality relations the main task is to ensure that
inter-nationality and nationality interests blend harmoniously, to develop and discover the ever new forms of linkage between them that are elicited by life itself.[13]

And in fact, before our very eyes, bilingualism is penetrating into the domain of
creative activity, i.e., the creation of cultural treasures.

Recently there appeared in print a collection of poems by V. Vladykin, with the
poetic title *Otchego poet tiuragai* [Why the Tiuragai Sings] (in the Udmurt language[b] *tiuragai* means lark). The appearance of this book has symbolic importance.
Its distinction lies in the fact that its contents (lyrical and philosophical reflections,
parables and poems) appeared in print simultaneously in Udmurt and Russian.
Without any doubt, this example deserves special attention. Examples of translation
of belles-lettres from some languages into many others are hardly rare in the history
of literature.[14] Somewhat less frequent, though already something of a tradition, are
works by national authors written in Russian. It is hardly necessary to mention in
this connection the works of Iu. Rytkheu, G. Khodzher, Iu. Shestalov, and many
others. There is yet another kind of example. The journal *Druzhba narodov* [Friend-
ship among Peoples] has published a novel by the Azerbaidzhani writer Ch. Guseinov with the subheading "translated from the Azerbaidzhani mother-tongue into
the Russian mother tongue."

Vladykin's artistry provides an example that stands apart from these others. His works are published not in translation from Udmurt into Russian, but, as it were, in the author's original variants of each work simultaneously in both languages. His very first literary reviewer[15] was able to conclude that bilingual creativity permitted this Udmurt poet to express his thoughts and feelings more expansively.

The example represented by Vladykin is, evidently, not an isolated one in our country. Edmund Günter, a poet from the Altai, writes in two languages, German and Russian. It would appear that between the two tendencies noted above—the tendency for bilingualism to spread and the tendency for reading habits to broaden (the habits of cultural consumption in two languages, in reading and in listening)—there is a direct link.

The growing spiritual needs of the bilingual reader have called into being a completely new type of spiritual creativity—bilingual creativity. This represents a manifestation of the dialectical unity between the national and the international in the domain of language and, at the same time, in the domain of culture. As for us, we face the task of assessing properly and thoroughly the interconnection between these tendencies.

Editor's notes

a. The Russian text says "all *Russian* peoples"—in the context, clearly an error.

b. The Udmurts are a Finnic-speaking people of the middle Volga region, organized in an autonomous republic within the RSFSR. In 1979 they numbered over 700,000 people, of whom 69% were reported as bilingual in Udmurt and Russian.

Annotated by Lubomyr Hajda

Notes

1. L. I. Brezhnev, *Leninskim kursom. Rechi, privetstviia, stat'i*, vol. 8 (Moscow, 1981), p. 44.

2. V. I. Lenin, *Polnoe sobranie sochinenii*, vol. 23, p. 423; vol. 24, p. 116.

3. Ibid., vol. 24, p. 295.

4. *Itogi Vsesoiuznoi perepisi naseleniia 1970 goda*, vol. 4 (Moscow, 1973, p. 5; *Naselenie SSSR. Po dannym Vsesoiuznoi perepisi naseleniia 1979 goda* (Moscow, 1980), pp. 23–27.

5. *Pravda*, May 21, 1981.

6. *Opyt etnosotsiologicheskogo izucheniia obraza zhizni* (Moscow, 1980), pp. 5–10 and passim.

7. Ethnolinguistic processes in Uzbekistan are examined in the article, M. N. Guboglo, "Tendentsii razvitiia natsional'no-russkogo dvuiazychiia. (Po materialam Uzbekskoi SSSR)," in *Polevye issledovaniia Instituta etnografii* (1976) (Moscow, 1978), pp. 12–23.

8. See M. I. Kulichenko, "Vklad KPSS v teoriiu i praktiku razvitiia natsional'nykh otnoshenii na etape zrelogo sotsializma," in *Aktual'nye problemy razvitiia natsii i natsional'-nykh otnoshenii* (Moscow, 1981), p. 49.

9. See Sh. R. Rashidov, *Iazyk nashego edinstva i sotrudnichestva* (Moscow, 1979), pp. 29–30.

10. V. I. Lenin, *Polnoe sobranie sochinenii*, vol. 24, pp. 294–295.

11. L. I. Brezhnev, *Leninskim kursom*, vol. 8, p. 45.

12. Ibid., p. 44.

13. See P. N. Fedoseev, "Zrelyi sotsializm i obshchestvennye nauki," *Kommunist*, 1981, no. 16, p. 48.

14. For more details, see *Mnogoiazychie i literaturnoe tvorchestvo* (Leningrad, 1981).

15. *Knizhnoe obozrenie*, May 15, 1981.

Factors and Tendencies of the Development of Bilingualism among the Russian Population Living in the Union Republics *

M. N. GUBOGLU

The study of the processes of bilingualism, especially of national and Russian bilingualism, when the languages of the non-Russian peoples of the USSR are combined with Russian, became one of the most important fields of Soviet science in the 1970s, as may be eloquently demonstrated by the sociolinguistic studies[1] of the Language Institute of the USSR Academy of Sciences and the ethnosociological studies[2] of the Institute of Ethnography of the USSR Academy of Sciences.

The works of a number of Soviet ethnographers, sociolinguists, historians, and philosophers have correctly demonstrated that the mutual character of linguistic contact in the USSR is sometimes only proclaimed.[3] However, until the present moment there has not been one special work in which this indicated "mutuality" has been examined on concrete, factual material of adequate scope and reliability.

One of the possible means to overcome this omission might be the study of the general and particular in the linguistic life of groups of Russian populations living in union republics. The relevance of this problem is connected not only with the necessity of narrow sociolinguistic studies, but also flows from the very linguistic life of the multinational Soviet society, which has perfected all aspects of the social processes at the contemporary stage of socialism, including national and linguistic ones.

The mastery of two languages, which is characteristic for some groups of Russians, is the result of the natural need to know the language of the nationality among which these groups live and work. Russian bilingualism is in its origin and function directly connected with the general linguistic situation that is characteristic for our multilingual state.

The leading tendency of ethnolinguistic processes in our country, as has often been noted in the literature, is the formation and functioning of the type of bilingualism in which the non-Russian population learns Russian. However, this does not automatically remove the counter necessity, of Russians to know the language of the nationality among whom they live. The voluntary mastery of this language by Russians, and using it in certain circumstances, is naturally dictated by rational and emotional needs. At the same time, in knowing the language of the nation among whom they are living, Russians cannot but feel a positive psychological attitude to their bilingualism on the part of the non-Russian population.

---

*Istoriia SSSR, 1987, no. 2, pp. 25–43. Russian text © 1987 by "Pravda" Publishers.

The adaptation of the Russian population to the languages of the native populations of the union republics is a constituent part of contemporary national processes, including as an important aspect the adaptation of Russians to a non-Russian environment. In the course of inter-nationality contacts with the local populations the Russian life style and culture are enriched by elements of the material and spiritual culture, the behavior, and certain habits and customs of the native populations.

As the journal *Kommunist* noted, "An important aspect of the linguistic problem is connected with the acquisition by Russians and other people of non-native nationality of the languages of the native inhabitants of the republics. This improves interpersonal relations and promotes adaptation to an environment of another ethnic type." [4] People in a bilingual situation in the union republics who react positively to the bilingualism of Russians also receive additional convincing evidence of the equality of languages, and the equality of all types of bilingualism. At the same time, the example of Russian–national-language bilingualism indirectly stimulates the further development of all other types of bilingualism.

The presence of Russians in a non-Russian environment gives a unique opportunity to examine the linguistic life of a Russian population in its "home" ethnic environment—within the RSFSR—and in an "alien" one—within other republics. In the RSFSR Russians are the majority of the population: 88.3% in 1959, 82.8 % in 1970, and 82.6% in 1979. [5]

The entire Russian population living in the union republics (23.9 million people, according to the 1979 census), just as the Russians living in the RSFSR, make up the Russian *etnikos*. At the same time that part of the Russians who live in one or another of the union republics also have additional traits and particularities evoked by a life of shared living and frequent contacts with representatives of the native populations of the republic.

The sources of Russian–national-language bilingualism are very old, connected with the first Russian settlement among the numerous non-Russian peoples in the various regions and areas of the country, from the western and southern borders to the shores of the Pacific and Arctic Oceans.

Thus, for example, the literature notes that according to mid-nineteenth-century sources, Russians living among the native populations of the Volga, particularly among the Tatars, Chuvash, and Mordvins, could speak well not only the language of their own nationality but also other local languages. Even now the language of the Russian population of the Volga and other regions of the country still preserve many words and phrases of the local populations. [6]

Russian–national-language bilingualism in the prerevolutionary period had three basic models of development. In the first, the ethnolinguistic life of Russians in a non-Russian environment developed through mastery of the non-Russian language up to the point that both languages (Russian and non-Russian) enjoyed stable use (after a certain time) in certain spheres of life. The second was that the acquisition of another language through the intermediate stage of Russian–national-language bilingualism led to the loss of the language of one's own nationality, and the establishment of a new monolingualism. Finally, in the third instance, the intermediate stage of bilingualism led to the loss of the acquired language and a return to the original monolingualism.

In the first years after the October Revolution, as part of the adaptation of the non-Russian population to Russian there emerged two types of bilingualism (national-language–Russian and Russian–national-language). This was an important component part of the essentially progressive process of mutual adaptation of nationalities. Later, in the years of socialist construction, the more widely that Russian was disseminated as the language of inter-nationality communication among the non-Russian population, the less objectively perceived was the need for Russians to know and use the languages of the native populations of the union republics. In the 1960s and 1970s the favored instrument of mass communication in the country was the wide distribution of national-language–Russian bilingualism.

Unfortunately, the censuses of the Soviet Union of 1920, 1926, 1939, and 1959 did not contain data regarding fluency in a second language. The lack of this information does not permit a full picture of the ethnolinguistic processes in temporal cross-section.

However, to establish the tempo and content of the ethnolinguistic processes of the Russian population of the USSR it is possible to apply a retrospective method, analyzing the dynamics of the numbers of bilingual people in the constituents of various age groups of the population.

Using the data of the 1970 census, we can refer to the ethnolinguistic portrait of those Russians who in the 1970s were 50 and older. Those who in 1970 were precisely 50 years old were born in 1920, while other representatives of this generation are even older. The period of their childhood is that of the most intensive socialization and ethnicization, which dates from the 1910s to the beginning of the 1930s.

Adaptation to the language of another nationality occured extremely unevenly among the nationalities in the first two decades of the twentieth century, without difficulty in a wholly non-Russian environment, and more slowly and narrowly in areas with a mixed national constituency. The basis for this conclusion is the data on various limits of bilingualism among people of the older age groups of many nationalities today. Thus, for example, the breadth of variations in scale of national-language–Russian bilingualism in the beginning of the 1970s among elderly Moldavians and Turkmens living outside their own republics is of a very striking size, 42.9% (see Table 1). In general, national-language–Russian bilingualism was much more widespread than bilingualism among Russians.

Russian bilingualism was basically represented by those cohorts of people who were born before the Great October Revolution and lived the first two decades of their lives in the 1910s and 1920s. In other words, their childhood, youth, army service, participation in the Civil War, the beginning of their productive and social and political activities took place in the period of transition from capitalism to socialism. These were years when under the leadership of the Communist Party wide circles of workers and intellectuals, including representatives of the non-Russian population, were drawn into national construction. The youth and first years

Table 1

Data from the 1970 Census on Russian–National and National–Russian Bilingualism in Various Age Groups of the Populations of Union Republics

| | Fully fluent in a foreign language (in %) | | | | | |
| | In the home republic | | | Outside the home republic | | |
Nationality	11–29	30–49	50 +	11–29	30–49	50 +
Russian	0.6	0.7	0.6	22.2	16.9	12.5
Ukrainian	57.7	45.5	20.4	43.4	43.3	40.5
Belorussian	74.7	66.5	37.5	39.6	39.6	33.6
Uzbek	23.4	23.3	6.6	32.3	29.7	19.6
Kazakh	38.5	62.6	24.1	56.9	56.8	40.9
Georgian	23.8	30.4	19.0	80.6	84.4	48.3
Azerbaidzhani	22.2	27.1	12.4	32.9	34.5	39.6
Lithuanian	54.5	49.4	22.2	53.7	62.3	52.4
Moldavian	49.4	47.1	25.9	57.5	50.6	52.4
Latvian	61.5	59.5	39.0	48.4	48.0	41.2
Kirghiz	37.1	31.9	6.7	14.6	11.8	29.7
Tadzhik	31.5	28.5	8.1	16.5	14.3	21.0
Armenian	30.3	38.9	20.4	44.8	54.2	42.0
Turkmen	25.3	26.9	8.4	10.3	11.5	9.2
Estonian	42.5	37.0	19.9	38.7	29.3	45.8

Note: We have corrected an apparent typographical error in one of the column heads, which in the printed version has "30–39."—M.B.O.

of civic maturity of this generation coincided with the active struggle of the broad popular masses to build the foundations of socialism. The developing industrialization, collectivization, and cultural revolution of these years activated all levels of the Russian and non-Russian population. These factors "shook things up" to a significant degree, made the generation an active one, bringing it to a broader and more open arena of inter-nationality communication. All of this led to broader inter-nationality contacts than there had been before.

The building of near-complete socialism in the USSR became an important watershed in the ethnolinguistic processes as well. This shows through vividly in the distribution of national-language–Russian bilingualism among those who in 1970 were between 30 and 49. The proportion of bilingual Ukrainians who were between 30 and 49 in 1970 exceeded the numbers of bilingual older people by 25.1% within the Ukraine and by 2.8% outside of it; among Belorussians the corresponding figures were 29.0% and 6.0%; among Uzbeks, 16.7% and 10.1; among Georgians, 11.4% and 36.1%; and among Armenians 18.5% and 12.2% (see Table 1).

Consequently, during the years of socialist construction serious advances were made in the linguistic life of the non-Russian populations. The contingents of people who know Russian or who consider it to be their native language among certain people constitute more than half the general population. Thanks to this there was also a significant change from an individual level to a mass one of national-language–Russian bilingualism. Among the Belorussians and Kazakhs this tendency appeared in its most energetic form, while it was weaker among others, such as for example the Uzbeks, Turkmen, and Tadzhiks.

At the same time there was a spread of bilingualism among Russians (see Table 1). The depth and scale of these processes in a temporal aspect maybe be evaluated based on the data on fluency in a second language among youth (11–29 years of age), the middle aged (30–49), and the elderly (50 and up). The greatest proportion of bilingual Russians (in a non-Russian environment) in union republics was found by the 1970 Census to be among youth. This indicator was almost twice as high as among those who were 50 or more in 1970, and 1.3 times higher than among those who were then between 30 and 49 (see Table 1).

This age group is the generation that was born between 1941 and 1959. The school years, meaning the period of relative ease for mastering a second language, was for most of this group the period 1948–1966.

It is striking, first how uniform, and second how relatively narrow, are the scales of distribution of bilingualism among all age groups of Russians who live "at home," meaning in the RSFSR. Unlike the growing tempos of widening bilingualism in the union republics, bilingualism of Russians within Russia itself has come in relatively uniform "doses" at all stages of the history of Soviet society.

It would seem at first glance that the mass adaptation of the native nationalities of the union republics to Russian and the significant widening of the frameworks of national-language–Russian bilingualism must to a certain degree produce the directly opposite trend, of the development of bilingualism among the Russians themselves, among whom this would naturally lessen the need to know the languages of the non-Russian nationalities. However, the census data do not support this. In fact, they suggest that in the union republics, parallel to the extensive development of national-language–Russian bilingualism, during socialist construction and thereafter, up to the present, there has been a synchronic broadening of Russian–national-language bilingualism. This trend was confirmed by the 1979 census, which fixed much wider frameworks of bilingualism among Russian youth aged 11–29 by comparison with the bilingualism of the elderly, or those people who in 1979 were 50 and older. A preliminary explanation of this situation is apparently that, inasmuch as the change of populations broadens the opportunity to learn a second language within Russian families which have long lived in a given territory, in addition to the fact that as the social functions of the languages of the native populations develop more actively, the greater becomes their contribution to the all-union treasury of material and spiritual values, the richer appears the fund of national cultures, the more strongly is felt the magnetism of national languages for those Russians who live in the union republics.

The synchronic development, by stage and by generation, of bilingualism among the Russians living in the union republics and of bilingualism among the indigenous nationalities may serve as another proof of the mutual character of the processes of bilingualism, at the base of which lies, first of all, the rigorous observation in the nationality policy of the CPSU of the Leninist principle of the equality of nations.

Russian–national-language bilingualism in the USSR is not dictated "from above." Its development and function shows with particular power the real need of all peoples of the USSR, joined into one friendly, fraternal family, to have reliable instruments of communication. Today, before our eyes, the practical needs of linguistic life give no few examples of the fact that just as with Russian, the non-Russian languages in a number of instances can also be rational and naturally evolved instruments of inter-nationality communication. The value of the non-Russian languages is growing as a result of an entire range of objective reasons, including the continuing development of the social functions of their literary languages.

Beyond any doubt, the further deepening of the political, social, cultural, pragmatic, and emotional value of the non-Russian languages is finding its ultimate, obvious expression in the dynamic tendencies of contemporary ethnolinguistic processes, in which the contours of Russian bilingualism are expanding. As a result, it is now possible to study the trends and factors of Russian adaptation to a second language, i.e., the appearance and function of Russian–national-language bilingualism.

In the 1970 census 3,876,668 Russians indicated that they were fluent in a second language, and another 203,769 indicated a native language other than that of their nationality.[7] In other words, four million people, or about 3.2%, out of the entire Russian population of the USSR were bilingual. In the nine years between censuses the number of bilingual Russians increased to 4,809,000 people who were fluent in other languages, and 215,000[8] with a native non-Russian language, which amounts to five million, or 3.7% of the entire Russian population of the country. Naturally, the census data should not be taken absolutely. The fixed statistical data on the frameworks of the ethnolinguistic processes among the Russian population conceal a great variety of types, forms, amd varieties of Russian–national-language bilingualism, deep inter- and intrarepublican, inter- and intragenerational differentiation in the levels of fluency in a second tongue, in scopes and frequency of its use, in the psychological nuances of its use and attitudes toward it. All of this requires special study.

Nevertheless, in general it is possible to say that in fact the real limits of bilingualism among the Russian population, particularly in the union republics, have obviously dropped. Here are some simple examples. According to the the 1970 census, 11.1% of the Russians in Moldavian cities were fluent in Moldavian. An ethnosociological questionnaire from 1971 revealed that the real scale of Russian bilingualism was somewhat broader. It turned out that, if one took not only "fluent," but also such degrees of mastery as "know it, but speak with great difficulty," "speak with some difficulty," and "speak it fairly well," then 52.1% of urban Russians were fluent in Moldavian, or almost 4.7 times more than the census data showed. In the middle of the 1970s, 78.2% of the urban Russians in the

Belorussian SSR had some Belorussian, of which 16.7% were fluent.[9] At the same time, the 1970 census, as is known, found only 19% of the Russians who lived in Belorussia to be fluent in Belorussian.[10] In other words, it may be assumed that the census "lowered" the real dimensions of Russian–Belorussian bilingualism within the BSSR no less than fourfold.

Apparently, similar trends existed in the other union republics. It follows that the census data about five million bilingual Russians is objective only from the viewpoint of their minimum representation.

Naturally, by comparison with national-language–Russian bilingualism, which increased from 48.7% in 1970 to 62.6% in 1979, the scale of Russian bilingualism looks significantly modest in both static and dynamic form.

No precise criteria for evaluating the real social significance and actual dimensions of Russian–national-language bilingualism yet exist, but it may be said that the present dimensions of Russian–national-language bilingualism nevertheless do not correspond to the real needs of the Russians and must be further developed.

The basis for advancing this hypothesis is the dynamic tendency of development of Russian bilingualism in the 1970s, which points to a direct need on the part of Russians to know a second language. Thus, with over-all growth of the Russian population of 6.5% between 1970 and 1979,[11] the contingent of people of Russian nationality who were fluent in any second language of the peoples of the USSR grew over the same period by 24.1%. In other words, the rate of growth of bilingual Russians was 3.7 times greater than the rates of growth of the overall population of Russians.

This tendency was particularly manifest in the linguistic life of Russians in a non-Russian environment, primarily outside of the RSFSR. Thus, for example, with general growth of the Russian population in the union republics (excluding the RSFSR) of 12.2%, the growth of bilingualism was 32.7%. Consequently, the need to know a second language was felt particularly strong in the union republics. This apparently explains the fact that the growth of bilingualism among Russians in a non-Russian environment proceeded 1.4 times more quickly than in the country as whole.

The faster growth of Russian bilingualism compared with the growth of their overall numbers that were characteristic for the 1970s are an objective indicator of the need among Russians to know a second language, and to realize that need. However, a single general look is obviously not sufficient to evaluate the full variety of form and function in Russian bilingualism. We will examine the geographic distribution of the basic contingents of bilingual Russian populations, which the census data permit us to do.

At the beginning of the 1970s, 84.7% of all bilingual Russians were concentrated in the union republics. By 1979 the concentration of the bilingual Russian population there had reached 88.8%. At the same time the number of bilingual Russians in the RSFSR, including those fluent in a second (non-Russian) language and those who called a language of a non-Russian nationality their second language, fell from

Table 2

Distribution of the Bilingual Russian Population in the Union Republics (from the 1970 census)

Republic	Fluent in language of native population no.	%	Native language not that of own nationality no.	%	Total no.	%	% of bilingual Russians in republic
Ukraine	2,368,527	25.9	136,790	1.5	2,505,317	27.4	76.5
Belorussia	193,262	20.6	14,762	1.6	208,024	22.2	6.3
Total	2,561,789	25.4	151,552	1.5	2,713,341	26.9	82.8
Uzbekistan	55,498	3.7	1,228	0.1	56,726	3.8	1.7
Kazakhstan	55,118	0.9	2,912	0.1	58,030	1.0	1.8
Georgia	41,679	10.5	2,419	0.7	44,098	11.2	1.3
Azerbaidzhan	38,581	7.5	583	0.2	39,164	7.7	1.2
Lithuania	82,447	30.7	5,940	2.3	88,387	33.0	2.7
Moldavia	55,277	13.3	3,669	0.9	58,946	14.2	1.8
Latvia	120,338	17.0	8,950	1.3	129,288	18.3	3.9
Kirghizia	12,832	1.4	381	0.1	13,213	1.5	0.4
Tadzhikistan	8,124	2.3	269	0.1	8,393	2.4	0.3
Armenia	11,354	17.1	356	0.6	11,710	17.7	0.4
Turkmenia	6,517	2.0	233	0.1	6,750	2.1	0.2
Estonia	42,063	12.5	5,268	1.6	47,331	14.1	1.4
Total	529,828	4.7	32,208	0.3	562,036	5.0	17.2
For all republics	3,091,617	14.5	183,760	0.9	3,275,377	15.4	100.0

625,800 to 563,800 people (or 9.9%), while in the union republics the numbers increased from 3,454,700 to 4,460,700 people, or 29.1%.

According to the 1970 census, the greater part of bilingual Russians had Ukrainian as their second language, which along with Belorussian was spoken by almost 83.0% of this population living outside the RSFSR (see Table 2).

In scale of distribution, in second place after Russian–Slavic bilingualism came bilingualism in the Baltic languages of Latvian and Lithuanian. In 1970 Russian–Baltic-language bilinguals accounted for 6.6% of the entire bilingual Russian population in the union republics. In third place was Russian–Turkic bilingualism, coming from Russian acquisition of the Uzbek, Kazakh, Azerbaidzhani, Kirghiz, and Turkmen languages. This constituted 5.3%. The percentage of Russians who were fluent in languages of the other native populations of union republics varied from the 0.3% of Russians fluent in Tadzhik to the 1.8% of them who were fluent in Moldavian (see Table 2). Since the necessity for Russians to know one language or another in relation to the general nature of the ethnolinguistic situation in each republic was not identical, the scales of distribution of Russian–national-language bilingualism also varied.

The development of bilingualism has been particularly extensive among Russians in the Lithuanian SSR. More than 88,000, or every third person of Russian nationality living in this republic, was by the beginning of the 1970s either fluent in Lithuanian or considered it his native language.

Close to this were development trends in the Ukraine and Belorussia. More than one-fourth of all Russians in the Ukraine were Russian–Ukrainian bilinguals, and a little less than one-fourth of the Russians in Belorussia were Russian–Belorussian bilinguals (see Table 2).

Naturally, the scale of Russian–Ukrainian and Russian–Belorussian bilingualism is striking. However, further explanation of what these data conceal is necessary. In the course of ethnosociological studies it was revealed that 10.0% of urban Russians in Belorussia speak a "mixture of Russian and Belorussian"[12] at work and within the family. This means that speech was in one of the two languages with a great admixture of elements of the other language. Phenomena of mixed language, in which there is violation of norms and elements from each of the two languages which are in contact, have also been noted by investigators in the Ukraine, where, for example, the mixture of Russian and Ukrainian languages is called "*surzhik.*"[13] Clearly this is not bilingualism, but rather double half-lingualism. As a result, the purity of speech is violated no matter what language is spoken by users of these "mixed languages." Unfortunately, this variety of speech (double half-lingualism) is also met frequently among certain groups of non-Russian population. This tendency must be overcome.

Noticeable positive results in broad distribution of Russian–national-language bilingualism were achieved in the beginning of the 1970s in Latvia, where the share of Russians fluent in the language of the native population was 18.3%; in Armenia this figure was 17.7%; in Moldavia, 14.2%; in Estonia 14.1 %; in Georgia, 11.2%. In the other republics the share of bilingual Russians did not rise above 10% of the entire Russian population (see Table 2).

A substantial role in discovering the trends in the linguistic life of Russians in the union republics is played by illuminating those changes which occurred between 1970 and 1979.

By contrasting the dynamics in the overall numbers of Russians with the development of quantitative parameters of bilingualism, we can draw certain conclusions about the general direction and character of ethnolinguistic processes among the Russians of the union republics. Thus, for example, the growth of the overall number of Russians and of the number of Russians speaking the native language of their nationality was on average identical in 1970 and in 1979. At the same time, both indicators were close in magnitude in all republics (see Table 3).

The only exception was Estonia, where the overall numbers of Russian population fell (by 18.2%), while the number of Russians claiming Russian as their native language rose (22.0%).

The more rapid growth of the number of Russians claiming Russian as their native language as compared to the growth of the number of Russians claiming a non-Russian language as native (see Table 3) reflects in general a good psychological situation, in which the Russians in union republics have not shown the slightest tendency to lose their native language and to move to the language of another nationality.

In certain republics this quicker rate of growth was very noticeable: 45.3% in Tadzhikistan, 40.0% in Kazakhstan, 28.0% in Uzbekistan, 22.6% in Latvia, and 19.7% in Turkmenia.

The ethnolinguistic situation in those union republics in which the transition of Russians to the language of the native population somewhat exceeds the rate of growth of the general population and the growth of people with the native language is of particular interest, such as Armenia (33.1%), Georgia (30.4%), Lithuania (6.3%), and Estonia (4.0%) (see Table 3).

As has been said above, in the 1970s interest among Russians in knowing the languages of the native populations of the union republics rose. Accordingly, the growth of the Russian population fluent in these languages as an average for all union republics was 2.7 times greater than the growth in the overall population of Russians and the numbers of Russians with the native language of their nationality, and 5.9 times greater than the growth of Russians with a native language not that of their own nationality (see Table 3).

With the exception of Kazakhstan, as well as Kirghizia and Moldavia, where the total number of Russians rose more quickly than the number of Russians fluent in the language of the native population, in all other republics it was the characteristic tendency that the tempos of "bilingualization" among Russians predominated, as compared to the rate of growth of their total numbers.

If we study the factors that act positively on the development of extensive tendencies for Russian–national-language bilingualism, it is inarguable that the experience of each republic is valuable. However, at the same time it is evident that one group of republics (Uzbekistan, Armenia, Belorussia, Georgia, and Estonia) exhibits particularly beneficial conditions for adaptation of Russians to the languages of the native populations, while on the other hand there is another group of republics (Kazakhstan, Kirghizia, and Moldavia) where the stimuli and factors that promote this trend are more weakly represented than in the first group.

Uneven rates of development of bilingualism among Russians in different republics has led to certain changes in the distribution of cohorts of bilingual people of Russian nationality. Toward the end of the 1970s the distribution of groups of Russian population who were fluent in the language of the native nationalities of the union republics remained largely unchanged. The percentage of Russian–Slavic bilinguals grew (from 82.8% to 84.1%), while the percentage of Russian–Baltic bilinguals fell (from 5.3% to 4.9%), as did Russian–Turkic bilinguals. Certain changes occurred in relation to the numbers of Russians who were fluent in one language or another.

In the Lithuanian SSR the scale of Russian–Lithuanian bilingualism continued to expand, by 1979 accounting for 37.6% of all Russians living in the republic. As a result, the groups of bilingual Russian population in Lithuania continued to

Table 3

Dynamics of Numbers and the Growth of Russian Bilingualism in the Union Republics in the 1970s (1979 as a % of 1970; 1970 = 100%)

		Russians		
		consider their mother tongue to be		fluent in the language of the native population
Republic	Russian population	Russian	other lang.	
Ukraine	114.7	114.9	103.8	131.8
Belorussia	120.8	120.9	119.5	172.4
Uzbekistan	113.0	113.0	85.0	175.9
Kazakhstan	108.4	108.5	68.5	72.2
Georgia	93.6	93.4	123.8	137.7
Azerbaidzhan	93.2	93.1	87.8	113.4
Lithuania	113.2	113.1	119.4	129.7
Moldavia	120.0	122.0	115.0	97.4
Latvia	116.5	116.8	94.2	130.2
Kirghizia	106.5	106.5	98.4	78.9
Tadzhikistan	114.8	114.8	69.5	130.8
Armenia	106.3	106.2	139.3	165.7
Turkmenia	111.5	111.5	91.8	112.0
Estonia	81.8	122.0	126.0	110.3
Total	112.2	112.3	105.5	132.7

lead, in comparison with the groups of bilingual Russians in other republics. In this connection the historical experience of Russian–Lithuanian bilingualism undoubtedly deserves more thorough, specialized study. It must be regretted that so far there is no possibility of comparing initial and final parameters of the appearance and function of Russian–Lithuanian bilingualism with the other types of Russian–national-language bilingualism, since in the 1970s no ethnosociological studies were conducted in which ethnolinguistic problems were a significant part of the program, including problems of bilingualism among the Russian population.

In the 1970s the percentage of bilingual Russians grew noticeably in Armenia (9.8%), in Belorussia (8.7%), in the Ukraine (3.8%), and in some other republics (see Tables 2 and 4), in addition to in Lithuania.

As a result, if in 1970 the variance between the groups of Russians occupying polar positions with, respectively, Russian–Lithuanian and Russian–Kazakh bilingualism, was 32.0%, then in 1979 it had grown to 36.9%. In a word, the diversity among Russian groups by republic did not lessen but rather grew. This trend is of fundamental significance, since, in the first place, it indicates that interlanguage processes and relations are not always and in all ways adequate as a linguistic phenomenon (economic, social, cultural, sociopolitical, and so forth), and in the second, it allows us to see a radical difference between the development of the national-language–Russian and Russian–national-language forms of bilingualism in the USSR.

Unlike that of national-language–Russian forms of bilingualism, the spread of which after all has ultimately led to an equalization of the non-Russian nationalities in their extent of adaptation of their representatives to the Russian language, Russian–national-language forms have spread, differentiating as they do. Nor should other tendencies have been expected. Probably there is no sense in demonstrating as wholly to be expected the unequal degree of the spread of bilingualism among Russians living in Kazakhstan, who constituted 42.7% [of the population of the republic] in 1959 and 40.8% in 1979, and in Armenia, where the percentage in the 1960s and 1970s never went higher than 3.2%, or in Lithuania, where Russians also were a small part of the republic's population: 8.5% in 1959, 8.6% in 1970, and 8.9% in 1979.

As a result, if the national-language–Russian forms of bilingualism, which largely develop from individual and small group forms into those for the whole people, lead to the establishment of forms of one type, then Russian–national language forms by constrast exhibit in their development a tendency toward differentiation. It is understood that we are speaking for the time only about the extensive side of the matter, that is, about the broad development of Russian bilingualism.

This tendency is far from accidental, since it shows a principal difference between national-language–Russian and Russian–national-language bilingualism, which in essence is that all nations and nationalities of the USSR have an interest in a single language of inter-nationality communication. "The mastery of Russian along with that of the language of one's nationality, which the Soviet people have voluntarily accepted as a means of inter-nationality communication, widens access to the achievements of science, technology, to domestic and world culture,"[14] says the new edition of the Program of the CPSU.

The necessity of knowing the one language of inter-nationality communication, despite all the possible variations of quality and quantity, nevertheless becomes a general category for all peoples of the multinational state. The necessity of Russians to know this or that second language develops completely differently. As a rule this need has a local, situational character and is defined in each concrete instance by the nature of the ethnolinguistic situation of the union republic in which the given group of Russians is living.

In connection with this, it would be helpful to recall once again that the path of each non-Russian population to common bilingualism in the one language of inter-nationality communication is more or less universal, while the path to bilingualism for Russians, particularly to one scale or another of its appearance, is differentiated. This conceals one of the most serious difficulties for the responsive management, if not of the entire course, then at least of the trends in ethnolinguistic processes among the fourteen groups of Russians in the union republics, and to a somewhat lesser extent the twenty groups of Russians in the autonomous republics.

The distribution of a second language among the Russian population of the union

Table 4

Distribution of Bilingual Russians by Republic (based on the 1979 census)

Republic	Fluent in lang. of native pop.		Consider mother tongue other than their national lang.		Total		As % of all bilinguals in union republic
	no.	%	no.	%	no.	%	
Ukraine	3,122,155	29.8	142,019	1.4	3,264,174	31.2	75.9
Belorussia	333,234	29.3	17,648	1.6	350,882	30.9	8.2
Total for Slavic-language republics	3,455,389	29.7	159,667	1.4	3,615,056	31.1	84.1
Uzbekistan	97,652	5.8	1,044	0.1	98,696	5.9	2.3
Kazakhstan	39,837	0.6	1,995	0.1	41,832	0.7	1.0
Georgia	57,420	15.4	2,995	0.9	60,415	16.3	1.4
Azerbaidzhan	43,766	9.2	512	0.2	44,278	9.4	1.0
Lithuania	106,954	35.2	7,093	2.4	114,047	37.6	2.7
Moldavia	53,851	10.6	4,221	0.9	58,072	11.5	1.4
Latvia	156,743	19.0	8,439	1.1	165,182	20.1	3.8
Kirghizia	10,137	1.1	375	0.1	10,512	1.2	0.2
Tadzhikistan	10,634	2.6	187	0.1	10,821	2.7	0.3
Armenia	18,821	26.7	496	0.8	19,317	27.5	0.4
Turkmenia	7,303	2.0	214	0.1	7,517	2.1	0.2
Estonia	46,415	11.3	6,641	1.7	53,056	13.0	1.2
Total for all others	649,533	5.3	34,212	0.3	683,745	5.6	15.9
Total for all republics	4,104,922	17.2	193,879	0.9	4,298,801	18.0	100.0

republics and the formation on this basis of Russian–national-language bilingualism proceeds under the influence of various factors. Interethnic contacts, and especially interpersonal contact by people of different nationalities, in various spheres of life, from those of production to everyday and family life, study in a common school, and many other factors, individually or in combination "assist" the Russian population to acquire a second language. Answering the survey question "If you know a second language, then indicate where you acquired it," Russians most often cite various forms of interethnic contacts as well as schools having non-Russian instruction.

As a whole the factors of distribution of a second language among the Russians under study can be joined into two groups.

Under the action of factors of the first group may be placed all forms of inter-nationality communication on the personal level, in which knowledge of a second language has come in a natural, almost elemental manner. Conditionally these factors might be called communicative, while the method of acquiring the second language under their influence might be called traditional, or elemental-communicative. This method is traditional in the sense that the history and practice of interethnic contacts shows countless instances of acquisition of a second language long before a second language began to be an object of purposeful study in some kind of educational institution, with the help of special methodology, textbooks, and aids. This method has significant merits, the chief of which is that it demands no additional manpower, material, or financial expenditures or resources of society in the solution of linguistic problems, or in the solution of those social and cultural problems which are closely associated with linguistic ones. The drawback to this method is that in the course of its realization, what is primarily learned is the lowest conversational form of the other language. Naturally this limits use of the second language primarily to everyday communication. Accordingly, the social and cultural significance of this type of bilingualism is lower.

The second group of factors, which as a rule are associated with the system of education (schools, secondary and higher educational institutions, and others), guarantee mastery of the second language in its literary form, and in an organized manner. This second method, also with certain reservations, can be called the modern method, or the organized method (or the school method, the textbook method, or the school and textbook method). In a number of case there are no insuperable barriers between these two methods. In fact, even in a general education school, along with mastery of the literary language habits of oral speech are acquired, and on the contrary the preliminary acquisition of the simple conversational form of the foreign language signiciantly eases its mastery in written form. At the same time along with the school sphere, some assistance in mastering the literary language may be provided by the republic's means of mass communication (the press, radio, television), organizing lessons in the national language and broadcasts in the language of the native population, particularly when these broadcasts are intended for an audience of non-native nationalities.

In order to imagine more fully the role of each group of factors in the development of Russian bilingualism, it is best to compare the development of bilingualism of representatives of various nationalities. We will take for our example Russians and Moldavians in the cities of Moldavia. The "contribution" of the elemental-communicative factors in adapting urban Russians to the Moldavian language exceeds by almost twice the role of study in schools and institutions of higher education. However, in adaptation of urban Moldavians to Russian it is the opposite, for the significance of the school factor is almost one and half times stronger than the role of these same elemental-communicative factors (within the family).

The formation of bilingualism among Moldavians is noticeably influenced by service in the army. This, incidentally, is one of the principal differences in the system of factors affecting the development of national-language–Russian and Russian–national-language bilingualism. However, since cases in which Russians study

Table 5

Factors in Distribution of a Second Language among the Russian and Moldavian Populations in the Cities of the Moldavian SSR (in %, based on data from a 1971 ethnosociological survey)

| Nationality | Elemental-communicative | | | | Organized | | |
| | | of which | | | | of which | |
	Total	contact	family	army	Total	school	secondary ed.
Russians of ages	36.2	26.2	10.0	—	20.0	18.1	1.9
18–19	38.4	24.7	13.7	—	43.8	41.1	2.7
20–24	29.8	20.5	9.3	—	37.2	33.0	4.2
25–29	32.5	24.2	8.3	—	24.9	21.7	3.2
30–39	37.7	25.9	11.8	—	19.4	18.1	1.3
40–49	37.0	28.8	8.2	—	17.3	15.6	1.7
50–59	41.6	33.1	8.5	—	12.7	11.3	1.4
60 and older	36.2	24.6	11.6	—	10.4	9.7	0.7
Moldavians of ages	58.1	32.7	11.0	14.4	62.0	53.9	9.0
18–19	33.3	21.4	11.9	—	95.2	84.5	10.7
20–24	42.2	24.3	8.0	9.9	91.1	75.2	15.9
25–29	54.2	24.4	11.3	18.5	80.7	68.9	11.8
30–39	63.1	34.2	11.1	17.8	64.9	56.0	8.9
40–49	71.7	39.9	10.7	21.1	38.3	33.0	5.3
50–59	73.4	42.3	16.3	14.8	26.0	21.9	4.1
60 and older	64.8	42.4	12.2	10.2	18.1	17.1	1.0

a second language in the same manner are extraordinarily rare, this must be excluded from the comparison.

The role of elemental-communicative and organized factors in Russian acquisition of the Moldavian language were not identical in the lives of various populations. Thus for example among Russian youth age 18–24, the action of organized factors were stronger than the influence of elemental ones. Among people of the middle and particularly of the older generation, on the other hand, the role of elemental factors was predominant (see Table 5).

The appearance of Moldavian–Russian bilingualism was defined primarily by the action of organized factors. This tendency is manifestly confirmed by the data in Table 5. The role of study in school and higher educational institutions was stronger than the role of elemental-communicative factors among urban Moldavians in the following age groups: 18–19, 20–24, 25–29, and 30–39.

The role of organized factors in creation of bilingualism varied noticeably by age in both the Russian and Moldavian populations. This show particularly eloquently against the background of the nearly identical role of elemental factors in Russian acquisition of Moldavian in all age groups. The variation between the extremes of age group in this regard ranges from 29.8% among youth 20-24 years old to 41.2% among those who were 50-59. This leads to the conclusion that the elementary-communicative factors "acted" more or less stably for a relatively long period time, at least for two or three generations of Russians living in the Moldavian SSR.

The organizational factor affected the linguistic life of the urban Russian population completely differently. Its effect on the development of Russian-Moldavian bilingualism among the elderly, that is among those who in the beginning of the 1970s were older than 60, was four times less than its effect on the creation of bilingualism of Russian youth aged 18-19 (see Table 5).

The role of organizational factors in the acquisition of Russian by Moldavians grows consistently stronger from the older to the younger generations. Thus, for example, the effect of study in school and higher educational institutions on the acquisition of Russian among the very youngest (18-19 years old) urban Moldavians was more noticeable (almost five times so) than among those who were 60 and over (see Table 5).

It is difficult to overestimate the significance of these data. They permit us with a relatively high degree of probability to define retrospectively the role of the organized (school and textbook) factor in distribution of a second language among Russians and Moldavians in various historical stages.

To judge by the data of the survey conducted at the beginning of the 1970s, the older generation of Russians living in Moldavia acquired Moldavian primarily by the elemental-communicative method. At least in the age group 50-59, the influence of this nonorganized factor was almost 3.3 times stronger than the influence of the school and textbook factor, while among those 60 and over, it was 3.5 times (see Table 5). The analogous means of acquiring Russian–Moldavian bilingualism also appears among the middle-age, though here the observable difference among 30-39-year-olds was 1.9 times more, while among 40-49-year-olds it was 2.1 times (see Table 5). Finally among Russian youth (18-19 years old and 20-24 years old) the predominance of the communicative factor over the school and text factor became the opposite (see Table 5). It follows that just before and just after the Great Fatherland War, that is, during the school years of those Russians who in the beginning of the 1970s were between 30 and 49 years old, or 50 and over, the influence of elemental factors was stronger than the influence of organized ones.

At the same time the ethnolinguistic fate of the middle-aged population (30-49 years) shows in the years of its early intensive socialization a lessening of the role of elemental-communicative factors and the growth of school and textbook ones.

Questions naturally arise: How much time was necessary for this restructuring? Which decade was crucial in the transition from fully elemental and disorganized acquisition to consciously offered assistance, and to the creation of defined conditions for the development of Russian–Moldavian bilingualism? And how persistent was this tendency?

A break in the ethnolinguistic situation came in the 1960s, the school years of those who in 1971, or the moment of the ethnosociological survey, were between 18 and 24. The conclusion that the 1960s were decisive and a radical departure in the development of Russian–national-language bilingualism because of the activation of the school factor in the ethnolinguistic processes of the Russian population of the union republics is convincingly confirmed by data from the 1970 census. The agreement of these two different sources (government statistics and the results of ethnosociological studies) is difficult to overestimate.

In fact, the "ceiling" of Russian–national-language bilingualism is represented by the bilingualism of Russian youths aged 16–19 years. In older age groups the scale of knowledge of a second language is much less. At the same time, the knowledge of a second language among Russians 11–15 years olds was 4.7 times greater, and among 16–19 year old 5.6 times greater, than among those 10 and under, which also leaves no doubts as to the significant role of schools as one of the organized factors in the development of bilingualism in the younger populations of Russians in the USSR (see Table 6).

The "school factor" looks entirely different in the development of national-language–Russian bilingualism, that is, in acquisition of a second language by representatives of the native populations of the union republics. National-language–Russian bilingualism tends to grow as the children of the native population grow older. The level of knowledge of Russian continues to rise even after completion of secondary school. A clear demonstration of this is the greater distribution of bilingualism among youth aged 20–29, as compared to younger groups (see Table 6). This tendency is characteristic for representatives of the native population of all union republics, with the exception of Moldavia, where historically the "school factor" came to full strength somewhat later than in the other union republics.

The growth of the role of schools in distribution of the Moldavian language among Russian students was a logical consequence of the universal strengthening of the social functions of the Moldavian literary language in many spheres of life, including in the system of schools and higher education.

At the same time it must be noted that the "equator" of the transition from the elemental-communicative method to the organized means of Russian-language acquisition for Moldavians were the first postwar years, that is, the school years of those urban Moldavians who in the beginning of the 1970s were 30–39 years old. Parenthetically, it was precisely this boundary that was one of the most significant in the history of the transition to systematic efforts to create and shape Moldavian–Russian bilingualism. This is illustrated sufficiently plainly by juxtaposing data on the role of the two groups of factors in distribution of Russian among Moldavians in the age groups 30–39 and 40–49 (see Table 5).

Both groups of factors, the communicative and the organized, appeared in different ways in creation of bilingualism among Russians and Moldavians depending upon their socio-occupational status.

In all socio-occupational groups of the urban Russian population, without excep-

Table 6

**Distribution of a Second Language among Young People
in the Union Republics (in %, based on 1970 census)**

Nationality	Full fluency in second language among residents of own union republic, by age group			
	0–10 yrs	11–15 yrs	16–19 yrs	20–29 yrs
Russian (except RSFSR)	4.4	20.8	24.8	21.8
Ukrainian	14.8	24.7	43.5	49.5
Belorussian	11.6	19.1	41.1	45.0
Uzbek	4.8	21.8	38.0	41.8
Kazakh	23.2	51.8	59.6	61.1
Georgian	49.0	77.6	81.9	81.8
Azerbaidzhani	8.2	24.7	36.3	42.3
Lithuanian	25.0	39.2	50.3	62.4
Moldavian	12.3	45.3	65.0	62.8
Latvian	22.1	36.8	44.6	55.4
Kirghiz	1.0	7.1	17.4	22.2
Tadzhik	2.2	9.7	19.1	23.8
Armenian	18.4	34.9	46.5	54.6
Turkmen	1.0	4.6	12.7	16.5
Estonian	18.1	33.2	37.0	40.8

tion the elemental-communicative factors played a much more noticeable role than did the organized ones.

Among urban Moldavian service personnel, and also unskilled physical laborers, having secondary and higher education, the role of communicative factors in acquisition of Russian was stronger than the role of organized ones. Noticeable here is a tendency toward weakening of the role of communicative factors and strengthening of that of organized factors according to the growth of the educational status of urban Moldavians. Thus, for example, taking account of the role of army service, the effect of communicative factors was almost twice as strong among unskilled physical laborers and just about equal among service personnel (see Table 7). Naturally, with the rise of education the role of educational institutions in developing bilingualism among Moldavians grew stronger.

It is to be expected in particular that the effect of lower and higher education as a factor in Moldavians' acquisition of Russian was stronger than all communicative factors taken together, including among specialists with a secondary education and middle-level managers, 1.3 times higher, while among specialists with higher education and upper-level managers it was 2.1 times higher (see Table 7).

Inasmuch as the effect of communicative factors on acquisition of Moldavian by urban Russians was similar in all occupational groups, it is evident that there is no

Table 7

Factors in Distribution of a Second Language in Socio-occupational Groups among the Urban Russian and Moldavian Populations of the Moldavian SSR (in %, based on a 1971 ethnosociological survey)

Nationality and socio-occupational groups	Factors						
	Elemental-communicative				Organized		
		of which				of which	
	Total	contact	family	army	Total	school	secondary ed.
Russians							
Physical laborers:							
unskilled	37.4	27.4	10.0	—	12.1	11.2	0.9
semiskilled	38.7	26.7	12.0	—	17.3	16.8	0.5
skilled	36.1	26.0	9.1	—	22.4	21.2	1.2
service	32.0	23.0	9.0	—	24.7	24.7	—
Specialists, administrators:							
middle-level	37.1	29.5	7.6	—	16.5	14.9	1.5
upper-level	33.7	24.7	9.0	—	22.3	17.6	4.7
Moldavians							
Physical laborers:							
unskilled	64.5	43.0	12.3	9.2	34.9	32.7	2.2
semiskilled	69.4	40.5	10.0	18.9	52.5	51.7	0.8
skilled	72.3	27.2	10.4	34.7	57.5	55.6	1.9
service	62.9	37.1	15.7	10.1	57.3	56.2	1.1
Specialists, administrators:							
middle-level	55.1	27.6	17.9	9.6	71.2	66.7	4.5
upper-level	45.0	23.2	10.0	11.8	93.4	62.6	30.8

connection between the socio-occupational status of a person of Russian nationality and his acquisition of a second (Moldavian) language in a natural way, in the course of interethnic contact. In fact, the difference between the extreme groups in this regard—semiskilled workers and service personnel—was 6.7% (see Table 7). Among Moldavians this difference between white-collar and skilled blue-collar workers was 27.3% (see Table 7).

It cannot be said that the role of the school factor was completely identical in acquisition of Moldavian by all Russian socio-occupational groups.

Among bilingual service personnel of Russian nationality, almost one-fourth indicated that they had learned Moldavian in school, while among bilingual unskilled laborers, school "assisted" every tenth to learn Moldavian (see Table 7).

Nevertheless there is probably no particular reason to imagine any proper connection between the organized factor and the socio-occupational status of the urban Russian population in the process of acquiring Moldavian. On the other hand, in the acquisition of Russian by Moldavians this connection is obvious. This is convincingly evident, in the first place, because the effect of education in schools and higher institutions in the acquisition of Russian by Moldavians was almost three times more noticeable in the group of specialists with higher education and senior management than among unskilled laborers, and in the second, because the significance of the organized factor grew correspondingly stronger from the group of unskilled laborers to skilled white-collar workers, from 34.9% among the first to 93.4% among the latter (see Table 7).

The effect of each group of factors (the elemental-communicative and organized) on the creation of Russian–national-language bilingualism appears to be complex. Most commonly, both groups of factors are interrelated and successfully complement one another.

Of the three basic processes which contribute to the development of national-language–Russian bilingualism—formation, distribution, and functioning—science and practice have grappled with the problems of how to manage the first two, formation and distribution. Successes in stimulating functioning are much more modest.

As for managing the processes of Russian–national-language bilingualism, it must for the time being be conceded that the successes are even more modest, in all three basic components.

In the union republics large-scale scientific, organizational, and coordinated efforts are constantly undertaken to popularize Russian. The particular scale of these efforts, one may hope, will produce an understanding of the growing role of Russian in accelerating the social and economic development of the country, in strengthening the coordination and mutual exchange of experience between union republics. It is not by chance that when the Plenum of the Central Committee of the Communist Party of Uzbekistan in October 1986 was considering the tasks of the republic's Party organizations for increasing the effectiveness of ideological work in light of the demands of the Twenty-seventh Congress of the CPSU, First Secretary of the Central Committee of the Communist Party of Uzbekistan I. B. Usmankhodzhaev, the director of High School No. 2 of Kuvin Raion in Fergana Oblast', Kh. Usmanov, and other speakers noted the impossibility of solving the problems of acceleration and development of the priority branches of industry that define scientific and technical progress without a thorough understanding of Russian. Participants in the plenum called on the Ministry of Higher and Secondary Specialized Education and the Academy of Sciences of the republic to draft a complex program, ''Russian Language,'' in order to generalize upon the experience accumulated in other republics and to make better use of it in the practice of teaching in the republic schools.[15]

At the same time they demanded the further systematic study of questions involving the teaching of the national languages in schools, and of training of teachers of the national language for Russian-language schools. Questions of the quantity and quality of studies on the methodology of teaching national languages (for students not of the native population) as a second language in the union republics need much greater attention.

There has not been sufficient study of the experience of propagandizing other national languages (Bulgarian, Gagauz, and Ukrainian in the Moldavian SSR, Abkhaz in Georgia, Armenian in Azerbaidzhan, Azerbaidzhani in the Armenian SSR, Tadzhik in the Uzbek SSR, and others), as well as of the languages of the native populations for Russians and representatives of other languages.

Publishing activity in the republics has been poorly studied. How many study aides have been prepared and published, including Russian–national-language phrase books; conversational, terminological, thematic, and encyclopedic dictionaries; texts that have been adapted for reading by people not of the native nationality, etc.?

At the same time, even a preliminary acquaintance with the degree to which representatives of Russian and other nationalities are supplied with aides for self-guided study of the language of the native population of a union republic indicates that there is not yet enough. The Russian–national-language phrasebooks which are published, in some few tens of thousands, do not last long on bookstore shelves.[16]

The goal of the majority of Russian–national-language phrasebooks is to help obtain a knowledge of everyday, conversational non-native speech, while people of the native population need more, to acquire Russian.

The sense and content of the language policy of the CPSU is to create conditions for satisfying the needs of all peoples of the USSR in the language of their nationality and in the one language of inter-nationality communication. Successes in this sphere are obvious and instructive, both in the sphere of real ethnolinguistic life and in that of scientific analysis of Soviet experience and the results of ethnolinguistic processes.

At the same time one of the important tasks in the study of contemporary national processes and problems in the perfection of socialism arises from the most recent documents of the CPSU, studies of special features of development and questions in the areas of the language, culture, and daily life of the non-native populations of the republics, including Russians living in non-Russian environments. In this plan the study of the complex of problems surrounding Russian–national-language bilingualism also acquires particular significance.

The tendency of the Russian population of a republic to have a growing need for the knowledge and use of the languages of the native populations should of course not be exaggerated or absolutized. Nor, however, should it be permitted to fall from view.

It is correctly stressed in the literature that "knowledge of the language of the native nationality is of great significance, appearing as a phenomenon of respect to the given people, to their culture, language, traditions, and practices."[17] Of course, this does not refer only to the emotional and moral side of Russian–national-language bilingualism. The rational side of the matter is also of extraordinary importance, i.e., use of the language of the native population in the speech activity of Russians, in the widening of their cultural and educational field of vision, in the raising of socio-occupational status, in overcoming negative nuances in the practice of inter-nationality relations.

The trend toward transition from the elemental-communicative factors, dominant in the past, to the predominance of educational and pedagogical factors deserves particular attention.

Combined with the aggregate of all objective conditions, the [general education] school and other educational institutions considerably accelerate the progressive development of modern ethnolinguistic processes. Few specialists doubt that the school plays the dominant role in the development of all national-language–Russian forms of bilingualism. In some republics, the role of the school in the distribution of a second language among different groups of Russian nationality—i.e, in the development of Russian–national-language bilingualism—albeit weaker than in the opposite case, has increased in recent years. Both trends deserve close attention in connection with the major turn toward the study of contemporary processes and with the reinforcement of the tie between the social sciences and the practice of modern ethnolinguistic processes. As the school's "burden" as an objective factor in the development of national-language–Russian bilingualism grows, so increases its day-to-day "responsibility" for the fate of the linguistic life of the nations, nationalities, and national groups, including that of bilingualism among the groups of Russians living in the union republics, and in a broader sense, for the fate of the sociocultural development of each nationality (from nation to national group) and of the entire Soviet people. However, since the elemental and organizational factors in no way operate in isolation from one another, the practical necessity arises of purposefully stimulating the development of each of the components contributing to bilingualism among Russians: skills, speech activity, and the psychological recognition of the need for a second language.

Yet it must be stated that our progress has been least visible precisely in this sphere—propagation of the languages of the native nationalities among non-natives. Moreover, the scholarly publications of some republics rarely mention the need for purposeful, convincing, and well-argumented propagation of the language of the native nationality. When efforts are being undertaken to create favorable conditions for learning the Russian language, it is quite right to raise the question of creating the appropriate conditions for representatives of non-native nationalities, including Russians, to learn the language of the titular nationality of the given union republic (offering lessons on radio and television, free and paid courses, making available special conversational aids, textbooks, etc.).

The main thing in these efforts in to find a sensible framework, corresponding to the actual needs of people of different nationalities, for the balanced interaction of the social functions of the languages of the peoples of the USSR and the language of inter-nationality communication in the various spheres of life.

Notes

1. See for example: Iu. D. Desheriev, *Zakonomernosti razvitiia i vzaimodeistviia iazykov v sovetskom obshchestve* (Moscow, 1966); idem, *Sotsial'naia lingvistika. K osnovam obshchei teorii* (Moscow, 1977); *Natsional'nalnyi iazyk i natsional'naia kul'tura* (Moscow, 1978); *Vzaimo-otnoshenie razvitiia natsional'nykh iazykov v sviazi s ikh funksionirovaniem v sfere vysshego obrazovaniia* (Moscow, 1982); *Iazyk v razvitom sotsialisticheskom obshchestve. Iazykovye problemy razvitiia sistemy massovoi kommunikatsii v SSSR* (Moscow, 1982); *Iazyk v ravitom sotsialisticheskom obshchestve. Sotsiolingvisticheskie problemy funktsionirovaniia sistemy massovoi kommunikatsii v SSSR* (Moscow, 1983); *Iazyk i massovaia kommunikatsiia. Sotsiolingvisticheskoe obsledovanie* (Moscow, 1984), and others.

2. See for example: *Sotsial'noe i natsional'noe. Opyt etnosotsiologicheskikh issledovanii po materialam Tatarskoi ASSR* (Moscow, 1973), pp. 230–272; V. V. Pimenov, *Udmurty. Opyt komponentnogo analiza* (Leningrad, 1977), pp. 93–112; *Opyt etnosotsiologicheskogo issledovaniia obraza zhizni (Po materialam Moldavskoi SSSR)* (Moscow, 1980), pp. 170–199; M. N. Guboglo, *Sovremennye etnoiazykovye protsessy v SSSR. Osnovnye faktory i tendentsii razvitiia natsional'no-russkogo dvuiazychiia* (Moscow, 1984), and others.

3. See for example: *Problemy dvuiazychie i mnogoiazychiia* (Moscow, 1972); *Puti razvitiia natsional'no-russkogo dvuiazychiia v nerusskikh shkolakh RSFSR*, 1979; M. I. Isaev, *Iazykovoe stroitel'stvo v SSSR* (Moscow, 1979); *Russkii iazyk v natsional'nykh respublikakh Sovetskogo Soiuza* (Moscow, 1980); *Russkii iazyk—iazyk druzhby i bratstva* (Baku, 1982); K. Kh. Khanazarov, *Reshenie natsional'no-iazykovoi problemy v SSSR* (Moscow, 1982), and others.

4. Iu. V. Bromlei, "Sovershenstvovanie natsional'nykh otnoshenii v SSSR," *Kommunist*, 1986, no. 8, p. 84.

5. Here and in other places in the text and tables, where not noted otherwise, calculations are made on the basis of census data from: *Itogi Vsesoiuznoi perepisi naseleniia 1970 g.*, vol. 4 (Moscow, 1973), pp. 9–11, 43–316; *Chislennost' i sostav naseleniia SSSR. Po dannym Vsesoiuznoi perepisi naseleniia 1979 g.* (Moscow, 1984), pp. 71–137.

6. See for example: T. S. Kogotkova, *Russkaia dialektnaia leksika. Sostoianie i perspektivy* (Moscow, 1979); E. D. Erdyneeva, *Dialektnaia rech' russkikh starozhilov Buriatii* (Novosibirsk, 1986), and others.

7. *Itogi Vsesoiuznoi perepisi naseleniia 1970 g.*, vol. 4 (Moscow, 1973), p. 20.

8. *Chislennost' i sostav naseleniia SSSR. Po dannym Vsesoiuznoi perepisi naseleniia 1979 g.* (Moscow, 1984), p. 71.

9. *Etnicheskie protsessy i obraz zhizni. Na materialakh issledovaniia naseleniia narodov BSSR* (Minsk, 1980), p. 206.

10. *Itogi Vsesoiuznoi perepisi naseleniia 1970 g.*, vol. 4 (Moscow, 1973), p. 193.

11. For more details on the dynamics of the Russian population, see: S. I. Bruk and V. M. Kabuzan, "Dinamika chislennosti i rasseleniia russkikh posle Velikoi Oktiabr'skoi sotsialisticheskoi revoliutsii," *Sovetskaia etnografiia*, 1982, no. 5, pp. 3–20.

12. *Etnicheskie protsessy i obraz zhizni (Na materialakh issledovaniia naseleniia gorodov BSSR)* (Minsk, 1980), p. 210.

13. G. I. Kasperovich, *Migratsiia naseleniia v goroda i etnicheskie protsessy* (Minsk, 1985), p. 114.

14. *Materialy XXVII s"ezda Kommunisticheskoi partii Sovetskogo Soiuza* (Moscow, 1986), p. 157.

15. *Pravda*, October 7, 1986.

16. See, for example: *Kratkii russko-altaiskii slovar'-razgovornik*, edited by T. M. Toshchakova, O. G. Sabashkina, N. A. Kuchigashieva (Gorno-Altaisk, 1961); V. P. Stashaitene, *Russko-litovskii razgovornik* (Vil'nius, 1961), 326 pp., second ed. (Vil'nius, 1968), 325 pp.,

sixth ed. (1986), 255 pp.; *Russko-tadzhikskii razgovornik* (Dushanbe, 1962), 128 pp., second ed. (1968), 127 pp.; Kh. Tokazov, *Russko-osetinskii razgovornik* (Ordzhonikidze, 1963), 234 pp., second ed. 1964, 234 pp.; *Russko-buriatskii razgovornik*, compiled by Iu. P. Boldonov, and U. R. N. Namzhinov (Ulan-Ude, 1964), 174 pp.; A. Reitsak, *Russko-estonskii razgovornik* (Tallin, 1966), 251 pp., second ed. (1972), 266 pp., fourth ed. (1978), 263 pp.; N. A. Ozolinia, *Russko-latyshskii razgovornik* (Riga, 1967), 190 pp., second ed. (Riga, 1971), 183 pp.; A. Dyrul, I. Etsko, and F. Kotel'nik, *Russko-moldavskii razgovornik* (Kishinev, 1967), 307 pp., second ed. (1971), 291 pp.; *Russko-tuvinskii razgovornik*, compiled by E. B. Salzynmaa (Kyzyl, 1968), 143 pp.; Z. M. Magrufov and T. N. Mikhailov, *Kratkii russko-uzbekskii razgovornik* (Tashkent, 1969), 79 pp; Kh. Magomadov, *Russko-chechenskii razgovornik* (Groznyi, 1971), 232 pp.; L. G. Zakhokhov and A. Kh. Sottaev, *Russko-kabardinskii razgovornik* (Nal'chick, 1972), 231 pp.; A. Gutmanis, *Russko-latyshskii razgovornik*, second ed. (Riga, 1979), 208 pp.; A. Amandurdyev, B. Amansaryev, M. Annanurova, and Kh. Kiiatkhanova, *Russko-turkmenskii razgovornik* (Ashkhabad, 1986), 119 pp.

17. *Aktual'nye problemy natsional'nogo i internatsional'nogo v dukhovnom mire sovetskogo cheloveka* (Baku, 1984), p. 199.

To Master Languages More Deeply *

The Commission on Nationality and Inter-nationality Relations of the Central Committee of the Communist Party of the Latvian SSR

The strength of our state was and is the unity of the Soviet peoples. The strategy of acceleration and the fundamental renovation of all sides of life demands even greater solidarity. The program of the Party is aimed at making sure each Soviet person possesses the feelings of friendship and brotherhood which unite all nations and nationalities of the USSR, as well as the high culture of inter-nationality relations, impatience for phenomena of nationalism and chauvinism, national limitation and national egoism, and for habits and practices which interfere with the communist renovation of life.

The Party resolves new problems of perfecting national relations in our multinational country on the basis of the proven principles of Leninist nationalist policy. One of these principles is the guarantee of the free development and legal equality of use by all citizens of the USSR of their native languages, as well as, alongside mastery of the language of one's nationality, mastery of Russian. Soviet people have voluntarily accepted Russian as a means of inter-nationality communication. It widens access to the achievements of domestic and world culture, to science, technology, and production, it allows the strengthening of a unified economic complex, the internationalization of state and social life, permitting the greater unification of the peoples and direct communication between people.

Parallel to this is growing the interest of people of the most varied possible nationalities in the study of the language of the native population of the republic in which they live. For the Soviet person, bilingualism is becoming an objective necessity and demand, and it actively serves the goals of the acceleration of society's development.

This tendency as the norm of life in the national republic is increasingly affirmed in the Latvian SSR. However, there are also some difficulties, on the one hand caused by the fact that national relations in the last decade have risen to a high new level, becoming more multifaceted, and on the other, by the fact that in practical activities these changes were not always taken into account, and emerging problems were hushed up.

The state of instruction and study of Russian in the republic in Latvian-language schools, and of Latvian in Russian-language schools, became the first question brought for the consideration of the Commission on Nationality and Inter-nationality Relations of the Central Committee of the Latvian Communist Party after it was

---

Sovetskaia molodezh', 7 August 1987, p. 1. Russian text © 1987 by ''Sovetskaia molodezh'.''

formed. The commission convened on August 3, opened by its president, First Secretary of the Central Committee of the Latvian Communist Party B. K. Pugo.

Speaking on the question were the First Deputy Minister of Education in the Republic, B. A. Kubulin, and the president of the State Committee of the Latvian SSR on Professional and Technical Education, Ia. A. Kaleisa.

Their reports, like the speeches of the commission's members, stressed that the most important direction of the schools' work is meant to allow the strengthening of inter-nationality communication in the growing generation, to realize the principle of bilingualism in the republic. Recently there has been a noticeable advance in the study of Russian in Latvian-language kindergartens, schools, and trade schools. Practically all charges of the kindergartens begin to study Russian beginning at the age five. An examination in Russian has been introduced in the eleventh class of general education schools, while study groups for the improved study of Russian are being formed in schools and special trade schools (SPTUs) that will not contain more than twenty-five people. The training of teachers has improved, as more than 85 percent of the teachers in this discipline have an advanced degree in philology. The Ministry of Education in the Republic has worked out new programs of Russian language and literature for the middle school, for study groups and special-interest groups. The material and technical base has been strengthened, and beginning next year the gradual introduction of new textbooks is planned.

The schools have many qualified pedagogues who achieve good results. The conference made note of the results of V. V. Golovenko's work in the Stuchkinskii Raion, as well as that of L. M. Kalinina, N. I. Chebykina, R. A. Potashe, and T. A. Fomina of Riga. The special technical school teachers E. I. Kaminskaia (of Cesis), A. L. Iansone (Valmiera Raion) and others have mastered well the intensive method of instruction of Russian and make active use of work outside the classroom for forming an interest in the culture of the Russians and other peoples of the USSR.

The best indicator of the work done is the students' knowledge of Russian. Analysis shows that the great majority of school children have mastered conversation and the bases of grammar: 35–38 percent of the students demonstrated optimal knowledge on tests, and only 0.13–0.18 percent have an insufficient level of knowledge. Nevertheless, unresolved problems make themselves felt. Almost a third of the Russian-language teachers in Latvian-language schools have no specialized education. There are shortages of qualified cadres in Aluksne, Valmiera, Kuldiga, Limbaži, Madona, and Tukum raions. There are still many middle schools where Russian-language instruction is conducted at too low a level.

An important aspect of the language problem is the adaptation of Russians and other nationalities living in the republic to Latvian. The necessity of the voluntary mastery of Latvian and its use in certain circumstances is conditioned by both rational and emotional demands. This helps people to adapt to an environment of another nationality, improves interpersonal relations, and as a result is met with a positive psychological response. A person who has two languages is made richer in material and spiritual culture, by having some practices and habits of another people.

As the conference participants noted, there has been some improvement in the teaching and study of Latvian in Russian-language schools. The textbooks are being updated in order to make their material more relevant. An experimental program is underway for teaching Latvian to children from five on. Some schools have created a good material and methodological basis. The graduating classes have an exam in Latvian. The graduates of teachers L. Ia. Griule and L. K. Kursite (Riga), and of M. P. Kamenskaia (Elgava) show good knowledge of the language.

However, partial successes cannot obscure the fact that many students, especially of the urban schools, have a weak practical knowledge of Latvian. The results of the examination have shown that only every fourth person who takes it has an optimal level of knowledge. About 3 percent of those taking the exam show clearly insufficient knowledge of Latvian.

The problem of preparing teachers of Latvian for Russian-language schools is critical, as only 25 percent of the teachers have higher education in this specialty.

To help teachers of Latvian and Russian the republic publishes a lot of intersting methodological material, an exhibit of which was arranged in the hall where the conference took place. Books published in Latvia are popular even in other republics. It was all the more amazing then to hear that many teachers, especially in the countryside, do not know about these editions.

The participants were interested in the experience of Jurmala in joint extracurricular work in Russian and Latvian. Work collectives of school children, Party and Komsomol gatherings and campaigns brought the teachers and the youths together as friends. As part of this they show a genuine interest in the culture of the fraternal peoples. Thus, Russian-language Middle School No. 5 has created a very popular Latvian folklore ensemble, and the Latvian-language Middle School No. 4 has founded a Russian drama circle. This experience though has not received the necessary dissemination.

The conference participants discussed how ineffective extra-curricular work, and the poor knowledge of the history and culture of the Latvian SSR of many teachers, their low level of pedagogic ability, hinder the deeper acquisition of Russian and Latvian. The Minister of Higher and Middle Special Education of the Latvian SSR, E. V. Linde, also told the participants what measures are being taken to correct the situation in the higher schools.

The role of the creative intelligentsia in forming the cultural demands of youth has always been large. Unfortunately, Latvian writers, actors, and artists are infrequent guests in Russian-language schools, while Russians and other nationalities are rare in Latvian schools. There would be a great emotional impact on school children if there were to be joint appearances, comments by a beloved poet on the work of his colleague of the other language, and might stimulate unfeigned interest in the culture of another people.

Problems of learning a language do not disappear when school is finished. Far from all graduates know Latvian, but it is precisely in their practical life, noted the Second Secretary of the Central Committee of the Latvian Komsomol, V. P. Parfenov, that youth feel a need to study it. "However," he said, "many difficulties spring up in the path of this desire. I encountered this personally. Having learned the minimum in a year, I wanted to learn how to master the language, but because of insufficient time I could not take the two-year courses, and there are no short-term courses with intensive language instruction, the existing textbooks and self-teachers are too complex, and there are no phonograph records to help students.''

The next speaker, chairman of the board of the Union of Writers of the Latvian SSR J. J. Peters, continuing this theme, proposed establishing a House of Language, where there would be courses on continuous offer. This House, where the best teachers with the help of modern technology could help those who wished to do so learn Russian, Latvian, and foreign languages, Peters envisioned not as a standard building, but as a kind of temple to the friendship of peoples.

An even more useful suggestion was made by L. M. Kalinina, a teacher at Zenta Ozola Middle School No. 5 in Riga, who proposed that the courses which are already in constant operation be set up in middle schools, on a self-financing basis, because there is a good material foundation and qualified teachers.

The attitude to studying languages is part of nationality policy. It is thus not surprising that the conference participants often did not confine themselves to the strictures of the question under discussion. Thus, the First Secretary of the Dobele Raion Party Committee, V. K. Avots, in analyzing the experience of teaching and studying languages in his raion, sharply pointed out the necessity of linking the study of languages, literatures, and history. Many of the speakers referred to problems of teaching the history of the republic.

Among these was the Vice-President of the republic Academy of Sciences A. A Drizul and the poet J. J. Peters, who in speaking about how to educate youth in the spirit of internationalism through the example of the Red Latvian Riflemen, noted the successful celebration of the seventieth anniversary of the Riflemen's transfer of allegiance to the Bolsheviks and proposed that May 30 be established as Day of the Revolutionary Rebirth of the Latvian Riflemen, as P. Stuchka called this historical event.

The deputy of the Political Directorate of the Red Star Baltic Military District, Major General N. F. Laguteev, informed the conference that Latvian youth called to the ranks of the Soviet army as a whole have good command of Russian, but the Latvians, like other nationals from the republic, have weak knowledge of the history of Latvia. Conference participants came to the conclusion that the primary cause of this is the insufficient hours of instruction devoted to study of the republic's history.

The rector of the State Academy of Arts of the Latvian SSR, I. A. Zarin, who voiced concern about the purity of the Latvian language, especially among the technical intelligentsia, pointed out the necessity of enlarging the publication of dictionaries and of improving the quality of translation, from Russian to Latvian and from Latvian to Russian.

The Secretary of the Central Committee of the Latvian Communist Party A. V. Gorbunov in his speech stressed the idea that dedicated development of bilingualism is and remains the key element of work in the sphere of nationality relations. At the present time particular attention is being paid, first, to mastery of the teaching and learning of Russian and Latvian in the educational establishments; second, to the creation of good possibilities for study of Russian and Latvian by the populace of the republic (preparation of phrasebooks, textual aids, dictionaries, free and tuition courses, lessons on televison, and so forth); third, to the guarantee of the principle of equality of languages in various spheres of life, of a balanced mutuality of the social functions of Latvian and Russian corresponding to the real needs of people.

The conference's concluding remarks were made by First Secretary of the Central Committee of the Latvian Communist Party B. K. Pugo. He pointed out the importance of getting public opinion to support bilingualism and the study of Russian and Latvian as an important means of developing the high common culture of people, and the high culture of inter-nationality communication. Much depends upon how correctly their position is elaborated by the primary Party organizations, the Party committees, the Komsomol, and the trade unions. They and the media of mass information and propaganda, the "Znanie" [Knowledge] Society, the cultural and enlightenment establishments, and the creative unions must foster respect and persistent interest in the culture and art of the Latvian and other peoples of our country. It must always be remembered that stimulating in children an interest in language study, in the culture and art of one's own people and of others, depends first of all on the attitude towards these questions shown by the family. Work with parents, helping them in the internationalist education of the growing generation is a responsibility of our specialists and the practitioners in the schools. Tact, mutual respect, attentiveness, and patience are vitally important in the creation of bilingualism. Everything must be done with complete naturalness. You cannot have excessive haste, but nor should there be foot-dragging in carrying out decisions—our work will be judged by concrete results.

The commission assigned the State Planning Committee, the Ministry of Higher and Secondary Specialized Education, the Ministry of Education, and the State Committee for Vocational and Technical Education to institute additional measures in the next three years which would prepare highly qualified teachers of Russian and Latvian for all general education schools and vocational and technical schools. The numbers admitted to the pedagogical institutes, to the philology faculty of the P. Stuchka Latvian State University, and to the Rezekne and Riga pedagogical schools in these disciplines must be increased. The intensity and efficiency of the study of Russian and Latvian languages must be raised, as must the mastery level of the teachers. The task has been set to find a way to increase school time for the study of Latvian in the Russian-language secondary schools. Study of Latvian must begin at age five in all preschool children's institutions where the level of training of the pedagogical personnel allows. In this regard the members of the commission expressed the opinion that it would be advisable to increase the minimum number of hours for language study in the younger classes, when languages are especially easy to learn.

The Ministry of Education and the pedagogical research institutes of the republic must guarantee realization of the principle of interconnectedness in language instruction as they prepare new textbooks for Russian and Latvian, to achieve broad incorporation in pedagogical practice of active methods of study, and must broaden the network of language labs.

The personnel must be trained and methodolgy found to support introduction of an exam in Latvian for the graduating class, or the class before graduation, of secondary general education Russian-language schools must be put in effect, beginning with the 1988–89 school year. The organs of public education must create Latvian language departments in all schools of the republic.

It was acknowledged that it is necessary to perfect the system of cooperation among communists, pedagogues, and students of Latvian- and Russian-language schools, to develop the practice of having joint working, creative, technical, and sporting student societies, special-interest circles, and sections, and to support the tendency toward creating schools with two courses of study.

The activity of the creative unions in the schools and professional-technical schools must be significantly increased to develop a lasting interest among students in the study of the culture and traditions of the Latvian and Russian peoples, and of other peoples of the USSR, and in recognition of the united international body of material and cultural values created by the Soviet peoples, making a holiday of language traditional.

The question of enlarging the numbers of books published in Russian in the republic, classic works of Latvian literature and contemporary authors, must be reexamined, and steps must be taken to satisfy the demand for various dictionaries, phrasebooks, and support materials for studying Russian and Latvian.

The State Committee on Radio and Television of the republic must revise radio and television broadcasts for preschool children who are studying Russian, and organize a new cycle of broadcasts for children and adults who wish to study Latvian. There were also tasks set for members of the press, to more widely propagandize the positive experience of studying Russian and Latvian in educational institutions.

The task was set to assist in all manner possible enhancement of the role of the family in introducing a deep interest in and respect for the cultural values, languages, traditions, and customs of the fraternal peoples.

Teachers must also learn. Exercises will be organized for them and for student teachers at which they will study the problems of nationality relations.

The conference participants considered the question in reference to letters received in answer to the commission's request to the residents of the republic to express their opinions and make concrete suggestions. The majority of letters were constructive, dictated by a sincere desire to raise the culture of inter-nationality communication in the republic. The authors of these letters were thanked by the commission members, since the broad and active participation and support of society, the open exchange of opinions, and discussion of various points of view are the most important preconditions for solving the problems which exist. However, there were also a few anonymous letters containing nationalistic and chauvinist attacks of ill intention, which naturally do not help in achieving this goal.

The conference noted that the close attention being paid to raising the culture of inter-nationality relations and to affirming the principle of bilingualism is not a short-lived campaign, but rather the fundamental policy of the Party. As General Secretary of the Central Committee of the CPSU M. S. Gorbachev stressed at the January 1987 Plenum of the Central Committee of the CPSU, "there is not a single major question which we could resolve, either in the past or now, without taking account of the fact that we live in a multinational state."

HOW MAY THE TURKMEN LANGUAGE BE STUDIED?

This is the question put to the editors by N. V. Alekseev, a reader from Ashkhabad.

"I have long wished to study Turkmen on my own, to learn to read, write, and speak Turkmen. The Russian–Turkmen and Turkmen–Russian dictionaries which are for sale are inconvenient. Wouldn't it be possible to get the proper authorities to put out a self-taught Turkmen course, on the model of the self-taught English course?"

The reader's question is answered by Sh. Gandymov, assistant director of the Makhtumkuli[a] Institute of Language and Literature of the Academy of Sciences of the Turkmen SSR:

"People who wish to study Turkmen by themselves are advised to use the existing Russian–Turkmen and Turkmen–Russian dictionaries and phrasebooks, as well as the textbooks on the Turkmen language from the Russian-language schools. There is a range of reference material—Russian–Turkmen and Turkmen–Russian pocket dictionaries, phrasebooks, and so forth—which is in the press and will soon appear. The creation of a self-teacher, of a television course, and of literature to help the student of Turkmen as a second language is under consideration by the republican program 'Bilingualism.'"

(From: *Turkmenskaia iskra*, 15 November 1987)

Editor's note

a. Makhtumkuli: the most famous Turkmen poet and philosopher of the eighteenth century.

7. Literature and National Culture

One of the longstanding premises of Soviet ideology is that the Party's nationality policy is leading to the "flourishing" of the national cultures of all the Soviet peoples. But what the official formulation ignores is the controversy over what the culture of a nationality is and who defines it—the native intelligentsia or Moscow? Party ideologists maintain that there is no implicit tension between Moscow's goals and those of the "progressive" intelligentsia in the national regions, and that opposition comes only from "nationalist extremists."

While Moscow has always sought to portray cultural relations between nationalities as harmonious, since the founding of the Soviet state there has been tension over official efforts to impose limits on artistic self-expression. By the mid-1930s the cultural experimentation of the early Soviet years had been replaced by a drive for ideological conformity. Soviet culture was to be "national in form and socialist in content"—a phrase first introduced by Stalin, but still a part of official parlance. During the quarter-century of Stalin's rule restrictions on the content of culture became more and more stringent, and repeated purges of intellectuals left cultural heritages warped and mangled beyond recognition.

The early Khrushchev years brought a brief "thaw"; publishing policies were loosened and some cultural figures were posthumously restored. But under Brezhnev the bureaucracy charged with supervising culture experienced the same stagnation that swamped others, leading to an unevenness of supervision. In some parts of the country controversial works were published and fallen heroes were unofficially rehabilitated, while in others writers considered nationalists were barred from publication and use of the local national language in the arts was sharply curtailed.

Since Gorbachev's ascent to power there has been great pressure from intellectuals to end the inconsistencies in cultural policy and, more generally, to allow much greater cultural expression. Prominent cultural figures throughout the country have taken advantage of *glasnost'* to challenge the assumptions of official cultural policy as it is applied to the various national communities of the country. Russian and non-Russian intellectuals have decried the misshaping of culture by bureaucrats who are more concerned with perpetuating acceptable ideological stereotypes than with allowing cultures to grow and form over time, in a way that harmonizes the cultural and historical past of a people with the realities of the present day. Some of the demands of the intellectuals are controversial. The rehabilitation of one nationality's heroes may mean that the villains in the history of another people are publicly acclaimed. Meanwhile, Party conservatives fear that increased freedom of artistic expression will lead inevitably to a decline of Party control.

Conservative Party ideologues feel most secure with statements like the one below by A. Karaganov of the Union of Cinematographers of the USSR, which depicts cultural relations as a harmonious, friendly process of mutual interaction under the benevolent supervision and direction of Russian intellectuals. Articles like this filled the pages of Soviet periodicals devoted to cultural issues during the Brezhnev era, and continue to be written even today. They are formulaic, praising the vision of the Soviet leaders past and present. They accentuate the positive role that the state has played in encouraging the development of national cultures while downplaying its negative or suppressive role.

It is true, as Karaganov writes, that Soviet cinema has become an important cultural outlet for the talents of non-Russians as well as Russians; as a new art form, film had no prerevolutionary legacy. However, until very recently the filming and release of movies was supervised by a cumbersome and conservative bureaucracy which subjected the ethnographic and historic interpretation of non-Russian directors to particularly close scrutiny, leaving some works on the shelf indefinitely. One such long-suppressed film was the controversial movie about Stalin, *Repentance*, by the Georgian director Tenghiz Abuladze. Film studios in many union republics— notably the Baltic republics, Georgia, Turkmenia, and Kazakhstan—were willing to risk the production of controversial films, even if there was trouble releasing them.

The creative leeway granted to writers in the non-Russian regions during the Brezhnev years tended to depend on the leadership of the cultural bureaucracy and artistic unions in the given republic, and whether the individuals in charge were sympathetic to efforts to reinvigorate the national culture. Thus, when Olzhas Suleimenov, the noted Kazakh poet, headed the Kazakh film industry in the late 1970s and early 1980s, a broad range of themes could be explored. Suleimenov, as the 1981 interview from *Literaturnaia gazeta* reproduced here shows, believed that intellectuals had a responsibility to rediscover and reconstruct the national past, and to guard it from distortion by historians. Without self knowledge, he felt, there could be no stable national identity. Suleimenov believed that his generation, born under socialism yet also directly tied to the prerevolutionary past, had a special responsibility to see that the Kazakh national identity be preserved. His criticism of Moscow's homogenizing policy was brash for the Brezhnev years, and would not have been permitted if Suleimenov had not enjoyed special protection from Kazakh party leader and Politburo member D. Kunaev.

Kunaev's protection led to Suleimenov's appointment as head of Kazakhstan's film industry when the poet was dropped from the USSR Union of Writers. The expulsion followed the outcry over publication of Suleimenov's controversial *AZ i IA* (literally A to Ia, the first and last letters in the Russian alphabet, but spelling "Asia"), a history of the period covered in the Russian chronicle "The Igor Tale" (*The Lay of the Host of Igor*) from a Turkic point of view. Other writers found the political situation in their home republics less hospitable.

Some, like the noted Kirghiz writer Chinghiz Aitmatov, were able to find publishing outlets in Moscow but not at home. The career of Aitmatov in particular was aided by the politics of literary "representationalism" (of the sort that is described by Barzudin in his address to the plenum of the Union of Writers, reproduced below), whereby Moscow's leading publishing houses were required to publish a certain number of works by prominent non-Russians each year. The careers of the most successful of the non-Slavic writers published in Moscow have always been boosted by official policies designed to demonstrate the achievements of Soviet nationality policy. The works of prominent writers like Aitmatov have been translated into dozens of languages and sent abroad to represent the USSR in various international forums. In the 1987 *Ogonek* interview reproduced below, Aitmatov refers with some embarrassment to his nonfiction writings from the 1960s and 1970s, which were largely devoted to praising Soviet foreign policy initiatives, as unworthy of surviving the test of time. But his willingness to do some public relations work for the Party gained him numerous advantages. Some were material, like his dacha in Kirghizia, or his receiving Pasternak's former dacha outside of Moscow (which has now been made a Pasternak museum, in response to a campaign led by Russian intellectuals).

Most interesting is the impression that Brezhnev's cultural bureaucracy seemed more tolerant of an Aitmatov, more willing to publish his works, than they typically were of Russians writing on similarly controversial themes. Aitmatov's novel *The Day Lasts More Than a Hundred Years*, published in 1980, dealt explicitly with the amorality of Soviet life. The hero of the novel, Edigei Dzhangeldin, warned that the destruction of historical consciousness led to the destruction of moral conscience, and argued that there was a role for faith in the modern world. This book received praise from Brezhnev (who must not have read it) for evoking rural themes and honoring the common man. Meanwhile, Russian writers were unable to write about similar themes for another five years.

This dual standard created a number of tensions for Soviet literary critics. Some, especially non-Russians like Mkrtchian, wrote in praise of the novel for raising important new themes in an evocative fashion. Others, especially Russian critics like Lakshin, were quick to look for weaknesses in the work, and treated it as a contribution to the inter-nationalist Soviet literature—as distinct from Russian literature. Lakshin obviously wants to create the impression that Aitmatov is less accomplished than a Russian writer. Although Aitmatov has written in Russian for about thirty years, Lakshin faults his use of Russian as sometimes stilted and artificial, and criticizes his depiction of Russian characters as two-dimensional.

Aitmatov became the subject of even more intense criticism by Russian literary critics after the publication of *The Executioner's Block*, which appeared in 1985 (and was recently issued in English translation under the title *Place of the Skull*). Many of the themes from *The Day Lasts More Than a Hundred Years* are repeated in the new novel. But in the new book, for the first time, Aitmatov's hero is a Russian: Avdii Kalestratov, a former seminarian in search of God. Kalestratov encounters drug-traffickers and other evils of modern-day Soviet life, and is defeated by them. The themes raised in the novel, which are mirrored in current discussions of social problems in the USSR, are themes which Aitmatov believed that he had the responsibility to raise (as he describes in the 1987 *Ogonek* interview). The publication of the novel encouraged others to raise similar issues in their writings and in discussions of the agenda for Soviet literature in the late 1980s and the 1990s.

While Soviet literature has always been charged with serving a social function, until recently writers were expected to publicize and praise the goals of the regime, —*not* to call for their modification. Writers today feel entitled to comment on the broadest range of reform issues in the USSR. Thus, Aitmatov has called for the creation of a new airline to compete with the state-owned Aeroflot, and the Georgian writer Tsitsishvili has criticized Gosplan for demanding excessive tea harvests at the expense of fruit and vegetable cultivation in Georgia.

At two recent plenums of the USSR Union of Writers (see the materials reproduced below) many writers made demands clearly related to nationality policy. Indeed, the complaints of the Russian and the non-Russian writers are sometimes in direct competition. Russians like M. Ganina and S. Kuniaev complained that non-Russian writers can explore historical themes and form societies for the preservation of their historical monuments without being labeled chauvinists, whereas Russians (and especially the *Pamiat'* group) are widely criticized for such activities. For their part, non-Russian writers complain that the central cultural bureaucracy is controlled by Russians, and that the artistic establishments from the national republics are given only a symbolic role in the cultural life of the country.

Barudzhin and Andreev (both from Moscow) and Beekman (from Estonia) complained of the second-class status that non-Russian writers are given in Russian-language publishing houses and journals. They cited the small printrun and the low esteem of the journal *Druzhba narodov* (Friendship among Peoples), the establishment of quotas for the publication of non-Russian writers by journals and publishing houses, and underinvestment in Russian-language translations of non-Russian classics. Others, like Ovanesian (Armenian) and Peters (Latvian), complained about the various ideological obstacles placed before non-Russian writers by cautious bureaucrats in the republics as well as in Moscow. Ever-vigilant against manifestations of national feeling, such bureaucrats would quash calls for the preservation of national languages or the creation of any sort of objective historical record. Oleinik (Ukrainian) made this point most forcefully when he argued that a historical period or cultural figure need not be judged "progressive" according to contemporary criteria to be recognized as having played a role worthy of recognition.

These speeches show that writers are now demanding—and playing—an expanded role in the process of restructuring Soviet society. But the problems that they are complaining of will not quickly disappear. The creation of expanded national language presses and the publication of new and better Russian translations of non-Russian works demand financial investment, at a time when the economy is severely strapped. While publishing houses have been granted much greater editorial authority, there is not yet much prospect of granting them financial autonomy, for the money they earn is needed elsewhere. A more complicated matter is the competing nature of the demands being made by Russian and non-Russian writers, and also by feuding neighbors such as the Azerbaidzhanis and Armenians or the Tadzhiks and the Uzbeks. When the goals of one community negate those of another hard choices have to be made, and the decisions can be expected to be both difficult and often arbitrary.

The Soviet Multinational Cinema *

Similarities and Differences

ALEKSANDR KARAGANOV

After the victory of the Great October in history there emerged in the broad expanses of Russia for the first time—as a voluntary union of equals—a multinational community of peoples, in which respect for the traditions and distinctive features of national cultures, mutual assistance, and reciprocity in relations among them were raised to the level of state policy.

The fundamentally new development of Soviet culture, including cinematography, is bound up with many historical factors and circumstances, among them the special role of Russia in the life of the multinational family of peoples of the USSR. It is well known that the Russian proletariat was the vanguard of the socialist revolution. And it is also well known that the culture of Pushkin and Tolstoy, Gogol and Dostoevsky, Glinka and Tchaikovsky, had acquired a truly universal historical significance already in the nineteenth century. Thus it is perfectly understandable and natural that such a mighty culture should exert its influence on the cultural development of the other peoples that united sixty years ago to form the Soviet Union. But this influence has nothing in common with the forcible Russification of peoples speaking other languages which was conducted by tsarism and which our ideological adversaries ascribe to the Soviet regime. It spreads not by command or order from above, but as a natural component in the life of national cultures under conditions of their full equality: generated by spiritual and esthetic needs, it does not impede but rather assists the development of the cultural traditions of each of the socialist nations. It is not only revolutionary internationalism of Soviet cultural policy that promotes this tendency, but also that which we call "the Pushkin principle" of Russian culture, exemplified by Pushkin's sensitivity to the style and spirit of other cultures, Pushkin's ability—in whatever he treated or translated—to preserve their distinctive charm and unique beauty. Contempt for national conceit and insularity, an internationalist openness towards people of other nationalities—these are the intrinsic qualities of the truly Russian worker, who is free from chauvinism and nationalism, and the most characteristic features of that part of Russian culture which is democratic and humanistic. This is the pinnacle of Russian culture. This is the living legacy inherited, continued and further developed by Soviet culture.

Of major importance in the establishment of the young national cinemas was the fact that their founding practitioners were trained at the Moscow All-Union State Institute of Cinematography or at the Advanced Courses for Directors and Script

---

*Pravda, 10 October 1982, p. 3. Russian text © 1982 by "Pravda."

Scenario Writers. Teachers of different generations at the Institute (as also the workshop supervisors at the courses), from Kuleshov and Eisenstein to Gerasimov and Kulidzhanov, constantly urged and continue to urge their pupils to learn from everyone who can teach them something, but to imitate no one. Learn but do not copy! Be yourselves! Be yourselves not only as creative individuals, but also as representatives of your culture! Of vital importance in the development of the ideologically unified but artistically varied film art of the socialist nations has been the practice of exchanging creative cadres. As we know from history, Alexander Dovzhenko, who began his great artistic career in the Ukraine, worked for many years at "Mosfil'm" [Moscow Film Studio] and exerted a strong influence on the development of poetic-philosophical films in all the republics. The name of Amo Bek-Nazarov is invariably mentioned by historians of Armenian, Azerbaidzhani, Georgian, and Russian cinematography. The creative work of Mikhail Kalatozov is linked to Georgian and Russian cinematography, that of Nikolai Shengelaia with Georgian and Azerbaidzhani. The work of a number of Moscow and Leningrad directors in the fraternal republics has been most effective in stimulating the development of the national cinemas and the professional growth of their creative cadres.

Practical cooperation, which takes the forms of sharing experience and artistic mutual assistance, continues. Larisa Shepit'ko produced *Heat* in Kirghizia (it is typical that the main role in this film was played by Bolot Shamshiev, who was subsequently to become one of the leading film directors in that republic). Georgii Danelia—a Georgian by origin, temperament, and directorial style—worked for many years at "Mosfil'm," enriching Soviet cinema with such films as *I Walk in Moscow*, *Don't Grieve*, *Mimino*, *Afonia*, and *Autumn Marathon*, which combine the best qualities of Russian and Georgian cinematographic cultures. The Lithuanian director Vytautas Žalakevičius produced *Liberty Is a Sweet Word* and *Centaur* at the "Mosfil'm" studio, and on his return to Lithuania wrote the screenplay for Almantas Grikevičius's powerful film *Fact*. The Kirghiz Tolomush Okeev made his talented picture *The Fierce One* at "Kazakhfil'm" [Kazakh Film Studio], Andrei Tarkovsky served as consultant for films by young directors in Odessa and Vilnius. Vija Artmane, Donatas Banionis, Gunārs Cilinskis, Valeriia Zaklunnaia, Ada Rohovsteva, Armen Dzhigarkhanian have given successful performances in films made at the Moscow and Leningrad studios.

In addition to these forms of contact and interaction may be mentioned creative conferences of cinematographers from the fifteen republics, plenary sessions of the Union of Cinematographers, seminars, and joint trips by practitioners of the film-arts from the various republics to large construction sites, factories, and agricultural areas.

At the outset, every one of the young cinemists was faced with problems that might be described in terms of a major theme in the film by Tolomush Okeev, *The Sky of Our Childhood*. In the course of the film, a helicopter lands on the field of Bakai, where the action takes place: September is approaching and it is time for the children to depart for school. It is not easy for them to part with the "sky of their childhood," with their familiar yurts and pastureland, and with their parents. But the school is in the city, and this helicopter, which has landed near their nomad camp, also represents life—its poverty, the sorrow of parting and joy of discovery, new encounters and friendships. When cinema was making its beginning in republics such as Kirghizia, its practitioners, like the heroes of the Okeev film, were faced with a choice: figuratively speaking, either to stay in their pasturelands or to board the helicopter.

In their "pasturelands" they faced the danger of turning their traditions into a conglomerate of frozen stereotypes. But the young practioners of the young cinema, who had received a modern education in the art of film education, had no desire to dwell on variations on the same themes of folklore and ethnographic symbols of their national style, though even now both folklore and ethnography are not infrequently employed in their films—no longer in the form of quotations or classroom recitations, but as contemporary, creatively assimilated motifs and tinctures hearkening to a distant past.

Aboard the "helicopters," on the other hand, it would not have been all that difficult to begin making films following ready-made models. For the youth early development of the new cinemas came at a time when cinematographers in other republics and other countries had already accumulated a fair store of experience, offering a great many models for imitation. And youth, after all, is always a time of apprenticeship, in many ways conducive to imitation and recapitulation. The young cinemists, however, strove to make use of helicopters without forgetting the pasturelands. Mindful of the fact that national traditions are not a code of laws but a process, they undertook, virtually from their first steps along the path of independent creative work, to employ the universal medium of the screen, accessible to all nations and nationalities. The newest achievements and discoveries of Soviet and world cinema become their own living possession, to be then enriched by national tinctures and resonances. This is what enables them to demonstrate the truth of national life in an impressive and throughly modern fashion. In the process, the best products of the national cinemas provide profound and finely nuanced examples of the living dialectic that marks the evolution of human personalities and relationships an important component of which is the maturation under socialism of the "primordial" national wellsprings of people's life.

The film *Daughter-in-Law* by Kh. Narliev is very much "Turkmen." But it has travelled throughout the entire Soviet Union and all over the world. And everywhere it was understood and well received, for in it, national, folk, and universal elements were combined and fused. Thanks to this fusion, the film's creators were better able to deal with their heroes' psychological problems on the current level of their social and moral development. The character of the main heroine (Maia Aimedova)—who remains faithful to her husband who perished in the war, and, touchingly, continues to care for her old father-in-law—reveals not only the moral strength of a Turkmen woman—rooted in centuries-old traditions and displaying, in its outward manifestations, a religious coloration—but also thoughts, feelings, and bursts of emotion engendered by recent social experience.

Old Makharashvili, the hero of the film *Father of a Soldier* by Revaza Chkheidze, is Georgian through and through. In manner of speech and dress. In plasticity of movement and gesture. And even in the fact that somewhere in Germany he barred the way to a vineyard with his own body when a young tank driver, his mind on the impending battle and not the grapevine, did not want to drive around it. But in his perception of life, his relations with his comrades-in-arms, his understanding of the nature and objectives of this war, he is very like the young tank driver with whom he clashed over the vineyard. Makharashvili, as played by Sergo Zakariadze, in social and moral terms is close to Alesha Skvortsov in *Ballad of a Soldier*, Andrei Sokolov in *The Destiny of a Man*, General Serpilin in *The Living and the Dead*, Sergeant-Major Vaskov and his girl fighters in the film *The Dawns Are Quiet Here* . . . , and the heroes of *Liberation*, the trilogy about Kovpak, *Ascension*, and *Twenty Days without War*.

Living examples of the development of national character as Soviet character are represented shown by the heroes of the films *The Taste of Bread*, *Some Interviews on Personal Matters*, *An Especially Important Assignment*, *This Is Your Son, O Earth*, *The Interrogation*, *Hope and Support*, and *The Train Stopped*.

At the root of these observed similarities and differences lies the all-pervasive influence of the people's practical experience in the social sphere. In the years and decades of socialist construction tremendous changes have occurred in the political and economic complexion of life and in the spiritual and moral makeup of people of all nationalities. These changes are inevitably reflected in the artist's approach to reality. Workers of the cinema welcome wholeheartedly the resolution of the Central Committee of the CPSU "On the Creative Links Between Literary Journals and the Practice of Communist Construction" which states in particular that: "For the art of socialist realism there is no task more important than to affirm the Soviet way of life, the norms of communist morality, and the beauty and grandeur of our moral values—such as honest work for the good of the people, internationalism, and faith in the historic righteousness of our cause."

In speaking about the development of cinemas in the fraternal republics, we are aware that each of them has its own unresolved problems, difficulties and shortcomings. For example, in Moldavia, Tadzhikistan, and some other republics there is a shortage of good scripts, and, not infrequently, mediocre ones are accepted for production for purposes of plan fulfillment, with inevitable consequences for the quality of the films.

The creators of some films that have come out in the republics become overly enamored with the decorativeness of their national styles, especially in their depiction of the past. This sometimes leads to bombast, concentration on the externals of style, and obfuscation of the essence of the action on the screen.

In contrast to such forcing of "national forms," some cinematographers mute the national principle with stylistic exercises that attempt to bring films up to "general European standards." Again, the result is a violation of artistic integrity. Again, there are barriers on the path of truth.

I have mentioned these extremes not to suggest finding a golden mean. What should be sought is not always to be found halfway between a delectation with the past and national exotica on the one hand and a faceless portrayal of life devoid of national and social features on the other. What should be sought is a dynamism in art, which reflects the dynamism of life and the socialist convergence and mutual enrichment of nationally distinct cultures.

Before our very eyes, national traditions are experiencing a new enrichment through the cinema. And this extends to subject matter as well. It is appropriate and natural—and profoundly consistent with the internationalist character of Soviet film art—that the Uzbek directors Malik Kaiumov, Latif Faiziev, and Ali Khamraev have turned to the subject of Afghanistan. It is likewise natural that documentary films on the construction of the Baikal-Amur Railroad should come out from the film studios of Ukraine and Georgia. Unfortunately, such treatment of life outside their own republic or of events taking place elsewhere in our country and the world in cinemas of the fraternal republics is not particularly frequent.

In some republics still, young people only rarely advance to position enabling them to undertake independent work, while the training of new experts (at the film division of the Kiev Theater Institute, for example), does not make the complex and rigorous demands on them that long ago have become a tradition at the All-Union State Institute of Cinematography.

For all their shortcomings, some of them mentioned here and others still unmentioned, and despite an abundance of unsolved problems, the truly remarkable development of cinemas in the fifteen fraternal republics has become an indisputable fact of life in the continuing evolution of world cinema, and constitutes yet another achievement of our Party's nationality policy. The basis underlying this development, both as a subject for portrayal and as a vantage point from which to view the realities of today's complex world, was and remains the life of the peoples now building communism, who of their own free will united sixty years ago to form the Union of Soviet Socialist Republics.

We Have Come to Act *

OLZHAS SULEIMENOV

What, exactly, is this "poetic character" one hears so much about today? Most likely, everyone construes it in line with his own life experience. Especially since this type of character is by no means limited to the literary field, but in fact appears in all spheres of human endeavor. The author is invariably present in the characters he creates, which is why it is only natural for an author to engage in a study of self-exploration. . . .

It took me five years to "hatch" my diploma in geological engineering. During the intersessions I wrote novels day and night. Then I entered the Institute of Literature. The study of literature now became a requirement. I immediately stopped writing prose. I became a perpetual visitor to the Lenin Library, where in a year I read through more geological literature than in my five years as student of geology. I wrote my study "The mechanics of formation of saline caps in the Embensk petroleum-bearing structure." I made, it seemed to me, a whole mass of discoveries in it useless to science, but extremely important for myself. Eruptions of creative joy would thunder through the silent halls of the library, inaudible to the outside world, but deafening to me. "A self-taught person"—that is a disparaging term. But what a delight it was to be one. I believe that only self-education can make a specialist.

Who knows, perhaps in five years of study at the Institute of Literature I might have become a good geologist, but already by the third year questions were raised about my staying as a student there. Some big wheel or other could save me. I went with my doggerel, written during classes on the theory of poetics, to The Poet. He looked through my notebook and said: "Do you have a profession? So, then, go and do some good. But don't write poetry. It won't come off." I left the Institute of Literature and published two books the same year.

By the time it was no longer necessary to "break through," with offers pouring in from various publishing houses, my poetry came less and less frequently from pen to paper. And even less frequently to mind. Does prohibition strengthen the will and permission weaken it? This was one among many reasons. But a significant one. Another was that I became fascinated by paleography, the history of writing and literary texts. Now I sometimes wonder: if historians had ever encouraged my first efforts, would I have dropped the business? Following the logic of my character, the simpler answer would be—yes. But then, I think, what might have happened is that some new creative mechanism would have come into force. We are always fascinated by troubled waters. This is another character trait of the type we are talking about.

Literaturnaia gazeta, 2 September 1981, p. 2. Russian text © 1981 by the USSR Union of Writers.

That is why even a most hospitable, most cordial welcome by the leading lights of historical linguistics would not have discouraged my desire to trespass on their territory. For me, the study of history and cultural interaction among peoples is no longer simply a passion, but a duty whose fulfillment is equally strongly stimulated by taboo.

Must one write verse to be a poet? I think not, if there are other means to bring harmony to the world. Weaving the best carpets, rescuing people ;om a burning house, smelting the best steel—are these not manifestations of a poetic worldview, or a poetic character?

But still, how pleasant it is to see and hold in one's hands one's own new book, still smelling of printer's ink! Recently, for example, I received a volume of my collected poems, *The Transformation of Fire* [Transformatsiia ognia], published in Paris—my second book translated into French by Léon Robel, my old friend, scholar and poet. If this book of mine, and the preceding ones, strikes a responsive chord among the readers—that is inducement enough for me to write poetry.

There is a view that literature is a solitary, cottage industry. At one time, I also would frequently counterpose literature, say, to film, in the belief that literature is created by an individual and the cinema by a collective. But now it seems to me that it may only be a first impression that it is a cottage industry. The writer is a factory plugged into a system of world industry, if by this one means world culture, heritage, and that which is being created today. A hack (in the negative sense of the word), is, on the other hand, a solitary handicraftsman, cut off from the world system. A writer's work can be divided into two stages: the stage of accumulation and the stage of unburdening. These stages are in a state of perpetual alternation. The stage of accumulation is more longlasting, more permanent, while output comes only infrequently. Material continues to be accumulated until it reaches some critical point— and then comes an explosion of creativity. The more fruitful the stage of accumulation, the more brilliant will be the revelation of a writer's gifts. The constant churning of ideas—that is the indispensable condition preparing the way for the explosion.

Even today, literature remains the most profound and vital factor in the nurturing of the spirit. The influence of the artistic word proceeds along very narrow lines of communication, spreading as if by capillary action through the very fabric of society. But act it certainly does. Happy is the poet who has the right to say: "I know the power of words. . . ."

A writer's life is the history of his own interaction—his conflict and his unity— with the reader. A book begins to exist from the moment it acquires a reader. The word "literature" translates from some ancient language, possibly Sanskrit, as "union in action." According to that notion, which is close to my heart and seems to me the only true one, literature is the result of interaction between a writer and a reader.

What interesting letters the mail brings sometimes. Some days, or even for a year, it happens, I virtually glow from a reader's words. I am thinking of someday publishing a collection, or rather a book, of selected letters—a self-portrait of my readers.

I met my first reader somewhere at the very beginning of my creative life. Since then I have always set my bearings by this person's taste, someone who, from my very first steps, has been both cruel and good to me, knew how to stimulate and excite my ideas and my ambition. I endured much from him, but it is him that I consider as my teacher. It was his reading of my first attempts that in many respects determined the direction my creativity took. He was able to find something unusual for himself in some, to my mind very simple line, and could demolish my most complex construction with a mere smirk, saying it was derivative. Years later, I began to be afraid meeting him. I thought that he had changed, lost his uncompromisingly high standards. I began to see him less frequently, and then our personal contacts broke off completely. But in my mind I still retain his youthful image.

I may be accused of counting on an unusual, in some sense elitist, reader. But even the notion is quite unstable and changeable, is it not? What Pushkin and Tolstoy wrote for the thousands is now beloved by the millions. On the other hand, Tolstoy's works written especially "for the people," and adapted to their level, no longer "work." The same may be said of some things by Mayakovsky or our own Saken Seifullin,[a] who intentionally wrote in a simplified language for the mass, then mostly semi-literate reader. Today we are inclined to be somewhat dubious about this part of our eminent writers' legacy—today, after all, everyone reads and understands even the most complicated books. But we (today so highly educated, so perceptive!) under no circumstances should forget the feats of Tolstoy, Mayakovsky, Seifullin and many others, who consciously "strangled the song in their throats." It is sad to see how some critics arrogantly dismiss the "utilitarian" literature of the greats and thereby impoverish and diminish their image. They simply deprive them of membership in their historical universe, view them apart from the circumstances of their times. To appreciate the nobility of the greats, it is necessary to be noble oneself.

Contemporary Soviet writers are more fortunate than their predecessors. Now every writer, however complex he may be in thought, style, or manner of writing, has his readers. There are as many different kinds of readers as there are writers. With such a splendid readership, whose current level of culture and discernment can "guarantee" full comprehension, a Soviet writer can let his talents unfold.

But here is a paradox. As a social phenomenon, the writer changes less than the reader. The great Russian literature of the nineteenth century considerably outstripped its readers. In the twentieth century, the opposite is taking place. There is a category of writers who lag behind their readers in education, culture, and level of thought. Today it is the reader who must bring the writer up to his level. Let me stress the point: the *writer*—who is his teacher. The bookshelves of every home are lined with world classics and we must fight for a place on those shelves.

Some time ago, one of my friends, a Russian poet, said: "Olzhas, why do you bother yourself with rubbish and waste your time deciphering graffiti? Come on, write verse, give poetry readings." I answered him: "You had your golden age of culture, the nineteenth century; someone had worked in your behalf. Our culture today is going through a renaissance, but in many respects also a birth. In culture we are today living through both the 19th and 20th centuries at the same time." Precisely for this reason, the mission of a Kazakh writer differs significantly, in scope and in direction, from tasks that face the Russian writer. We have to be enlighteners, illuminators, and even something of luminaries.

To take an example, our historiography was poor. But we, Kazakh men of letters, wrote historical novels and verses, rummaged around in archives, trying at least in this way to prod our historians, to give them some direction where to look, show them the areas they should study. Essentially, the immense period prior to the twentieth century in the life of my republic remained without supervision or system-atization. I spent twenty years on historiography, which I considered absolutely essential for the normal functioning of the body that is contemporary culture.

Some scholars tried to persuade me that our past was the pitch darkness of barbarism. But I wanted to find in my past such men of encyclopedic stature as Al-Farabi.[b] I know that the relations of my people with other peoples were formed not only on the level of crude actions, but also on a cultural and humanistic plane. This knowledge is extremely necessary to us today, when our life is unthinkable without such fruitful cooperation and interaction with all peoples inhabiting this earth. We desperately need the historical examples of moral goodness, mutual assistance, and life together.

One of the salient features of the poetic character is impatience. The creative impatience of a man who wants to see the results of his efforts right now, today, in the time allotted him by nature and fate, who wants to help the impetuous development of the self-consciousness of the society that gave him birth. This impatience prob-ably inheres in the character of many, including mine. Narrow specialization contra-venes our nature. We try to apply our efforts wherever we might be useful.

I write books. I am impelled to by my awareness that literature can harmonize so actively and so quickly one's macrocosm and microcosm. I am involved in Kazakh cinema, since our cinema is underdeveloped. If it was opera that lagged behind, I probably would have gone on to "work" as a baritone and a tenor combined. But we have splendid singers, the best in Central Asia.

In *The Book of Clay* [Glinianaia kniga] there is one character, Koten. I do not like to reread my own things. Except for *The Book of Clay*—from my point of view, the most successful. I reread it with pleasure, it reveals a potential I had not seen before, it seems to develop together with me. I never worked on anything with such enjoy-ment. He had the habit of interfering in other people's business affairs. He tried to inject his views into everything, even things about which he understood nothing. But he is a product of that impatience and lack of indifference which I value in people. Koten was impatient to get on with living, he was constantly in action, he was always trying to force people to be happy. He taught a roofer how to cover a roof, a land reclaimer how to dig ditches properly, soldiers how to fight, sovereigns how to rule, executioners how to cut off heads. He had no patience for ineptitude, even in his enemies. There is always something of the author's personality in the character of a literary figure. I too should like to wage a universal struggle with ineptitude, to exorcise from man the demon of servitude and all the other petty demons like cruelty, ignorance, mendacity; I cannot wait to see in man compassion as his Supreme Emotion, distinguishing him from his fellow creatures, that which makes him a Man.

If talent and goodness are to be seen as a people's achievement, then ineptitude, ignorance, and indifference must be viewed today as a people's loss, as social defects. In every individual case, literature rouses the reader's talents by developing the culture of his emotions and ideas. It promotes society's spiritual progress. These truths need repeating all the more frequently because now, in the era of film and television, a growing danger threatens the book. But we have still managed to read Pushkin, Dostoevsky, and Tolstoi. The generations after us will only have "seen" them. Today there is mounting evidence which allows, for example, a generalization like: television movies are able to popularize and virtually enshrine as classics any mediocre prose, but the true classics, as a rule, they deprive of readers.

Film and television are not able to cope with those social tasks which literature alone could undertake. They operate superficially, on the surface of consciousness, not in its depths. The danger that the video arts pose to the book unfolded over the past two decades, just when my generation was learning to "stand on its own two feet" in literature, and this circumstance made its mark on our fate.

Voznesenskii, Yevtushenko, Rozhdestvenskii in Russia; Drach and Korotych in Ukraine; Aripov and Vakhidov in Uzbekistan; Kanoat, Sherali, and Kirom in Tadzhikistan; Marcinkevičius and Mikuta in Lithuania; Vācietis, Ziedonis, Auziņš in Latvia—all of us belong to that genetic stratum in literature which not too long ago was called the sixties generation. All of us want to be writers who are both national and international, we are all members of one team, though each has his own specific aims. We are marginal personalities, who were born on the border of at least two cultures, and we are all both a bridge between them and a conduit of mutual influences. We represent world culture in our own, and our own culture in world culture.

We were one of the most active generations in Soviet literature. Someone before us said: "We come into life to act." This applies precisely to us.

The steadfastness and fortitude of our generation is being tested now, today. Some kind of critical moment is looming, maybe even the mid-life crisis. A slowdown in output is perceptible, the tendency to socialize weakens a bit, and sometimes personal concerns begin to prevail over the social. Plus the experience of disillusionment, distress, and failures—all this weighs on the shoulders and on the pen. Soon it will be clear—are you a sprinter or long-distance runner, how long a span of time has been allotted to your strength, the reserves of rage, anger and goodness with which you entered literature, the energy of ideas that once pushed you onto this path. There is a wise Kazakh saying: "On a long trip take with you long thoughts." How great a distance are your ideas meant to travel, where does this path lead—to a precipice or to the next road? All these are questions of the moment. They stimulate thought, they force you to test yourself in various genres—after all, verse cannot express everything you have amassed. The euphoria of youth is gone. What may be forgiven the novice is not forgiven the professional. (Let me note parenthetically that I, too, have conceived an idea for a prose work. There are many themes in the conception which cannot fit into verse form. I am writing screenplays, doing scholarly research, preparing an etymological dictionary called "A thousand and one words," writing a study about the origins of the Old Turkic script.c) This is the typical experience of a member of our generation in literature. We are not standing at a crossroads, we are in motion—although our movement is less noticeable than before, since it is no longer in a straight line.

Artists in Japan used to have the following custom: sometime before turning forty, when a creative person came into his own, he changed his name and began over again under a pseudonym. If his work continued to arouse interest, it meant that he had succeeded as an artist, it meant that it was not his name that worked for him, but he worked for his name. It would do us good to adopt this practice—what if suddenly all writers after the age of forty changed their names! Only I fear that the critics would be at a loss: whom to praise and whom to intimidate? It is hardly a secret that for many of them the main criterion is the name.

If literature is an activity for the good of the people, it is a wonderful way of life for many, including me—the only one possible. And wherever the curve of poetry may take us, we always return to literature.

Recorded by S. Taroshchinaia

Editor's notes

a. Saken Seiufullin (1894–1939): Kazakh poet, considered one of the founders of socialist realism in Kazakh literature. An early supporter of Bolshevik rule, Seiufullin was arrested and died during the purges.

b. Abu Nasr Muhammad b. Tarkhan al-Farabi (870–950): one of the outstanding medieval Muslim philosophers. His works, written in Arabic, combined Aristotelianism with elements of Neo-Platonism, and were important in the transmission of classical philosophy to medieval Europe. Of Turkic stock, he was born near Farab, now in Chardzhou Oblast of the Turkmen SSR.

c. Presumably the Old Turkic runes, known from a small number of mortuary inscriptions on steles in Central Asia and Mongolia, dating from the 7th–9th centuries.

Annotated by Lubomyr Hajda

Discussing Aitmatov's Novel "A Blizzard Waystation" (The Day Lasts More Than a Hundred Years) *

(Moscow: "Molodaia Gvardiia," 1981)

Because Mkrtchian discusses the novel so elliptically, it seems useful to synopsize the plot, which consists of three levels. The surface plot begins with the death of Kazangap, a railroad worker, and concerns the attempt by his friend, Edigei, to bury him in the traditional tribal burial ground, some distance away. The novel gives a detailed account of traditional mourning and burial practices, including an obvious Muslim interment. The novel's next layer is a social history of the USSR from collectivization on, as retold in Edigei's reminiscences as the funeral party rides toward the burial ground; these include an account of Abutalip, a war hero and excellent teacher who dies when arrested on false charges during the Stalin era. The final layer comes in two tribal legends, one of a mother, Naiman-Ana, who goes to seek her captured son, only to be killed by him because he has become a mindless slave; the other is an account of an old singer, Raimaly-aga, who is killed by his relatives because he falls in love with a young woman, Begimai. Interspersed with these stories is a science fiction plot of first contact with an alien civilization, the Lesnogrudtsi, who are so advanced that the Americans and Soviets decide jointly to encircle earth with a system of defensive automatic space weapons (called Operation "Obruch" [Ring]), to prevent anyone from entering or leaving.—Ed.

The Donenbai Bird

LEVON MKRTCHIAN

Chinghiz Aitmatov turned fifty in December 1978. I had a chance to go to Frunze for the celebration, but at the same time I had to make a trip to Bulgaria. When I entered Auditorium 136 of Sofia University for a meeting with students on Tuesday, 12 December, Aitmatov's birthday, someone had written carefully on the board, "Chinghiz Aitmatov is fifty." I am not speaking of the student audience now in order to discuss the universal fame of the writer. That very same day, 12 December, at an international conference in Sofia it was discussed with pain and bitterness how "the world now spends more than a billion dollars a day on arms" (*Pravda*, 13 December 1978). This startling figure makes one think, wondering at the mindlessness of mankind. . . . And when I had read Chinghiz Aitmatov's novel *The Day Lasts More Than a Hundred Years*, I remembered this black billion they had

---

Literaturnoe obozrenie, 1981, no. 10, pp. 36–43. Russian text © 1981 by the USSR Union of Writers.

discussed in Sofia, and then later I recalled Auditorium 136 of Sofia University.

In his novel Aitmatov talks about—or shouts about—the possibility of a catastrophe on earth. (Those daily billions bring that catastrophe nearer.) The novel is journalistic. Journalistic qualities of prose are generally mentioned when people want to say that even though something is not glittering with artistic merit, it is necessary and important.

"A lot of people write sharply now," a famous Armenian mathematician says. "The trick is to write both sharply and artistically."

The comment is a just one. Aitmatov's prose is journalistic though precisely because it is artistic.

I ran into Aitmatov in June 1980, in Moscow. The manuscript of the novel had been read in *New World* [Novyi mir], and though it was not yet published, people were already talking about it. I asked to have the manuscript for a day (luckily we were living in the same hotel). I was particularly interested in this novel because I knew that Aitmatov had taken as its epigraph some lines from the Armenian poet Grigor Narekatsi, "This book is in place of my body, These words in place of my soul . . . " I read the novel in a single sitting. The next morning at breakfast, when I told Aitmatov that the book was written with an enormous sense of personal responsibility for people, he began to talk about Dostoevsky.

"I was rereading *Crime and Punishment*. Two old women are murdered, and from the point of view of everyday logic, one of them is a truly worthless and harmful old witch. As you read though you see that after this murder not only is it impossible for Raskolnikov to live, but impossible for you yourself to live. In the modern world though everyday there are murders a thousand times crueler and bloodier. How important it is that the modern writer is able to shake his reader like that, to force him to stand up with his entire being against injustice, murder, and violence."

We were talking of Dostoevsky, but Aitmatov was also speaking of his new novel and its sources. I also see Aitmatov in the letter he wrote me, where he discusses Grigor Narekatsi's *Lamentations* [Kniga skorbi]: "Don't think" that I have been wasting time on nothing. I read *Lamentations* and tried to keep myself from total destruction before the inarguable Narekatsi . . . Narekatsi is 'awful' for us because of his unthinking maximalism, his inhuman ability to subject himself to the pitiless judgment of a higher, eternal office, the judgment of conscience, of responsibility before God." (2 February 1978).

Aitmatov values his forebears (and his forebears are Kirghiz and Russian cultural figures, as well as figures from world culture) when they are tormented by the same things that torment him, when they struggle toward the same things he struggles for.

Of late there is a great deal of talk about the death of the world. To some people it even seems that to speak of the world's impending doom, of the need to save mankind and the world is a rule of good manners.

Turgenev's Pigasov precisely and vividly characterizes the noble lady who loves to talk about the things which upset all the best people. "Well, Daria Mikhailovna," Pigasov answered with irritation, "I think that in any case it would be easier for you to live without truth than it would be to live without your cook Stepan, who is such a master of bouillon making!''

I often recall this acid comment. Bouillon lovers, too, know that man does not live by bread alone . . . .

Aitmatov's novel *The Day Lasts More Than a Hundred Years* is dedicated to the most serious problems of the modern world.

Recently the students of Erevan University asked Mikhail Dudin[b] what he would say to all mankind, if he had the opportunity.

"I would repeat Pushkin's words," Dudin said, "or Pushkin's sigh, really . . . 'When peoples join into a great family, what rends them asunder is forgotten.'"

Mikhail Dudin's open letter to Aitmatov was the first response to the novel *The Day Lasts More Than a Hundred Years*. The Russian poet is tormented by the same problems as is Aitmatov:

> Never satiating its maw with food,
> The twentieth century gnaws itself
> Chopping, chopping at the Tree of Life
> Like a pitiless woodsman . . .
> And this tree is ever more compliant
> Not following the laws of nature.
> The bark cracks, the roots grow weak,
> The dusty leaves rattle.
> Oh, Great Reason, you might forbid
> That at least the last branch be cut,
> But all science's branches
> Develop appetites,
> Science acts as madame,
> But time does not reproach the madame.
> In the battle for a better Today
> The future is everywhere in flames . . .

Mikhail Dudin, the author of these lines, could not help but write them; he had to write an awed letter to Aitmatov after reading the novel *The Day Lasts More Than a Hundred Years*.

For Dudin, for Aitmatov, just as for all of us, Pushkin's dream, Pushkin's sigh, is extraordinarily important now: ". . . what rends them asunder is forgotten."

In one of Aitmatov's books there is an idea that memory is conscience, that a man who loses his memory loses his conscience. In the novel *The Day Lasts More Than a Hundred Years* discusses how a man deprived of memory is no longer a man.

The Zhuan-zhuan (even the sound of their name has a hint of insects, of swarming masses), having seized the land of others, turn the people into slaves. They stretch a *shiri*, raw camel hide, over a freshly shaved head. The camel hide dries, crushing the head, and the man either dies or loses his memory, becoming a *mankurt*.

Because of Aitmatov's novel, this word—*mankurt*—will enter the language, if it has not done so already. Now we know how to call people who have lost their memory. The word is found—*mankurt*, the one who "only recognizes his masters, just like a dog."

The *mankurt* can't remember his own name, Zholaman, or the name of his father, Donenbai. He doesn't recognize his mother Naiman-Ana. And when he killed her, "her white scarf fell from her head and in the air turned into a bird, flying off crying, 'Remember, who are you? What is your name? Your father is Donenbai! Donenbai! Donenbai!' (This name Donenbai, the sound, seems to contain an echo. When you say Donenbai you can hear it ringing round, Donenbai, Donenbai . . . nenbai. . . .)

The legend of the Donenbai bird is a key one for the novel. Legends and myths have become an almost obligatory attribute of modern prose. However, for eastern literatures, which have a parable-like, exhortatory manner of composition, the use of legends is a tradition. Aitmatov's legend (which goes back to *Manas*, the Kirghiz folk legend) has a deep philosophical meaning and function. The legend organizes the deeper, secondary and tertiary levels of the novel's content. The legend illuminates, explains, and makes modern the plot, the actions, and characters of the heros, Sabitzhan, the two Tansykbaevs . . .

Even Edigei's camel Karanar (who is a full-blooded hero of the book) has a direct connection to Naiman-Ana and the Donenbai bird. The breed-mother of Karanar ("here's a case of genes working to the maximum") is the same Akmaia, the white-head she-camel which belonged to Naiman-Ana. . . . In Karanar's fury is the cry and memory of the breed. The power of instinct in his case is the logic of living nature, of life. Karanar is a reproach to people, people like Sabitzhan. "We live for our fannies, so that what we put in our mouths will be a little sweeter," Sabitzhan says in a moment of honesty. His most treasured worries are all that same "boullion," and the memory of the tribe is all a side issue . . . .

Operation "Obruch" (read that as *shiri)* in light of the legend acquires a tragic sense, as does the whole line of the extraplanetary civilization of the Lesnogrudtsi, as well as the bitterly written pages about the danger which hangs over the world because of reactionary forces. We know what all this leads to (the medicine is a hundred times more frightful and worse than the disease), to those billions wasted on arms that the Sophia conference discussed, to the anti-human, mindless decision to start mass production of the neutron bomb, of death.

There is a lot written about Aitmatov's novel; but it is discussed and argued about even more.

"For you the main thing in the novel is the bite, the cosmic problems," our Amo Sagiian complains, "but I think that Edigei is the main thing, and Kazangap and Abutalip. What kind of people are they? A god-forsaken station, arid, deserted . . . Even the trains don't stop there. . . . 'In order to live in the Sary-ozek stations you had to have spirit, or otherwise you would rot.' And Edigei and Kazangap live there without complaint. And how Aitmatov loves them! "

You know that prose fails when writers don't love their own heros. In order to write a good novel, you must love the people you write about very, very much. I am convinced of that . . . Kazangap has died, and Edigei speaks of him as God might: "It must be that the water and salt set aside for him at birth had run out." Why has none of us spoken of Lake Sevan[c] as Kazangap has about the Aral Sea[d]: "Whatever the land is worth, the Aral Sea is worth as much. Now it is drying up. So what is there to be said of the life of man?" This remark by the elder of Armenian poets, Amo Sagiian, seems to me to be important. However, the cosmic plot (of necessity abstract, though there are some touching details; for example: "[the extraplanetary] old men seem to get grey just as ours do") makes concrete, fills out the societal and political sharpness of the novel because it has the most direct relation to Edigei, to Kazangap's burial, and to the funeral procession. In general, as Aitmatov has shown, everything that happens on earth and in space has some relation to us, influences our lives, conditioning it.

The conflict (nature and technology) is given in the very beginning of the novel. A hungry vixen in search of food runs to the railroad tracks. When the train comes though, "a monster with running fires," the vixen flees, "hugging the ground in fear." Later, seeing the rockets rising into the sky on gigantic tongues of flame [as the system of defensive satellites is put into orbit—Trans.], Edigei suddenly recalls the vixen that had run along the railroad tracks. "It was just the same as for her, when that whirlwind caught her in the open steppe. . . ." The conflict on earth grows to become a conflict in space. Here it is only hinted. In the end of the novel you feel more acutely the vixen's naïveté; she "ran off on a big circle in the steppe, having decided to come up to the tracks in another place, where the trains didn't run."

The novel's final scene ("The sky crashed down on his head, yawning wide in balls of boiling flame and smoke . . . The man, the camel, and the dog, these simplest of creatures, ran mindlessly away . . . No matter how long they ran though, they were just running in place, for each new explosion enveloped them in flames of universal light, and surrounding thunder . . .") is illumined from the depths of memory about Noah's Ark. There it was the world-wide flood and Noah and his Ark . . . Here it is universal fire and Edigei with his camel and dog . . . A natural catastrophe, no work of man, and a catastrophe which, alas, *is* the work of man . . .

After reading Aitmatov's novel and the story of Burannyi Edigei's life, I thought of Pavel Korchagin.[e] There is something of Korchagin, something strong in Edigei Zhangeldin. Edigei's life is also an example of how steel is tempered. Of Edigei's same breed is the deceased, Kazangap Asanbaev: "Once they fought the drifts for two days straight, never stopping, trying to keep the track clear of snow. At night they brought up a locomotive with lights, to light up the area. And the snow kept coming, and the wind whipped it around. You clean in front of you, and behind you a new drift has already begun. And cold? That wasn't the word—your face, your hands, everything swelled up . . ." Towards morning, when the trains could pass, the departing workers whistled rudely as farewells to Edigei and Kazangap: "Hey, idiots, go suck the big one!"

The stern school of life did not break Edigei. Strong and wise, he stands firmly on the earth of his fathers, helping those near him stand too. Edigei has a friend, a Russian, Afanasii Elizarov, who knows the Sary-ozek desert. In Edigei's difficult moments Elizarov helps and supports him . . . This image (though it is only hinted at in the novel) is dear to me. In our republics we know many Russians who are totally committed to the history and culture of one people or another, who have devoted their lives to their second motherland. . . .

Edigei is morally severe, morally healthy, which gives him the right to say: "And it is given to me in such an hour to think as though you might think, creator." Health, and especially moral health, is as the ancients said, is a condition of preserving the image, just as disease destroys the image of man. Much of what Edigei says should be remembered: "What kind of people are these? Everything on earth is important to them, except death! If death is nothing to them, then it must be that life has no value either." Or "The best thing a man can do for other people is to raise worthy children in his own family. . . ."

Edigei has earned the right to judge and teach others. For his WORD (for the word is the deed) he has paid his life.

Edigei's love for Zaripa' is also a test, after all. A married man falls in love with a woman driven by fate, loves her children and her disastrous life. His love is doomed, just as love was doomed in the old legend about Raimaly-aga and Begimai. But the songs of Raimaly-aga show that Edigei is correct to love. Tortured by paradoxes, he found himself in songs. And his love for Zaripa is very like a song, infinitely sad and pure: "And the Earth floated in her circles, washed by the higher winds. Floating about the Sun and turning on her axis, she carried within her at that hour a man up to his knees in snow, in the middle of a snowy waste. No king, emperor, or other ruler would have fallen to his knees before the wide world, reeling at loss of state and power, with a despair greater than that of Burannyi Edigei in the day he was parted from the woman he loved . . . and the Earth floated on . . ."

These words of Aitmatov's are like a song themselves, a lofty model of the love lyric. Where he needs to, Aitmatov writes like a true poet. "The trains in these lands ran from east to west and from west to east . . ." This refrain, so significant, so rich with meaning (everything is compared to movement, with the constancy of motion, and everything, the entire novel, the people, the events, are keyed to movement . . .) gives the novel a definite musical, poetic character.

The image of Burannyi Edigei reminds me of yet another parable (comparison makes clear), that of Job. Much as with Job, one wants to say to the working, struggling Edigei that "He will yet fill your lips with laughter and your mouth with exclamations of joy."

The guarantee of that is Edigei Zhangeldin himself, the hero of Chinghiz Aitmatov's novel *The Day Lasts More Than a Hundred Years.*

Erevan

Editor's notes

a. The quote reveals that Aitmatov uses informal address in writing to Mkrtchian, suggesting that they are personal friends.

b. Dudin is a Russian poet.

c. The only large body of water in Soviet Armenia, and a symbol of national pride. The water level has dropped precipitously in recent years because of Soviet water-diversion schemes.

d. The Aral Sea is Kazakhstan's large body of water. Irrigation diversion has caused the water line in this lake to recede as much as a hundred kilometers in some places, and the water level has dropped more than twelve meters.

e. Hero of Nikolai Ostrovskii's *How the Steel Was Tempered*, one of the classic heroes of socialist-realism.

f. The wife of Abutalip. Mkrtchian refers to a crisis in the novel: Abutalip has been arrested, torn from his family, and Edigei is surprised to find his concern to help Zaripa becoming a passionate love which he can not control.

Of Home and the World

V. LAKSHIN

Events in literature occur rarely, and generally in spite of expectations and prognoses.

I think that Chinghiz Aitmatov's novel *The Day Lasts More Than a Hundred Years* has become such an event, important not only for the author, promising new inspiration in literature. Not because this work is perfect in all respects (there are superficial and weak sides to it), but because it shows a new scale of artistic thought, which is enough for which to be grateful to the author.

The literary historian and critic love to use the measure of decades, the sixties, the seventies. . . . This is like a carpenter's folding ruler. The living movement of art fits poorly into the chronological frameworks intended for it. Here though it is laughably precise; the eighties begin, and the line separating us from the preceding decade is set very sharply, for with Aitmatov's novel literature is raised to a new platform of observation.

This is even more obvious because the seventies have not brought an abundance of successes. Two great themes have been the soul of the postwar literature, the war and the village. There were discoveries here, and a shattering truth which gradually took root in our hearts and minds. The inexhaustibility of these themes is clear, and until recently we saw vivid attempts to speak in new ways about what was already known. From Vasil Bykov and Baklanov to Viacheslav Kondrat'ev, from Belov, Abramov, and Mozhaev to Vladimir Lichutin, this was absolutely original plowing, but still in the same field. For an entire decade literature continued to talk out what had not yet been said about the village and about the war. Particularly about the village, the native, central Russian area that is now referred to by the arid word "*Nechernozem'e*."[a] The northern and Siberian villages too.

Of course for literature the village was never just an external theme. In a traditional peasant country like Russia, if you recall the nineteenth century, the very traditions of culture, the national spirit and visage always stood in close dependence on the earth and the peasant hut. Dostoevsky's peasant Marei and Tolstoy's old man Fokanych are only the obvious surface, and not yet the main thing. The shadow of the Great Village fell across the pages of all the beloved Russian books, no matter what they depicted, whether palaces in the capital or city taverns, the railroad or the monastery.

A hundred years passed, and many great, tragic events came to pass in our land before the middle of the twentieth century, when the former, backward Russia became a multinational mighty power and industrial nation with a predominantly urban population. And literature began to bid farewell to the last old women and old men, the embodiments of the past Russian peasant virtues. For a long time our major pain and major poetry was connected with the village. So much of the burden fell on it during the last war, and after, to say nothing of earlier times, that literature was grateful to bow before the sacrificial victories of the village. And this leave-taking was not easy. This was "the long good-bye," to use Yuri Trifonov's words, "the lost bow" to a beloved theme, to use the words of Viktor Astaf'ev.

Social experience and recent history (which is especially strong in Belov's *On the Eve* [Kanunakh] and Zalygin's story "On the Irtysh" [Na Irtyshe], peasant speech, rituals, habits, and characteristics were recorded not just with living naturalness, but with filial love for "the little motherland," for that clump of earth where the author, himself long a city-dweller, once lived and grew up. The tribulations of the village were lamented with so much energetic sympathy and sadness, it was as if for the last time.

At the end of Fedor Abramov's marvellous village chronicle, in the novel *Home* [Dom], a wooden horse, once the best decoration of the wooden hut from which it was torn and a souvenir of the Priaslin family's nest, kills Liza, the author's beloved heroine, while her brother Mikhail, a hard-working man from the post-war years, can find himself no place in the new generation of village people. In Rasputin's *Farewell to Matëra* [Proshchanie s Materoi] the old village which had been inhabited for generations disappeared under water, drowned by an artificial lake, a dramatic image which lingered long in the consciousness.

In that circle, though, exhaustion of themes and images could already be foreseen. True, the heart of "village prose," in Rasputin's works and in Astaf'ev's *Tsar-Fish* [Tsar'-ryba], contained one more poetic resource, the conflict between what might be called "Tsar-Nature" and its proud enemy, man, who from time immemorial has been impatient to seize nature's blessings.

However, in recent years the feeling has begun to arise that literature was standing in place, as if once more to look about and catch its breath. Belov's "Harmony" [Lad], V. Afonin's stories, Lichutin's stories of the north all tried to record the tiniest details of the face of the disappearing Russian village, picking over every detail of daily work routines, of celebrations and rituals. This though was no longer the joy of becoming acquainted, but rather an elegy of parting, at times with a touch of the museum curator's fussing.

The events of the past few years, in the nation and in the world, at the same time made it necessary to seek new horizons; the sensation of time and space had clearly changed. In addition the frameworks of realistic detail and poetic ethnography, the rights for which were so hard won within recent memory by A. Iashin in his *Wedding in Vologda* [Vologodskaia svad'ba], became very narrow. The past and the future wanted to live in the present, while space moved from the native clot of land, the hut, fields, and wells, to universal visibility of country and of the whole globe, a world which the technology of communication and air travel had made sharply smaller in girth.

It was lyric poetry which first felt the inspiring and foreboding change of scale, as Bulat Okudzhava sang:

> While the earth yet turns
> And the light's still bright
> Lord, give every man
> What he is without . . .

In face of a threat of the destruction of all life, the end of human culture on earth, it seemed as though everyone required a different measure.

Aitmatov's novel does not come to us alone. It seems as though one characteristic of literature of the eighties will be a freer and more inspired attitude to the two basic categories of life, time and space, and as for style, that the workaday descriptive prose will be interspersed with the poetry of legend and stylization, by the new life of utopia, fantasy, and tale-telling.

One experiment in this manner is still memorable, Vladimir Orlov's novel *Danilov the Violist* [Al'tist Danilov], in which a modest orchestra musician finds a demon within himself and so with a twist of his magic wrist bracelet can transport himself to other "layers" and "spheres." It was amusing to see him hovering above the Ostankino television tower. However, some readers thought that the author had not written or printed everything, while others thought he had printed too much, and those who read the entire long novel on the whole were disappointed. They agreed that this was an imitation of Mikhail Bulgakov, fruit of a playful and promising, but clouded fantasy. Parenthetically, that Orlov's experiment was not an accident was confirmed in my view by Anatolii Kim's[b] talented story "Lotus" [Lotos]. The theme of a son's last farewell to his mother is not a new one, recently explored very strongly by Rasputin. In Kim though, there is a different law of prose at work, decorated with the poetry of the east, and there is no everyday here. The story's hero is Lokhov, who has come to say good-bye to his mother, to look again into her reddish pupils, see the dying light in her eyes, and to put a bright orange, cut into sections like the flower of a lotus, into her feeble, wrinkled hand.

That image might seem excessively pretty, even artistic; the orange is exotic and excessively bright in the grey hovel on the Sakhalin shores where the mother is dying. We have before us the confession of a sincere man in search of himself, deeply wounded by a feeling of guilt. Lokhov had long forgotten his mother, leaving her alone for the sake of his life and his art. And perhaps his last gift is a bit awkward in its considered beauty, but this handmade "lotus" contains his pity for his mother and grief for her unrealized fate.

The author writes that "Lokhov saw that his mother wasn't up to him. And what is called the soul of man, and what they had told him since childhood does not exist, now stood clearly before him." On the threshold of death there rears up a cluttered mottled heap of days already lived, and suddenly the immortal part of the soul, which is usually blocked out by the details of everyday life, begins to mourn that it never found embodiment. In Kim's story the soul is in close similarity with nature, with the clouds, the dying steppe, the animals and grass. The author is possessed by the idea of the unity of all that lives; he feels the "unbelievable pain of grass being transformed into a living, moving being" and he guesses the silent dialogue between the man and the otter, sticking her wet whiskered face out of the water.

Here too is the mother fleeing the Germans along war-driven roads, children in her arms; running with her are wild boars, hares, foxes, all of them feeling their kinship in time of trouble. The entire life of this woman, who once had been young and ready for happiness, who had survived the war, lost her husband, been poor for ages, worked as a stoker, then had gotten old, destroyed by paralysis, this life appears in the light of some sort of expectation, of suffering for unfading beauty. The lotus flower which the son makes from the skin and pulp of an orange is a poor and belated sign for her.

Kim's prose arises from the mottled links of dreams, visions, and memories not to depart from the substance of life, but in order to approach it more closely. As the author remarks, "When a person who has outlived his life begins to depart for eternity, WE, our attention focused on the life which remains to him, can enter his life at any instant of time, without interrupting its flow." This transition from "I" to "we," the union of man and mankind which is most obvious at the moments of birth and death, fascinates the young writer. He believes in art's ability to touch the main secrets of life. His word too is not subject to material or means, seeming to have an enchanting power of its own, to possess poetic self-sufficiency. It might even be said that A. Kim's phrases, which are so light, melodious, and flowing, contain the danger that they will be heard in spite of or oblique to their sense. The author misuses such adjectives as "diamond-like" and "nacreous," which does not add to his artistic style. Still, on the best pages of the story, shining from within like an eastern gem, the word is well adapted to conveying dreams, spiritual revelations, and visions which widen the narrow experience of everyday.

Kim does not need the viola player's bracelet for his imagination to overcome time and space. Thus on the ocean shore, in the place of the hut where his mother is dying with a lotus blossom in her hand, he sees a city of the twenty-first century, the bay faced with a wall of colored concrete. The clouds floating in the sky, the noise of the ocean, the smells of the Manych steppe all reflect for him a single world soul. In this light the first, significant phrase of the story becomes more understandable, something almost like an epigraph. "If WE all inhale at once, Earth's air will rise up in a hurricane never before seen." Some sort of new artistic world-view, even if it is still disjointed, feeling its way blindly, is knocking at our door.

The writer Vladimir Krupin, who would seem outwardly not to resemble Kim in style in his story "Living Water" [Zhivaia voda] discloses a sudden similarity in his satiric story. He too is talking about a soul which has belatedly decided to understand itself, though his is a tragi-comedy. Krupin's hero is the peasant Aleksandr Kirpikov, stableboy and watchman, a curser and a drunk, a person far from the poetic, nearer in fact to the opposite. However, possessing sixty years of life and a beloved grandson who likes to listen to fairy tales, Kirpikov in Krupin's story suddenly quits drinking. This event, which at first glance seems insignificant, has astounding consequences for the entire region, least of which is the disappearance of the customary "universal equivalent," often more reliable than money, the bottle of transparent, stupefying liquid. (It used to be that for a half-liter Kirpikov would use his horse to plow potato patches for the whole village). In the people's minds there also occurs a dangerous confusion.

Russians aren't a hasty people. In the fairy stories the hero Ilia Muromets sits thirty-three years to be summoned to his exploits. Kirpikov too comes to his realization late. As though he has waked up to understand that he has lived his life without having learned anything significant about it, Krupin's hero locks himself away from family and neighbors in his root cellar. In this domestic "Diogenes's barrel" he begins to ponder life. He begins to get a taste for history and archeology as he digs the earth beneath himself.

Kirpikov honestly wants to know why he lived, why in general people are born and come onto the earth. He has but one fount of wisdom, a tear-off wall calendar. However, making use as well of his own observations, it is also possible to reflect on the numbers of people on earth who are born and who die daily, and what Americans landing on the moon means for mankind. Thinking about things which seem useless, this home-made philsopher achieves self-respect, paying no attention to the knocking on the floor above and the displeasure of his wife Varvara, who doesn't understand him any better than Xanthippe understood her genius husband Socrates.

What joy this happiness of invention is! Krupin shows the danger of vodka not through contrite exhortations that excessive drinking is a bad thing, but through the opposite, a utopia of vodka's disappearance. The author's saucy, ironic, mocking imagination points us toward the tradition of the folk tale. In Russian folklore heros are healed and revivified by "living water." The village that Kirpikov lives in has grown used to regarding vodka as 'living water,' but Krupin offers a dangerous competitor, in thought, knowledge, and self-knowledge, all of which have their own intoxicating power.

A bad example is infectious. Kirpikov's neighbor Vasia Ziukin finds a spring in his basement that has the purest possible water, a miraculous fluid which simultaneously makes people younger and cures them of vodka. Not only does this entire village which Krupin has invented stop drinking, but the peasants of Viatsk prepare to take their experience with sobering up the population to the entire nation, and then maybe even the entire world. A Russian likes a problem with a little scale; Vasia Ziukin is working on the problem of "sobering up the planet." This grandiose plan fails only because the offices in Moscow cannot agree on a sale price for "Ziukin's crystal water" and so, to be safe, seal up the spring.

The whole charm of this "Russian utopia" is that it is based on the most realistic possible everyday life of a small modern village, somewhere between countryside and city. Unlike Kim and his Oriental flowering of style and frothiness of phrase, Krupin's prose grows from the tradition of the "shaggy dog," the everyday anecdote. Krupin hears living speech beautifully, not the stylized speech of The Old

Village, which in some books by the "village writers" already seems an imitation, but rather the dialect of the village which is thoroughly saturated with the influence of the modern city. Expressions like "penny-piles of hay wallowed in the mist" and "they swatted up the yard" are neighbors to the announcement that "Science proceeds exponentially," or sentiments like "now you're cutting" or "a nightmare like" or "if you can't hang out, hang it up."[c]

Krupin's ironic utopia is a modern fantastic, with a taste of aluminum and plastic, blended with the poetics of a folk tale, sometimes gay, sometimes bitter, and ever full of life. Ivan the Fool[d] is by tradition the wisest person, while clowns and jesters turning somersaults always tell the public the truth to their face.

The wafting of another time, the shoots of a new understanding of life exist in Krupin and in Kim, but so far they are evident most significantly in Aitmatov.

Perhaps what acts most directly on the reader in *The Day Lasts More Than a Hundred Years* is the author's artistic symbolism. The endless, lifeless expanses of the Sary-ozek desert, the "middle lands" of Asia, are portrayed magnificently, cut as they are from end to end by rails running east to west and west to east, binding in thin steel bands an earth whose curve can almost be seen (these bands, changing their visage, will several more times appear before the reader). Across this desert there straggles towards the ancient cemetery of Ana-Beiit the bizarre funeral cortege of old Kazangap—Edigei riding a black camel, followed by a tractor-drawn cart bearing the relatives, then a back-hoe, to dig the grave and finally, the red mutt Zholbars, who has attached himself to the procession. This picture sets firmly in the mind's eye, as though we had seen it on the movie screen. The mighty, handsome Bactrian Karanar, with his two towering black humps, is so portrayed as to be far from the least important poetic image of the book.

A camel is an extremely effective picture against the background of a modern space center! About fifty years ago there was a photo in all the illustrated journals, of a train racing across the desert, with a caravan disappearing on the horizon. The camel seemed a symbol of the exotic Asian past, which was now outlived forever. But here he moves, gently shaking his black humps at every step, mastering the spaces of the Sary-ozek desert with his powerful legs, the handsome Karanar, while the sky above the desert is etched with rocket contrails, a madly complex technology is at work, and contact is being made with civilizations from other worlds. The one, though, does not replace the other, as human reason is wont to think, as it races on ahead.

Aitmatov thinks and writes on a large scale. In parts the author's execution might be criticized, which should not be passed by in silence, in order not to seem biased. The image of Elizarov seemed false, programmatic to me, as did the poor shadow cast by Edigei's wife or the once-mentioned administrative head of the station, who are as incompletely sketched as the two astronauts, one Soviet, one American. They are more signs of thoughts and assistants to the plot than they are images. The novel's language also gives ground for criticism at times. This is far from Aitmatov's first book to be written in Russian, without a translator, and he writes well. Sometimes he writes marvellously, modestly and precisely: "Clattering the train gradually slowed, bearing the shimmering shadow of motion and the flying dust above its cars.'' You see something like this, believing it in a second, without problems.

Aitmatov though is seeking new resources in the language, and strains sometimes to boast of rare and unusual word combinations; sometimes too he uses words imprecisely or inappropriately, and is sometimes attracted by jargon, all of which endanger the value of his story, sometimes with journal-ese, sometimes with rarities of folk Russian. The very first page of the novel is astonishingly thick with them, apparently the result of special attention and thus seeming artificial; you see such things as ''verge-ward'' and ''thither-ward wind'' and confusion of a verb meaning ''weave'' with a similar one meaning ''to wiggle the ears.'' Any one of these words, of course, might be used without criticism, but their concentration on certain pages of the story (and on others their violation of smooth literary speech) is disturbing, like something artificial, born in the ink-well.

Parenthetically, this is true not only of Aitmatov, for whom Russian is after all a second language. The element of native language is the living air which we breath. And if that air is short of the oxygen of fresh, real words, then the reader will suffer from ''nitrous'' word effacement (like ''the stern winds of time'' or a ''good, steady, friendly family'' or ''he turned to his work,'' and so on). However the excessive thickness of nonce words and rare words can also seem like a language super-saturated with ''oxygen,'' like breathing through a mask. When in giving a portrait of his heroine Aitmatov says ''her skinnied shoulders'' it is new, expressive, and well said. When, however, right afterward are remarked her ''never-to-be reversed wrinkles'' this is an obvious miss. Such phrases as ''the toothy maw squeaked'' or ''not up to stretching a leg'' or ''took up the study. . . of the place'' or ''the ghost of war still reeled on their heels'' or the use of ''utilitous'' where a simple ''useful'' would do show that a little extra effort by the author or the editor would not have been amiss.

Still, this is not just expressive Russian, but also vivid national prose. The reader remembers that the author is a Kirghiz and the main heroes are Kazakhs.

The recent infectious success of masters of foreign literature, such as the Japanese Kobo Abe and the Colombian Gabriel García Márquez, has also confirmed how strongly the reader is influenced by the very latest social problems when attached to a national essence, often with a bit of history and ethnography. Aitmatov's novel bears the living breath of the East, the burning air of the Central Asian deserts, the icy wind of the Sary-ozek in winter. Nor is this exotic local color or a simple external ornament, all these landscapes so unlike the usual, the strange names, the beautiful legends which from time to time interweave the story. The very intonation of the story, the psychology and speech of the heroes has something particular, inexpressibly attractive, something which in flitting across the face like a smile gives the uniqueness, the personality of the nation.

In part this can be guessed in that particular wise delicacy, a characteristic of Eastern poetry, with which the author describes the love his hero, a married man, feels for the wife of his comrade. Here Aitmatov does not take refuge in psychological descriptions and internal monologues, which would have been false in application to a man of simple and strong feelings such as his Edigei. The poetic background and oblique parallels to the hero's emotion tell a great deal. When the time comes to speak of Edigei's consuming love, to let his love song spill forth, the author interrupts the action with a legend about the old singer Raimaly-aga and the young girl Begimai, who had fallen in love in spite of all obstacles, and who were separated by force. Edigei though is not a flesh-free romantic inspirer, and in order to convey the power of the passion which rages in him, and which he carefully suppresses, the author as if in exchange creates the memorable picture of the rut, the reproductive frenzy of the blackhumped beauty Karanar. The savage whistle of the quirt which the master uses to subdue his beloved camel is an externalization of the passion he has crushed within himself, his despair at learning that Zaripa and her children have left the settlement forever. This is but one example of the nationally decorated figurative language, a portion of the artistry of the whole picture.

Perhaps, though, the main thing in the novel is the scale of time. There are four time levels in the book: ancient patriarchal time, with the power of legends and tales, root traditions and poetic mythology; the first post-war years with their problems of daily living, hard heroic labor and phenomena of lawlessness, the fear of denunciations and an unshakeable belief in the existing order; a time close to ours, in many ways better organized and better fed than those, but with signs of pragmatism and indifference among the younger generation; and finally, an imagined time that seems to be but an arm's length away, the near future of the space age. Throughout the story, now weaker, now rising again, there is a note of alarm. The common everyday matter of the death and burial of old man Kazangap is a *"memento mori"* which touches everyone, flying above the steppe like the gigantic shadow of the black wings of the white-tailed vulture.

Aitmatov finds the sore point in each of the four times, an episode or image which is in artistic "focus." For the patriarchal antiquity this is the legend of the *mankurts*, and the terrible punishment of losing your memory. For the recent historical past and the beginning of the fifties this is the story of the arrest of the teacher Kuttybaev in a settlement lost in the desert. For the present it is the barrier which arises in the path of the funeral procession to the tribal burial ground, the barbed wire which surrounds the grounds of the space center. And for the near future which flows from the present, this is the utopian story of the discovery out in space of a planet with a higher and more humane civilization than that of earth, and the solidarity of earth's governments in their attempt to defend themselves against its influence.

All these rays, streaming from the past, present and future, Aitmatov focuses on one figure, the rail repairman Edigei, from a minute railroad siding in the middle of the Sary-ozek desert. The village, the regional center, the settlement . . . A vast portion of the population of our country lives in something no longer village and not yet city, and it is good that major literature has noticed this world. After all the life of the people does not take place solely in village fields and Moscow boulevards. The hero is described in the best traditions of Russian literature's attention to the common, ordinary working man. The usual impression of a city-dweller on the road is that there are a lot of these figures, dressed in dirty workclothes or greasy coveralls, flitting for a second in the window of the express train as it passes water towers, rail crossings and switching booths. How often our imagination flies after them, wondering what sort of unfamiliar life is being led there. Aitmatov helps us to look at that life, and to look too into the man who in the recent past has enthusiastically been called a "bolthead."*

Edigei Burannyi is not a thinker, not a philosopher or poet; he is the most ordinary workman possible, reliable and honest. Such people support the world. However, he has his own understanding of life, firm and solid, and how otherwise could he live a life on a clot of earth which has only the rails disappearing into the distance, the six pre-fab houses bearing a number, not a name, and his own hand-made house, plus Kazangap's adobe? Edigei is a man of the people's fate, but the fate of the people is neither smooth nor clean; "from saddle bags and prison lags," as the saying puts it. Aitmatov's book places the bitter, sweaty, coarse smell of life beside the most tender possible Oriental poetry.

Yes, he is a reliable fellow, and has always been so, not used to sparing himself; after the war, when there was no other means of doing it, using nothing more than a scraper, working almost by hand, working to exhaustion, to a heart attack, he cleared the track of snow drifts so that the trains could run. "The young will laugh; they are old idiots who wasted their whole lives, and for what?"

In fact, for what? Is habitual reliability really such a good thing? That in fact is the point, that Edigei's attitude to labor and to duty, as he understands it, gives the hero endurance, independence, and power such as most men cannot boast. You cannot help but admire him when he pulls the train's emergency brake; he is not afraid to say everything that he is thinking directly to the administrator's face, and he will go to the end of the line for what he considers to be the truth.

Edigei's virtues are old-fashioned, as is his faith. He doesn't go to the mullahs, but he prays, in his own way recognizing a relationship to some higher, faultless power. He has spent his life among animals, birds, weather, and winds, in the loneliness of the desert, and he senses nature to be the measure of everything. The soul of the dead man departs into nature, dissolves in it, and seems almost to become, this soul of old Kazangap, the shape of the vixen who picks her way along the slope of the railbed dike.

Edigei is courageous. He lives in the full power of his soul, but he does not drive from himself the thought of inescapable death, as is the habit of city people of small soul or great self-content. "Poor things, they are dead!" he thinks, listening to speakers at normal funerals. Death enters the book not as the plot for burials, but as a philosophical theme. To remind every man of the end of existence is to take a high point from which to evaluate thoughts, contemporary affairs and earthly fates. Edigei's attitude towards his ancestors, to the earth and the cemetery, cannot be separated from his attitude to people and to work. They all are a part of the same morale of duty. Today's literature is pulled toward a rejection of flat empiricism and business-like pragmatism, to disbelief in a soul, to attention only to the immediate, the close, and the most directly practical of questions. It also rejects red-cheeked self-content; we know everything, can do everything, and understand everything. Without being noticed there is apparently a new consciousness being formed which is more exacting, in that its scale is the age, and its place of action is the entire world, but which is also more modest and self-reflective, as there is so very much more still to understand and learn. The riddle of death must be solved, the further goals of life, and the justification for appearing on this earth. Can it be that we were born simply to burden the earth with our presence for six or seven decades, especially in some forsaken settlement in the middle of the desert, and then to rot, often as not leaving neither voice nor trace?

This is why Edigei needs faith in simple things, in truth, in his labor and in conscience. He seeks truth, disturbed by the arrest of his guiltless comrade, the teacher Kuttybaev, and he insists on his right to bury old Kazangap in the tribal cemetery. This is what leaves the reader with the impression that this is a man, a personality, whose life cannot simply be reduced to the harness of labor from dawn to dusk. A man cannot work as Edigei works, without self-consciousness and an active will for justice. The self-consciousness and strong conscience of labor are inseparable, nor are they sold on the open market.

Among the utopian portraits of the near future which occupy Aitmatov's imagination there is one which he depicts with especial sarcasm, the bureaucratic dream which Sabitzhan expresses while getting drunk at his father's wake. This secretary to an administrator, with an office of his own, has quickly forgotten his father, asking everyone to drink "to our health," to "the health of the government" the author portrays with unfeigned hatred. Modishly posing in conversations about robots and biotechnology Sabitzhan dreams about a time when science will force everyone to do everything by "commands from above," with the help of biotechnological signallers, making them sing, dance, work, love, fight, and die. These conversations about robots and bio-tech are unexpectedly similar to the ancient method of the Zhuan-zhuan for depriving a man of his memory, covering his head with *shiri*, a cap made from the skin of a milking she-camel. This ancient legend is the nerve cluster of Aitmatov's book. The cap as it clamps on the head, squeezing his head, makes a man into a creature without memory or gratitude, capable of forgetting his father and killing his mother. The name of such a creature, fit only for obeying, for the labor of a slave, is *mankurt*.

There are not many instances in literature when a word discovered or invented by a writer passes over into life, travelling from mouth to mouth. Once it happened with the word "nihilist," which Turgenev invented, and with the word "martinette," which the dramatist Ostrovskii discovered. "Akh, you unlucky *mankurt*!" I heard recently as I got into the metro. A young man was chiding his friend. The word has become separated from its author, has begun to live on its own, because even before Aitmatov there was an important, if not so precisely named understanding of the loss of memory, about the past, about those near, about a break with tradition.

The *mankurt* does not wish to and is not able to think; he is a fulfiller of orders, indifferent to the pain of another. In this sense not only Sabitzhan is a *mankurt*; a *mankurt* is also the "hawkeye" who interrogates the teacher. A *mankurt* is the young lieutenant from the space center security (Tansykbaev, just like the "hawkeye"—are they just namesakes, or father and son?) who does not let Edigei and his burial caravan come in to the tribal burial ground. The defensive hoop is also a *mankurt*, the space girdle which helps the powers of earth to try to wall themselves off from an apparently higher level of civilization. Aitmatov's idea, if we have properly understood the author, is twofold with great respect for the earth, for the faith of the ancestors, respect for the native legends and old traditions, the people's experience of the millenia, with which it would be dangerous and frivolous to break. At the same time though there is an openess to the new, a freedom from preconception, a trust in bold innovation which astounds the imagination.

In order to go forward with assurance, the eyes must not be closed to anything, and everything must be remembered. How does Tvardovskii' put it?

> In vain they think that memory
> Does not value itself,
> That time like a cassock will cover
> Any past, any pain.
> That the planet flies hither and thither
> Counting out days and years,
> And that nothing is exacted from the poet
> When behind the ghost of injunction
> He is silent about the things that incinerate his soul . . .

Everything must be remembered, the poetic and the monstrous and the beautiful and the cruel in the history of the native land. Only in that way is it possible through an accumulation of years and thousands of kilometers to feel what one has in common with other people, with humanity. With those people who once lived on your earth and with those who are living now, in other lands. World history has begun to be studied from one end to the other, and the globe of earth has become like something transparent and fragile. The world isn't as big as it once seemed; this is our common home. The trains across the Sary-ozek go from east to west and west to east. And sometimes it seems that the people of all times are contemporaries, that the people of different tribes are all of one tribe. A narrowly local, egotistically national consciousness finds no support from the artist. That does not mean that he loves his native region the less for it. Yes, in his native home there is a great deal that is difficult and undecided. Nor are thoughts about the fate of all the world a flight from the native yard, whether in Berdiaika or Pekashin or the Boranly-Burannyi siding. Simply one's own walls and roof should be examined more than ever before as a part of the entire world. The life of the home depends upon what is accomplished in the world. The world though also depends directly upon what happens in the home.

The same thing is true with the scale of time. One may love or not love one's era, but it is important to understand its place in the chain of generations. Before you came, people lived, suffered, thought about human happiness for many centuries, and probably they were no dumber than us. After you too the generations will live, complaining about their age or else considering their time to be the very best, the most fruitful. Aitmatov helps us to understand with a new clarity that:

> We are in the middle of the historical path,
> We are at the crossroads of the universe.

Not all readers like that side of the novel, which in theme and instrumentation recall the science fiction genre. In fact, we lack here the fullness of life described, as we had in description of the desert, the camel, the people of the Burannyi siding. This is more a quick charcoal sketch. However, though it is weaker than other pages in artistry, this line of the novel seems in no way to be superfluous. It gives the book scope, as we already said, giving the possibility to look at the earth as though we were on a different planet, from where she looks "no bigger than a car tire." By the same token though a point which is not even on the map, the siding Burannyi, becomes a whole special world, where even now probably some Edigei or other is driving in spikes that have worked loose or is shifting the ties.

I think that it is not just in Aitmatov, but in all literature that this new consciousness of space and time are growing. I tried to point its traces in the works of Kim and Krupin as well. To any attentive glance such traces will also be evident in the most recent works of Zalygin,[g] Abramov and Rasputin.[h]

If Earth and man are fated to remain whole in the tempests of world history, are not to go blind in an atomic explosion or perish in a black pulverizing whirlwind, then probably people of the twenty-first or twenty-second century will be accustomed to viewing our planet as their home, a united whole. That is why it seems significant to me that Soviet literature has once again spoken to the people not only in alarm for the fate of mankind as a species, but also with the dream of universal brotherhood, with the attempt to examine the contemporary world and its course from some distant peaks.

Editor's notes

a. Non–Black-Earth zone.

b. Anatolii Kim is of Korean ancestry, though he writes in Russian.

c. These are approximations in sense of colloquial expressions Lakshin is remarking as unusual in literature. Until very recently (1985-1986) it was not common for Soviet slang to be printed.

d. Ivan the Fool: a stock folk tale figure in Russia.

e. Literally, "a little screw."

f. Andrei Tvardovskii: a popular Russian poet of the Soviet period, and the editor of *Novyi mir* who was responsible for publishing Solzhenitsyn.

g. Zalygin: prominent writer and critic, since 1985 editor of *Novyi mir*.

h. Abramov and Rasputin: the two most prominent members of the "village" prose movement.

The Price of Enlightenment
From Moscow to Cholpon-Ata *

Ogonek's Special Correspondent Feliks Medvedev
Speaks with Chinghiz Aitmatov

*The telephone call came at nearly midnight: "I am ready to begin the conversation,"
he said slowly. "If you want, come see me."*

*I raced through Moscow in a taxi, to the writer whose name is known throughout
the whole world, and thought feverishly for the umpteenth time about what I would
talk to him about. What? What? It seemed to me that our readers know everything
about Chinghiz Aitmatov; after all that quantity of things written about him is many
times larger than what he has written himself. There are studies of all of his works,
whether "Dzhamilia" or "The White Steamship" [Belyi parakhod],* The Day Lasts
More Than a Hundred Years, *or* The Executioner's Block *[Plakha], and more than
one book tells of his artistic and personal fate. Every period of his creative life has
been studied and set up on the proper shelves. He has given countless interviews,
although he has often complained about this "extravagance." What could the writer
say about himself or his work that would be new?*

*"But the measure of life," I thought to myself, "is unfathomable. Even if
Chinghiz Aitmatov had met with journalists yesterday, then today is a new day, and
with it a new facet of life, new concerns, new doubts. Particularly in these days,
when every hour that we have lived is especially weighed on the scales of history,
when every moment might be equal to an epoch. And millions of people listen to the
voice of the respected writer and artist; he is valued and trusted."*

*And Chinghiz Torekulovich immediately began talking about the most important,
most painful, most serious . . .*

At last we have been enlightened, we have wiped our eyes clear, looked back, and
seen the yawning emptiness. It is frightening to think
what would have happened to us if we had continued on as before, when
work was replaced with ritual empty words. Up until recently many ideas about life
were expressed with the aid of clichés, with interjections that set your teeth on edge,
about the most progressive society in the world, the most educated reader, about the
unchangeable avant-garde essence of all that touched on the idea of "ours, the Soviet
way." In that sweet self-deception we dulled the sensation of the real and concrete,
trying not to notice that the world around us had overtaken us by a number of
lengths. And the goal ceased to be the obligatory "today's generation of Soviet
people will live in communism . . ." A profanation, monstrous voluntarism. . . .

---

*Ogonek, 1987, no. 28 (11–18 June), pp. 4–9. Russian text © 1987 by "Ogonek."

Our goal, communism, moved further away. Even worse, many of the postulates even of socialism were distorted.

Please tell us why in The Executioner's Block *you decided to use the theme of narcomancy, which not long before had still been forbidden, and at the same time to pose the problem of the spiritual emptiness of man? Did you sense the approach of some kind of cardinal changes in society?*

Yes, there perhaps was an internal presentiment. However, narcomancy in the given instance is only part of it. Let's talk about the main point. In the last few years I always felt that we were suffering through some ungifted period of history, and that very soon there would have to be some enlightenment, or insight. It can't be that we've all become that stupid. . . . You'll agree that what is happening today is that enlightenment. Slowly, but surely, we are removing our shackles of self-satisfaction, self-flattery, and arrogance. There are no more deliberate assertions that we have achieved something or other, that we have surpassed somebody.

Chinghiz Torekulovich, when we spoke in January 1984, for some reason I remembered your words that (I am quoting you) "Real history is only beginning now, and only now will it become clear, absolutely obviously clear, how mature our society is, how fully it can become master of all that it has achieved, of all that it possesses . . . and we must win, and this will be an unheard-of victory." It seemed to me then that you had a particular subtext for these words. I repeat, this was January of 1984, not April of 1985, and not 1986.

You know, I always sensed, as it appears many did, some sort of monstrous lack of democracy, and at times, its complete absence. Even today we are not ready for its proper application. Democracy is something very responsible, which is bred into generations. And it does not come from being able to say everything in writing and aloud; this is more the superficial approach. Democracy in action is first of all a most complex process of patience with and respect for one another, of each layer of society for the others. This is an unbelievably difficult, in some ways dramatic process of forming a new view of the fate of society.

Since that democracy which we always needed existed mostly on paper, I think that only now will the real meaning of socialism become sensible. I think that in general the higher goal of everything on earth is realized only through democracy. Any political system can be called whatever you want, but if it does not provide a basis for the liberation of the spirit nothing will come of it. The meaning of happiness can be personal, separate, and individual, but there is also such a thing as the happiness of society. Thus the happiness of socialism can come only when there is complete and clear democracy, penetrating all spheres of life, of human existence.

Such a period has already partly existed in our history, after the Twentieth Party Congress. Literary critics consider that it was precisely those years that were decisive for your writing, since after all between 1956 and 1963 you wrote Tales of the Mountains and the Steppes *[Povesti gor i stepei], which won the Lenin Prize.*

Yes, I am thankful to fate for those years, that I lived and worked then. Those six or eight years were worth a great deal. It was then that the pleiad of writers formed who even now are the main leading force of contemporary literature. It's good that they were young then. I was young too. This allowed us to preserve inside ourselves a sense of internal worth and hope, over long, long years.

Happily, today the curtains have again been pulled back, and if in those years there was a vague sense of hope, then today we are at a time of conscious no-return in the changes that are under way. And that's why in the fields of literature and art I am waiting for real volcanic explosions. It seems that after Valentin Rasputin,[a] who is fifty now, there is a sense of some kind of emptiness in literature, in the generations after him. Both in Russian and non-Russian literature something has stopped, slowed down. . . . Potential possibilities have disappeared for the formula "and the word was God."

Now though, I think, there has come a propitious time for big discoveries. And if tomorrow there should appear a big novelist or poet to astonish us, this will be as it should. Let him crowd us off the scene. We will take this as a phenomenon we have long awaited.

This process doesn't seem so easy or painless to me. The idea of "tomorrow" for affirming democracy seems to be a lengthening process. And not all writers clearly understand and sympathetically accept what is going on "outside." It was not without reason that Mikhail Sergeevich Gorbachev in one of his recent speeches used the term "settling of accounts," already become a negative idea, meaning matters far removed from real art.

This is worthy of regret and contempt, since to use literary relationships to settle some sort of personal or group accounts is a fruitless path, long ago known and unable no matter what happens to lead to productive achievements. Vainglorious, artificial people thirsting for personal popularity and glory, and even more so writers of this sort, are disgusting. They poison life for themselves and for others. It has long been remarked that hatred lessens a man. This is what should be remembered. I know young people who are shrivelled with hate and envy for others. I also know people who have lived long years on this earth, but who all the same have not managed to gain any wisdom for their old age and so approach everything vindictively for their chronic unproductivity, punishing everyone and everything, including nursery-school-age children. It has long been time for all of us to understand that our life is indeed short, and that the longer you live, then the more you should understand this as the highest good fortune, and not as the means for some belated assertion of the self, at any price. Lessening oneself with hatred, envy, and rancor makes a man the slave of night, and not the creator of light.

Is it true that your father, Torekul Aitmatov, and his brothers Ryskulbek and Alemkul, all village activists, were repressed in 1937? I only just learned about this.

Yes, it's true. Exactly half a century has passed, and it's still hard to think about it. I have never said anything about this publicly, so you might say this is my first mention of it. I don't want this fact to be incorrectly interpreted by people. But even if there had not been such a thing, I would still have resisted the "rod" of the cult of personality. Even now many people don't understand what enormous damage he caused Soviet society. The cult of personality caused a unrecoverable, maiming loss to the shape of socialism. For too long we were in the trap of the authoritarian regime created by Stalin, and only now, almost thirty-five years after he is gone, have we begun to free ourselves and force out of ourselves the slaves of the cult of personality. Only now has society really begun to overcome the heavy burden of that gloomy epoch. And doing so comes at no little price. After all there are even today a lot of followers of the past. They don't want to see anything, and they don't want any changes. Thus if we manage once and for all to free ourselves from the complexes of the past, this will be the great achievement of restructuring, both political and spiritual.

I listened to my partner in conversation and understood how he is excited by the processes occurring in the country. All the concerns of restructuring he suffers as a son would, close to the heart. I could sense how much he had thought through, suffered through, and worked out. He is a man on the scale of the government, a Hero of Socialist Labor, a deputy of the highest law-making body of the country; he speaks of concrete things with understanding, thinking about what has to be changed to improve our life. He spoke of isolated facts, and generalized a great deal, analyzing and drawing conclusions, with inspiration and passion. I did not interrupt him, did not stop him with my own questions, and it seemed to me that his conversation with me poured out in a passionate. . .

. . . *monologue*
about the most important issues of the day

I always think about the paradox that in creating socialism, in giving preference to everything that comes from the collective, from collectivism, we have lost a great deal of that which concerns individuality, the individual, the "selfness" of man, if one can put it like that. One must begin from the point that if the I exists, then all the rest is the world. As they say today, this is the major loss! For a great deal, and in a great deal. For the quality of labor. For relationships of man with man. For the valuation of his creative constructive potential.

The value of the personality itself is not set with us, is not defined. And we ignore these problems, free ourselves from them, as if we didn't notice them. They meanwhile have accumulated, ripened, have begun to tell on the relationship of man to the government, the government to man, man to the collective. All of this taken together demands resolution through what we now call by the word "restructuring." Restructuring is a broad idea. Some people think that restructuring refers only to organizational matters, the shuffling of cadres; others think it has only to do with technological, technocratic problems. For me, though, the most important aspects are the social ones, of the mutual relations of people, the individual, and society.

Personality, the individual, and the state. I am not a scientist, not a sociologist, and approach these problems empirically, you might say. And it seems to me that this should be discussed in a more qualified manner. We've had enough dogmatics, and formulas made up beforehand. We've already had a great many of both dogmatists and formulae, who slowed our forward progress, and we must move away from the levelling, the effacing, the standardization. Universal standardization in the name of the collective is murderous.

We are people, and our entire life, no matter what we do in it, is made of everyday existence, quotidian concerns. Part of society makes something, another part uses it, and between them there is the sphere of service. Everything is collectivized. It used to be that man could get by with a natural economy, relying primarily on himself. On his work, his property, his land. Nowadays everything here is different; the government takes on all concerns.

On the one hand such an approach is a phenomenon of the principles of socialism, but on the other hand I am disillusioned by the fact that we have not been able really to organize many spheres of our existence. Take housing for example.

If before a man used to take care of his own housing, trying to keep it up and improve it, so that he treasured every nail, now people only sit waiting for a comfortable, ready apartment. Of course, resources are diverted for this, there are branches of industry for construction. On the one hand, this situation makes life easier, but on the other hand, we have not been able to make this housing feel like home, make it comfortable and inseparable from ourselves. Look at what goes on in the entry ways, in the lifts, on the landings! What have we turned our homes into? Into highrise barracks? It is as though we are living, taking revenge upon ourselves for something. But why are we punishing ourselves, that is the government, for taking upon ourself this unheard-of obligation? The hell with it, it can't really be that the old philistine saying is correct, "Do no good, and you'll get no evil." We haven't learned how to live in big apartment houses, haven't learned how to preserve our own abode. In addition we build our homes poorly. In the very beginning of a project we permit errors and clumsiness, we don't think projects through, and then during construction many elements of the project are ignored. Then the whole thing is done entirely slap-dash, to get rid of the project as quickly as possible.

The new microregions which we see in Moscow are flowers, the best of our contemporary construction. Go to provincial cities, oblast centers. Even from the train you can see the astonishing disorder in the construction of our new housing. And housing after all is our life. No matter how much we talk about it, no matter how much we scold one another, everything stays where it is, without changing. Nothing happens, nothing changes. I fear that the younger generation does not even suspect that man is meant to worry about his own dwelling from birth. Young people think that everything exists, all prepared. Just hand over the keys!

The second problem is transportation. This problem is depressing, year after year. I will begin with the longest-distance form of transportation, aviation. I have and have had occasion to be in other countries and use a wide variety of airlines, so I am well aware of what good aviation is. And I don't see any signs of progress in our own air service. Today this is a drab, crowded, nerve-wracking way to ship people from one place to another, in very poorly organized conditions. Domodedovo Airport[b] in summertime, for example, looks like a picture of a disorganized evacuation of refugees from some natural disaster or a war. Our airports, just like our train stations, have turned into hopelessly crowded, chaotic collection points for passengers. Where is there any sign of higher civilization here? And here I must say that personally I think that Aeroflot will never fix any of this by itself. A competing firm has to be created. Maybe Aeroflot should be divided into two halves, each half given means and its specific possibilities, and so force the two to compete, to make it so that the wages of the entire flight staff, all the service personnel, depended upon the quality of their work.

I am even more depressed that the air fleet is aging visibly, that very little is replaced. I can give a number of examples. For many years, the frequency of Asian flights, from Frunze to Moscow or Alma-Ata to Moscow, have not been increased. The fleet is replaced very slowly. And the flow of passengers is rising steadily.

The air fleet is growing increasingly decrepit. Even superficially. I am speaking as a passenger. Flies and cockroaches have infested the airplanes as badly as in communal apartments. Once I asked a stewardess, "How come you don't do something about the cockroaches? They're everywhere." She said, "What do you want from us? We don't have time to disinfect the airplanes because they are constantly in the air. The flight crews are replaced, the passengers are replaced, but the same machines go back and forth." I began to get suspicious whether in such conditions the necessary safety precautions are being taken. I also think that the planes are overloaded, jammed like nowhere else in the world. I don't see such merciless crowding in the airplanes of other companies.

And when we speak of the fact that in capitalist production the main thing is profit, or the pursuit of profit, to be honest, I don't see a difference in this case. They have the pursuit of profit, we have pursuit of the plan, or in other words profit, no matter what.

Until recently, though, Aeroflot was some sort of elite organization which a mere mortal could not criticize. So this often caused the soul to ache, since we all have to use aviation. Contemporary man simply cannot get by without aviation. Aviation has entered into our flesh and blood, into our daily existence, into our everyday plans. Only with the aid of aviation can we have time to do anything, in the tense tempos of modern life. And it is precisely in this link so vital to life that see an ever greater weakeness.

Now about city transportation. Its condition is beyond any criticism. Everything is overcrowded, the metro, the buses, the trolleys, the trams. And not just in Moscow either, but everywhere, no matter where. The flow of passengers grows, and the means of movement lag behind. Transportation stresses affect people's ability to work, their moods, and their relations with one another.

The West also encounters similar problems, but there they are saved by an enormous fleet of individual transportation. Our own is in no way comparable with it.

And how about our roads? In the cities and between the cities, they are village roads, country roads. Compared with the roads that exist in other parts of the world, these aren't even roads. Here too we have no end of work to do.

So then from day to day we somehow get used to everything, put up with it, get angry, but get used to it, endure, and accept it as our unchanging lot. Why?

The schools are in many ways in a piteous condition, medical service is horribly poor, trade is on the level of the Stone Age. . . .

I am not grumbling. I am analyzing, I want better. Where are we to turn? Many think that labor must be better organized, that people must work better. I understand that this is very important. I think though that this is not the main point; the main point is where to get the means to overcome all this, to get a start on the standard of living. After all the state budget isn't made of rubber. Raise the pay in the service sector? Impossible. Raise prices for goods and services? Probably that is possible. But then wages have to be raised, and you get a vicious circle from which we must at all costs free ourselves. After all each generation is as mortal as each of us, and a man should live in conditions worthy of a man.

Thank God there's no war, as people say. But why then year after year do many problems of life, government and society remain unresolved, or worse still, grow deeper. Probably we don't think about them much. And if we do think about them or talk about them, then it is not always substantively. Why? Within each of us there is a dogmatist, each of us was to some degree "concussed" by the epoch of Stalinism, trained not to think or act without sanctions from above.

Many of my colleagues try to find answers in some sort of scholastic, politicized judgments. It is simple to say that socialism has potential advantages, but it is much harder to discover them in action. And how are we to do this? Not every person can answer. How are we best to liberate our scientists, theoreticians, technicians, sociologists, and economists from the inertia of demagogy and conservatism that has been sown in their heads?

I think that restructuring must resolve many of the problems I have mentioned. At least I'd like to believe that it will help solve them.

Chinghiz Torekulovich spoke of our many economic difficulties. Although everyone has the minimum necessary to live, has a roof over his head, has work, and people live without fear of unemployment or unexpected social upheavals, this is not what is under discussion. What is, the writer reasoned, is that given our progressive social structure, given our enormous expanses, our incomprehensible resources, our leading accomplishments of science and technology, we could be at the head of all civilization.

We began to speak about the July Plenum of the Central Committee of the CPSU, the most important recent event.

The plenum must in many ways change our ideas about the future of the economy, about our whole lives, pondered my partner in conversation. This is a revolutionary plenum. Both in the report and in the speeches restructuring was victorious, crushing the snail, the old cart that for many years had stood in the way of change, slowing movement.

Chinghiz Torekulovich grew thoughtful.

If you want, I'll say one thing, that with my mind I understand that we still have not achieved such a sufficiently high level of production that the military expenditures don't tell so obviously as they now do on the life style of Soviet people. . . With my mind, that is, not my heart. . . After all, we are all asking the same banal question today: how could it happen that a semitrained young amateur pilot, a boy, in spite of everything, managed to overcome all the barriers of our defensive systems and land calmly on the Holy of Holies of our Fatherland, Red Square?[c] The guilty have been removed, of course, but still? . . .

It seems to me that a great deal could be solved if we were to find a way to resolve the foreign policy problems. If only the world could come to agree that an endless military race is senseless. After all, we have long said to one another that we mustn't bother one another, provoke each other, challenge each other to duels . . . the world is on the edge of a nuclear apocalypse. So what point is there in these mutual snubs and warnings? Of course if we look back we can see the mistakes caused by the short-sightedness of our foreign policy even comparatively recently. How we wish that our peace initiatives, which are prompted by the full logic of life, would find an answer on the other side.

Not long ago, during the visit of U.S. Secretary of State George Shultz to Moscow, it happened that I and a few other writers had the chance to meet with him. He was very interested in what *glasnost'* means in the USSR. This question agitated him a great deal, because the former stereotype of how to meet with us had been broken and had become a negative in use. Shultz asked us a lot about *glasnost'* and restructuring, about whether we believe in the widening prospects. As we told him about all this, answering his questions, we convinced him, and it seemed to me that for some space of time we managed to convince him that the best result of the twentieth century would be for the West and the East to find a common language and end once and for all the possibility that ideological differences might be settled with war.

If a government figure of the calibre of Shultz could waver, even for a minute, an instant, could think about the truth of our understandings of the future of peace on earth, that means that we must use every last possibility in order to agree not to fight with one another.

I must note here that the conversation with Chinghiz Aitmatov which had begun in Moscow was moved, continued first in the airplane, then in Frunze, and then on the shore of Lake Issyk-Kul, which is three hundred kilometers from the capital of Kirghizia. This is where the tiny town Cholpon-Ata is, the place of "labor and inspiration" for the writer. Nor was this just a holiday trip, or just one more trip to his native soil that he took, inviting me and Ogonek's photo-correspondent Dmitri Baltermanets.

Many people already know about Aitmatov's peace activism. He is the initiator and organizer of the so-called "Issyk-Kul Forum," the first meetings of which our journal reported fully. In October 1986 the most visible representatives of world culture came here, to the shores of Issyk-Kul, scientists, politicians, writers, artists. They came to the USSR as Aitmatov's personal guests. When they returned to Moscow they were received by M. S. Gorbachev.

Thus was formed one more new movement of intellectuals in the struggle for peace, for the survival of mankind, for the preservation of civilization. Before and after the formation of the Issyk-Kul Forum Chinghiz Aitmatov travelled a great deal about the globe, organizing and formulating his initiative.

This time the general secretary of the Great Britain–USSR Association, David Roberts, and the extremely popular western writer (his novels are also widely known here in our country) John LeCarré had come to the USSR for personal contacts with the world-famous writer and warrior for peace. Aitmatov met them in Moscow and set off with them on a trip to Kirghizia.

I was able to see for myself the meaning and significance of Aitmatov's initiative. It was obvious how the personal participation of the writer in informal contacts on all levels seemed to broaden the idea of the role of personality in the modern world.

I spoke to Chinghiz Aitmatov about how having recently exaggerated it, we then undertook almost to deny the role of personality in history. But now, today, we understand that we can reconstruct our life in all its manifestations from economics to culture, only if we rely on the energy, initiative, and talent of prominent people, talented people.

Such as Dr. Sviatoslav Fedorov, for example, who by the way is a member of the editorial board of [Ogonek]. I know him a long time. They write about him a lot now, using his organization of things as an example, but I understood that this was an unusual man back when no one said anything about him and he was proving to all and sundry how we must work, how production must be organized in conditions of socialism, and how any task must be perceived as a deeply personal one. Particularly in so fine and complex a business as medicine.

When we speak of restructuring, we cannot fail to speak of talented people, organizers, movers. But in doing so we used to omit one important factor—personal self-interest. I am certain that until we create an atmosphere of personal self-interest everywhere, very many of our beautiful ideas will remain unrealized. Yes, personal self-interest is vital, the same thing that we unjustly rejected right after the revolution, putting everything over onto collective initiative, collective psychology. Where there is a good self-interest a man will become creative, will become skilled. However, we generally shrug at each other, why do I have to do thus-and-so, let someone else do it. This gives birth to a chain reaction of regression, of inertia.

Many people think that restructuring has hit the provinces and the territories far from the center only with its weaker side. Do you see the fruits of restructuring in Kirghizia, for example?

Of course. People are thinking differently, the demands are wholly different. There no longer is the freedom from consequence, the indifference that existed even recently. It no longer is possible for some groups to enjoy unearned comforts.

Can you name a simple person, so to speak, who has appeared in the recent past, during the process of restructuring, as a leader, as a true restructurer of life?

I can. The shepherd Tashtanbek Akmatov.[d] Probably there are many workers like him. But this man is astonishing. He is a shepherd-thinker, a shepherd-manager. Everything he does is thought through, is admirable in advance. He approaches his goals fully armed with knowledge and experience. He is an undoubted example of leadership among farmers.

The word "glasnost'" comes from the word "glas," "golos," or voice. Thus it seems that today we ought to have before us those who have a voice, meaning the writers, literary people, and journalists, all those who can offer a voice, can speak out, can speak to the people.

Yes, of course, in literature *"glasnost'"* is as necessary as air. But I understand *glasnost'* not just as a voice; I have my own interpretation of this. *Glasnost'* is one component of freedom. The second component is the calculation and result of *glasnost'*, meaning of the opinion and desires of the majority. It is this which forms the beginnings of freedom. Without the factor of freedom it is not possible in today's world to develop, to perfect, to achieve the heights of productivity. Of course journalism and popular writing are the very first reactions to what is occurring, and the very first attempt to influence reality. A book or serious literature fulfill their functions, but they have one set of possibilities, while popular writing and journalism are another matter entirely. Sometimes, at certain periods, it is precisely popular writing which can mean more than serious fiction. I think that now is such a period. Newspapers have become so popular that people get up early in the morning to queue for them. During this sort of social agitation the responsibilitiy of journalism grows many times larger. Usually we understand responsibility in its legal sense, or Party sense, or work sense, meaning that responsibility is a limitation, an interdiction. I understand responsibility in a different way, as the responsibility to use one's own opinion to form the opinions of others.

Progress has always developed through obstacles of some kind. It is not possible to move toward progress hiding things or forbidding them, hushing things up or putting them under taboo. It is better once you have met difficulties on the road to suffer through them and overcome them, and then move farther in the consciousness of society.

I think that if our journalism and popular writing will refuse the many ways of falling silent and will find the strength within to portray man and his time freshly, newly, clearly, cleanly, and truthfully then this will help all of us find ourselves in restructuring.

Speaking honestly, Chinghiz Torekulovich, before the epoch of glasnost' did you consider yourself a practitioner of it?

More or less . . .

Why?

It always seemed to me that I approached what I was depicting in a principled and honest way. Still, it now seems that I might have put new scenes into *The Day Lasts More Than a Hundred Years* and *The Executioner's Block*, ones that I was forced either not to write or to remove from the works because of censorship or other prohibitions. Yes, today I might redo something, make some points sharper or stronger. . . . But I am not going to do so now. What is once created, let it remain as it is.

I will repeat though, that today for the writer, including for me in part, is a remarkable time to write about what it is vital to talk and write about. And I want to, to write without looking back.

Don't you think that too many critical articles and generalizations have appeared in our press, or is this the norm of today? Isn't there some sort of excess here?

I don't see any excess. Society must have a sense both of self-irony and of self-criticism. After all, not long ago we couldn't even make jokes about ourselves—that was considered blasphemy. There was no self-criticism, and we became more and more self-satisfied, because we wanted and demanded more and more praise, self-satisfied admiration of ourselves. Although we ought to know that words aren't the main thing, but rather deeds, that you can't ride far on declarations alone, we still tried. We tried so hard that labor productivity dropped in the last decade to an almost critical point, which now shows catastrophically in our economy.

That is why we must boldly and decisively talk out loud about all negative phenomena of life. It is better that we should tell the whole truth about ourselves. . . .

Can you imagine that the process of democratization of society might stop and everything will revert to what it was?

What, to the cult of personality again?! To the diseases hidden inside society? To violation of elementary human rights? To inertia? Never! This must not happen. The logic of life is such that the guarantee of development is to move forward. If we stop that means that we will again be moving backward. Isn't that right?

Yes, stopping would kill everything.

And that would be a catastrophe for everyone. I don't think that our society has powers that are still greatly interested in stopping, in returning to the past. Even the bureaucracy which we curse today in all grammatical cases, as they say, from head to tail, and see it as the root of all evil, even it is not interestred in this. I don't think that the bureaucracy is its own enemy. . . .

But what do you think, can there be limits to democracy?

The limits to democracy? Freedom and discipline. No matter how paradoxical this may sound, I cannot picture freedom without discipline and discipline without freedom. These ideas are as necessary to one another as they are different one from the other. Freedom is as dangerous as it is beautiful. When it is perverted. When there is no freedom, people demand it; when there is, they pervert it. I consider this to be ingratitude to whatever or whomever gave them this freedom, who won it.

But isn't there a certain "debauch of democracy" in the existence and activity of the organization "Pamiat'," [e] which in its origin and intent, so to speak, is a useful and necessary organization, but which recently has become an instrument of chauvinism and anti-Semitism?

If it's a debauch, then it isn't democracy.

I think that we still have not learned how to use the fruits of democracy. For example, we have had introduced the competitive form of election of candidates for administrative posts and responsibilities. Naturally one candidate is chosen and just as naturally another drops away. I have noticed that the second one, the candidate who didn't get all the way through the competition, immediately becomes inferior somehow, despised. How can we do that? A moment ago he might have become the head of the collective and now he's suddenly thrown to one side, his authority now minimal. Is this really proper? The candidates who don't make it all the way to the finish line are worthy people, who must be seen as the cadres of restructuring. They must be put to use, not treated with the sort of indifference worthy of Ivans who don't remember their kin.

You said that you sensed some changes in society before you started The Executioner's Block. *What presentiments do you have now, and are they connected with your new work? What is it about, if that's not a secret?*

It is still difficult for me to formulate this presentiment, but it exists. Perhaps it is the hope that we will be able to withstand the trials we are currently enduring. This is a great self-examination, an examination of the future. I understand what the cost of withstanding it might be. It is not easy to refuse the familiar and irresponsible self-flattery, the falsehood, to learn not to avert our eyes from truth. Unflattering criticism and the condemnation of shortcomings are almost always connected with tension and difficulties. And we have freed ourselves from self-examination for such a long time.

If I am going to write something now (and I have already begun a new novel), then it will be connected with this presentiment of mine. With the cost of examination. . . .

Among the many other zones and spheres forbidden for discussion until recently were questions of the inter-nationality relations among the peoples of our country. We were afraid to talk aloud about something that seemed to some people to be a nasty topic. However, at the recent plenum of the Union of Writers of the USSR many speakers devoted their frank speeches to the national question. They spoke with alarm about the fact that, for example, the number of schools and educational institutions in the republics in which the teaching is conducted in the native languages is growing ever smaller. They spoke too of so-called provincial nationalism. What do you think of all this, Chinghiz Torekulovich?

Yes, for us, for a multinational country, this question is of supreme importance, not permitting ambiguities or delays. I will begin by saying that somehow we have recently begun to speak and write less about the real qualities of socialism, as opposed to the momentary ones, about the superiority of the socialist system. I am not in agreement with this. The virtues of socialism have been demonstrated to the entire world. It is impossible not to agree with this. Among these virtues I would say first of all is the equal opportunity for all national groups to develop economically and culturally.

In fact the very idea of "man" has been raised under socialism, has grown and achieved status as a universally acknowledged social criterion. During the years of Soviet power we have lost, on the one hand, the governing estate, and on the other, the serving estate. Man has sensed his right, his significance on the earth. It makes me happiest of all and I am proud, we must all be proud, that over seventy years we have worked untiringly so that in an enormous multinational state all peoples without exception could feel their full worthiness.

When I am abroad, if the need arises, I unfortunately cannot boast there, let's say, about some kind of technical things, that is, about material products, but I always say with pride that we, the Soviet people, have learned how to live like people.

Of course we often use the word "internationalism" in vain. We should preserve the treasured and sacred significance of this term. We can build new factories, achieve new heights in production, can accomplish a great deal in the material sphere, but the internal unity of our peoples, once broken, is very difficult to restore. This is why each of the peoples and national groups living in the Soviet Union must take care to have a protective attitude to the idea of the friendship of peoples, the brotherhood of peoples. In the last few years certain rough spots have appeared in the national question. In my view this is connected with the fact that the contemporary international process to a significant degree is taking place against a background of growth in the national self-consciousness of peoples. This process seems two-fold. It would even seem that these ideas would contradict one another. But in conditions of socialism a growth in national self-consciousness is to be expected along with the strengthening of the inter-national community of nations. This process we must preserve.

In general the so-called national problems are in great part what I would consider the mirror reflection of our petty world. Look, you and I were at one of Frunze's special schools when the English writers met the schoolchildren. We saw the angel-pure faces of the children, who were thirsting to learn something new from new people, in part about England. What trust and beauty shone from their eyes, and I was frightened—it was involuntary, but I was frightened, wondering what would happen if the wrong seeds were sown in the souls of these children, not the proper truth, but some distorted one. What a tragedy that would be. Then I thought how much effort has to be expended in order not to mislead the younger generation with the same contentious national problems, both in the international arena and in the domestic one. It is very easy to lead them astray, easy to tear the fine threads of the community of people of various nationalities.

The problem of international education is one of the most complex since here among us it has become wholly cliché-ridden, transformed into stereotypes on the level of invocations and slogans. We load down little children, schoolchildren who thirst to learn all they can from grownups, with phraseological ballast without revealing the essence and significance of the necessity in life of the very idea of "internationalism" in concrete examples and situations which personally affect their families, environs, towns, regions, and republics. What our poor teachers say does not last and isn't understood by the children. Reports, salutes, slogans, and loud phrases take the place of a vivid, living example.

Now, about literature. There's no such thing as "non-national" literature. Every word springs from a national source of some sort. Yes, one man can know several languages, another knows only his own native language, and many know two languages. Even before we came along the world had nations, countries and regions that lived, got along, influencing one another and enriching one another. Our time though, and our country in this regard are absolutely in a unique position. We have become the proving ground, as it were, of a great experiment, in which we have thrived. I consider this experiment to be one of the main achievments of our society, as compared with what is going on in the world. No matter where you look, there are unresolved, dead-end mutually antagonistic problems everywhere—terrorism, killings, hostage-taking, bitterness, hatred. In the Middle East, in Africa, in Europe. And the reasons for all this are linguistic and racial prejudices.

Thank God, this cup has passed us by. And we have created the earth's largest multinational structure. People will ask, what about China, or India? Yes, but the people who live there are close in cultural, ethnic, and economic levels. In our country, however, there took place the union of the most various possible linguistic cultures, of peoples who were at the most various possible social stages of development, and all these living elements had to find a common denominator. Now we have an "equalization" of the potential possibilities of various peoples and nations. However, to think that this question is already solved forever, as we were told in the past decades, that no problems remain, would be naive. Even worse, it would be dangerous. Every nationality evolves, develops, raising its national consciousness higher. I will put it like this—this is not to be feared. What must be feared is unnecessary and dangerous interpretations of this growth, invented suspicions and the self-interested attempts of certain people to make the situation worse in the attempt to make a career.

It is natural that one of the main aspects of internationalism is linguistic policy. If we used to speak of this with reservation, we now must announce directly that for a lot of regions, including first of all Turkestan,/ we must look toward bilingualism as the most fruitful path of development. All of the nations living in the Turkestan region are closely connected to one another, in which may be felt the role of Russian language and culture. Our life is so interwoven spiritually and economically that we cannot limit our existence to only one national language, either in the republic, or in the national republics. This is pointless and useless. On the other hand, if it were proposed that we throw the national languages aside and take as our weapon only one, in this case Russian, then this would be an inferior and unilateral solution.

In this sense history itself suggests a beautiful approach, which to some degree has been approved—bilingualism. In my view, all regions should have a constitutional guarantee of full coexistence of the language of the native population parallel to Russian. What do I mean by full? That the local language must have all necessary conditions for use and development. This means not only an infrastructure of press, radio, television, and media; those are a given. It is even more important to look to the roots, where the language is formed, at what age? There must be kindergardens and schools where the national languages are studied as the basic language, but at the same time Russian is studied from the very earliest years. Bilingualism will on the one hand guarantee the preservation and development of the national language, and on the other hand guarantee knowledge of Russian. Such a process is wholly feasible, something of which both the children and their teachers are capable. Bilingualism must be seen as a new historical phenomenon, as the cultural achievement of the end of the twentieth century. The culture of bilingualism will give new potentialities to the spiritual development of our peoples. This will be like the two wings of a bird, when every man in the national republics has two languages—his own mother tongue, and the common national language, Russian.

I repeat though that this is a complicated question. Many dogmatic thinkers do not want to accept and understand this. Not in the localities, not in Moscow. Unfortunately there are forces in the people themselves and it commonly happens that they negate themselves. They engage in self-slander. This I call national nihilism. Since national nihilism isn't mentioned in the press, is not condemned, and no one ever utters imprecations against it, certain people think that they are playing a game they can neither lose nor be punished for. Some of these "players" for their own selfish ends create a halo of "supernationalism" for themselves.

A normal, sensible solution to the problem would come from a consideration of the languages and establishing what I would call a protocol of internationalism. Just like a protocol in diplomatic relations, where everything is laid out in advance, how things are to be. This protocol of internationalism must be set up in a legislative form, establishing the equality, the equal value and significance, of the given languages in official circulars, in the methodology of study and education, and in the practice of daily life. This protocol must observe equality in everything, great and small. In inscriptions, in slogans, in announcements, in public speeches. Today, after all, we don't observe this rule anywhere. In some republics you won't find Russian signs, in others you couldn't find the national elements, their symbols, in the daytime with a lamp. This may seem petty, but such things make up a monstrous mosaic.

I think that all problems and difficulties of national relations should be regarded as normal, treated patiently, and there's no obligation immediately to see in this no more and no less than phenomena of nationalism. After all many people are frightened by this bugbear; people are warned and accused and followed. Many administrators in the localities are afraid to give speeches in their native language, because they fear being accused of nationalism. The point after all isn't what language you are speaking, but what you are saying, what you are thinking. . . .

Everyone understand that things are exactly so, but the thirties, the Stalin years, still sit in everyone's guts, and so everybody tries first and foremost to be safe.

I have heard the expression "national plank." That is to say that every republic has writers who cannot overcome the height of the national plank, and the readers take these as prophets in their own land. Neither the reader nor the writer of this type wants to look at matters more broadly. For them the main thing is what is theirs, what is close to the blood, even if it isn't great, just so long as it is theirs. . . .

This is an artificial posing of the criteria. If such writers and readers exist, then I am certain that new young forces will appear, to step over any artificial thresholds.

Chinghiz Torekulovich, why did you begin to write in two languages?

What pushed me to it? Several reasons. In the beginning to write in Russian was simply an unconscious instinct of self-preservation. Since the level of criticism and its criteria all suffer from narrowness and aggression in the localities, the author can sometimes find it difficult in such surroundings. Labels are hung on him immediately, and there is unjust criticism, and studies of the writer are begun. In the Moscow literary atmosphere the approach is broader, the views are more enlightened. You know, if one of the big leaders of a republic at a meeting were seriously to interpret a young author's story about the unhappy fate of a village dog as a story about the fate of Soviet man, and were to demand punishment, well, what more is there to say? So I began with the Moscow editorial boards. To get firmly set up in the center was my first instinct.

It seems to me though that the Kirghiz reader must understand your works more deeply, more finely, since everything the stories are about is close to that reader, familiar.

If you were to take the ordinary reader, a proper, well-intentioned person, then he would be precisely the same as a Russian reader. He also loves to read things that are written with insight, with art. I sense this. And I trust both the Kirghiz and the Russian reader. There is, however, a medium associated with literature that tries immediately to give a negative response, and often with a political brand at that. By publishing my things in Moscow I avoided such criticisms.

Chinghiz Torekulovich, doesn't it seem to you that certain of your works in their day were written about topical issues, and that they haven't withstood the test of time?

I could probably confess that my nonfiction was written topically, as were my speeches and interviews. As they say, what is is what is. However, insofar as I could, I understood that even in popular nonfiction pieces you have to figure on holding the warmth a long time. I tried as much as I could to figure on "longer."

But how long can a work of art last?

Well, that's a very complicated question. And I doubt whether anyone could give a precise answer and foretell which work of art was going to last a long time, and which would die quickly. Every concrete work of art has its own fate, just like the fate of the writer. At the same time there are general laws of art, literature, culture. There are laws of this historical formation or that. A new attempt, built on new principles, to evaluate literature was undertaken in our Soviet era. All that was created was tested by the method which we called socialist realism. I am not against this term, because the problem isn't with the term, but with the reality. You can talk about socialist realism or critical realism or magical realism, or any kind you like. It is important that the work of art be of full value. However, how a novel will come into being, or a poem or a drama, and what its fate will be in the future is not something which can be predicted.

I don't share the announcements from the tribunes and the victorious exultation that the social-realist method has let us open a new epoch, a new era in art, that all of our literature and culture is supposedly unique and unusual. This is not true. Yes, we undertook a very deep and powerful attempt to change the essence and significance of art. I think that there are definite stages when art can be predetermined for definite layers, definite classes, for a definite cultural layer of society. This is the novel of daily life, describing events which people know well, and the readers become like witnesses and participants in this or that historical fact or episode. However, art can achieve another, and as it seems to me, higher level when it acquires a universal significance. This is already a new horizon. Then art addresses not only the details of daily life, not only what is occuring in reality, but it also addresses myth, legend, large philosophical generalizations, and large historical depictions, which relate what is depicted not only to the realiaties of some small region and defined environment, but tries to extend it to all human existence. Perhaps our literature is only now trying to take this step. In saying this I am not trying to cross out the past of our art. We have had large and interesting achievments. At the same time, however, we must honestly and frankly say that we have expended a great deal of effort, and perhaps in vain. Though this is not entirely correct. What happened in our art was one of the great experiments, and not every experiment can be crowned with absolute victory. We had our successes, and our errors. And these errors are now entering our experience.

It is difficult to measure what is not measured only linearly. Though who is to say, literature too has periods of dying. . . . Look for yourself, you can see everything ages. Much of what we read and were in awe of in the fifties and sixties today is already passing into oblivion. Other readers have arrived, with another psychology and a different life experience. I foresee that this assertion of mine will call down on me a heap of criticism by scholars and literary critics, who have suffered all these ideas into existence in their own way, coined them, but their studies don't always convince me. I hope they won't be offended by what I say. Scientific theories are unquestionably necessary, in order to find some explanation for processes under way. Today, in connection with the fact that we are living through a profound process of internal examination, it seems to me that the science of literary criticism must renew itself, change and restructure. The conservatives of our literature now are primarily the critics.

Can you name works of the forties and fifties which have not withstood the test of time?

I think that each of us makes his own conclusions in this sense.

Then what hasn't grown old?

Very little. A great deal has passed through the sieve of time into oblivion. What remains? *Quiet Flows the Don* of course, a mighty step in the development of our literature and artistic thought. This is one pole of folk epic literature, sprung from the roots of life. At the other pole, I would say, is the prose that is refined, and perhaps that is its value, that it has a dense intellectual level—Bulgakov. Between these two poles you can lay out some things which still move the reader.

What about Tvardovskii?[g]

It's harder for me to judge poetry. Of course Tvardovskii is great, both as a craftsman and as someone who expresses large social suffering.

Nabokov has entered the literary realm, the arsenal of the reader's perception. How do you evaluate this?

I look at it this way. Nabokov and other names that have been returned to the reader are all wheat from the same sheaf. The sheaf of Russian literature. Even what Nabokov wrote in English, that's still Russian literature. That some will like him and some not, that's a different matter. After all, we aren't used to reading that sort of Russian literature. By the way, it seems to me that we have invented our own criteria for evaluation and we use them regardless of the fact that they don't correspond to the general understanding. Because of these, there are a number of claims against Nabokov, but nevertheless I think that he is a major artist of the word, and an extremely interesting stylist.

I like Bunin[h] better though. He is closer to me and more understandable. He has more musicality, and I sense the warmth of his word almost physically. Nabokov has a refinement. But the one here doesn't replace the other, doesn't reduce the significance of the other. The more varied the palette, the richer literature is. Thus I think it was proper to return Nabokov to the lap of our literature.

My favorite question: Gauguin said, "In art I am correct." Can you say the same thing about yourself?

Yes, I can say that. That is, I do not want to say that I have achieved some sort of pinnacle of art and everything that I have done is an absolute *chef-d'oeuvre*, but I am right in that I consider beauty to be justice and evil ugly.

Do you have your own laws of art?

I haven't thought about this, what my laws are, and how I set them for myself. But there is a basic, common human understanding of what is good and what is bad.

Do the torments of creation exist for you or not?

To me this is something wholly subjective. Let's talk about something else.

Such as?

I greatly envy [the writer Valentin] Rasputin. He is defending Lake Baikal, which is worthy of having later generations be grateful to him forever. Just for that, to say nothing of the fact that he is a talented writer. Unfortunately I have two concerns of that sort. Our Issyk-Kul also demands quick decisions, cardinal efforts, because agricultural needs are taking every last drop of water which should fall into Lake Issyk-Kul and refill it. More than sixty rivers and streams that used to fall into the lake now don't make it to the lake shore. And the lake is inexorably silting up. We all realize this, talk about it, write about it, including me, in part, but we cannot overcome our own economic needs. Nobody has personal responsibility for the lake, so to speak. Just as when people have personal responsibility for not meeting the plan. This is the contradiction between quotidien needs and eternal ecological problems. We are in a blind alley with this. Glancing at the lake, seeing how it silts up and shrinks, I remember another lake, also one of the holy relics of the people, that of language. If powerful new rivers, in the form of new generations, don't flow into the language, if they don't succeed in mastering their native tongue, if they have no facilities for it, none of the necessary childhood institutions and schools, then this is a silting up of the language, which is; if not an ecological impoverishment, then a national one. Up until now it wasn't done to talk of such things, we couldn't talk about them. But when we began to discuss them aloud we felt how great was the inertia of the past. And another problem, this one already catastrophic. The problem of the Aral Sea. I can't separate the Aral from Issyk-Kul, just as I can't separate Baikal from these biggest water reservoirs of our country. I am happy though that Baikal has its defenders and interceders. The catastrophe of the Aral is largely the fault of man. It is our agriculture, the cotton monoculture which has literally produced ecological devastation, because in striving so long for harvests, we are killing the Aral. Yes, they say that a lot of cotton went and is going for export. I understand the necessity of convertible currency for the government. But somehow or other there has occurred an enormous ecological catastrophe—a sea is disappearing, has receded from its shores more than forty kilometers. All this has become a devastated zone, a desert. Which has caused climatic changes, social poverty, disease, and a poisoned atmosphere. We tried to warn the responsible governmental organs about a lot of this, but without success. The Kazakh writer Nurpeisov, a very important prose writer, and knowledgeable about the Aral, has written a long sketch about this. For three years no one would publish this piece, and still won't. And during this time a great deal has been lost forever. I also want to talk about the responses to *The Executioner's Block*. Until recently the acceptance of the work of this or that writer often used to begin with the flattering feed-in of one critic, and then it was like all one wave. Someone would sound the horn and all the organs of the press would sound their opinions in their turn.

The polyphony of the most various possible voices and disagreements tells us that a time of broad democratic judging of all works of art has arrived. And I think that the first test balloon was *The Executioner's Block*. A literal tidal wave of the most varied, sometimes diametrically opposed readers' opinion washed over it. However, I can tell what comes from deep understanding, from sincerity, and what comes from the superificial and tendentious. That is, I see behind this the most varied possible motives, including ill-intentioned ones, but at the same time I see the high arc of critical thought, and in a professional sense that pleases me. I am not afraid of broad discussion and the stormy boil of passions.

I also get the sort of reader's letters that you can't read in a single sitting. They contain our pain, our worries, propositions. They discuss what could not be discussed among us for many long years.

Chinghiz Torekulovich, the Issyk-Kul Forum is continuing its work. Today its working participants are you, David Roberts, and John LeCarré. Not all of our readers know about the forum, about this new initiative in the struggle for the future of mankind. Tell us about it.

I consider that this trip of ours is a shoot, a runner from the Issyk-Kul Forum. In the past it rarely happened that official contacts became warm personal ones. This is also not just a process of getting acquainted, but also one of mutual enrichment, enlightening one another about our cares and worries. I am very pleased that John LeCarré, whom I didn't know much about as a personality, has expressed interesting observations, views which in many instances coincide with my own. Yes, we are not philosophers or scientists, but we consider that the state is now so powerful that man finds himself fully under its dictate. Of course, the collective and the individual are eternal, because man cannot live all by himself. And various socioeconomic structures arrange this relationship in various ways. Nevertheless, there still does not exist anywhere an ideally founded basis, the essence of which is the happiness of every separate individual. This cherished goal contains the meaning of human existence, the worth of human life. How are we to reach it? The artist must think about this, propose ways to achieve this goal. This was the subject of one of the discussions with LeCarré. The second conversation was a meditation on the phenomenon of secretiveness in the modern world. The author has written a novel on this theme. What is secretiveness? Who needs it? Of what proportions? We understand that since there are various political systems governmental secretiveness is an unavoidable thing. But it's bad when secretiveness becomes a self-contained phenomenon. It seems to me that we sometimes love excessive secretiveness. There are people who make themselves privileges out of this, putting themselves into a particular position. And then secretiveness must have a certain apparatus around it, and that apparatus has to have another around it, and so on to infinity. In any society this ground produces a definite stratum, which pursues its own benefits and goals . . . I am speaking about this openly, and it is possible that there will be people who are guarding secretiveness who will hate me for this openness. I remember that until recently we used to keep all our space flights secret. People were photographed from the back, the cosmonaut reporting to someone or saying goodbye to someone who we saw only from behind. I think, though, that this was a secret only from us, and those who needed to know, knew everything.

When and where is the next meeting of the Issyk-Kul Forum?

Peter Ustinov has proposed a meeting this fall, in Geneva. You see, the founders of the Issyk-Kul Forum agreed to meet not less than once a year. Our agenda is open, we don't set it in advance, and we don't try to direct our conversations in advance. Every participant brings his own attitude to contemporary difficult problems. And in the discussions we represent ourselves most of all.

I think that the Issyk-Kul Forum is one of the signs of *glasnost'*. No one bothers us, no one controls what we talk about. Or what we don't talk about. This is a big achievement, I would say, one of the new, definite freedoms of our day. There are people who talk about freedom a lot, but don't do anything about it. It seems to me though that many people do not even understand what freedom is. Others think that freedom is when everything is permissible, that whatever comes into your head you can do or say. In fact, this is wrong. Freedom is the acquisition of new spiritual expanses, a new step in the moral and social perfection of man.

Many impressions remain from the trip to Kirghizia. Outside of the interview there were Chinghiz Aitmatov's reflections on other, no less important problems of our life today, and of our recent past. For me this was a conversation with a man who analyzes life in his own way, who thinks deeply about its processes, and who is offering a path to its positive restructuring.

I saw Aitmatov among people who trust and believe him, both as a writer and as a man. For in him, in his life and his art, in his social activism, are reflected the dislocations of our time, and its tragic essence.

The highly powerful flow of contemporary life must concern each of us, or so I thought in those days. As it concerns Aitmatov in absolutely everything, from philosophical discussions with a very famous English writer and fatherly murmurings with his daughter Shirin, who accompanied her father on his journey, to admiring the mountainous beauty of the Zailii Alatau and the bursts of weighty memories about the fate of his forebears at the cemeteries we visited. As it concerns the most important thing in his life, his books, and that which is born in the writer's soul, the creator of new works.

When I was already getting ready to go back to Moscow, tired from the interesting and difficult journey, having discussed, or so it seemed, everything on earth, I decided to bring my hero to earth and so asked him about his most memorable moment of childhood, that time when there was nothing, or almost nothing, and his entire fate had just begun, was just coming together, beginning to form. Chinghiz Torekulovich began:

There was such an episode in my life, and I have already talked about it a bit, but I will recall it again, since in a literary biography such things must be returned to. It is very important what a person first remembers in life, when it is, and what it is.

I was five when I first served as a translator, and a piece of boiled meat was my first "honorarium." This happened at summer herding in the mountains, where, as usual, I was with my grandmother. The kolkhozes in those years were just getting on their feet, had just begun to get organized. In our *dzhailoo*ⁱ there had been a mishap. A thoroughbred stallion which the kolkhoz had bought not long before had suddenly died. In broad daylight he fell down with a swollen belly and breathed his last. The herders were upset because the stallion was expensive, of the Don breed, brought from distant Russia. They sent a messenger to the kolkhoz, and from there to the raion center. And a day later a Russian came to us in the mountains. He was tall, with a red beard and blue eyes, in a black leather jacket, with a field sack at his side. I remember him very well. He didn't know a word of Kirghiz, and our herders didn't know any Russian. There had to be an investigation, to find out the causes of the animal's death, and to make out the documents. After a quick think, the herders decided that I would be the translator. I was standing in the crowd of children, staring solemnly at the newcomer.

"Let's go," one of the herders said and took me by the hand. "This man doesn't know the language. You translate what he says, and then we'll tell you what to tell him."

I was shy and frightened. I pulled away and ran to grandmother in her yurt, followed by a whole crowd of friends, who were seized with curiosity. A little while later the same man came up, to complain about me. Grandmother was always gentle with me, but this time she frowned sternly.

"Why don't you want to talk with the newcomer? Big people are asking you to do it, maybe you don't know Russian?"

I was silent. My friends hid behind the yurt, wondering what next.

"What, are you ashamed to talk Russian or ashamed of your own language? All languages are the gift of God, so don't fuss, come on. . . ."

She took me by the hand and led me off. The children followed again.

In the yurt, where they were already boiling mutton in honor of the guest, there was a big crowd. They were drinking *kumys*.ʲ The visiting veterinarian was sitting with the village elders. He remembered me and smiled.

"Come in, little boy, come here. What's your name?"

I muttered quietly what it was. He patted me.

"Ask them why this stallion died," he said, taking out paper to make notes.

Everyone got quiet, waiting, and I was frozen shut, couldn't say a word. My grandmother sat down, confused. Then an old man, our relative, took me on his knee, hugged me, and whispered confidentially and very seriously in my ear.

"This man knows your father. What will he tell him about us? Will he say how poorly the Kirghiz are raising his son?" Then he said loudly, "Now he will talk. Tell our guest that this place is called Uu-Saz. . . ."

"Uncle," I began timidly, "this place is called Uu-Saz, or poison meadow . . ."
Then I got braver because I saw how happy grandmother had become, and the visitor, and everybody who was in the tent. My whole life I've remembered the synchronous translation of this conversation, word for word, in both languages. The stallion had apparently poisoned himself on poison grass. When asked why the other horses don't eat this grass, our herders explained that the local horses don't touch it, knowing that it is inedible. That is what I translated.

The visitor praised me, and the elders gave me a whole piece of boiled meat, hot and aromatic. I dashed out of the yurt with a triumphant expression. The children surrounded me in a flash.

"Great! Terrific!" they were in awe. "You spout Russian like water in a river, never stopping!" In fact I had talked haltingly, but the children liked understanding things as they wanted to.

We immediately ate the meat and ran off to play.

Editor's notes

a. Valentin Rasputin: prominent Russian writer, author of *Five* [Piatero].

b. Domodedovo Airport: the main airport in Moscow for flights to the eastern parts of the Soviet Union.

c. Reference is to the 1987 unauthorized solo flight across the Soviet border by the West German youth Mathias Rust, who landed his plane in Red Square. This event precipitated a major shakeup in the Soviet military leadership.

d. Tashtanbek Akmatov: President of the Supreme Soviet, Kirghiz SSR, the first shepherd appointed to that post.

e. *Pamiat'* [Memory]: an unofficial Russian nationalist organization dedicated to preserving the cultural and racial purity of the Russian people.

f. Turkestan: the prerevolutionary name for Soviet Central Asia (excluding the Kazakh steppe). In the 1920s Soviet officials divided the area into five republics with five national languages, reducing the potential for political and cultural cohesiveness.

g. Andrei Tvardovskii: editor of *Novyi mir* during the Khrushchev "Thaw." He was a popular poet and creator of Vassilii Terkin, a comic soldier Everyman.

h. Ivan Bunin: the first Russian writer to win the Nobel Prize in literature, he left Russia after the revolution.

i. *Dzhailoo:* term for summer pasture site of nomads.

j. *Kumys:* a beverage made from fermented mare's milk.

From the 1987 Plenum
of the USSR Union of Writers *

Literature and the Present

Speech by Boris Oleinik (Ukraine)

I too used to grow alarmed at times, comrades, wondering whether we weren't talking nonsense, blithering away a beautiful idea. After all, there seem to have appeared rather a lot, not only of nightingales, but also roosters of restructuring, for whom the main thing is to keep singing, and never worry whether the sun comes up.

Happily, and to the honor of all that is healthy and businesslike in our society, words are already being realized in concrete ways, as today's presentations by V. Karpov, M. Alekseev, F. Kuznetsov, N. Gilevich, and G. Baklanov demonstrate.

The most visible positive leaps are in the economic sphere. They are least noticeable in the administrative, scientific, and creative spheres, where voids and gaps may be covered over with posters and semantic tightrope-walking. Even so the wind of renewal is felt even there, not as dynamically as might be desired, but still. . .

And here I catch myself for inertia, for stamping with a flourish a still-glowing matrix of fresh-cast chunks of social and political material into the trembling tissue of culture in general and literature in particular. After all, Lenin warned that "The cultural question cannot be resolved so quickly as the political and military ones. . . . by the very nature of the business you need a longer period, and you must get accustomed to this longer period in considering your work, showing the greatest persistence, firmness, and organization." This is true, we might add, if only because the defining natural characteristic of literature is continuity. The very best intentions for the most progressive changes can lead to wholly regrettable consequences, if even one link in the system of continuity be broken. After all, the new thinking which we are proclaiming far and wide today is contained in the very biology of every work of art, if it is truly one of talent, since the artistic vision is the same thing as seeing the future. In the opposite event this is only an illustration of the past.

If the literary process even of the past twenty years, infected with the virus of stasis, is examined from this vantage point, then real writers, even if not all of them, always struggled honestly for the renewal of society, for the democratization of social relationships, insisting on their sacred right to tell the people the truth, defending nature and historical monuments, defending the purity of their native

*Literaturnaia gazeta, 6 May 1987, pp. 2 and 10. Russian text © 1987 by the USSR Union of Writers.

sources, fighting for the establishment of Leninist norms, and for giving to the people works by authors unjustly silenced or simply forgotten. It would seem as though this is their shining hour. After all, they have toiled bravely for it, and not in conditions of the greatest comfort, often earning bruises as their rewards.

But things have somehow come out that the mechanism of democracy for which they had suffered, the loudspeakers of *glasnost'* have begun to be used with force by those people who in the time of stasis did not especially distinguish themselves for activity. Nor did they particularly stick out in the sphere of creativity. Paradoxical as it may seem, in their harmonious chorus the voices of those who initiated restructuring are gradually getting lost. This wouldn't matter, were it not that certain soloists step forward onto the tribunes and up to the microphones of radio and television with the air of people coming from another planet to introduce order and reason into our solar system. Using the vocabulary of crisis, flailing at all and sundry, they often go so far to the right, or so far to the left, that they just about disappear. The slightest mention of the obvious distortions that endanger the very essence of restructuring is immediately attacked as an infringement upon democracy. Immediately, not even pausing for air, they quite democratically attempt to frighten their opponents by declaring what amounts to a "holy war." If, for example, this concerns me personally, then I can accuse my opponents of elementary unprofessionalism; trying to frighten a front-line party committee secretary "fed at spearpoint," for whom heightened battle-readiness is a natural condition of body and spirit, is an empty waste of time and ammunition.

As a line-soldier of literature I may permit myself a joke, but it is not a joking matter when under cover of a renewal of values artillery fire is opened, aimed straight at the people who define the level of our multinational literature.

Sinner that I am, I thought that such things were achievements only of our region, but unfortunately I was mistaken. It turns out that similar things also occur in Russia and in the other fraternal republics. And a certain pattern to it immediately makes you wonder, for the attacks are strongest precisely on the brightest figures. Perhaps because they are visible from afar?

There is, of course, an element of jealousy. Since time immemorial the ordinary has not forgiven nor will it ever forgive real talent. Talent disturbs the ordinary as a background, for its bright light shows in particular contrast to the other's greyness. In this case the saying that "white begins but grey wins" is particularly apropos. However, if it were only the mechanism of jealousy that was at work, then sooner or later everything would fall into the proper place; during any reconstruction the constant measurements remain the same, and a lack of talent cannot be compensated for even by UNESCO.

It is something else which puts one on guard: that in demanding with justice that missing links in the spiritual line be resurrected, that the unjustly silenced be returned to the people, we sometimes try not to join these valuables to existing ones, but rather to exchange them or replace the ones which we have already acquired over the decades. Sometimes we even oppose one to the other. Besides, is absolutely everything worth being assimilated? Over "there" they curse us for our excessive obsession with ideology, but it is we, not they, who recall that there are values which transcend all ambitions, that there are common human priorities, among which the greatest is life, for the preservation of which our side made a most noble proposal— that we enter the third millennium without nuclear weapons. This also concerns the preservation of the surrounding natural environment.

Yes, we are obligated to incorporate into our spiritual potential those same unrealized values at home just as we are those which arise outside of it. Each republic can present its melancholy roll. For example, back in the 1960s we tried to publish some works of Vladimir Vinnichenko, a man with a complex, multifaceted, and politically uneven fate. This important writer has a complex meaning on the creative level as well, particularly in works from the prerevolutionary period, which are to a significant extent progressive. One of his stories, for example, describes a man who has suffered for the Ukraine, and who, winding up in prison for his excessively violent separatism, upon learning that there are also Russians serving sentences in this institution, organizes a demonstration under the slogan "Russkies Out of Ukrainian Jails!" It would be difficult to find more killing ridicule of nationalism in its heaviest, most metallic form!

Thus with a well-intentioned analysis to dissipate the errors, this author is worthy of publishing. So too the work of Academician Iavornitskii about the history of the Zaporozhe cossacks, and the codex of chronicles, and much, much more. Much more, but not everything. After all, in every self-respecting country there exist fundamental points of world-view which have become part of the very nature of society, and that which is organically inimical to that society is of course rejected, if the society does not wish to change, or betray, itself.

For example, Gippius never concealed her absolute rejection of the October revolution. Further, she never betrayed her nature even in the very heaviest hour of our Motherland, when the fascists invaded. I am certain that as a complete personality, in her own way, Zinaida Nikolaevna herself would object to our clumsy attempts to bring her work into the cultural values of the land of the Soviets, to which she was inimical to the end. Nevertheless, we are trying. . . .

We are accused of maximalism and intolerance, which we are told is a result of our late industrialization, our nonparliamentary development, the costs of tribal and communal atavism, and, very nearly, blood feuds. But then take Knut Hamsun, a classic not only of his own country, but of world literature. Norway certainly cannot be accused of late industrialization, ideological intolerance and the rest. Yet Knut Hamsun was condemned to the sternest penalty for collaboration with the occupiers by the Norwegians themselves, who took no account of the fact that he was a classic, or that he was well over eighty. Even more, Hamsun's son renounced his father.

We might mention Ezra Pound, too, who is not among the weakest handful of poets, but whose collaboration with Mussolini is not forgotten (nor is it likely to be forgiven). This means that there are crimes which cannot be bought off with the coin of talent, even of the purest metal—treason, trampling on the very nature of things, on a country's beliefs, its people's holy things. Independent of worldview and degree of industrialization. What is the source here of these up-swells of a lackey's psychology, this servile desire to have some third-rate visiting foreigners think we have characters of liberal views? Sometimes in order to earn a condescending clap on the shoulder and a grudging "okay!" we are prepared to give way to those who in demanding of us that we drop our complexes about ideology without themselves giving up even a micron of their own ideology, defend it with talent. At least the one elementary feeling of self-worth should be preserved, for they will simply cease to respect us, not just as ideological opponents, but even as equal colleagues. This must be said aloud, for *glasnost'* must be for all, and of equal power in everything.

Unfortunately, *glasnost'* is often selective. For example, every writer from any republic has the natural right to confess his love for his people, his roots. This is beautiful, for our Soviet patriotism isn't grown hydroponically, but rather in real national soil. But when our Russian colleague extoll his native land with precisely the same natural filial love, often there arise whispers and hints at all sorts of great-power and simply governmental "isms." What is this, comrades? Who has given us the right to doubt the internationalism of a great people who in their disinterested generosity after October assisted many peoples to become literate, to organize an academy in every republic, while to this day in its modesty it does not have one of its own?

The same stereotype of someone's origin makes the natural desire of a Ukrainian to develop his native language provoke an almost traditional reaction—"Oh, oh, they're stirring!"—and then there follow the corresponding traditional terms. However, Lenin, in the "Resolution of the Central Committee of the Russian Communist Party (Bolsheviks) on Soviet Power in the Ukraine," viewed the Ukrainian language as the most important means of communist education of the working masses and called for every effort to be made to resist attempts to give the issue secondary importance.

At the same time in certain of our regional centers the number of Ukrainian schools is approaching zero. This has happened not through the fault of someone else, but through our fault. . . . However, you know perfectly well to whom our enemies ascribe these errors. And so it is that we ask our Russian brothers to help us bring Leninist order to this sphere as well. As for the Russian language, we are simply unable to imagine ourselves without it. Russian gives us the opportunity to communicate and get to know one another in our multinational Fatherland. Thus we value it from childhood, just as we do our motherland's *mova.*[a]

All of these problems must become the provenance of *glasnost'*, and a challenge I address first and foremost to the central press, which sometimes tries to avoid it. For example, for several months I have not been able to publish anything about the Chernobyl' atomic power plant, where it is proposed (they say perhaps already was proposed) to build a third line. Today, on the melancholy anniversary, it is more worthwhile than ever to wonder whether we have weighed everything in undertaking this risky step.

By the holy laws of "the sense of a single family" we are responsible to each other. We are equally responsible for our own people and for every people that lives under the sky of Leninist fraternity. Life has taught us this throughout the entire seventy years since October; thus has our multinational Soviet literature raised us!

Speech by Olzhas Suleimenov (Kazakhstan)

In considering the theme of the plenum, "Literature and the Present," we understand that events in life and in literature do not happen all of a sudden. They are prepared by the entire movement of the joint development of society and personality.

I support the pathos of B. Mozhaev's speech. Our nation is truly broad, with many faces, and the rate of restructuring is not the same everywhere. This is natural, unfortunately. It is enough to compare the repertoire of certain journals from the capital with the contents of our local and republic-level journals to understand that creative freedom and *glasnost'* are spreading about the country with various . . . braking rates. For example, in Moscow and here at the plenum voices are heard demanding a halt to publication or the banning of publication of works by writers of earlier years. In our republic, on the other hand, attempts to publish the verses of the best poets of the 1920s and 1930s, who were repressed without cause, are ending with the same hue and cry as always. So I am wondering, what would happen if the Muscovites suddenly really do get fed up and they stop publishing or the list is stopped. Then our Makzhan and Shakarim[b] will be even farther back in the line. And for how long? After all, the first attempts to publish them began in 1956. We don't have so many great poets that we can afford to squander their fates and work so wastefully.

I will repeat what I said at the congress,[c] that a great culture makes even its lesser figures bigger, because it is great. A little culture tries to bring down even its greats, because it is little.

What has changed now? In the republic a great deal has, in the social sphere. The moral situation is changing, as is the economic. Ideology ought somehow to precede restructuring, but as always with us, it is remaining where it has always been, snugly against our ear. People are constantly checking with Moscow, but as before they don't hear us. The absence of a dialogue of equals for so many decades has distorted the direction and development of spiritual culture.

In preparing for my report for the Ninth Congress of Writers of the republic [Kazakhstan], held in April of last year, I read several score of the stories and novels which had come out over the five years, in Russian and in Kazakh. Various books, about various things, but there was one thing common to them all. The cast of characters in nearly all of them was mononational. In life we work in multinational collectives, but this reality is steadfastly not reflected in literature, which unintentionally fosters an isolationist consciousness. One book stood out for the natural multinational nature of its heroes, *Region in Uprising*, by Musrepov, who died in 1985 after finishing the novel, the work of his entire life. He was the last master from the pleiades of founders of Soviet Kazakh literature. His book, about how the Kazakh working class arose and grew in a union with the Russian proletariat, is like a legacy to continue this important work. The basic theme of the works of all our mighty quartet of prose writers—M. Auezov, Mukanov, Mustafin, and Musrepov—

was that alone we can do nothing only together can we. But why has this idea grown feeble, come to nothing in the books of the last generation?

After the congress we had a round-table discussion in the journal *Expanse* [Prostor],[d] at which Russian, Kazakh, German, Uighur, and Korean writers for the first time spoke frankly about these things. Then a plenum was convened to discuss this question. On 12 December [1986] there was even a discussion in the secretariat of the leadership of the Writers' Union in Moscow, on the "International Theme in the Literature of Multinational Kazakhstan." We did not speak about any alarming disorder in our society, nor did we see one; rather, we spoke only of the disorder we had noticed in our literature.

A few days later, 17–18 December, there occurred the disturbing events in which the sense of disintegration first appeared as a mass phenomenon.[e]

After Chernobyl[f] everyone knew the exchange, "What are the chances of an accident at an atomic station?"; "One in a million." In Kazakhstan we consoled ourselves with the same sort of metaphors, that we were "The Land of a Hundred Languages," "The Laboratory of Friendship among Peoples." Then suddenly, a breakdown. The energy of the collapse burned everyone. And now we recognize with pain that internationalism is not a given, but the fruit of painstaking, everyday work. This is a job that does not forgive carelessness.

This bitter lesson must be studied in every writers' organization of the country. Not formalistically, but with an understanding of the necessity of learning to live in conditions of democracy in a multinational country. We must not pretend that what happened was a sad local misunderstanding. The reaction of collapse has long been shaking the large capitalist countries. Ideas of ethnic isolationism, alas, don't know any territorial limits. Their limits are in the consciousness of man, that is, in that sphere which responds to the power of the word. And in speaking about the strengthening of social justice we probably ought always to take account of the action of the factor of national justice. Although the nationality question itself has been resolved in the country, problems of inter-nationality relations exist, and as things turn out, it seems they are rather sharp. We must be prepared for the possibility that in a setting of the acceleration of the development of democracy centrifugal forces might come to life, and it is literature which can speed them up or stop them.

M. Alekseev has introduced a good example for a song, in which that which is common seems to overcome the personal: "My address is no house or street . . ." In fact, what is there good about a man who has neither a street nor a house? Perhaps the songwriters wanted to express not a nihilistic attitude to their smaller homeland, but rather just pride in their large one, our common one. During the war we felt our international unity more keenly. The fate of the country always depended upon the strength of that unity, and the writers of those years never lost sight of the supreme task, educating the Soviet man, a patriot of the entire nation. That was a war of internationalism with nationalism, which was the particular ideological category which distinguished the Great Fatherland War from the thousands of wars which preceded it in history. Our generation was reared in that same spirit; we came into literature in the beginning of the 1960s, when the term "Soviet people" was still recognized as our own self-designation. Then over the years the category of the Great Fatherland has grown weaker, so it is not as strong or vivid in us, as much as it has sundered our consciousness into a plethora of little motherlands. Wasn't it this that became the spiritual support for the philosophy and practice of regionalism, self-interested protectionism, old-boy networks, and local boosterism which appeared so actively in our social life in the 1970s and 1980s?

These prejudices that are fatal to an international consciousness came to life neither suddenly nor in one place; their appearance must be seen as a result of the weakening of class community in all of society, so the disease of nationalism can appear in any region. Local freedom from these ills does not remove the seriousness of the problem. The ailment must be cured patiently and over time, not driving the disease deeper inside; it must be cured by drawing the entire country into the process of democratic public healing.

I recall V. V. Karpov's[f] intonation in that part of his report where he departed from his text and began to speak of children. Tenderly and a bit despairingly, even enviously, he spoke of how his grandchildren would not have to restructure. Our grandfathers and fathers also hoped that we would live in a cloudless time, for which hope they bore all the burdens and sacrificed themselves. However, that their sacrifices be not in vain, we again today take on ourselves this most heavy burden of both the past and our own time.

The restructuring of society today is the growth of the country, a growth by leaps, as the dialecticians say, of economy, morals, and civic intelligence. But in order to make our children and grandchildren happy, we today must be happy too, in order to give them a legacy not just of hardships and insults. We must be victorious in the battle with lies, slander, and the baseness of prejudice. We want to believe that this is our last, decisive battle with the bland bureaucratic swine who will continue to try to divide us using old and time-proven methods.

Editor's notes

a. The Russian text used the Ukrainian word for language, *mova*.

b. Poets of the late nineteenth and early twentieth centuries who wrote in part of religious themes.

c. The congress of the Writers' Union held in June 1986.

d. *Prostor* is the Russian-language organ of the Union of Writers of Kazakhstan.

e. Reference is to the riots in Alma-Ata which accompanied the replacement by G. Kolbin of Kazakhstan's party First Secretary D. A. Kunaev.

f. V. V. Karpov: first secretary of the USSR Writers' Union

From the 1988 Plenum
of the USSR Union of Writers *

Speech by Iurii Andreev (Leningrad)

It is of course a delightful psychological peculiarity of literary people to have heightened emotional responses in judging phenomena.

It is disturbing, though, when there are situations in which this emotionalism begins to resemble some enormously heavy iron maiden which destroys very real, fundamental truths. For example, when I hear today that we don't have a united Soviet people, I can't help but remember *The Lay of the Host of Igor*. After all, the significance of that extremely great book is to call all the little princes and princelings together for unity and solidarity in the face of a great threat.

The "Poet's Library" [Biblioteka poeta] series, whose editorial board I represent, has prepared a plan to create a body of 160 volumes to present the best that has been created by the creative genius of all the peoples of our country. We will publish the remarkable Belorussian poet Gusovskii, who in scale is fully comparable to both Shakespeare and Petrarch. We will prepare a collection called *Epos of the Peoples of the North and the Far East* [Epos narodov Severa i Dal'nego Vostoka], which will be a monumental discovery on a planetary level.

Thus it can be said that I began with the good part.

But now here's the first difficulty. During the war the smaller series of "Poet's Library" didn't publish for three years, and now, during the period of restructuring, it also has not published for three years. Why? Because our printing plant simply can't handle the publishing.

The editorial board of "The Poet's Library," which is supposed to publish 400 books, consists of five people. If with the greatest intensification of powers we publish as we are able to, this process will last 40 years. This unquestionably is an irritating attitude to the very great cultural fund that "The Poet's Library" represents.

The members of our advisory board—Likhachev, Kanoat, Dudin, Gamzatov, Isaev, and others—have written a letter about the impossibility of this type of cadre situation and have appealed to the very highest levels.

We have received the extremely kind answer that they sympathize, that it can not be permitted to lose such colossal spiritual treasures, but in the given instance we should turn to the secretariat of the directorate of the Writers' Union of the USSR.

After all, everything might have been done differently. Why, really, should the President of the Council of Ministers Comrade Ryzhkov or the Minister of Finance have to decide questions of the state of the publishing house where we know the state of affairs much better? What is this sort of hierarchy for? For example, we need one

---

*Literaturnaia gazeta, 9 March 1988. Russian text © 1988 by the USSR Union of Writers.

person in the editorial office, an assistant editor, who could work with our thousand-plus poets and translators. We don't have such a position. When we ask about getting one, they tell us that this can be decided only on the level of comrade Ryzhkov. Our publishing house brings in millions of rubles in profit, but we can't spend thousands of rubles a year to get the specialists that we need to publish this collection of 160 or 400 great books.

Now I will address the representatives of the republics who are sitting here. Expert opinion has shown, dear comrades, that up to 80 percent of the books which we want to publish are poorly translated.

What is to be done? Of course they have to be republished, retranslated. And here we appeal to you, dear comrades! Look at what we must publish from your republics and create a bank of interlinear literal translations, so that we can go to the very best poets, so that the chef d'oeuvres of the spirit of your people can become an achievement of the whole country, of the whole world. Right now in the "Sovetskii pisatel'" [Publishing House] we have 20 million rubles in profits that aren't doing anything. We don't know what to do with them. So that the heavy burden of paying for new translations won't be on the publishing house, we ask that you permit us to use this fund to improve the translations of our great all-nationality collection. This would be the correct thing to do.

Speech by Sergei Baruzdin (Moscow)

Relations among nationalities probably always have been and will be in the future the most complex, most delicate, most sticky, and most finicky.

Yes, we were the first to make a revolution of social justice, yes, we transformed backward, multinational Russia, the "prison of nations," as Lenin called it, into a world-leading country, highly developed and highly cultured, where every people and every person received equal rights and obligations.

The party and people, who were mostly Russian, spared neither means, nor physical effort, nor spiritual warmth for the sharp uplifting of the social and living standards of the former tsarist borderlands. However, after the death of Lenin, as in many other areas of life, in the sphere of national relations we began to take as if what we desired was real. In other words the national question was considered resolved once and for all.

Having pronounced internationalism and the friendship among peoples to be the basis among our society, we began to forget that there can be no understanding the international without the national, that the friendship among peoples doesn't mean the friendship of all the surrounding peoples for the one in the middle, but rather equal respect for all peoples, no matter how big or small.

Now I don't want to throw yet another stone at Iosif Vissarionovich, for we have already done extremely well at putting all our sins of yesterday and today off onto Stalin, but the truth and *glasnost'* demand that we say that distortions of national policy began back in those years, the 1930s. On the one hand there was the purely formal show of national cultures and literatures, for effect, and on the other, a forced leap in the direction of fusing[a] peoples, national groups, and languages.

It was then that the bureaucratic approach to the resolution of the national question appeared, and the strange idea of the "elder brother"[b] was born, both in propaganda and, alas, saddest of all, in our literature.

The pompous image of the "elder brother" went on to migrate from literature to literature, from book to book, like some form of obligatory character. Perhaps we were not sufficeintly mature then to understand that this idea was equally insulting for the "elder brother" himself and for his "younger brothers." However paradoxical it may seem, it was also at that time that the idea of "fraternal literatures" appeared too, meaning all fraternal literatures except Russian.

Our *Friendship among Peoples* [Druzhba narodov] [c] was founded in 1939, a living affirmation of this. Right up until 1966 it published all authors save Russian ones. The journal was weak, last of all the publications of the Writers' Union, and it's embarassing now even to name its print run. Among writers it was dubbed "the fraternal grave."

Also, publishing policy has little importance in the improvement of nationality relations. The tendency of so-called representationalism in literature was also born in the 1930s. In the Supreme Soviet and other organs of power this is normal and proper. But is it normal in literature? In the meantime all publishers' plans began with and still begin with this postulate. For example, the publishing house "Sovetskii pisatel'," not just in the past but even today, publishes sixty percent of its books by Russian authors, and forty percent of its books by writers from the republics. Why? Maybe the present year, which was planned in advance, doesn't have sixty percent good Russian books, but there are more good books from the republics, and another year maybe the other way about? No, the plan is the plan.

And further, if we are going to talk about representationalism of all our literatures in publishing plans, wouldn't it be better, instead of something new and dull, to republish some things that have withstood the test of time? And not on the republic level, or even the all-union, but on the world level.

Of course the Russian and Russian-language reader has 5–10 names of writers who are, as they say, above the competition. Here too there is a definite paradox. I will mention three names, though I could name more—Chinghiz Aitmatov, Grant Matevosian,[d] and Ion Drutse.[e] They were valued first of all by the all-union reader, and not the local, republican reader. And also not their local fellow writers.

I remember what a large number of attacks on Chinghiz Aitmatov were relayed to Moscow in Khrushchev's day from many Kirghiz writers. And Grant Matevosian was not recognized not only by the official powers of local significance, but also by many of his comrade writers. The same can be said of Ion Drutse.

Now is the right time to say a few words about criticism too. For at least three decades, and maybe more, we have declaimed the proposition that our brother literatures influence and enrich one another. But where and when has our criticism said anything concrete about this?! The critics can't say anything about it, except perhaps Russian critics, though they too are limited, because they are embarassed to criticize works by writers in other languages. Every critic from the union or autonomous republics limits his discussion to the literature of his own republic, in a complete break from Soviet multinational literature, including Russian. With very few exceptions. Here I could name Algimantas Bučis and five or six others, but not more than that. They don't change the situation. And after all, isn't the discussion of one's own literature in connection with all-union literature a sign of internationalism?

Recently, since the April Plenum of the Central Committee of the CPSU and the Twenty-seventh Party Congress, we have restored to Russian literature a few undeservedly forgotten names. These names are those of repressed writers, emigré writers, and finally the manuscripts of still-living authors whose works for one reason or another were not published for decades. This, believe, me, is not sensationalism, but the movement of truth.

But why is this process moving so slowly, or not moving at all in our republics? I know an enormous number of timorous editors who seek agreement from party and state authorities: Can the name of this writer be mentioned at a meeting, or not yet? Are these still the old bureaucratic obstacles?!

On the other hand, the Gorno-Altai Oblast' Party Committee and the writers' organization have made the first step. An unusual anthology of Gorno-Altai literature has come out which includes all the undeservedly forgotten names. . . . Every last one of them, from the repressed to the mistaken.

But what about our other republics? They ask us, *Friendship among Peoples*, to reestablish historical literary justice! We are pleased to try, but you don't tell us how to do it. In the last two and a half years of restructuring I don't recall a single suggestion of this sort to the editors. I am also speaking about this to show one more time how difficult it is for restructuring and *glasnost'* to penetrate even our literary life.

Our criticism and literary studies must entirely refuse to be "local," to reject the regional approach to their literature. The literature must be written into the general process of development of our multinational literature, with all its achievments and obvious faults. In turning to history we must refuse sloganeering about how all peoples and national groups truly voluntarily united with Russia. Incidentally, this thesis is not the fault of Stalin's day; it was invented much later than Stalin.

Yes, some were voluntary, but others were by force. Russia was the prison of nations. That should not be forgotten. So why should history be forcibly reworked? It is another matter that after the October revolution all these peoples gained.

The events of recent years—Alma-Ata, the Baltic region, Iakutiia, the Crimean Tatars, the ripe problem of Nagorno Karabakh—all are disquieting symptoms.

And I think that here we have a common responsibility along with our ideological services, our Party leadership, and our scientists that these problems, just like many others, are now in a state of stagnation. And this stagnation is, alas, still not overcome in all spheres of our life.

At the last Plenum of the CPSU Central Committee, in February [1988], M. S. Gorbachev very precisely and clearly laid out a program of improving our internationality relations. Further, even more important, he spoke of culture as the necessary environment for all our multi-faceted activity, the economic, political, social, and the simply human.

Editor's notes

a. A reference to the Leninist goal of *sliianie*, the fusion of peoples.

b. During Stalin's rule and continuing through the Khrushchev years there was frequent mention of the positive role played by the Russian "elder brother" in fostering the cultures of the non-Russian nationalities.

c. *Druzhba narodov:* the literary journal.

d. Grant Matevosian: the noted Armenian writer.

e. Ion Drutse: the noted Moldavian writer.

Speech by Vladimir Beekman (Estonia)

Real, unfalsified internationalism grows from mutual respect, which in order to be born requires as a minimum that we must know one another. So let us ask ourselves the question whether we know each other well, in order to achieve real mutual respect, not just government pretend. I would answer in the negative. And the cause here is not someone's ill will or national limitation, but a range of objective conditions, on which I would like to linger.

To really get to know a writer undoubtedly requires having his books in print and available. We have a catastrophic lack of such books. To try to replace the book with some kind of oral literary almanac is a hopeless business, especially today, when the era of reading huts and collective reading shelves has long since passed.

The journal *Friendship among Peoples* is truly struggling to embrace the unembraceable. But judge for yourselves: there are twelve issues a year for all fifteen union republics, not counting the autonomous republics. You can't even publish a smattering from each republic every year, to say nothing of a novel. But then there are good harvest years, when all at once there are two or three or even more deserving, very interesting works that appear in some republic, and what happens if that occurs in more than one at the same time? Then there are waiting periods again, and "movement in stages," and in the meantime new things are coming along, and something is put off until later and then is forgotten entirely, fallen out of the field of vision.

The all-union channels for publication in Russian of works by national authors have remained on the level of the 1940s and 1950s, when *Friendship among Peoples* became a monthly, and since then they have neither widened nor deepened, and here it is almost the 1990s. Our national literatures have grown immeasurably in these decades, but unfortunately not in the eyes of the all-union reader, who in practice is still deprived of the opportunity to be convinced of this in good time. We still know each other too little.

And what are we doing ourselves, or are we hoping that someone up above will solve all our problems and take away all the complaints? As much as we can, we in Estonia are trying to do something, publishing the Russian-language journal *Tallin*, and creating a special editorial board of literature in Russian in the republic publishing house "Eesti raamat." However, our feeble journal comes out once every other month, in 8,600 copies, so there isn't much that we are able to publish, and it is hard to count on it reaching a broad public. The Russian editorial board of the publisher also has problems. Its possibilities are to a significant degree blocked by central orders from the USSR State Publishing Committee [Goskomizdat] for publishing large print-run editions of so-called high-demand literature, which have been created to satisfy the all-union book famine for Russian-language literature. We fully understand the need here, but it would be good if there were some discussion about using the republic's not-overworked printing powers for now the massive Moscow orders, though they are probably profitable for the printers, are mercilessly blocking the way for first publication of translations of Estonian literature. Not long ago M. F. Nenashev announced from this tribune that Goskomizdat USSR doesn't obligate any republic to do these editions. In the republic Goskomizdat they insist on something the opposite. So we have Ivan pointing at Peter. But this is good for somebody, after all, and it clearly isn't the writers. That's why it seems to us that for some reason restructuring is going slowly in the Goskomizdat system, despite the printed hearty speeches by certain of its administrators.

But even first publication in Russian is only half the matter. It is useful for putting the work into international literary circulation. But if we want a book that deserves to become at least somewhat known to a broad circle of readers, large numbers also have to be printed. Considering the scale of our country and the demand for fiction, this is a far from simple task. The limited number of yearly reprints by the "Khudozhestvennaia literature" Publishing House, half of which are classics, even with so-called mass print runs, can only satisfy the demand to a minor degree.

I speak about this because I wish to raise the question of the role to be played in international literary connections of what is probably our only publication whose usually print run corresponds to the demands of the present day. I am speaking of the *Novel-Gazette* [Roman-gazeta].[a] In our view, it long ago departed decisively from any literary mission and is guided in its work by mysterious principles which only the editors know. It is our melancholy experience which impels us to these thoughts. In all the postwar decades, or for practically all of the existence of Estonian Soviet literature, the *Novel-Gazette* has found room for only four works by Estonian authors. Perhaps we would have remained quiet if these proportions were just. However, when we have of late often encountered data in the press which show that certain authors, beloved of the editors, have been published in this journal twelve or fifteen times in the same period, our innocent provincial minds refuse to understand it.

All that I have said above leads to the question, hasn't the time come to create a new central press, which we could conditionally call the press of the friendship among peoples? Maybe even with its own literary journal? We, at least, say that it has.

Editor's note

a. *Roman-gazeta:* a journal that reprints whole novels in newspaper columns and on newsprint.

Speech by Maiia Ganina (Moscow)

Like the majority of Russian intellectuals, I was raised from childhood with the awareness that hatred of any nation first of all destroys the person who hates. Whenever I went on business trips to Uzbekistan, Kazakhstan, Khakasia [sic], Lithuania, and so forth, I always learned a hundred or hundred and fifty words and phrases, so as to be able to talk and ask for things. In Uzbek when I learned *"chiroili kuzlar,"* or "beautiful eyes," I remembered the Russian for "bewitching" and "charming" [words that come from Turkic roots—Ed.]. It was pleasant to discover a kind of primordial, pre-Tower of Babel, connection which, whether we wish it or not, unites us. The word for an old trade route, which Belorussian preserves, *gostinets* [which means "hotel" in modern Russian—Ed.], or the ancient path along which trading guests were welcomed into our lands from other lands, carressed my ears, while at the same time I was disturbed that Russian had lost this word, which undoubtedly it had once shared, thoughtlessly exchanging it for the words [of foreign origin—Ed.] *"magistral"* and *"chausée."*

I am talking about this in such great detail because everything else I am going to say might give some people an opportunity to hang around my neck a label that is current today.

I think that the time has come to begin to discuss the emotional coloration which the word "Russian" has acquired in the past decades, both among us here in the country and abroad.

One Georgian writer sent me a letter of five hundred pages, in which, seeking my sympathy, he accused the Russians of a number of sins. He also wrote that some time ago there suddenly appeared the idea of making Russian the "main" language of Georgia. I'm not surprised at that; you can find almost anything today from those unforgettable days of stagnation! But go down any Moscow street and ask any passer-by you come to, "Listen, do you want Russian to become the main language of Georgia?" I don't think I have to tell you the answer. . . "Whatever language the Georgians want, let them have it."

Every year news comes from the republics that the number of national-language kindergartens and schools is falling. Language is the blood of a people, where its history and culture are imprinted genetically. However, the main point of this criminal game is presented to people as, look, those Russian scoundrels want you to change your national identity, they want to russify you. It is possible that some Russian bureaucrats are in fact guilty of this, but the main fault, in my view, must rest with the bureaucratic "national" scoundrels, who are anticipating desires "from above."

Because of historical reasons the unifying language of the Soviet Union is Russian. Armenians talk to Uzbeks, Latvians talk to Georgians in some sort of "Russian esperanto" which has a vocabulary of from one hundred to five hundred words, maximum a thousand. While Russian has more than two hundred thousand words!

I never answered my Georgian correspondent. I lacked the wisdom to answer. I could only have written one thing, that let's suppose that Georgian or Lithuanian or Uzbek became the state language, the main language, instead of Russian. My "Great

Russian pride'' would not suffer from this at all! The opposite, in fact. After struggling to learn five hundred words and the essential grammar, I would take great comfort in the thought that now my native Russian had finally became a zone of preservation and would become once again as pure as it had been in the beginning, as pure as we can suppose Armenian and Georgian are today. No longer would people encroach on the complexity of Russian, on the ancient words it contains which can't be understood by those who out of two hundred thousand words know five hundred and think that the remainder aren't necessary.

And the last thing. Like many of you, not long ago I read Vasilii Grossman's novel *Life and Fate*. I luxuriated in the tragic polyphony of sounds and colors arising from everyday events of the Battle of Stalingrad, I agreed with many of the author's philosophical mediations about what should exist in our society and what is fundamentally impermissible and criminal.

However, after rereading the prison-camp scenes I noticed that Grossman's political prisoners are primarily Jews. They are not idealized in any way, with their mistakes, delusions, and weakness. At the same time the bad criminals, who keep the barracks in fear, who kill those whom they don't like at night, are all Russian. Of course, we can understand the author; when your bones are crushed, then it seems like that pain is the only one in the world.

But there was my uncle Aleksandr Ganin, my father's second cousin, first director of the gold searches in Bodaibo, who was repressed in 1937, shot, and then fully rehabilitated in 1956.

The woman who is coming down the Vitim River to the mainland, from prison, the heroine of my story, a woman whom I had seen with my own eyes, was a Russian, imprisoned for being late to work, and who spent many years in those places. There were quite a few like her in the prisons, for "gleaning," for being late, for an anecdote, for an angry word. . . Half of Russia was dumped into the forests of those regions, worked in the ore pits, in the mines, suffered hunger, cold, degradation, and terror. In Siberia, on the Pechora River, in Kolyma, in Magadan, and in the so-called Dal'stroi.[a] . . . Among them were Jews, Ukrainians, Belorussians, Georgians, Armenians, and Uzbeks, but the majority of those imprisoned by Article 58[b] were Russians, even if only because then Russians were more numerous.

Aren't the Russian people too often and too easily accused of the sins of the Georgian Stalin, the Georgian Beria, the Jew Kaganovich, the Russian Khrushchev (who also was far from free of errors!) and Brezhnev . . . Put on them the mistakes and crimes of power! Not crimes of the people. No single people, as a whole, can be criminal.

I will not be mistaken if I say that each of us, no matter what nation he belongs to, if we have worked and lived honestly, without compromising, without damaging the soul, has to have felt the heavy hand of time upon him.

Editor's notes

   a. Dal'stroi: a ''company'' formed in the 1930s to develop the Soviet Far East, which consisted almost entirely of forced labor.
   b. An article of the criminal code used for condemning political prisoners.

Speech by Stanislav Kuniaev (Moscow)

I was alarmed not long ago to read in Valentin Rasputin's meditations these words about the present day: "Art . . . is beginning to mock what was holy for people. It has come to a state where the idea of 'motherland' or 'patriot,' 'memory,' or 'history' are increasingly interpreted in a nationalistic vein."

Rasputin was looking clearly ahead, for which he immediately paid for making that kind of pronouncement; a few days later *Izvestiia* tried to put Rasputin himself into a nationalist vein, distorting his views to make them seem as though they were influencing a few extremists in the group "Pamiat'."[a] And this was said about Rasputin, who all his life has defended not some little group, but the patriotic movement of all the people.

What labels do we hear most often now? "Chauvinism," "nationalism," "Great Power" and ":Black Hundred." . . .

They have even been dragged into the light by *Ogonek* and *Nedelia* and *Komsomol'skaia Pravda* and *Moscow News*.

In the pages of *Knizhnoe obozrenie* [Review of Books] the poet Iurii Kuznetsov was called "a Black Hundred."

To achieve their ends in the polemic, *Komsomol'skaia Pravda* and *Nedelia* descended to publishing anonymous denunciations in articles by Rassadin and Losoto, and in their selections of letters from readers.

Thank God the law has finally been adopted which obligates anonymous letters to be carefully ignored, so that now, I hope, this practice will end.

Juggling with these kinds of labels isn't new. At one time the leading Russian poet Pavel Vasil'ev was labelled as part of a group of writers, after which his fate was decided.

Does our bitter historical experience really teach these hotheads nothing?

Here's Fazil Iskander[b] publishing his poem "Ode to Fools":

> There are different kinds of fools.
> One's lyrical
> Publicly beating his chest
> Almost always patriotic
> But drinks a little too much

Here you have patriotism and stupidity tied into some kind of knot. Evtushenko publishes his poem "Russian Koalas," scolding the Russians for having built "blast-furnaces, blooming mills, and caisson dams" while being spiritual "snoozers" who kept silent during the repressions. Does our poet really not know that Magnitogorsk and the Kuzbass were largely built by former peasants who had run away from the villages because of famine and forced collectivization?

So why, if he has called himself an "internationalist" so many times, did he not write "Soviet koalas" in this instance? There's "internationalism" for you, Evtushenko-style.

We have to create a mutually respectful atmosphere for discussions, in which we can fruitfully discuss the most difficult themes.

One of the most visible writers of the West, Lion Feuchtwanger, was once asked what national strain his literature belonged to. He replied, "I am a German by language, an internationalist by conviction, and a Jew by feeling." That's the frank answer of a free man. And now let's imagine that one of our critics were to say something of the same sort. What a noise there would be! And poor Feuchtwanger would become either a "Black Hundred" or a "Zionist," however *Komsomol'skaia Pravda* thought best. No, we still have not grown up enough for real socialist pluralism!

The January *Znamia* for this year published a dialogue between G. Kh. Popov, Ph.D in economics, and Nikita Adzhubei.[c] It has many interesting observations and interpretations of history, which sometimes are sensible, but which other times demand rebuttal. The main idea is whether it isn't harmful to certain nationalities of our country to widen the work to preserve the historical memory. The co-authors caution that 1) "whoever values the memory only of his own people sooner or later will begin to justify everything in the world" and 2) "what is to be done, when the memory of one people collides with the memory of another people?"

But no matter how "uneven" the process of resurrecting historical memory, it nevertheless is a good thing, against a background of memory-loss and denationalization.

The coauthors even recall the battle on the Kalka to construct this absurd utopia: "If the Mongols had lost that battle, their horde might possibly have rolled off into the steppes and fields and memory of them would have disappeared. . . And another 'Pamiat'' could have raised a sign on the site of the battle in honor of the victory over the Russians. Is that logical? But a question arises here: how do the present residents of those regions feel about the attempt to establish such a monument?"

All of this historically false proposition reminds me of Lev Tolstoy's conversation with an English journalist who went to Tolstoy to ask, "Look, you preach nonresistance to evil, but imagine if you go into a forest and a tiger attacks you, wouldn't you resist?" Tolstoy threw up his hands, "Mercy, old man, where are you going to get tigers in Iasnaia Poliana?"[d] There is an obelisk on the Poltava battlefield from Peter's time, a tribute to the bravery of Carl II's troops, and in 1812 the French raised a monument to their fallen in Borodino. And the residents of Poltavshchina and Borodino regard that as normal. So when *Znamia* poses the dilemma of immortalizing the historical signs of Russia's path into Siberia or the monuments of the native peoples living there, there is but one answer, both the one and the other must be immortalized, and build our history on this fundament of mutual respect.

Such dialogues as that in *Znamia*, which seem to be oriented in advance to the worst side of things, talk about some form of threat, most often in the figure of Russian chauvinism. But I recently read the polemics on this theme very careful and nowhere was there a single fact indicating that the Russian patriotic movement has as its goal a struggle with the historical memory of the Ukrainian, Tatar, Armenian or other destructive forces of denationalized greyness.

The *Znamia* authors exclaim, ''But then every people should create its own 'Pamiat'' society.'' That is, if we permit it to the Russians, then others will want it too! But what harm is there in relying on trust, wisdom, and *glasnost'*, on the constructive forces of national and spiritual life?

Not long ago in Gor'kii I saw a memorial tablet which said that here ''lived the great revolutionary people's poet, T. G. Shevchenko.'' Everything there, except the one word ''Ukrainian.'' This wasn't the fault of Russians, but of the power-holding stratum there who don't even want to give back to their own native town its ancient and glorious name of Nizhnii Novgorod.

Aleksandr Blok once wrote a profound poem in which after enumerating all the sins of the Russian national character, he nevertheless suddenly ended with the words, ''Yes, and as such, my Russia, you are dearest to me of all lands.'' Note, not ''best of all lands,'' but ''dearest.'' . . . It isn't done to say of a mother that she is better or more beautiful than other mothers. She is the dearest of all.

It was precisely that feeling that Gilevich's words here breathed, and Iakubov's, Mushketik's, and Ovanesian's.

Only by unifying the uplifting powers of every national cultural movement may we save the unique historical and natural floodlands of Chernigova and the famous Georgian grapevine and the Aral Sea. To save them from the national-nihilistic class which seems to be a government within the government. Thus we shall unite all the rising currents of our national forces into one channel, in the name of the future.

Editor's notes

a. *Pamiat'* (''Memory''): an organization of militant Russian nationalists which became very active politically in the 1980s.
b. Fazil Iskander: the noted writer from Abkhazia.
c. Nikita Adzhubei: presumably Nikita Khrushchev's grandson.
d. Iasnaia Poliana: Leo Tolstoy's estate, located near the city of Tula.

Speech by Rachii Ovanesian (Armenia)

As far as I remember, this is the first time the directorate of the Union of Writers of the USSR has convened with an agenda of this sort.

It seems to me that the happiest period of friendship among our peoples was the cruel years of the Great Fatherland War. In those years, when the question of the Motherland's life or death was being decided, our peoples showed how quickly they could master Russian, or to be more precise, the language of destroying the enemy, they showed how correctly and succesfully they found the paths of brotherhood and how equal they were. The danger threatening the Soviet Union made them a real, large, and united family. But when we say ''Soviet people'' we almost always forget that the adjective ''Soviet'' has more a political character than a national one. The multicolored bouquet of Soviet peoples may not be painted with one color, for there are no Soviet people. There are Soviet Russians and Soviet Uzbeks and Soviet Moldavians. There is no Soviet language, but there is Armenian and Tadzhik and

Georgian. There is no Soviet republic, but there is a Soviet Ukraine and a Soviet Latvia and a Soviet Kazakhstan. And when we say Soviet man or Soviet people we are characterizing their citizenship and political orientation. However, each of the Soviet peoples has its own history and culture and language and character and a significantly unique tradition.

Belonging to the various nationalities absolutely does not interfere with the biography and fate of a Soviet man. Spared from the tsarist satrapy by Lenin's will, the peoples rejoiced, proud that as Armenians and Georgians and Belorussians and Ukrainians they had gained freedom and become sons in a multinational family. However, not too many years after the revolution this natural feeling of love for one's own nation, that is for its language, history, geographical location, and historical biography, began to be regarded suspiciously and cautiously. I well remember the terminology of ideological and political accusations that developed in the 1930s. Where the forces of the intelligentsia and state and political figures in the center were accused of left or right deviations, in the national republics the most common accusation was the black spot of being accused of nationalism.

Take Armenia, just as an example, where all those repressed were accused of just that. Even illiterate peasants. Leaping over the four war years, the accusation of nationalism again appeared in the postwar years.

If you are in a gloomy mood, that means you're a nationalist. If you talk about preserving the water in Lake Sevan, that means you're a nationalist. If you introduce a motion to create a national circus troupe, you're a nationalist. If you sent your child to an Armenian school, that means you are already close to politically unreliable. I beg you to believe me when I say that even Maxim Gorky was accused of Armenian nationalism, accused in our Armenian press only because in the essay published in *Our Achievements* [Nashi dostizheniia] he mentioned the cruel oppression of the Armenian people by Ottoman Turkey.

Now our Soviet leadership and our intelligentsia are concerned about the cleansing and saving not only the ecology of the natural environment, but also the moral and political ecology of the recent past. Having endured bitter, irreplaceable losses, we are happy today that the Phoenix bird of justice has once again sprung from the ashes, no more to burn its wings in the flames of lies and falsehood.

In this epochal movement of the economic, social, scientific, technical, and ideological restructuring of our country a new approach and new understanding of the development of national culture is of grandiose significance. I should like to exchange a few thoughts with you in this regard. The February 1988 Plenum of the CPSU Central Committee considered the very important question of secondary and higher education, which is the underlying basis of the succesful progress of society. This is one of the most important programs of our time. My first thought has to do with the national-language secondary school and the hours allotted to teaching the social disciplines—language, art, literature, native history, and native geography. The student of the national-language secondary school is obligated to master two languages, his native one and Russian. However, he is also obligated to know a foreign language, and in the autonomous republics and regions he will also have to know the language of that region or republic. Very few hours are allotted for the study of these four languages, and they are not distributed in a logical order. This is also true of the hours allotted to the hours for literature.

(The speaker then discussed the necessity of improving the teaching of native history in the schools.)

Making the central Ministry of Enlightenment into a union-republic ministry has some drawbacks. Of course the general level of the modern technical and precise sciences must be guaranteed in all schools of the country, but for certain subjects in the humanities, in my opinion, it is necessary to take acount of the national character of the school.

A true writer is a banner-carrier of internationalism, and true literature is a banner of internationalism.

Such is the essence of real literature in all times. For more than two centuries already, the Armenian people, through the lips of its famed sons, has preached fraternal love for all its neighbors and for distant peoples. I would say that the spirit of internationalism, along with the chord of patriotism, has sounded at all stages in the history of our literature.

Both this plenum of writers and all the facts of the recent past in the sphere of national culture, national and state construction, just and unjust things in the past understanding of national relations provide abundant material for the preparation of the upcoming Plenum of the Central Committee of the CPSU. We are obligated to our party, and to General Secretary comrade M. S. Gorbachev, who in the global complex of international and internal affairs is working so tirelessly, honestly, and courageously on the problems of nations and national relations, which so evoke and adorn the great idea and content of real socialism.

Speech by Ianis Peters (Latvia)

The national factor today must be not a weak stimulus, but a strong one for the process of democratization, *glasnost'*, and restructuring. The enemies of restructuring are already trying to present the growth of national self-consciousness by the peoples of our country as a wave of nationalism, and in their analyses they are dangerously close to our enemies, who hasten to ascribe wordy labels to this phenomenon, taken from the terminology of the sad past.

According to the 1979 census, 53.7 percent of the population in the Latvian SSR belonged to the native nationality. It must be admitted that because of forced migration the demographic and ecological balance of the republic was violated, which in turn affected the psychology of the Latvian population, evoking an active movement to defend the national language, national culture, and ecological environment. Of course it is not at all difficult here to make use of an impermissible forced device and so present this tendency of self-preservation as nationalism.

I categorically reject this criminal act.

Or maybe there are forces which have an interest in seeing the word "Russian" compromised in the eyes of the people? And maybe these forces were born in the same epoch as Stalinism? And if this is true, then this must be discussed out loud, as was done by G. Popov, doctor of economics, in his conversation with N. Adzhubei, published in the first issue of *Znamia* for this year [1988].

Today we must take account of the social erosion caused by extensive management, with its characteristic irresponsible attitude to personal fates. As a result of "enticements" people were torn from their historical roots by, the exhausting collectivization of the non–black-earth belt, ending up in the Baltic area, where other traditions had been developed for centuries.

In order not to be understood negatively, I want to stress that I include in the basic population of the Baltic area people of all nationalities who respect the culture and language of Latvia, Lithuania, and Estonia. Not even knowledge of the language is necessarily the defining factor; the most important thing is observation of the traditions, the way of life, the knowledge of the history and fate of any people. It must be confessed that for the time being bilingualism is successfully developing in Latvia only among the native population, while many residents of other nationalities remain monolingual.

However, no one should be singled out for criticism here. At one time people were told, help us to develop our economy, we welcome you to our republic. And people responded. But what were immigrants to the republics offered, in our republic, let's say? What spiritual riches? Apartments? Yes, but that's about it. Although that's not such a little thing, often even significantly more than the native inhabitants got. But after all people were asked to help, they were torn from their environments and what were they given in return? Shouldn't the administration of the republic have had the full responsibility to provide the new arrivals with the opportunity to study, for example, Latvian, Estonian, or Kirghiz, to learn the history of the country's culture, the country which had become home not only for the immigrant, but also for his children?

On the initiative of the Writers' Union of Latvia, the Latvian State University has organized the Soviet Union's first group of students from all the union republics who are studying Latvian in Riga. These young people have not yet distinguished themselves in any way, yet they have already been filmed for a newsreel, have been on television and written about in newspapers. This speaks of society's attempts to have a nationality policy of a new quality. Unfortunately we have come to all this only now, and again at a high price. We have woken up and are asking, how could it happen that it is precisely because of the national factor that restructuring is suffering a heavy test?

It must be admitted that we often judged the state of internationalism solely according to "concerts," where the brightly dressed sons and daughters of all the union republics danced and sang. The life of the people though, as is known, is not a concert and not a meeting of the translators' section of the Writers' Union.

Today we are living in a new time. A new time means too renewed relationships not only in the economy in internal and external politics, but also in ideology, as well as in questions of the autonomy of the republics in the spheres of culture and education.

(The speaker emphasized the importance of the young knowing history, the Leninist

positions of our national policy, which is precisely where the real and the socialist lie).

After the revolution in Soviet Russia there were more than 200,000 Latvians, and at the Thirteenth Party Congress seven percent of the delegates were Latvians. In 1923 there were 130 Latvian libraries and reading rooms in the Soviet Union, 150 schools, 200 clubs, and later the Petr Stuchka Central Latvian Club was founded, with 12,000 members, and there was a Latvian pedagogic technicum. In the minorities divisions of Leningrad State University and the Herzen Institute there were Latvian faculties. The Latvian enlightenment society "Prometheus" might also be mentioned, which had a publishing house, a printing plant, and a bookstore. There were several Latvian newspapers and journals in the Soviet Union. What am I trying to say with all this? Only that we have a large common history, which cannot be buried along with the lawlessness of the personality cult. This history has to be remembered, in order to convince youth that there is no other path for us but a return to the Leninist tradition, creatively united with the present moment.

In the restructuring of national relations the bureaucracy will, of course, take a temporizing position. However, isn't the bureaucracy to blame for the appearance of today's situation? Bureaucracies of all times have a great deal in common. Please permit me to end my speech with a characteristic example.

The great Latvian poet Rainis for a time in the 1920s had the post of Minister of Education in the administration of the Latvian bourgeois government. Then he actively supported the creation of schools for the national minorities and defended the Belorussians living in Latvia against denationalization. And, can you imagine it, the opponents of Rainis's humane idea said that "Belorussian nationalism in Latvia" had been invented by the poet himself. It seems that to the bureaucrats of the day the Belorussians of Latvia were just a fantasy of the poet, that there was no such people. But isn't the fantasy of a poet sometimes much more true than reality, than the version the bureaucrat insists upon, which even though it doesn't correspond to reality, is nevertheless beneficial to the bureaucracy itself?

Speech by Mukhtar Shakhanov (Kazakhstan)

The story is told how many years ago one of the leaders of our republic passed through Chimkent. Kazakhstan was suffering a hard time then. Hunger had taken a great many people from this life. People surrounded his railroad car and waited patiently. Finally he came to the door of the car. Those gathered there, interrupting each other, told him what was bothering them. The highly placed guest kept a significant silence and, raising his hand majestically, he waited until there was complete silence. Slicing the air three times with his hand, he said repeatedly "The plan! The plan! The plan!"—and slammed the door.

This kind of bureaucratic dictum for the economy, at the expense of morality, has come down even to our day and has led to the impoverishment of peoples' spiritual world, has damaged the feeling of internationalism. Now as never before we feel the sharp need for international unity as the fundamental basis of relations between peoples and between nations. And so it is absolutely necessary to speak about everything in our lives, particularly about history.

In connection with this I wish to say that the work of such of our writers as Shakarim, Magzhan Zhumabaev, Akhmet Baitursunov, Zhusupbek Aimautov,[a] and others still awaits objective critical evaluation. But why speak of them when we still have not established a true idea of the work of our contemporary Olzhas Suleimenov?! His book *AZ and I* [Az i Ia] came out in 1975, and was met by sharp criticism. Why is it, now when other works that were once forbidden are coming out, that *AZ and I* can't be republished? I don't say that there aren't omissions in the book, and a polemical choice of materials. But after all the author put a great deal that was new into the book, and took account of the criticism. To forbid it solely with a careerist-bureaucratic flourish of the pen could cause serious harm to the international connections of literature in our multinational Motherland.

For long years we used nature irresponsibly and soullessly, and now nature has begun to avenge itself upon people. As proof we can point to the fate of Lake Baikal, Lake Ladoga, Lake Sevan, Lake Balkash, the Aral Sea.

We aren't sitting with our arms folded. The Committee on Problems in the Aral and Balkash of the Writers' Union of Kazakhstan is doing a lot of work, and proposes different variants of getting out of the situation which has come about. There is the same kind of committee in Uzbekistan as well. For the time being however, society is powerless. The time has long since come to create a state commission under the leadership of the Central Committee of the CPSU, which would contain representatives of society, journalists, and scientists, the best minds and specialists in the country.

A year ago I was able to speak at the Komsomol congress of Kazakhstan, about how the revolutionary holidays are conducted. When I look at the identical columns, I would like to see people holding portraits of Chernyshevskii, Hertzen, Pushkin, Shevchenko, Abai, Toktogul, the heroes of the Paris Commune, portraits of the ardent revolutionaries of our epoch, Dzerzhinsky, Lunacharsky, Frunze, Furmanov, Mayakovsky, Khamza Khakimzade, Ryskulov, Ordzhonikidze, Shaumian . . . after all, there were no small number of those for whom life itself was the revolution! And the roots of our friendship, of our unity, are in the revolution.

I should like to end my speech with these lines,[b] in which my hero, an old man, says:

In Kzylkum from ancient days to now
Camel thorns grow And tumbleweeds too
And so
The thorn roots, stretching for the water
Go down forty meters and more . . .
When the windstorms come
And the clouds drive the sand
The rootless tumbleweed
Dashes before the wind
Rolls here and there about the steppe

While the camel thorn
As though nothing has happened
Is always in its customary place!
Such is the power of roots.
And a person from his earliest years
Is in a bad way if he has no roots.
Everyone
Must have
Besides parents
Four roots, like four mothers:
a motherland,
a mother tongue,
a mother culture,
a mother history . . .
And all of them
In the single face
Of one's own mother.
When you love your roots
And value them,
You understand the pain and love
Of everything and everyone,
You get the same feeling for
another land,
another tongue,
another culture,
another history . . .

Editor's notes

a. Kazakh poets labeled as nationalists in the 1920s. Some of the works of Shakarim are now being reprinted.

b. The poem does not rhyme or scan in Russian.

Speech by Georgii Tsitsishvili (Georgia)

I would be insincere if I did not say that [Writer's Union First Secretary] V. Karpov's report, where he talks about the fraternal literatures, caused me a certain dissatisfaction. The report had almost no generalizing conclusions and the characteristic tendencies of the national literatures today were not characterized. It seems to me that when reports of this nature are prepared, the secretariat of the directorate of the Union of Writers should do more consultation with the republic unions. Georgian literature suffered in the report, and as for Abkhaz and Ossetian literature, they were not even mentioned.

It must be said that our plenum is proceeding on a high level, that it is without doubt a success.

I do not intend to fill in some blank spots. I want to touch on just one side of the most important problems of modernity, the problem of inter-nationality relations.

I think that it would be self-deception to consider the national question to be already decided. We have decided it methodologically, we have found a path to a modern and promising solution, and have put the basic principles of its solution into life in a practical way. On this path we have achieved unquestioned successes in liquidating national inequality, in creating the conditions for the universal development of all peoples. But this doesn't exhaust the national question, since national relations receive, which means that they demand constant care and continual improvement. For that reason we were pleased to get the news that a special plenum of the Central Committee of the CPSU will be devoted to this issue. The most obvious harm that can be done to the mutual understanding and unity of the Soviet peoples will come from the voluntaristic actions, without economic or social sense, of a few people, those whom comrade Gorbachev has called "paid functionaries," some administrators of the huge enterprises and central departments, who often ignore the desires and needs of the union republics and regions of the country. After all, the fate of some important government business in some republic or other, in a region or an oblast, often depends upon the single penstroke of a functionary in a central office.

For more than two decades the leadership and society of Georgia have spoken out against the planned quota for tea leaves, demonstrating that the maximum we can harvest in a year is only 300 to 350 thousand tons of tea (when the planned quota is for 600–650 thousand tons), but without success. This has told miserably on the quality of the once-famed Georgian tea. In November of last year they finally lowered our quota, but during the long litigation Georgian tea lost its former reputation.

Or another example. The republic leadership even today cannot convince Gosplan SSR that it is impossible to develop livestock breeding in regions of intensive tea and citrus production.

For more than thirty years the republic has been unable to reverse the wastefulness of the all-union departments and convince them that central Georgia should not be planted with sugar beets, but rather with fruit production, since the conditions for it are there.

I have cited these examples in order to support comrade Gorbachev's thesis about how the rights of the republics must be strengthened, including in representation in the central government organs, and that it is vital to overcome the domination of paid functionaries, organizationalism, and bureaucratism by giving part of the central organs' power to those beneath them, in order to free the lower organs from the necessity of checking their every step with the bureaucracy above them. It must be admitted that this is the most acute question of national and governmental construction.

Mutual understanding among nationalities is also seriously endangered by the one-sided, tendentious speeches of certain central press organs. A painful number of volunteer journalists have appeared who go from Moscow to all ends of the country to seek out so-called "necessary materials." These correspondents don't overburden themselves by trying to clarify the ethnic composition of the people about whom they are writing. How many times have we had to read articles and sketches in which indigenous Georgians—Svans, Adzhars, Mingrelians[b]—were discussed as though they were representatives of some nonexistent nation.

I will not hide that some publications in *Sovetskaia kul'tura, Trud, Moscow News, Komsomol'skaia Pravda,* and *Ogonek* caused sharp unhappiness in the broad populace because of their incompetence and tendentious quality. On the other hand, under the protection of *glasnost'* and democratization, local demagogues have also raised their heads. They are trying wholly to deceive public opinion, sending letters everywhere, accusing their fellow countrymen of all possible sins, beginning with nationalism and anti-Party attitudes. Among them, unfortunately, there are also writers. The Georgian Union of Writers has decided to speak sternly with such people, and has already taken measures in this direction.

Our propaganda in the area of the national question is impermissibly out of date, and still has not freed itself from blather, sloganeering, and empty phraseology. When things were especially bad for us, our propaganda then reminded us of the shining heights of communism. The constant stress on the future devalued the present.

What must be stressed is not the distant future, but the present. The life of our people can become wholly trouble-free and truly happy in the very near future, if we fulfill the intentions connected with revolutionary transformations.

Editor's note

a. Svans, Adzhars, and Mingrelians: ethnic communities that are related to and are largely being absorbed by the Georgians.

Speech by Boris Ukachin (Gorno-Altai AO)

The growth and development of any national culture depends a great deal upon the leadership of the local Party and government organs, such as, let's say, the first secretary of the Party obkom. In the 1960s the first secretary of the Gorno-Altai Party obkom was Nikolai Semenovich Lazebnii. It was his idea that almost caused them to close the only national-language secondary school we have in the oblast, the forge which has shaped the greater part of cadres in the autonomous areas. In proving the enormous role of this school in preparing such specialists as agronomists, engineers, doctors, and teachers, we will talk about contemporary Altai literature. After all, almost all today's best-known and actively working prose writers and poets of the Gorno-Altai are graduates of this national-language secondary school.

The Gorno-Altai Autonomous Oblast was formed in June 1922. In those distant and difficult days we had several oblast newspapers; (not just one, like now), appearing in Altai and in Russian. There was a national publisher on the budget of the then oblispolkom [executive committee of the regional soviet], publishing textbooks, widely translating fiction and poetry by Russian and Soviet classic writers, the books and articles of Marx and Lenin, and first books of local authors. Yet at that time the entire Gorno-Altai had not a single member in the Writers' Union of the USSR, nor in the Journalists' Union or Artists' Union.

Even in the most difficult years of the entire country, during the Great Fatherland War, we in the autonomous oblast had our own publishing house. Today we do not. Our publishing house has now become a division of the Altai regional book publishers. If you can imagine it, for fiction we are allotted only four titles for twenty-three members of the Union of Writers. Let's look at this from the viewpoint of the Leninist nationality policy of our government. The ''Altai'' book publishing house does not publish a single textbook for the national-language schools and is reluctant to accept books translated from Altai into Russian. Our writers primarily publish translations of their works in Moscow.

I ask the secretariat of the directorate of the Writers' Union of the USSR and the RSFSR to, first of all, assist us in establishing independent publishing houses in all the autonomous oblasts of the RSFSR. If such houses are reestablished, then it is vital that these publishers must have Russian editors too. When the regional publishers were closed the Russian writers who lived and who live in our provinces also suffered.

For more than twenty years the Gorno-Altai writers' organization has agitated for the creation of an almanac, to come out once every other month, with a total volume of sixty folios (1920 pages).

We ask for help in publishing a children's journal in Altai, such as *Murzilka*. We consider it abnormal to deprive children of the possibility of reading books in their native language. Children whose parents work in the far-flung livestock-breeding areas of present-day Gorno-Altai are deprived of the elementary benefits and basic comforts of life. They live and study in the most difficult possible conditions of a nomadic or seminomadic lifestyle. They have neither radio nor television.

I understand that this will mean a loss for our national publishers. But I wish to pose one more extremely important question: in speaking of economic viability and self-financing are we going to smother the languages of our lesser and greater peoples, their unique and ancient cultures?

In finishing my speech, I would like to say, dear friends, let us not forget the wise words of Aleksei Maksimovich Gor'kii, that the quantity of a people does not affect the quality of its talents. How many wonderful talents the numerically smaller peoples and national groups of our truly multinational country have given to Soviet literature!

8. Religion and National Culture

Since the time it took power, the Communist Party of the Soviet Union has pursued policies designed to curtail the power of religious authorities and the influence of religion on the population. Atheism has always been a part of the Party's ideology. Following Marx, the Party avows materialist explanations of phenomena and argues that religious hierarchies use their claims concerning the hereafter to retard social progress and preserve the power of the dominant economic forces here on earth. Accordingly, one of the goals of Soviet "internationalist" education is to inculcate an atheistic world view in young people; antireligious propaganda is used to build upon this training.

Officially church and state are separate in the Soviet Union. However, only religious organizations that are sanctioned by Moscow are permitted to operate, and even they may not open churches, train clerics, or print religious materials without permission from a state board of overseers. The rights of religious believers were separately provided for and allegedly protected in the current and previous constitutions. These rights include rights of worship (for adherents of recognized faiths) in licensed religious facilities, but not the right to propagate their faith.

New legislation on "freedom of conscience" has been promised which will increase the discretionary authority of officially recognized religious establishments to train clergy and open new houses of worship and also better protect the civil rights of religious believers. However, the Soviet leadership is not disavowing the idea that relations between church and state are to be governed by Leninist principles; what they are doing is simply instituting a new interpretation of Lenin's writings on this topic. Indeed, in the most recent Soviet writings on religion it is suggested that the current Gorbachev policies regarding religion are truly Leninist, while those of Gorbachev's predecessors were not. But in fact, the policies that have been applied to believers and to both state-licensed and unofficial religious organizations have varied greatly over time and from faith to faith.

Immediately after the Bolshevik takeover, all ecclesiastically held properties were nationalized, religious institutions were forcibly closed, and clerics were harassed and arrested. In the early 1920s, as a part of a broader policy to gain popular support for the regime, a more tolerant policy was briefly pursued. But in the late 1920s religious officials were again attacked and arrested, churches and mosques were seized and oftentimes destroyed, and religious education was banned. The antireligious campaign heightened in intensity throughout the 1930s, but was halted during World War II when the Party tried to mobilize religious and national loyalties in support of the war effort. Shortly after the war official religious organizations were again subjected to much stricter supervision, and a large-scale antireligious campaign was launched in the newly annexed territories (the Baltic region, the Western Ukraine, Moldavia, and part of Belorussia).

This campaign was moderated somewhat under Khrushchev. During the Brezhnev years antireligious propaganda became increasingly ineffective. Those charged with designing and implementing ideological education seemed to be more concerned with symbolic exhortations than with actually seeing that policies were being successfully implemented. The articles below by Biskup and Nosovich are good examples of the types of antireligious propaganda characteristic of the Brezhnev period. One is a scurrilous attack on a church that has no legal recognition; and the other a "scientific" attack on religion in general.

"The Radio Mouthpiece of the Uniate Clergy" by Biskup is intended to discredit the Ukrainian-language broadcasts of the Vatican Radio and to condemn the activities of Ukrainian Uniates more generally. The Ukrainian Catholic (Uniate) Church was banned in 1946, following the arrest of virtually all its prominent clerics on charges of treason for having supported the anti-Soviet resistance movement in the western Ukraine during the war. According to official Soviet accounts, in 1946 the newly appointed clerical leaders voluntarily agreed to join with the rival Ukrainian Orthodox Church, dominant in the eastern Ukraine, an Eastern rite church under the jurisdiction of the Moscow Patriarch. The Biskup article both misrepresents the history of the postwar period and tries to explain the continued identification of western Ukrainians with the Uniate church solely as a result of foreign machinations. The author reduces the western Ukrainians' ties to the Catholic church to nothing more than anti-Soviet nationalist sentiment, wholly discounting the long religious history of the region.

This article is typical of many that have appeared in publications designed to reach Ukrainian and Lithuanian audiences over the past decade, when the activities of the Vatican have been of particular concern for Soviet antireligious propagandists. Polish-born Pope John Paul II has been far more attentive to the needs of Catholics living in the USSR and in Eastern Europe than were his predecessors; at the same time, his background has increased the influence of the Papacy in these areas. Likewise, throughout the 1980s virulent attacks have been made against other unrecognized churches, particularly Protestant evangelical churches. These attacks have also tended to focus on Western "infiltration" of seditious religious ideas and materials across the air waves and borders of the Soviet Union. Moreover, the attack on the Uniate church has continued almost unabated, with Moscow's support, at the very time that most religious communities in the USSR are being permitted to play a new role in public life.

The Nosovich article "Culture and Religion" is an example of the more passive side of antireligious propaganda. It is designed to clarify Soviet policy toward religion for a Soviet audience (in this case the Russian-language reader in Estonia), who it is assumed has been misled about policies in this area by Western propaganda and by those who still hold "bourgeois world views." Nosovich depicts Soviet leaders as sympathetic to the need for a spiritual culture and as interested in preserving the physical representations of the spiritual culture of the past. But he then goes on to try and "scientifically" demonstrate that because of its covertly antiegalitarian political and economic agendas, religion is not a source of a true national culture, or even the basis of a genuinely supportive spiritual culture. His main argument is a standard one in Soviet antireligious literature: no great religion (Christianity, Islam,

Buddhism)* can be the basis of a national culture because its ideology is internationalist and its practices subsume or warp popular national traditions. He depicts Christianity as a force that hindered culture and enlightenment rather than encouraged it. Nosovich maintains that the Church monopolized talented artisans, writers, and educators and forcibly directed their talents in a particular direction, artificially restricting art and hindering the development of science. Communism, according to Nosovich, is the liberator of these talents.

The current Party leadership has tried to distance itself from the types of antireligious propaganda that were characteristic of the Brezhnev period, considering them generally ineffective because they do not engage the cultural realities of Soviet life. Propagandists are now being urged to accept the fact that religion and culture have been fused through time, and that even nonbelievers have respect for the religious traditions of their ancestors. Thus, combatting the influence of religion requires better knowledge about the prevalence of religious practice and the fusion of religion and culture. This task is assigned to Soviet antireligious propagandists (whose ranks include sociologists of religion as well as party ideologues), and to Soviet scholars of related specialties, such as historians, ethnographers, and orientalists.

Soviet ethnographers have long studied the religious practices of the various Soviet peoples, and their research builds on the legacy of prerevolutionary Russian ethnography as well as research from the Soviet period. G. Snesarev, a contributing scholar for over fifty years, is one of the foremost ethnographers studying Islam. His thesis is that mass religious practices help create cultural continuity. He argues that pre-Islamic practices survived the conversion to Islam, albeit in altered form, and that this transformed faith has continued to be transmitted, again with alteration, even after decades of Soviet antireligious propaganda. Snesarev's thesis as to the tenacity of Islam led to his scholarly disgrace in the late 1930s, and his works went unpublished for nearly twenty years. His research was considered controversial through the early 1970s. But in the late 1970s and early 1980s his conclusions were no longer viewed as threatening, because he emphasized that the doctrinal side of Islam, the formal teachings about the faith, were dying out, and that even Islamic rituals were becoming more and more attenuated from generation to generation.

However, in the late 1970s and early 1980s data from the major Muslim regions of the USSR (from Central Asia and Azerbaidzhan in particular) were increasingly at odds with the conclusions of Snesarev and most other Soviet ethnographers. As glasnost' encouraged the more accurate reporting of social practices throughout the country, it became clear that the practice of Islamic rituals, particularly those marking birth and death, was virtually universal. Moreover, as was true in Muslim areas worldwide, people born in the post–World War II period were showing a marked interest in learning about and practicing their faith.

Soviet scholars and other observers had mixed reactions to reports of these developments. Some, like Igor Beliaev, a prominent Soviet journalist who specializes in covering the Muslim world, expressed great concern over the course of the

---

*As we will see in the next section, Judaism poses a special problem for the Soviet authorities because Jews are considered a nationality, and retain that status even if they do not practice their faith.

revival of Islam which he witnessed in the USSR. His two-part article "Islam and Politics" is representative of a strain in Soviet thinking that views Islam as a critical countercultural force which impedes social and economic development and poses the potential for political unrest in the Muslim regions of the USSR.

While there is lots of evidence that Islam has grown in popularity in the Soviet Union in recent years, there is almost no concrete evidence as to how widespread this religious revival is. While Beliaev attacks Western scholars who claim that everyone of Muslim background must be considered as having some sort of active identification with the faith, Beliaev offers no concrete data on how to define a Muslim or on the numbers of believers in the USSR. All he says is that the number of practitioners of Islamic rituals is growing, and the study of Islamic doctrine is spreading as well. This information is confirmed by a number of other sources, as is Beliaev's argument that this religious revival has the tacit support of the local and republic communist parties in the Muslim regions. The disagreement among Soviet experts is as to what sort of threat this poses. Beliaev implies that Islam is potentially a seditious ideology, one that falsely fuses religion with nationalism and thus undermines internationalist ideals. However, many who are knowledgeable about Soviet Islam, particularly those such as Talib Saidbaev who are themselves of Muslim background, do not accept Beliaev's conclusions as to the dangers the revival of Islam poses. In his rejoinder to Beliaev's article Saidbaev argues that while religion and nationalism are strongly intertwined in the Muslim areas, this need not undermine Moscow's economic or social goals for these regions. Islam, Saidbaev maintains, does not have a predetermined social structure; the Islamic heritage of many Soviet nationalities need not retard their economic and political integration.

Those who share Saidbaev's views maintain that while traditional culture in Muslim areas hinders economic and social development, this culture is based on a whole complex of values and will not be transformed simply by attacking religion. In fact, many scholars privately argue that the local communist parties' tacit toleration of the perpetuation of Islamic practices probably increased popular acceptance of Moscow's economic and political policies, as local officials were able to present the CPSU as sharing the values of the community and not being hostile to them.

Party ideologists who have come to prominence under Gorbachev do not seem to accept such arguments. In the last few years Islam has been identified as a major cause of the retardation of economic and social development in the Muslim regions, and the toleration of religious practice by local Party officials is taken to be yet another sign of their corrupt behavior. To date, while there has been pressure to end the clandestine teaching of Islam in the universities, no major crackdown on Islamic religious practice has been conducted. If Moscow were to decide to translate its rhetoric into just such a policy, it would risk provoking a major confrontation with its Muslim populations.

The antireligious policy being pursued by Gorbachev and his followers does not treat all religions uniformly. The prevalence of Islam is viewed as troublesome insofar as it undermines the regime's reform program. On the other hand, Gorbachev has permitted a beneficent attitude to be shown toward religion when this seems to be in the interests of advancing his political goals. Thus, at the time of the riots in the Nagorno Karabakh, prominent Armenian religious leaders were encouraged to speak out and try and calm the population. Similarly, the republic Party organizations in the Baltic region have been displaying a more moderate attitude toward religion. The elevation of the first Lithuanian cardinal in over three hundred years was treated officially as an occasion for national pride. Catholic officials are permitted to appear at public events, as encouragement to Lithuanians to accept Gorbachev's policies as broad enough to meet their national and cultural aspirations. Party officials in Estonia and Latvia are also trying to make common front with religious officials to advance the goals of the Gorbachev reform program.

The biggest change in attitude toward religion has been with regard to the Russian Orthodox Church. Russian nationalists both inside and outside the Party had long been pressuring for the Russian Orthodox church to be given a more respected official position. They have looked to Gorbachev to advance their interests, and he in return has sought their support for his reform program.

The thousandth anniversary of the baptism of Russia provided an occasion for an official reevalution of the role of the church in the development of Russian culture. The tone of the public celebration of this event and the descriptive materials published about it portray Russian Orthodoxy in more positive terms than at any time since World War II. The discussion of religion in the interview with Dmitri Likhachev, the leading Soviet authority on medieval Russian history, raises the prospect that in the near future the Russian Orthodox Church may come to play a far more active role in official Soviet life than it has previously.

In sharp contradiction to official Soviet antireligious propaganda like that written by Nosovich, Likhachev boldly states that Christianity provided the spiritual strength which led to Muscovy's greatness, and that Russian Orthodoxy is an integral part of the Russian cultural heritage. Christianity is credited with being a force of cultural enlightenment, a creator of beauty and a source of encouragement in the development of natural science. Likhachev implies that Marx falsely condemned religion because of the negative social role played by religion during Marx's lifetime, but he claims that religion need not always be a retrograde social force. Likhachev admits that the Russian Orthodox Church played a negative role historically in Russia because it chose to unite with the Romanov monarchy at the beginning of the nineteenth century, but he maintains that Russian Orthodoxy can play a positive role in fostering spiritual life in the Soviet Union if the proper separation of church and state is maintained. Christianity, he argues, diminishes national insularity and encourages the spread of internationalist values. Thus Likhachev seems to be setting the stage for a formal rapprochement between the Party and the Russian Orthodox Church.

Gorbachev appears to be pursuing a risky strategy with regard to religion, showing greater tolerance toward some of the national churches of the USSR when this seems likely to increase support for his overall reform strategy, but showing less tolerance toward those faiths whose practices he regards as unsuited to his reform program. The danger of this strategy is that it may increase feelings of differential treatment and contribute to the growing sense of popular unrest, particularly in the Muslim republics.

The Radio Mouthpiece of the Uniate Clergy *

A. BISKUP

In their attacks on real socialism and on the communist scientific-materialist world view, bourgeois ideologues make extensive use of religion and the Church, with whose help they seek to instill in the masses illusory notions of the perpetuity and inviolability of the capitalist system, and to inculcate anticommunist views in them.

The Vatican, the world center of Catholicism, occupies a special place among those religious organizations of the West that march under the banner of clerical anticommunism. For many years now the Vatican has flowed with the mainstream of anticommunism, fully supporting the reactionary circles of the clerical emigration, including the so-called Ukrainian Catholic Church (UCC),ᵃ an ecclesiastical-political grouping created by those reactionary clergy of the Uniate Church—which had self-dissolved in the Ukraine—who emigrated to the West. The pretentious self-assumed deisgnation of "the Ukrainian Catholic Church" has no connection with reality, either in terms of church administration (the UCC has not a single parish in the Ukraine) or canonically (the Uniate, Greek Catholic Church of the Ukrainians is officially called the Eastern Catholic Church of the Slavic-Byzantine Rite).

After World War II the Vatican, in concert with imperialist reactionaries, under-took urgent measures to save the remnants of the Uniate Church and to bolster its position abroad. In an atmosphere of frenzied anticommunist and "cold war" propaganda, numerous ultra-right-wing organizations and associations appeared on the political arena of capitalist countries, among them the émigré organizations of Ukrainian bourgeois nationalism and the Uniate Church.

The traditional anticommunist stance of the Uniate Church abroad opened its ideologues a path to the mass media of the West, allowing the Uniate clericals to take a quite active part in the ideological diversions of imperialism. Of late one may observe attempts to bolster the influence of Uniate clerical propaganda not only on a substantial part of the Ukrainian working emigration, but also within our country. Various channels are used for this purpose: postal communications, international tourism, cultural cooperation,etc.

Vatican radio broadcasts occupy an important place in ideological diversion against socialist countries, especially its "Ukrainian Division," whose programs are edited by the ideologues of the Uniate Church abroad, mainly the Uniate Basilian Order, and currently broadcast fourteen times per week.

The Roman Curia attaches great importance to radio propaganda, as evidenced by the fact that the programs of the Vatican radio are broadcast in thirty-three

---

Zhovten', 1982, no. 11, pp. 81–84. Ukrainian text © 1982 Zhovten'.

languages, including sixteen languages of the peoples of socialist countries. The Vatican today has one of the most powerful radio transmitters in the world, more than 500 kilowatts strong and with a rotating antenna. In 1966, Pope Paul VI, on the occasion of the relocation of the radio station to a new site (the Vatican radio station began operations in February 1931), declared that everything necessary had been done for the Vatican radio to improve its programming and to maximize the effectiveness of its broadcasts to those countries where atheistic propaganda was conducted. As of that same year, 1966, the "Ukrainian Division" of the Vatican radio, after a reorganization and expansion of its staff, initiated daily broadcasts in the Ukrainian language.

In February 1980, Pope John Paul II paid a visit to the Vatican radio station and also its "Ukrainian Division." On his instructions, the radio station stepped up its propaganda, especially in the languages of the Soviet republics: Russian, Ukrainian, Belorussian, Lithuanian, Latvian, and Armenian. For this purpose, the time allotted to radio broadcasts in these languages was doubled and anticommunist insinuations and gross attacks on scientific atheism were intensified. Thus began the preparations for the 50th anniversary of the operation of the Vatican radio station. The culmination of this jubilee was a solemn liturgy celebrated by Pope John Paul II in the Sistine Chapel on February 12, 1981, for the staff of the radio station, followed by meetings with various groups from the respective divisions of "Radio Vatican."

Fabrications and distortions, slanders and lies—these, the most common and "infallibly" true techniques of bourgeois propaganda, according to V. I. Lenin (V. I. Lenin, *Collected Works*, Vol. 31, p. 210), have been used by Uniate radio saboteurs for more than forty years. The first transmission of the Vatican radio in the Ukrainian language took place on December 14, 1939, and was arranged at the request of the Uniate Metropolitan A. Sheptyts'ky. At the very time when a new life was just taking shape on Western Ukrainian territories, reunited with the Soviet Ukraine within the USSR, the Vatican radio began to broadcast programs full of crude anti-Soviet slander and lies, calling for a struggle against "godless Bolshevik" power. One of the broadcasts reported the arrest and execution of Metropolitan Sheptyts'ky by the "godless Bolsheviks." Within a few days this "sensation" burst like a balloon, but the slanderers in the Vatican did not even contemplate issuing a correction to their own fabrications and continued to broadcast anti-Soviet falsehoods.

A whole flood of foul slander and malicious insinuations was released by "Radio Vatican" and its Uniate toadies on the occasion of the decision by the Lvov synod in 1946 on the self-dissolution of the Uniate Church.[b] Ever since, the Vatican radio has continued to repeat its fabrications and malicious distortion of the facts about the events that brought the Uniate Church to utter bankruptcy in the Ukraine.

As the main task of its broadcasts to our country the Vatican radio proclaimed the spread of evangelical ideals and the popularization of the Catholic faith. But its endlessly advertised supra-class character, noninterference in politics, and "high spiritual purpose" are used as a cloak for political propaganda at whose root lie class hatred for the socialist system and Marxist-Leninist ideology and a denial of the scientific-materialist world view. This is especially typical of broadcasts in the Ukrainian language. On the air the ideologues of the Uniate Church abroad behave with insolence, deeming it unnecessary to maintain diplomatic reserve and discretion. The programs of the Ukrainian Division continue to pour forth crude and primitive anticommunist attacks, using the trite propagandistic clichés from the days of the Cold War.

An analysis of the Uniate clerical radio propaganda aimed at believers in the Ukraine shows that it is concerned first of all with falsification of the policies of the CPSU and the Soviet state regarding religion and the Church and with discrediting socialist democracy. Fabrications are persistently disseminated about the "persecution" and "harassment" of the faithful in our country, the closing of churches, the lack of freedom of conscience, etc. Deliberately falsifying the situation of religion and the church in the USSR, as well as Soviet legislation on religious cults, the Uniate clericals try to stir up the hostility of world public opinion to real socialism, which allegedly is unable to satisfy the religious needs of citizens or to create normal conditions for the fulfilment of the principles of freedom of conscience. With the help of such falsifications, the Uniate radio saboteurs hope to incite religious fanaticism among their listeners in the Ukraine, to arrouse among the devout dissatisfaction with the policy of the Communist Party and the Soviet government, and to make of them a political opposition to the socialist system, undermining it from within.

Material anti-Soviet in spirit is broadcast on purported "insidious plans of Moscow to destroy the UCC" which is said to have gone "underground and now lives in modern-day catacombs," and about "the fabrications" of Soviet propaganda which ascribes to the Uniate Church collaboration with the fascist occupiers. It is constantly stressed that the UCC was liquidated by force because of a particular hostility of Soviet power to the Uniate Church, while the Lvov synod of 1946 is called "a Bolshevik synod," which, it is said, lacks any legality. The Uniate bishops, who had been sentenced for collaboration with Hitler's fascists and the OUN bandits,ᶜ are defended in every conceivable way.

Anti-Soviet insinuations are systematically disseminated not only in special broadcasts, news programs, and radio surveys of the bourgeois clerical press, but are even introduced into religious sermons and pastoral messages from the Uniate bishops. Archbishop I. Buchko, Metropolitan M. Hermaniuk, Bishop M. Marusin, and Metropolitan M. Lubachivsky, have often come on the air with anti-Soviet slanders. The last-named was recently appointed by the Pope as coadjutor (successor) to the aged Cardinal J. Slipi. The Easter pastoral message which Lubachivski broadcast on the Vatican radio in April 1980 was filled with crude anti-Soviet attacks. Since this message was Lubachivski's first public address in his role as coadjutor, it may be regarded as the programmatic statement of the future head of Uniate church abroad.

Uniate clerical radio propaganda falsifies scientific atheism, and tries to disparage its fundamental principles of class character, scientific nature, and humanistic essence. Attacks are made on the scientific-materialist world view and on materialist scholars from the positions of neo-Thomism, the official philosophy of Catholicism, while the religious world outlook is defended and justified. The clericals try to lend a semblance of "rationality" to their criticism of materialism and atheism through blatant falsification and disregard of generally known scientific facts, artful casuistry and sophistry. A typical example of such falsification is the broadcast of January 23, 1980, in which it was said that "science has demonstrated that our solar system came into being six billion years ago, the earth five billion years ago, and life on earth three billion years ago. Yet the materialists claim that the world is eternal, even as it has been established scientifically that the universe had a beginning." Here is a blatant interchange of the concepts "the solar system" and "the universe" in the expectation that the unenlightened listener will not notice.

Much of the programming is devoted to refutations of scientific atheism, and the disparagement of its social and moral significance. Uniate clericals endeavor with all their might to discredit materialism and atheism, declaring that the philosophical resources of materialism are insignificant, that materialists are alienated from life, and cannot, allegedly, hold their own in combat with idealism and religion. Atheism is declared to be "the sickly product of a miserable segment of humanity, a sickness of the soul," "no atheist knows true happiness, for without God man cannot be truly happy." It is asserted that "atheism is an unnatural phenomenon and religion a natural one," and the practice of atheist education is distorted. Without any justification it is asserted that "the whole struggle against religion and the huge expenditures for atheistic propaganda have been in vain; religion has not disappeared, and on the contrary, a rebirth of religion can be observed" in our country. Young people allegedly do not to believe in communist teaching, "which is devoid of spiritual content, yet steeped in class consciousness," and youth are said to be searching for Christian truths and ideals. While showing their contempt for scientific atheism, which, according to their claims, is devoid of any scientific rationale, Uniate clericals baselessly reject the atheistic implications of scientific discoveries. They reserve a special hatred for Darwin's theory of evolution, which they declare unprovable and false, and even though "simple-minded materialists may have latched onto it," nevertheless "as far as thinking people are concerned, Darwinism has long been dead." Similar declarations are made about Academician O. I. Oparin's theory on the origins of life on earth, and about the atheistic implications stemming from the conquest of space, etc.

At the same time, in their struggle against materialism and atheism the clericals more and more frequently appeal to scientific authority, trying to harness it to strengthen religious faith. Thus they claim that the latest achievements of science not only have been incapable of undermining belief in God, but on the contrary, they corroborate all the more the existence of a supernatural world. The favorite technique of the Uniate clericals to "prove" the possibility of congruence between science and religion is to exploit the names of great scientists. In the broadcasts of the "Ukrainian Division," one may quite often hear references to views imputed to Newton, Ampère, Edison, and other scientists that allegedly testify not only to their conscious religiosity but even to harmony between religious notions and scientific facts. Yet the clericals purposefully "forget" that independently of scientists' volition, and not infrequently despite their subjective convictions, the discoveries they made in the natural sciences have become arguments against religion, exposing the inadequacy of various biblical assertions about nature. Engels wrote in this connection: "No one is more cruel to God than the natural scientists who believe in him" (Marx and Engels, *Works*, Vol. 20, p. 41).

These pseudoscientific broadcasts are meant for unenlightened listeners who lack firm scientific-materialist convictions.

In recent times, Uniate clerical radio propaganda reveals ever more clearly a tendency to conduct, under religious guise, propaganda on behalf of Ukrainian bourgeois nationalist ideology. In broadcasts entitled "The history of the church in the Ukraine," the history of the Ukraine and of Vatican–Ukrainian relations is presented in clerical and nationalist terms, the activities of such chieftains of the Uniate Church as Potii, Kuntsevich, Shumliansky, Sheptyts'ky, Voloshin, and others, are celebrated, the "leaders" and ideologues of Ukrainian bourgeois nationalism—Petliura,[d] Vinnichenko,[e] Grushevsky, Bandera,[f] and others—are variously glorified, and the OUN bandits are proclaimed "Ukrainian heroes."

An essential ingredient of the Uniate broadcasts is their demagogic protestations of the allegedly national character of the Uniate Church, which, it is said, has always been and still remains the only defender and protector of the national and cultural distinctiveness of the Ukrainian people. Appeals to support the Ukrainian faith— that is, the Uniate Church, and not the Orthodox Church, which is alien to the Ukrainian spirit and Ukrainian history—continually flow from the Vatican radio. Uniate radio saboteurs persistently repeat long-refuted bourgeois nationalist myths about the exceptional religiosity of the Ukrainian people, their natural gravitation to Catholicism, etc. In this manner, despite the Vatican's official condemnation of racism and nationalism, Uniate clericalss in their broadcasts continue to promote a nationalist ideology in religious garb and preach not only religious hostility but national hostility as well.

To spread bourgeois nationalist ideas the Uniate clericals also exploit meetings of Pope John Paul II with the Uniate hierarchy abroad and with believers of Ukrainian origin, as well as the Pope's speeches in Ukrainian. It is specially emphasized that Moscow addresses believers and their churches in Russian, while the Pope speaks to the Ukrainian people in Ukrainian. In this connection they have resuscitated the hoary Uniate legend about the Papacy's special solicitude for the Ukrainian people and concern for their "long-suffering Church." To propagandize religious and nationalist views, days or weeks of prayer for the "persecuted Church and people of the Ukraine" are proclaimed, and, using pilgrim's icons of the virgin, "prayer campaigns" are conducted "for the Ukrainian people and the deliverance of the Ukraine from the godless Bolshevik yoke."

There is one other distinguishing characteristic of the entire hierarchy of the Uniate Church abroad and the "Ukrainian Division" of the Vatican radio. It is impossible to find in any message of the Uniate hierarchy appeals for a cessation of the arms race, or for establishment of peaceful and just relations among peoples. On the contrary, the Uniate bishops seek to obstruct every attempt to implement the principles of peaceful coexistence and support those who promote a return of mankind to the era of the "Cold" War. Uniate radio saboteurs eagerly transmit information about attempts by reactionary forces in the West to undermine detente, while at the same time portraying apologists of imperialism and aggression as peacemakers and champions of human rights.

It may seem incomprehensible how in our day the directors of the largest Catholic radio center can give the Uniate clericals access to the microphone, with their frenzied anticommunism, especially since in the past two decades the Vatican had demonstrated a realistic approach to the problems of coexistence with the world of socialism, the preservation and strengthening of peace on earth, and detente. The leaders of the Catholic Church renounced their straightforward policy of leading a "crusade" against communism, and have refrained from crude attacks on the theory and practice of Marxism-Leninism. However, the ultraconservative part of the Catholic hierarchy, who have close ties with imperialist circles, continue their "holy war" against communism and openly support the aggressive policies of imperialism.

The leaders of the émigré Uniate Church belong to this camp of the ultraconservatives. The deep crisis of clerical and other varieties of anticommunism has exacerbated the contradictions between the "renovators" and the ultraconservatives regarding methods of combatting communism. This fact finds its reflection in Vatican radio propaganda. The official Vatican shrouds its anticommunist position in a religious idealist fog, confining itself to subtle innuendos and generalities. Ultraconservatives, on the other hand, have transformed the broadcasts of the "Ukrainian Division," and indeed some other divisions that are staffed by reactionary émigré clericals, into a mouthpiece of flagrant anticommunism. Uniate clericals use the Vatican radio to incite the remnants of the Uniate Church in the Ukraine, provoke former Uniate clergymen, monks and nuns to extremism, and attempt to revive the Uniate Church in our country.

However, the propaganda of crude, straightforward anticommunism, or anticommunism more subtle and shrouded in a religious fog, cannot hope for success among the working masses, for it is directed against their fundamental interests and built on lies and fabrications. The more Uniate radio saboteurs try to fill the airwaves with anticommunist venom, the more they discredit religion and themselves in the eyes of religious believers.

Editor's notes

a. The Ukrainian Catholic Church was outlawed in 1946 in favor of the rival (and more firmly pro-Soviet) Ukrainian Orthodox Church. The former, which is a Uniate church, i.e., in communion with the Roman Catholic Church and subordinate to the Pope, was directly linked to Ukrainian independence movements while the latter was under the jurisdiction of the Moscow Patriarch.

b. The Lvov (Lviv) Synod of 1946, which announced the dissolution of the Uniate Church, was held after the arrest of all of the Ukrainian Catholic bishops as well as many other clerics.

c. The OUN (the Organization of Ukrainian Nationalists) was formed in 1929 by Ukrainians living in Polish-held territory to advance the cause of an independent Ukraine. Initially pro-Nazi, the group fought both the Germans and the Soviets. Their resistance efforts continued until the mid-1950s.

d. Simon Petliura: leader of the short-lived Republic of United Independent Ukraine (1918–1920).

e. Volodimir Vinnichenko: a writer; leader of the Ukrainian Social Democratic Party, he chaired the General Secretariat of the Ukrainian Rada in 1917.

f. Stefan Bandera: leader of the right-wing faction of the OUN. He was arrested by the Germans after he declared an independent Ukrainian state in Lvov in June 1941.

Annotated by Lubomyr Hajda

Culture and Religion *

V. NOSOVICH

"The false notion about usefulness of religion, which, in the opinion of many, is at least able to control people, derives from the pernicious prejudice that there can be *useful delusions* and that truth can be dangerous."—P. Holbach[a]

At the All-Union Scientific-Practical Conference on "The Intensification of the Ideological Struggle on the World Arena and the Political Education of Workers," held in October of last year in Tallin, among other problems considered was the important one of religious falsification of the history of culture. The fact is that in recent years, the anticommunist campaign conducted by imperialist forces in the West has made extensive use of religion, exploiting, among other things, interpretations of the various periods in its history. One of the stereotypes promoted by this campaign is the claim that socialism is hostile to spiritual culture, if only because it is bent on a struggle with religion, which is supposedly the womb of culture, its main integrative element, and a vital precondition for its development. Not eschewing even the crudest distortions of the true state of affairs, the ideologues of anticommunism try to convince public opinion that the communist parties of socialist countries, and above all the Soviet Union, are conducting a policy of ruin and destruction of outstanding cultural monuments of the past, most of which allegedly owe their origin to religion and the activities of religious institutions.

It must be admitted, however, that our response to these slanderers and falsifiers has at times lacked the requisite militancy and consistency. One reason for this state of affairs stems from a certain lack of clarity in facing methodological problems connected with the assessment of the role of religion in the history of human culture. In some recent publications one can meet the notion that religion had a positive impact on the historico-cultural process, particularly on the development of national cultures. To be sure, no serious evidence is adduced to support this contention, and cannot be adduced, for there is none. The argument is supported only by references to the long duration of religion and to the great importance of monuments of specifically religious culture in our cultural heritage.

But to assess the role of any phenomenon by the criterion of the length of its duration is meaningful only when the social role this phenomenon played over that period is made clear. The specifically social role of religion, as Marxist-Leninist science has proven conclusively, consisted and still consists in providing the ideological justification for the inhuman living conditions of the toiling masses, and thus

Kommunist Estonii, 1983, no. 6, pp.81–89. Russian text © 1983 by "Kommunist Estonii."

in maintaining social injustice. "The yoke of religion over mankind," V. I. Lenin wrote, "is only a product and a reflection of the economic oppression existing within society."[1] Make-believe recompense for social impotence and fabrications about illusory happiness in the next world—this is what constitutes the essence of religion in the exercise of its social role. Not for nothing did Karl Marx define religion as "the opium of the people." All the other functions of religion, including the educational and cultural, not only never played an independent role, but on the contrary, always served its narcotic function. More plainly put, the Church supported culture, art, literature and philosophy only to the extent that they supported the concept of God and the transcendence of life in the next world. This same position is maintained by religious organizations even today.

Over the past two decades, in many if not most capitalist countries, there has occurred a significant quickening of religious life, and not only due to stepped-up activities of religious organizations. Bourgeois philosophers and sociologists even speak of a "religious boom," a "religious revival," a renaissance of religious consciousness. And in fact, alongside the mainstream denominations, religions of the "new coming" have been sprouting literally like mushrooms after a rain, while fascination with Eastern mysticism, astrology, and magic has reached epidemic proportions. And moreover, among adherents of this new religious wave a very high percentage are from the so-called middle class. What is the reason for this phenomenon?

Capitalist society is in principle unable to manage without a false, and in the first instance a religious, comprehension of its own being. In a society afflicted by incurable social ills and torn by irreconcilable class contradictions, the need for a religious "opium" becomes especially intense in times of crisis. This is all the more true at the present stage in the general crisis of capitalism, which has become significantly aggravated as a result of the scientific-technical revolution. The crisis of overproduction, the energy and financial crises, the degeneration of institutional authority, organized crime and drug addiction, and a homogenized mass culture lacking spiritual content engender a dissatisfied, sick consciousness and a complex of social inferiority. From this stems the search for a way out, along the easiest well-trodden road, the path of religion.

Clergymen in the capitalist world cleverly exploit the soulless, formal, and functional nature of interpersonal ties and relations in their societies. The alienation of people from one another limits the potential for satisfying a most important need, the need for social intercourse. And it is true indeed that informal social intercourse, and sincere, emotionally rich relationships are one of the most important values in human culture. But what does religion provide?

The so-called world religions (Buddhism, Christianity, Islam) do indeed proclaim the principle of equality and call for observance of elementary moral standards. Equality, however, is fixed only in relation to an invented object—God—while existing social and class inequalities are viewed as an unimportant side of life. It is for this reason that the association of people within a religious community, an association that creates the illusion of fullness of spiritual life, promotes the preservation of social inequality in those spheres that are its actual determinants (economics, politics, and culture).

From this it follows that religion, of its very essence, is in no position to play the role of some supraclass integrator, or a custodian, not to say creator, of cultural values. Thus, any positive assessment of religion's historico-cultural mission is based either on ignorance of the real historical process or on deliberate falsification.

Objectively speaking, such an interpretation of history corresponds to the notion of a single cultural stream, maintained by modern theology. Thus, Catholic ecclesiastical figures propound the unity of the historical experience and culture of the European peoples, stemming allegedly from the commonality of their religious—and more precisely, Christian—perception of the world and the value system which this religion proclaims. European culture (in itself a vague concept) is said to have originated in Christianity, and hence any weakening of this religion's influence and prestige is fraught with fatal consequences, not excluding a real danger of downfall of European civilization. It is not difficult to guess against whom the cutting edge of such arguments is directed. Against the socialist countries and against Communist ideology, of course, toward which the Catholic Church has never concealed its hostility. The call for the evangelization of Europe from the Atlantic to the Urals follows from this premise.

An analogous view on this question is maintained by Protestant theology and current bourgeois sociology of religion, whose founder was the most eminent bourgeois sociologist of the early twentieth century, Max Weber.[2]

In his book *The Protestant Ethic and the Spirit of Capitalism* he attempts to prove that it was precisely the distinctive features of Protestant ideology and its attendant mode of thought which thus gave rise to bourgeois culture and such traits of bourgeois psychology as thrift and faith in the boundless possibilities presented by the principles of calculability and computability. Thus, capitalism is made out to be the offspring of Protestantism. In fact, everything is the other way around. Protestantism is the offspring of capitalism, the adaptation of religion and the Church to the interests of the bourgeoisie.

Capitalist private ownership of the means of production, the type of exploitation it entails, and the drive for maximum profits transform "cold cash" into the main guidepost in life and the main value in bourgeois culture. Weber admits this and even considers it most likely that the culture and values of humanism may be destroyed by the sheer weight of the totalitarian-bureaucratic system of government in the bourgeois state; nevertheless, he sees precisely in religion the paramount driving force of history and the main bulwark of personal liberties.

In its assessment of the role of religion in the development of culture, Orthodox theology follows methodologically the same point of view as Catholic and Protestant theology. Its fundamental thesis is that "all culture emanates from the church." To Christianity is attributed the role of the main producer of culture and the principal source of the synthesis of all its varieties, thanks to the sense of the sublime, the moral, and the beautiful that this religion inculcates in man. From this claim follows its corollary: the struggle with religion is a struggle with culture.

It would seem improbable that in our times such ideas and opinions should enjoy currency and support, and not so infrequently. Every truly educated man knows that the history of all denominations represents an unending struggle against the upward-striving human spirit, an unbroken chain of infringements on reason and humanity, an unending propagation of superstition and obscurantism. (For example, the famous religious reformer M. Luther spoke openly of reason as "the devil's whore.") And truly, it required uncommon courage and fearlessness in periods when religion held absolute dominion over the minds and lives of men to raise the banner of defiant struggle against its tyranny. It is well known how over the course of centuries the Church paid back those who raised this banner—with the most savage persecutions, frequently culminating in the physical destruction of these people. The "Holy" Inquisition alone burned at the stake or let rot in prison millions of people, among them great thinkers and scholars, and similar practices occurred both in the history of Orthodoxy and in the history of Protestantism, though on a somewhat smaller scale. All told, as the eminent biologist E. Haeckel[b] observed, the number of those who perished in the persecutions of the Papal Inquisition, in the Christian wars of religion, etc., greatly exceeds ten million. "But this number pales," he wrote, "before ten times this number of unfortunates who became moral victims of priestly power and oppressions, before the countless multitude of those whose capacity for spiritual growth was crushed, their guileless conscience racked by torments, their family life ravaged."[3]

No one today can calculate how many priceless works of ancient literature, art and other cultural monuments were burned or otherwise destroyed, especially when Christianity was moving into ascendancy. One thing is known: a great number.

Churchmen try to suppress all this, for otherwise it would become more difficult to find credulous people to parrot their old wive's tales about a "European culture which grew out of Christianity." It is perfectly clear that theories about religion's "civilizing" mission are designed primarily for people who are poorly versed in problems of cultural history.

In the theological interpretation of the role of religion in cultural history much is made of the proposition that the religious and national components of culture coincide, or, more precisely, that religion underlies national culture as its deep structure. From this it follows that religion is supposedly an essential component of national identity, the embodiment, as it were, of national distinctiveness. In recent years this precise claim has been used with special urgency in anticommunist propaganda as well, with the primary purpose of inciting nationalist sentiments and destabilizing the union of socialist nations. But in the process, one perfectly obvious fact is deliberately passed over in silence: religions, at least the world religions—Christianity, Buddhism, and Islam—cannot serve as the embodiment of any national distinctiveness if for no other reason than because they are, so to speak, transnational.

The anticommunist ballyhoo reached an unprecedented scale in connection with the sixtieth anniversary of the formation of the USSR. It was persistently maintained that atheistic upbringing and the religious policies of the Soviet state, by undermining the religious values of, say, Orthodoxy, Catholicism, or Islam, undermine at the same time the forms in which our country's national cultures are preserved and passed on.[4]

Unfortunately, such notions, maliciously disseminated by religious figures in the West, not infrequently strike a responsive chord and find backing among the least mature segments of our people. These ideas impress particularly those who generally tend to exaggerate the role of national factors in culture and are alarmed, as Academician G. Naan of the Academy of Sciences of the Estonian SSR correctly points out, at the rapidly declining weight of ethnic (national) factors in people's spiritual culture under conditions of the scientific-technical revolution, as an ever-increasing role in culture devolves on science.[5]

Consequently, our task is to expose the anti-scientific constructions devised by theologians regarding the role of religion in the development of national cultures, constructions which today carry an overt anti-Soviet and anti-socialist bias and thus coincide with like machinations of imperialism. It is essential to conduct a resolute struggle against all attempts, including those by churchmen, to inflame the nationalist prejudices of some individuals, and to prevent even the slightest deviation from Leninist principles in our nationalities policy. Here we must bear in mind, as the General Secretary of the Central Committee of the CPSU, Comrade Iu. V. Andropov, said, that economic and cultural progress of all the nations and nationalities in our socialist federation ''is inevitably accompanied by a growth of their national self-consciousness. This is a natural, objective process. It is important, however, that natural pride in one's achievements not be transformed into national arrogance or conceit, that it not generate tendencies toward isolation or disrespectful attitudes toward other nations and nationalities.''[6]

But even in our country notions about the religious roots of national cultures are cultivated. The crowning laurels here belong to the Orthodox and Catholic clergy. They always place an equals sign between such traits as Russian and Orthodox, Lithuanian and Catholic, etc.

The motif of religion's preeminent role in national culture has come to occupy a most important place in the activities of the Russian Orthodox Church in the last few years in connection with the recent 600th anniversary of the Battle on the Field of Kulikovo[c] and the approaching millennium of the Christianization of Rus'.[d] In publications and sermons devoted to these illustrious anniversaries the claim is made that the Orthodox Church fostered the cultural, national, and state consolidation of Rus'.[7] When speaking of the greatness of the Russian people, the theologians stress their spiritual beauty, which purportedly found its most striking embodiment in the numerous righteous ones, ascetics, and saints, in those who are called ''earthly angels'' and ''celestial men,'' etc. It is they who supposedly pointed the way to light, to good, to life's truth, they who were the salt of the Russian earth, etc.

In principle these claims in no way differ from the already mentioned constructs of Western theologians about the ''civilizing'' role of religion. Here again, one can only repeat that religion never played any positive role in the story of man, not in primitive preclass society (tribal religions), nor in antagonistic societies (national religions). Nor did Orthodoxy as a national religion play any positive role in the fortunes and culture of the Russian people. These and all similar claims by churchmen are nothing but pure falsification of the true state of affairs, and a gross manipulation of the facts, their being turned upside down.

As evidence that the Orthodox Church supposedly was a champion of enlightenment and culture will be cited, for example, the fact that the Christianization of Rus' was accompanied by the spread of literacy. Yes, to be sure, the introduction of Christianity into Rus' was undoubtedly a progressive occurrence, but only to the extent that along with Christianity and the ''sacred'' scriptures came the penetration of elements of the higher Greco-Byzantine culture and the gradual spread of literacy. The Church itself advocated literacy only insofar as it was necessary for divine services and for the reading of saints' lives and the Bible. And it is not the Church by any means that should be given credit for the fact that in time a secular, nonecclesiastical literature made its appearance or that scientific learning began to spread. This happened not because of, but despite the church.

Christianity in general and Orthodoxy in particular made every effort to keep the people in bondage and servitude. And the ''sacred'' scriptures served this end perfectly. ''With the help of the Bible,'' Engels said, ''were sanctioned royal authority, by the grace of God, and meek obedience, and even serfdom.''[8] Precisely here is to be found one of the reasons why the Orthodox Church, as a faithful servant first of princely authority and later of the autocracy, waged a constant, at times simply frenzied and savage struggle against the dissemination of ''impious'' scientific and nonreligious books, and when book printing appeared—it came out against it as well. Together with the tsarist government the Orthodox Church bears responsibility for the cultural backwardness of prerevolutionary Russia and for the benightedness and ignorance of most of the populace.

The confines of a journal article do not allow a detailed exposé of the Orthodox Church's reactionary role in public education and the development of culture and science. And there is evidently no great need for such, since no one even the least bit familiar with history and Russian literary classics lacks for evidence and facts that demonstrate convincingly that religion is the enemy of science, education and true culture. Let us cite only one more of the ''Acts'' of the clergy in the not too distant past, when in Russia there already were functioning universities. So what did the clergy do but demand that at these educational institutions ''all the postulates of scholarship be based not on intellectual but on religious truths.''

Also ridiculous and absurd in this light, to say the least, are churchmen's claims that the various righteous ones, ascetics, saints, etc., pointed the way to light, to good, to the truth of life, that they were that salt of the earth which defined the spiritual makeup of the Russian people. Well, to begin, just as a point of information, let us mention that in the Christian Church the number of saints is reckoned to exceed 190,000 in all, most of them also recognized by the Orthodox Church. And what a motley crew they are! Prophets, and apostles, and martyrs for the Christian faith (as modern scholarship has shown, many stories about the martyrs are simply fiction), and kings, and princes, and religious obscurantists—those moving spirits of the

Inquisition and, in Russia, ferocious persecutors of the Raskol'niki[e] or simply nonconformists, and all the more of atheists—and "fools for Christ," "seers," hysterics, etc.

There is no question that in Russian monasteries, hermitages, and solitary retreats there were individual religious fanatics who in God's name wasted away and mortified their flesh, and made countless prostrations before the icons, or that there were "ascetics" like Tolstoi's "Father Sergei." But what do they have in common with the true spiritual profile of the Russian people, or with that truth and liberty they sought over a period of many centuries?

But there is another side to the story as well: in those same Orthodox, as in the Catholic, "quiet cloisters" there flourished not infrequently drunkenness, gluttony, debauchery, extortion, greed, and other vices. The secular clergy, and mainly the parish priests, covered themselves with no less glory in this regard. The people's true attitude toward these "pastors" is well expressed by the great Russian literary critic, revolutionary democrat, and enlightener V. Belinskii,[f] in his famous letter to Gogol[']: "Our clergy are held in universal contempt by Russian society and the Russian people. . . . Who is the subject of the Russian people's ribald tales? The priest, the priest's wife, the priest's daughter, and the priest's hired hand. Whom do the Russian people call a doltish breed, or big-bellied stallions? The priests. . . . And is not the priest in Russia a representative for all Russians of gluttony, stinginess, servility, and shamelessness?"[9]

Thus there are no grounds to speak of some positive influence exerted by the various "saints of God" on the formation of the Russian people's spiritual makeup and spiritual culture. And it could not be otherwise, for all else aside, the Russian people on the whole, as Belinskii quite justifiably observed, are a "profoundly atheistic people. Among them there is still much superstition, but not a trace of religiosity. . . . Mystical exaltation is not in their nature; they possess too much common sense, clarity of mind and realism for this, and herein lies, perhaps, the greatness of their historical destinies in the future."[10]

This last observation, we might note, is simply staggering for its profound perspicacity and the ability of the "impassioned Vissarion" to foresee for this people—under conditions of Nicholas's brutal tyranny,[g] in the midst of their crushing misery and degradation—their great destiny in world history, without the help of God and not in His name, but in the name of man and in the name of man's liberation from class, economic, and spiritual oppression.

Here it is appropriate to mention the total confidence in the liberation of the Estonian people from every form of domination by the Lutheran clergy expressed by the compiler of the Estonian national epic and writer-author enlightener F. R. Kreuzwald.[h] He wrote: "Sooner or later there will come a time when only fools and perhaps some isolated hypocrites will dance to the pastor's tune."[11]

That time arrived a little more than sixty-five years ago, when a great cleansing storm, the October Revolution, swept through our country. It is already long ago that real socialism became firmly rooted and a scientific, materialist world view triumphed. The bright hopes of progressive thinkers for a society of atheists, built on the principles of goodness and justice, on faith in man's creative powers and his ability to comprehend in strictly scientific terms his own past, present and future have come true.

As has already been mentioned, in our own times there still are people who have a positive view of the role religion played in the development of human culture. In this instance we do not mean the relatively small numbers of mostly elderly people caught in the snares of religious prejudices, but the youth. Thus, according to the results of surveys conducted over the past three years, some 40% of first-year students in the Russian division of the Tallin Polytechnical Institute considered the impact of religion on culture to have been beneficial. But if a substantial part of first-year students think like this, we may assume that among the youth who have not embarked on a higher education the proportion holding such views would not be smaller. As corroboration we may cite the fact, for example, that results similar to those at the TPI were also obtained in a survey of philosophical attitudes among seniors in a number of Leningrad secondary schools. It would seem that it is no coincidence that in recent years for some young people religious paraphernalia—crosses, icons and even religious literature—have become fashionable status symbols, and that there is a noticeable fascination with religious rituals, as evidenced, for example, by an increase in the number of baptisms.

Among the reasons for youth's incorrect understanding of the role religion has played in the development of culture, and also for their fascination with "religio-cultural games," is undoubtedly the low level of general instruction in the humanities in our schools, a poor knowledge of history in general and, more particularly, the history of religion and its role in the development of human society. We do a poor job of bringing youth to an understanding of Lenin's words that "any flirtation even with a godling is a most inexpressible abomination."[12] Atheistic upbringing and education has not yet acquired the character of an all-pervasive operation, it fails to permeate the whole curriculum in secondary and higher schools. As yet it still looks like disjointed criticism of religion in history and social science textbooks, while the courses in scientific atheism at institutions of higher learning are not sufficiently reinforced by the philosophical component of instruction in such basic sciences as physics, chemistry and biology. In other words, we are dealing here with a limited breadth and depth of atheistic knowledge on the part of youth, and frequently, therefore, with its insubstantiality that borders on ignorance. As they come face to face with historical facts in which the religious and national-cultural components appear to be in unity, and at the same time feel the effects of religious propaganda conducted by church and church-oriented circles, many young people begin to accept appearances for essence and the religious forms of cultural values for their content.

Of course, a proper clarification of these interrelationships and the conduct of scientific-atheistic work as a whole, is by no means an easy matter. To put everything in its proper place, as they say, requires a profound knowledge of the subject, broad erudition, a mastery of pedagogical skills and, most importantly, Marxist-Leninist methodology. It requires a rigorously class approach and strict adherence to the principles of historical method.

Over a period of many centuries religion and its attendant rituals did indeed form a stable part of most people's lives and the basis of their world view, their ethical and aesthetic values. The Church itself, to use the picturesque expression of Voltaire, was opera for the people. It was at the same time a school in which the priest played the role of teacher in the ordinary sense of the word, and, even more importantly, the role of a teacher of life. The best architects, painters and sculptors of their times created splendid monuments of religious art. Great composers wrote music for divine services. All this led to the creation of a kind of artistic-cultural synthesis with the capacity to make a strong emotional impact, even on nonbelievers. What lends Tallin, let us say, and its architectural composition their unique charm? The religious edifices first of all, of course—the Oleviste (St. Olaf), the Nigulist (St. Nicholas), and Holy Spirit Churches and the Toom Cathedral. Can one imagine Novgorod without the St. Sophia Cathedral and the Iur'ev Monastery, or the pictorial art of Rus' without the icons of Feofan the Greek, Andrei Rublev, and Dionisii?[i] Of course not.

The very earliest books—the Hindu Vedas, the Tao Te Ching, the Judeo-Christian Bible—are examples of religio-philosophical literature. Incunabula (early printed books), also, in their vast majority belong to the genre of theological or liturgical literature. Among these are a partially preserved book in the Estonian language—a Lutheran catechism, published in 1535, and the first Russian incunabulum—the so-called *Lenten Service Book*, published in 1532. In 1981, our republic observed the 350th anniversary of Estonian book printing. And the same picture emerges. The first books published in Tartu in 1631 were the works of Lutheran theologians, just as the *Apostol*, printed by Ivan Fedorov[j] in 1564, is an example of Orthodox theology. And we cannot forget that the Slavonic writing system itself (the Cyrillic alphabet) was the product of the Orthodox priests Cyril and Methodius.[k] Many such facts could be cited from any people's history.

Historically religion became most closely intermeshed with other types of cultural activity, and at some historical point largely subordinated them to itself, turning them into handmaidens of the Church. Thus it is not surprising that from all this an unsophisticated man might easily conclude that human culture is derived from religion.

If, however, by culture we understand the totality of spiritual and material values created by society, then religion itself represents a type of culture. To explain its true, i.e., social, role it is necessary to define, first, the specific features of religion as a type of culture, and secondly, the place that religion occupies in the structure of culture as a whole.

Let us consider then, the specific character of religion as a type of culture. One of the most important elements of religion is a system of ritual acts—ceremonies, celebrations, all that which is called worship. The distinctive character of ritual ceremonies lies in their detachment from all other types of social activity, their deliberate contraposition to everyday life. This is, so to speak, activity for activity's sake, "pure" activity. In actual fact, however, the main function of worship is to communicate religiously significant, i.e., ideological, information. Thus Catholic and Orthodox divine services possess a kind of theatricality that is able to satisfy in some measure people's aesthetic sensibilities. But this aspect plays an ancillary role, being used primarily to lend Christian preachings and teachings greater expressiveness and thereby increase their efficacy. All other types of culture, once they have come under the influence of religion, are drawn into the system of worship, and in the process lose their independent function and gradually become a mouthpiece for religious ideology.

Religion is the most conservative form of social consciousness. This is quite understandable. The very notion of God as the creator of the world and absolute regulator of everything in existence deprives man of the possibility to introduce any modifications into the divine plan for the universe. This attribute of religious ideology is most strikingly embodied precisely in the forms of worship. And it is precisely in this sphere of activity, where direct contact between priests and the faithful takes place, that any changes, not to speak of innovations, occur infrequently. When at the present time theological thinking tries to find ways to update its doctrines, wraps itself in the mantle of defender of scientific thought and social progress, and makes urgent efforts at modernization, this finds practically no reflection in divine services. These remain the same or virtually the same as they were centuries ago. It is, however, precisely worship that is of paramount interest to the clergy since this is the primary medium through which they exercise their influence over the faithful.

Thus, the main characteristic of religion as a type of culture is the dogmatic, conservative method of propagating religious ideology and belief in the supernatural.

Let us now turn to the question of how religion functions within the framework of other types of cultural activity, and to the problem of its influence on them.

As we have already said, the very fact of such an influence is not in doubt, as is easily ascertainable by simple observation. Indeed, in some historical periods this influence was so powerful that the religious element formed the deep structure of culture. This was particularly typical of feudal society when religion dominated man's view and perception of the world, and religious institutions could employ even legal sanctions to regulate cultural processes. Decisively important here was the cultural polarization resulting from the corporate class nature of society. Most of the cultural values being created (fine arts, literature, science and philosophy) were the monopoly of the ruling class and its intellectual elite, including the clergy. Even so, the popular masses remained, of course, the primary creator of culture, though to a significant degree in covert fashion, so to speak, since their illiteracy deprived them of access to such important sources of information as, for example, books, to say nothing of opportunities for an education indispensable for cultural activities.

Social and spiritual oppression, and, in its wake, benightedness, ignorance, and degradation of the masses created a situation in which cultural values reached the mass consumer largely in the form of religious worship and through the channels of religious information.

It should be clear from the foregoing how mistaken those opinions are that attribute an exalted cultural mission to religion and religious institutions. Religious forms of regulating the cultural process inevitably impoverished its potential and its content. In his analysis, for example, of why the Russian pre-Renaissance (late fourteenth–early fifteenth centuries) failed to develop into a Renaissance, Academician D. S. Likhachev considers the most important reason to have been the power of the Church organization, which, with the help of the state, suppressed heresies and anticlerical movements, and abetted the destruction of the cultural importance of the city-communes of Novgorod and Pskov.[13] The Church is not among those least to blame for the fact that the formation of a secular culture was so drastically retarded. Indeed, Russian literature, theater, music and painting developed as independent forms of society's spiritual life for the most part only in the eighteenth century. The same applies in even greater measure to scientific and philosophical thought, which the clergy in that period regarded as the inspiration of the devil and a most grievous sin.

But perhaps the Church exhibited concern for the creation of superior spiritual values within the spheres of its exclusive influence. It might appear that such examples as the creative work of Feofan the Greek, Andrei Rublev, and Russian icon-painting in general, would serve as confirmation of this view. But then it is no secret, first of all, that the extreme importance of their works was brought to the attention of the world not by the Church, but by the Russian artists of the late 19th century, and only then did the Orthodox clergy itself become involved in their popularization—naturally, in its own fashion, presenting them primarily as talented spokesmen for Orthodox ideology. But there is more. According to ecclesiastical and theological standards in this matter, it would be totally incomprehensible why the old Russian icons exhibited in our country's museums should give aesthetic pleasure to nonbelievers and atheists. The same can be said of the chorales and requiems that are performed in concert halls.

The whole point is that true culture and high art are broader, more powerful, and in their content richer than religious culture. That is why, in particular, the process of emancipation of culture from the dictates of religion that occurred in the West during the Renaissance led to an unprecedented flourishing and enrichment of the whole spectrum of cultural life. The path of true cultural progress lies through the ruins of all forms of religious ideology and worship that fetter its development.

The aforesaid does not at all mean that the main line of development of socialist culture consists in a total rejection of those stages that preceded it, on the grounds that they frequently were subjected to the influence of religion. The dialectic of all processes, including social ones, consists in the fact that the negation of the old is simultaneously the acquisition of the positive features of the preceding stages of development, which, albeit in a transformed state, are nevertheless incorporated into the new quality. Continuity, therefore, is not only an absolutely necessary feature of the development of culture, but also an important methodological principle for regulating the spiritual life of socialist society.

From its very beginnings our socialist state has followed a policy of care for the cultural legacy of our Fatherland and the world, a fact reflected in appropriate legislative acts. In the implementation of its cultural policy the CPSU proceeds from Lenin's teaching about the two cultures in every national culture,[1] and therefore opposes cultural omnivorousness and any objectivist, ideologically neutral assessment of a cultural heritage. In particular, the Party has criticized recent attempts to idealize certain aspects of life in the past and, in the process, to "rehabilitate" the role of religion in the history of our Fatherland. In his address, "Sixty Years of the USSR," Comrade Iu. V. Andropov emphasized that "the spiritual legacy, traditions, and everyday life of every nation contains not only what is good, but also that which is bad and obsolete. From this premise follows yet another task—not to preserve these bad elements, but to emancipate oneself from everything that has become antiquated and goes counter to the standards of Soviet communal life, socialist morality, and our communist ideals."[14]

The harm that may result from any lapse into patriarchal ways consists in the creation of conditions for a revival not only of religious, but also nationalist prejudices.

In conclusion, let us emphasize again that the current ideological situation demands not only criticism of religion and unmasking of the religious falsification of the historico-cultural process, but also a consistent struggle to transform the principles of a scientific world view into a system of convictions, a struggle to strengthen the social role of the values that characterize the socialist way of life and culture. This is all the more necessary now that activists from various religious communities have been intensifying their activities, even to the point of violating Soviet law. Here is just one example. Last year, a group of young Baptists carried out a series of "raids" of the student dormitory at the Tallin Polytechnical Institute, where they would distribute brochures and leaflets (which were prepared or acquired in violation of the laws dealing with such matters), urge students to listen to recordings of church services which they had brought with them, and invite them to religious services, especially those conducted for young people at the Oleviste Church.

The atheistic education of the students at the Tallin Polytechnical Institute is fostered, for example, by the "Atheos" club, whose members not only try to expand their knowledge of scientific atheism and materialist philosophy, but also participate in sociological surveys dealing with various aspects of the state of religion in Estonia. In Tallin there is also an extragovernmental, so to speak, club of atheists which does some important and useful work as well. All this, of course, is well and good, but clearly not enough. It is essential that well-thought-out atheistic propaganda become an inseparable and organic part of the educational activities conducted by every Party organization, as required by the resolution of the Central Committee of the CPSU "On the Further Improvement of Ideological and Politico-educational Work."

The highest goal of our efforts to build a communist society is the formation of a new, thoroughly accomplished and highly educated man. His characteristic features are a scientific world view, moral maturity and integrity, high standards of professional and humanitarian culture, and active involvement in life. And this requires, all other things apart, the emancipation of man from all religious prejudices. Religion, by its very essence, is in opposition to science, advanced culture, social progress, and real humanism, which, according to Marx, is identical with social humanism.

Editor's notes

a. Paul Holbach (1723–1789): French philosopher and encyclopedist, a vigorous proponent of atheism.

b. Ernst Haeckel (1834–1919): German biologist and an enthusiastic propagator of Darwin's theory of evolution, which he also attempted to apply to problems of philosophy and religion.

c. The Battle on the Field of Kulikovo in 1380 marked a significant Russian victory over the Mongol-Tartar forces of the Golden Horde and an important step in the consolidation of power by the principality of Moscow.

d. The official reception of Christianity in Rus' is usually dated to 988, when the population of Kiev was baptized at the instance of St. Vladimir, the grand prince. Conflicting interpretations of this event by Soviet authorities and the Russian Orthodox Church in the USSR, as well as by Ukrainian Orthodox and Catholics abroad, are certain to turn the upcoming Millennium celebrations into a political, and not merely religious, event.

e. *Raskol'niki*, or Old Believers: religious dissenters who broke with the official Orthodox Church in Russia over the reforms initiated by Patriarch Nikon in the 1650s. They were subjected to harsh persecutions by the state and the established Church, which continued sporadically even through the nineteenth century.

f. Vissarion Belinskii (1811–1848): the leading Russian literary critic and publicist of the nineteenth century.

g. The reign of Nicholas I (1825–1855) was a period of extreme political reaction and considerable repression in tsarist Russia.

h. Friedrich Kreuzwald (1803–1882), frequently styled the father of Estonian literature, was most notably the compiler of the national epic, *Kalevipoeg* (published between 1857–61).

i. Feofan the Greek (ca. 1340–ca. 1405), an emigrant from Byzantium, Andrei Rublev (ca. 1360–1427), and Dionisii (ca. 1440–ca. 1502): icon painters, whose works are considered the most celebrated examples of the art form in Russia.

j. Ivan Fedorov (ca. 1510–1583): the founder of book printing in Russia and Ukraine. Forced by outraged scribes to flee Moscow shortly after the appearance of the *Apostol* in 1564, Fedorov found more hospitable ground for his printing enterprises in the Ukrainian territories of Poland-Lithuania.

k. Sts. Cyril and Methodius (ninth century), apostles to the Slavs and originators of the Slavonic rite of Eastern Christian worship. Cyril's name is associated with the invention of the alphabet (Cyrillic) in use among most Slavs to this day.

l. The reference is to Lenin's view, expressed in the article "Critical Remarks on the National Question" (1913), that every nation possesses two cultures—a democratic culture and a bourgeois culture of the ruling classes.

Annotated by Lubomyr Hajda

Notes

1. V. I. Lenin, *Polnoe sobranie sochinenii*, vol. 12, p. 146.
2. See G. Korf, *Kritika teorii kul'tury Maksa Vebera i Gerberta Markuse*, Moscow, "Progress," 1975.
3. *O vere i neverii*, Moscow, Politizdat, 1982, p. 144.
4. See M. Gol'dberg, M., "Neproshenye popechiteli," *Nauka i religiia*, 1982, no. 11.

5. See Gustav Naan, "Mnogoobrazie edinogo," *Kommunist Estonii*, 1983, no. 1, p. 32.

6. Iu. V. Andropov, *Shest'desiat let SSSR*, Moscow, Politizdat, 1982, p. 13.

7. See *Zhurnal Moskovskoi Patriarkhii*, 1980, no. 9, p. 5.

8. K. Marks, and F. Engels, *Sochineniia*, vol. 7, p. 368.

9. V. G. Belinskii, *Izbrannye filosofskie sochineniia*, Moscow, Politizdat, 1948, vol. 2, p. 516.

10. Ibid.

11. F. R. Kreitsval'd, *Izbrannye pis'ma*, Tallin, 1953, p. 190.

12. V. I. Lenin, *Polnoe sobranie sochinenii*, vol. 48, p. 226.

13. See D. S. Likhachev, *Kul'tura Rusi vremeni Andreia Rubleva i Epifaniia Premudrogo*, Moscow-Leningrad, Akademiia Nauk SSSR, 1962.

14. Iu. V. Andropov, *Shest'desiat let SSSR*, Moscow, Politizdat, 1982, p. 13.

Sheikh Yusuf Hamadani *

G. SNESAREV

It is quite natural that sheikh[a] Yusuf Hamadani should occupy an honored place in the hagiology of Khorezm[b] and all Central Asia: it was he who introduced Sufism[c] to Central Asia, and it was to his school that many prominent Sufis, who form the main contingent of local saints, belonged.

Yusuf Hamadani is a historical personage; we know the dates of his life (1048 or 1049 to 1140) as well as many biographical details. The life of this ascetic, though rich in incidents of various kinds, is nothing really exceptional. Biographers describe him as an outstanding Muslim. According to one account, "In his lifetime Yusuf Hamadani read the Koran ten thousand times; memorized 700 works devoted to the word of God, law, interpretations of the Koran, and traditions concerning the Prophet; held discussions with 213 sheikhs; . . . converted 8,000 idolators to Islam; those whom he caused through his admonitions to repent their sins and set out on the path of righteousness are beyond number."[1] Moreover, according to his disciples, he made the pilgrimage to Mecca and the holy places thirty-seven times, always on foot.

One can only marvel that after all this he still had time for those pursuits which these same biographers say were his main occupation—farming and shoe making. But let us leave the incredible number of pious deeds ascribed to our sheikh on their own conscience, and turn our attention specifically to his missionary activities. However, doubtful the number of persons (8,000) he converted to Islam, certainly exaggerated many times over, for us it is significant for it testifies to one of the vital functions of Yusuf Hamadani and other such Sufi sheikhs. They were among the main bearers of Islam to Central Asian lands. And Yusuf Hamadani clearly excelled in this field.

The Islamization of Central Asia and adjoining regions extended over whole centuries, but it began soon after the rise of Islam. V. V. Barthold noted that "Muslim propaganda was at work in the steppes as early as the Umayyad period,"[2]—i.e., no later than the eighth century. And by our sheikh's lifetime (11th-12th cent.) the "steppe" had already "moved" close to the main Islamic centers of the time; thus Yusuf Hamadani, and other missionaries like him, did not have to venture into the depths of Asia: Khorasan itself,[d] the main arena of Yusuf Hamadani's preachings, was already inundated by masses of newcomers from the north, only recently still shamanists.

We know that he won many followers in Bukhara and lived quite long in Samar-

*Nauka i religiia, 1984, no. 12, pp. 30–32. Russian text © 1984 by the All-Union "Knowledge" Society.

kand, where he was also held in great esteem. We may assume that it was in this period that Sultan Sanjar[e] sent his epistle to the sheikhs and notables of Samarkand in which he wrote: "It has become known that the God-devoted elder Yusuf Hamadani has achieved perfection, but we do not have the opportunity to call on him." Sanjar then goes on to say that he is sending 50,000 dinars for the general upkeep of the dervishes[f] and asks Yusuf Hamadani to blessing for this war with Suleymanshah (also a Seljukid, the son of his brother Muhammad—G.S.).[3]

Yusuf Hamadani died on his way to Merv, and that is where his tomb is located. The celebrated Sufi poet Jami[g] (15th cent.) wrote about it. V. A. Zhukovskii inspected it at the end of the last century, and afterwards began to gather information about Yusuf Hamadani. The tomb has survived to this day. However, our expedition has discovered yet another grave of Hamadani's—in the settlement of Besh-Mergen, at some distance from the main centers, past or present, of Khorezm. But from conversations with the local inhabitants it turned out that the Khorezmian "bookmen," people more or less conversant with theology and Islamic traditions, do not consider it the true burial place of Yusuf Hamadani. Ataullah, the mullah of the mosque in Hankin, who was able to name the sheikh's dates with a fair degree of accuracy, said that Yusuf Hamadani spent only three days in Khorezm and that this is only his *kadamjo* (literally: "place of his step," i.e. a spot where he had set his foot). Yusuf Hamadani's Khorezmian tomb was also identified as a *kadamjo* by Said Ahmed-hoja, an old man living immediately next to it. He explained to us that this place is "very powerful in its holiness, more powerful than other places." But on the whole, the Muslims of Khorezm still believe that Yusuf Hamadani rests in Besh-Mergen.

It is curious why Yusuf Hamadani's cult in Khorezm should be centered in such a remote spot. For if the renowned sheikh had actually spent time in Khorezm, his followers should have received him with honor in Gurganj, the capital of Khorezm. But in none of the centers of eleventh–twelfth-century Khorezm—not in Kunia-Urgench, not in Birun, not in Khiva—did we find any trace of the famous sheikh's sojourn there, not even a hint of his memory. We came to the settlement of Besh-Mergen by chance, never expecting to find ourselves within the zone of one of the most enigmatic cult complexes in the hagiology of Khorezm.

This so-called "tomb" of Yusuf Hamadani can in no way compare with the lavish mausoleums raised in Khorezm over the graves of the saints Palvan-ata, Sultan-bobo, or Türebek-hanim. A rather primitive frame structure coated with clay, resembling an ordinary dwelling home, with a flat roof, it does not even have the usual domed ceiling. True, the dimensions of the *stug*—ritual banners placed against the back wall of the *mazar*[h] and rising far above the rooftop—make a strong impression: most of them are tree poles cut off at the root, with flags attached and wreathed with votive ribbons left by the pilgrims.

In a neighboring kishlak we gathered a considerable amount of information from the local sheikhs about the history of this tomb and the cult of Yusuf Hamadani. Subsequently this was all rechecked and the gaps filled out. The material thus collected allows for the conclusion that this cult is among the most original in the hagiology of Khorezm, one in which are intertwined the myriad ways that the cult of Muslim saints developed.

Most interesting for us was the report about an annual *sayl*—a celebration at Yusuf Hamadani's *mazar*. Various celebrations attended by large crowds have taken place at the *mazars* of saints elsewhere in Khorezm as well, but only at two (of those Yusuf Hamadani and sheikh Mukhtar-vali) were we able to record any specific features in the ritual, in people's behavior, and in the role played by the popular saint himself.

The *sayls* celebrated at these two *mazars* had nothing in common either with orthodox Islam or with canonic hagiology; they were nocturnal gatherings of people indulging in boisterous and rather disorderly merry-making, with, as almost all our informants relate, quite loose relations between men and women—which, of course, absolutely does not accord with the traditional standards of Islam.

This is in significant ways a unique phenomenon, but there is every reason to believe that detailed knowledge of it will soon disappear from the memories of even the older generation. That is why we shall go into it in some detail, for many aspects of these celebrations will undoubtedly attract the interest of scholars of religion.

The *sayls* held at the *mazar* of Yusuf Hamadani attracted people from the most diverse, often quite remote, corners of Khorezm. Yunusjan-ishan (born in 1907), a villager from Besh-Mergen where this *mazar* is found, who reckons himself as one of its custodians, told us in detail about the ritual of this celebration.

The *sayl* was held in September, when everything in the fields and gardens was ripening. Whole families came to the festivities, settling down by "localities," according to their origin—guests from Khiva in one place, those from Urgench in another, those from Tashauz in still another, etc. The festivities began on Thursday at noon, and people, therefore, tried to arrive in the morning; the *sayl* reached its peak about four o'clock, and ended past midnight at about two.

There were no special supervisors and within each "locality" order was maintained by its own *yashuls* (elders). Every community brought its own foodstuffs and cooking utensils.

The festivities were not interrupted for prayers. The mullahs, if such were present, simply sat there and watched, without performing any of their responsibilities. If anyone wanted to pray, they would withdraw aside. The main attraction of the *sayl* was "*tomosho*"—diversion. Here would gather musicians, singers, *mask-harabozes* (clowns), *dorbozes* (tightrope walkers), and *kurchakchi* (puppeteers). First to perform were the musicians and singers, then followed by the *kurash*—a wrestling contest organized "*tarap ma tarap*" (one side against another). Then the young boys would dance. But there were no ram fights, so beloved in Khorezm, or the customary dog fights, or goat fights at this celebration. At two o'clock Friday morning everyone quickly dispersed, even ran off, if they had not managed to get a seat on time in one of the carts.

This strange, long vanished celebration at the *mazar* of Yusuf Hamadani was also described for us by the inhabitants of kishlaks in the vicinity of the Kyat fortress. Let us cite here some of the most interesting testimonies to supplement what was already said about the *sayl*.

We learned, for example, that toward morning the sheikh Yusuf would emerge from his grave. Some informants said that he was displeased if people by that time had not yet left, but others offered a different explanation: Yusuf would watch the gathering and make merry together with the people, for this saint loved merry-making.

Old men told us that the sheikhs attached to the *mazar* would seek permission from the Khan of Khiva to hold the *sayl* and made large profits from the celebrations. "All these things were not right, according to the laws of Islam," said one of our informants, a representative of the local Muslim clergy. Indeed, he stressed in no uncertain terms that the *sayl* held at Yusuf Hamadani's *mazar* had nothing in common with the orthodox religion.

There was one unique feature of this festivity, already mentioned earlier, that does not in any way conform with the traditional customs, rooted in the people's everyday lives and confirmed by the standards of the Muslim religion. Yunusjan-ishan told us about it:

"The *sayl* at the *mazar* of Yusuf Hamadani was attended by men, women and children. Here women mixed with the men and never covered their faces. In fact, it was mainly women who came to these *sayls*. Elsewhere, at other *tois*, *i* the women sat separately from the men. Barren women used to come here both to take part in the *sayl* and at the same time to make a *ziarat*—a pilgrimage to the saint's grave. The saint was pleased with whatever gave pleasure to those who gathered here. He was *kichirimli* (i.e., forgiving—G.S.) and gave people great latitude."

Babajan (65 years old) a villager from the kishlak told us: "There were love affairs at the *sayl*, sometimes even leading to murder. I remember a case when a husband killed his wife because he discovered her with another man."

How did the saint view this free behavior of men and women? "The saint was a simple man," said the elderly Saur-bobo, explaining this permissiveness. "Merry-making at the *sayl* was forgiven for the saint himself was merry," the local inhabitants told us. Instances of free behavior by men and women occurred during celebrations at other *mazars* as well, but other saints did not forgive this, and punished such behavior; people knew that and were careful, but at Yusuf Hamadani's *mazar* there were unusual things going on in August and September and none was punished for it. That means that the saint forgave it."

The specific behavior of men and women at this *sayl*, and its special and unusual nature, so far removed from Muslim orthodoxy, may be considered as a late survival of ancient feasts of the harvest and fertility, connected with magic rites, orgiastic in character.[4]

Some conjectures about the origins of the Khorezmian *sayls* will help to clarify the evolution of the cult of Muslim saints, including the Khorezmian variant of the cult of Yusuf Hamadani. We will say something about this later, in the conclusion.

But to conclude the story of the *sayl* at Yusuf Hamadani's *mazar*, there should still be mentioned one strange custom about which we had never heard before. This was the "*arava tirkash*"—the coupling of the carts. This entertainment can be described as follows. Two carts were fastened together with thick poles (one behind the other) and to this vehicle was harnessed one solitary horse. As many as twenty people (some informants cited an even higher number) would find a place on the carts and the poles, among them young women performers and young men. One of them would carry on his shoulders a *bacha*—a young boy dancer, who by movements of his hand imitated a dance. In the first cart sat a musician with a *surna*.[5] The vehicle moved slowly, occasionally pushed by those participants in the fun who were on foot, or they might try to drag it up some elevation, for example, a bridge over a canal.

No one was able to make sense of this custom; the orthodox mullahs with whom we spoke were very negative about it. Perhaps at one time it had a sacral meaning, but what was it? As yet the mystery remains unsolved.

The image of sheikh Yusuf Hamadani is, perhaps, the most unusual and complex in Khorezmian hagiology. At first glance everything is the way it is supposed be: a revered ascetic, by no means an ordinary Sufi sheikh, but the founder of the Central Asian school of mysticism, comes to be numbered in the company of Muslim saints. But that is only at first glance. The unusual begins with the *sayl* described above, with all its enigmatic components. The supposed tomb of Yusuf Hamadani reveals that the cult had even older roots from which it underwent further development: this tomb was a kind of Mecca to which flocked the mentally ill from all over Khorezm in the hopes of being healed.

The mentally ill were also brought to other *mazars* in Khorezm, but the *mazar* of Yusuf Hamadani's was, so to speak, a "specialized hospital." Here is what Yunus-jan-ishan, the resident of Besh-Mergen, mentioned earlier, had to say on the subject: "Sheikh Yusuf Hamadani is a healer of the insane (*jinni*). That is his specialty. To Sultan-bobo[6] they might bring three or four insane people a year, but here it would be forty or fifty every month—from Kunia-Urgench, from Kungrad, from Tashkent. They would live here around the *mazar* in mud huts or with acquaintances in the kishlak. The violent ones would be brought in restraints."

Jamal Mahmudov from a *kishlak* near Shavat told us: "When *jinnis* would be brought to Yusuf Hamadani, the sheikh of the *mazar* would know how to approach such sufferers, and would put chains on the violent ones. Some *jinnis* would immediately go away: this meant that the saint did not wish to help them, but those he wanted to cure remained. On the fortieth day the chains would fall off by themselves; afterward such *jinnis* later would visit the *mazar* of their own free will. No one recited prayers over the sufferers; in such cases there was no praying at all. The *shifo* (healing) would come simply from staying in the *mazar*. The sufferers would sit on the ground, they would be given food and water, and if the saint wished, the sufferer would be cured. . ." We heard many stories from old men about cases of healing of the insane at Yusuf Hamadani's *mazar*.

The materials gathered in Khorezm have clearly shown that the cult of Yusuf Hamadani is closely tied to complex pre-Islamic beliefs and rituals that we call shamanism (today, of course, it survives in quite degenerate form, but it cannot be said to have totally disappeared). Furthermore, Yusuf Hamadani, that respected Sufi sheikh, has been transformed into a *pir*—a patron of shamans and people suffering from various nervous disorders or mentally retarded. Here I would like to recall the quite unusual belief distinguishing Yusuf Hamadani from the other numerous saints of Khorezm—that during the *sayl* the saint would emerge from his grave and observe the entertainment of the revelers. This superstition is unique, possibly related to the peculiar nature of his cult.

Here is an interesting story related by Vapa Vaisov, who used to be acting sheikh not even at the *mazar* of Khamadani, but far from it, on the right bank of the Amu Daria, at the *mazar* of Sultan-bobo:

"There would be *parkhanis* (shamans) around the Sultan-bobo *mazar*, but they would not obtain a *potiya* (blessing—G. S.) here. For that they would go to the *mazar* of sheikh Yusuf Hamadani. When a man became a *jinni*, it meant that the *jinnis* and the *peris*[j] had 'closed the lock' and the key to this lock was Yusuf Hamadani." We were told roughly the same thing by Yunusjan-ishan from Besh-Mergen: "Sheikh Yusuf Hamadani still in his lifetime subjected all the *jinnis*, *peris*, and *devis*[7] to his will, and shamans and *parkhans* came to his grave to receive *his blessing*. It would sometimes happen that *jinnis* who were being treated at the *mazar* of Yusuf Hamadani would become *folbins*—shamans. In their sleep they would hear the words: 'You should become a *folbin*!'"

Those of our interlocutors who represented Yusuf Hamadani as the patron of shamans gave us perhaps the most detailed description of the shamanist system of any we obtained in Khorezm. And one more piece of evidence remains to be mentioned. There is a belief that the teacher of Yusuf Hamadani was Lukman-Hakim himself, who in the Islamic word is considered as the founder of the science of healing. According to tradition, he was a contemporary of the first people on earth, and around him "gathered all the medicinal plants to place themselves at his disposal."

For an explanation of the way the cult of Muslim saints developed in Khorezm the cult of Yusuf Hamadani is interesting in two respects.

We have here, of course, the quite banal process of canonization of well-known Sufi sheikhs of the distant past, one that continued practically to our own day, when added to the list of saints would be the most ordinary *ishans*—heads of small provincial communities of a totally vulgarized type, and virtually devoid of any of the religio-philosophical elements of early sufism.

But another aspect of the cult of Yusuf Hamadani is much more noteworthy, even if our suggestions must remain hypothetical. It would seem that in the period when the Islamization of the population of Khorezm and the surrounding steppes was reaching culmination, and ancient beliefs were finally being pushed out from consciousness and rituals to be replaced by new objects of veneration proper to Muslim teachings, it was this cult, by virtue of sheikh Yusuf Hamadani's eminence and his role in the religious life of Central Asian peoples that replaced on the territory of Khorezm some major pagan object of veneration, connected with the fertility cult and with shamanist notions and rituals that had taken deep root among the ancient inhabitants of Khorezm.

Everything would suggest this: the strange location of the cult's epicenter, in a remote spot in an oasis, and the unusual nature of the celebrations (*sayls*) at the *mazar*, which preserved elements of magical eroticism, and in particular the functional nature of the *mazar*, linked to shamanism and its rituals whose object was the healing of the mentally ill.

To identify this ancient object of veneration any more precisely is now impossible. Whether it was one of the divinities of the Mazdean pantheon, or an even more archaic "great spirit" of a shamanist belief cycle, it is difficult to say. It seems probable that once there was located here a center of an ancient fertility cult, a cult whose survivals in Khorezm, that true repository of ethnographic and archaeological antiquities, may be found everywhere, in the most diverse spheres of life. There is also another possibility: that the cult of Yusuf Hamadani came to be identified here with some shamanist center, a sanctuary where the shamans underwent the rite of initiation. For the given period in the history of Central Asia such a substitution would have been typical. There can be hardly any doubt that the numerous saints and patron *pirs*, belief in whom was widespread not only among craftsmen but in every other professional milieu, in time replaced the pre-Islamic divinities and spirits who had analogous functions of patronage, but were banished from mind and ritual life in the process of Islamization of the population of Central Asia.

Editor's notes

a. Sheikh: a Muslim honorific, applied especially to religious teachers, scholars, and heads of religious communities.

b. Khorezm: a country on the lower course and delta of the Amu Daria, that at times, and especially during the twelfth century, constituted an important power in western Asia. Among its major centers at various times were Gurganj (Urgench), Merv and Khiva. Much of the territory is now in the Uzbek and Turkmen republics.

c. Sufism: a mystic trend in Islam that emphasized asceticism and communion with God through contemplation and ecstasy. The sufis were among the most important bearers of Islam to Central Asia.

d. Khorasan: an extensive country south of the Amu Daria and north of the Hindu Kush (now mostly in Afghanistan), that in the eleventh-twelfth centuries formed part of the Great Seljukid empire.

e. Sanjar (1086–1157): the last sultan of the Great Seljuks.

f. Dervish: member of a religious (sufi) fraternity.

g. Jami (1414–1492): a mystic and last of the great classic Persian poets.

h. *Mazar*: tomb (Pers.).

i. *Toi*: feast (Pers.).

j. *Peri*: fairy, the beneficent obverse of a *jinni*.

Notes

1. V. A. Zhukovskii, *Drevnosti Zakaspiiskogo kraia. Razvaliny starogo Merva*, St. Petersburg, 1894, p. 172. The biographical details from the life of Yusuf Hamadani have been taken mainly from this work.

2. V. V. Bartol'd, *Turkestan v epokhu mongol'skogo nashestviia*, in: *Sochineniia*, vol. 1,

Moscow, 1963, p. 316. The Umayyads were an Arab dynasty (661–750).

3. See V. A. Zhukovskii, *op. cit.*, p. 171.

4. This question is examined in detail in the book G. P. Snesarev, *Relikty domusul'-manskikh verovanii i obriadov u uzbekov Khorezma,* Moscow, 1969, pp. 303–306.

5. A type of wind instrument.

6. A sanctuary on the right bank of the Amu Daria near the Sultan-Ouizdag mountains; it was discussed in *Nauka i religiia* 1983, no. 8.

7. Spirits with whom the Central Asian shamans "dealt."

Islam and Politics *

IGOR BELIAEV

"There are differences of principle between our materialist world view and Islam. Does this mean, though, as some Western politicians think, that many Soviet Muslims are under the influence of their fellow-believers from other countries who are still carrying on an undying struggle against socialism?"

—*A. Mikhailov, student*

City of Gor'kii

According to the lunar calendar of the Muslims' religion, this is the year 1407. A large number, it would seem, but some theologians are inclined to stress that this is a young religion, and therefore, they say, full of untapped potential. In comparison, for example, with Buddhism and Christianity, which have long ago passed that age.

The Muslim factor

A great deal is said, written, and thought about Islam nowadays, for various reasons and in various connections. And not just by those who do so by virtue of their main business—the Muslim *ulema*, interpreters of the Koran, or Christian theologians and religious figures from other religions. Recently there has been an obvious growth in interest on the part of university professors, the world's scholars, intelligence people, and journalists. It is a curious and even remarkable connection, isn't it? The connection has grown ever more noticeable since the second half of the 1970s, when the influence of Islamic fundamentalism increased, there was a movement to return to the sources of the faith of the prophet Muhammad, and the scope of international terrorism grew. . . Once again it is worth recalling this at first glance inexplicable connection between orthodox religion and the terrible scenes of open war against guiltless people (after all, kidnapping of hostages has become almost a political business, painted in the colors of Islam). I confess that this connection disturbs me more and more, just as does the interest in Muslims shown by the Western intelligence agencies. Particularly when you consider that there are today more than 850 million people who profess Islam, living in many countries of the world.[1]

Every religion, Islam included, appeared and grew because it served people as a

---

Literaturnaia gazeta, 13 May 1987, p. 13, and 20 May 1987, p. 12; with a response published 10 June 1987. Russian text © 1987 by the USSR Union of Writers.

kind of means for understanding the world and, of course, for resolving everyday human problems; and sometimes, at least in the first stages of man's existence, without interfering with the natural development of things. No one would think to argue that algebra, trigonometry, chemistry, geography, and philosophy did not appear and prosper in the Arab countries and other states of the East after the birth of Islam. Naturally I do not argue that they appeared only because of Islam either.

However, it is just as obvious that with the passage of time Islam and its predecessors, Buddhism and Christianity, just like other religions not of world stature, grew more and more conservative. Standing on the border between the past and the present, Muslim reformers like Muhammad Abduh[a] and Jamal al-Din al-Afghani[b] (whose works are well known here) tried to modernize or, more precisely, adapt Islam to the conditions that existed in the lands of the foreign East, especially in the Arab countries, in connection with the stormy growth of capitalism. After all, other religions also had reformations, each in its own time and in its historic conditions. Consequently, conclusions about the progressiveness or conservatism or the authoritativeness of a given religion or faith are always relative. Everything depends upon the conditions in which people live. And one thing is clear: that the religiousness of the broad masses of the population is most often directly proportional to the degree to which social problems are unresolved.

One example. Soon after the announcement that socialism was the goal of the Egyptian social revolution (in July 1962), President Nasser stopped using ritual phrases in his speeches like "In the Name of Allah, the gracious and merciful." Then, a while later, he began using them again, and journalists noticed this. I asked the President about the reasons for this return to Islam.

"I am for the triumph of science in explaining what happens around man and with a man. Religions, partly including Islam, are receding. I am for the triumph of science. However, science still has not demonstrated its correctness in the minds of many millions of Egyptians. They believe in the teachings of the Prophet Muhammad. Am I really to ignore this incontrovertible fact? In a number of situations I use the postulates of the Koran, such as for example those which forbid large landholdings, the charging of interest for loans, and some others, for purposes of religious transformation. What is bad about this?"

Nasser did a great deal for the modernization of the most famous Muslim university, al-Azar in Cairo. In part he introduced a lay administration (the rector is named by the state), created a science faculty, and a women's faculty. In a word, he brought this religious educational institution, where students from all the Muslim countries study, closer to life on earth.

The revolutionary changes brought to Egypt by President Nasser also evoked skepticism from the Muslim religious authorities. However, this was not open opposition! The sympathies of the believers, who were mostly illiterate and backward, but who could see and feel sharply that the social revolution which was then occuring on the banks of the Nile truly answered the interest of their lives, were on the side of Nasser. It was also, if you wish, a most interesting historical phenomenon.

Sometimes one hears that interest in Islam is almost entirely a product of the 1979 Islamic revolution in Iran. But is it true? Yes, and no. Yes, because the "Iranian factor," which made itself felt in the most unexpected ways, helped strengthen interest in Islam throughout the world. And no, because the turning of millions of Muslims to their mosques with prayers for assistance in solving their daily tasks began decades earlier. In 1969–1970, when I was in Cairo and Damascus, I noticed that in comparison with the spring of 1967 there was a great increase in the number of people praying on Friday. The mosques could not hold all the people who came for secret communion with Allah. The police would close off the streets and squares in the middle of the capitals, because they were filled with believers. Was this growth of interest in Islam connected to the people's disenchantment with the deep social transformations then taking place in Egypt and Syria? I am convinced that they were not. For illustration I will remind you that the social revolution was dominated by a leftward tendency. The persistent growth of influence of the working class in Egypt and Syria was always making itself felt, and laws appeared that strengthened the role of the working class in society. So why did the number of people praying in the mosques of these and other Arab countries continue to multiply?

Primarily because the Egyptians, Syrians, and Palestinians, like all Arabs, who after the war with Israel in June 1967 were in national prostration (their self-respect and pride had been rudely stomped upon before the eyes of all mankind), took ever greater account of the fact that those who then stood at the head of the Arab world were not in a position to offer the masses a realistic program for successful military and political resistance to aggression and imperialism. Egypt, Syria, Jordan, Lebanon, and Iraq, which had taken upon themselves the main burden of confronting Israel and the United States, suffered continuous new defeats. The social revolution in the Arab countries proved to be seriously deformed. Seeing no prospects for a war of national liberation, the Arab masses and the youth went to the mosques! An extreme crisis of political leadership began in the Arab world, growing sharply worse after the death of President Nasser in September 1970. It continues to this day.

Now one hears about how there was a purported crisis of "secular nationalism," that the socialist slogans which President Nasser advanced in 1962 failed, that the entire experience of the Egyptian social revolution proved unattractive, and so on. In my opinion such remarks do not take account of the time factor. Egypt in the beginning of the 1960s, despite the reforms already introduced, was a very backward country. Recall its economy, its conservative social structure, the low level of literacy in the many millions of its populace. To redirect, to radically transform everything at once, was naturally not within Nasser's power; even with the help of the Soviet Union and other socialist countries. And how many years did life and history give him to introduce even the fundamental transformations? Five is all, from July 1962 to June 1967! Yes, had any of his opponents who now talk about "the failure of Nasserism" been in Nasser's place, they would not have been able to do more. Less, yes, but no way could it be more!

I consider the Arab masses' turn to the mosques after they had suffered the national catastrophe of 1967 to be even proper. It is the nature of people to seek an easy path to salvation. When things are especially hard, then they seek salvation in religion. Especially there, in the foreign East. Only later did the Arabs, primarily the Palestinians, take up arms. After all, the alternative was shameful capitulation, throwing themselves on the mercies of the United States and Israel.

Old ideas in a new way

Scarcely had the events in Iran shaken the stability of the Shah's regime and begun to threaten the interests of the United States in that country, in the Gulf region, in the Middle East and in Africa, when attention to Islam grew even stronger. Everywhere. Every year a million new followers of the teachings of the Prophet Muhammad appeared on the African continent. In Washington and in London, though, the attitude to Islam became ever more specific, or, to be precise, more subversive. Z. Brzezinski, the national security adviser of then-U.S. President J. Carter, reacted to the "Islamic explosion" in his own way. Having perceived Islamic fundamentalism as a "bulwark against communism," Brzezinski announced in an interview in the *New York Times* that the United States should applaud the rising forces of Islam. He found it wholly tempting to have the Americans make use of the fact that Islam seemed to be in ever sharper conflict with the allies of the Soviet Union; for example in Syria, Libya, and South Yemen. And to lessen Soviet influence, all means are good. So the President's adviser expressed support for the old British idea of creating governments and regimes in the Near and Middle East with the participation, and even under the control, of the "Muslim Brotherhoods."

I will explain what is being discussed. The Muslim Brotherhoods were created in 1928 with the support of London. The English, as is always the case in such instances, appeared to stay to one side, but their people in Cairo prepared a new, carefully conspiratorial political organization for confrontation with the truly national forces that were agitating for the immediate liberation of the country from British rule. First and foremost they were prepared to struggle for power under religious, Islamic slogans. There were anti-English actions enough among the leaders of the Muslim Brotherhoods, even more than enough, but this situation did not disturb those who stood at the source of the association. The opposite in fact; the conviction that the Brotherhoods would be able to splinter and weaken the true nationalists was almost absolute.

The 1950s brought the English a series of catastrophes in the Arab world, especially in Egypt. The revolution that began there in July 1952 led first to the banning of the Muslim Brotherhoods, and then four years later to the English departure from the area of the Suez Canal. The military wings of the Brotherhoods were disbanded, the leaders punished, and the association went underground.

The Muslim Brotherhoods became active very soon after the 1967 war. Now they are active in 30 states of Asia and Africa. It was they who Brzezinski chose to play the "Islamic card" against the Soviet Union. He, a graduate of McGill, the Jesuit university in Canada, already thought then that religious manipulation, especially of Islam, on a global level, would not only guarantee the defense of U.S. interests in an area from Pakistan in the east to Morocco in the West, but would give the possibility, naturally in favorable circumstances that had still to be created, of exploding an "Islamic bomb" in the Soviet Central Asian republics.

Developing the idea, there appeared in Washington in 1979 an official strategic report on the problems associated with the "Islamic games," which in part directed that along the southern borders of the USSR there had to appear special, top-secret Muslim organizations oriented toward disruptive activities within our country. They were prepared to make use of Soviet citizens who lived in the places traditional for Islam.

Those were the plans! Not only to surround the Soviet Union on the south with ideologically hostile governments, but also to begin to create conditions for the explosion of a Soviet "Muslim bomb"! Am I exaggerating? Judge for yourself, reader.

In December 1979, right after the just-mentioned report, the coordinating committee of the National Security Council of the United States gave the "green light" to disruptive broadcasts by the radio stations "Liberty" and "Free Europe" in Uzbek and other languages of the Central Asian republics. In addition it was specifically directed that the broadcasts were intended primarily for believers, for Soviet Muslims. But not exclusively . . .

In January 1980 President Carter informed the Senate that he had ordered a report on Islamic fundamentalism, not for some research program, but for use against the Soviet Union. The *Washington Post* then announced that the White House had directed the CIA to prepare a special report about this political phenomenon. Note, political, not religious!

Moment of truth?

I am not convinced that Islamic fundamentalism, which its leaders say is a return to the sources of the faith and the purity of national culture, is some kind of "new nationalism." I think that something else is involved here. Those who know what they are doing, with a feeling for the changing situation, are manipulating this movement, whether they are regional activists or secular politicans, trying if not to seize power in their countries then at least to influence them very strongly. To the benefit of those who stand behind them.

One of the peculiarities of the gathering popularity of Islamic fundamentalism is the multiplicity of its movements and organizations. And often of an extremist nature. There is literally a horde of them! And they continue to multiply. Many of them are secret, deliberately made deeply conspiratorial. Their structure very much recalls Masonic lodges; it seems to me that the time has come to speak of Muslim, "green" Masonry.

Have you heard of a secret organization called "Hojati"? I think not. It has been active for more than forty years in Iran, having as members Muslim clergy, diplomats, soldiers, high government officials, arms dealers, the heads of the secret services, businessmen, bankers, and technocrats. In a word, the flower of the

Islamic republic. "Hojati" maintains extremely close contacts with two English Masonic lodges, "Austrum Argentsium" and "Golden Dow in Water." The circle of its interests is wide, from banks, trade, and the Teheran Bazaar to secret purchases of American, Israeli, and other arms, the acquisition of modern electronic equipment, spare parts for the F-14 fighters that are in the arsenal of the Iranian army. "Hojati" actively supports Iranian lobbies in the United States, although its leaders are doing everything possible to make Iran broaden and strengthen its political connections with Western Europe, primarily with England! This then is the main goal of the most influential Islamic organization, hidden from the "uninitiated." Once again I would point out that as soon as you begin to discuss Iran, you immediately run across "English tracks"!

I confess that we know too little about the Muslim Brotherhoods who are gathering strength in the Islamic countries. A great deal that goes on in their organizations we, alas, can not see . . . In addition, something that should give pause has been happening in the past fifteen years, the appearance of offshoots of the Muslim Brotherhoods. Many offshoots! Often wholly respectable and even educational offshoots. For example in Kuwait, where I had a very lively discussion for many hours with the "Brethren," there passed before me an endless succession of representatives of the then legally existing "Al-Muzhtamaa al-izhtimai" (Social Organization), spelling each other in discussing the matters at hand. Before the start of the discussion I asked my opponents, "Do you consider us Soviet atheists to be "*mulkhidini*," or "buriers of the faith"?

Once the English had worked very hard to instill this nonsensical idea in the Arab consciousness. "No, we don't," said the first secretary of the society, Ibrahim Shati, after thinking a bit, looking me in the eyes.

What didn't we argue about! In part they asked me about the situation in Afghanistan. Reminding them that the *dushmany*[c] had killed five thousand mullahs (!) for nothing more than their loyalty to the Kabul government, I stressed that the limited Soviet military contingent which had entered the country on the request of the legal government was defending the mosques of Afghanistan. Against the "brotherhoods," the *dushmany* . . .

Where are they, these directors of the fates of many hundreds of thousands of believers who have joined their fates and the future of their countries to the Muslim Brotherhoods? In the West! However, paradoxical it may seem, the greater part of their administrative centers and other fundamentalist associations and societies are quartered in Munich, Aachen, and Hamburg (in the Federal Republic of Germany). There are Muslim centers in Paris and London. The most important of them are secretly connected with Israel. The CIA, MI-6, the French secret services, and the Mossad each have departments for working with the Brotherhoods. West Germany, the United States, England, and France all publish literature on Islam. The organizational structure of the Muslim Brotherhoods is wholly unusual. "Below," in the localities, they work in fives or threes. Each is unquestioningly subordinate to a sheik appointed by the high spiritual leader of the association, who in his turn is subordinate to a "link" who has contact with the leaders. The orders of the superiors are obligatory for execution. Disobedience is punished by death. Assembling the Brotherhoods when there is an alarm, or for conveying important information or action directives, is the prerogative of the sheiks. The assembly point is the mosque, or sometimes at conspiratorial secret addresses, for example in coffee houses or stalls in the bazaar, carefully hidden from the eyes of the curious. The discipline of members of the Muslim Brotherhoods is astonishing. During the discussion in Kuwait, Ibrahim Shati had only to raise his hand for the argument, no matter how hot it had been, to stop immediately. In place of the frowning faces there appeared smiles, and tea bearers mysteriously popped up from somewhere . . .

How dangerous are the activities of the Muslim Brotherhoods? In Afghanistan the great majority of *dushmany* are brethren. One of the fans of the association, the recently deceased American Richard Mitchell, once remarked that "The Muslim Brotherhoods are the West's most reliable and most promising move . . ."

I would ponder the evaluation of this serious American orientalist. Mitchell looked to the roots of things. And was surprised at nothing. Including the fact that the much-discussed "arc of crisis" is directed at the Soviet Union!

I am convinced that for the majority of our readers, such a turn in the conversation about the "arc of crisis" and its position on our Caucausian and Central Asian borders is not unexpected, for which reason I want to recall one more very cautionary judgment.

On the way to Beirut in 1981, where I was then working as a correspondent for *Literaturnaia gazeta,* I happened to speak with the famous Iranian political figure Jalal ad-Din al-Farsi, who in 1980 had been one of the candidates for the presidency in Iran, for which he had serious chances. However, an unexpectedly revealed circumstance interfered: that his father was an Afghan citizen. Farsi had carefully hidden this. When this fact became the object of publicity, he had to withdraw his candidacy and not stand for president. Imagine what would have happened had that fact remained hidden. The head of Iran could have been a citizen of Afghanistan! But this, as they say, already had nothing to do with the matter. We spoke in Arabic, so that there is no chance of a misunderstanding. Among the questions that were put to me that morning was the following:

"Why doesn't the Soviet Union get its soldiers out of Afghanistan?"

"How is it that this question is suddenly so important for you? After all, you are Iranian and have to know the real reason that our soldiers are there."

"It's very simple," Jalal ad-Din al-Farsi replied. "We made an Islamic revolution in Iran, and we consider it our task to turn it into a worldwide Islamic revolution. For that reason an Islamic revolution in Sunni Afghanistan is necessary. Your military presence prevents that. The revolution in Iran is a Shiite one, and the Shiites are sectarians, a minority in the Islamic world. After an Islamic revolution in Afghanistan the real worldwide Islamic revolution will begin. It will be more powerful than the French Revolution and all other such precursors. And then (sic!) we will inspire a third Islamic revolution . . ."

"Where, if it isn't a secret?"

"In your Central Asia," he said, then looked challengingly at me . . .

Both what I heard from the Iranian and Mitchell's passing observation about Western reliance on the Brotherhoods, it is not difficult to note, have one and the same projection.

In the Soviet Union every person who believes in the teachings of the Prophet Muhammad has the opportunity to observe all the commandments of the Koran. The mosques, of which there are 365, are open and full of worshippers, which even our most passionate opponents admit. Among the Turkmens, Tadzhiks, Uzbeks, Kazakhs, and Azerbaidzhanis there are many believers. Of course there are not 60 million, or even 45 million, as the Western experts on Islam affirm. Who are they relying on, those in the United States, and especially in England and Western Europe, who very much want to become witnesses tomorrow to an "Islamic march" from Central Asia and Azerbaidzhan to Moscow?

Yes, between Marxism-Leninism, our materialist world view, and Islam there are differences of principle. I was often reminded of this by many people in the Arab countries and in Iran. True! But something else is true as well. Those same people in the end agreed that even with all these differences, in these troubling times it is important to think about what is common to all mankind, about common experiences, which excludes playing the "Islamic cards," which Washington and London continue to dream about. It is not destructive games that the believers need. In an atomic age new thinking is necessary. People must have mutual understanding in support of life, not death; there is the path to salvation. The only path.

We are for the peaceful activities of the Muslim clergy as was recently demonstrated in Baku. The Soviet Union is correct to count on understanding of its approach to the problem of Afghanistan, in part to the far from abstract question of who was threatening whom there. Moscow decisively rejects playing any "Islamic cards" on our southern borders.

Washington, London, Paris, and Munich nevertheless continue to play these cards, and are inclined to think that there are already some results. Thus, according to the London *Times* (the newspaper published a special study of this), many Soviet citizens belong either to secret Sufi organizations or to the association of the Muslim Brotherhoods.

Itis reasonable to doubt the reliability of this very sensational account by a respected English newspaper. Perhaps it is only an assertion? Parenthetically, some people have already made such an assertion. However, how is it possible not to pay attention to something in the *Times*? Immediately there arose a number of questions; "what is what" in Sufism and are there Sufi organizations? Are they involved in politics or only in Islamic mysticism? . . .

The facts speak for themselves

Just two separate facts, which at first glance don't seem to be connected.

In Tashkent, at the republican special communications center, where parenthetically a number of well-educated people work, "strange" messages began to appear on the bulletin board almost every day. Some of the workers, including members of the CPSU, were inviting their colleagues to various . . . religious activities. This impressive bulletin board was prepared on the orders of the administrator in charge of the network, of course a member of the CPSU, S. Tairov. The actual texts were drawn up and their posting was supervised by another member of the CPSU, the courier M. Kadyrov. So here was senior dispatcher S. Tursunov (a young communist and secretary of the network's Komsomol organization) inviting people to the home of his late father-in-law for a memorial gathering at which prayers would be read. I would point out especially that the ritual is a Muslim one, so what was meant was reading the Koran. The driver T. Iusupov, also a member of the CPSU, invited his fellow workers to celebrate the Islamic holiday ''Sunnat-toi.''

And no one was disturbed by this public dissemination of this kind of message. The opposite, in fact, since for some time some of the workers have come to regard these notices as an integral part of the social life of the organization. Are you surprised? You shouldn't be. Or at least that's what the secretary of the network's party organization, K. Khikmatullaeva, thought, who peacefully failed to notice the appearance of these announcements. When, however, trouble broke out about the workers' interest in Islam, the assistant to the supervisor N. Vakhabov took those Muslims who had been ''distracted'' by religion under his protection. At an open party meeting which had just considered means for improving ideological work in light of the decisions of the Plenum of the Central Committee of the Uzbek Communist Party, Vakhabov emotionally, heatedly, even passionately characterized the signs of communists' participation in Islamic rituals and prayers as ''slander'' and called everyone to fight . . . the slanderers!

Fact two. In the Turkmen SSR a few years ago there appeared burial sites which became the objects of pilgrimages for believing Muslims. I didn't wonder why this kind of ''little *haj*''[d] pilgrimage was occurring, but I did want to find out what these new ''holy'' places were. It turns out that these suddenly ''holy'' burial places were for deserters who, for religious reasons (?!), had refused to serve in the ranks of the Soviet Army during the Great Fatherland War.

Can you imagine my surprise at hearing this? To be frank, though, my surprise grew even greater when I heard some new details. The asphalted roads leading to these burial sites were paid for by the kolkhozes. And the transport of pilgrims to these sites was also organized by the kolkhozes, at their expense. Meaning that just as with the incident at the Tashkent network, members of the CPSU in charge of expensive enterprises naturally knew that they were financing Islamic rituals!

I run to exclamations because it seems to me that only exclamation points are in some part able to fix emotionally and stress the astounding reality, that in our Central Asian republics there are facts becoming known which are literally frightening. There is already a very receptive environment there, a kind of Islamic infrastructure, whether you call it religious or national. Why is it that the question has to be put like that?

Primarily because the ''Islamic cards'' rely on this infrastructure. In Washington, Paris, London, and Munich, where the foreign centers of the ''Muslim Brotherhoods'' and other Muslim organizations are active, it is precisely in this infrastructure that reliable points of support are sought.

The Voice of America, Radio Liberty, and Radio Free Europe devote 90 percent of their broadcasts in Uzbek, just as in the other languages of Central Asia, to Islam. Yes, precisely Islam. Nor should it be thought that the studios of these radio stations are staffed by some sort of cranks who have no idea of their audiences. The opposite, I would make bold to state, since these very experienced gentlemen do not directly attack the CPSU or Soviet power in our "Muslim" republics. The basis of their programs is essentially the Islamic education of their audience, with a carefully considered content and very attractive format. Then, gradually and in no way obtrusively, they develop a taste for things such that the spiritual, the religious will come to the fore, or more precisely, the Islamic. Yes, it is the study of the Prophet Muhammad.

I would add that it is not only the United States that directs radio broadcasts at Soviet Central Asia and the Caucasus with an "Islamic accent" in the national languages of our republics. On the Iranian-Soviet border alone there are 38 (thirty eight!) radio stations broadcasting about Islam and the "Islamic revolution." The goals of their broadcasts are openly disruptive, even though the broadcasts purport to be about the Muslim religion. That means that assertions about the export of the "Islamic revolution" are not propaganda!

Everyone knows that in the Soviet Union religion is separate from the state, but no one here is forbidden to believe in Allah or Christ. Here, though, some unexpected things begin, to which it is wholly useful to pay some attention.

Today in Central Asia and Azerbaidzhan, the lower Volga and the Urals, and in some other places where Islam was traditionally practiced, there now operate so-called "parallel mosques." Of which there are more than 1800! What kinds of sermons are read in them and who is reading them, only Allah knows. It should be stressed here that to build a small mosque, if even just in a part of a house, is not complicated. Neither the Koran nor the prayer rules of the believers demand the observation of any particular or hard-to-observe rules. Thus people will learn of the appearance of an active mosque in, let's say, an Uzbek or Kazakh village only very slowly.

There are also believing Muslims in Moscow, who gather fairly regularly in Izmailovo Park. Also to discuss Islamic problems.

I am always having to stipulate, "in the places where there are believing Muslims." In some cities and towns the Muslim societies can also be numerous. Characteristically they have open mosques, while Muslim organizations exist and function openly, with open access.

Another question thus inescapably arises: if everything is so easy, then why have there suddenly appeared "parallel" mosques? If in this village or that, some regional center or city there arises an interest in Islam, wouldn't it be wiser and more far-sighted to legalize these parallel institutions as quickly as possible? A great deal would immediately become clear, both for the local authorities and for the believers.

One hears that too often the national customs of the Uzbeks, Tadzhiks, Turkmen,

Kazakhs, Azerbaidzhanis, Tatars, and other Soviet citizens are mixed, sometimes intentionally, with religious practices. Parenthetically, the word "*adat*" in translation from Arabic means "habit, custom, ordinary practice." We, however, interpret it solely as a religious term, which causes a misunderstanding. It is exactly as though someone very much wants other people, especially the non-Muslims, to consider religious rituals as national customs. How easy it is to deceive yourself and others! In part by swearing that all national customs are some how or other connected with Islam, that this connection is almost organically a part of this people or that. Thus to subject them to any kind of criticism, or even worse to condemn them, is taboo! Try to argue with an approach like this, for example . . .

Kalym [bride price], the five-repeat genuflection (or prayer) passed off as physical exercise (!), observation of the Muslim fast (which in Central Asia is called *uraza* and in other parts of the Soviet Union is called *ramazan*), other Islamic holidays, especially the holiday of sacrifice after the completion of the fast, have all been written about and studied. These works are available everywhere. So I am puzzled by the indifference of some party committees to the growth of Islam. For example, in Dzhizak Oblast the restoration of a mosque cost 500 thousand rubles. And the party oblast committee knew about it, but had no response!

But let us return to customs. I am not rediscovering America if I stress that for many centuries the churches and mosques were the inventors and sustainers of custom. How does a precise understanding of what predominates in a given custom, the national or the religious, help? Why is it important? Primarily because it is easy to overdo things and cause people irreparable insult and offense. However, "underdoing" things is also risky . . .

A few words about terminology and names. Somewhere in the Kara-Kum there is a village with the name of "Islam." I heard a radio broadcast about it myself, and would not have misused double-meanings there. In this case, where there is no necessity, I would have refused to use the first and last names which in translation meant "religion of Muhammad" and "light of religion," "light of Islam". . . Of course, that would have been voluntary. People might object that such was the custom there, but I would ask, the custom for whom? When? I think that my opponents would find it hard to answer this question.

I have long been aware of the vocal-instrumental group "Yalla." I have no idea where this name came from, but I do know that in translation from Arabic this name means "O, Allah!" No doubt people will object that the name of the group has nothing to do with this interpretation. I am happy to concede that, but if some name or other can be interpreted as something have a direct relation to Islam, then the name should be pondered well! Otherwise someone could use the name ambiguously. Is it worth permitting such things?

Rumors or reality?

It is known that among the clergy of Central Asia and other places where Islam is traditional in the Soviet Union, there are many interesting people. I know some of them, having seen something of them when they were very young, studying in al-Azar in Cairo, in the world-famous Islamic university. Recently, during a trip to the Persian Gulf nations (in November 1986), the group of Soviet cultural figures included two Muslim hiearchs, the imam of the Tashkent mosque and the director of the Mir Arab *medresseh* [religious school] in Bukhara. The first is a little over forty, the second about fifty. They were received with interest and, I should like to stress, with great respect in Kuwait and the United Arab Emirates. I got interested in their attitude towards Soviet power.

"We co-exist," they answered. . .

I was satisfied with the answer. In fact, these Uzbek Muslim figures, occupying important places among the clergy of the republic, don't think about entering into conflict with the authorities. So why am I suddenly mentioning this?

Here's why. . . In reading the latest books on Islam written by Western orientalists and journalists I have noted their ideas about a "Muslim opposition" which they said exists in the Soviet Union, about the suppression of Islam in the areas where the teachings of the Prophet Muhammad are traditionally distributed. Is this chance? I don't think so.

Earlier I already spoke of how some Western experts and wholly authoritative organs have argued that the Soviet Union already has Muslim organizations, certain sects, "brotherhoods" and societies. Underground, of course. Otherwise the London *Times* would not print communiques about this sort of activity.

I would not want anyone to get the impression that it is enough for some Western newspaper to print something for there to be something to worry about. I will begin by saying that the *Times* printed that article several years ago. I stress too that the London newspaper as a rule does not knowingly publish trifles. We should also consider that the English have a marvelous knowledge of Islam, its impulses, trends, and its secret organizations like the Muslim Brotherhoods. This is far from being a compliment. Knowledge of the infrastructures of Islamic societies once allowed the British powers to influence them.

Today it is worth remembering recent history. For example, the divisions of India and Palestine in 1947 were carefully prepared on religious lines by the English. The result? The India–Pakistan conflict and the Israeli–Arab conflict brought about by the divisions continue to this day. To London's benefit. And there is no end in sight to these conflicts. In 1980 interested imperialist circles provoked the Iran–Iraq war, a religious and political conflict within Islam. To it too there is no end in sight. History shows that religious wars are the most difficult to end. Directing them into any kind of channels for political solutions is an extraordinarily complex task.

Who else knows that there is a Muslim underground in the Soviet Union? I have before me the voluminous study of Sir Edward Mortimer, *Faith and Power: The Politics of Islam*, published in London in 1982. Reading it I had to acknowledge the erudition of the author, for which reason I could not read his passages about Soviet Muslims without attention. Sir Edward is honestly amazed, wondering why the believers of Azerbaidzhan don't revolt, on the model of their fellow Shiites in Iran. He discusses the "Muslim opposition," and puts his hopes not on the clergy of the republic but on the supposed anti-communist attitudes of the same Sufi brotherhoods that the *Times* wrote about. The crystallization of their attitudes, Mortimer noted, has proceeded especially quickly in the last fifteen years.

Militant Sufism is active in the North Caucasus, according to the Englishman. It is less noticeable in other areas of the dissemination of Islam in the Soviet Union, for example in Tataria, Bashkiria, and the lower Volga.

There is a curious and even characteristic trait emerging in Sufism. At its roots this Islamic mysticism, as those who know the religion of the faithful interpret Sufism, is Shiite. Thus its spread (I shall speak about its nature and forms a bit later) should, it would seem, provoke attacks and even resistance by the Sunni authorities. But it does not. In places where Islam of the Sunni type is traditional in the Soviet Union, Sufism does not encounter any difficulties; primarily, or so Mortimer says, because adherence to Islamic mysticism aids the dissemination of the religion of the faithful.

Another book, in my opinion, also deserves close attention; this is *Holy War*, by Wilhelm Dietel, a West German journalist who travels a great deal in the Near and Middle East. He was in Afghanistan, was interested in the work of the counter-revolutionary groups there, knew many of their leaders. The structure of these groups has a great deal in common with that of the Syrian Muslim Brotherhoods. He reports on a conference of the *dushman* leaders, which took place under the aegis of the Brotherhoods. Dietel in his book gives a somewhat unusual definition to the Sufis, the Islamic mystics, calling them dervishes.

In Dietel's opinion the Muslims of the Soviet Union have succeeded in the battle for religious freedoms. Here is the point of view he would have us accept: "As soon as Islam, which is now hidden in the wings, breaks out into the mainstream, and the aggressive fundamentalists begin to rebel, the Kremlin will have a new Poland, and this time within its own borders."

I do not think it was a coincidence that at a 1986 international conference of Muslims in the United States there was a call to set the task of separating Central Asia from the Soviet Union and creating some kind of independent Islamic state (!). Obviously those in Washington who would play the "Islamic cards" think that the time for action has already come. Along with the present hand of playing cards it is interesting to note that the players already have a concrete political task of a disruptive nature set before them. Its point is to complicate the situation in the Soviet Central Asian republics, and nothing less! In another recently published book, *Shi'ism and Social Protest*, edited by J. Cole and N. Keddie, stress is placed on the Soviet Shiites, in part the Ismailis who live in the Pamirs (more than 100 thousand people), and on the fairly strong influence of the idea of Islamic revolution.

Dietel too, after he was in Afghanistan, answered that "There are underground forces there."

Where is "there"? Dietel clarifies.

"On the other side of the southern border (of the Soviet Union). . . . From members of some *dushman* groups (or as Dietel calls them, "*mujaheddin*") I heard that connections had already been made with relatives and friends on the Soviet side. They even told about attacks on southern targets. Of course it was very difficult to get confirmation of this in Moscow. One of the leaders (of the *dushmany*) told me, 'We have already taken the battle to the land of the *shuravi* (the Soviet Union)!'"

Nonsense? Unfortunately, no! I will remind you of known facts. As the central press announced, on 8 March of this year Afghan *dushmany* shelled the border village of Piandzh. On the night of 9 April, east of the village of Moskovskii, the *dushmany* attacked our border troops. There were casualties. The inspiration of this obvious demonstration raid was Mir Muhammad, a relative of Bashir, the head of the Afghan bands called the Islamic Party, which are active in the province of Takhar. It is of course ridiculous to think that an attack by these pretenders to the role of "new Bashmachi"[e] could cause any loss to the Soviet Union. However, if what happened to the village of Moskovskii is seen as a signal that the war against the *shuravi* (the Soviets) is widened and already taken to their side, then what occurred may be seen in a different light. The lies of the heads of the *dushmany* acquire a more sinister meaning. Obviously the organizers of the "Islamic card" in Washington can not be dissuaded, even if they are hasty. . .

Have you heard of *taqiya*? This is something fairly common among Shiites, when some of them say publicly that they are renouncing Islam, when in fact they remain true believers. That is *taqiya*; it is used primarily to create illegal organizations. In Azerbaidzhan, let's say, where there are hundreds of "parallel" mosques, the sectarians are all very active, declaring themselves to be atheists (this is especially true of Sufis).

The youth who took part in the well-known December events in Alma-Ata[f] were also manipulated by Muslim fanatics and Sufis, who had infiltrated the student body. I mean senior students and even professors. What is alarming about this? It is alarming that many young people, not even knowing anything about the 16 December Plenum of the Central Committee of the Communist Party of Kazakhstan, were easily able to subordinate themselves to certain forces which would not risk talking about themselves out loud. And they appeared at the site of the events already bearing clubs . . .

Is this "Muslim opposition"?

The answer is yet to be seen. However, some people in the West certainly want things to be exactly so. I have before me an interview with Alexandre Bennigsen, an authoritative expert on Islam, published at the end of January in the Paris weekly *Le Point*. According to this Frenchman, Islam today is more destructive for communism than for Western democracy; it is an enemy to the East and only then to the West. Among those who provoked the demonstration in Alma-Ata, Bennigsen too singles out the Sufis; even though, according to him, they are primarily active in the North Caucasus, particularly in Daghestan, and in Central Asia and

Azerbaidzhan . . . I will admit that Bennigsen is obviously exaggerating. But for what purpose? In order to create a misleading picture. The goal is that same one, to prove that an Islamic infrastructure not only exists but is active.

How do the Sufi brotherhoods function? As secret organizations, frequently under the cover of so-called "business clubs." Further, Beningsen says, "outsiders" still have not infiltrated them in the territory of the USSR, meaning people from outside the cordon. So where are they to recruit their new members in these brotherhoods? Primarily from among youth and the intelligentsia. Naturally, none of the Sufis openly oppose Marxist-Leninist ideology and Soviet power. Although. . .

Sufism is ever more actively propagandized among Soviet Muslims. There is an "Islamizdat"[g] which fairly widely retypes and xeroxes publications on religious topics. Cassettes with recordings of the holy Islamic texts and of Islamic authorities are distributed. I would not be surprised to hear that some of these cassettes reach Tadzhikistan and Uzbekistan from over the borders, and thereafter they can reach the rest of the Soviet Union.

How seriously can Bennigsen's assertions be taken? It seems that it is time to pay some attention to them. Particularly as he goes too far in his thinking. The French expert even discusses a possible worsening of the situation. Of course we are only speaking of his assertions. However, he and other Western experts have a great deal, even too much, that is unsettling, and indicative that we ought to study Islam very carefully here at home. And in no event should the Muslims be allowed to use religion to the detriment of our Fatherland, the Union of Soviet Socialist Republics!

Editor's notes

a. Muhammad Abduh (1849-1905): a Mufti of Egypt, who is often considered the father of Arab nationalism.

b. Jamal al-Din al-Asadabadi (1838-1897): a Persian Shiite who adopted the name al-Afghani in his effort to spread Pan-Islamic philosophy.

c. *Dushmany:* anti-Soviet Afghan fighters.

d. *Haj:* pilgrimage to Mecca, a journey which every Muslim is obligated by the tenets of the faith to make at least once in his life.

e. *Basmachi:* the name the Soviets use to describe their armed opponents in the Central Asian uprisings of the 1920s and 1930s; it has a very negative connotation in Russian.

f. Reference is to the riots in Alma-Ata in December 1986 following the appointment of G. Kolbin to replace D. Kunaev as first secretary of the Communist Party of Kazakhstan.

g. "Islamizdat": unofficial (and hence illegal) presses distributing Islamic materials.

Note

1. The Organization of Islamic Conferences (OIC), founded in 1969, has 46 states; in 28 of them Islam is the state religion. Muslims live as well in the USSR, in Azerbaidzhan, Kazakhstan, Uzbekistan, Kirghizia, and Turkmenia, as well as in the Tatar and Bashkir ASSRs, in the North Caucasus, and in certain other regions of the country which are places for the traditional spread of Islam.

Resonance

I read the article by I. Beliaev "Islam and Politics," published in *Literaturnaia gazeta* (nos. 20 and 21, 1987) with extraordinary interest. The timeliness of this article is difficult to exaggerate. After all, even for experts there are still many blank spots in the study of the influence of Islam on contemporary political, social, and economic processes.

In fact, the program of scientific studies of the problems of modern Islamic studies includes the publication of an enormous number of monographs and collections on the history and ideology of Islam, on its position in foreign countries and regions, but it does not include a section offering the study of Islam in the USSR.

Beliaev's concern about the "restoration" of Islam's influence on the spiritual life of those peoples who professed Islam in the prerevolutionary period is near to me and understandable. I would say even more, that science still has not worked out the question of the reasons for the reproduction of Muslim rituals and traditions in conditions of socialism, the attraction of Islam for apparent nonbelievers, the identification in the social consciousness of the religious and the national. To explain these phenomena solely by the activity of the religious organizations and clergy contradicts the Marxist understand of religion, which demands a wide consideration of religion's social and historical condition.

It is impossible not to agree with such of Beliaev's concrete proposals as that, for example, the "parallel" mosques should be legalized. The small number of officially registered mosques (a little more than one percent of the prerevolutionary number) in no way corresponds to the number of believers and is nothing more than make-believe.

At the same time the author of the article writes of the existence in the Soviet Central Asian republics of "a kind of Islamic infrastructure." This is an exaggeration. Islam plays no role in the economy, in policy, in the law, in the educational system of the region, although at the same time it unquestionably occupies a certain place in social psychology, influencing the world view and life values of many people.

It is also impossible to call Beliaev's clearly ill-considered proposal about changing toponyms and personal names which have a "Muslim" etymology successful. In the interests of fairness it would also be necessary to rename a great deal outside of Central Asia as well. Studies have shown that, for example, the most common "Islamic" name of the past, Fatima, now stands almost thirtieth in popularity for newborn citizens of Samarkand, while names that in the past were very rare are coming to dominate, such as Ilkhom (Inspiration), Gairat (Energy), Guzal (Beautiful), and so on.

Beliaev's attempt to find a mention of Allah in the name of the popular group "Yalla" is aggravating, for this authentically Turkic word has since pre-Muslim times meant a joking dance song in the Uzbek language.

Beyond doubt Beliaev's article helps the correct understanding of the strength of

Islam in modern society, outside our country and inside it. It is no secret after all that ordinarily we most often understand an ideological struggle as something that does not concern us personally, as a function of political and state mechanisms. However, Beliaev convincingly demonstrates how deeply this struggle has entered into our daily lives, showing the means and colossal technological arsenal that propaganda hostile to us possesses. For me personally, as a student of Islam, the article was a reason once more to evaluate critically what we have at our disposal in this implacable struggle.

Professor Talib Saidbaev, PhD
Director of the Institute of Philosophy and Law,
Academy of Sciences, Uzbek SSR

Preliminary Results of a Thousand-year Experiment *

A Conversation with Academician D. S. Likhachev

Dmitrii Sergeevich, what we don't want is that this conversation should be as round and "anniversarial" as the date itself, the millennium of the Christianizing of ancient Rus'.ᵃ What shall we begin with?

With the question of the role of the baptism of Rus' in the history of the fatherland's culture. I think that it is with the baptism of Rus' in general that the history of Russian culture may be begun. Just as with Ukrainian and Belorussian culture. Because in general culture goes back to the Stone Age, to the Neolithic or the Paleolithic Ages. But the characteristic traits of Russian, Belorussian, and Ukrainian culture, the East Slavic culture of ancient Rus', go back to that time when Christianity replaced paganism.

Christianity is a written religion, which introduced Rus' to a highly developed mythology, to the history of the European and Near Eastern countries. There occurred a union with the culture of Byzantium, which at that time was the most advanced country. In addition this occurred when Byzantine culture was at the peak of its flourishing, in the ninth to eleventh centuries.

So, remind us how this occurred . . .

Rus' saved the Byzantine emperor Vasilii during the uprising of the Varda Foki. Vladimirᵇ sent Vasilii II and Constantine VIII a six-thousand strong troop of hand-picked soldiers, Varangian-Rus', who put down the uprising. As a result of this, apparently, Vasilii II promised to marry his sister Anna to Vladimir. However, when Emperor Vasilii II and his sluggish co-emperor Constantine VIII grew more secure on their throne, Vasilii II forgot about his promise, decided not to keep it, because his uncle, Constantine the Noble, forbade Byzantine emperors to take foreigners into their families, and especially pagans. Doing so he referred to an inscription on the altar in Sofia which said that members of the imperial family could not marry foreigners. Vladimir though was able to demonstrate his right to do so by military force.

He besieged Korsun—a Greek town which is now within Sevastopl'. Korsun fell and, according to tradition, the prince was baptized in the Korsun baptistry, which by the way still exists.

Then Vasilii II gave his sister to Vladimir I, and in the dynastic scheme Rus'

Ogonek, 1988, no. 10 (March), pp. 9–12. The interview was conducted by Andrei Chernov. Russian text © 1988 by Ogonek.

was elevated to an unprecedented stature, becoming related to the imperial house of Byzantium. Vladimir Monomach[c] was also a descendant of the Byzantine emperors. Out of a barbarous power on the edge of the world their suddenly appeared a power with a world culture, a world religion, which was immediately made plain with the flourishing of ancient Russian culture. This unusual flourishing is visible in the construction of Sofia in Kiev, which even today is the central architectural complex of the city.

And for almost a thousand years the Oranta of Kiev, the mosaic of the Madonna of the Unbreakable Wall with her hands raised in prayer, supports the arch of the temple. And the smalt of which she is made has not darkened or fallen despite the succession of centuries and the destruction in the mother of Russian cities.

Let's remember the Sofia in Polotsk, the central temple there. And the Novgorod temple of Sofia. No matter how many skyscrapers they build alongside, Sofia will remain the center of Novgorod, but not of some other city which is alien to our culture. Then there is the Salvation church in Chernigov, which even today is the center of Chernigov. Ascension Cathedral in Vladimir is the central sanctuary in its town. Everywhere temples sprang up that had no equal among our neighbors in size or in beauty; after all at that time the Czechs, the Moravians, and the Poles were putting up little rotunda-topped churches, while to the east of them was a great country with big churches, with frescoes, mosaics, remarkable icons, and a remarkable literature. For example, Ilarion's *Tale of Law and Blessings*. This is an exceptional work, because Byzantium had no such theological-political works. There there were only theological tracts, while here there was historisophical, political speech which affirmed the existence of Rus', its connection with world history, and her place in world history. This is an astonishing phenomenon, just as the Chronicles are an astonishing phenomenon. Then there are the works of Feodosii Pecherskii, then Vladimir Monomakh, who in his "Testament" combines high Christianity with pagan military ideals. Thus Rus' immediately became a world power, and Kiev was a rival for Constantinople.

I should like to point out to our readers how alive for people of the time were the connections of cultural tradition. If we don't, as Pushkin put it, "rouse the dream with heart-felt strength," then we won't notice that the famous Iaroslavna may be compared with that same Madonna of the Unbreakable Wall in Kiev, for after all with her passionate prayer Iaroslavna also supports the scorched walls of Putivl. This coincidence is even more important because in 1185 the only city which was taken by the Polovtsians fell after two watchtowers collapsed with people on them, unable to bear the weight of the defenders. And that means the walls between the watchtowers. And the hands which Iaroslavna raised to the Wind, the Dnepr River, and the Sun are invisible supports for the wall. After all did the troubadors make these same comparisons of Mary in the twelfth century? And wasn't Iaroslavna helped by the Old Testament Rachel, for after all Iaroslavna's Lament is filled with quotations from Rachel's Lament: "On the Dunai Iaroslavna's voice was heard . . . In Ram the voice was heard. Weeping and wailing and many cries. " *The Old Russian reader did not require commentaries of these "similarities.*" *It is a lot more difficult for us . . . But how did it happen that Rus' passed out of the learning stage so quickly and joined world culture with rights of equal dialogue?*

I think it was because there was an extremely rich basis, in the form of folklore, in the form of a developed legal system. "The Russian Truth" was apparently created before the Christianization of Rus'.

That means the soil was already prepared?

The soil was already prepared by the great route from the Varangians to the Greeks. After all Rus' controlled the northeastern European route. In the twelfth century it moved to the west, but two centuries earlier the great route from the Varangians to the Greeks was founded. And Christianity comes precisely along that route. It is not for nothing that the legend was created that the Apostle Andrew travelled this route. It was here, in Khersones (the same as Korsun), in Kiev, and in Novgorod, in these two centers of Rus', that our Christianity arose, on that great route. It appears already in the pagan troops which attacked Constantinople. If in the 911 treaty with the Greeks Rus' is represented primarily by pagans, then by 944 Christians predominate as signatories.

The names make that clear?

No, it is simply indicated in the treaty. If you read in the Chronicles about the treaty of 944, it says that the Rus' Christians swear in their church in Il'ia, while the Rus' pagans swear by their gods in Kiev. Rus' was an astonishing power which united Finno-Ugric peoples and Turkic peoples and Iranian peoples, and eastern Slavs. This may be seen in the names, and in the names of the gods. What is Mokosh'? The Mokosh' tribe. What is Perun? That's the Finno-Ugric Perkun. We had Veles or Volos, Stribog . . .

There are others too in The Lay of the Host of Igor[d] *. . . Khors, Dazhd'bog.*

So Rus' needed political unity all the more. A few years before accepting Christianity Vladimir tried to create a pantheon of pagan gods. But it didn't work.

You mean not long before his baptism Vladimir tries to "introduce" paganism, but in an ordered form. Why didn't it work out?

I think that the reasons here are completely objective, that paganism was chopped up among many places and tribes. And it was possible to unite only the surface of paganism, but not the entire religion as a whole. Besides, this was a religion without a developed written compoenent, and also telling was the isolation of paganism from all of Europe, from Byzantium.

In other words, paganism was all right at home, in your own field?

Precisely, in your own field. And up to that time paganism was really all right, since even paganism has its own moral system. And a very important one. There is a remarkable new book by Marina Mikhailovna Gromyko called *Traditional Norms of*

Behavior and Forms of Association Among Russian Peasants of the Nineteenth Century (1986) [Traditsionnye normy povedeniia i formy obshcheniia russkikh krest'ian XIX v.], which demonstrates that every ritual contains a certain moral norm. What for example is *toloka*? That's communal work by the entire village. But in Christian Rus', at that stage of economic development when the need for communal work lessened because the peasant controlled his own land and could work it himself, *toloka* was transformed into a form of assistance for poor families, those which had no head of the family.

Does the name of the ritual come from the verb toloch' *[to pound or crush]?*
Yes, but remember too what the pagan allies in *The Lay of the Host of Igor* are called? They are mentioned in Sviatoslav's dream.

Tolkoviny.
See, that's how the pre-Christian Slavic village united during the time of a *toloka*. And as for the so-called "dual faith," I think that it is a scholar's myth. Dual faiths are impossible, because you can't believe in both pagan gods and be a Christian at the same time. It's impossible.

That means that a person doesn't believe the one or the other?
Or that he's lying.

Or that he believes in Christ as one more pagan god.
Inasmuch as paganism was fractured, Vladimir destroyed it in a fairly peaceful way. He pushed the idols into the water after they had been standing in Kiev only a few years. People cried over them and forgot them. Note that they weren't chopped up or burnt. They were seen off with honors, in the same way that an icon destroyed by age will be put in the water, trusting its fate to the river. And that's all. ancient gods left. However, paganism in agricultural and domestic moral forms exists even now. One example is the belief in house spirits [*domovye*].

Even Mokosh' is alive in the people's consciousness. My mother spent the entire war as a young girl in a village in Tver' and heard how the Ivanovs live richly, that at night Mokush' (as they called him) brought grain into their barn. The peasants still remember Mokosh'-Mokush' now, though by all laws the god hasn't existed for more than a thousand years. But who speaks of the dual faith of modern peasants?
And this Mokosh' doesn't contradict Christianity at all. You remember how Dostoevskii's Raskol'nikov bows down to the earth at the crossroads, asking the earth's forgiveness? There are scientific studies of bowing and confessing to the earth.

That's how the "strigol'niki" bowed and confessed right up to the twentieth century.
They used to ask the earth's pardon when the plow bit into the earth. People sang a song to say "forgive me, nurturing earth, for scratching your breast."

Agriculture was built on respect for the earth, faith in the earth.

And Christianity didn't touch that, since otherwise how was one to live, to grow bread?

That's not a dual faith, but a particular love for the earth.

I would even take the risk of proposing that the very term "dual faith" comes as a result of scorn for the peasant life-style, as a result of an active failure to understand the structure of peasant agriculture, domestic existence, life.

It's a term from the nineteenth century. Here's something else that's very important. Let's go back to that same *toloka*. In order to help other people, people dressed in their holiday clothes, sang gay songs, and decked their horses out. Then they held races, games, and feasts. It was a holiday. Help and charity were not forced from people. Not a heavy obligation, but a holiday ritual, that's what the *toloka* was. Just like belief in the might of trees. Let's remember the holy groves of Rus'. Peryn' was a holy grove, perhaps the last one, which right now is dying in Novgorod because of government inattention. It was constantly supported and cared for by the people of Novgorod, while now there is some sort of camp, for tourists or Young Pioneers, and people are trampling Peryn'. . . . Belief in trees, in their healing power, is so important! What we are trying to inculcate right now with all possible scientific means was all achieved with life, with beliefs. A tree is alive, and if you live under a big oak tree, you will live a long time, because the tree will give you part of its strength. Isn't that true? And Christianity took all that. Trinity Day is a holiday of everything alive.

Dmitrii Sergeevich, here's that holy Tree of the World, they most ancient axis of creation, right in your office. I mean the tree on the shoulder of the middle angel in that reproduction of Rublev's "Trinity." Now on that day the Orthodox churches are decorated with green branches. And not long ago the Moscow biologist G. V. Sumarukov established a chronological table of Igor Sviatoslavich's escape from captivity, and it turns out that in The Lay of the Host of Igor *Igor bids the Don River farewell precisely on Trinity Sunday, while the Donets River "spread for him its green grass on its silver shores beneath the canopy of a green tree"! And that same tree bends down to the earth in lament when trouble comes to Rus'.*

In one of my books I reproduced an old Russian icon in which the trees bow down to the Madonna. And remember the ikon with Vlasii, who replaced the pagan Volos, where there are horses of diferent colors. Horses like flowers.

How painless was the change from Volos to Vlasii?

I think this process took place more or less painlessly. Because the Volkhv uprising of 1071 was caused first of all by hunger, and not to defend the old gods. The Volkhvs were convinced that some kinds of witches kept grain under their humpbacks, and that their humps had to be unstitched in order for there to be grain. So the uprising wasn't purely religious, but economic.

But for the sake of fairness apparently we have to remind our readers about the

Christian homilies on paganism as well. When pagan rituals and morals entered in contradiction with the morals of Christianity, the church took a severe position. The view of the pagan gods was that they were the founders of the tribes, which the author of the Chronicles shared. And there was a view that they were devils, which was shared by many later church writers. But was it really so rare that a warring Christian behaved like a true pagan, and in his struggle with superstition himself fell into cruel superstition?

Princely behavior in the world was defined for a long time by the pagan codex of honor and glory. The ideal of the soldier was not Christian, but pagan. That's what it stayed. Vladimir Monomakh recounts how many campaigns he completed, how quickly he reached Chernigov from Kiev. He boasts about it.

And that's not Christian behavior.

No, not Christian. But very similar to the behavior of Sviatoslav who went about "unburdened with his own burdens" and ate what came along, horse meat or the meat of wild animals, or just a sliver of something, kept under his saddle, carried with him. And he slept on his saddle blanket. That's the ideal of a pagan prince. I repeat, we don't know the details of the advanced pagan cult. We know the rituals, but they were different in each locality. And we know the ethical norms of paganism.

A book came out last year that argued that the author of The Lay of the Host of Igor *was a pagan. Why is that impossible?*

It's impossible simply because at the end of the poem Igor goes to the church of the Blessed Virgin of the Tower, and the entire poem is steeped in Christian spirit. That was already noted by Karl Marx, although he was not a specialist on the "Igor Tale."

But people will answer that Karl Marx wasn't a specialist, and the end was added on by a monk!

So then everything was added by a monk! The "Igor Tale" makes clear that the pagan world view was not forgotten in the twelfth century. However, it was understood in the form that was also characteristic for the eighteenth and nineteenth centuries, when the writers referred to the pagan gods of antiquity as definite symbols. Those "arrows of Stribog" that the author of the "Tale" uses are no longer on the religious stage, but rather the esthetic stage of religion.

Let's say even further that reminders of the pagan gods and pagan attributes only show in the poet when he speaks of the past of the Russian Earth, or how this past defines the tragedy of the present. The poet contrasts pagan splintering with Christian behavior and the Christian unity of the motherland. For that reason, in addition to Virgin of the Tower church there are two Sofia churches, the one in Kiev and the one in Polotsk. To continue your thought, Dmitrii Sergeevich, the poet shows how following pagan moral norms, however, attractive they may be, leads to tragedy for the great grandchildren of Dazhd'bog.

They no longer believed in the former gods as gods. However, the ecological system of paganism was also accepted by Christianity.

Let's note that this is a world-wide process. M. I. Steblin-Kamenskii, who studied the art of the northern European "skald," wrote that after the Christianization of Ireland and Scandainavia mention of the pagan gods disappeared for a hundred and fifty years, then right in the epoch of the "Tale" they once again come into poetry, but already in a different capacity.

Paganism is not a negative magnitude. It is a definite cultural value which after the acceptance of Christianity doesn't lose its value, but is raised to the height of another world view. There are some lines in one of the Psalms, "Every breath praises the Lord." The pagan understanding of "every breath" here is raised to a level unreachable by paganism.

Sergei Sergeevich Averintsev has a beautiful book, The Poetics of Early Byzantine Literature *[Poetika rannevizantiiskoi literatury], in which the author shows, in part, that Christianity was a way out of the spiritual and intellectual dead-end of antiquity. That dead-end was fully evident to the writers of antiquity at the beginning of the era.*

Things among us were a bit different. Simply the government could not live with different beliefs. After all, Christianity is accepted at the moment when Valdimir has united Rus'. One must speak not of a way out of a dead end, but of government necessity, which paganism was not in a position to guarantee. Vladimir's government was not sustained by a police system and not just by a military system. This was a multinational state, which made it so necessary to have an international religion. After the baptism of Rus' Istvan I (Stefan I) introduced Christianity into Hungary, where before that it had existed only in places, among the Slavic tribes who had taken Christianity from Cyril and Methodius, the great Bulgarian preachers. Istvan introduced the western form of Christianity, uniting Hungary by force, as Karl the Great before him had baptised the Saxons by force of arms. No weapons were required for us, though. Among us this process was fairly peaceful. What is very important here for understanding the eastern variant of Christianity? Take Patriarch Fotii, the same one in whose day Askold and Dir unsuccessfully attacked Constantinople, who in sending the Bulgarian prince Boris Mikhail several missives said that truth may be known by beauty.

It seems to me that a thousand years later one of the great western physicists said that if the formula is beautiful, then it is reliable.

You see? Just as how you can't change anything in a human face, if this is a healthy and beautiful face, so for Flotii the true religion is recognizable by beauty. And Vladimir's emissaries, sent to various countries in search of the true religion, when they returned they told the prince that he must accept precisely the Greek faith, since they had seen beauty among the Greeks.

But could Vladimir really have known Flotii's words?

Whether he knew it or not, everything was shot through with this. Including the decision of the emissaries, which of course weren't as laconic as they are presented in the chronicles.

That means we can trust the chronicles?
We can. Even if we doubt the sending of emissaries and the trip and the argumentation of merits, how can we not trust the choice itself? The main argument was the churches, which, with their living, true beauty, were overpowering. Vladimir was concerned about the construction of churches, but Istvan I of Hungary was not. In the same way Poland and Moravia, which took Christianity from the West, were not so concerned. Vladimir, however, built and built and built. He invited the Greeks in. He created an entire network of crafts, which later influenced all of Russian culture. This shows in the primacy of the aesthetic moment over the philosophical one. Who are the best Russian philosophers? Derzhavin (in his ode *God* [Bog]), Tiutchev, Dostoevsky, Vladimir Solov'ev. Even Chernyshevskii struggled to be a writer. It is possible to argue about who is good and who is bad, but the Russian philosophers were all writers and artists. And "mental vision in paints"—those are icons. What is our very greatest treatise of the beginning of the fifteenth century? Rublev's *Trinity*.

Dmitrii Sergeevich, I would like to be a bit more detailed about this. They told us that Gagarin had flown, but he didn't see any god. Perhaps for a child growing up in an atheist family this might be a convincing argument. But is it possible to call such atheism scientific, if the believers know that the icon is "a depiction of likeness," so that from the visible image he might ascend to that which, as a Byzantine philosopher puts it, "has no sensible form"?
In the drive for beauty and the comprehension of the world through beauty there were superiorities, but there was also a disadvantage.

Right now "Nauka" publishing house has a collection that includes an article about the monogram "INTsI" inscribed in the colonnade of Rublev's Trinity. This is a shortened notation of what Pontius Pilate had written on the cross. The left column has "I," the right one has "N," and together they make "Ts," while the last letter coincides with the same "N."[8] Such graphic contractions are to be found in the old Russian books. Rublev's mongrams are constructed so that the smallest destruction of proportions would kill it. And now a few decades later the icon painters don't see it, they rationalize Rublev's architecture. But perhaps the most amazing thing is that Rublev's secret writing is not an end in itself, but a key to a philosophical picture of the world.
There was no university education in Rus', but the country was literate. Very literate. At one time that was demonstrated by Academician A. I. Sobolevskii, using signatures on documents, and now it has become clear from excavations in Novgorod. We are no longer surprised by the writings on birchbark. There were no universities, but art didn't lag behind the West at all.

And it follows a unique path.

Unique in what? Our churches are gay, and decorated. This may even be some sort of element of the East, if you like. Or, more precisely, and an element of jolly beauty. Orthodox Christianity is the gayest Christianity. Remember how Tiutchev puts it, "I love the Lutheran service"? However, the poet stresses the gloominess of this service. You'll notice that the Catholic churches are also severe in their grandiosity. While the Russian church, thanks to its light, vivid, shining iconostasis, thanks to the humanized structure of the space, its cosmism, and the gold of fire is simply beautiful. And light.

Let's stop at at least one monument. Last summer I was astonished by the Savior-Transfiguration Cathedral of the Mirozhskii monastery in Pskov. The restoration is finished there and the mid-twelfth century frescoes are presented in their full magnificence. And Christ ascends toward the cupola on a multicolored rainbow, while rays of light from the narrow windows support him. From the same sort of window a ray stretches from the archangel to Mary. And the old Russian masters violated the canon and painted the composition of Purification in mirror-fashion. By departing from the letter, they achieved having Mary drawing the youth into the center of the church, where he is already sitting on the throne as her grown son. This would be understandable to every woman of Pskov, how she had brought her own child here, so had Mary done at some time. Why was it understood? Because the road from the city is laid out from right to left, from the south to the north. And the entire northern part of the church tells about death, while the southern speaks of resurrection. And the cave with the buried Lazarus before our eyes turns from a black pit into a green tree. Thus the most hasty first glance will tell that pagan and Christian beliefs are intersecting here, that this is an attempt of genius, to make an explosion in an animated and inspired cosmos. There is no picture of the Last Judgment. Instead there is the descent of the Holy Spirit upon the apostles. You look around, wondering where the Last Judgement is, but it's there, inside you, inside your soul, because the Judge is already sitting on the throne directly before you. What astonished me most of all was that the church was painted by Greek and Russian master craftsmen together, but they created not an ensemble of frescoes, but a united story, of which I know nothing analogous.

It must be said that Rus' was never cut off from other countries. She subsumed Byzantine culture and western culture and Scandinavian culture and the culture of her southern neighbors, the nomads. Because her basis was unusually strong. What a language we had before the influence of the churchly, bookish language! How amazing in conciseness and beauty were the princes' addresses to their troops and the speeches at the princely congresses! This was not folkloric tradition, but oratorical, oral tradition, which was unusually strong.

Dmitrii Sergeevich, I would like to touch on the role of the monasteries in the Christianization of Rus'.

The role of the monasteries is extraordinarily interesting. We are accustomed to thinking that culture develops primarily in cities. In fact from the very beginning the *smerd*, or peasant farmer, becomes a *krest'ianin* [peasant], meaning a *khristianin* [Christian].[*h*] In the very old chronicle the *smerd*s are mentioned only once. That means that in the peasant environment Christianity spread very rapidly. And this would have been impossible with the help of the sword, but possible with the help of paganism itself, which become Christianized and made Christianity comprehensible. The *smerd*s, or simple peasants. saw Christianity as a continuation of their own paganism, but it opened new horizons, and they were ready to accept these new horizons. Rus' understood that besides circular calendar time, there is also horizontal time, into which the neighboring people were drawn. Or let's say vertical time.

The circle became a spiral?

Yes. Christianity among us began to develop along the great route from Variag to Greece because the people saw foreigners here, foreign goods, they knew about the existence of other peoples. And here there comes the understanding that history is not limited to the local burial mounds, that there is a history of all mankind. The Slavs had writing, but it was a disorganized one. The scribe Khrabor talks of how the Slavs wrote with lines and cuts, but without order. For the first writing they used either their own signs or even Greek letters. As a sign that, for example, this vessel holds wine of such and such a sort, while this one has grain. With Christianity comes a writing of another and very high class. This was writing with order, with punctuation and division into words, with a defined grammar. This is a writing system of a literary language and a very rich literature. The most complex ideas appear, which means that the language was prepared to accept the Christian idea, to accept writing. And here is where the role of the monasteries is noteworthy. How were new lands taken over? They were taken over by monasteries, where first and foremost they were occupied with writing. The thing most pleasing to God was the letter. That's why in the movement of Christian culture to the north the monasteries are formed first. Iaroslavl' is Savior-Transfiguration monastery. Vologda is Kirillo-Belozerskii monastery. And there primarily is where writing develops. Then Valaam. And there is a letter there too. Then the Solov'ev Islands, and the same picture there. The monasteries had enormous book-copying workshops. The book conquered new territories. It is clear now that books were taken to Siberia and they conquered Siberia. It wasn't so much the weapon as the book.

Let's mention at least the so-called Zyrian Trinity, an icon with an extensive inscription in the Zyrian language, made by Stefan of Perm', the Zyrian enlightener. It comes to us from the fourteenth century, and can be seen in the Vologda museum.

The monasteries were built out in the country. The Kiev Cave Monastery was outside of town and Trinity-Sergius, the most important center of Russian book production and the mother of many Russian monasteries. Our section of old Russian literature in at Pushkin House is studying the book-producing centers of ancient Rus'. It is absolutely clear that book production takes places on the periphery, and that the peripheries are engaged in enormous book activity. If people write in buildings today, five story and twenty story ones, then they use to write in forests.

But could there have been a Russian literature before Christianity? What do you think of the "Vlesov Book"?

It's a fake. It's obvious when and how this primitive falsification appeared, and why it became popular in the White emigrant environment. The "Vlesov Book" is of no interest. Let's talk about something real . . .

If Rus' was baptized by fire and sword, as some authors say, why was there no restoration of paganism during the three centuries of Tatar control?

The Tatar-Mongols who conquered Rus were polytheists, and polytheism is strong in that it recognizes new gods. Khan Batyi [Batu]^i was religiously tolerant. When the Tatar-Mongols took Mohammedanism [Islam], that was when Dmitrii Donskoi's^j holy war against Mamai began. Mamai's campaign was not just another campaign, but the campaign of Islam against Rus'.

By the way, that was understood by contemporaries. In the stories of the Kulikovo cycle it says that Mamai was not going to destroy the Russian towns, but rather seize them and rule them. That is he set the task of occupying and enslaving Rus, of muslimizing it. And the transition of the Mongol-Tatars to the settled control of Russian cities.

That's when Dmitrii needed the support of Christianity, and he turned to Sergii Radonezhskii, who was the major authority in the Russian peasantry. Why? Because he shared all the peasant's work. Sergii Radonezhskii is the Russian analogue of Francis of Assisi, he had the same attitude to nature, to birds and animals . . . This is a Christianity of poverty, proceeding from poverty and closely tied to the people. Francis though was a hundred and fifty years earlier and in fact lived on alms. Sergii didn't work at poverty, he worked at simple peasant labor. For a peasant Sergii Radonezhskii was more authoritative than the metropolitan, than the church in Moscow or wherever.

But why does a Moscow prince go to him?

Dmitrii had to have a militia. For the first time in Russian history there was the need to mobilize the people's militia of peasants. And the prince went to the main authority of peasantdom and Christianity. For them Sergii was the head of the people. And Sergii Radonezhskii broke the church canons . . .

He gave Dmitrii two monks . . .

Not just monks, but *skhimniks* [those who had taken the very strictest monastic orders—Trans.]. And that doesn't mean that he gave two hero knights. Two knights, no matter who they were, would have meant nothing in such a battle. But they created the conviction among the troops that this was a holy struggle, that those who died in it would go to heaven, that this battle was not simply killing for the salvation of the motherland, but was a holy war. They went to defend their land, for which reason they destroyed their barges behind them on the Oka River. They had crossed and they would not go back. They would stand there, on the soil of Riazan'.

And die there, having strengthened the Russian soil with their blood. It is not for nothing that the very idea of Russia appears in the end of the fourteenth century. Let's remember that Andrei Rublev also painted his Trinity "in praise of most excellent father Sergii" and, as Epifanii puts it, "so that by seeing the Holy Trinity fear in this world will be destroyed."

Sergii Radonezhskii was the conduit of certain ideas and traditions, connecting the unity of Rus' with the church. The princes quarreled and brought the Tatars onto Russian land, as the Polovtsians had been before them. There was a constant on-going struggle for the great princedom, for the title of great prince. The church though was united. That is why the major idea of Rublev's Trinity is the idea of unity, which was so important in the gloom of our division . . . Dmitrii Donskoi began not uniting territory but by a national and moral unification. That was what was remarkable about this Moscow prince who came to head the Russian troops. And Moscow gained from this in the eyes of all Rus'. It gained not because, as people try to prove, it stood in especially advantageous trade routes, but because in this extremely complex situation it made supreme a policy of uniting the Russian lands. That is Moscow gained spiritually.

But there are economic laws!

We have incorrect, vulgarized ideas about economic laws. These laws of course are the basis of everything, but when they lead to a spiritual enlightenment, at some point the spiritual begins to play a major role. Moscow was not stronger economically than were Tver' or Novgorod, but she proved spiritually stronger. If Novgorod did nothing for the unification of Rus' because it was a republic, the Metropolitan of All Rus' moved to Moscow, and Moscow became the symbol of spiritual unification.

Was the church schism of the seventeenth necessary? Were Nikon's reforms unavoidable and needed?

They were necessary to some degree, but they could have been otherwise. Moscow had become the center for the Ukraine and Belorussia as well, and for that reason the Orthodox church had to have a single ritual. The initiator of the schism was Nikon, because he replaced the old two-fingered way of crossing one's self with the new three fingered one. At that time the rituals among the Greeks, as it was said in Rus', were "defiled," there was much "innovation," while Russia preserved the traditional ways. It would have been possible to find some sort of compromise decision, but Nikon took the side of the Ukraine to join it and Belorussia to Russia. The Ukraine had the three-fingered crossing "which had come from the Greeks." It is now clear that in many instances the Old Believers were correct, so that, as we know, the Nikonites had to fake certain documents. In addition Nikon had an extraordinarily cruel nature. Just like Aleksei Mikhailkovich, who also had a hard character. It's not an accident that he was the father of Peter. Nikon and Aleksei began to introduce uniformity with extremely cruel measures, which strengthened the schism in the Russian church. There's an example of the role of personality in history for you.

When does that historic moment come when the spiritual seeking of the flower of a nation parts ways with the pronouncements of official orthodoxy?

I think that a very large and negative role was played here by the seminary system of education. In the nineteenth century noble education was replaced by seminary education. And noble culture was replaced by that of the *raznochintsy*.[*] The culture of Dobroliubov and Chernyshevskii. The *raznochintsy* were main conduits of atheism, because their educational foundation was the seminary, however, paradoxical that may sound. The seminary killed enthusiasm for the apparently out-moded church dogmas. When a person comes too close to holy things and ways, the holy loses the charm of the holy. The church became too everyday, too simple for the intelligentsia of the *raznochintsy*. There was something of the village, something out-moded in the church. There was also something from the theater, where the roles and actors are known in advance. Further our seminaries, just like the Catholics, had discussions, someone took the role of atheist or heretic and students took up the roles passionately simply in a youthful spirit of opposition. Their atheism was provoked by the administration and the instruction. The major reason of course was that the entire civilized world in general was become atheist. That means both Europe and America. The appearance of materialists was a consequence of the development of the science of the day. There is a scientific spirit, which differs in different times. Let's say that in the period of the Renaissance science was visible, because Italy formed the Academy of the Lynx's Eye. At that time the main sign of a learned man was a precise eye, able to note the petty details of daily life and what is in heaven as well, like stars in a telescope for example. Then there comes the period of the mathematicization of science and the explanation for phenomena from the phenomena themselves. So you get the formula man is what he eats. All kinds of Bazarovs appear. Bazarov is a general European phenomenon, because science was suffering through a period in which God was not necessary. Then later, already in the twentieth century, in outer space and the inner space of the atom we discovered various obscure phenomena and now a scientist can also be a believer. We know of many such instances.

But in the beginning, in the sixteenth and seventeenth centuries, when the conflict between science and the church was born, when western European scientists in cassocks had to go against the church's picture of ther world because of scientific facts, doesn't the fault for the conflict seem to lie with orthodoxy itself? After all the monk Copernicus challenged the geocentric systems of the pagans Ptolemy and Aristotle.

Of course. But the scientist of the nineteenth century also thought that a little bit more and the building of science will be completed, and everything will be explained. That was so up until the appearance of the Mendeleev tables, when there arose a million new questions. After Mendeleev's tables there is the possibility of atomic physics. And the expanding universe, and a great deal more.

Whole branches of modern science have grown out of the religious searches of the medieval scientists. For example the attempt to count how many angels could fit on the head of a pin gave rise to integral and differential calculation, to the theory of "eroded multiples." Much of what science consigned to the archives as superstition is being considered in the end of the twentieth century to be a flowering of pre-scientific thought.

A great deal comes from an insufficiency of imagination. The systems of Copernicus and Galileo did not attack church dogmas. The earth could remain the center of the universe even as it turned about the sun. Simply a more complex mathematical model had to be built. After all the sun itself moves in outer space.

And to finish this theme, we have a rupture between the development of personal religious thought and its opponent, scientific atheism. The critic of religion in our country frequently gets out of it by claiming religion is beneath all criticism. Taking advantage of this opportunity, I would like to talk about the necessity of a special publication, some sort of "Dialogue" in which scientists, theologians, philosphers, poets, and writers would speak with equal right. In that way at least we could free ourselves of prejudice, find common position points. And at least no longer carry on polemics in separate planes, not hearing or understanding one another. So, when exactly did the ideology of official Orthodoxy become a spiritual brake in the development of the nation? From where do we count? From Nicholas's formula of Autocracy–Orthodoxy–People? Or earlier? Why were the Decembrists primarily believers, and the raznochintsy *weren't?*

I think a great deal depended on Peter I.[l] Although Peter himself loved the Orthodox service and sang in the choir and was in no way an atheist. Peter's reforms were a continuation of Nikon's reforms and led to a terrible drop in the authority of the church. If a confessor is deprived of the right of a secret confession, if a priest is obligated by a government order to inform on his congregants, then what kind of authority can the church have? This is where Old Believerism flourishes. It flourished not so much under Aleksei Mikhailovich as under Peter I[l] and Nicholas I.[m] And already there was nothing to be done. Nicholas I's role in all this was very negative; his drive against the Old Believers in many ways destroyed the economy of Russia. The most substantial and hard-working class were the Old Believers. Old Believers created industry in the Urals. Nicholas I's laws against them destroyed Russian metallurgy. Under Catherine and Alexander I the Russian artillery was first in the world. Russia was the leading country in quantity and quality of workable metal. If you ask the archeologists who dig in the field of Borodino, they will tell you that the difference between Russian shells and French shells is immediately obvious. The Russian ones have a different quality of casting, they don't have any bubbles. Russian cannons of the old castings seized by the British still stand in many English and Scottish towns. Even today the English admire the casting of these cannons.

Under Nicholas though Russia began to fall behind.

All the same, why was the Uvarov-Nicholas formula of Autocracy-Orthodoxy-People greeted with such disgust by the Russian intelligentsia?

Autocracy could not be identified with Orthodoxy. I won't try to judge how guilty the churches were in this, although Metropolitan Fotii and others were guilty. The guarantee of authority for the church is its separation from the government. The church and the state were interwoven, and all the faults of the government fell on the church. That formula destroyed the Orthodoxy of the day, or at least splintered it. The church must be separate from the state. A thousand years ago Christianity became the state religion of ancient Rus' and united Rus', and later Russia, Belorussia, and the Ukraine. This was a strength, but it was also a weakness. The church subordinated to the state wasted its spiritual freedom, its freedom of conscience. Its future was predetermined, since if you were a believer, that meant you were a monarchist. But Christianity isn't an ideology, either bourgeois or socialist. It is a world view plus ethical norms of everyday behavior, in life.

In the last fifteen years or so the word "spirituality" has flicked through the pages of our newspapers. It is used in an extremely mundane sense and is contrasted with aspirituality . . .

I don't know what "spirituality" means in its journalistic sense. The word is used lots of ways, but no one defines it.

So what is it, a phantom word? An ersatz word?

I understand it like this: if the term is intended to mean the life of the mind, intellectual life, then its level is in fact falling. Intellectual interests are falling, people read less philosophy, classics, fiction, real poetry. Feuilletonism is intruding into poetry. This is a bad thing. The intellectual side which is so strong in Pushkin, Tiutchev, Fet, in the poetry of Vladimir Solov'ev and Aleksandr Blok is now much weaker in our most popular poets. Poetic feuilletons, meaning poems which unmask or extoll some event of public life are being substituted for poetry. By the way, this also happened with Nekrasov. Even so though Nekrasov knew how to raise a feuilleton up to the level of poetry, which today's poets don't.

The contribution of Russian Orthodoxy to the defeat of fascism is not to be doubted. Why though are there no vivid church monuments to this, or do we simply not know these works?

Where could they have appeared, if they didn't publish Platonov and Nabokov? And anyway the general decline also affected the church.

But nevertheless in the 1970s many of my contemporaries turned to religion. The civic realization of personality was very much more difficult for those who did not wish to take part in yea-saying or careerism...

I can't agree with you here, Andrei Iur'evich. When a person goes to the church out of modishness or simply for a change of worldview, this is also a lie. The church is not just a change of world view, it is a change of how you live, of your habits. For the believer the everyday too must be religious, with observation of the fasts and holidays and so forth. But many people went to the church out of a feeling of protest against official lies. And that too contained an element of lying. Christianity does not demand just a Christian worldview, but actions as well. Without actions faith is dead. And there were no actions.

To have faith means to act? But in the 1970s the press raised the alarm that Komsomol members were baptizing their children. And the Orthodox priests even began to talk about a second baptism of Rus'.

A very imprecise expression. There was Christianity in Rus' before the baptism of Rus', before the acceptance of Christianity. Princess Olga was baptized and there was Il'ia church in Kiev. The baptism of Rus' was the official acceptance of Christianity by the state, the union of church and state. It is impossible to speak of a second baptism of Rus', because it would be a misfortune for the Christianity, to join church and state. The opposite in fact, the church must be wholly separate from the state, in order to develop freely and be religious in the full sense of the word. In general social progress comes with freedom, with enlargement of the sector of freedom. I wrote about that in my article "The Future of Literature," which is reprinted in my three-volume collection. The sector of freedom grows along all lines, while the sector of the church's freedom to the degree that the church renounces its dependence on the government. What dependence? To be either encouraged or discouraged.

One of the questions which is particularly disturbing today: why can't a Christian be a nationalist or a nationalist be a Christian?

That's an easy question. Because Christianity is a universal religion, equally a religion for Negroes and Chinese. Christianity is a great religion to the degree that it is an international one. If it becomes a nationalist religion, it ceases to be itself. I don't wish to name the religions which are closed within one people. There are a few of them, but that is the big deficiency of these religions.

Dmitrii Sergeevich, what is the major conclusion of the jubilee of the Russian church?

That the church shouldn't meddle in the affairs of the state, and the state shouldn't meddle in the affairs of the church. This mutual independence was already defined by Vladimir I. A great deal remains to be done, including overcoming the timidity of the bureaucrats. Here's a small example. At the Vyrskii Postal Station Museum near Gatchina, someone is afraid to put a cross on top of the restored clock tower. Also superstition? Finally, the Bible must be published, because the Bible is the code of modern art. That means that not only the believer suffers from the situation, but the atheists as well. We are nourishing patriotism, but we don't know the extremely rich old Russian literature, which after all is inaccessible without knowledge of Christian problematics. This is the cause of speculation and sects and

God knows what else. We can only hope that the situation can be put right, if we are not afraid of dialogue.

Editor's notes

a. Rus' is the name of the Kievan state which lasted from the ninth to the thirteenth centuries.

b. Vladimir ruled 978–1015.

c. Vladimir Monomach ruled 1113–1125.

d. *The Lay of the Host of Igor* ("The Igor Tale"): epic twelfth-century poem which tells of Prince Igor's unsuccessful campaign against the Kumans.

e. This would be World War I and/or the Russian Revolution and Civil War.

f. *Strigol'niki*: roughly "the tonsured"; a Christian sect.

g. All of this discussion depends upon the shape of the Cyrillic letters.

h. These words are related in Russian: *khristianin* is Christian, *krest'ianin* is peasant.

i. Khan Batu: son of Chinghis Khan, crossed the Volga to lay siege to Russian territory in 1237.

j. Grand Duke Dimitri: ruled 1362–1389; called Dimitri Donskoi because of his defeat of the Mongols at Kulikovo Pole [field] on the Don.

k. *Raznochintsy:* individuals of no definite social class; for example, children of clergy or civil servants who did not follow their fathers' professions.

l. Peter I, known as Peter the Great, ruled 1682–1725.

m. Nicholas I ruled 1825–1855.

9. Patriotism and National Exclusivity

In order for the USSR to be a stable political system, Russians and non-Russians alike must be trained to be loyal and patriotic citizens. Political socialization begins in childhood, as Soviet schoolchildren are taught loyalty to the Communist Party and the Soviet socialist way of life. Initial patriotic training is quite general, but as the students progress to secondary school they begin formal training in Party history, Marxist economics, and scientific atheism. Male highschool students are additionally required to take specialized military preparation courses.

The program of socialization devised by the various educational authorities in Moscow makes little distinction between Russian and non-Russian students. Official literature refers to the "Soviet people—a new historical community," but the reality of the political socialization process is that people are trained to be loyal to a Russian-dominated state. The necessary teaching materials are mostly in Russian and, while technically "internationalist," they present Soviet history from a decidedly Russian point of view. Official histories defend Russia's acquisition of non-Russian territories as positive by definition, because it allowed other nationalities to enjoy the benefits of socialism and communist rule.

However, as we see in the concluding sections of this book, the elaborate political socialization network has failed to convince all citizens that their political interests are being adequately protected and that they are living in a truly "internationalist" society. Part of the explanation of this failure lies in the nature of the socialization experience to which non-Russians have been subjected.

The materials used in political socialization have always drawn a fictitious picture of conditions in the USSR, describing things as the Party wanted them to be perceived rather than as they really were. This is particularly true in the area of nationality relations. Dashdamirov's *Pravda* editorial on "Soviet Patriotism" is a good example of the type of materials that were written on patriotic themes during the Brezhnev years. In this article Dashdamirov asserts the existence of the "Soviet people" as an accomplished fact.

In fact his argument is more moderate than many made in the 1970s and early 1980s. Dashdamirov, an Azerbaidzhani who heads the propaganda department of the Communist Party of Azerbaidzhan, implicitly rejects the claim, made by some, that the Soviet people have formed a new ethnic community. He writes of the continued existence of distinct nationalities in the USSR, although he asserts that they now have common values, goals, and cultural traits because they are all part of a uniform nationwide social system.

Dashdamirov's analysis has a two-faced quality about it, demonstrating that party ideologists in the non-Russian regions recognized the potential politicization of the national problem well before *glasnost'*. On the one hand, Dashdamirov exaggerates the degree of ethnic consolidation that has occurred with his assertion that the

"Soviet people" have a single new personality type—this in the face of the published conclusions to the contrary by Soviet social scientists. On the other hand, he claims that Soviet patriotic education has fused the national and the international, and warns in a veiled fashion that nationalist sentiments can be aroused if "progressive" national traits are not appreciated. While Dashdamirov stresses how important it is for all Soviet young people to be successfully indoctrinated with patriotic values, he does not raise the discussion beyond the level of platitudes. He offers no standard for differentiating between "progressive" or acceptable national traits and unacceptable "chauvinistic" ones, nor does he discuss the special problems of socialization for national minorities.

The political socialization of Russians and non-Russians alike took on new immediacy in 1979, when the Soviet Union invaded Afghanistan and began a decade-long involvement there, committing massive numbers of troops of all nationalities. The war revealed the existence of a number of deep-set problems in Soviet society, and helped to exacerbate them as well. Soviet officials have had to confront growing problems of military desertion and draft evasion, not only on the part of Muslim troops asked to fire upon their ethnic kinsmen and co-religionists, but among Russian troops as well. They have also had to reabsorb and provide for hundreds of thousands of returning veterans scarred physically or psychologically by their experiences.

In addition to the particular problems created by the war in Afghanistan, there are a number of more general difficulties specific to the deployment of national minorities within the military which will continue to be troublesome even after the war. Many conscripts have inadequate knowledge of Russian, the language of command in the military; many, especially those from Central Asia and the Caucasian republics, have deficient physical and technical skills as well. Non-Russian soldiers are considered more difficult to socialize for military service, a problem compounded by the underrepresentation of non-Russians in the officer corps, and their loyalty is not taken for granted.

These problems have taken on new salience as the ethnic balance of the Soviet Union shifts and the number of non-Russians slated for conscription increases each year. Central Asians and Caucasians, now comprising more than one-quarter of the annual call, can no longer be assigned to construction brigades *en masse*. Special programs designed to increase technical skill levels, improve language proficiency, and provide better socialization have been introduced in all these republics, but they have had only limited success. More disappointing still have been the results of new remedial programs designed to increase the number of non-Slavic officers in the armed forces. Few Central Asian and Caucasian youths are willing to pursue careers that will take them away from their home republics for most of their adult lives. Many of those who do seek admission to military academies are turned away or dropped mid-course because of academic deficiencies.

By late 1986 and 1987, Soviet authorities began to admit the existence of all these problems, although references to them tended to be buried in lengthy speeches. But by 1988 *glasnost'* had proceeded so far that even problems within the military were being openly discussed. Many of these (such as the widespread and often violent practices of hazing) had little to do with nationality as such; but the problem of ethnic violence within the military and the generally poor preparation of Central Asian and Caucasian conscripts were discussed with unprecedented frankness. Still, the overwhelming majority of articles about military service continue to be devoted to praise of the heroism of the fighting forces in World War II and in Afghanistan as well. This is particularly true of coverage in Central Asia, where the republic press, and the Komsomol press in particular, is used to popularize military service. The articles "Portrait Gallery of Internationalist Soldiers" and "When a Son Returns Home" are typical of this coverage, praising the heroism of Central Asian soldiers in the multinational Soviet armed forces, and depicting the gratitude of the peoples of Afghanistan for their sacrifices. Both articles try to show how the linguistic and other obstacles that Central Asians face in the army can be overcome.

In general, coverage of the Afghanistan war, even at the time of the Soviet retreat, has tried to downplay the negative. The heroes in both of our selections are wounded, but neither dies. Similarly, accounts of the difficulties of returning soldiers, such as the article "Young Reservists Club," attempt to minimize the alienation experienced by the veterans and stress instead the positive role they can serve in preparing others for military service. Coverage of these issues in other regions of the country, especially in the Baltic republics, has been franker about the difficulties, but the majority of articles still depict military service (and the reception given returning veterans) in glowing terms.

But once the withdrawal from Afghanistan was completed, it became possible to call for military reforms without being branded a traitor. Calls for "restructuring" in the army have originated in all parts of the country, but nowhere have efforts to redefine the nature of military service been as systematically pursued as in the three Baltic republics. Here the question of military service has become firmly intertwined with the national question. Each of the national fronts has called for the formation of national military units which will have as their primary responsibility the defense of the national republic. Similar views have been expressed in Armenia and Georgia as well.

The recent dramatic rise in nationalist sentiments in the USSR has given the Party notice that for political socialization to succeed, it must be conducted in new ways and transmit new messages. But the Party is not sure of its footing here. This confusion has been apparent since the Alma-Ata riots of December 1986, when hundreds, perhaps even thousands of Kazakh students and young workers rampaged through the streets of the Kazakhstan's capital to protest the appointment of a Russian from outside of the republic, G. Kolbin, to replace Kazakh party leader and Politburo member D. Kunaev. In a real departure from past practice, coverage of this event acknowledged the existence of interethnic conflict in the USSR. Moscow tried to discredit the riots as the actions of the corrupt and disgruntled. However, the subsequent wholesale reexamination of nationality policies and political socialization programs indicates official awareness of the seriousness of ethnic tensions.

A Central Committee resolution demanding the overhaul of internationalist education in Kazakhstan, reproduced below, blamed the existence of political, social, and economic problems within the republic on the corrupt Party practices of the past. Better internationalist education and the appointment of honest officials are proposed as remedies; but there are no concrete suggestions as to how internationalist education could be improved to reduce ethnic tensions. A follow-up resolution from the Communist Party of Ukraine, also reproduced below, is equally vague; it indicates the authorities' continued reliance on formulaic statements. This has been particularly true in the Ukraine, home of the country's second largest national group. The Moscow leadership has not known how to deal with the potential challenge of a resurgent Ukrainian nationalism, and so has grudgingly allowed the Brezhnev-era party leader Shcherbitsky to remain in power. The hope seems to be that fear, and continued operation of the party patronage system, will keep the situation in check.

In general, Moscow has been reactive in the area of nationality relations. Policy changes occur only in response to vocal public protest. And while the conditions of *glasnost'* have certainly broadened the public debate on the rights of nationalities, most of the concessions that have been made are still largely symbolic ones. This is particularly true with regard to the treatment of small groups that do not have national territories.

In recent years Moscow has substantially eased the restrictions on the emigration of Jews, but there have been no substantial changes in attitudes. The practice of the Jewish religion, like others, is regulated by the state. But Jews are also considered a nationality and have been assigned a national "homeland"—the Birobadzhan Autonomous Oblast, on the Mongolian border in the Soviet Far East. Moscow maintains that Jews have the same rights as all other nationalities, and denies that there is officially practiced anti-Semitism in the USSR. Jews may ask to leave the USSR to be "restored" to their national community in Israel, but this makes them Zionists, and Zionism is considered a reactionary internationalist doctrine which represses the expression of the legitimate national aims of the Palestinian people. Thus, the Soviet press publishes articles like "Roots," reproduced below, attacking Jews who want to leave the USSR, and also depicting the disappointment of Jews who have reached the West. A similar policy is followed in the publication of highly critical articles about the emigration to West Germany of ethnic Germans, who, during World War II, had been deported en masse to Central Asia and Kazakhstan from their home regions along the Volga.

A number of other nationalities were also deported to the east during World War II, including the entire Crimean Tatar nation, who had their autonomous territory dissolved. Throughout the 1980s they campaigned actively for the full restoration of their civil rights and the return of the Crimea to their control. Andropov absolved the Crimean people of charges of disloyalty during World War II, but he was unwilling to meet the more substantive of their demands. After Gorbachev took over, Crimean Tatar activists became more outspoken and visible. In the summer of 1987 they organized a series of public demonstrations in Moscow and in Tashkent.

In keeping with the policies of *glasnost'* these demonstrations were reported in the press. But, as exemplified by the article "There Are No Waves Without Foam," which was widely reprinted throughout the USSR, the press coverage was used in an effort to discredit the Tatar activists. This article describes the Crimean Tatar demonstrators as misguided, manipulated by Western propaganda, and out of touch with the goals of the majority of the Crimean Tatar people.

In reality, the Tatar protests reflected the sentiments of a substantial part of the Tatar community, and Moscow recognized this by forming a special commission of the Supreme Soviet, headed by Andrei Gromyko, to investigate their demands. The results of this commission, published below, responded to only the most basic of the protestors' demands. The Crimean Tatars were granted increased cultural autonomy both in Central Asia and in the Crimea (which is now part of the Ukrainian SSR). But, except for the creation of several thousand agricultural jobs designated especially for them, the Tatars were given the same rights of settlement in the Crimea that any Soviet citizen enjoys; that is, they have the right to move there if available housing and jobs permit. In effect, this means that the overwhelming majority of Crimean Tatars are barred from settlement in their ancestral homeland.

The commission based its decisions on the premise that, whether or not boundaries were justly drawn in past, the historical reality of their existence justifies their continuation. Thus, there could be no question of even considering restoration of the Crimea to Tatar control, as this would violate the rights of the Russians and Ukrainians who have now lived there for nearly fifty years. This same premise is being applied by Moscow in the efforts to regulate ethnic tensions in the Baltic region and in the dispute over Nagorno-Karabakh in the Caucasus.

Soviet Patriotism *

A. DASHDAMIROV

In the process of building a new society over the sixty-year period of development of the multinational Soviet state, a new Soviet man has come into being. He is a conscientious worker, a man of high political culture, a patriot, and an internationalist—reared as such by the Party, by the heroic historical experience of our country, by our whole order. The patriotism and internationalism of the Soviet man embodies the ideals and principles of socialism and communism, and a single socialist way of life common to all the nations and nationalities of the USSR.

I

Social practice of our day has borne out Lenin's prescience that socialism would create new—international—forms for man's communal life. The victory of the socialist order, the securing of equality of peoples and their ever closer integration within a united federal state—all this has led to the elimination of former conflicts among the nationalities. The radical changes in relations among the nationalities over the last sixty years show that the nationality problem in the form that we inherited from the past has been solved once and for all.

The establishment of relations based on friendship, mutual assistance, and comradely support—a fact without precedent in history—through which dozens of nations and nationalities have been forged into a single Soviet people, has led to the formation and maturation of a personality fundamentally new as an historical type. Its principal features are determined by the collectivist relations prevailing in a society of developed socialism.

A single social system, common ideals, goals, and interests, joint labors, and a shared historical destiny have forged among Soviet people of different nationalities a common ideological orientation and similar traits of character and moral makeup. The new type of personality developed in our multinational society has assimilated the advanced internationalist qualities of the victorious working class at the same time that it preserves the best features and traditions of each nation and nationality. There has occurred a genuine spiritual emancipation of the worker from what once were ethnic outlands, a transformation of his national consciousness, an eradication of the insularity and limitations of his social life.

The scope and intensity of interethnic processes taking place as a result of the expanding collectivization of socialist production and scientific-technical progress are such that they put their mark on the intellectual and moral makeup of nearly

Pravda, 29 December 1982, p. 2. Russian text © 1982 by "Pravda."

every individual. International features permeate more and more thoroughly the consciousness, psychology, way of life, and customs of millions upon millions of Soviet people, producing in them a profound sense of spiritual kinship with all the peoples of our country and a sense of participation in the affairs and achievements of our multinational state as a whole. The formation of the Soviet man—a patriot and internationalist—serves as a touchstone of the maturity of our society and a measure of the solidarity of the Soviet people as a qualitatively new, historic community of people.

The quintessential reflection of the high degree of unity already achieved between the individual and the society is the consciousness and sense of internationalist fellowship within the single Soviet people that has developed over the whole course of our lives. This is one of the most important social and political traits of the Soviet man. The transformation of socialist nations and nationalities into constituent parts of the new historical community has led to the organic linkage of the individual's national and international relationships, his international and national identities.

The increase of international, class, and universal human elements in an individual's development does not, of course, signify an eradication of his national features. National identity constitutes a real, stable, and variegated link between an individual and society, reflected in his consciousness, way of life, and value system. When he participates in the building of communism, the Soviet man finds sustenance for his endeavors both in internationalist and in progressive national traditions. As he assimilates the values of his own people, these are transmitted further through broad social intercourse among nationalities; as he absorbs the values of other nationalities, especially an internationalist world view and political consciousness, these in turn enrich his own culture and way of life. As he enhances his republic's achievements through his own labors, he advances to the well-being and progress of our common great, socialist Motherland.

II

The patriotism of the Soviet man is the true embodiment of the dialectical unity of national and international elements in the life of our society and the life of the individual. The patriotism of workers, who won their socialist Fatherland in the course of the proletarian revolution and the subsequent radical transformation of society, today represents the highest sociohistorical type of patriotism. It expresses the individual's relationship to his socialist Motherland, to the culture, history and traditions of his people—from working-class ideological and political positions, the positions of proletarian internationalism—which have become the common property of all the classes and social groups. These have all become imbued with Soviet patriotism by virtue of the social and ideological-political unity achieved in our society, the internationalist unity of our goals and revolutionary ideals.

Socialist patriotism finds its realization in labor exertions, in selfless devotion to the interests of the Motherland, in readiness to defend her freedom, independence, and dignity, in strivings to increase her glory and prosperity. These qualities clearly describe the Soviet patriot and reflect the vital activism of his life. Love for his republic and a natural attachment to his national language and culture are for him inseparable from his love for and devotion to the multinational socialist Fatherland and the entire Soviet people. His Motherland is not only "the land of his ancestors" but the whole Soviet land.

History has shown that Soviet patriotism and devotion to the socialist Motherland are a guarantee of the invincibility of the Soviet state and an active, driving force of social progress.

Does this mean, however, that further development of patriotic consciousness among Soviet people should be allowed to take its own course? Of course not.

The proper planning of patriotic education assumes not only the propagation of all-Soviet norms, traditions and achievements, but also a clear and precise appraisal, from communist positions, of distinctive national features, values and customs, as well as an uncompromising struggle against any transgressions or errors in the area of nationality relations, against any manifestations of alien views or practices— whatever form these may assume and however insignificant their incidence.

To be a patriot means to love one's people and its culture. However, every nation's spiritual legacy, traditions, and way of life contain not only that which is good, but also that which is bad or obsolete. It is important not to preserve what is bad but to emancipate oneself from everything that has become antiquated or conflicts with the norms of Soviet society, socialist morality, and our communist ideals.

The struggle against distortions of patriotic values, against attempts to inject into Soviet patriotism elements alien to its nature and to insinuate into modern social consciousness backward, conservative petty-bourgeois and patriarchal ideas under a "patriotic" mask, continues to be relevant. A false understanding of the "purity" of national culture, remote from any concern for its fruitful development, and advocacy of obsolete forms of culture and way of life under the banner of "preservation of traditions"—how remote this is from the ethics of socialist internationalism, how incompatible with the nature of true patriotism!

Reliance on the internationalist social and spiritual experience, friendship, and fraternal support of other peoples is a vitally important precondition for the successful advancement of every socialist nation. Every living and developing culture interacts closely with other cultures. Interrelations among nations and reciprocal processes of cultural influence and enrichment spread through the very tissues of peoples' social and spiritual life, like a network of capillaries, and are inseparable from their present, and particularly from their future.

Historical experience is an important source of a people's social and spiritual energy. Without a profound knowledge of one's own history and its scholarly interpretation, and without learning lessons of a class nature from past events, no successful progress or increase in the material and spiritual riches already created can even be contemplated. Only the Marxist-Leninist theory of the historical process provides a true understanding and a total picture authentic of a people's history and enables us to uncover the true content and to ascertain the meaning of all its phenomena and events. More than that, it is only socialism and Soviet rule that have placed at the workers' disposal the tremendous spiritual riches accumulated by different peoples in the past and made them the common property of all nationalities.

Alongside the steady rise in the workers' education and culture and the intensive development of mass communications, media, and propaganda, there is a growing interest in historical problems of one's own and other people, and in the history of our whole country. It is important to satisfy this interest and to present people with the best, most valuable findings of historical and ethnographic scholarship. These will provide them with realistic conceptions of their people's past and the historic origins of the distinctive features of their traditions and culture, as well as teach them how to relate properly the values of the past to the tasks facing them in the present and their aspirations for the future, how to integrate the national with the international. This is among the most important means of fostering the internationalist and patriotic education of the broad working masses.

III

In our country, which has entered the stage of a developed socialist society, it is everyone's patriotic, civic duty to take an active part in the building of communism and the implementation of the programmatic tasks advanced by the Communist Party. The principles and sentiments of patriotism are an effective force in the struggle against everything that forms an obstacle on the path toward communism. To show that indifference to the common interest, political apathy, perfunctory work habits, manifestations of a private-ownership psychology and morality, and any deviations from the norms of socialist communal life are incompatible with our ideals, world view, and way of life, and to maintain an uncompromising attitude to any shortcomings or negligence—is this not, in its very essence and nature, a patriotic task?

The main thing, as V. I. Lenin taught us, is not to close one's eyes to difficulties, to find the proper means to surmount them, and to concentrate all our efforts on finding solutions to the vital problems of our society's development.

Soviet patriotism is a dynamic patriotism, rooted in the vibrant activism of revolutionaries—transformers and builders of a new life. It finds expression in the Soviet people's active involvement in labor and politics, and in their real personal contribution to the country's economy and culture. The more sustained a man's exertions—the greater his initiative, ingenuity, and creativity, the more spirit he brings to his endeavors—that much more strikingly are manifested his qualities of a patriot and internationalist.

Every Soviet person has a right to be proud: our society is the first in the world where socialist fellowship as an attribute of relations among people is a vital principle that is becoming more and more deeply entrenched as a behavioral norm. There is no doubt that gradually all the social and moral "sore spots," those lingering vestiges of the past that clash and interfere with the principles of this fellowship, will be eliminated. It is the lofty duty of the Soviet man, as a patriot and internationalist, to wage an unremitting struggle for the total triumph of those norms that typify the socialist way of life and social discipline, and for the enhancement of a sound ideological-moral climate in society and in all aspects of work and daily life.

The propagation of the values and ideals of Soviet patriotism and socialist internationalism can not, of course, be confined to expounding on these concepts, but must be closely bound up with life and people's daily concerns. Neither patriotism nor internationalism can be internalized "in a flash," or memorized like poetry or multiplication tables. They are both internalized and tested in deeds—from the heroic to the trivial and prosaic. It is essential that the influence of the ideas that are embodied in Soviet patriotism be constantly strengthened in the process of the workers' communist education. This applies especially to the rising generation: for youth lacking direct experience of the class struggle, patriotic education serves as the cornerstone and the core of their education, both political and moral.

A concrete manifestation of Soviet patriotism is the Soviet people's unremitting struggle to implement the resolutions of the Twenty-sixth Congress of the CPSU and the May and November (1982) plenums of the Central Committee of the CPSU. A striving to work creatively, with initiative, and a constant quest for the new—this is Soviet patriotism in action, this is love for the Motherland which inspires people to heroic accomplishments in their labors.

We are faced with "an enduring mission of abiding importance," observed the General Secretary of the Central Committee of the CPSU, Iu. V. Andropov, in his report "Sixty Years of the USSR," "and that is to educate the Soviet people in a spirit of mutual respect and friendship among all the nations and nationalities of our country, love for their great Soviet Motherland, internationalism, and solidarity with workers of other countries." Indeed, our people's great high-mindedness, their firm solidarity behind the Communist Party and indissoluble internationalist unity form the life-giving source of our society's strength.

Service in Afghanistan

Coverage in the Republic Press

Portrait Gallery of Internationalist
Soldiers: El'murod Alovakov *

He was born in 1962 in the kishlak*a* of Shirgovad, in Vanch Raion. After finishing secondary school he entered the Kurgan-Tiube filial of the T. G. Shevchenko Daghestan State Pedagogical Institute.

From 1982 to 1984 he served with a limited contingent of Soviet soldiers in the Democratic Republic of Afghanistan. For his model fulfillment of his international duty he was awarded the order of The Red Star and the medal "For Valor."

In the life of every man there are many difficulties. True, some people strive to escape them, while others accept them as their duty. El'murod Alovakov always went directly to the test himself. After school he enrolled in the faculty of Russian language and literature. His friends tried to talk him out of it, saying "you can barely speak Russian." But El'murod always insisted, "I want to speak well, which is why I have decided to study here." Two years later, another move against the current. The institute behind him, he had epaulets on his shoulders and boots on his feet: The army. Why?

"I just felt that I had to go through this," Alovakov explains today. "No, I didn't need this for self-affirmation. Even back then I wasn't a milksop. I was first degree in judo and I had taken prizes in competitions of the republic's higher education establishments. I simply felt that I had to go where strong fellows were needed."

El'murod Alovakov asked to go where it was heaviest, to Afghanistan. His Russian language lessons helped, as did his attraction to fighting. He got into various scrapes, which his boldness, physical strength, and his cleverness got him out of. For example, once he tracked the head of a band of *dushmany*b for about seven kilometers through the mountains. However, big muscles aren't the only thing. El'murod also understood this quite well. Afghanistan taught him to value a man's spirituality most of all, to value selfless friendship.

. . .

They lay beneath a small bridge, Alovakov, Golubev, and Simchenko.c They were separated from the battalion medical point by a broad strip of rocky ground, which was wholly under enemy fire, from where their commander, Senior Lieutenant

---

*Komsomolets Tadzhikistana, 16 August 1987, p. 3. Russian text © 1987 by "*Komsomolets Tadzhikistana*."

Zhenia Krivchikov was returning fire. Their platoon was surrounded. And then, step by step, the *dushmany* tightened the circle. Each of them beneath the bridge had thought more than once about how they ought to save their last grenade for themselves. It was even more painful though to think that in these desperate moments they could not be beside those who were fighting over near the battalion medical point. Then they left their cover. None of the three cared anymore that they had to run through a band of heavy fire, because it was more important to be together with the other guys.

* * *

The platoon broke out of the *dushman* encirclement. Now, every year, the participants of that battle gather on Paratrooper Day in Tashkent. And once again they recall March 1984 to the smallest detail. Their company stayed another week in the mountains, defending a strategic tunnel, which prevented the *dushmany* from getting a caravan of gold through which was intended for buying guns in Pakistan. There was not a man in the company who escaped a bandit's bullet or shrapnel fragment. El'murod too was wounded. The medical battalion point returned the metal they removed from each soldier's body as a souvenir, and somebody got the idea to weigh it—for the whole company there was almost ten kilograms.

Comrades in arms . . . Many of them are missing from the traditional gatherings in Tashkent. The Muscovite Andrei Golubev will never come, nor will Andrei Simchenko from Arkhangel'sk. They died in that uneven battle. Hundreds of kilometers now separate them too from their Afghan friends, with whom they had to fight side by side. In one of the kishlaks El'murod met an old man whose chest already bore two Soviet medals "For Valor." It turned out that these were rewards for the assistance which he had often given to the Soviet forces. Once by sending the *dushmany* on a false trail he helped an entire sub-unit to get out of an encirclement.

Such meetings are not forgotten. And how could you forget? A year ago E. Alovakov had a son, whom he named Sherafgan. A pretty name. Translated into Russian it means "Afghan tiger."

A. Lunin

Editor's notes

   a. *Kishlak*: small native village.
   b. *Dushmany*: Soviet term for Afghan rebels.
   c. Golubev is a Russian name; Simchenko is Ukrainian.

When a Son Returns Home *

They are talked and written about a great deal. Understandably! Internationalist soldiers! In reality though these are everyday simple guys, our sons, brothers, someone's father or husband. As a rule they aren't talkative. They are distinguished more by modesty, reserve, humanity, and . . . And something else! Something not so common for us in the struggles of daily worries—a frank hatred for injustice, for dishonesty in any form, for disrespect for human dignity, for phenomena of evil, and they have some kind of special measure of a man's worth, which only they understand.

When you look these guys in the face (still boys, of an age to be in the Komsomol), when you listen to them and look into the bottomless sorrow of their eyes, then a great deal becomes understandable. Yes, they had to learn about war not from films, books, or tales.

They hastened to save the Afghan people, under the fire of the *dushmany*, to save their homes and property, their lives, often without sparing their own lives. They had to taste the pain and bitterness of losing friends and comrades.

* * *

"Head of the military detail during the watch is Ensign Faratov," the voice of company commander Captain Katkov[a] carries from the courtyard. "During this duty I order you to pay particular attention to . . ."

I have a good view of Shirin Faratov, slender, as ever tidy and erect, with two rows of ribbon on the left side of his uniform, smoothly fastened down with a sword belt. Shirin and his comrades leave the courtyard, and I continue to stand at the window and think about him and those like him, all these soldiers of the Fatherland, living and dead, all those to whom we the living are obligated for peace on earth.

* * *

"Comrade passengers," the flaxen-haired stewardess has appeared in the cabin of the airliner, "in twenty minutes our airplane will be landing in Manas[b] Airport. Welcome to the capital of medal-winning Kirghizia, the city of Frunze! Please fasten your seat belts. The captain and crew wish you a gentle landing."

Shirin was glued to the window. There it is, home. Greetings, Motherland! The years of service are behind; ahead lies the sight of parents, brothers, sisters, friends. For a moment the face of his mother flashed before him, like a vision. In his sudden burst of emotion he so clearly imagined her eyes, and remembered precisely how they had filled with tears and worry when she saw him off to the army. That was in April 1981. The whole family had seen him off, but he had walked to the edge of his native village with his mother. She had hugged him there, pressed him to her breast, and cried. Shirin, yesterday a tenth-grader, embraced her heaving shoulders and comforted her tersely.

Komsomolets Kirgizii, 16 December 1986, p. 8. Russian text © 1986 by "Komsomolets Kirgizii."

"It's nothing, mama, everything will be all right. Take care of yourself, mama, and don't worry. I'll do my service, like in the song, 'Two winters, two summers . . .' I'll do my service like you have to, and then I'll come back . . .''

"Hmm," the elder Faratov, Ali Binalievich,[c] Shirin's father, coughed then. "That's enough, wife. You're not seeing him off to war. Look at Guli, El'dar, and Fazli, they all did their service. This one will come back too." Then he added more seriously, "Don't wail, I know how you are . . . This is your favorite, the youngest, that you're seeing off. You're spoiling him!"

Shirin knew that his father was grumbling like that for greater gravity. He understood that his father loved him no less than his mother did, only male pride did not allow him to show weakness in front of other people.

"It's time," the father gently parted mother and son, and then suddenly embraced both of them tightly. "Gul'peri, don't, it's . . . don't be upset . . . listen, your son said that everything would be all right. Let him say goodbye to his brothers and sisters."

Neighbors came over, and uncle Farat, his father's elder brother.

"Well, that's it. Good luck to you. Serve well. Don't shame the Faratovs," he said, embracing his nephew and giving him a sturdy kiss. Then Shirin said goodbye to his neighbors, gave a quick hug to Madina and Tomina, his twin sisters. "Grow, little ones," he said, then leaped nimbly into the back of the *kolkhoz* truck and knocked on the cab to the driver, "Let's go!"

Right to the bend in the road Shirin stood in the bed of the truck, waving his hand, saying goodbye to everyone. On the little rise, just to one side of the rest he could see the little figure of his mother and his distraught sisters, who were wildly waving after him and shouting something. But Shirin couldn't hear anything. He waved his hand for the last time, and they disappeared from sight. A lump of some sort blocked his throat. He coughed like his father, then leaned across the edge of the bed to shout at the driver, "Step on it, brother, or I won't be on time for the army!"

"You'll be in time," the driver said, "You'll get your fill of service. . ."

Now Shirin straightened up in his seat, his spine aching from the long, tedious ride.

"They were fifteen then," he said aloud. "They're probably brides by now. . ."

"What are you talking about? What did you say?" His neighbor, an old man, asked him, glancing respectfully at the medal glittering beneath his open great coat, "For Battle Merit."

"Oh, nothing. I was just thinking about my sisters," he smiled broadly at the old man, who could not take his understanding glance from the medal.

On the ground spring was raging with apple blossoms, field poppies, and sweet green grass, like a thick-pile carpet generously laid before people's feet by nature. And the golden sun floating up from the mountain heights of Ala-Too, flooding the whole visible space with its gentle, caressing and warm light, as though greeting the arrivla of another peaceful day. One more peaceful day, for the sake of which Shirin and his friends had gone into battle.

* * *

The sub-unit commander Ruslan Sultanovich Aushev (now a major, and Hero of the Soviet Union) was extremely laconic when putting the task before his personal staff in that night of 9–10 November 1981, which Shirin Faratov remembered so well. "Comrades!" he addressed the officers and soldiers. "We have received information that a band of *dushmany* is moving into Afghan territory from the Pakistan side."

On the map he showed the direction of the band's movement, marked it with a pencil, then continued. "Our job is to move up to the border crossing point along with the Afghan soldiers, meet the bandits, and destroy them. I know that there are many young soldiers among us, who have never been under fire before. This should not bother them though. At their side will be experience soldier comrades. This will be a battle baptism for the new recruits. We must meet and destroy the enemy. And we will do so. The time we move out will be announced later."

It was exactly these words by the battalion commander that Shirin remembered, because among those untested newcomers was himself, the sergeant of a mortar platoon, who had nothing under their belts save book study.

Shirin didn't sleep that night. He tossed from side to side. All kinds of thoughts came to him. Again he recalled home, the truck taking him to the city to the induction center, his relatives and friends, his sisters waving after him, and his mother, whom he could see so long on the little rise.

The signal to move out was unexpected even though everyone had mentally prepared himself for it. The sub-unit set out to fulfill its military task.

For two days they moved among the narrow ravines and gulches. Shirin looked at these mountains, so unlike his own blue Tian-Shan mountains. Bare stony enormities rising one after another, with an occasional tree in the infrequent villages, which looked as though they were dying out, so few were the people in them.

"The *dushmany* have the people good and frightened," Shirin was told by the gun-layer Gulakov, with whom he had become friends. Shirin couldn't help but agree. Sometimes at the short halts the little boys that seemed to be everywhere would run up and ask for bread and sugar. As soon as they received their treat, they would disappear behind the clay-brick walls of their wretched hovels, where the scolding voices of their elders could be heard. In one village the soldiers saw a wooden plough near one dwelling.

"They don't really use a log like that to work the earth, do they?" somebody asked.

"Figure it out yourself," Shirin replied. "There's nothing else around, and they wouldn't have the money to buy it if there was. This is a poor people."

Shirin could see on the faces of his fellows how clearly they were understanding the poverty of a social system in which some people enjoy all the blessings of civilization, and others, the majority, lead a beggar's existence and live in the Middle Ages, without elementary possibilities or rights.

"It's better to be dead than to live like that! You call that living?" Gulakov said.

"The people don't want to live like that anymore, but these *dushmany* won't let them build a new life."

"These *dushmany* wouldn't get anywhere," Bakhtiiarov, the loader, entered the conversation. "The people would straighten their heads out in a hurry for them, but those stinking devils get help from all the scum out there, they give them weapons, and what weapons!"

At the beginning of the second day's march, when the unit had begun to stretch out in a narrow ravine that looked like the Latin letter V (what the geologists call a V-shaped valley) grenade and machine gun fire began up ahead, first rifle and machine gun fire, the rapid chatter of the machine guns, then the explosions of grenades.

As soon became clear, the scouts had stumbled onto the *dushmany* and had begun a fight immediately. The enemy had the edge, because they occupied both steep sides of the ravine, had a good field of fire, and had pinned the scouts to the ground with dagger-like machine gun fire.

"Mortarmen! Take the front position. Aim . . . At the enemy. . . Volley! Fire!" the commands rained down. The coordinates worked precisely and well. Echoes roared around the mountains and the explosions of mortars repeated many times, laying in ever tighter among the *dushmany* scatterd on both sides of the ravine. The mortars fired and fired.

Shirin saw along the right slope how the motor rifles were following the fleeing *dushmany*. But they were being hit head on by a hidden enemy machine gun.

"Faratov!" the commander of the mortar crew shouted with pain in his voice.

And Shirin cruelly and coldly shot mine after mine until the machine gun stopped. He once again saw the motor rifles running forward, heard their multi-voiced "hurrah!"

Unable to stand the mortar fire the *dushmany* were running in a pack for the safety of the top of the slope, where they could drop behind the other side and once again continue to shoot at the attackers. Here though the last of them would find his fate.

When the last shots had echoed their last and silence descended, Shirin dropped to the ground, tired, his face black with soot, his hands shaking and unresponsive. He couldn't smoke; the matches kept breaking. "Here," Gulakov held out a burning cigarette, then wiped the sweat from his face. "All the same, we took it. You hear that we didn't lose any of the mortar crews?"

"We didn't," Shirin sighed, pulling on the cigarette, "but the riflemen . . . listen, how long did that take?" When he found out that it was three hours, he didn't believe it. "I thought it was an eternity . . ."

The assignment was accomplished. In this cruel fight the bandit band was completely destroyed.

Shirin and his fellow novices really did receive their baptism of fire in that battle. And each of them suddenly understood clearly that they would have no peace, until they did everything that was in their power to make it so no one on the earth ever shot. They understood something else too, that peace has to be fought for, swinging with all your might and resources, before it's too late. So as not to let people like these *dushmany* or their protectors come in and have their way, people for whom nothing is sacred. People who once again want to plunge the people into a bloody battle. "Who are you?" Shirin was looking at a bearded lad, dressed in a Turkish-style robe, not the cleanest either, whose black hair that pushed out of his turban was crusted with blood. He lay on his back, his arms flung wide, on the bank of a mountain stream, right where the bullet had found him. Alongside was a rifle of English manufacture. His eyes stared motionlessly into the endless grey sky.

"Who sent you to kill? Maybe they forced you to it, and maybe you forced other people to do it. Who taught you to kill, and why? Why couldn't you live peaceably on this earth?!" Such thoughts did not leave Shirin as he stood by the corpse. "Well, you sowed death, firing at my comrades. It was you, not them, who first raised his hand against them. And you find what you were looking for, you got what you deserve."

Shirin would never forget the animal baring of teeth, the mouth twisted into a savage snarl, the blood-filled eyes of a hashish smoker of one 27-year old *dushman*. In pure Russian he shouted at our soldiers when they captured him in one of the battles, saying he hated us with the wildest hatred. He was going to shred us, cut us up into little pieces if he was able to survive this and continue the fight against us.

"That vermin has had good training," Shirin thought, but answered him aloud, looking him in the eye, "You're playing the devil because you aren't going to continue anything. The Afghan people will never stand behind scum like you, because you are against the people . . . And anyway you don't have a motherland and you don't belong to any people. You're a whore and a wretch, even if you did learn to speak Russian."

Shirin couldn't help wondering what that sort of enemy might be able to do if he weren't opposed. How much misery one like that could spread. And we have no right to forget that.

He remembered the veterans' stories about the cruelty of the *dushmany*, even to their own people. Once in winter, during a retreat, fearful of just retribution for their actions, a group of *dushmany* that our soldiers were pursuing chased out old men, women, even children to clear snow in the mountain passes, just to save their own skins. Later our soldiers found the villagers dead, frozen like statues, up to their necks in snow.

The struggle continued, and Shirin stood in the ranks of those who did all that they had to to defend the accomplishments of the April revolution. He remained a soldier of his Fatherland, a solder-internationalist, who fulfilled his duty.

*   *   *

Two memorable events took place in Shirin's life in May 1982. First, he was put up for a government honor, the medal "For Battle Merit," and second, he was unanimously accepted into the Komsomol, accepted right after a hot battle in which he and his comrades had stood firm and conquered. And the best recommendation for his entrance into the Komsomol was the staunchness and courage he had shown in that battle. The withering heat of forty plus degrees [centigrade] and the burning Afghan wind was making itself felt, making for incredible thirst. Sweat covered the faces of the soldiers, who had already been moving an hour and a half up the difficult rise of one slope of a ravine. "Enough! Fall out!" the commander ordered. People flopped on the burning earth, breathing heavily. The long climb into the mountains with heavy packs was telling, as was of course the altitude.

Over the pass there was a descent no less difficult, which also took a lot of time. But all that was behind them. In the evening shadows they came to the dispatching point for the motor rifle company, whose duties included helping the Afghan troops blockade the *dushmany*, in case they tried to break out of the ravine. The guys were happy to see their own people, and the others didn't hide their feelings either.

"The mortar men are here, now we'll have our own fire!"

. . . Shirin looked at the glowing numbers of the commander's watch. Ten minutes more. A whole ten minutes of silence! And then what? Unknown. . . . Somehow his mind would not grasp this combination of an apparently peaceful world and the temporary silence of the moon-washed mountains, the black spots of nearby low-growing shrubs, the indolent babble of the stream tumbling water, and the agitated sense of waiting, brought on by the impending battle.

And it began, the battle! A battle to remember for Shirin and his friends in arms. At first from the north they could hear the deafening explosions of shells, among them the sharp clatter of high-calibre machine guns and the buzzing of automatic weapons. The noise of the battle beginning was seized and multiplied a hundred-fold by the mountain echoes, growing until it seemed that the battle was right next to them, then dying down for a second, pulling off to some as-yet unseen field of battle.

More than an hour passed, but there was no movement at the exit from the ravine.

"They're strong in there, looks like," the commander come over to Shirin. "Soon our 'guests' will be arriving."

As if to confirm his words at the mouth of the ravine there appeared three trucks with dimmed headlights, their backs full of *dushmany*. The forward truck moved slowly toward the stream, right where it made a small bend and flowed smoothly out of the ravine into the small mountain flat. The soldiers had good visibility in the moonlight, could see how a man jumped out of the truck cab, quickly crossed the stream, then once again returned to the center of the shallows and waved his hand, saying to come on, then pointed out the ford. When the first truck was almost across the ford and the second was up to its wheels in the middle, the mortar crew began to shell, supported by machine gun and automatic weapon fire from the motor rifles.

Shirin saw first one truck, then the second burst into flames, like a torch. The scattering bandits jumped into the water, falling under the fire of our soldiers. The third truck hid back in the ravine, while from its bed ripped disordered machine gun fire, carbines echoing. But then everything became unexpectedly quiet.

"Hang on now, boys," the commander called. "They'll be coming now, on the attack.

And come they did . . .

Somewhere out of the dark of the night began to explode *dushman* grenade launchers with implacable hatred from the opposite slope, and from where the shrubs were blackest the enemy's machine guns shot like a rain of lead. The *dushmany* came in wave after wave at the motor rifle's position, shrieking wildly, firing their machine guns and automatics as they ran, throwing grenades. They were met by the strong, accurate fire of the motor rifles, suppored by vollies of mortar fire. Neither side was worried about preserving its supplies, and a constant roar stood over the mouth of the ravine. But the *dushmany* kept coming and coming.

The tension of the battle was so great that none of the soldiers noticed tha dawn was coming on. There was a short breather.

The commander of the motor rifle company called to ask, "Fellows, can't you cover the bandits' machine guns?"

"It's dangerous," the mortar company commander answered. "The distance between the mortars and the *dushmany* isn't more than a hundred fifty meters, and your riflemen are in between."

"Give it a try, guys," they heard in the receiver. "Think up something. I'll remeber it forever! These machine guns are like a sty in my eye!"

"We'll try," the mortarmen replied.

"There you go, thanks! You're real countrymen . . . I know what you mean, anyway. . ." And he hung up. Shirin looked at his commanding officer and said, "Let's try a medium charge, huh?"

"Give it a try," he nodded in reply.

Soon though the *dushmany* began another attack, with even greater cruelty and impudence. They advanced almost erect and shouting something in their own language. Letting them get nearer, the riflemen began to mow this scum down mercilessly with machine gun and automatic, and then in a single burst they got up and ran to meet the *dushmany*. The *dushmany* could not withstand the blow and ran away, suffering heavy losses. Once again though our soldiers ran into the same machine guns that the commander of the motor rifle company had spoken of before.

"Ekh, the bastards!" Shirin could not contain himself, and so gave the command, "Medium charge! Get the bastards' machine guns! Fire!"

A minute later the observer told them that the enemy's machine guns were destroyed. But Shirin could see that for himself. Shouting "Hurrah!" the riflemen were chasing the *dushmany*, no longer pinned to the ground by the deadly fire of the machine guns which Shirin had destroyed. The commander of the motor rifle company came over to the mortarmen.

"You made my day! Good for you, lads!" he shook everybody's hand. "You didn't waver . . ."

It was only about two hours later that the *dushmany* were able to recover and take up the attack again. The riflemen answered their fire less and less frequently, conserving their fire. The *dushmany* got bolder. They set up a loudspeaker close by and began to broadcast to our troops: "Russians! Surrender, we won't touch you. We know that there's not many of you!"

"Comrade assistant commander!" Gulakov addressed Shirin. "Give me the command, and I'll stuff that down his throat!"

"Take it easy," Shirin looked at him. "It's not worth wasting a mortar on just one *dushman*. Let him have his fun. Time is on our side. You can tell the boys that help is on the way. They radioed from headquarters.''

Shirin knew that he was lying, but he wanted to encourage his comrades any way he could, even that way. He could still hear the alarmed voice of the company commander about how they had mined all their positions.

Someone's voice came over the speaker.

"Hey, you red dogs! Surrender! In five minutes it'll be too late! We are going to destroy you all!''

"You see, Gulakov,'' Shirin went over to him, "That's already a little more concrete. They're expecting more bandits to come visiting.'' And he laughed. "You wanted to wasted a mortar on him, and they're going to be coming this way themselves. In five minutes. So let's talk about it then.''

"Here they come,'' Shirin looked at the opposite slope, where *dushmany* were descending in relays toward the mouth of the ravine, while out of the ravine itself was heading a mass of bandits, straight up and straight for the position of the company. They were crossing the river, skirting the corpses. They stopped for a moment and then with a savage roar of "Allah akbar!"[d] they rushed forward.

"What a brain you are!'' Shirin couldn't help thinking about the commander of the riflemen. "You did right to plant the mines in time.''

Antipersonnel mines began to explode among the shouting crowds of *dushmany*. They had fallen into the trap. The riflemen raked them with short but accurate bursts of machine gun and automatic fire. Nor did the mortarmen hang behind, sending mortars into the shrieking throngs. Everything was chaos. The shouts of the *dushmany* and of our troops, the explosions of the mines and grenades, the desperate fire of automatics and machine guns. The *dushmany* concentrated their fire on the mortar men.

"Fire! Fire!'' the mortar platoon commander shouted. And in this thunder and noise Shirin and his soldiers friends could hear other noises as, motors growling, shooting on the run, tanks began to move toward the mouth of the ravine, the infantry running too.

In October 1982 when he was with a group of other soldiers being presented battle orders by their Motherland, the assistant commander of the mortar platoon and Komsomol member Shirin Faratov answered clearly, "I serve the Soviet Union!''

On his chest glittered the medal "For Battle Merit.'' And then he returned to the ranks.

*   *   *

Shirin asked the truckdriver to stop near the village. He wanted to look at his village from the same rise on which his mother had stood when she saw him of to the army.

He didn't have time though even to go halfway there before he noticed two small figures coming from the last house, on the edge of the kolkhoz field, running toward him. More with his heart than his head he knew that these were his sisters.

"Shirin! Shirin!" they shouted. "Our Shirin has returned!"

He was thunderstruck for a moment, then went quickly toward them; then, suddenly unable to contain himself, he also ran. "My girls! My sisters!" he embraced them, not hiding his joyous tears. "Look how big you've gotten, and how pretty!" The three of them walked down the street of the village, the noise they were making brought the neighbors out.

"Greetings, Shirin!" they said. "Glad you're home! Gul'peri and Ali will be overjoyed. Their son has come home."

"Oy!" Gul'peri shrieked, coming through the gate of the house and noticing her son coming toward her. "Shirin! My son, my baby boy . . . you've come back alive!"

"Alive, mama," he hugged her to his breast, then calmed her. "Listen, don't cry. Greetings, mama!" And he kissed her. He kissed the woman to whom he owed his life, the woman who had carried him beneath her heart so that he might have an honorable life on this earth!

His father came up, informed of his son's arrival at work.

"Hmm," he coughed at the stoop, seeing Shirin. "Let's see you, come on, let's have a look . . ." He looked approvingly at the shining medal. "So . . . not bad, eh? A man's word, not bad, eh, mother? Well, greetings, son!"

"Greetings, dad!" Shirin hugged him.

And there was something in that strong masculine embrace which only passionately loving and faithful hearts can understand!

While the women cleaned the house and got the food ready for the evening of celebration, father and son went to the steam baths.

"I haven't steamed like this in ages, dad," Shirin thrashed himself stoutly with his besom. "Our bath house . . . wonderful!"

"Ehhh," the father replied, flattered. "I made it special with your brothers just for this. You won't find a bath like this in our whole village, and as for that Afghanistan of yours. . ." He laughed happily. There in the bath, as they were towelling dry, Ali asked, feigning casualness as he noticed scars on his son's arms and legs, asked, "What about wounds?"

"I had some, dad," his son answered simply. "Plus shrapnel in my head . . ."

"Is that what you got the medal for?"

"No, dad, not for that. I'll tell you sometime . . ." Then, looking in his father's eyes, he said, "Don't tell mama about it . . . please, dad . . ."

"Hmmm," the father looked at his son approvingly. "When the time comes she will find out herself . . ."

A few days later Shirin told his family that he had rested enough and he didn't intend to sit around any longer doing nothing.

"So where have you got it into your head to go, if it's not a secret?" his father asked.

"The army!" came the reply.

"My son!" Gul'peri moaned. "Is there a shortage of places where you could work? How come the army's got such a hold on you?"

"I can't, mama, try to understand," he looked at her. "I can't do without the army . . ."

So a few days later the soldier-internationalist became a soldier in the internal troops of the Ministry of Internal Affairs of the USSR. And once again began for him the everyday army life to which he had decided to devote himself.

*   *   *

One day, coming home from work, Shirin noticed his mother was upset for some reason. She laid his supper, then sat silently by him as he ate, thinking her thoughts.

"What's on your mind, mama?" Shirin asked, thanking her for the meal.

"You didn't listen to your mother," she sighed. "Didn't I say, don't go into the army, didn't I say there's got to be other work?"

"What are you talking about?" Shirin put an arm around her shoulders.

After hestitating a moment to answer, she took a sealed envelope out of hre apron pocket and gave it to him.

Shirin opened it. There were orders inside. The military committee was summoning Shirin. He looked at the date; the summons was for today. He had to go.

"This is just an order, mama," he looked at her gently. "And you got all upset . . . They want to talk to me at the military committee . . . I'll go round right now, and that's all . . ."

"That's what I mean, that it's orders," his mother kept it up. "That's why my heart is worried."

"Don't worry, mama!" his voice came in from the courtyard, along with the rattle of the motorcycle. "I'll be back soon."

But Shirin returned only in the evening. He rolled up to the house, killed the engine, opened the gate, and pushed the machine into his courtyard. He noticed his father and mother on the porch. Shirin understood from their looks that they were worried, so he hurried to reassure them.

"Everything's all right! I'll tell you in a second . . ."

"Tell us, son," Ali looked at his son. "Your mother has just about looked the eyes out of her head, waiting for you . . . what did the military committee want?"

Shirin sat down across from them, unable to supress a smile.

"Don't worry, everything is all right . . . just they wanted to congragulate your son . . . seems they gave him the Order of the Red Star. . ." "My baby boy!" Gul'peri flung herself at her son's neck and burst into loud tears. "My boy!"

"Hmmm," the father got up from the table and embraced his son. "We're supposed to rejoice, and here she's crying. . ."

"But, son," his mother looked scoldingly at him, "why didn't you tell us anything about it? Instead, just like that, a medal! You thought that your mother wouldn't notice your wounds. Ekh, children . . ."

"I told you so," he pressed his son's head to his breast. "When the time comes, she'll find out about it herself . . . Well, for the medal, a father's thanks . . . I'm proud . . . but don't get a swelled head," he finished, more for the benefit of the younger ones, than in fact.

"Why didn't you write that you had been wounded? That you had been put up for a medal?" Gul'peri still insisted.

"I didn't wnat to upset anybody, mama," her son looked at her guiltily. "And as for the medal . . . why say anything about it in advance? Being put up for it still didn't mean that I would get it. So why get everyone all worked up in advance? Anyway, it wasn't for the medals that I was out there with the guys, mama, understand that. . ." And some kind of melancholy about that distant and irretrievable time now behind him, but uneffaceable from his memory, lay across his face. Gul'peri noticed it.

"Don't get upset, son, if I say something wrong. . ."

"Oh, mama. . ."

In a triumphal ceremony, beneath the unfurled flag of their unit, the military commissar awarded him the battle order of the Motherland. And when the award ceremony ended, he was surrounded by officers and soldiers. Each thought it his duty to congratulate the soldier. Shirin smiled, thanked them for the congratulations, untiringly returning the firm masculine handshakes.

"Good boys," the military commissar noted with pride. "They wouldn't let you down."

"That's for sure!" the unit commander affirmed.

* * *

The years will pass. But never will the the deeds and names of all the internationalist soldiers, especially those who took upon their shoulders the fundamental burden of battle with the *dushmany* rabble, be forgotten in the grateful memories of the defenders of the April revolution. One such was a simple fellow from a Kirghiz village, a Soviet soldier, a Komsomol member, now a communist, Shirin Faratov. He has tied his fate permanently to military service, so that the world might always be peaceful! Nothing but peace!

P. Ergunov

Editor's notes

a. Faratov is a Central Asian name, Katkov is a Russian one.

b. Manas: the hero of the Kirghiz people's most famous epic poem.

c. A redundant form of the patronymic, showing Arabic practice (Ali Binali means Ali, son of Ali) and Russian administrative practice, which requires that Binali become Binalievich, the suffix being Russian.

d. Allah akbar: "God is Great," an Islamic prayer, indicating that the *dushmany* believe they are fighting a Holy War.

The Young Reservists' Club *

Very recently such a sign appeared on the door of Room 13 in Classroom Building 7 of the Medical Institute, and the Club itself has existed only a few months.

When we are asked to share our experience of founding a club and people ask what we began with, we answer honestly, "with a discotheque!"

My friends and I were at the discotheque in the locomotive depot. We stood around, looked things over. . . . So many young people there, and nothing but music around, everywhere, so there was no time to stop or talk or think. We went over to the disk jockey and introduced ourselves. "We are students at the medical institute who served in Afghanistan. If you want, we could talk to the people here . . ."

That was our first appearance. We didn't expect ourselves that people would listen to us as they did, and how many questions they would have! Then there was a meeting with first-year students of the institute, where we talked about what army duty is like, and how to prepare for it, what to study. And again there were a lot of questions from the kids who have yet to serve in the army.

These meetings did a lot for us too. We sensed the attention and trust with which they listened to us; we could feel our responsibility. That's when we had the idea of gathering all the guys who had fulfilled their internationalist duty in Afghanistan and setting up a club for young reservists. They were very understanding about our idea in the institute's Party committee and Komsomol committee, and the military faculty helped us check our list of students in military reserve.

The backbone of the club was made up of fellows who had fulfilled their internationalist duty in the limited contingent of Soviet soldiers in Afghanistan. At that time the club's agit-brigade of seven men took part in an agit-train of the Central Committee of the Turkmen Komsomol, called the "Leninist Crew," which went to Bakharden to speak to students at the agricultural institute and to the foreign language department of the medical institute. The club made up a display in its room with the theme "Each Generation Has Its Field of Battle."

We soon understood that speaking to audiences was only part of the larger military-patriotic work that the club should do. After all, there are 67 of us in the club. Some first-year students who had not served in the army became members— A. Akmuradov, M. Iarogyshev, B. Purliev, and others. So it looked like the club would be growing in the future. This was a force that needed to have a use found for it, that we had to know how to organize proper work for. How was this to be done?

This was also discussed at a conference that took place at the end of December, in Minsk, on the military and patriotic education of young military reservists. This was the first time there had been such a meeting, and many questions were resolved there. It was memorable for its excellent organization, the subjects of the speeches, and for the heated discussions. We talked about what reservists could do to bring the country's military and patriotic work up to the necessary level.

Komsomolets Turkmenistana, 27 January 1987, p. 2. Russian text © 1987 by "Komsomolets Turkmenistana."

We representatives of Turkmenia had to blush when Air Marshal I. I. Pustyga said in his speech that the majority of inductees from Turkmenia don't know the construction of an automatic weapon, don't know the simple movements of parade drill, and have such poor knowledge of Russian that they are very slow to learn the habits of military service.

I had not intended to speak at Minsk, but after these words I sent to the podium a request to be recognized. I was very upset. I talked about how we young military reservists had to do all we could to correct the situation, and that we were ready to, only we didn't know how and where to begin. The work is new, not only for us in the institute; other clubs in the country don't have experience yet, or recommendations for methodical changes. In my speech I asked each speaker to give me his room number and I gave mine, proposing that we talk. Fellows came, or I visited them, and sometimes we talked right through the night. We recalled Afghanistan, but we thought more about how we were to set up work on military and patriotic education of youth, given our experience and possibilities.

We came back from Minsk and got the club members together to tell them about the meeting. The club includes guys with the widest possible variety of military specialties. We thought about how to convey our experience to those who are preparing for army service, to teach them how to overcome the first difficulties and get accustomed to new conditions and attitudes. We decided to set up special interest circles in the schools, "Young Rifleman," "Young Paratrooper," and so forth, to help the instructors of introductory military preparation. We are also thinking how to help the teenagers who have been cited in inspections for youthful offenses.

We have a lot of plans. Right now we are buys with the direct setting up of the club room, since this is its face, its business card. We want to make it so that the very first visit will interest the guys in our displays, photographs, exhibits, which means they will be interested in our work.

We have a lot of books about Afghanistan, the Great Patriotic War, army service, all donated to us by veterans, writers, and poets. We brought a lot of these gifts home from Minsk. We found the addresses of students of the medical institute who are now in the ranks of the Soviet Army. The main thing is that we've begun. The club gets letters from students in Chardzhou and Nebit-Dag requesting us to share our experiences, tell them how to begin. Our [female] assistants, the students Gul'nar Annatulaeva and Maiia Baigaeva, answer this correspondence.

. . . Each person who comes to the club for the first time is taken to a symbolic eternal flame. A red lamp mounted in a star illuminates the words "A moment of silence . . . but life is endless." This ritual doesn't leave anyone indifferent. That's the main thing. Actual with people, to educate them to love their Motherland, to make eternal the memory about those who gave their lives for her, this can not endure indifference. And we are waiting for people who cherish the slogan of the club for young soldiers, "To Be a Soldier Even in Reserve!"

A. Rakhmanov,
President of the "Young Reservists Club"
Turkmen State Medical Institute

In the Central Committee of the CPSU *

The Central Committee of the CPSU passed a resolution "On the Work of the Kazakh Party Organization in the Internationalist and Patriotic Education of Workers."

The resolution notes that in the years of Soviet power, and with the assistance of all the fraternal republics, the Kazakh SSR has achieved significant successes in economic, social, and spiritual development. Today the republic is a large industrial and agricultural region. A true cultural revolution has been completed, and a scientific and creative intelligentsia has been created. Among the multinational population, on a firm foundation of socialist internationalism and common basic interests, have emerged relationships of equal rights, trust, and mutual respect. At all stages of socialist construction the workers of Kazakhstan exhibited high Soviet patriotism, faithfulness to the Leninist principles of internationalism and the friendship of peoples.

At the same time the former leadership of the Central Committee of the Communist Party of Kazakhstan and many Party committees of the republic committed serious errors in realizing national policies and significantly weakened the work of internationalist and patriotic education of the workers. They failed to take account of the rapid growth of national self-consciousness, and did not find timely and correct resolutions to problems which arose. At a certain stage the Party organizations for all practical purposes stopped the struggle with manifestations of chauvinism, nationalism, and regionalism in the economic, cultural, and spiritual spheres. This had a negative effect on the socioeconomic and cultural development of the republic.

At the end of the 1970s and beginning of the 1980s Kazakhstan's contribution to the economic complex of the country as a whole began to correspond less and less to the republic's growing economic and scientific potential. Phenomena of stasis seized all branches of the economy and all spheres of social and political life. The tempos of production dropped sharply, and the qualitative indices of economic development got worse. In the last two five-year plans Kazakhstan had the lowest growth rate of gross national product and labor productivity in the nation. Phenomena of isolationism and parasitism grew more frequent. Many forms of industrial and agricultural production, needed in other republics, were systematically not supplied to the common fund.

Plans of social and cultural construction were constantly disrupted. The food supply grew worse. Principles of socialist justice were violated. The scale of theft of socialist property, pilfering, and bribery grew to be significant. Drug addiction and drunkenness flourished. All of this created an unhealthy moral atmosphere, gave birth to undesirable phenomena in inter-nationality relations, and caused alarm, misunderstanding, and concern among communists and all honest workers.

Partiinaia zhizn', 15 August 1987, pp. 6–11. Russian text © 1987 by "Partiinaia zhizn'."

The resolutions of the Central Committee of the CPSU repeatedly pointed out serious deficiencies in the development of the economy, the low level of Party and government discipline, and lapses in ideological and political work to the Party committees of Kazakhstan. However, the necessary conclusions were never drawn in the republic. Ostentation and vainglory continued to flourish, achievments were exaggerated, results were not examined critically, and failures and shortcomings were hushed up. In this way a false image of the true state of affairs was formed, and a part of the cadres began to show feelings of national egoism and self-satisfaction.

The ruling organs of the republic alienated the national cadres of the working class, the main bearers and carriers of the ideas of internationalism, from purposeful formation. The proportional weight of Kazakhs among industrial workers fell, particularly in the coal and metallurgical branches. Few young Kazakhs enter the professional and technical schools (PTUs) or the specialized secondary schools which prepare cadre for the leading branches of industry. At the same time the network of institutions of higher education and their affiliates spread without sufficient reason. Once they entered these institutions the Kazakh youth had advantageous conditions; protectionism flourished, principles of entrance procedures were violated, and grades were inflated. The preparation of specialists goes on without regard for their demand. As a result posts which do not require secondary or specialized higher education are held by a significant number of workers with diplomas.

Gross errors of cadre policy caused enormous damage to the internationalist education of workers. The decisive factors in cadre selection and advancement were often not qualities of politics, ability, or morals, but rather of nationality, birth, home region, and personal loyalty. In an atmosphere of group exclusivity and mutual guarantees many of the key posts of Party, state, and administrative organs, as well as scientific and educational institutions were given to careerists, time-servers, and yes-men. A portion of the cadre suffered moral decay.

The necessary representation of all those nations and nationalities living in the republic was not guaranteed in the various levels of the social and political structure. The Party and state administration was formed with national distortions, as were the organs of justice and the institutions of science and culture; the creative unions were packed, the Party was accepting people and nominations for national honors on the bases of nationality. These violations, as well as inattention to the needs and desires of certain national groups,[a] led to the departure of parts of this population from the republic, particularly from the Guriev, Dzhezkazgan, Kzyl-Orda, Semipalatinsk, and Tselinograd oblasts.

The Central Committee of the Communist Party of Kazakhstan, the oblast, city, and raion committees of the Party, had not examined the basic questions of Party organization for internationalist education for years, and no in-depth analysis of processes was under way. Scientific works, literary works, and works of art often idealized the past of the Kazakh people, and there were attempts to rehabilitate bourgeois nationalists.

At the same time the revolutionary past of the peoples of Kazakhstan and their struggles to establish Soviet power and socialism were essentially silenced. Friendship among peoples was basically only talked about and the fraternal assistance given to establish and develop Soviet Kazakhstan was mentioned only at celebration of important dates. Tendencies toward national isolationism grew stronger, contacts with fraternal republics were curtailed, tending to become mere show, and there was in practice a lack of the businesslike exchange of experience of real competition.

In the republic there was in fact an extended battle with the feudal ways of the *bais*, with patriarch and clannish practices. Work to show the reactionary essence of Islam, its attempt to preserve antiquated traditions and ideas, to strengthen national isolationism, was not actively undertaken. In many regions there has been a reawakening of religious activity, and the influence of the clergy on various aspects of the life and daily habits of the population is growing stronger. The Party organizations are amenable to administrative workers and communists who take part in religious rituals, justifying this as a local practice.

Education of youth has been strongly overgrown with formalism and bureaucracy, with empty didacticism. The Party leadership role of Komsomol organizations has weakened. The processes taking place in the sphere of youth, particularly in student collectives, has not been analyzed deeply. The number of youth travelling to all-union sites of intensive construction has fallen. Military and patriotic education is in an abandoned state.

Serious errors and miscalculations in the work of the republic's Party committees has led to the growth of nationalist phenomena which were not only not halted when they should have been, but were hushed up or explained as common hooliganism. The Central Committee of the Kazakh Communist Party did not give even the 1979 Tselinograd nationalist demonstrations a critical political evaluation. The disturbances in December of last year in Alma-Ata were also a manifestation of Kazakh nationalism.

The creation of the unhealthy situation in the social and political life of the republic, including in the sphere of national relationships, was in large part made possible by the unprincipled position of the *buro* of the Central Committee of the Kazakh Communist Party, and by gross violations of th norms and principles of party leadership by former first secretary of the Central Commitee D. A. Kunaev. The style of his leadership began to show subjectivism, to violate collegiality, to increase the role of yes-men and curriers of favor. Family ties took over, and in his immediate circle there were several people who abused their positions for personal gain.

The Central Committee of the CPSU considers the departures from the norms of Party life committed in Kazakhstan and the violations of Leninist principles of national policy to be impermissible. Today, when revolutionary processes of renewal are seizing all sides of life in the society, the timely solution of problems arising in the sphere of national relations acquires the greatest significance. Any appearance of chauvinism or nationalism, of national isolationism or boastfulness must be seen as an infringement upon the very greatest achievement of socialism, the fraternal friendship of peoples, and the international unity of Soviet society.

It is noted in the resolution that work to improve the situation and introduce order has lately been under way in the republic. However, this work has not yet acquired the necessary scope or depth, and not all links of the republic Party organization have taken active part in it. The government organs, the trade unions, and the Komsomol, the creative organizations and institutions are all restructuring slowly.

It is considered vital that the Central Committee of the Kazakh Communist Party, the oblast, city, and raion committees of the Party and the primary Party organizations immediately take the most decisive measures to eliminate insufficiencies in the international and patriotic education of the workers, and to complete the further development of national relations.

The Central Committee of the CPSU stressed that internationalism in deed, not just in words, must appear first and foremost in the growth of Kazakhstan's contribution to the whole of the country's economic complex and in the continued rise in realization of the republic's scientific and industrial potential, as well as in active participation in the solution of problems common to all the peoples.

The Central Committee of the Kazakh Communist Party and the Soviet of Ministries must develop and put into effect concrete measures which in the next few years will overcome static phenomena in the economy, will unconditionally fill the food production quotas, and achieve a sharp rise in quality, and make up the debts permitted in supplying goods to the all-union fund. Phenomena of cronyism and nationally superior attitudes must be decisively ended. The strict honoring of supply agreements, especially of interrepublican ones, must become the operating norm of every production collective.

The rational exploitation of labor resources must be guaranteed. Particular attention must be paid to the future strengthening of national cadres in the working class, especially in the leading branches of industry. Interrepublican exchange of cadres, and the participation of workers and specialists in the opening of new regions, must be widened. Real competition must be organized, and the exchange of experience with workers' collectives, towns, regions, and oblasts of the fraternal republics.

The development of the social and cultural spheres must be developed purposeflly and persistently. The responsibility of Party committees, Soviet and trade union organizations, and production administrators must be increased for the creation of the necessary labor and living conditions, for the realization of the program of housing and support services construction, and for improvement of the food supply and medical assistance for the population.

It is proposed to the Party committees of Kazakhstan that, governed by decisions of the January (1987) Plenum of the Central Committee of the CPSU, they radically restructure the entire system of work with the cadre, to give it a truly democratic character. It should be guaranteed that every Party organization make full use of the rights of the Party rules in resolution of questions of cadre. *Glasnost'* is to be developed by all means possible, and the opinions of workers are to be more fully taken account of in the nomination of administrators, with a widening of the list of candidates. Protectionism must be decisively rooted out, as must the selection of workers by reason of connections of tribe, clan, place of origin, or friendship.

The necessary representation of all national groups and nations living in the republic must be achieved in administrative organs, the Party and government apparatus, and the social organizations, though without haste or a mechanical approach. The preparation of administrators in the Party, the government, trade unions, and the Komsomol, as well as of economic administrators, and ideological cadre must be improved in the area of Marxist-Leninist thought about nations and national relations and of the national policies of the CPSU. The study of these problems must be organized in all links of political instruction and economic education, as well as the seminars and courses for retraining of cadre. Every administrator and communist must systematically bring to life Leninist nationality policy, serving as an example of how to fulfill one's international and patriotic duty.

The Central Committee of the Party considers that one of the main areas of organizational and political work among the masses must be the teaching of firm internationalist convictions and patriotic feelings. It is very important to give this task a systematic character, perfecting its scientific bases. On-going tendencies and processes in the sphere of national relations must be analyzed deeply, the situation evaluated realistically, and account taken of particularities of various categories and groups of the population.

All means of propaganda and mass political work must show vividly and profoundly, with concrete examples, the historical achievements of the resolution of the national question, the role of international fraternity in the fate of the Kazakh people and the development of Soviet Kazakhstan. The objective character of the process of deepening the internationalization of all spheres of social life must be convincingly explained. Constant concern must be shown for the satisfaction of needs of life and culture of all the nations and national groups, and problems which arise must be resolved promptly. The necessary conditions for the further development of national–Russian bilingualism must be created.

It was directed that it is vital to pay particular attention to the organization of international and patriotic education among the scientific and creative intelligentsia and among youth. A high cultural level of inter-nationality contact must be taught, as well as a respectful attitude toward the history, language, and ways of fraternal peoples. The ability to approach all national problems from class positions must be elaborated. The struggle against nationalist attitudes, feudal habits of the *bais*, clan and tribal traditions, and religious prejudices which have a negative effect on national self-consciousness must be waged aggressively and actively. The enemy's falsifications of the nationality policy of the CPSU must be strenuously exposed, as must the attempts of bourgeois propaganda to sow discord among nations and national groups.

The Central Committee obligated the Party and government organs of the republic to achieve better preparation, distribution, and use of specialists, taking into account perspectives for the social and economic development of Kazakhstan. They are to elaborate means to upgrade the specialization of institutions of learning, to put the network of schools in order, and to close filials, faculties, departments, and laboratories which do not have qualified cadre of scientific pedagogic method and the necessary material bases. They are to eliminate protectionism, bribery, and other negative phenomena affecting entrance into institutes of higher learning.

They are to improve the role of the course of education and study in institutions of higher learning, in technicums, colleges, and general schools in the formation of a scientific world view and of the ideological and moral development of citizenship among youth. They are to raise the level of social science teaching. They are to strengthen an atmosphere of friendship and mutual aid in multinational student collectives. They are to develop the initiative and self-reliance of student youth in resolving all questions of the organization of study, of socially useful labor, free time, and daily life. They are to arrange regular meetings of the administrative staff of Party and state organs with the teaching staffs, professors, and students.

They are to strengthen the Party's administration of the Komsomol. They are to facilitate the wide participation of youth of all nationalities in the all-union construction sites of the five-year plan. They are to develop tourism, as well as contacts of sport and culture with other republics.

They are to improve the role of the Academy of Sciences of the Kazakh SSR in solving the practical problems which the economy will face in accelerating scientific and technical progress in the republic.

They are to assure the more active participation of social scientists in the elaboration of the actual problems of the struggle against nationalist and other negative phenomena, in the preparation of concrete recommendations for Party, government, and economic organs. They are to improve coordination with the scientific establishments of the nation in studying problem areas in nationality relations. They are to study the history of the Kazakh SSR and of Russian–Kazakh relations from consistent Marxist-Leninist positions. They are to reexamine the textbooks of schools and higher educational institutions concerning the history of the republic, in order to illuminate objectively the events of the past and historical personages.

It is proposed to improve the Party leadership of creative organizations and unions. They are to strengthen the local-level Party organizations in the creative unions by using talented and socially active representatives of the artistic intelligentsia. They are to offer all possible support to people in the literary and artistic sphere to create new, significant works that use class and Party positions to reflect the reality and meaning of Leninist national policy, and of the events and phenomena of the reality and the past of the Kazakh people, and of those who are acting to strengthen the friendship of peoples in the USSR.

Particular attention must be paid to deepen the processes of mutual enrichment in national cultures. To this end there must be a regular program of theatrical presentations, concerts, art exhibits, and film festivals of the republics and autonomous regions. The repertoires of professional collectives and artistic amateur groups must include more heroic and patriotic material, and more works by authors in the fraternal republics. The role of museums in propagandizing the unity of Soviet peoples in their common struggle for socialism must be raised.

They are to take real measures to strengthen law, discipline, and organization in various spheres of republic life. They are to use all means of Party and political influence and administrative action to achieve the decisive elimination of corruption and money-grubbing. The role of workers' collectives is to be increased in the battle with pilfering, drunkeness and alcoholism, and drug addiction. They are to strengthen the administrative organs with cadre and to permit them scope in guaranteeing the strict observance of laws, citizens' rights, and the principles of social justice.

The Central Committee of the union republics, the territorial and oblast committees of the Party recommend that the state of labors to achieve the recommendations of the Twenty-seventh Congress of the CPSU and of the January (1987) Plenum of the Central Committee of the CPSU be deeply analyzed in the realm of national relations, and that effective measures to strengthen the international and patriotic education of various groups of the population be defined and realized. To this end they should make active use of preparation for the seventieth anniversary of the Great October Socialist Revolution and the sixty-fifth anniversary of the formation of the USSR.

Editor's note

a. The groups referred to would be Russians, Ukrainians, and Germans.

In the Central Committee of the Communist Party of the Ukraine *

The Central Committee of the Communist Party of the Ukraine discussed the question "On Measures to Realize in the Republic the Directives of the Twenty-seventh Party Congress and of the January 1987 Plenum of the Central Committee of the CPSU in the Sphere of Nationality Relations, Toward the Strengthening of Internationalist and Patriotic Education among the Population."

It was noted in discussion of this question that the Party committees, Soviet organs, and social organizations of the republic are carrying out work appropriate to bring about the Leninist nationality policy of the Party, to educate the population in the spirit of Soviet patriotism and internationalism and of its implacability toward any nationalistic phenomena. An atmosphere of friendship among peoples, of equality and mutal trust, of respect for the national sentiments of people has grown firm in the Ukrainian SSR. Measures are being taken to more fully satisfy the sociocultural demands of the population, with consideration for its national makeup, its demands in the sphere of education, culture, literature, and art, the mass media, book publishing, and cultural hobbyism. The representation of all nations and national groups living in the republic is guaranteed in replacement of party ranks, in the formation of Party, soviet, and civil organs, and in the promotion of cadres.

Constant attention is paid to the development of Ukrainian socialist culture. The works of Marx and Engels have been published in Ukrainian, in 50 volumes, and those of V. I. Lenin, in 55 volumes. The Ukrainian Soviet Encyclopedia has been published in Ukrainian and in Russian, in 12 volumes; the *History of Towns and Villages of the Ukrainian SSR* has appeared, in 26 volumes; the *History of the Ukrainian SSR* is published in 10 volumes, the *History of Ukrainian Literature* in 8 volumes. The classic works of Ukrainian literature and of the brother literatures of the peoples of the USSR are in print, as are the works of contemporary Soviet authors. Work has begun on the *Index of Monuments of History and Culture of the Ukrainian SSR*. The publication of multi-volume fundamental works is a convincing proof of the development of the Ukrainian language and of the growth of its social role; some examples are *Contemporary Ukrainian Literary Language*, *History of the Ukrainian Language*, *Dictionary of the Ukrainian Language*, and *Dictionary of Old Ukrainian*.

At the same time questions arise in the conduct of nationality relations, demanding deep, systematic study and timely, well-considered reaction in an internationalist context, and the taking of necessary measures. Not all work collectives pay the necessary attention to fostering in people a spirit of the high responsibility of every worker to achieve the general tasks of accelerating the socioeconomic development

Komsomol'skoe znamia, 15 August 1987, p. 1. Russian text © 1987 by "Komsomol'-skoe znamia."

of our country, for the strict observation of contractual obligations to other brother republics; insufficiencies are permitted in preparing cadre for them, in the organization of contacts between heads, in the exchanges of experience. Such negative phenomena as bureaucratism, abuse of office, violation of the principles of socialist justice are not being overcome with sufficient decisiveness and so give rise to local chauvinism and the recidivism of petty-bourgeois national psychology. Recently society has been raising a range of questions of a national and cultural nature, in some publications and speeches, in letters to the Central Committee of the CPSU, the Central Committee of the Communist Party of the Ukraine, the Presidium of the Supreme Soviet of the Ukrainian SSR, in letters to the editors of newspapers, magazines, television and radio. In part these questions direct attention to the narrowing sphere in which Ukrainian is used, the decline in the level of how it is taught and studied in school, violation of the linguistic status of Ukrainian theatres, and the fall in numbers of films released in Ukrainian. The linguistic demands of the non-native national groups have not been fully satisfied. As the decision of the Central Committee of the Communist Party of the Ukraine notes, the work of a range of Party organizations has not overcome a formalistic approach to the organization of patriotic and internationalist education. Many Party, Soviet, trade-union and Komsomol workers, ideological *activists*, and economic managers have not grown beyond understanding the national processes as problem-free, often avoiding workers' questions, avoiding reasoned explanation of the substance and achievements of the nationality policy of the Party. Scientific studies poorly explain the new tendencies and phenomena of nationality relations, in international development, and do not elaborate concrete, practical recommendations.

The Central Committee of the Ukrainian Communist Party has directed the oblast, city, and raion committees of the Party, the Ukrainian trade-union council, the Central Committee of the Ukrainian Komsomol, the corresponding ministries and institutions to analyze the condition of nationality relations in depth, as well as the state of internationalist and patriotic education of the population, in light of the resolutions of the Twenty-seventh Party Congress and the January (1987) Plenum of the Central Committee of the CPSU, and the recommendations made by the Politburo of the Central Committee of the CPSU in its resolution about the work of the Kazakh republic Party organization; it has also directed that practical measures be taken to improve this work in all work collectives and educational institutions. To strengthen the education of the population in the spirit of the friendship of the peoples of the USSR and of great responsibility for completing the tasks set for the whole country, increasing the republic's contribution to the unified economic complex of the country, to guarantee that the seventieth anniversary of Great October be worthily met, and the establishment of Soviet rule in the Ukraine, and the sixty-fifth anniversary of the formation of the USSR.

The Central Committee approved a broad complex of measures aimed at strengthening propaganda for Leninist nationality policy, for perfecting inter-nationality relations, as well as patriotic and internationalist education of the population, improving the teaching of Ukrainian, Russian, and other languages of the peoples of the USSR, the more complete satisfaction of social and cultural demands and needs of the population, with consideration of its national composition. Practical steps were noted to rid this work of its existing insufficiencies.

Along with the guarantee of all conditions for in-depth study of Russian as a medium of international communication, a series of measures are planned to permit elevating the level of teaching and study of Ukrainian in secondary schools and institutions of higher education. The Ministry of Education and the Ministry of Higher Education have been recommended raising the quality of preparation for teachers of Ukrainian lanaguage and literature, to perfect the study programs in these subjects, to widen the network of schools (and classes) with more in-depth study of Ukrainian language and literature, for schools with Ukrainian to create courses of study in which experienced pedagogues and the writers of new educational materials (textbooks, anthologies, teacher's guides, dictionaries, and handbooks) take part. and to examine the manner in which "days" of the native language and literature are conducted. Preschool establishments in which Russian is used are to acquaint children with the works of Ukrainian folklore, literature, and art.

The responsible ministries and institutions are directed to supply the schools and preschools with record and tape collections of lessons in Ukrainian and Russian language and conversation, to prepare educational films to help the pedagogical collectives, including video cassettes and cartoons.

The necessity of improving the linguistic culture in the operation of government organs was stressed, as was the need to observe the principle of Russian bilingualism in carrying out social functions, in production, in agitprop work, in television and radio, and in advertisements and announcements.

Measures were indicated to strengthen the material basis for international and patriotic education of the population. In part, it was proposed that a specialized bookstore, "Friendship of Peoples," be established in Kiev in the October Palace of Culture of the republic's cultural, educational, and methodological "Friendship" center; it was also proposed that a monthly social, political, and literary journal be created (*Suzir'ia*), that the publication of books and release of films be expanded, taking account of the nationality requirements of the population, that libraries be established which contain books of literature in the national languages. It was ordered that programs be elaborated to develop the traditional national artistic enterprises, to restore and make use of historical and cultural monuments, and to perfect translation.

In order to raise the level of political culture and to better supply the social and cultural needs of the non-native national groups measures were examined to strengthen all educational work, to widen the preparation of the cadre in education and culture for regions where such populations live compactly. It was proposed that long-term cultural and educational programs be elaborated, taking account of questions of native language study, publication of literature, the creation of ethnographic and artistic collectives, assuring rental of films in national languages, the activization of touring concert programs which take into account the population of national groups, and the development of progressive national traditions and rituals.

It was noted that collaboration with publishers in the union republics and socialist countries should be improved, for joint publication of texts and methodological materials in the languages of the non-native populations that live in the Ukrainian SSR, and to supply this literature through the network of the "Friendship" stores.

The Central Committee of the Communist Party of the Ukraine obligated the Party committees, Soviet organs, and ideological organizations to assure the supply of profoundly thoughtful and systematic propoganda of the pressing questions of the nationality policy of the CPSU and the Soviet state, of ideas of the friendship of peoples of the USSR, of Soviet patriotism and internationalism. All questions arising in the sphere of international relations should be decided in the spirit of *glasnost'* and the observation of principle; at the same time the necessary resistance must be shown to any appearance of bourgeois nationalism or chauvinism, to national limitation or exclusivity, to attempts to analyze events of the past or the role of historical personages without concern for class positions.

Departments of the Central Committee of the Communist Party of the Ukraine, Party committees, the responsible ministries and institutions, the Party organizations of the creative unions were all recommended to take constant care for the forging of ideological, class, and internationalist feelings and development of citizenship on a high level, of the creative activity of writers, journalists, composers, artists, architects, theater and film workers, to inform them regularly about the pressing questions of the political, social, and economic development of society, about the realization of principles of Leninist nationality policy in the republic, and to confirm a demanding, comradely atmosphere in evaluating phenomena and facts of the literary-artistic process.

It was declared necessary to deeepen counter-propaganda aimed at unmasking the disruptive activities of overseas Ukrainian bourgeois-nationalist, Zionist, and clerical centers which speculate on problems of nationality relations, trying to sow discord among the nationalities of our country.

The Presidium of the Academy of Sciences of the UkSRR, the ministries of Education and Higher and specialized Secondary education of the UkSSR were recommended to elaborate a perspective, comprehensive plan of study of questions of nationality relations and of internationalist patriotic education.

Roots *

A. PRAVOV

Among the former Soviet citizens who are now returning to the Motherland or who have announced their intention to return, a large percentage are people of the creative professions—writers, poets, composers, film people, and scientists. Why? What makes them leave the "blessed, wealthy West" where they tried so hard to get, and return to where there is neither "freedom nor the goods necessary for living"? Probably this question interests many readers of Western newspapers and journals, who are used to getting information about the USSR as a country with a "nondemocratic regime," which Soviet citizens will readily leave at the first opportunity.

In order to answer, probably, it is necessary first of all to find out what once moved these people to leave. The reasons vary. This was discussed, in part, at a press conference in Moscow, at the press center of the Ministry of Foreign Affairs of the USSR by seven representatives of the creative professions who had returned to the Soviet Union from the United States and Canada at the end of last year [1986].

The musician Taras Kordonskii sought a more complete satisfaction of his need to play rock music in the west. The artist Iurii Galetskii and the theoretical mathematician Iurii Chapovskii simply wanted to see something of the world. Film director Rashid Atamalibekov, who before leaving had worked at the Mosfil'm film studio, said that the reason for his departure to the west had been conflict with the administration of the film studio, which insisted on a substantial reworking of a film he had made. The desire arose to "slam the door."

Among those who left were also people who had believed Zionist propaganda, and there were those who considered themselves "unappreciated geniuses," who supposed that in the West "justice would triumph." Perhaps the decision to leave was not always dictated by unbridled ambition. In some instances the reason was conflict between a talented person and a bureaucrat. Thus, one way or another, not only people who were working at the so-called "entry level" went to the West, but also some genuinely important artists, popular in the USSR and abroad.

Here can be felt the comparatively recent negative phenomena in the cultural and artistic sphere, which today have been judged in principle. As M. S. Gorbachev said at the January Plenum of the Central Committee of the CPSU, "in the activity of the creative unions there was a lack of principle, of scrupulousness, of real concern about the development and support of talents. . . . And at the same time conventionalism and formalism flourished, and there was extreme intolerance of criticism."

Today, many of those who had gone to the West, who appeared at the press

---

*Sovetskaia Kirgiziia, 8 February 1987, p. 3. Russian text © 1987 by Sovetskaia Kirgiziia.

conference, say that their decision to return is explained in many ways by the positive processes of restructuring which are now under way in the Soviet Union. There are also a number of reasons which forced these people to reexamine their positions, to recognize they had once committed a fateful error.

"Face to face you'll never see, it's more visible from afar." These lines of [the poet] Sergei Esenin, which every Soviet person knows from childhood, were introduced at the press conference by the poetess Olga Gross-Pavlova, who had returned to her native Moscow from New York, where she and her husband, the composer Anatolii Dneprov, had lived several years. Gross-Pavlova talked about how a creative person is in an absolute vacuum when he is torn from his native roots. It is difficult for him to accept another form of life not only because the form, in his opinion, is incorrect, but also because it is alien to him. The poetess supported her words by saying that not one of the important Soviet people of art and literature who were in the West had created a work worthy of himself. All their best work had been done in the Motherland. According to Olga Gross-Pavlova all the "geniuses" who had left the USSR for the United States had quarreled with one another, their characters had been spoiled, and they were all extremely bitter.

Rashid Atamlibekov said that none of the Soviet cinematographers who were in the West could express himself or create a worthy work of art. The film directors Gabai, Bogin, and Bronshtein were without work. Mikhail Suslov, who once had been a famous camera man for Mosfil'm studio, was barely able to film one or two advertising spots.

The artist Iurii Galetskii said that a great deal disturbed him in the West, where he had lived nine years, but he was especially unable to put up with the flow of lies of anti-Soviet propaganda.

He said, "The culture of Russia is consciously deformed in the United States, and its successes are hushed up. This descends to genuine Russophobia. I was ready to hear criticism, but constructive, not malevolent criticism, with constant irony."

The composer Anatolii Dneprov feels that he could not reconcile himself to the approach to art in the United States. "Art there is a business," he said. "For me, where business begins, that's where art ends."

Taras Kordonskii almost immediately realized the mistake he had made in deciding to leave. He considers that the rock music people of the United States have formed a closed clan inaccessible to others, which even the most talented musician "from outside" almost cannot break into, to say nothing of people of modest abilities. Kordonskii didn't even try to work at his beloved business in the United States. "The only thing I know now," he says, "is that I'm never going to sing songs in a foreign language."

What are these people going to do now, having returned to the Motherland? What can they expect? They are not yet ready to talk about definite plans; too little time has passed since their return and they are not yet oriented. But they agree on one thing: they want to work at their favorite activities and be of real use to the country which, as Iurii Chapovskii says, turns out to be their one true Motherland.

The Crimean Tatars

There are No Waves without Foam: On the Visit of a Group of Crimean Tatars to Moscow *

V. PONAMAREV

I have before me telegrams and letters. Communiqués from Central Asia, the Crimea, Krasnodar Territory, and other places where Crimean Tatars live and work. The news about the creation of a commission at the highest government level was received with satisfaction here, for the commission is assigned to examine an entire complex of questions. Meetings are taking place in many towns and villages, at which the businesslike and serious approach to the resolution of complex problems is discussed, as is the actual situation in the Crimea, about the need of a certain time for the state commission to work. At these meetings, which take place in conditions of complete openness and sincerity, people understand the situation and urge balance and responsibility.

The teacher Refat Gozhenov says, "When I spoke in Tashkent before the people who had sent me to the capital, the great majority agreed that we must firmly and calmly support the government's efforts. At the same meeting, though, there was a rabblerouser, who had been sent by a small group of extremists, who refuse to work with the authorities and advance embarassing political demands, openly struggling for "help" from abroad. This was Nariman Kadyrov, who tried to convince people that they are being deceived. However, he was not able to inflame people's passions. The provocateur was turned away and asked to take himself back to those who had sent him.''

Such was the story in Tashkent, but it must not be thought that this was a sad exception or an atypical showing of imbalance on the part of certain citizens. There are no waves without foam. On top of the combers always swim up those who in the sense of citizenship are not pulled down by a total weight more than simply the personal, the self-interested.

For example, not long ago in Moscow appeared a group of residents, most of them from Krasnodar Territory. Pronouncing themselves the sole and authorized representatives of the Crimean Tatar people, they began a public demonstration with provocative slogans, sent petitions with ultimata to state and party organs, conducted press conferences for foreign journalists, and did other things meant to inflame passions around the question which is being examined by the government commission.

A certain Reshat and Mustafa Dzhemilev and some people close to them are trying to manipulate this group. In order to create the appearance of "wide support," they quickly stirred up the arrival of a group of young people, and even

---

*Izvestiia, 30 July 1987, and Kommunist Tadzhikistana, 4 August 1987. Russian text © 1987 by "Izvestiia."

women with children. This "initiative group" based itself in the apartments of Moscow acquaintances, who played the role of instigators, relaying through certain excessively "credulous" foreign correspondents information which was far from the truth, and in the end interfering in the calm atmosphere in which the questions posed were being discussed.

Playing on the national feelings of people, feeding them false information about the measures the government was taking, Reshat Dzhemilev (jailed more than once), the self-proclaimed writer Eskander Fazylov, Dr. Fuat Abliamitov, who had abandoned the sick, led these visitors to Moscow out onto the street. How great though was the surprise of these people when they could not find this "trio" among their numbers. Dzhemilev proved to be "in the middle of GUM [the state department store in Moscow], by the fountain," while the other two, as they later explained, suddenly "came down with migraines" . . .

Worked up to the limit by the exhortations of the extremists, the women and young people obediently signed the petitions and protests. Against what? Against the truth set down by TASS? Nevertheless, what happened, happened. History cannot be remade in any direction. The facts of collaboration by bourgeois nationalists with the German-fascist occupiers are well known, just as well known as the injustice of the wholesale deportation of the Crimean Tatars.[a] But it was precisely mention of these traitors who had been direct participants in the destruction of their fellow countrymen, of Soviet citizens of various nationalities, including Crimean Tatars, of wounded and captured Red Army soldiers which these "envoys" rejected as an insult to the entire people. These are old tunes! In a time of *glasnost'* there can be no half truths. No one can redo history to his own taste and comfort. No one can be permitted to lump swine and honest people into one bunch, as Dzhemilev and some of his companions would like to do.

The country knows and remembers everything. It remembers and reverse two-time Hero of the Soviet Union Sultan Amet-Khan, the Heroes Abraim Reshidov, Taifuk Abdul, Seitnafi Seitveliev, and Uzeir Abdurmanov. It remembers the full cavaliers of the Order of Glory, Seit-Nebi, Abduramov, Leonid Veliliaev, the generals Abliakim Gafarov and Ismail Bulatov.[b] The people will never forget Alime Abdennanova, the legendary Soviet spy, organizer and leader of an anti-fascist underground group in the Crimea, who died in the torture chamber of the Gestapo, and who was posthumously awarded a battle order. Nor will the nation forget the thousands of other glorious names of Crimean Tatars who defended their socialist Fatherland as common soldiers.

The people and the nation speak with respect and pride of the Heroes of Socialist Labor E. Aliev, D. Zinabatdinov, M. Chachi, and others. So too the names of many other Crimean Tatars who are academicians, deputies, leaders of republic organs, Party and soviet workers, leading figures of production, writers, scientists, important figures of culture and art.

But we know too about the "spiritual brothers" of Dzhemilev in New York, among who are the hack writer Memet Muedinov, of the former pro-fascist rag *Azad Krym*. Today he is called Sevdiar, as *Pravda Vostoka* has already described, writing about how this "spiritual brother" of Dzhemilev and other fascist hangers-on fought for the victory of the "thousand-year Reich" and who in 1942 greeted Hitler as "the great liberator of peoples from Bolshevism." It was to this "brother" that Dzhemilev sent a congratulatory telegram on the occasion of his seventieth birthday, expressing servile hopes for the achievement of their "common goals." Are these the same that Dzhemilev is trying to achieve today, speculating on certain questions and trying to stir up interethnic strife and passions?

It is plain from the communiqués of the foreign agencies that the enterprising "initiators" regularly closet themselves in the apartments of a certain Grigoriants and of Senderov, where a small circle of foreign correspondents especially given to sensationalism gather. Every day from these secret "press conferences" distorted information is issued for the West about conversations between Crimean Tatar citizens and representatives of the higher Party and soviet organs, inventions about the lives of the Crimean Tatars, pretentious announcements, denials, and so forth. It has become ever clearer that these self-proclaimed leaders are little concerned about the fate of the Tatar people, that they are most attracted by the thought of possible scandal and the desire to help certain western circles interfere in the beneficial processes now underway in the Soviet Union.

Attempts to pressure the government-created commission are only slowing examination of the question, as has already been said. This is well understood by all those who today are decisively distancing themselves from the extremists. Residents of the Crimea well know, for example, that Muksim Osmanov, who enjoys the respect of his countrymen, has sternly condemned any approaches to foreign representatives, considering that this question is wholly internal to our country.

Appealing to *glasnost'* and democratization, a clutch of extremists are literally gagging those who would express opinions differing from theirs. Honest representatives of the people who would tell people the truth about measures taken by the Party and the government are driven from Moscow by highly refined techniques of psychological pressure and persecution. For example these extremists are demanding absolute submission to the majority, but to which "majority"? To that same majority that Dzhemilev has gathered about him. In this way a group from the Fergana valley were driven from Moscow. A letter from Seiran Useinov is being passed hand to hand among the Crimean Tatars, about how the very same people who are shouting so loudly about *glasnost'* today on the squares of Moscow tried to deprive him and other honest citizens of the right to a voice.

Still, you can't hide the truth from people, and some of the people who recently gave their blessing to their friends for a trip to Moscow have upon learning of the unseemly, to put it gently, behavior of the leading band of extremists demanded that their countrymen return home immediately, so as not to dishonor their people further. They have also sent numerous agitated letters and telegrams to the capital, to the Central Committee, and to the newspapers.

"A small group is inciting the Crimean Tatars who are in Moscow to illegal acts which shame our people. They are trying to appeal to the West, they spread rumors, and they spread doubts and distrust among people about the steps taken by the Party and government to resolve the Crimean Tatar question. Meetings and gatherings conducted jointly in workers' collectives in Uzbekistan by representatives of the Crimean Tatars and Party organs condemn the actions of the extremists,'' says a letter from Central Asia, where the majority of Crimean Tatars live. They are demonstrating an understanding of the complexities of the problem, as well as balance and responsibility.

The best statement, perhaps, about the campaign of slander undertaken by the extremists against those who are appealing for calm and dialogue without threats and provocations, was made by one of the acknowledged authorities among the Crimean Tatars, the Communist and journalist Timur Dagdzhi, in his open letter. He calls those who are trying to usurp the right to represent the entire people the "Dzhemilev company." Can it really be, he asks, that in order to satisfy their immoderate ambitions these people must slander others? Not only Dagdzhi himself was slandered, but also Rollan Kadyev, a university teacher from Samarkand, and many other Soviet citizens. What hasn't been said of them, as long as it soiled them and spread distrust and disbelief about them. Dagdzhi recalls how suspicious personages in the Fergana valley began suddenly to gather signatures on a demand to the authorities to put him behind bars . . . for having contact with the West. The vile devise of provocateurs! Now the "Dzhemilev company" is inventing various tales about the school teacher Refat Godzhenov, the engineer Izzet Izetdinov, and others, in order to cause doubts among people about their honesty and respectability. Who, asks Timur Dagdzhi, are these Dzhemilevs working for?

He writes that the people have always sent the best of the best to Moscow—communists, leading workers, veterans of the war, Heroes of the Soviet Union. "And I don't understand Fuat Abliamitov," Dagdzhi writes, "who proposed Mustafa Dzhemilev as a candidate to represent the people. Dzehmilev has been convicted several times; since when has it become prestigious among us to have a record of convictions?" Dagdzhi complains, with reason.

Don't these very questions conceal the answer?

Timur Dagdzhi, appealing to the Crimean Tatars in his open letter, reminds them, "Today, when truly revolutionary processes are taking place in the country, we must be very vigilant, and not submit to provocations. . . . At this moment of responsibility to try to give our problem some sort of inimical, anti-Soviet Islamic character means to throw a shadow on the Crimean Tatars, to threaten the chance of a positive decision of our question."

A whole series of letters asks why our organs for the preservation of rights have remained on the sidelines in all this. Can it really be that the numerous well-known cases of slander, incitement, and even provocation are not a violation of public order? Why must democracy and legality give way before phenomena of license? These questions, I think, are wholly justified, but I also think that to call these extremists to order, to rein in the rabble-rousers so as not to permit them to torpedo the peaceful and weighty dialogue, especially in so delicate a sphere as that of nationality relations, is the business first and foremost of the Crimean Tatars themselves.

Editor's notes

   a. Reference is to the deportation during World War II of the entire Crimean Tatar nation from their home region to Central Asia.

   b. Those named are Crimean Tatars who were heroes during World War II.

The Report of the State Commission *

The state commission created to examine questions raised in appeals by some Crimean Tatar citizens reports on what it has done.

Numerous meetings and conversations with representatives of the Crimean Tatars have been held in the Presidium of the USSR Supreme Soviet and in local party committees and state agencies. Large groups of people of this nationality have been received by the Andrei Gromyko, president of the state commission. Localities with dense populations have been visited repeatedly by senior officials of the Presidium of the Supreme Soviet and the Council of Ministers of the USSR. Working groups made up of Crimean Tatars and administrators from republic and regional party and state organs have been constantly involved in the commission's work.

The commission has been carefully examining incoming requests, complaints, and proposals. The relevant bodies have decided to lift all restrictions that infringed upon the rights of Crimean Tatars, to guarantee their complete equality with other Soviet citizens, including in questions of choice of place of residence, work, and study. Since the middle of 1987 some 2,500 Crimean Tatars have been granted residence permits and have gotten jobs in the Crimea. Sovkhozes and other economic organizations are being established to increase employment opportunities. They are being allocated farm machinery, prefabricated homes, and building materials.

Measures have been adopted to more fully meet the social and cultural needs of the Crimean Tatars. Additional conditions have been created to develop their national culture and opportunities have been broadened for study of their native language in the schools of Uzbekistan, Krasnodar Territory, Crimea Oblast, and other areas. The circulation and extent of newspapers and radio and television broadcasting in their native language have been increased.

The commission is continuing work in this direction, strictly controlling the implementation of the planned measures, which are being met with understanding by the Crimean Tatars and by all Soviet people.

The overwhelming majority of people of this ethnic group are working calmly and conscientiously in all sectors of the national economy. At the same time certain citizens' groups from among the Crimean Tatars are trying by various means to hamper the implementation of positive measures, insisting that the first thing to decide is the question of creating Crimean autonomy. Doing so they ignore the fact that the present administrative-territorial division of the country, which came into existence many decades ago and which has been affirmed by the seal of the Constitution of the USSR, is what permits successful solution of the tasks of economic and

*Pravda, 9 June 1988.

social development of all the nations and national groups in the country.

In the postwar period significant demographic and social changes have taken place in the Crimea. The population has grown from 780,000 to nearly 2.5 million, or nearly threefold. In composition it is multinational, with an overwhelming predominance of Russians and Ukrainians. A resolution of the USSR Council of Ministers clearly defines procedures concerning residence and the issuance of residence permits to citizens, regardless of their nationality, for the Crimea and other health resort areas of the country.

Taking into account all these circumstances, the commission has reached the conclusion that there are no grounds for a Crimean autonomy.

The Communist Party of the Soviet Union, pursuing the Leninist course of nationalities policy, proceeds in its practical activities from a considered accounting of the interests of every nationality and national group and of the Union of Soviet Socialist Republics as a whole.

10A. Nationality Relations in Conflict: The Baltic Republics

The administration of the Baltic republics has always posed special problems for Moscow. The three main national communities in the area—the Latvians, the Lithuanians, and the Estonians—have existed as distinct peoples for several hundred years, and their principal cities have been centers of culture and learning since the Middle Ages. Historically, the Latvians and Estonians were influenced by German culture and joined the Lutheran faith, while the Lithuanians, whose history has been linked with that of Poland, are Roman Catholic. Imperial Russia's acquisition of the Baltic territories proceeded slowly, but was complete by the beginning of the nineteenth century.

All three of the Baltic nations experienced strong national resurgence in the nineteenth century, and took advantage of World War I and the Russian Revolution to declare their independence. At the end of the war, after Germany's defeat, the Versailles Conference recognized the existence of Latvia, Lithuania, and Estonia, and all three were admitted into the new League of Nations.

After unsuccessful efforts to establish communist regimes in the Baltic states, the Bolsheviks recognized the three republics in 1919–20 while retaining guarded hopes of eventually reclaiming them. In 1939, as part of the Ribbentrop–Molotov Pact between the Soviet Union and Nazi Germany, Hitler recognized Soviet territorial interests over the Baltic republics (as well as the western parts of the Ukraine and Belorussia which had been incorporated into Poland in 1918–20). Once the Germans were in control of all the areas immediately to the west of these territories, the Soviets were free to act.

In June 1940, under threat of a Soviet invasion which was sure to result in thousands of civilian casualties, the governments of Latvia, Lithuania, and Estonia were forced to resign and hold elections in which only Communist candidates were permitted to participate. In August 1940 the new governments called for the dissolution of their respective sovereign states and for the incorporation of their territories as union republics in the USSR. The new republics were quickly subjected to the full force of Stalin's political, economic, and social policies. Nationalist leaders were deported en masse, as were landowners, "kulaks," religious and cultural leaders. The Baltic republics were occupied by the German army from mid–1941 until 1944, when they were captured by the Red Army and reincorporated in the USSR. The reacquisition of the Baltic republics was followed by a new wave of arrests and deportations.

Nationalist sentiments have remained strong in the region, stimulated in part by activities of the large émigré communities comprised of people who fled Soviet rule.

Moscow has kept a close eye on events in the Baltic, and has traditionally named as the senior officials of these republics members of the titular nationality who had been born or raised in Russia. While outwardly showing no confidence in the loyalty of the Baltic peoples, or even the dependability of the communist parties in these republics, Moscow has always demanded strict adherence to the official Party line that the Baltic republics were voluntarily joined to the rest of the USSR through democratic elections. The republics' official histories, textbooks, and museums all laud a fictitious popularly supported "June revolution of 1940," and condemn the still-remembered nationalist governments of the interwar period as anti-popular bourgeois anachronisms.

Throughout the period of Soviet rule, Party ideologues have endeavored to socialize the Baltic population to accept Soviet socialist rule as superior to political independence. The propaganda is varied, but pieces about the positive achievements of socialism are far outnumbered by articles designed to discredit the historical legacy of the independent Baltic states. This negative propaganda is intended to counter the broadcasts of Radio Liberty and the Voice of America. Typically, such pieces describe how Western intelligence agencies enlist "traitors" and "fascists" drawn from the émigré community in their efforts to overthrow popularly supported Communist Party rule in the three Baltic republics.

Some of the anti-national propaganda is quite sophisticated; an example is the article reproduced below on "The Youth Problem in the Lithuanian Emigration" by K. Malinauskas. The author tries to convince his readers that the survival of the Lithuanian people and Lithuanian culture depends upon decisions made by Soviet Lithuanians, as the Lithuanian community in emigration is only a generation away from assimilation. The conservatism and anti-Soviet attitudes of the older genera- tion of Lithuanians in exile are blamed for poisoning the attitudes of younger people. The Lithuanians of the USSR are counseled to strive more aggressively to change the attitudes of their relatives abroad, who should be encouraged to send their children to the Lithuanian SSR, both to learn their national language and culture and to acquire a more positive orientation to the USSR.

The article, written in 1981, downplays all the practical problems of receiving foreign guests or of getting permission to travel abroad. Only since 1987 has there been much opportunity for families to be temporarily reunited, now that Soviet citizens have been allowed to receive and send invitations to sponsor or make visits abroad. While there are complaints that procedures for obtaining visas or purchasing foreign currency need to be further simplified, the policy seems to have been positively received. However, it has not led Lithuanians or Latvians or Estonians to accept unquestioningly the virtues of Soviet rule. Quite the opposite has been true.

Glasnost' and the policies of "restructuring" have provided an opportunity for Baltic nationalists to challenge the nature of Soviet rule within their republics, and the relationship between Moscow and the national republics in general. In 1987–88 the call for political change in these areas grew from an appeal by a small group of activists who enjoyed latent public support, to a mass political movement. Official attitudes have changed as well. Initial public protests were strongly condemned in

Moscow and in the republic press, but as the scale of the protests mounted Gorbachev sought ways to use them to gain support for his own reform program. Despite the resistance of some in the leadership, Moscow has been willing to allow local policies to be modified to meet some of the Baltic republics' demands. But many of the goals of the political reformers go far beyond the scope of change that Moscow is likely to tolerate.

The cycle of protest began with demonstrations organized in the capital cities of the three Baltic republics for August 23, 1987, to mark the anniversary of the signing of the Ribbentrop-Molotov Pact. A number of accounts of these demonstrations are reproduced below, and their tone is uniformly negative. The demonstrations are termed the product of provocation by anti-Soviet Western propaganda; the demonstrators are depicted as dissolute and corrupted youths unrepresentative of the attitudes of their generation. The articles also refer to incitement by religious extremists, and imply that the majority of religious believers were not supportive of the demands of the demonstrators (note the description of a Mass continuing uninterrupted in "Who Are They?"). The demands of the demonstrators themselves were never stated, only refuted. The official Soviet history of the annexation of the Baltics is reiterated, the Stalin-era deportations are at least partially defended, the regime's policy toward religion is reaffirmed, and the argument that the Baltic republics have been "colonized" by Russians is rejected.

Despite official resistance to the use of public protests to attain political demands, increasingly frank discussions about problems of nationality relations began to be held in gatherings of intellectuals and educators and even in meetings of Party and state officials. Some of the early impetus for these discussions came from the organization of republic-wide committees on nationality relations and the problems of internationalist education, which proposed that lower Party and state organs and educational institutions open up dialogue on these questions. As noted in the previous section of this volume, this initiative was a response to the Kazakh riots in Alma Ata in December 1986.

The atmosphere of *glasnost'* created a perception that the boundaries of public debate had been expanded. After the outbreak of ethnic violence in Azerbaidzhan and Armenia, it became vividly apparent that the old formulas of nationality policy had failed to regulate interethnic conflict. Gorbachev promised the convocation of a special session of the Central Committee of the CPSU to deal with nationality questions and called for a debate on proposals for political reform to be introduced at the Nineteenth Party Conference. Many in the Baltic republics took this as a charge to create their own agendas for political, economic, and cultural reform, and officials accordingly licensed a major expansion of public debate. Not all are fully comfortable with this situation. "Positions Without 'Opposition'" from the Moscow publication *Sovetskaia kul'tura* describes problems created by the refusal of the state press service of Lithuania to fully cover a wide-ranging debate on nationality issues that occurred at a May 1988 meeting of the Vilnius Party organization.

But generally the Party organizations in all three Baltic republics have tolerated and sometimes even supported efforts by national intellectuals to create coherent agendas of reform, in an effort to keep these initiatives for change under some sort of Party supervision. Moscow has tried to maintain the credibility of the CPSU by retiring the old leadership of the Baltic party organizations and replacing them with new first secretaries who are willing to work with the reformers. But the demands of the nationalist reform movements can not be met simply by a change in the local Party leadership.

The Estonian Front for Glasnost', organized in May 1988, was the first independent mass organization formed in the USSR. Its well-publicized reform program includes a call for complete financial autonomy for Estonia, the limitation of Russian in-migration to the republic, recognition of Estonian as the state language of the republic, and complete cultural autonomy. By mid-summer of the same year a Front for Glasnost' was organized in Latvia.

In June 1988, the Union of Writers of Latvia invited representatives of all the other creative unions to join them in sending a resolution to the delegates to the Nineteenth Party Congress. This resolution, reproduced below, was published in all of the republic newspapers after a delay of some ten days. If they were to be put into effect, the changes proposed in this document, which have received at least partial support from the Central Committee of the Communist Party of Latvia, would fundamentally transform the nature of Soviet rule in the republic. The resolution calls for Latvia to be granted international recognition as a sovereign nation and recognition as a sovereign state among free states of a Soviet Union. Citizenship in Latvia would carry with it responsibilities distinct from Soviet citizenship, such as the need to be fluent in Latvian. As a people with a sovereign state the Latvians would have a responsibility to protect their existence and their culture and regulate their schools. They would oversee not only in-migration, but even military detachments and the functioning of the KGB on their territory.

Similar demands have since been made by Lithuanians, who organized their own national front in October 1988. The Lithuanians' demands go even further, and include a request to issue their own money and enter into independent trading agreements with foreign powers. To date little has been done to implement these demands.

Throughout most of 1988 Moscow adopted a wait-and-see attitude toward the Baltic republics, neither rejecting nor endorsing their demands, and saying little more than that the reform movements must act within the confines of the Soviet constitution (a *de facto* rejection of demands to issue currencies or receive foreign legations). The republic Party organizations are proceeding gingerly to begin implementing some of the points of the reformers' agendas in order to sustain credibility among the population. In late June, as the document "On the State and National Symbol of the Estonian SSR" records, Estonians were permitted to display the flag of the former independent Estonian government, though not at official state occasions. The Latvians and Lithuanians soon received similar privileges, and the traditional city flags of Riga, Vilnius, and Tallin were also restored. In October 1988 Latvian became the official language of the Latvian SSR. Since Russian remains the language of inter-nationality communication there, the impact of the new legislation is still more symbolic than real.

In August 1988 large mass demonstrations were permitted to mark the signing of the Ribbentrop–Molotov Pact. The largest gathering was in Vilnius, where over a hundred thousand people gathered to hear addresses by Party officials, writers, and church figures. The speeches were reported in the press. The press also reported on the gathering in Tallin, where speakers demanded that Moscow admit it had acquired the Baltic republics through military conquest. More dramatic still was the publication of the Ribbentrop–Molotov Pact, complete with the secret protocols that permitted Soviet takeover of the Baltic states. This document (whose existence Moscow continues to deny) was published first in an Estonian-language journal and then reprinted in numerous publications in all three republics.

The political agenda in the Baltic republics had shifted dramatically by the late 1980s. Republic Party officials, with Moscow's consent, have entered discussions about the introduction of local self-rule. The constitution of the Lithuanian SSR has been amended to state explicitly that the laws of the republic are to take precedence over the laws of the USSR when the two are in conflict. Moreover, the Lithuanian Supreme Soviet approved a declaration of sovereignty which condemned the unlawful way in which Lithuania had been incorporated into the USSR. The threat of a mass movement for independence is in the air. Accounts of the August 1988 demonstration indicated that some protesters did indeed carry signs calling for national independence. By the end of that year the long-outlawed pro-independence parties were active (in the Latvian case, illegally). The resounding victories of nationalist-front candidates in the elections to the Congress of People's Deputies in the spring of 1989 only fed the popular determination to push for complete political self-determination. Meanwhile, the republic communist parties must struggle to both articulate the local agenda and to maintain some semblance of loyalty to the CPSU.

But the redefinition of political life in the Baltic republics is far from an accomplished fact. Many in Moscow continue to argue that the Baltic republics cannot be treated differentially, and that to permit financial autonomy, not to speak of political self-rule, in republics of the USSR would undermine rather than strengthen the goals of the Gorbachev reforms. And there are strong critics within the Baltic republics themselves, especially among the large Russian population. In all three republics Russian opponents of the national fronts have banded together to form "internationalist" fronts, with platforms asserting that Soviet citizenship must apply equally from republic to republic, that Russian must remain the sole official language everywhere in the country, and that Russians must remain free to settle anywhere in the USSR.

Meanwhile, the demands for change continue to escalate, even including calls for national independence (accounts of the August 1988 demonstrations reported that some protesters carried signs to that effect). Party officials counsel that historical realities must be accepted; that independent Latvia, Lithuania, and Estonia have been gone for more than five decades.

The dilemma is clear, but the solution is not. If some sort of effective political compromise is not implemented whereby more power devolves locally, then pressure for permanent severance from Moscow is sure to increase. But for Moscow to allow the three Baltic republics to function as semi-sovereign states would mean the total transformation of the Soviet constitutional system, a step which not even the most reform-minded member of the Politburo would be willing to contemplate. Yet anything short of this is unlikely to satisfy local demands. Moscow continues to vacillate between the twin horrors of a resort to military force to suppress popular resistance movements or allowing the Baltic republics to secede from the USSR in everything but name.

The Youth Problem in the Lithuanian Emigration *

K. MALINAUSKAS

In recent years one of the major concerns in the life of the Lithuanian emigration as an ethnic group has been the problem of their youth. Even the most recent generation of emigrés, those who found themselves abroad during the years of World War II, is rapidly aging and giving way to new generations. There is a growing conviction in the Lithuanian emigré community that its vitality and historical continuity will depend, first and foremost, on the extent to which its young progeny adopt and develop further various elements of the national culture.ᵃ

Several articles in Soviet scholarly literature have dealt with the youth problem in the Lithuanian emigration. Among them are the works of J. Aničas, which examine the activities of the clerical emigré youth organizations, problems of ideological-political upbringing, and the education of youth in Lithuanian language and culture (cf. "The system of clerical upbringing of youth in the bourgeois Lithuanian emigration, 1945–1972," Lietuvos TSR Moksly akademijos Darbai/*Trudy Akademii nauk Litovskoi SSR* [Proceedings of the Academy of Sciences of the Lithuanian SSR], Series A, 1973, no. 4 (45); "The crisis in the system of clerical upbringing of youth in the bourgeois Lithuanian emigration," in *The Ideological Struggle and Youth*," Vilnius, 1972; "The crisis in [emigré] Lithuanian education," *Literatūra ir menas* [Literature and Art], 1979, no. 10). V. Kazakevičius, in the course of his examination of the correlation between national and democratic features of the Lithuanian emigration, has demonstrated that the "conflict of generations" is essentially a manifestation of the contradictions in bourgeois society ("How many paths are there? Some observations on the paths and wanderings of the Lithuanian youth abroad," *Nemunas* [The Niemen], 1977, no. 7, p. 52). Problems of the assimilation of youth have been examined by A. Balsys, S. Laurinaitis, and L. Petkevičiene (A. Balsys, "On foreign soil trees wither" *Šviesa* [The Light], 1976, no. 1; S. Laurinaitis, "On the other side of native shores," *Nemunas*, 1969, no. 3; L. Petkevičienė, *Socio-cultural activities of progressive Lithuanians in the USA in 1933–1940*, Vilnius, 1969).

* * *

In bourgeois society, emigré ethnic groups are not homogeneous in terms of social class. They reflect the features of the society in which they live. They include, on the one hand, working and democratic strata, and, on the other, reactionary strata. This is what gives rise to contradictory processes among the emigrés.

In the last few decades, a crisis has arisen in emigré ethnic life. The reason for this

---

Kommunist (Vilnius), 1981, no. 8, pp. 38–46. Russian text © 1981 by "Kommunist."

lies in the quantitative and qualitative changes in emigré social life. Among the youth the process of assimilation has intensified. In the USA, where the overwhelming majority of the most recent emigrés settled (more than 30,000), there were in 1960, according to the American press, 402,346 Lithuanians, of whom 121,475 had been born in Lithuania, while in 1970 there were 330,977 Lithuanians, of whom only 76,000 were born in Lithuania. More and more frequently complaints are being voiced in the emigration that there is no one to replace the aged newspaper and magazine editors or leaders of amateur artistic groups and community organizations, and that the level of national consciousness and the active involvement of emigré youth are declining.

These are attempts in the emigration to stimulate youth organizations, and studies are conducted to determine the views of young people, their position on political and ethnic issues, their feelings about the country of their residence and about Lithuania. Considerable variances and conflicts between parents and children have appeared in the Lithuanian emigration on such issues, evidenced by disparities in ideals, attitudes and value systems. It has been found that representatives of the older generation more frequently isolate themselves within a restricted ethnic environment, and are more conservative and dogmatic than the general public of the given country or their own children. This ethnic isolation was for the older generation a psychological weapon, a kind of refuge from the threat of assimilation. In the meantime, young people, as they became increasingly integrated into the economic, political and cultural-spiritual life of the country of their residence and accept its values, become increasingly attached to it. About two-thirds of the parents polled declared that they set a higher value on Lithuania than on America, and the remainder that they felt equally about both countries. Meanwhile half of the students polled felt equally about both countries, while one-third preferred Lithuania and one-sixth—America.

Young Lithuanians have surpassed their parents both in terms of education and social status. At the same time their ethnic involvement is diminishing. Obviously this process was affected by the older generation's particular and idiosyncratic interest in politics, its conservatism, and antipathy toward democratic self-government. For this reason their children have shunned them.

A poll of graduates from the Montreal Saturday school in Lithuanian language and culture showed that 41% never participated in Lithuanian ethnic activities. More and more young people are drifting away from the Lithuanian press. In 1956, 16% of Lithuanian students had not read a single Lithuanian book, while in 1960 this figure reached 28.7%. In 1972, a survey was conducted among 455 young people participating in a congress of Lithuanian youth abroad. And what were the results? 41.6% had not read a single Lithuanian book in the preceding year, while 25.5% had read only one. 10.4% had not read a single Lithuanian newspaper or periodical. The older generation makes considerable efforts to maintain Lithuanian radio programs. However, 20.4% of those polled do not listen to them. To be sure, a fairly significant portion of young people does listen to Lithuanian music.

The survey results strongly suggest that at times young people regard the ethnic isolation that is being forced upon them and the desire of their elders to limit themselves to the Lithuanian world as an obstacle to broader horizons in science and art, to the wide realm of social intercourse. One may even hear the view that customs or a language that is imposed by force, even if they are used, can become hateful. For these reasons one increasingly meets in the emigré press calls for the generations to enter into a dialogue, for a rejection of tendentious and one-sided assessments of Lithuania's historical past, for an acknowledgement of Soviet Lithuania's great economic and cultural achievements and for an expansion and strengthening of ties with her.

Young people do not want to live merely on a sentimental yearning for the past, to follow obsolete traditions and struggle for antiquated ideals and a verbal patriotism. Lithuania, for those young people who have never seen her, often remains an abstraction and for this reason young people have their own perspectives on the facts and the historical situation that has evolved. On the other hand, they themselves more and more frequently express the notion that ethnic distinctiveness is linked with a broader participation in the public life of their new homeland, that it is necessary to make one's contribution to the latter's culture and in this way bring glory to Lithuania. Moreover, young people are alienated by the discord, dissensions, and intolerance exhibited by people of the older generation.

In rejecting the reactionary ideology of bourgeois emigré leaders, young people often times simultaneously reject everything connected with Lithuanian ethnic life. Nihilistic attitudes in this regard are promoted also by the bourgeoisie of the ruling nation which extols its own culture as being universal and deprecates the cultures of ethnic minorities as a symbol of conservatism.

The preservation of specifically ethnic attributes depends to a significant degree on one's world outlook. The bourgeois emigré press has also noted that young people need shining and inspiring ideals, but the bourgeoisie does not possess these. Relying on bourgeois ideology it is impossible to deal successfully and over the long term with the ethnic problems of the emigration.

*   *   *

The children of Lithuanian emigrés—educated on the one hand in the country of their residence and unremittingly under its influence, but on the other hand raised by their parents in the spirit of Lithuanian culture—in a certain sense find themselves in a conflict situation. Life, in objective terms, brings its own influence to bear and draws them into the mainstream, while their parents, with great exertions of will-power, strive to keep them within the orbit of the Lithuanian world and instill them in a Lithuanian consciousness. Hence a considerable number of young people are faced with such questions as: "Who am I, an American or a Lithuanian? To which culture do I belong? What am I aiming for? How am I to behave and what national path shall I follow?" In short, there arises the problem of national identity.

In the midst of one's own people, the entire ethnic environment and socialization process promote a natural resolution of this problem. Since emigrés are scattered all over the world, however, their linguistic and cultural environment is not conducive to the formation of a national identity. Emigrés are not united even by political interests. Divided by various political parties which strive to advance their own class interests, emigrés do not even have a single unified ideal. In consequence emigré Lithuanian youth has even greater difficulty discovering their national identity.

Various criteria for defining ethnic affiliation have been propounded in emigré circles, but at their heart remain the perception of Lithuania as the emigrés' motherland as well as the Lithuanian language and national consciousness. Quite widespread is the notion that Lithuanian language and literature are the main attributes of Lithuanian national identity by which Lithuanians identify one another, and that therefore the main focus of attention should be directed at preserving the Lithuanian language in order to forestall absorption by other peoples. Some emigrés regard their role and function as serving Lithuania through their creative efforts and in this way contributing to her cultural potential in the future.

Obviously, all this does not mean that the majority of Lithuanian bourgeois emigrés approve of the current course of Lithuania's historical development. Most often they are ill-disposed toward the socialist system and all the more toward the current internationalist nature of interrelations among peoples in the Soviet Union. In discussing problems such as freedom, happiness, national culture and independence, many emigrés continue to maintain bourgeois class positions.

* * *

The problem of ethnic continuity in the emigration is closely linked to issues surrounding ethnically mixed families. Initially such families were viewed as a fact or promoting assimilation, and consequently evoked disapproval and even hostility. Reality, however, is more powerful than wishful thinking or any prohibitions. The Lithuanian emigration is not sufficiently compact or numerous to provide favorable conditions for extensive daily contact among its members. In many countries, Lithuanians are racially indistinguishable from the bulk of the populace, while having mastered the language of the land, they are hardly distinguishable even in cultural features. Thus, in the absence of negative ethnic stereotypes, ethnic antipathies, or other psychological or linguistic barriers, ethnic factors in the choice of spouse play a negligible role.

Already in the early 1940s, mixed families constituted one-third of the total number of families in the American-Lithuanian emigration (L. Petkevičiené, *Sociocultural activities of progressive Lithuanians in the USA in 1933–1940*, p. 15). In 1972, in their responses to a sociological survey 34.4% of young people declared that the nationality of a prospective spouse was unimportant. In actual fact, youth is even more susceptible to assimilation. Increases in the number of ethnically mixed marriages are typical for emigré groups of all nationalities.

Under the circumstances, the Lithuanian emigration is trying to find a compromise. There are proposals that those who set up ethnically mixed families not be "stricken from the rolls" of the Lithuanian community, but rather be assisted in every way to preserve and develop features of Lithuanian culture. The emigré press now more frequently opposes discrimination against mixed families and manifestations of mistrust and intolerance toward them. At the same time, there is greater stress on instances when the non-Lithuanian partner in a mixed marriage learns Lithuanian and becomes actively involved in the cultural life of the Lithuanian ethnic community. The art historian A. Rannit married a Lithuanian and not only mastered the Lithuanian language, but even wrote a master's thesis on Čiurlionis[b] and continues to publish articles on his creative work. The American professor R. Sealy translates Lithuanian literature into English. Even before the war, the Swiss A. Senn, who married a Lithuanian, not only mastered Lithuanian to perfection, but has even done a considerable amount of work in the field of Lithuanian linguistics.

Nevertheless, in a foreign environment the vast majority of those who form ethnically mixed families assimilate quite rapidly.

* * *

Language is one of the burning issues in the community life of the Lithuanian emigration.

The role of the native language in the life of any ethnic group is extraordinarily important. N. Kulikov, who has written about the Russian emigration, notes that: "Language recreates the spiritual image of one's native kin, provides the means of grasping its poetic essence, nourishes feelings of national conciousness and dignity, and, as it were, summons up and illuminates the image of the motherland, making her lovingly dear to those of her children who, through the vicissitudes of life, have found themselves in foreign lands" (N. Kulikov, *The Honor and Dignity of the Russian Name*, Moscow, 1973, p. 18).

Since a significant number of young people oftentimes regard English as their native language, while the number of ethnically mixed marriages is also increasing, there are attempts to supplement the concept of ethnicity with subjective psychological factors: i.e., national consciousness, sentiments, etc. Not only those who speak Lithuanian, are to be considered as belonging to the Lithuanian ethnic community, but also those "who think or feel Lithuanian" and show a willingness to take part in one form or another in Lithuanian social and cultural life.

As experience has shown, the objective components of ethnicity (language, traditions, way of life, etc.) change more rapidly than ethnic consciousness. Language is not the sole attribute of a national ethnic group. The Soviet scholar L. Fursova, who studied Canadian immigrants, concluded that the principal determinant of a national ethnic group is the ethnic self-consciousness of the immigrant. "The main indicator of assimilation", writes the author, "is a change in ethnic self-consciousness." Even an immigrant who has lost his language may feel that he has not yet lost his nationality, and a sense of Canadian patriotism frequently coexists with the immigrant's ethnic self-consciousness" (L. Fursova, *Immigration and the National Development of Canada, 1945-1970*, Moscow, p. 389). An analysis of the ethnic life of Lithuanian emigrés shows that second or even third generation emigrés preserve their language or ethnic consciousness.

In the emigré communities, all possible efforts are made to excite interest in and impart love for the Lithuanian language, and to maintain its social functions as broad as possible. There is an emphasis on the scientific value of the Lithuanian language, with roots deep in the Indo-European linguistic community,[c] and glorification of the beauty of Lithuanian.

The Lithuanian emigration has been forced to adapt to its new environment, and first of all, learn the language of the country (mainly English) as an essential means of communication with non-Lithuanians. But the children of immigrants—born and bred in the new country, completing their secondary or higher education there, exposed to the influence of mass media, and developing broader personal contacts—increasingly master the language of the new country to the point that it serves as their main mode of communication and thinking. For the young generation the language of their country of residence gradually becomes the native language, while their former native language becomes increasingly remote until it merely functions as the language of "domestic" use, that is, the language of communication with one's own family and a narrow circle of Lithuanian relatives, friends, and acquaintances.

It has been found that even among the middle-aged, the inner drive to speak Lithuanian tends to disappear, and that the Lithuanian language is often used only on solemn occasions or at conventions—that is, at official functions where it is necessary to "demonstrate" one's affiliation with the Lithuanian nation. Gradually even an intellectual interest in the Lithuanian language is disappearing.

In the emigration there are (or were) a number of specialists in Lithuanian, either working as scholars of the Lithuanian language or as its popularizers in the emigré community: P. Skardžius, A. Salys, and others. Nonetheless young people in considerable numbers are completely forgetting the Lithuanian language. In England, 90% of Lithuanian youth no longer knows Lithuanian. The foreign language is spoken more and more frequently even in the home. According to some data, only 3.7% of the youth speak with their peers solely in Lithuanian, 12.5% more frequently in Lithuanian than in the language of the given country, 37.3% use Lithuanian and the language of the given country to the same extent, 40.5% speak mostly in the language of their country of residence, while 6% speak only in that language.

With a decline in the number of people who know Lithuanian, the readership of Lithuanian books, newspapers, and magazines is also diminishing. As a result, the quantity of Lithuanian books and periodicals being published is decreasing and—one may expect—will continue to decrease, eroding in this way the objective basis of Lithuanian culture. Even now there are anxious laments in print that the works of the best writers, published in editions of several hundred copies, are gathering dust in warehouses or garages.

As a counterweight to lingusitic assimilation, there has appeared the advocacy of bilingualism. It is said that bilingualism is a valuable skill that is not only nondetrimental to the individual, but promotes intellectual development, broadens ones's horizons, and expands and deepens life experiences. A person fluent in two languages possesses a key to the treasure-house of two cultures, and at the same time has greater opportunities to use his talents for the benefit of both cultures. It is asserted that bilingualism can only do good rather than harm to a child. Great attention is devoted in emigré periodicals to the family as the basic institution that transmits the most important ethnic attributes —language, customs and other spiritual values—to the young generation.

Another way of teaching the Lithuanian language to the rising generation is provided by schools of Lithuanian language and culture and Lithuanian-oriented education in general.

*   *   *

Increased attention to Lithuanian education in emigré circles can be dated to the 1950s. It was widely assumed that this would constitute a major means of warding off assimilation, facilitating the training of new people to replace aging editors and community leaders, and thereby ensuring the continuity of Lithuanian cultural-ethnic life. Considerable financial resources and human energy are expended on Lithuanian schools in which children on Saturdays study their native language and literature, the history and geography of Lithuania, and elements of folk art according to specially prepared syllabi. Special textbooks and manuals are published.

The first schools of Lithuanian language and culture were established in the late 19th and early 20th centuries. Until 1969 there were three Lithuanian high schools in the emigration. In 1969, which had been proclaimed the year of Lithuanian education, the Lithuanian high schools in the USA and Italy were closed, as were some other educational institutions. At the present time there is only one functioning Lithuanian boarding school in West Germany. Its diploma is recognized by educational institutions in West Germany since it provides an accredited general course of study in additon to special courses of instruction in Lithuanian language and culture. In 1977 this high school had 70 students. In 1958, in the whole of the emigration there were 144 educational institutions offering various types and levels of instruction in Lithuanian subjects, with a combined enrollment of some 10,000. In 1967 there were in the emigration about 100 schools with 5,700 students. And ten years hence? According to various press reports, in 1978 in the whole of the emigration there were only 53 Lithuanian schools with some 3,150 pupils. In the USA in the 1966–67 school year there were more than 50 Lithuanian educational institutions with 3,740 pupils, while in 1977–78 there were only 30 schools with 2,041 pupils. Lithuanian schools in the USA are attended by only one-third of Lithuanian youth.

Education in Lithuanian language and culture is organized comparatively more successfully in Canada, where it enjoys material support by local government. But even there, for example, one of the largest schools in the emigration, the Maironis School in Toronto,[d] which had 620 pupils in 1966–67, had only 231 by the end of 1978. In Australia in 1968 there were ten Lithuanian schools that conducted their work on weekends, with 428 pupils, as well as four higher courses in Lithuanian language and literature with 83 auditors; by 1978 only five Lithuanian schools with 150 pupils remained.

In recent years, with great difficulties there has been some renewal of education in Lithuanian language and literature in South America, where after World War II governments had suppressed the cultural life of various ethnic groups. For example, in Sao Paulo there were in 1976, 44 pupils in the Lithuanian school of whom half were unable to express themselves in Lithuanian. In Argentina in 1978, there were three Lithuanian schools with 80 pupils, while there were 50 pupils in the single Lithuanian school in Venezuela in 1976.

In the majority of schools pupils may be divided into three groups: (1) those without any knowledge of the Lithuanian language; (2) those with a poor command of the language, and (3) those who speak Lithuanian fluently. The Lithuanian schools in South America suffer from a shortage of textbooks and teachers, and their financial basis is weak. The quality of the work in the schools is declining. Some graduates of these schools are unable to read or speak Lithuanian. The youth are also disaffected by the dull and old-fashioned methods of instruction in the Lithuanian schools.

The emigré press notes that the main task of Lithuanian schools should be the teaching of the Lithuanian language. However, children do not spend much time in a Lithuanian school, and for an ordinary young person it remains merely a peculiar episode in his life. It cannot compete with the official schools of the country, which leave a young person with a body of knowledge and a requisite basis for leading an independent adult life.

At the present time, Lithuanian language and literature are taught in the USA in two universities in Chicago, as well as at Fordham, Kent, and Sacred Heart Universities. Yet even here a lack of interest on the part of Lithuanian students is apparent. At the University of Illinois at Chicago in 1972, when this course was first introduced, the enrollment reached 101 students, while in 1978 there were only 29 students, despite the fact that some 300 Lithuanians attend this university.

It is not easy in a foreign land to preserve one's native language, or obtain even a minimum of knowledge about one's native land. The press sees the chief reason for the decline in Lithuanian schools as the indifference of parents. Young people are also dissatisfied with the cultural level of these schools. The decline in the number of Lithuanian schools and pupils is a reflection of the gradual estrangement of the Lithuanian emigration from its ethnic life and the weakening of the self-consciousness of Lithuanians as they become increasingly absorbed into the country's dominant culture.

A breakdown in their own ethnic education is noticeable among many emigré ethnic groups. The Lithuanian emigration is no exception. In the schools of Lithuanian language and culture pupils are frequently educated in a religious spirit[e] and instilled with antisocialist and anti-Soviet attitudes.

Young people of the Lithuanian emigration are not very eager to study the Lithuanian language, and the pleas of their elders to learn Lithuanian are frequently seen as one more unnecessary burden, for they see no practical use for this language. There are no extensive contacts with Lithuania which could sustain ethnic enthusiasm. For this reason progressive emigrés strata attach particular importance to courses in the Lithuanian language organized by Vilnius University and to children's summer camps in Lithuania, where they have the opportunity not only to gain better knowledge of the Lithuanian language, but also to become acquainted with Lithuania, its culture and its people. A way out in the emigration's struggle against assimilation is the establishment of close ties with Lithuania. At the time of a 1968 poll, almost all respondents declared that it was essential to maintain contact with Soviet Lithuania. Gradually the emigration is being forced to abandon its pretensions to represent Lithuania and the interests and will of the entire Lithuanian people.ᶠ Newspapers of a liberal orientation are also speaking out in favor of extensive cultural cooperation with Lithuania, though they often recommend that such contacts be used for the propagation of anti-Soviet ideas.

* * *

Many of the features in the pragmatic life of the emigration can be attributed to incorrect theoretical premises. In the works of many emigré ideologues one can meet with the notion that the Lithuanian emigration constitutes a community of the same nature as a nation. This is an inaccurate assertion. Lithuanians abroad represent a national minority, and their problems are the problems of a national minority.

Of course the emigration, owing to their historical past and memory, perceptions—that is, a certain shared life experience prior to emigration—traditions and language, as well as consciousness, does preserve some ethnic elements and features of the Lithuanian nation. However, present-day Lithuania is developing on new economic and ideological-political foundations, and its social structure has also changed. Little by little the cultural and psychological differences between Lithuanians in Lithuania and Lithuanians abroad are growing. In this respect the emigration is a part of the former Lithuanian people, and this part frequently still lives in an illusory past. At the same time, Lithuanians abroad are in actual fact taking root in the new soil of their adopted countries and increasingly assuming the features of those societies. The emigration is like the two-faced god Janus, whose one face looks back into the past and lives in it, while the other lives in the present and looks toward the future.

As they scrutinize the ongoing process of assimilation, bourgeois emigré activists frequently make only narrow appeals to the emotions and sentiment. The cement which binds people together, in the opinion of bourgeois ideologues, is more emotional than economic or social in nature. Not infrequently, in the spirit of their idealistic tradition, they attempt to explain the crisis in emigré ethnic life by the lack of good leaders. The youth however, is to a growing extent of the opinion that in the struggle against assimilation it is essential to unify the entire emigration and struggle not against individuals but against a pernicious environment, and to create a climate conducive to inter-Lithuanian fellowship.

Bourgeois class bias and limitations of an idealist methodology hamper any successful resolution of the most basic problem in emigré social life. The bourgeois emigré leadership seeks to steer young people onto an anti-Soviet course and set them in opposition to socialist Lithuania. However, without life-sustaining links with Lithuania the emigration faces the threat of even greater assimilation. The problem of ethnic continuity in the Lithuanian emigration is indissolubly linked with sociopolitical and cultural progress as a whole.

The bourgeois emigré press virtually ignores the differentiation of the emigration in terms of social class as well as the fact that every social stratum has its own particular economic, political and spiritual needs and interests. The contrast of spiritual and material values as a whole is typical of all philosophical and sociopolitical thinking in the Lithuanian bourgeois emigration. In the process, the daily, "worldly" needs and interests of rank-and-file representatives of the emigration are not considered.

Seldom are emigré voices raised in protest against the inattention to acute social problems, or in complaint against the disregard of material, practical workaday or moral aspects of problems in the emigration. It may also be said that, paralleling the disregard of people's material needs, the self-contained nature of the Lithuanian community is often abused for purposes of profit, and that well-being frequently stills the voice of national consciousness.

A lack of understanding of the dialectic of class and national interests in social life, or, indeed, their conscious rejection has led the bourgeois elements in the emigration to present themselves as the sole spokesmen for ethnic interests and needs, and leaders of ethnic life, while they declare the theory and practice of communism to be incompatible with a defense of national interests or with the fostering of national culture and consciousness. This domination of bourgeois class interests and mutual competition are pushing the Lithuanian emigration toward dissension and divisions, not only ideological and political, but also organizational.

Within every class or social group of a society, the resolution of nationality problems has its own nuances. In a class society, ethnic problems have a class nature, and to resolve them "wholesale," without taking into account the interests of different social strata and individuals, is impossible. Young people in different historical and cultural circumstances understand their ethnic problems in different ways. On their class and national orientation will depend the future of the Lithuanian emigration as an ethnic group abroad.

Editor's Notes

a. For purposes of context and counterpoise, see the concise information on Lithuanian communities abroad (history, organization, statistical data, etc.) in the English-language *Encyclopedia Lituanica* (6 vols., Boston, 1970–1978), especially the articles "Emigration" (vol. 2, pp. 149–153) and on individual countries, entered alphabetically except for the USA, which appears in the Supplement section under "Lithuanians in the United States" (vol. 6, pp. 434–451).

b. Mikalojus Čiurlionis (1875–1911): composer and painter, probably the internationally best-known Lithuanian cultural figure.

c. Lithuanian is indeed among the most archaic of Indo-European languages, and for that reason holds a place of importance in historical and comparative linguistics far out of proportion to the relatively small number of its speakers—a matter of considerable national pride for many Lithuanians.

d. Named after Maironis (pseud. of Jonas Mačiulis) (1862–1932), a Roman Catholic priest and a leading poet of the Lithuanian cultural rebirth.

e. The Lithuanians are in their vast majority Roman Catholic, and much of their community life abroad, including schools, is connected with ethnic Lithuanian parishes.

f. The reference may contain an allusion to the fact that many Western countries, including the United States, have not recognized the annexation of Lithuania by the USSR, and continue to recognize the diplomatic credentials of the surviving consular representatives appointed by the independent interwar Lithuanian government.

Annotated by Lubomyr Hajda

The Summer 1987 Protests

Coverage from the Soviet Press

To an Alien Script: "Manifesters" Incited by Western Radio Broadcasters Try to Read Latvian History *

It seemed as though he was even a little insulted that he got permission to leave the Motherland so quickly. What else could have displeased 21-year-old Roland Sila-raups, who had grown up in Soviet Latvia and who had first made his noise as a participant in the so-called Latvian human rights group "Helsinki 86"? The views of this ten-person group all come to the same thing—to separate Latvia from the Soviet Union.

Both Roland and his supporters, clearly from what they are fed by western ideologues, think that Latvia was occupied by the Red Army in 1940. The interpretation of historical facts to reach this conclusion is very free, for they "forget" that detachments of Red troops entered Latvia because of a treaty of mutual aid in the threat of fascist aggression. The former Foreign Minister of bourgeois Latvia Wilhelm Muiters, who took part in the negotiation and signing of the mutual aid pact between Latvia and the USSR of 5 October 1939 writes in his memoirs that, "after the collapse of talks in Moscow between England, France, and the USSR the last hopes were gone that the western nations would support our neutrality. We remained alone." That Red Army troops were in Latvia at the disposal of her government was also announced by radio on 17 June 1940, by Karlis Ulmanis, head of the bourgeois republic. Today's champions of "freedom" from the Helsinki-86 group also close their eyes to the fact that the legal establishment of Soviet power in Latvia in 1940 was proclaimed as result of the vote taken by delegates of the people's *seim* [parliament]. Even Roland Silaraups couldn't deny this, when he talked with me. However, as he admitted it, he immediately went off on another tangent, as though he had been specially trained to; "Here I have no freedom to express my views, to achieve justice."

With these words the voice of this thin but sturdy lad takes on tragic tones. Let his unproven supposition remain on his conscience. Even his anti-Soviet activity (the dissemination and progandizing of literature hostile to our nation, which is forbidden by the Constitution of the USSR), for which Silaraups, though he did received five years' deprivation of freedom, was pardoned after a year in prison. Since February of this year, after his return to freedom, Roland has basically worked nowhere, but before, in his own words, he made a decent living at VEF. Apparently

---

Komsomol'skaia pravda, 26 August 1987. Russian text © 1987 by "Komsomol'skaia pravda."

500

though he then decided that he could "earn" more doing something else. And so on 14 June at the monument to Freedom a flower-laying was organized in honor of the dead, presented as a kind of demarche to demonstrate lack of agreement with the facts of history.

Why at the monument to Freedom? Because it was erected during the period of bourgeois Latvia, in 1935, so the monument can be used as a sort of symbol. Which in fact is what the organizers of the flower-laying did, taking advantage of the long absence of any information whatsoever about the monument, even in guidebooks to the city.

The center of Riga. Here on a small square, on a high plinth, stands a sculpture which raises three five-pointed stars in her upstretched hands, symbols of the historical territories of Latvia, Kurzeme, Vidzeme, and Latgale. Below bas-reliefs depict the fighters of the 1905 revolution, their clashes with punitive detachments, the battles of the Red Latvian Riflemen with German occupation troops and with Bermondt's bands in 1919, at the Riga railroad bridge. Along the edges of the monument are sculpture groups representing Labor, Science, Family, and Defense of the Fatherland. Money for the monument was collected, as they called it, from the whole world. The sculptor Karlis Zale though, at one time lived in Petrograd and was one of the first to enter into realizing Lenin's plan of monument propaganda. He created monuments to Dobroliubov and Garibaldi, and as A. Lunacharskii[a] describes him in his memoirs, he was one of the best.

However, no one reminded the youths about the history and meaning of the monument with the beautiful words interspersed among the stones, "To the Fatherland and Freedom." Thus all kinds of whispering became possible: "Look, the Motherland statue there is even facing the West . . ." Not the Daugava River, with which the history of the Latvian people is closely connected, but rather to the West . . .

I happened to be a witness to the events of 14 June. Before that day various radio stations,[b] making use of the services of Roland, were summoning people to mark this day with a demonstration. We can explain briefly. In 1941, eight days before Germany attacked the USSR, officers with pro-fascist inclinations, reenlisters from the former Ulmanis army, agents, members of the fascist organization "Perkonirusts" who had acted illegally, were all sent out of Latvia. However, at the same time there were also guiltless people who suffered—and not just Latvians either, but also Russians, Poles, and others. As well as the members of their families.[c] A significant part of these people returned to their native places in the middle of the 1950s, as Soviet citizens with full rights. It is on these tragic mistakes, tragic not just for Latvia but for all the people of our country, that members of the group "Helsinki 86" are trying to speculate today, with the support of foreign radio centers.

So, what took place that day? There was a bicycle race to start at the monument to Freedom, the crown of All-Union Bicycle Sport Week, at 3 PM. At precisely the same time a group wishing to place flowers on the monument arrived. It was spitting rain. The cyclists though were optimistically turning their pedals, going around the monument and moving further down Lenin Street. Naturally during the time of the cycling holiday the area around the monument was blocked off. Then the participants in the action decided to wait. They gathered on Bastion Hill, a rise in the city park, which is nearby. On the hill the orators with their badges "Helsinki 86" gave their speeches, pseudopatriotic in nature, but more will be said about this in a moment. I remember a moment when someone among them, apparently not sharing the opinion of the speakers, tried to speak. He was not permitted to get near to the little rise in the center. People gathered over several hours on the rise and in the tree-lined alleys around it. Under the guidance of Roland Silaraups and Eva Bitenietse, who was wearing a national costume, the people moved toward the monument to Freedom. Naturally no one interfered with this advance. They laid their flowers, sang folk songs, including songs of the Red Latvian riflemen. Nothing criminal. It was only in the night that some young bucks appeared at the monument with flowers, shouting and running, and so disturbing the public order. Naturally the hooligans were called to order by members of the militia. Then for several days white and red carnations and roses appeared at the monument, repeating the color compostiion of the bourgeois Latvian flag. These little scenes were common, as some one of the "heroes," as they probably styled themselves, made for the monument with their flowers, generally picked right there in the flower beds. The "brave lad" was then applauded grandly, people looking around proudly, as if to say "look, one of ours!" Bravado, you might say; is it worthy of attention?

And what does youth itself think about all this? I asked Ziedonis Chevers, the first secretary of the Kirov Raion committee of the Riga Komsomol (the center of the city, where the monument to Freedom happens to be located) to help me find young people who had taken part in laying flowers at the monument. This wasn't difficult for him, as he enjoys a deserved authority among the youth of the area. The summer of last year the committee appealed to boys and girls to help clean up the abandoned basements of the old city. The workers of the Komosomol raion committee, as well as their first secretary, without obligation worked alongside the youths in their spare time.

Over the year scores of buildings were cleaned. In many others the work is still going on. In the future these are going to hold special interest clubs, sports halls, youth cafes. Ziedonis and I went to one of the basements where students, school kids, young workers, and students at the technical institutes (PTUs) gather in their free time. Ziedonis is well known here. There are debates here, on the most pressing of issues, and amateur films are shown, various ensembles perform, young artists and sculptures exhibit their work, and finally there are discotheques. In a smallish hall among these ancient walls we met Aigar, Ugis, Gatis, Artis, and Inese. We decided to speak frankly, especially since three of the boys had been at the monument on 14 June. My new acquaintances were all of an age with Roland Silaraups, who in an open letter to the republic Latvian newspapers had written, "We understand that you can not and do not want to understand or evaluate the group "Helsinki–86" objectively. However, we will leave the freedom to evaluate this question to the Latvian people themselves, the majority of whom are now learning to come to their own independent conclusions, without being lead." Where does this assurance of

Roland's come from? No doubt from the fact that so far nothing substantive has been said about his group in Latvia. Is it enough simply to call them "extremists"? So let's leave the evaluating to the youths themselves.

Aigar: "I went to the monument about three. I knew what would be there. I was told that "Voice of America" had announced it."

Gatis: "In my family there are people who suffered during the resettlement. They went to the monument to Freedom, because it had been built by the entire people, and people travelled to Riga especially to bring offerings to the monument."

Here is how the youths describe the slogans on Bastion Hill, among which were such as "Youth must stand in our ranks," "The sacrifices of the Red Latvian riflemen were in vain," and "We want only truth but do not wish revenge." There were also comments about the "colonization" of Latvia . . .

Ugis: "Not everybody who placed flowers that day thought about the meaning of what they were doing. Many people just came for the show of it."

Aigar: "On Bastion Hill there was one moment when a group began to shout that there was no reason to wait until the end of the bicycle marathon, that we should go to the monument immediately. Probably they wanted that so that the radio could announce that the demonstration was broken up by the militia. It was good though that the majority understood the situation correctly, so that the provocation was unsuccessful."

This CONVERSATION took place while the tracks were still hot, as they say. Many of the events of those days are now understood in a different way, of course. The problem however, remains. And first and foremost the problem lies in the philistine way in which inter-nationality relations are understood in the republic.

A reminder, by the way. Historically it has worked out that, unlike in neighboring Estonia and Lithuania, members of various nationalities have lived here for a long time. On one street, in one building, Latvians, Russians, Poles, Germans, Jews, Belorussians, and Lithuanians have lived as peaceful neighbors. People from the national regions of Russia have studied in the Latvian higher educational institutions. I am flattered to admit that my famous countryman Stepan Shauman[d] studied at the polytechnicum, but did not receive his diploma because he took part in the revolutionary movement and was expelled from Latvia. He was guilty of struggling for the happiness of all the peoples of Russia who were exploited by the tsarist government. It is bad to forget the internationalist past of the republic; unfortunately, it is happening.

Why? The young people themselves give as reasons an insufficiency of civility, the lack of knowledge about history among the Latvians and, the lack of knowledge of Latvian of the Russian-speaking population. Sometimes there is also a lack of desire to study it. You will agree that someone who grows up in a republic, who studies ten years in a school, and who can't put two words together in the local language can easily cause anger. It is important to know how to respect the people among whom you are living, to respect their traditions. These subjects used somehow to be left to one side, and weren't particularly bothered with. Nor can you solve them on the fly, either. These things must be considered at all times. In the republic this question has begun to receive more constant attention. Thus for example there recently has begun a commission on inter-nationality relations in the Central Committee of the Latvian Communist Party.

"We are accustomed to interpreting international education as something like having the Russian and Latvian classes conduct a joint evening, and that's it," says Ziedonis Chevers. "One evening won't give you anything."

A common task, common labor brings people together, gives no opportunity for nationalistic chauvinism to appear. How often have I witnessed various squabbles in the city buses or overcrowded trains; someone steps on someone else's foot or jostles someone. Immediately "offensive" words fly, with explanations of nationality. We are reduced to that! And believe me, it is in great part from such little trifles that the nuclei of mutual hatred grows. From living offenses on the bus! But what may be said, for example, of a man who after visiting the famous ethnographic museum (in which one can see how the peasants of various districts of Latvia lived a century and two centuries ago) could scratch on the wooden strut of a mill "Beat the Russians!"? Local nationalists attempt to use such pitiful scratchings as proof of the hatred for Russians which is supposed to exist in "enslaved" Latvia. One of the organizers of the flower-laying demonstration was Roland Silaraups. By all appearances he decided that this gave him sufficient political baggage to get abroad.

"I know that reliable people will meet me in West Germany," he told me a few days before his departure.

Wasn't he also confident because he could rely on more than his own just deserts, on certain facts of his biography as well, such as that his father was a former SS member and his uncle was a *Polizei*?

By the by, several of the Helsinki group had been convicted of crimes. For example, one of the founders of the group, Raimonds Bitenieks, was stopped in 1983 in an attempt to cross the border with his daughter Eva, who then was only fifteen. At nineteen (remember?) she was already dressed in a national costume and was heading the "demonstration protest"! It appears she likes to be in the center of attention. Nor is she the only one.

Roland's example makes it clear that the scandal that blew up on the short waves around their action was to the benefit of the group members. Particularly since in Latvia almost no one knows about "Helsinki 86," or knows about it only by rumor. The aura of mystery in fact dissipates like smoke once the real goals of the "rights advocates" are understood, which is to present themselves in a profitable light for the western provocateurs. It was not by chance that immediately after Roland's departure for Vienna at the end of July a press conference was arranged for him.

So who remains active in the group here in the Motherland? Janis Barkanis, convicted in 1981 of attempting to cross the border, convicted in 1983 for anti-Soviet agitation. Or the "elder" of the group, Edmund Tsirvilis, sentenced to ten years in 1945 for betraying the Motherland. He was arrested when he was dropped into our country as part of a troup of paratrooper-diversionists . . .

These and other "accomplishments" apparently do not disturb those who promise them every support in the West. So we can only be curious about one thing, how Roland is going to defend liberty, national values, and the traditions of the Latvian people from the other side of the cordon?

At the end of his life's path, grown wiser from the years he had lived, the former Foreign Minister of bourgeois Latvia Wilhelm Munters affirmed that, "I have no doubt in the correctness of the choice of the Latvian people. I will not hide that not everything in my native Latvia seems to me to be as it ought . . . However, I am convinced that the preservation of the living strength of my people, her growing well-being, her peaceful life, and the guarantees necessary for these are assured."

The "how" was announced in the press, the flower-laying of 23 August in Riga, at the monument to Freedom, to mark the anniversary of the nonaggression pact between the USSR and Germany. Speculating on people's ignorance about the real historical situation in 1939, for almost the entire month "Radio Free Europe" and "The Voice of America" summoned the peoples of the Soviet Baltic to mount anti-Soviet demonstrations. Members of "Helsinki–86" took active part in this. The day and hour of the demonstration were set—the 23rd, at 5 o'clock.

That Sunday, long before the appointed hour, almost two thousand people gathered at the monument. Some came simply to look at the event, others in obedience to the radio stations, and only a third group, merely some individuals, tried to stir up the people to an open anti-Soviet demonstration. Precisely at 5 o'clock a group of people under the leadership of A. Silaroze gathered at the very base of the monument. Silaroze began with a demagogic challenge to strengthen Latvian friendship with real Russians. Soon, however, flowers, bourgeois trappings, and the chant "Freedom for Latvia!" gave testimony as to the real inclinations of this group. The emotions which they stoked with the skills of actor's devices clouded the reason of some people, who had no idea who it was that was leading them. They need reminding.

Silaroze, a singer in the Latvian Opera and Ballet Theater, once convicted of encouraging minors to immoral acts, clearly enjoyed being in the center of attention. In order to understand the reasons for this vainglorious desire, it must be said that this year Silaroze was prepared to mark festivally his fiftieth birthday in the theater, but the artistic soviet failed to find any particular accomplishments which would permit Silaroze to be feted on the stage. So the singer set up his own jubilee in one of Riga's palaces of culture. . . .

Naturally the militia reacted to the provocations and hooliganism of the ringleaders. Particularly obstreperous violaters of the civil order were taken to the departments of internal affairs. However, no one interfered with the laying of flowers, which continued until 7 p.m.

I spoke with people of various ages that day. In general they were little aware of what was happening, about the true face of the group "Helsinki 86." This ignorance was and continued to be used by the enemies of our country, those hostile to a socialist Latvia. To sow discord and distrust among peoples, to use any method to undermine the accomplishments of socialism is their real goal, which they were not able to disguise.

The people of Latvia are also convinced of this, for they once directed their representatives in the people's *seime* to ask the Supreme Soviet of the USSR to permit the republic to enter the Soviet Union. On 5 August 1940, a joint session of both houses of the Supreme Soviet of the USSR granted that request.

K. Markarian[e]

Editor's Notes

a. Anatoly Lunacharskii: Lenin's Minister of Enlightenment (Education).
b. Reference is to the Voice of America and Radio Liberty.
c. Reference is to the arrest, deportation, and in some cases execution of "nationalists" and other alleged "traitors" by the Soviet Secret Police.
d. Stepan Shauman: One of the early Bolshevik leaders in Azerbaidzhan.
e. The author of this article is an Armenian.

Why the Noise? *

In the street and on the bus, in the cafe and in the store the events of 23 August at the Statue to Freedom are being discussed today. What is insulting is that some people take the position in these conversations of observers, as if to say, I wasn't demonstrating myself, but I also don't think that those who gathered "to make some noise" did anything terribly bad. In an atmosphere of *glasnost'*, they say, each is free to state his opinion openly.

Which is precisely where the shakiness of the position becomes obvious. The populace of Latvia was forewarned by the Soviet mass media that the western intelligence agencies were preparing their next provocation against the USSR. After perverting the sense of a historical document, the Soviet-German non-aggression pact, the organizers of the hostile action tried to ignite nationalistic attitudes in the Baltic republics, including among the Latvian population. Like moths to a flame there gathered at a time set in advance by the foreign "directors" of this farce fans of causes and fans without them, people who love to make noise, cause scandals, and at any price "be famous."

Well, and Ianis Barkans, Maris Ludvik, Ianis Rozhkalns all became famous in Latvia. It hardly seems though that a proper, honest fellow would have taken pride in the fame of a traitor to the Motherland, of a criminal and seducer of young souls. It was precisely on youth that the provocateurs relied as they prepared for their little noise-fest in the center of our capital.

The major feeling which I have as I recall the events of 23 August is shame for those of my countrymen who gave in to the unctuous blandishments of the radio announcers and for those who today are pretending that this has nothing to do with them. I am also offended that our youth don't know our own history sufficiently, the history of their native republic. This deserves a special conversation.

I am lucky. I first became acquainted with many pages of the history of Latvia and

Sovetskaia molodezh', 26 August 1987.

the entire country hearing stories from direct participants, our forebears, the Red Latvian Riflemen[a] and infantry guardsmen of the Great Fatherland War. Whenever the conversation came round to relations between nationalities, these men never grew tired of repeating that Latvian and Russian in difficult moments always helped each other, saw one another not simply as helpers, but as brothers in arms in the struggle for a better future.

However, not everybody knows about the past from the lips of participants. This means that the history course in schools must be accessible and clear. For now certain important periods in the life of the people are skirted in silence, and this vacuum is what the "bestowers of liberty" who have feathered soft nests in the West, as well as their local yes-men, hasten to fill in. Everyone must constantly remember this if they are working with education of youth. Far from last among them are the specialists, historians, philosophers, literary critics. . . .

Not long ago I finished the historico-philosophical faculty of the Stuchka Latvian State University, and soon I will enter my first auditorium in the new capacity of teacher. I won't disguise it, I am seized with anxiety every time I try to imagine this moment. And not solely because a new stage of my life is beginning. The conditions in which we live today require me and other teachers to show a particular tact in illuminating historical events. It is not manipulation of facts, not silence, but the open discussion of complex phenomena of civic life that is the sole reliable path to the hearts and minds of the young.

A. Freimanis, Instructor and Student
The Stuchka Latvian State University

Editor's Note

a. Pro-Bolshevik Latvian forces, the praetorian guards of the Bolsheviks.

The Opinions of Young Rigans *

Dainis Zelmatis, energy sector welder of the Straume factory: The tendentious reshuffling of real historical facts, the open instigation of hostile radio voices, and then agitation in the streets among the first groups of adolescents that turned up to "Come on, come make some noise." Dirty? Disgusting! And take a look at the organizers of the mob themselves—E. Tsirvelis, a former fascist diversionist, Ia. Rozhkalis, an open anti Soviet. And they try to lead others! The young must know who is what.

The calculation of "those behind the cadres" was simple and cynical, to interfere in the internal affairs of our country. Of the Soviet Baltic. Of Soviet Latvia. The events didn't quite have the resonance that the West had so counted on. An inarguably significant number of Rigans rejected the demonstrators, didn't listen to them, as the healthy social organism always reject what is unnecessary. I myself am a

---

*Sovetskaia molodezh', 26 August 1987.

member of the Komsomol and want to say that the history of Soviet Latvia is a history written on a blank page by our own contemporaries, the Red Latvian Riflemen like Peteris Grishko, Peteris Shmidre, Iakov Damburg, whose work we, the Komsomols of the 1980s, are continuing today. Attempts to "plant" a blot on our history are clearly doomed to failure.

Marite Lasmane, a seamstress of the service group "Rigas Modes," Zigurd Klia-vins, Komosomol secretary of "Rigas Modes," Marite Darge, senior craftsman of atelier No. 6, "Rigas Modes": What kind of "demonstration for freedom" can we talk about if obvious hooligans, not content with shouting provocational slogans, had armed themselves with the arsenal of a genuine pogrom, from knives to spiked braclets and home-made clubs? They interfered with normal traffic on the city streets and on the sidewalks. Order was restored. However, we think that the rank of Komosomol workers must draw some conclusions for themselves; a part of the young were attracted by the demagogic hostile challenges of the provocateurs and for these hours became a "mob." The fog of momentary error is already dissipating and the young heroes will surely regret their tricks. The Komsomol leaders of a range of schools and technical schools (SPTUs) should review their work with their youngsters, keeping in mind that no simplification or stereotypes can be permitted here.

Unsuccessful Provocation *

In these days there were also types who wanted to ruin this Sunday, to make it not a day of rest and pleasant visiting, not a day of sport and labor, but a day of hatred and slander. For some time "radio voices"[a] inimical to our government had been broadcasting the news that on August 23 there would be a demonstration in Vilnius, in their words, in memory of the Molotov-Ribbentrop pact. The time and place of the gathering was constantly repeated, the anti-Soviet content of the demonstration was savored, and it was averred that the demonstration would signal the Lithuanian people's disagreement with the historical revolution of 1940, the establishment of Soviet power, and Lithuania's entry into the Soviet Union. This was nothing less than the instructions of diversionary centers about how we here in Lithuania have to behave, how we are to think, what values we must hold dear. And of course somebody had to rise to the bait and swallow it. . . .

At noon a group of people inclined to extremism came to the monument to Adam Mickiewicz.[b] Another two or three hundred of the curious gathered—it was a nice day, so why not stop and have a look, if you were passing by.

When they understood that no more people were coming, the speeches began. Apparently they were well rehearsed, since the speeches were practically identical to the texts broadcast by the diversionist radio centers. One of the speakers, N. Sadunaite, in fact even admitted that she kept contact with activists who live in the

---

Komsomol'skaia pravda, 25 August 1987.

West and slander our country, especially with a certain Algis Klimaitis, a professional provocateur. And so what? The spiritual connection between local extremists and foreign ideological diversionists has long been clear! Although the speeches alternated with religious songs (for which a conductor turned up—the organist from the Mikolish cathedral A. Bumbulis), they weren't dedicated to love for your neighbor or mutual understanding. Plain historical facts were distorted, hysterical hatred of our contemporary life and other nationalities was expressed. Things went so far that it became necessary to defend the "good name" of such Hitlerite collaborators as Bishop Brizgis. . . .

Our people are taciturn, but even the most patient of the audience assembled by chance began to show displeasure as they listened to the ridiculous slogans and shouts of protest. Who do they represent? Who asked them to speak in the name of the whole Lithuanian people? The religious extremists were not able to stir up a mass "action." Some people joined the group, some left. In the cathedral of Saint Anne next door the usual service went on.

Representatives of the press of capitalist countries came to Vilnius and had the opportunity to talk freely with people. How honestly and conscientiously they will depict this Sunday in Vilnius is a matter of their honesty and professional ethics.

Editor's notes

  a. Refers to broadcasts by Radio Liberty, and Voice of America.
  b. The nineteenth-century Polish nationalist playwright and poet.

Who Are They? *

One of the most passionate servants of the will of foreign "directors," and the main organizer of the mob of 23 August, is Nicole Sadunaite. Taking cover in religiosity, this 49-year-old woman has chosen as the main goal of her life open anti-Sovietism and the dissemination of nationalistic ideas. She was condemned to three years in prison and three years in exile in 1975 for fabrication and distribution of anti-Soviet literature. In her places of incarceration she tried to organize various enemy actions and spread slanderous inventions about Soviet reality. N. Sadunaite's main goal is naked self-proclamation. In a book published abroad she depicts herself as a martyr for freedom of conscience and the faith, one of the main fighters for human rights in Lithuania.

The organist from the Mikolish cathedral, Alfonsas Bumbulis, has long been known as a religious extremist. However, to him the cathedral is first and foremost a cover for the distribution of nationalistic ideology. A. Bumbulis's favorite activity is the gathering of signatures on invented demands and the inflaming of nationalist attitudes.

The youngest of this band is the 27-year-old sexton of the Kiaukliais cathedral, Robertas Grigas. Having grown up in a family of religious extremists, he has taken

---

Komsomol'skaia pravda, 25 August 1987.

part in illegal gatherings of nationalists. With other renegades he composed and distributed a manifesto calling for struggle against Soviet power. He is also known as a "poet" among nationalists, as the author of poems lauding participants in the nationalistic underground which was active in Soviet Lithuania after the war, and their bloody deeds. It should be noted that not one of them has ever worked for the benefit of society, nor has produced anything, whether in the sphere of material production, or of cultural or spiritual life. They receive their bread from foreign nationalistic center, financed by the CIA. They are ticks on the healthy body of our society.

Also taking active part in the mob of 23 August were Taurage resident Liaonas Laurinskas, Ionas Petkiavičius from Shiauliai, Vilnius resident Ionas Pratusiavičius and others, earlier convicted of state crimes and antisocial activities and former participants in nationalistic bands.

Position Without "Opposition" *

Comments from the Plenum of the Central Committee
of the Communist Party of Lithuania

The Vilnius–Vilnius City Party Committee report to the Lithuanian Communist Party Central Committee plenum was practically five months in preparation. During this time scientists did sociological research and meetings were held with veterans, the creative intelligentsia, young people, and members of informal associations. The manner in which the capital's gorkom conducts ideological and class education, and nurtures patriotism was analyzed by Communists from many other regions of the republic. Such thoroughness and painstaking care are explained not only by the fact that the Party committee of this multinational city had not been heard at plenums of the republic Communist Party for more than twenty years but also, and more pressingly, by the topicality and relevance of the theme. A most important, most fundamental, and vital issue was at stake, the friendship, unity, internationalism, and patriotism of the peoples and the problems of present-day relations among nationalities.

All of us still remember the events of last 23 August, when nationalistic elements and clerical extremists tried to organize a large-scale anti-Soviet action in the city, which had previously been trumpeted by foreign radio "voices." And it has to be said that bourgeois propaganda at times does find a response among politically immature citizens. However, this time the city's working people did not support the action, and it failed. At the same time it must be considered that the efforts of a group of anti-Soviets did expose serious shortcomings in the ideological education work of not just the city Party organization but of the republic one as well.

By now it is clear that not everything in national relations was or is as satisfactory as we might wish. That is why the concern and desire to critically analyze the state of national relations were understood and appreciated by those in the hall.

"The nationalities question and the level of national relations are always closely tied to the economic and social aspects of life," E. Maiauskene, First Secretary of Kaunas's Leninskii Raion Party committee, said. "We have seen this for ourselves in our work many times."

This proposition by Elena Eduardovna gave many who spoke after her grounds for reflection, since we still often analyze the nature of national relations in isolation from real life, governed at times by outmoded theories and dogmas.

In this respect the experience of Vilnius can be a good example for the whole republic Party organization. The plenum named many labor collectives at plants producing fuel equipment, electrowelding equipment, radio measuring instruments,

---

*Sovetskaia kul'tura, 14 May 1988. Russian text © 1988 by Sovetskaia kul'tura.

construction and finishing machinery, both "Plasta" and others, where tangible improvements in solving production, housing, and consumer problems have done more to affirm social justice and strengthen international friendship than Panegyrics about "consolidation, prosperity, and fusion."

"Internationalism and patriotism," as O. Burdenko, director of the Vilnius radio measuring instrument plant, said, "submit least of all to planning and computation in terms of percentages and numbers. They become flesh and blood for a collective when people feel the pain of others as their own, when they give shelter and everything necessary—from baby coats to umbrellas—to the scores of families who suffered in the Chernobyl disaster, when they worry about internationalist servicemen," when they don't leave veterans of war and labor, or even just lonely old people without attention." One could continue painting a positive picture, but then O. Buinauskene, leader of the arable section of the S. Neris Kolkhoz, spoke. "Perception of the Russian people as the 'older brother,' molded in the Stalin era, offended our national self-esteem and made our culture seem secondary. . . . And it is not the Russian people who are to blame for our failure to restore a healthy national equilibrium within our republic. We ourselves, our leaders and certain figures in our culture and art, are to blame for the fact that up to now we have gathered the crumbs of the history of our people and their literary and cultural heritage. We know how preparations for the 1000th anniversary of the introduction of Christianity to Russia are going. The more modest but for us no less significant jubilee of the 600th anniversary of the advent of Christianity in Lithuania was conveyed as a purely negative event for our people and culture. Antireligious propaganda on this score merely roused the passions of religious extremists, who immediately tried to play off the Russian against the Lithuania people. . . ."

Here we had a Communist openly, honestly, and sincerely expressing her position, asking questions that are far from easy, to put it bluntly. This sharp speech was clearly a surprise to many people. It was perhaps the clearest expression of the principled rejection of the "figure of silence" which has already done so much harm to the delicate sphere of national relations. There were many such speeches made at the plenum, sharp, prodding people to think and urging them to take action. Understandably so, because recent events show that the fate of restructuring and the level and nature of our future life depend directly on the extent to which democratic relations among people and among Communists of different nationalities become organic. That is to say, restructuring in society and restructuring in national relations must advance in tandem. But it seemed as though two approaches, two attitudes to the problem under discussion made themselves felt at the plenum: on the one hand, the desire to delineate phenomena frankly and without dramatization, to thoroughly investigate the causes of shortcomings, to carefully analyze them, and to build practical action on this basis; and on the other, the desire to close one's eyes, to disregard the new approach in the sphere of national relations to the complex problems of international education generated by *glasnost'* and the democratization of social processes, and to continue to accept the desired as fact already. Was that not why you find behind the generally correct words of some speakers about "prosperity, fusion, and a single family'' you find the same old standard approaches, truisms, and, as a result, covering up of painful problems?

Another approach appeared too. Some people clearly wanted to see the roots of nationalism primarily in people's minds rather than in events. This in practice sometimes leaves the social conditions which give rise to and sustain national prejudices and help maintain nationalism as a phenomenon unrevealed. There were also those who wanted simply to theorize on the topic of international education in isolation from actual practice, which, it cannot be hidden, seemed and sometimes still seems like a desire to avoid solving actual problems and to shift difficult work onto others. A. Matsaitis, first secretary of the Lithuanian Komsomol Central Committee, described in his speech how this shows up in practice.

''. . . Today, in evaluating the state of ideological work critically, it has to be admitted that many chronic problems exist here. We have repeatedly talked, for example, about how important efforts to inform the public are. We must have an accurate idea of what is happening around us, in the republic and in the country. Young people today are interested in the economy, in ecology, the protection of monuments, and in question of international cooperation. However, the leaders of our ministries, departments, and scientific institutions decline to give any direct answers to these topical questions. We still do not know how the how particular decisions of interest to young people and the public are discussed and made. Unfortunately, apparatus workers and propagandists are ill-prepared for open dialogue with young people. . . .''

After the plenum we talked with many of its participants. After all, what was the plenium for the life of the republic Party organization, a real event or just routine? Iu. Nekrošius, a poet and chairman of the republic State Committee for Publishing Houses, Printing Plants, and the Book Trade, expressed the common view: ''I felt a movement of fresh ideas at the plenum. Previously we were several steps behind in solving many questions, including national questions. Many people at the plenum, however, discussed this problem from various angles. Different opinions and approaches did clash, I think, but one thing is indisputable, that it is essential to actively support energetic people who are seeking to on-going processes and to carry out renewal and restructuring.''

Unfortunately, the plenum's spirit and atmosphere was not reflected in the report published in republic Party newspapers. The honestly, openness, principle, and *glasnost'* for which the advocates of restructuring fought at the plenum seem deformed in this report. The critical fervor, straight talking, and nonstandard approach to the problems of international and patriotic education, in short, everything that differentiated position from position at the plenum, all were ''edited out.'' Incidentally, after the speech by V. Eemelianov, editor of the newspaper *Sovetskaia Litva*, we could not contain ourselves and congratulated him colleague to colleague on a very principled and competent speech which proposed discussion of the complex problems of bilingualism, so-called everyday nationalism, historical truth, and national relations. To be honest, we would have withheld congratulations if we had only read the summary of the speech published in the newspaper he edits. Speeches by A. Maldonis, chairman of the Union of Writers Board, A. Matsaitis, first secretary of the republic Komsomol Central Committee, and others were likewise "tidied up." Nor will the excerpts from the speech by O. Buinaiskene which we cite by us be found in the report prepared by the republic news agency (ELTA).

How is this to be understood today, at a time of extensive development of *glasnost'* and democracy? What is the point of the omissions, of this measuring out of "good" and "bad," and, finally of the painting over and smoothing out of sharp corners? Does it benefit the cause? This out-of-the-ordinary event in the life of the republic party organization deserved to have the Communists and all the working people of the republic learn about it in full and feel that fresh wind that blows when opinions clash, stances come into collision, and routine is shaken up.

R. I. Songaila, first secretary of the Lithuanian Communist Party Central Committee, and Iu. A. Skliarov, chief of the CPSU Central Committee propaganda department, took part in the plenum's work.

E. Govorushko and V. Matonin

Editor's Note

a. "Internationalist servicemen": a term for those who have "fulfilled their internationalist responsibilities" through service in Afghanistan.

Resolution of the Plenum of the Latvian Union of Writers *

With the Participation of the Directorates of the Unions of Architects, Designers, Artists, Cinematographers, Composers, and Theatrical Workers, Journalists, and Experts

From the departments of the Central Committee of the Communist Party of Latvia

The plenum of the Directorate of the Union of Writers of the Latvian SSR that took place 1–2 June, with participation by leaders of the other artistic unions of the republic, demonstrated the high level of social activism and civic concern of the artistic intelligentsia of the republic in deepening the revolutionary character of restructuring. The discussion at the plenum, the sharp criticism of phenomena of stagnation, analysis of their causes, various approaches and proposals for renovating all sides of life in our society, for the democratization of Party and state activity are all practical expressions of affirmation of *glasnost'*, of democratic forms of expression of views of representatives of the artistic and scientific communities. The theses, opinions, and proposals contained in the resolution of the plenum reflect the viewpoint of the directorate of the Union of Writers and the administrators of the artistic unions of the republic about important problems of the development of the Latvian socialist nation. Their opinions and constructive ideas deserve all possible support, and consideration in the practical work of Party and government organs, and ideological establishments. At the same time a number of proposals set out in the resolution are for purposes of discussion and are difficult to agree with; they must be attentively analyzed considering the confluence of republican and all-union interests, calculating the interests of residents of all nationalities, categories, and levels of the republic's population, as well as the social and political consequences of the measures proposed in the resolution.

This is the task of scientists and competent specialists in the various branches of the economy, considering the opinions of the workers' collectives. Their conclusions will be published and submitted for the consideration of the administering Party and state organs of the republic.

The materials of the plenum of the directorate of the Union of Writers of the republic are an important impulse toward activating social and political thought, towards decisively overcoming stereotypes in ideological work, towards solving pressing problems of the economic, ecological, demographic, socio-political and spiritual development of the republic. The constructive ideas of the plenum will find

---

Sovetskaia molodezh', 11 June 1988.

their reflection in the conception being elaborated of the social and economic development of the republic to the year 2005.

RESOLUTION

Having heard the reports of members of the artistic unions of the Latvian Soviet Socialist Republic, as well as of the specially invited experts, on the theme "Current Problems of Culture in Soviet Latvia on the Eve of the Nineteenth All-Union Party Conference," the plenum draws the following conclusions, poses the following problems, and makes the following constructive proposals:

That at the given historical stage radical reforms in the economic sphere, *glasnost'*, democratization, and the new way of thinking which permits the transformation of the face of socialism and which answers truly scientific organization and ethical ideals must be considered primary and decisive. That the course of restructuring must be considered the sole guarantee both of the society of the entire USSR and of the national statehood of every union republic.

That support must be given to the initiative elaborated as a result of the policies of General Secretary of the Central Committee of the CPSU M. S. Gorbachev, with maximum participation to realize it in life.

That appeals against the course of restructuring, democratization, and *glasnost'* are to be regarded as attacks against socialism, internationalism, the national rights of the peoples, and the rights of every individual citizen.

That in the process of restructuring consistent efforts of society for the radical reorganization of the electoral system and the further democratization of life in the Party must be supported, and the role of the soviet of people's deputies must be raised in a cardinal way, in full realization of the measures promulgated in the Theses of the Central Committee of the CPSU, to turn the soviets into organs having full rights for conducting government business.

That proposals to also elevate non-Party members to administrative work be supported.

That in elaboration of historical conceptualizations Stalinist interpretations must be decisively renounced, for they continue to cause harm to the Soviet people, including the Latvian people, and Latvian history. It is established that Latvia's entrance into the Soviet Union and the meaning of its existence in the makeup of the USSR was compromised by conditions of the cult of Stalin's personality.

That the attempt made after the Twentieth Party Congress [1956] to return Latvia to a more or less sovereign economic and social policy was cut short in 1959 by purported unmaskings of so-called nationalism, which strengthened even more the extensive development of the economy in the republic.

That in this connection the proposal made at the May (1988) Plenum of the Central Committee of the Latvian Communist Party to reevaluate the contents and conclusions of the July (1959) Plenum of the Central Committee of the Latvian Communist Party be supported.

That truth must be learned to be faced, no matter how difficult and bitter it may at times be. Otherwise all our hopes of today are inescapably doomed.

Aspects of the status and rights of the republic

That the Leninist conception of the union republic be resurrected in legal practice and in daily practice. It is to be considered that apart from the general formulations of the constitutions of the USSR and of the Latvian SSR the governmental rights of our republic have not found precise definition and explanation in the legislature. The participation of the Latvian SSR in the economic and social development of the USSR is not proceeding on bases of parity of a sovereign state within a union of free states, which has led to the result that the native population of Latvia, the Latvians, are becoming a national minority within the boundaries of their own ethno-geographic territory.

Since this sort of minority position is occurring for the first time in the age-long and heavy history of the Latvian people, we urge that the preservation and development of the Latvian nation be considered one of the priority tasks of the Latvian Communist Party. In executing this task the republic leadership and every individual citizen must at the same time guarantee observation of the principles of internationalism and respect for the rights and human dignity of citizens of all nationalities who live in Latvia.

That in acknowledging the status of rights of a citizen of the USSR, the status of rights of a citizen of the union republics must also be elaborated.

That the situations in which rights provided by the Constitution can not be used because of the lack of a corresponding law which would define the means of realizing these rights must be eliminated.

That strict regulation and control of the process of migration be achieved. The case of each person (and his family) who is invited to come work in Latvia from another republic must be decided by the local councils, with definition for the organizations and establishments of the payments which will wholly cover all expenses for his social and communal needs. Expenses must also be guaranteed by quotas in construction.

In the name of creating political restructuring we urge the government of the Latvian SSR and the USSR to actively establish a policy and diplomacy which would make the status of the republic such that in practice Latvia would be internationally recognized as a sovereign and national state in the composition of the Soviet Federation. Entry of the Latvian SSR into the UN, UNESCO, the Olympics, sporting and other federations is to be achieved, with the right of participation in political, cultural, scientific, and sporting forums, including the use in doing so of the state and national symbols of our sovereign republic.

That the Supreme Soviet is to be sent proposals for the concrete solution of this question.

That the radical expansion of all forms of cooperation with Latvians living in other republics and abroad is to be considered self-evident and necessary, and that a body of the press be published in Latvian and Russian for Latvians living in other republics of the USSR.

That in the governmental makeup of the Latvian SSR there be created a full-time position of Minister of Foreign Affairs, freed from other work, as is the case in other union republics.

That government-supported posts for correspondents in some large political and cultural centers overseas be given to representatives of the Latvian press, radio, television, and film.

That accreditation of the press, radio, television, and film industry of the Latvian SSR during visits by foreign leaders and delegations to Moscow and other cities and republics of the USSR be considered necessary and obligatory. That the same be true for using Latvian media workers for publicizing visits by state delegations of the USSR to foreign countries.

That citizens of the Latvian SSR be given the right to freely choose to work and study abroad.

That in achieving these solutions this idea expressed in the Theses of the Central Committee of the CPSU for the Nineteenth All-Union Party Conference is to be relied upon: "Decentralization and the maximal transfer of many administrative functions to the localities is relevant to all forms of our national states and autonomous regions. Necessary here is unflinching observation of the clauses of the Constitution of the USSR and of Soviet laws, which guarantee the rights of union and autonomous republics, autonomous regions and areas."

That the Council of Nationalities of the Supreme Soviet of the USSR be transformed from a purely representational body into a functioning parliamentary organ, which could in fact represent and defend the interests of the nations and national groups and which could oppose those measures which threaten the existence of a native population, or its equality, and which could guarantee the true national statehood of a republic in the body of the Soviet Federation.

That public opinion in the sphere of nationality relations be constantly studied, and that society be openly and regularly informed of it.

That census materials about the population in all aspects be widely published in the press.

It is proposed that a clause be inserted in the Constitution of the Latvian SSR (as there is in the Constitutions of the Georgian, Armenian, and Azerbaidzhani SSRs) affirming the status of Latvian as the state language of the republic. Russian must be used, as it is at the present time, as a means of inter-nationality communication, both in the republic and in the USSR as a whole. However, the language of the native people must also become a means of inter-nationality communication.

That mastery of other languages must be considered an indicator of professional aptitude for work in state and Soviet institutions, especially in branches connected to the social sphere, in the fields of health care, in schools, and in institutions of preservation of public order.

That the possibility to obtain elementary and professional education (middle and higher, in all specialities studied in the republic) in Latvian be fully guaranteed.

That the possibility to use Latvian in all spheres of the material and spiritual life of the republic, including business and manufacturing be guaranteed, which would create a basis for the existence and development of all functional styles of the Latvian language.

That the possibility to receive an education in one's native language be guaranteed for representatives of all other nationalities living in the republic, by opening schools or classes in places of concentrated population. Social organizations and cultural centers should be created to handle cultural problems for the Russians, Ukrainians, Belorussians, Poles, Jews, Lithuanians, Gypsies, and citizens of other nationalities who are permanent residents of the republic, including Latgals[a] and Livs.[b]

That measures be taken to overcome the cultural and social isolation of the non-Latvian population of the Latvian SSR. All possible support should be given to forming a sense of patriotism for one's own republic, for the organic growth by all national groups into the culture of Latvia, and for the conscious study of the history of Latvia and its cultural traditions, with respect for them.

That a state law guarantee the proposals above.

That based upon the experience of the republic, the mechanical and artificial expansion of the number of schools with bilingual instructional groups be stopped, reorganizing them only in those instances in which parents express the demand for them. The results of such schools should be studied, analyzing the effects of creating such schools upon the formation of nationality relations.

That, taking account of the fact that the Latvian Red Riflemen were the first and most conscious part of the Red Army, and to establish the preeminence of internationalist traditions in the Armed Forces, the possibility of creating a military configuration on the territory of the Latvian SSR (as a subdivision or military school) be considered, which would guarantee the function of Latvian language and Latvian culture alongside Russian.

This configuration could be formed from youth fluent in Russian and Latvian.

That in the political life of the republic, in the mass media, and in ideological work, attempts to replace objective study of concrete facts and events with irresponsible accusations of nationalism be eliminated.

That ideological activity which does not analyze social and national dissatisfaction among broad social layers, in order to explain and eliminate causes of economic, demographic, and ecological deformations, or which presents them as being the results of foreign propaganda or the idea of restoring capitalism, be considered unacceptable and incompatible with the principles of *glasnost'*.

That attempts to present the appearance of national problems as the negative consequences of the policy of restructuring be combated.

That the legislative power be separated from the executive. That a system of financial relations be created which guarantee the soviets the necessary funds for their activities.

That statistics of crimes and other violations of rights be given full publicity [*glasnost'*], systematically publicized, so that society might actively and effectively participate in elimination of these negative phenomena.

That the legislation about appealing the decisions of people in positions of responsibility be changed, to offer the right to contest in court the decision of any collective body, as well as the right of administrators of any rank to defend in a judicial procedure their right to work (in the event of illegal termination, to initiate a suit to be returned to work, and so forth).

That the Supreme Soviet of the Latvian SSR be asked to control more effectively the activities of the Ministry of Internal Affairs and the Committee of State Security [KGB], as well as of the military divisions of the Army, the Navy, and the border guards, who affect the legal interests of the republic (in economic life, in the sphere of preservation of nature, and so forth). The legislature should precisely define the concept of the state secret, its contents and limitations.

That the proposal of the Council of Ministers of the Latvian SSR to the Council of Ministers of the USSR to repeal the resolution of the Central Committee of the VKP(B) and the Council of Peoples' Commissars of the USSR from 14 May 1941 and of the Central Committee of the VKP(B) and Council of Ministers of the USSR from 29 January 1949 about the administrative deportation of certain population groups from the republics of the Baltic, the western Ukraine, and western Belorussia as illegal, contrary to the Constitution of the USSR, and unfounded juridically and morally be supported, since this resolution was the basis for further repressions and demanded an enormous number of innocent victims. The necessity of a legislative act which would forbid deportation is also pressing.

That in the interests of establishing historical truth the society of the republic be made familiar with the secret protocol of the pact signed by Ribbentrop and Molotov on 23 August 1939.

Rehabilitation of undeservedly repressed victims of Stalinist policy should also organically embody social censure of concretely guilty people and those who carried out the repressions, where necessary by bringing them to criminal culpability. These people should be deprived of the social privileges accorded them, their titles of honor, and their rights to be symbols of the achievements of Soviet power (for example, in the names of cities, streets, schools, and so forth).

That the factual inviolability of postal functions, correspondence, and telephone conversations by guaranteed. That a broad circle of readers be given access to the materials in the special holdings in archives, museums, and libraries, as is provided for by state laws.

That the period of validity for all documents of Party and government be defined. At the end of this period documents should be sent to the archives, where they must also be accessible.

The economy and preservation of nature

For almost fifty years Latvia was seen primarily as a territory on which it was profitable to establish efficient productive forces. The concept of the postwar development of industry relied upon a unilateral economic policy, in which the development of production outstripped the means of production, relying as well upon urbanization of the republic.

This policy of industrial organization brought irreplaceable losses to the cultural sphere, significantly slowed development of the social infrastructure, and slowed the pace of growth of the population's well-being.

Primitive technology, absurd standardization, and universal integration, as well as unlimited industrial programs led to vulgarization of the goods produced by industry, to their moral and technological shoddiness. The policy of extensive development continues. In 1987 population growth because of interrepublic migration was 18,800 people.

In bringing about restructuring of the economy, city-building, and agriculture of the republic, it is necessary to:

—introduce the principles of economic self-sufficiency and the mechanisms of effecting it also in its regional aspect, undertaking its existence on the scale of the union republic;

—reconsider the necessity for and basis of new construction or reconstruction of industrial plants of all-union allegiance in the republic, particularly in Riga, Jurmala, and Liepaia, taking into consideration resolution number 567, 18 June 1981, of the Central Committee of the CPSU and the Council of Ministers of the USSR, "On Limiting Industrial Construction in Large Cities." Any extensive expansion of production connected with use of additional work forces should be forbidden;

—in planning capital investments in development of industrial branches or departments, the priority of interests of the whole complex of territorial development should be guaranteed;

—in correspondence with the new economic conditions, plans should be perfected for the regional planning of the republic, for the development and location of productive forces, directed at the sharp improvement of the ecological and social situation in the republic and to limit the population of Riga, for the control of which a commission of experts should be created;

—relying on the traditions and achievments of industry and agriculture, on the highly developed scientific, technological, cultural, and social potential, and taking account of the whole departmental structure of the republic, it is vital to consolidate industry and in the future to develop technologically complex industries of small volume, using nonconsumptive technology and a highly qualified work force oriented to production of modern and competitive goods;

—alongside the development of large-scale industrial production there must be support for the quality work of craftsmen, as a model and school of the logic of things. The lost experience of the people should be compensated for by creation of an Institute of Culture in the National Environment, which would systematically study the problems of craft, design, and architecture, and which would supply real scientific information for the organization and management of industry;

—it should be defined that the natural development of the republic's economy must rely exclusively on local labor resources. Taking account of the sanitary condition of Riga and the situation in housing construction, Riga must also limit the allocation of housing to demobilizing military personnel and to other categories of citizen equal to them, as has already been done in Moscow, Leningrad, Kiev, and the resort cities of the Caucasus;

—allotment of land in Jurmala for building all-union departments must be stopped, as well as any construction in the seacoast zone of the Baltic Sea within the territory of the republic. Using the means of the republic's budget, recreational facilities presently belonging to all-union departments should be bought up and transferred to the holdings of the republic;

—the existing policy of construction should be reexamined and radically changed, guaranteeing formation of functional and aesthetically valuable environments of habitation, aesthetically expressive, of quality, and answering the needs of man, both in the cities and in rural areas;

—in effecting the above measures on city-building in the general plans for the republic's economy provision, must be made for city-building and architectural sites separate from and truly independent of construction complexes, making them subject to the Council of Ministers of the Latvian SSR;

—in agriculture, farm holdings must be given full independence in their fulfillment of government orders, so that as a result all administrative regulation may be rejected and state purchases may be fully guaranteed, with the help of the levers of price formation;

—the main masters of the land must be the council of people's deputies, who must themselves make decisions whether to accept or reject the orders of higher executive committees, ever preserving for themselves the right of veto;

—in the event of the bankruptcy of a kolkhoz or sovkhoz, or in the event of their liquidation following a referendum of its working members, the land should be transferred to the disposition of the local soviets, with the right to rent the land out. The creation of cooperatives of free renters is to be supported.

In farm holding family succession should be supported, with transfer of land for rental in life and with the right of inheritance. The form of agriculture traditional for Latvia should be guaranteed, its structures in agricultural production be resurrected, and included in the socialist cooperative movement. The mechanism of competition should show which form is most vital, family succession, cooperatives, or the present form of production, under state allegiance.

Taking account of the experience of the Academy of Sciences of the Estonian SSR, the Academy of Sciences of the Latvian SSR is asked to arrange a competition for the optimal method of transferring the economy of the Latvian SSR or all there Baltic republics to principles of economic self-sufficiency and self-financing.

In the Latvian SSR industrial production has developed thoughtlessly, without consideration for the ecological particularities of the region and its cultural and historical character. To supply industry raw materials are imported and the work force is mechanically enlarged. Use of outdated industrial technology has lead to having only an insignificant part of all resources be processed into ready products, while the greater part of these resources is lost as various byproducts which soil the air, soil, and water. About 400,000 tons of sulphur compounds precipitate onto the republic, which leads to degradation of the soil, rapid corrosion of metals, destruction of forests, and causes human illness.

The situation is threatening to become catastrophic, making it necessary to judge the activity of the Council of Ministers and Gosplan of the Latvian SSR in the sphere of social and economic development to be obviously unsatisfactory and in need of cardinal reexamination.

In this connection it is necessary to:

—take care, keeping in mind that the economy of the Latvian SSR is a constituent part of the economic complex of the USSR, that the national riches, above all natural ones, are used in the interests of the native population;

—prefer to develop the tendencies of the economy which do not contradict international conventions and our cultural and economic type;

—stop the gigantomania of urbanization, to develop a scientifically founded program for the ecological recovery of the republic, as well as a general conception of the development of productive forces, submitting them for the consideration of the public of the republic;

—widen the scientific search for solutions to regional ecological questions, working directly with the countries of the Baltic basin and concretizing international obligations as fixed in treaties for the Baltic Sea and the basin as a whole. Considering the catastrophic degree of pollution in Lielupe, the mouth of the Daugava, and the Bay of Riga, a system of preserves and game reserves must be created, and until the full exploitation of cleansing devices to stop the expansion of Rigan factories already begun, which is proceeding in contravention of the resolutions of 1982 and 1984, and at the same time the people guilty of violating the indicated resolutions of the Council of Ministers of the USSR should be brought to indictment;

—elaborate and put into effect a directed program to widen forest management, beginning with the present condition of the forests and relying upon an ecologically founded structure of foresting;

—systematically deflect the extensive ambitions of the all-union departments which in violating the rights of the local soviets, laws, and ethics, combine expansion of production and construction of new plants in the cities with a dramatically intensified ecological situation;

—forbid construction of any industrial plant which does not have the necessary anti-pollution devices;

—forbid use of chemical substances whose toxic effects are unknown or which has not had set the maximum allowable measure of their concentration, as well as those toxic substances whose concentration in the natural environment is not defined;

—regularly publish all data on the degree of pollution of the environment in every territorial subdivision.

Optimization of the environment must be considered the main strategic direction in the business of health care of people.

—study and define the ecological impact and economic need for construction of the atomic energy station in the Liepaia region, and of the Ekabil hydroelectric station. Plants which threaten the health of people and the environment must be closed.

Health care, education, culture

Inasmuch as the health of the people to a predominant degree (90%) is defined by the social and economic situation of the republic, the manufacture of food products, construction of housing, and systematic preservation of the environment are to be considered the most important factors in this area.Health care of the people, just as their education, is to be recognized as the most important areas, demanding much greater resources (including hard currency) than they are accorded at this time.

Health care should be decentralized, leaving as the right of the republic the formation of systems corresponding to local conditions and traditions.

A fund to help young and large families should be established, so that the demographic situation in Latvia can be improved.

Independent inspectors unaffiliated with any departments should be created for determining the ecological, medical, and sanitary condition of the environment and of food. The conclusions of these inspections must be considered obligatory and of high priority to implement.

In all the schools of the republic, no matter what the language of instruction, the educational subjects should be taught according to teaching plans elaborated by the Ministry of Education of the Latvian SSR, following a unified program and unified textbooks.

The humanities should be strengthened in education, so that the schools may assist in maximum development of a child's personality.

In order to guarantee true bilingualism identical conditions for the study of Latvian and Russian should be established in all schools.

The autonomy of the republic's higher educational institutions in educational and scientific work should be established. The programs of study in the higher educational institutions should be confirmed in the republic, taking account of their national traditions and regional particularities. Broad possibilities to get higher education abroad should be guaranteed.

Any changes in manufacturing capacities must agree with the real possibilities for preparing middle- and upper-level specialists. The higher educational institutions of the Latvian SSR should prepare specialists primarily for the needs of the republic.

It is proposed that the Riga Polytechnical Institute be named for Friedrich Zander, pioneer of Soviet rocketbuilding and the sphere of cosmic navigation, in order to stress the historical preeminence of and raise the prestige of the Riga Polytechnical Institute, which is the oldest polytechnicum in our country.

The councils of scientists of the republican higher educational institutions and the Academy of Sciences should have permission to award scientific degrees without subsequent confirmation by the higher credential commission of the Council of Ministers of the USSR.

The financial resources for developing the social sciences and the humanities should be sharply increased, which is vital for the spiritual potential and growth of national self-awareness (economics, philosophy, ethnography, the history of culture, art history, and so on).

A Center of Latvian Culture should be founded in Moscow.

The higher educational institutions should have introduced a course on the history of culture which would particularly examine questions of culture in Latvia.

In the sphere of fisheries, which is a historically traditional industry for the Latvian people, a school of sea fishing should be established, with Latvian as the language of instruction, to guarantee the fishing kolkhozes local personnel.

The Riga Maritime School and one of Riga's main streets should have the name of Krishiianis Valdemar, founder of the Imperial Russian Maritime School, returned to them.Incompetent and bureaucratic administration in the spheres of culture and art, primitive understanding of ideological tasks, and financing on the principle of "what's left over" have significantly retarded the development of national culture, creating a critical situation of material bases in the theaters, in the plastic arts, in printing, in libraries, and in other cultural institutions, as well as in the solution of other problems.

The policy of constantly reducing the number of titles printed and increasing instead the numbers printed of certain titles has reached the utter limit, creating a threat to the people's supply of necessary books.

Cooperation with religious organizations in the spheres of culture, ecology, the peace movement, and others should be encouraged.

The possibility of any interference in the work of writers by censorship should be removed.

The right of every citizen to public defend his own opinion should be acknowledged. In this connection, in light of the new thinking and democratization, it is proposed that Resolution N. 29 of the Council of Ministers of the Latvian SSR from 29 January 1988 (*Gazette of the Supreme Soviet and Government of the Latvian Soviet Socialist Republic*, 1988, no. 10) be reconsidered.

Every writer should be considered responsible to his own conscience and to his readers.

It is proposed that any person in a position of responsibility who in his own administrative or bureaucratic interests interferes with *glasnost'* in the press, on the radio, television, or in film-making should be brought to account.

*   *   *

The task of the current plenum is to formulate and present for discussion by society the pressing problems of our life, as well as to make proposals for solving them.

The contents of this resolution should be brought to the attention of delegates to the Nineteenth All-Union Party Conference and to the attention of General Secretary of the Central Committee of the CPSU, Mikhail Sergeevich Gorbachev, in a letter sent in the name of the creative unions of the Latvian SSR and the experts specially invited to this plenum, affirmed with the personal signatures of the plenum's participants.

The newspaper *Literatura un Maksla* should be given the full text of this resolution for publication.

Requests should be made of republic and all-union newspapers to print the text of this resolution and materials from the plenum, of radio and television to broadcast them, and that a separate book be published, to acquaint the creative unions of other republics with these materials.

All the constructive things said by collectives, initiative groups, and individuals should be generalized, included in the documents of the plenum, and conveyed for further distribution to the Central Committee of the Communist Party, the Presidium of the Supreme Soviet, and the Council of Ministers of the Latvian SSR.

Riga, 2 June 1988

Editor's notes

a. The Latgals are a culturally distinct group of Latvians, traditionally Catholic, speaking a dialect transitional between Latvian and Lithuanian.

b. The Livs (Livonians) are a Finnic minority in Latvia.

Order of the Presidium of the Supreme Soviet of the Estonian Soviet Socialist Republic

On the State and National Symbol of the Estonian SSR

The state symbol of the Estonian SSR is established by the Constitution (Fundamental Law) of the Estonian SSR.

Orders of the Supreme Soviet have confirmed the matters of the state seal, the state flag, and the anthem of the Estonian SSR, execution of which is to be undertaken by the responsible persons and citizens.

Symbols in cities and regions (city emblems, traditional signs, and so on) are to be established by the executive commitees of the corresponding local soviets of people's deputies.

Taking account of the numerous requests by citizens, social organizations, and workers' collectives of the republic, it is proposed that the national symbols of the Estonian SSR, other than state symbols, be the traditional combination of the colors blue, black, and white, cornflowers, and the barn swallow.

Based upon the above and the proposals of the working group on questions of citizenship and the state symbolism of the Estonian SSR, formed on the instructions of the Presidium of the Supreme Soviet of the Estonian SSR on 19 May 1988, the Presidium of the Supreme Soviet of the Estonian SSR *orders that:*

1. the historically created combination of the colors blue, black, and white be acknowledged as the Estonian national colors;

2. the cornflower and the barn swallow be acknowledged as the Estonian national symbols;

3. establishment of means of adopting and defending the national symbols is to be considered necessary.

President of the Presidium of the Supreme Soviet
of the Estonian SSR, E. Riuitel
Secretary of the Presidium of the Supreme Soviet
of the Estonian SSR, V. Vakht

Molodezh' Estonii, 25 June 1988.

1OB. Nationality Relations in Conflict: Nagorno-Karabakh

The history of relations between the Armenians and the Azerbaidzhanis is a troubled one. Tensions long predate the current dispute over whether or not the Nagorno-Karabakh Autonomous Oblast (NKAO) should be transferred from the Azerbaidzhan SSR to the Armenian SSR. This is a conflict over territory; but it is also the fight of an ancient but small Christian nation which has always seen itself as threatened by the surrounding large Muslim human sea.

The Armenians, who had a united state as early as the second century B.C., claim the oldest state church in the world. They became Christians in the fourth century and developed their written language at about the same time. Armenians flourished during the reign of the Byzantine Christians, but were subject peoples during the rule of the Turkic Muslim Seljuks and Ottomans. In the seventeenth century the eastern third of Armenian territory, including the religious center at Echmeiadze, came under the control of the Persian Empire.

Two hundred years later, in 1828, the Russians conquered this territory, which corresponds roughly to the present Armenian SSR. The remainder of Armenia, including the city of Erzurum, remained under Turkish control. As internal pressures in the Ottoman Empire grew in the late nineteenth and early twentieth centuries, so too did anti-Armenian sentiments. Armenian sources claim that several hundred thousand Armenians were killed in Turkey between 1894 and 1896, and another 1.5 million people were slaughtered in the 1915 massacre. While some say that these figures are too high, there is no question that the Armenians were murdered and forced from their homeland by the Turks, and that these actions created indelible anti-Turkic sentiments in the collective memory which are passed from generation to generation.

The massacres led to a mass migration of Armenians from eastern Turkey, and many of the migrants settled in Russian Armenia, where they were free to settle anywhere in Transcaucasia they could find work. Large numbers of Armenians moved to the Georgian city of Tiflis (now Tbilisi) and to the newly Russianized old Turkic city at Baku. Others settled in the countryside, where Armenian farming communities were oftentimes interspersed with Turkic ones.

The Azerbaidzhanis did not consider themselves a distinct nationality until the Soviet period, but Muslim, Turkic-speaking Caucasian tribesmen have been living in what is now Azerbaidzhan since the tenth century. Present-day Azerbaidzhan was the home of an ancient Persian-speaking population. But after the Arab conquest the local population, now converted to Islam, began to absorb growing numbers of Turkic-speaking tribesmen. By the fifteenth century the mass of the population was

Turkic-speaking, although, as adherents of Shiite Islam, they maintained a cultural affinity to Persia. (Until 1813 Persia held most of the territory; there is an irridentist Azerbaidzhani community in Iran even today.) The Turks of Transcaucasia experienced a cultural revival at the end of the nineteenth century. The majority of the intellectuals allied with the Musavat party, which called for the creation of an independent Muslim (rather than Azerbaidzhani or Turkic) state.

The period following the Civil War in Transcaucasia was one of short-lived regimes and shifting alliances. The Dashnaksutiun, the Armenian national party, declared independence from Soviet Russia in 1918, but, denied foreign assistance, they were defeated in 1920. The situation in Azerbaidzhan was more chaotic. The Musavat was briefly in control in 1918, and then again in 1919–20, having received first Turkish and then British support. But their authority was never accepted by the local Armenian population. In March 1918 the fall of the Musavat government in Baku led to the slaughter of Muslims; two months later, the fall of the Dashnaksutiun led to the massacre of the Armenian population of Baku.

The Bolshevik takeover of Azerbaidzhan in 1919–20 led to a renewal of ethnic violence. This time the fighting centered in three territories whose possession was disputed between Soviet Armenia and Soviet Azerbaidzhan: Nakhichevansk, Zanzegur, and Nagorno-Karabakh. At first, in 1920, the newly formed Moscow-dominated Soviet government in Azerbaidzhan recognized Armenian claims over the three regions. However, in January 1921, as Azerbaidzhani participation in the new Bolshevik government was broadened and Muslim nationalist protest to Bolshevik rule increased, the Soviet government in Azerbaidzhan petitioned the Caucasian Bureau of the Russian Communist party for control of these territories. The Azerbaidzhani request was first refused but a day later granted, supposedly at the behest of Stalin, then Commissar of Nationalities. Nagorno-Karabakh became an autonomous oblast in 1923 and Nakhichevansk an autonomous republic in 1924, but these territories have remained part of the the the Azerbaidzhan SSR. From the time of the formation of the USSR in 1922 until 1987 the territorial boundaries of the Soviet republics were not subject to debate. Over time the Armenian population centers became completely integrated into the economy of Azerbaidzhan, and Azerbaidzhanis moved into many formerly Armenian territories, including Nakhichevansk. But, although sublimated, tensions between the two communities remained. Armenians and Azerbaidzhanis were often called upon to work together, but they lived in separate neighborhoods, did not intermarry, and socialized as little as possible. Yet there was no official recognition that the "friendship of peoples" in Azerbaidzhan might be precarious.

The 1983 addresses of then Azerbaidzhan Communist Party First Secretary Bagirov and Academician Fedoseev to an all-union conference on nationality relations convened in Baku are typical of the Brezhnev period. Both speakers point to Azerbaidzhan as an example of the successes of Soviet nationality policies. Fedoseev diagnoses "racism" as a characteristic of capitalist society and explicitly notes that "predatory border conflicts" do not occur in communist societies.

But in early 1988 it became obvious that the communist parties of Azerbaidzhan and Armenia had not succeeded in channeling the nationalist sentiments of their respective populations, and that the antipathy between the Armenians and Azerbaidzhanis remained keen and violent. Moreover, it also became clear that the leadership of the communist parties of both republics, and of the Nagorno-Karabakh AO, defined their responsibility as first and foremost to protect the interests of their co-nationals, even when this placed them in conflict with the interests of the rest of the country.

This led to a situation in which the leaderships of two union republics became pitted against each other and—more seriously yet—against Moscow. The dispute over the Nagorno-Karabakh quickly became a constitutional crisis and a test of Gorbachev's authority. It showed how the application of "democratic principles" can lead to the formulation of irreconcilable political agendas. It demonstrated that violence can be the fruit of unsatisfied rising expectations—violence severe enough to require the persistent use of force. What is worse, it has led to a situation that seems to have no obvious solution.

In January 1988 the government in the NKAO sharply reduced the availability of primary education in the Armenian language. This increased the local Armenians' perceptions that the republic government in Baku intended either to assimilate them culturally or to drive them out of the territory. With strong support from political activists and party officials in Erevan, the Armenian capital, the Armenians in Stepanakert, the capital of the NKAO, began a strike to protest the cultural and economic policies of the local Party organization and the Azerbaidzhan Communist Party leadership in Baku. This strike grew in intensity. By mid-February the economy of the oblast was at a virtual standstill, with provisions for the Armenian population being trucked in from the Armenian republic. On February 20, the Supreme Soviet of the NKAO appealed to the supreme soviets of Armenia, Azerbaidzhan, and the USSR to allow them to secede from Azerbaidzhan and be joined to Armenia.

The strike movement now spread to Armenia, and virtually shut down the capital city of Erevan. Moscow recognized that it must act, and on February 23, NKAO Obkom first secretary V. Kevorkov (an Armenian by nationality, but seen as a creature of Baku's will) was dismissed and replaced by G. Pogosian, considered more sympathetic to the population's aims. Special troops of the Ministry of Internal Affairs (MVD) were sent to Erevan and Stepanakert to try to put a lid on the protests, which by then had erupted into street brawls on a number of occasions, and senior Politburo members were dispatched to Erevan, Baku, and Stepanakert to investigate the situation.

On February 26 Gorbachev himself issued a strong personal appeal, reproduced below, which was published in all of the local newspapers on the following day. He called for calm, defended the cultural rights of national minority communities, and promised the appointment of a commission of the Supreme Soviet of the USSR to examine the question of the transfer of the NKAO to Armenia. While Gorbachev criticized extremists on both sides, the fact that he attacked the leadership of the NKAO and even raised the question of possibly shifting the NKAO to Armenian control, outraged many Azerbaidzhanis who then took matters into their own hands. Word from Agdam Raion (which borders on the NKAO) of the deaths of two Azerbaidzhani youths at the hands of Armenians reached the industrial city of Sumgait (located near Baku) and sparked two days of rioting, culminating in a bloody rampage of Azerbaidzhanis through the city's Armenian quarter. Thirty-one Armenians were reported dead; informal accounts increased this figure tenfold (Armenian activists still claim that the official figures are much too low).

The Sumgait riots began a new phase in the crisis. Soviet press coverage of the situation changed. While previously the press downplayed and even suppressed mention of the problems in Stepanakert and Erevan, now Moscow chose to report on the events, hoping to diminish the potential effectiveness of foreign and other unofficial sources of news. Initial accounts tried to minimize the severity of the social unrest, and in the first days after the Sumgait riots official reports made no reference to the savagery of the violence. While later accounts did note the deaths of thirty-two residents (one Azerbaidzhani was killed), the reports from early March (examples of which are reproduced below) tried to minimize the widespread nature of the riots, attributing them to "hooligan" elements who would be rooted out and punished, and stressed that the situation was under control. Subsequent reports noted that peace had been restored in Sumgait only after the arrival of some fifteen tanks. Other accounts covered the migration of thousands of Armenians from Sumgait to Armenia.

By mid-March, as noted in the report of the Central Committee of the Azerbaidzhan Communist Party reproduced below, much of the blame for the riots was placed on the indifference of the Sumgait Party organization and city government, and on the behavior of the local militia. The senior leadership of Sumgait was soon dismissed, and later even dropped from the CPSU membership.

Rioting continued in both Stepanakert and Erevan throughout the month of March. The two television addresses given by then Armenian Communist Party First Secretary K. Demirchian, reproduced below, give some sense of the growing sense of crisis and of the Party's inability to stop the growing nationalist-inspired momentum for change in the republic. Armenian intellectuals, instrumental in the creation of the unsanctioned Karabakh Committee, kept up the pressure for return of the territory. Demirchian complained of the "bias" of the official Armenian press; it was proving difficult in both Erevan and Moscow to recruit Armenians who would write "objectively" about events in their republic.

On March 21, *Pravda* published an allegedly staff-written piece—"Emotions and Reason," reproduced below—which attempted to discredit the Karabakh movement and blamed the strikes in Erevan on opponents of *perestroika*. But no sooner was the piece published than the one Armenian coauthor of the article, Iu. Arakelian, held a news conference with Western reporters in which he disassociated himself from the article. Searching for Armenian intellectuals willing to speak out against the demonstrators, Moscow had to turn to R. Kaplanian, an elderly playwright (who died in summer 1988), whose viewpoint would not be seen as credible by most Armenians. In an article in *Sovetskaia kul'tura*, Kaplanian wrote of the debt of the Armenians to the Russians who, he implies, loved them like a father who gives selflessly to an adopted child.

Baku's coverage of events in Stepanakert was also partisan. Articles like "The Economy of the Mountain Region," which argues that NKAO is fully integrated with the economy of Azerbaidzhan and that its residents enjoy a higher standard of living than those in the republic more generally, have been frequent in the Azerbaidzhani press. Azerbaidzhani journalists like those who prepared the piece "Working Rhythm" note the insensitivity of the Armenian strikers in Stepanakert to the hardships that their work-stoppages are inflicting on Azerbaidzhan's residents and Soviet citizens more generally. Moreover, they assert that the NKAO can be successfully reintegrated into Azerbaidzhan and that the Armenians and Azerbaidzhanis can learn to live together successfully, if the guidelines developed in the March 24, 1988, joint resolution of the Central Committee of the CPSU and the USSR Council of Ministers are followed.

This resolution, reproduced below, expressed sympathy for the demands of the Armenian population of the NKAO for greater cultural autonomy, and mandated an improvement in their economic and social situation. However, it did not support Armenian demands for secession of the territory from Azerbaidzhan. Moscow saw this resolution as a formula for the settlement of the conflict, and when Armenians continued to strike in both Erevan and Stepanakert, the Party position toward the Armenians began to harden. By March 31, the threat of force brought demonstrations in Erevan to an end, while they continued in Stepanakert until April 6. As the articles "Meetings After the Demonstration" and "Reportage" show, central press coverage of events in the Nagorno-Karabakh and Erevan continued to blame the origins of the conflict on Azerbaidzhani efforts to attain cultural hegemony in Stepanakert, but Armenian "extremists" came under increasing attack for furthering the conflict and for bringing the economy of the Armenian-dominated territories to a stand-still.

While special forces of the MVD remained in place in both Erevan and Stenakert, the situation stayed relatively peaceful for the next six weeks. Then, in mid-May, strikes and mass rallies calling for the "return" of the NKAO were again organized, and Armenian displeasure was fueled when it was announced that the first of the Sumgait defendants had received a fifteen-year term. The Azerbaidzhanis organized their own demonstrations to counter those of the Armenians, possibly with official support, although this was of course denied (see the Azerbaidzhani "Appeal"). Both the Armenian and Azerbaidzhani authorities tried to convey the impression that they were in control. However, the Armenian Party organization was unable to quell successfully the public disturbance, and the Azerbaidzhani Party leadership (in spite of official accounts of wayward militiamen being disciplined, and busts of Lenin being erected) were not seen as credible representatives of Moscow's goals for nationality policy.

On May 21 Gorbachev used the renewal of disturbances in both republics to dismiss Demirchian and Bagirov, the respective Party first secretaries of Armenia and Azerbaidzhan, whose leadership he had been critical of for several years.

S. Arutiunian, an allegedly reform-minded member of Armenia's Communist Party leadership, and A. Vezirov, an Azerbaidzhani diplomat who had spent the last twelve years outside of his home republic and so owed no local debts, were named as their replacements.

The appointment of new first secretaries did not change the positions of the two republics on the disposition of the Nagorno-Karabakh. In mid-June, Armenia's Supreme Soviet again called upon the Azerbaidzhanis to "return" the NKAO, and again the request was refused. By this time, as the article "Today in the Nagorno-Karabakh" shows, Moscow had become quite critical of the Armenian strike movement and, more surprisingly, was willing to admit its inability and the inability of the local party organizations to manage the situations in Stepanakert and Erevan effectively.

Nonetheless, the near total loss of control seemed to harden Moscow's position that Party policy would not be shaped by violent demands. In early July, an armed siege at the Erevan Airport was broken by force, and one demonstrator was killed by the police. Then the MVD made a sweep of Erevan and seized dozens of homemade bombs. Shortly thereafter, on July 18, at the session of the Supreme Soviet of the USSR, Gorbachev delivered a speech which was highly critical of both Armenians and Azerbaidzhanis. He granted that the rights of the Armenians in Nagorno-Karabakh had been violated, but he strongly condemned the Armenian strike movement as an unacceptable form of political protest. Moreover, he asserted the same principle that had been cited with regard to the claims of Crimean Tatars: that the territorial boundaries of the USSR would not be redrawn in order to right past wrongs. The NKAO would remain part of the Azerbaidzhan SSR.

Gorbachev has been willing to use increasingly larger concentrations of force to back up this policy. The reinforced presence of MVD special troops brought a temporary end to the strike movement in late July and early August. However, the return to work was a brief one. Public sentiment in Armenia hardened as a result of the July decision of the Supreme Soviet. In mid-September strikes resumed in both Erevan and Stepanakert, closing the factories, schools, banks, and food stores, and halting public transportation. The organizers of the renewed strike movement felt betrayed by Gorbachev, and many called for Armenia to secede from the USSR. Such public protest is clearly unacceptable, and on September 19 it was announced that martial law had been imposed, first in Stepanakert and a day later in Erevan. Although Soviet officials quickly qualified this statement with a claim that "special conditions" prevailed, and not martial law as such, the distinction is a semantic one, as rights of assembly are now severely restricted and a strict curfew is in place.

Yet the strike movement was not defeated, although many enterprises had returned to work. The political demands of the Armenians remained unmet, and their sense of grievance continued to grow. In November and December 1988 renewed violence broke out, in Baku as well as in Erevan and in the NKAO. Eventually, after over a week of riots and protests, the imposition of martial law succeeded in quelling the disturbances in Erevan and Baku. But the situation in the NKAO remained so tense that in mid-January 1989 the CPSU and the Council of Ministers of the USSR announced the suspension of the NKAO Supreme Soviet and the supersession of the local party by a "special commission" appointed by Moscow to rule the fractious area.

The "special commission" was composed of Russians, Armenians, and Azerbaidzhanis who were said to be sympathetic to the need to increase economic investment in the area and allow greater cultural and political autonomy for the local population. The "peace" that was introduced proved tenuous. By mid-May the population of the NKAO was again on strike, with support from striking workers in Erevan. Moscow remains at a loss as to how to resolve the situation permanently. The solution taken in the Baltic republics—the promise of a future redefinition of political and economic relations—cannot be employed here, for the Armenians are demanding that Moscow intervene against another union republic. Moscow cannot meet Armenian demands, nor have they managed to discredit them. The longer the Armenian demonstrators disrupt daily life, the more Moscow's authority to assert control is undermined, not only in Armenia but also in the national republics more generally, making the prospect of future violent confrontations a certainty.

Current Problems in Nationality Relations *

The All-Union Conference in Baku, December 1983

Speech of Comrade K. M. Bagirov

Dear Comrades!

The formation of a new man and his well-rounded, harmonious development are among the most important programmatic goals of the Communist Party. Toward this end, the mighty economic, social, and spiritual potential of developed socialism and all the resources of education and enlightenment, ideology and propaganda have been mobilized. A special place in this endeavor belongs to Soviet science, whose task it is to carry on in-depth and comprehensive studies of the tendencies and principles of the formation and development of the socialist personality, to ascertain and realize all the potentialities inherent in our society for social and spiritual progress, and for perfecting the conditions and substance of life and work of the Soviet populace.

And so we are pleased that such distinguished scholars, specialists on the nationality question and problems of the personality have gathered in the capital of our republic, the city of Baku. Together with the scholars in this hall there are also writers, composers, and artists. It can truly be said that all aspects of ideological activity which the Party has defined as an important front in the struggle for communism are represented here.

Allow me, dear Comrades, on behalf of the Central Committee of the Communist Party of Azerbaidzhan and the government of our republic to extend to the participants at the All-Union Scientific-Practical Conference on "The Dialectic of the National and International in the Spiritual World of Soviet Man" a warm and cordial welcome to Azerbaidzhani soil, and to wish all of you productive work, new creative successes, and great achievements.

The participation of Petr Nikolaevich Fedoseev, Vice-President of the Academy of Sciences of the USSR, in the work of the conference occasions satisfaction. An eminent Soviet scientist who has made outstanding contributions to the elaboration of philosophical problems of the present day, Petr Nikolaevich has rendered invaluable assistance to the development of social sciences in all the fraternal republics, including Soviet Azerbaidzhan. We regard the participation of Academician P. N. Fedoseev in this conference as a fresh manifestation of concern shown by the general staff of Soviet science, the Academy of Sciences of the USSR, for the elaboration of the most important current and long-term problems of social science. We express our gratitude to Petr Nikolaevich for coming to Azerbaidzhan and participating in a

Bakinskii rabochii, 7 December 1983.

conference which we are sure will provide a fresh stimulus to the development of social sciences in our republic.

We are glad for the attention shown to the All-Union conference by the Department of science and educational institutions at the Central Committee of the CPSU, represented here by the senior official of the Central Committee of the Party, Vladimir Anatol'evich Georgiev. We are grateful to the Department of science and educational institutions for the continuous attention and help extended to our republic in fostering the development of science, education, and general enlightenment.

Taking part in the work of our conference are secretaries of the Central Committees of the union republics, and krai and oblast committees of the Komsomol. This is entirely as it should be: the internationalist and patriotic education of youth is one of the most important aspects of the formation of the new man, an active builder of communism. We are grateful to the Central Committee of the Komsomol for its warm interest in the organization and proceedings of the Scientific-Practical Conference, and expect that the recommendations generated by the conference will yield practical results in the internationalist and patriotic education of youth, and the inculcation in them of an active attitude to life.

The principal organizer of our conference is the Scientific Council on Nationality Problems of the Section on Social Sciences of the Presidium of the Academy of Sciences of the USSR. Headed by the prominent Soviet scholar, Academician Iulian Vladimirovich Bromlei, Director of the Institute of Ethnography of the Academy of Sciences of the USSR, the Council plays an important role in organizating and conducting research into nationality and internationality processes in the period of developed socialism, and publishing fundamental works on these questions. An important part of its activities is the holding of all-union conferences on these issues. We express our warm appreciation to the Presidium of the Academy of Sciences of the USSR and to the Council on Nationality Problems for having again selected the capital of Soviet Azerbaidzhan, a city of glorious revolutionary internationalist and labor traditions, as the site of so impressive a conference. Baku has for a long time provided lofty examples of proletarian internationalism in action and of the enormous creative force of friendship and brotherhood among peoples, a force that ennobles the working man.

Besides scholars, other participants in the conference include cultural figures, practical workers in ideology, and Party, Komsomol, and trade-union workers. It would seem that such a combination of workers in the realm of science and culture, of those who work on problems of the personality and those who organize ideological work and the education of the populace—in the first instance of the rising generation—can and must enrich both theory and practice, and, most importantly, contribute to an elucidation on a broad and comprehensive scale of such an infinitely complex and multifaceted problem as the spiritual world of man and the dialectic of his international and national ties and relations.

Such an approach to the task at hand, a consideration of the indissoluble link between theory and practice, between ideological work and real problems of life is prompted by the ideas and resolutions adopted at the June (1983) Plenum of the

Central Committee of the CPSU and the speech delivered there by the General Secretary of the Central Committee of the CPSU and chairman of the Presidium of the Supreme Soviet of the USSR, Comrade Iu. V. Andropov. Recent Party documents and the speeches of Comrade Iu. V. Andropov, especially his address "Sixty Years of the USSR," provide a profoundly scientific basis for dealing with both immediate and long-term tasks of nationality policy at the stage of developed socialism, defining the main areas of scientific-theoretical and ideological activity in the sphere of nationality relations and the patriotic and internationalist education of workers. We are faced with the challenge of studying the entire system of nationality relations in their broadest scope from the inter-republican to the personal level, from the realm of economics to that of psychology, from planning and prognosis to the practical implementation of scientific recommendations. At the forefront of these problems increasingly appears the topic of the individual personality and its place and function in the development of nationality relations and the strengthening of friendship and brotherhood among the peoples of the USSR. This is clearly demonstrated by this conference, its subject matter, and the lively interest with which it is followed by such a wide circle of researchers and practical workers of the most diverse backgrounds.

The problems which you are called to discuss are of great social and practical importance. Indeed, they are dictated by the most important tasks facing our society at the current stage of its development: the intensification of material production, the social and cultural advancement of our country, the further perfecting of the socialist way of life, the strengthening of friendship and brotherhood among the peoples of the USSR, the reinforcement of the international unity of the new historical community—the Soviet people. Especially important today are such rapidly evolving processes as labor cooperation among socialist nations and nationalities, the sharing of material and spiritual values among them, and the convergence and interaction of national cultures. These processes imbue the spiritual world of Soviet man with a rich content and endow his life with vigor and variety.

The Soviet state has acquired a truly unique experience in cooperation among dozens of nations and nationalities, and national and ethnic groups. This experience has already enriched and continues to enrich the universal historical practice of the revolutionary national liberation movement, and should be subjected to thoughtful analysis and critical examination.

The experience and achievements of the Soviet land is composed of the attainments of all its regions and republics. The path of the Azerbaidzhan people within the family of fraternal nations of the USSR has also been marked by historic achievements. The attainments of the workers of Azerbaidzhan offer clear and tangible evidence of the successful implementation of the Leninist nationality policy of the Communist Party and the untiring paternal solicitude concern of the Central Committee of the CPSU and the Soviet government. Our cumulative experience also deserves the close attention of scholars and calls for some serious generalizations.

Soviet Azerbaidzhan is a multinational republic which represents a united and cohesive international collective of workers. The Communist Party of Azerbaidzhan, faithful to Lenin's legacy and the principles of proletarian internationalism, consistently implements the nationality policy of the Leninist party and conducts considerable, wide-ranging work in the area of internationalist and patriotic education of workers.

We aim to encompass in this work all spheres of life, from the economic to the spiritual. In practice, the Party organizations of our republic take into account the multinational structure of the population, showing concern for the economic and sociocultural development of all the nationalities, encouraging their active participation in our social and political life, untiringly pursuit of an internationalist course in their cadre policy as they select and place cadres with due regard for the national composition of the population.

An important aspect of this work is the expansion and deepening of industrial and economic, sociopolitical, and cultural relations of the Azerbaidzhani people and the workers of our republic with all the fraternal peoples of our country—above all, with the great Russian people. The most important task toward which the efforts of the Communists in our republic are directed is the strengthening among the workers of their internationalist convictions, their internationalist attitude toward life, their consciousness and sense of belonging to the one great Soviet people. This is a vast and complex undertaking. And in this undertaking a place of prominence belongs to social scientists of our republic, who have been called upon to investigate national and international processes currently taking place, to analyze and draw generalizations from the rich experience of economic and cultural construction—the experience of putting into practice the norms and principles of socialist internationalism.

And one more point. In all its organizational and political and ideological work the Communist Party of Azerbaidzhan proceeds from the assumption that the formation of the new man is not only the most important goal, but also an indispensable precondition for communist construction and for the wholesale adoption of a Leninist style of work—a style that is businesslike, creative, innovative, and permeated with high-mindedness—a precondition as well for the adoption of an implacable attitude toward everything repugnant and contradictory to norms of socialist morality and a collectivist way of life. The experience accumulated by the communists of Azerbaidzhan testifies to the fact that an uncompromising struggle with negative phenomena, vestiges of private property psychology, philistine morality, and backward and obsolete traditions and customs, not only facilitates a fundamental regeneration of the moral-psychological climate and moral-political environment, but also strengthens the internationalist spirit that reigns in our republic.

The June Plenum of the Central Committee of the CPSU has called for organic linkage between developments in science and the requirements of practical work. Ideological work must rely on well-founded recommendations that reflect the latest findings of scientific research. This is one of the most important conditions for efficiency and efficacy of educational and political work among the masses. It is precisely from these positions that we attempt to assess the relevance and theoretical and ideological significance of the problems that are to be the subject of discussion at this conference. It is a question of making sure those national and international factors that have taken shape in the socialist society produce a more complete and more effective impact on personal improvement. It is a question of harnessing the enormous spiritual riches of dozens of nations and nationalities of our country to the fullest extent for the spiritual enhancement of each person, regardless of his national identity. It is a question, finally, by fostering Soviet patriotism and socialist internationalism, of increasing the labor and political participation by citizens of the socialist society and expanding even more the historic creativity of the masses.

Communist convictions and an enormous vital energy, a high level of culture, a rich store of knowledge and the ability to apply it to creative use—these are the distinguishing qualities that define Soviet man as a new historic type of individual. The most important among these remarkable qualities are an ardent patriotism and resolute internationalism. Our task is to find ever newer ways and means for perfecting these qualities and ever newer forms for their mass development.

Comrades! Your conference will examine a broad and complex range of current problems in nationality relations and the spiritual life of Soviet man. Discussion of these will doubtless enrich scientific research and bring it closer to the needs of practical work, as well as facilitate the development of a new important area—the study of the problems of the personality within the system of nationality relations. For this we have the indispensable fundamentals: Marxist-Leninist theory—a living guide to action and to creative work—and the policies of our Party and its programmatic positions. For this we also have highly qualified cadres of scientists and practical workers.

In conclusion, dear comrades, allow me once again wish you every success in your great and important work whose aim is the further social and spiritual progress of the Soviet man. (*applause*)

Speech of Academician P. N. Fedoseev

Esteemed Comrades!

In the Soviet multinational state the question of the relationship between the national and the international in people's consciousness and way of life has an exceptionally great significance. It is necessary all the more to emphasize that multinational as well are all our union and autonomous republics which make up the great Soviet Union. Thus in Azerbaidzhan, besides the indigenous nationality, there live many thousands of Russians, Armenians, Ukrainians, Georgians, Jews, Tatars, Avars,[a] Lezghins,[b] etc.

It is fitting, it seems to us that this conference, arranged on the initiative of the Scientific Council on Nationality Problems jointly with the Central Committee of the Communist Party of Azerbaidzhan, should take place in the city of Baku, with its glorious international traditions.

Allow me, on behalf of the Academy of Sciences of the USSR and its President A. P. Aleksandrov, to greet the participants at this conference who have gathered here in the hospitable capital of Azerbaidzhan to discuss one of the most crucial problems of contemporary social development and spiritual life.

The workers of this republic, led by the Party in organization, achieved considerable successes in the 1970s, both in their economic tasks and in combining economic activity with large-scale ideological work on a broad scale, including work with regard to the internationalist education of workers.

In his speech, Comrade Kiamran Mamedovich Bagirov presented an impressive picture of the great achievements of Soviet Azerbaidzhan in all areas of life. We extend hearty congratulations to the communists and all the citizens of the republic for their great labor successes.

Present-day Azerbaidzhan provides a concrete example of the efficacy and fruitfulness of the Leninist nationality policy and gives vivid testimony to the enormous creative force of friendship and fraternal cooperation among the peoples of the USSR.

Internationalism is manifested in our daily lives, in the constructive labor and in the lifestyle of Soviet people. It is a noteworthy that in all oblasts and raions districts, in many enterprises and on collective farms, in many establishments and institutes, people of different nationalities live and work together in harmony, like brothers, and on the basis of mutual assistance achieve ever new success in socialist construction.

Mutual respect and mutual trust among people of different nationalities on the job and in everyday life, mutual assistance among multinational work collectives, and a genuine internationalism in human relations—these are the indispensable features of a socialist way of life.

The construction of a developed socialist society in the USSR is a historic achievement for all the peoples of our country and all its nations and nationalities. In our fraternal family of nations the economies of all the Soviet republics have expanded greatly and the task of equalizing their levels of economic development has been largely solved. In our mature socialist society we see the successful development of a single economic complex, created through the common efforts of all the peoples of the USSR.

Soviet people of different nationalities are united by the community of their spiritual life, by their common world outlook and Soviet socialist culture. The common international culture of all the socialist nations incorporates the best progressive achievements and values of the national culture. The contribution of each nation and nationality to the common Soviet culture increases steadily in proprtion to the development of their own national socialist cultures.

We can observe the remarkable achievements of the Azerbaidzhani people's artistry from ancient times down to the present day in the republic's museums of history, literature and art, in theaters and concert halls, and at the carpet exhibition. It is important to note that in the works of masters of literature and art are reflected the spiritual world of the new man and the ideals of friendship and cooperation among peoples.

An important factor in promoting inter-nationality contact and solidarity is represented by Soviet science, which has reached a high level of development in all our republics. The republican academies of science, along with the All-Union Academy, are a source of national and all-Soviet pride. I should like to take this opportunity to note the great contribution made by the scientists of Azerbaidzhan to the development of Soviet science and technology.

The international and the national in the consciousness and way of life of Soviet people are not two disconnected and separable principles. The national becomes incorporated in the international, while the international manifests itself in the life of each socialist nation and nationality. One who ignores national traditions and features cannot be an internationalist. Similarly, one who underestimates or deprecates the international tasks and common interests of the workers cannot be a patriot.

Anyone who considers himself to be an internationalist but disdains national interests and features is in fact actually not an internationalist, but a cosmopolitan. Anyone who divorces patriotism from internationalism inevitably slips into national narrow-mindedness and nationalism.

An all-Soviet patriotic pride and a love of one's own nation and one's own republic become organically fused in Soviet patriotism. Thus in its very essence Soviet patriotism is international, for it is based on the principles of friendship among peoples and international solidarity.

With the growth of social homogeneity among all the nations and nationalities in a developed socialist society, stemming from the progressive convergence of socialist classes and social groups, processes of internationalization of all public life intensify. On this basis occurs the process of further convergence and close cooperation of all Soviet peoples and the strengthening of their inviolable fraternal friendship. At the same time, under conditions of mature socialism there is an acceleration of processes of the comprehensive development of socialist nations and their cultures, unfoldment of their full potential, and the establishment of indispensable conditions for the full flourishing of all that is national. However, the all-inclusive flourishing of nations on the basis of the Leninist nationality policy leads not to individuation, but to their ever closer unification. Such is the dialectic of national and international relationships in the developed socialist society heading toward communism.

Of course this unity of the national and the international was effected at an advanced stage of sociopolitical and ideological unity achieved by our society, namely, at the stage of developed socialism. It is this stage that the ideals and goals of the working class become the ideals and goals of the whole people, and class interests merge with the interests of the entire public.

The CPSU, while it remains the party of the working class, is becoming as well the party of the whole people. The Soviet people, as a new historic community, embodies the social and international unity of people belonging to all nationalities.

However, one cannot ignore the fact that vestiges of presocialist structures in people's consciousness and way of life not infrequently find expression in a national narrow-mindedness and conceit, in ethnic prejudice and bias. Nor can we for one moment forget the hostile activities of imperialist centers, which strive to inflame nationalist prejudices and undermine friendship and cooperation among our peoples. The CPSU devotes unflagging attention to the consolidation of friendship and cooperation among peoples of all nationalities and the strengthening of socialist internationalism.

In this connection it is important to intensify our propaganda to publicize the achievements of socialism in solving the nationality question and to show more fully and concretely what great blessings Soviet power has brought to the various peoples. It is justly said that comparisons offer clear and persuasive testimony. We all, and with us our foreign friends, rejoice in the outstanding achievements of the peoples of the national republics of the Soviet Union, be they Azerbaidzhanis or Armenians, Turkmens, Uzbeks, or Tadzhiks. But we also know the cruel fate that befell their kinsmen who, as a result of predatory wars or arbitrary frontier demarcations, found themselves on territories of bordering bourgeois or feudal states. Our peoples are sensible and aware of the good fortune that is theirs to live and work in the Soviet Union, under the sun of socialism, and they bless destiny they do not find themselves outside the borders of our socialist state.

To continue the comparison, we can recall that not so long ago millions of Belorussians, Ukrainians, and Moldavians languished in the grip of injustice and poverty under the rule of Polish lords, Czechoslovak magnates, and Romanian aristocrats. The liberation of our compatriots and the reunion of the fraternal peoples of the Ukraine, Belorussia and Moldavia enabled these new Soviet citizens, in a matter of three or four decades to reach the heights of a developed socialist society and to achieve the all-union level in their economy and culture.

The same may be said of the Baltic peoples, torn from their Soviet Motherland in the difficult years of civil war and foreign intervention and made totally dependent on world capital. The victory of the popular masses over the bourgeois and landowning forces and the establishment of Soviet power in Lithuania, Latvia, and Estonia in 1940 led as a natural consequence to their voluntary entry into the USSR. With the fraternal assistance of all our peoples, the Soviet republics of the Baltic region quickly made up for lost time, overcame their former backwardness, and in the postwar years, despite the enormous losses that followed the invasion by the fascist barbarians, moved to the forefront of socialist construction.

Historical experience has shown conclusively that the internationalism evinced by socialist states in their domestic policies by its very nature extends to their internationalist foreign policies and their relations with fraternal socialist countries and the workers' liberation movement worldwide. The Soviet Union consistently pursues a Leninist policy of peace and friendship among peoples, a policy of international solidarity of workers and peaceful coexistence of states with differing social systems. The peace program elaborated and consistently followed by our Party has had an enormous impact in mobilizing all peace-loving forces in the struggle against the threat of a new world war and a thermonuclear catastrophe.

The entire history of capitalism, especially at its imperialist stage, testifies to the fact that racism, chauvinism, and oppression of unequal races and nations inside a country are inextricably linked to a great-power, hegemonist policy in international relations, a policy of diktat, plunder and aggression, a policy of enslavement of other countries and peoples, a policy of wars of aggression. It is no happenstance that in the United States in recent times acute outbreaks of racism and racist pogroms have coincided with a wave of militarism and war hysteria. One and the other are fruits of the reactionary policies of the present U.S. administration, which represents the most extremist tendencies of monopoly capital and, in particular, the military-industrial complex. American imperialism today has become particularly aggressive, having chosen the path of an unbridled arms race and preparation for a "limited" "protracted" nuclear war, and in this way exposing the world to the catastrophic threat of the destruction of civilization and the death of the greater part of mankind.

With the help of military power and the threat of its application, Washington and its allies are making every attempt, at any cost, to turn back history, to halt the growing process of social renewal throughout the world, and to preserve or expand the influence of state monopoly capital on all continents. Shaken by internal contradictions and antagonisms, imperialism seeks to extricate itself by way of confrontation and violent conflict.

To achieve their imperialist aims and establish world hegemony, the ruling circles in the United States are expanding their military presence in various regions of the world and are interfering, even with armed force, in the internal affairs of other states and peoples. The deployment of new American nuclear middle-range missiles in a number of countries in Western Europe constitutes a particular danger to the cause of peace in Europe and all over the planet.

The attitude of the Soviet Union and all Soviet people, including Soviet scientists, toward the adventuristic actions of the United States and its NATO allies was unequivocally expressed, to countrywide approval and support, in the Declaration by the General Secretary of the Central Committee of the CPSU and chairman of the Presidium of the Supreme Soviet of the USSR, Comrade Iu. V. Andropov. "The Soviet Union and other countries of the socialist community," Comrade Iu. V. Andropov emphasized, "cannot close their eyes to the fact that Washington has proclaimed a 'crusade' against socialism as a social system, nor to the fact that those who just issued the orders for the deployment of new nuclear weapons at the doorstep of our home are basing their pragmatic policies on this reckless premise."

Our country is taking all the necessary measures to safeguard the security of the USSR and our allies. All calculations on the part of the US to achieve military superiority over the USSR are futile. Our country will not remain defenseless in the face of any threat.

Nevertheless, as Iu. V. Andropov emphasized, the Soviet Union remains committed, as a matter of principle, to a policy of cessation of the arms race, especially in nuclear armaments, to reduce and, ultimately, completely eliminate the threat of nuclear war. The Soviet Union will continue to make every effort to achieve these noble aims.

This, comrades, is fully in keeping with the principles of internationalism and the interests of all humanity.

In conclusion, allow me to express my sincere thanks to the First Secretary of the Central Committee of the Communist Party of Azerbaidzhan K. M. Bagirov for his invitation and interest in the conference, for his active participation in the preparation and proceedings of this scholarly forum, as well as to wish, on behalf of the Presidium of the Academy of Sciences of the USSR, productive work to the participants. (*applause*)

Editor's notes

a. The Avars: a Sunni Muslim Caucasian tribal community, the majority of whose members live in western Daghestan.

b. The Lezghins: a Sunni Muslim Caucasian tribal community, the majority of whose members live in southern Daghestan.

M. S. Gorbachev's Appeal to the Workers and the Peoples of Azerbaidzhan and Armenia *

Dear Comrades,

I appeal to you in connection with the events in and around Nagorno-Karabakh.

The question has been raised of the transfer of this autonomous oblast from the Azerbaidzhan SSR to the Armenian SSR. An acute and dramatic nature has been imparted to this, which has led to tension and even to actions which go beyond the law.

I will state frankly: The Central Committee of the CPSU is concerned with this development of events, which is fraught with the most serious consequences.

We do not advocate evading a frank discussion of different ideas and suggestions, but this must be done calmly, within the framework of the democratic process and legality, without permitting the slightest harm to the internationalist solidarity of our peoples. Serious questions of the people's destiny can not be left to the rule of primordial forces and emotions.

It is very important to assess one's anxieties not only in the context of local conditions but also with due regard for the processes of revolutionary renewal that are under way in the country.

Yes, there are unresolved problems in our life, but the fanning of feuds and mistrust between peoples only hinders their resolution. This would run counter to our socialist principles and our morality, counter to the traditions of friendship and brotherhood of the Soviet peoples. We live in a multinational country, moreover, all the republics, many of our oblasts, and even cities and settlements are multinational. The meaning of Lenin's nationalities policy is that every person and every nation should be able to develop freely and that every people should be able to satisfy its needs in all spheres of sociopolitical life, in their mother tongue and culture, in customs and beliefs.

Socialist internationalism is the source of our tremendous strength. The genuine fraternity and unity is our path.

The great Armenian poet E. Charents expressed it well, addressing Soviet Azerbaidzhan: "In the name of immense past suffering, in the name of life granted to us among victories, in the name of a friendly and creative union—we send greetings, greetings to a fraternal people."

How this is echoed by the words of S. Vurgun, great son of the Azerbaidzhani people: "We live not as neighbors but within each other. The peoples long ago took from each other fire for the hearth and their daily bread."

No mother would consent to her children being threatened by national feuds

---

*Komsomolets, 27 February 1988.

instead of firm bonds of friendship, equality, and mutual assistance and the truly great acquisition of socialism.

Many shortcomings and difficulties have accumulated in the Nagorno-Karabakh Autonomous Oblast. The new leadership of the oblast must take urgent measures for the rectification of the situation. The Central Committee of the CPSU has made clear recommendations about this and will follow firsthand their fulfillment.

For now the most important thing is to concentrate on overcoming the situation which has come about and resolving the specific economic, social, ecological, and other problems which have accumulated in Azerbaidzhan and in Armenia; in the spirit of the policy of restructuring and renewal being implemented throughout our country.

The traditions of friendship between the Azerbaidzhani and Armenian peoples which have formed over the years of Soviet power must be cherished and in every way strengthened. Only this approach corresponds to the genuine interests of all the peoples of the USSR.

You know that it is intended to devote a plenum of the Central Committee of our party specifically to the development of national relations. We have to discuss a wide range of questions in this very important social sphere and, on the basis of the fundamental gains of Lenin's nationalities policy, to outline ways for the concrete resolution of social, economic, cultural, and other problems.

You and I are all Soviet citizens, we have a common history, and common victories, and behind us lie great labor, misfortunes, and losses. We are engaged in the great cause of restructuring, on whose success depends the fate of socialism, our Motherland, and of each of us.

I appeal to you, comrades, to your consciousness and responsibility, to your prudence. We will perservere also in this trail of our Soviet internationalism and in our unshakable faith that only in an amicable family of all our peoples can we secure our society's progress and the prosperity of all its citizens.

I call on you to display civic maturity and restraint, to return to normal life and work, to observe public order.

The time for reason and sober decisions has come.

On Measures to Accelerate Socioeconomic Development of the Nagorno-Karabakh AO of the Azerbaidzhan SSR in 1988-1995 *

Resolution of the Central Committee of the CPSU and the Council of Ministers of the USSR of 24 March 1988

The Central Committee of the CPSU and USSR Council of Ministers note that with the fraternal assistance of all the peoples of the Soviet Union, the Nagorno-Karabakh Autonomous Oblast has achieved considerable successes in social and economic development; the economy has been guaranteed a stronger material and technical base. In the last three five-year plans alone the volume of industrial production in the oblast has increased more than three times, while agricultural production has increased 1.5 times. Participation in the republic and all-union divisions of labor has increased substantially in the oblast and integrative processes are actively developing. Provision of housing, hospitals, libraries, and clubs for the population has improved.

At the same time, the efficiency of social production has recently tended to fall off; the plans for capital construction and commissioning of housing are not being fulfilled. Development of the social and cultural sphere lags behind the population's increasing demands. In many labor collectives discipline has gotten worse and responsibility for the fulfillment of production plans and of contractual obligations for goods has diminished. The inconstant work of the oblast's enterprises is having an adverse effect on the state of affairs in the economy.

These shortcomings are caused by a weakening of the administrative and organizational role of local and republic-level Party and state bodies. Their slow restructuring in conditions of expanding democracy and of implementation of radical reform in management of the economy and of a drop in the level of party-political work among the masses.

In order to ensure the further social and economic development of the Nagorno-Karabakh Autonomous Oblast and to eliminate the noted shortcomings, the Central Committee of the CPSU and the USSR Council of Ministers have resolved as follows:

1. The Central Committee of the Communist Party of Azerbaidzhan and the Council of Ministers of the Azerbaidzhan SSR, the Nagorno-Karabakh Autonomous Oblast Communist Party Committee, and the Nagorno-Karabakh Oblast Executive Committee and other Party and state bodies and primary Party organizations in the

---

Komsomolets, 31 March 1988.

oblast are to intensify political and organization work in mobilizing working people to implement the decisions of the Twenty-seventh Congress of the CPSU, the CPSU Central Committee June (1987) and February (1988) Plenums, and the Party's course for restructuring and accelerating socioeconomic development on the basis of utilization of the achievements of scientific-technical progress and advanced experience and intensification of social production.

Education of working people and the entire population in the spirit of internationalism, fraternal friendship, and mutual assistance must be considered the primary and immediate task, and the slightest manifestations of nationalism or lack of respect for the national feelings of representatives of various peoples must be resolutely suppressed.

Constant attention is to be paid to the economic and social development of the Nagorno-Karabakh Autonomous Oblast. In 1988–89 USSR Gosplan, the USSR State Committee for Science and Technology, and the USSR Academy of Sciences must elaborate a comprehensive plan for the economic and social development of this oblast, up to 2005, which will foresee the complete development of its productive forces. It is necessary, as of 1989, to elaborate and embark on implementation of a range of measures to accelerate the development of the social sphere, providing a 40% increase in the volume of housing construction in the Five-year Plan so that by the year 2000 every family will have a separate apartment or its own house. It is necessary to insure by 1995 the basic transition to one-shift teaching in general educational schools, for which 9–10 schools will have to be built.

Plans for 1989–90 and the Thirteenth Five-year Plan period are to include construction of an 850-seat Palace of Culture (in Stepanakert), a 400-bed oblast hospital with a clinic handling 600 patients per shift, a Pioneers' Center, a city library, and also housing and other social facilities in accordance with Appendix No. 1.

2. In 1988 the USSR Ministry of Communications and the USSR State Committee for Television and Radio Broadcasting are to elaborate for implementation in 1988–89 a range of measures to provide the population of Nagorno-Karabakh Autonomous Oblast and adjoining areas with high-quality all-Union television broadcasts and also the transmission in that region of the full complement of Azerbaidzhan and Armenian television broadcasts (with the possibility of relaying local television as part of these broadcasts).

3. In line with the wishes for Armenians living in the Azerbaidzhan SSR, the USSR Ministry of Culture and the Azerbaidzhan SSR Council of Ministers are to consider the question of setting up an Armenian drama theater in Baku, and elaborate and implement a range of measures on further work to restore and renovate historical and cultural monuments on the territory of the Nagorno-Karabakh Autonomous Oblast, using Armenian craftsmen and restoration specialists in this work.

4. The USSR State Committee for Publishing Houses, Printing Works, and the Book Trade in the Twelfth Five-year Plan is to carry out the reconstruction of the printing plant in Stepanakert and raion centers of the Nagorno-Karabakh Autonomous Oblast and to expand the production of printed material in Armenian, with

a view to satisfying the needs of the oblast's populace for this material.

5. The USSR Ministry of Civil Aviation is to consider in 1989 the question of reconstructing the airport in Stepanakert (including providing it with modern radio navigation equipment) to take larger passenger aircraft and, if necessary, submit the relevant proposals when the draft plan for the Thirteenth Five-year Plan period is being prepared.

6. In order to improve water supplies for the population and to develop irrigation farming in the Nagorno-Karabakh Autonomous Oblast the USSR Ministry of Land Reclamation and Water Resources and USSR Gosagroprom are to insure that plans are made in 1988–90 for a reservoir on the Badarachai River with a capacity of 30 million cubic meters, to be basically constructed in the Thirteenth Five-year Plan period, with the first phase to be commissioned in 1993.

They are also to consider a proposal to plan and construct a reservoir of 20 million cubic meters on the Karkarchai River during the period of the Thirteenth and Fourteenth Five-year Plans and adopt the relevant decision. In 1988–90 they are further to allocate to the Azerbaidzhan SSR Main Administration for Land Reclamation and Water Resources Construction additional centralized state capital investments funds of about twelve million rubles to draw up planning estimates and documents, and carry out preparatory work for the construction of reservoirs on the Badarachi and Karkarchai rivers, as well as the requisite material and technical resources. They should allocate to the "Azselkhozvodoprovodstroi" association the centralized state capital investments required in order to complete the construction of the Karabakh aggregate water pipeline on the territory of the autonomous oblast in 1989, and also to ensure a centralized water supply for all rural population centers in the future.

The Azerbaidzhan SSR Council of Ministers in the Twelfth Five-year Plan is to institute measures to guarantee Stepanakert and raion centers in the oblast with a regular water supply.

7. In order to improve food supplies for the population and insure the processing and storage of agricultural raw materials, the USSR Gosagroprom and the Azerbaidzhan SSR Council of Ministers are to provide in 1988–94 for the construction agro-industrial complex facilities in the Nagorno-Karabakh Autonomous Oblast.

8. The USSR Ministry of Grain Products is to insure in 1989 the drawing up of planning and estimates documents, and in 1990–91 the construction of a mixed feed plant in the settlement of Askeran with a capacity of 250 tons of mixed feed per day.

9. In order to further improve transportation services for the population of the Nagorno-Karabakh Autonomous Oblast, the Azerbaidzhan SSR Council of Ministers is to elaborate and confirm in 1989 a scheme for the development of general-purpose highways and farm roads in this region and to set up the corresponding structural subunits to insure a 50–100% increase in highway construction. The reconstruction of the 75-km. Goris–Lachin–Stepanakert highway is to be carried out in 1988–90.

10. The USSR Ministry of Power and Electrification is to insure a reliability of

the electrical supply for productive, cultural, and consumer facilities in the Nagorno-Karabakh Autonomous Oblast and the Azerbaidzhan SSR Main Administration of Power and Electrification is to be allocated the requisite machinery and mechanisms for construction and reconstruction of equipment in the power grid.

11. The USSR Ministry of the Gas Industry is to put in its 1989 plan assignment to the "Aztransgaz" association the task of constructing a gas branch pipeline to the settlement of Gadrut (as part of the Fizuli–Dzhebrail gas pipeline), and to insure in 1989 the planning, and 1990–91 the construction, of a Mir–Bashir–Mardakert–Kelbadzhar gas branch pipeline.

When elaborating draft plans for the economic and social development of the USSR in 1989–90 and for the Thirteenth Five-year Plan USSR Gosagroprom is to include the construction of gas branch pipelines and 550 km of gas supply systems in Nagorno-Karabakh Autonomous Oblast population centers.

12. The Azerbaidzhan SSR Council of Ministers, in conjunction with the relevant USSR ministries and departments, is to elaborate and implement a range of measures providing a 50–60% increase in industrial output in the Nagorno-Karabakh Autonomous Oblast by the end of the Thirteenth Five-year Plan, including a 160% increase in machinebuilding output and a 30–40% increase in gross agricultural production, as well as a considerable increase in the production of consumer goods and construction materials.

Allocation of capital investment funds for these ends is to be planned, as are the subsequent work, the financial and material resources, and the creation of a modern material and technical basis for repair, construction, motor transport, and highway organizations, providing them with the requisite machinery, mechanisms, and equipment.

13. In order to ensure rational employment of the population and the development of the industrial potential of the Nagorno-Karabakh Autonomous Oblast, the USSR Ministries of the Electrical Equipment Industry, of the Electronics Industry, of the Radio Industry, of Light Industry, and of the Forestry Industry are to plan, construct, expand, and restructure subsidiary enterprises and their branches in 1988–94.

These ministries are obligated to give the local soviets in the autonomous oblast funds on a quota basis for the development of the social sphere and community services facilities.

To insure that this work is done in an economic manner the USSR Ministries of Light Industry and of the Timber Industry, are to give the Azerbaidzhan SSR Ministry of Light Industry and the Azerbaidzhan SSR Ministry of Forests and Wood assistance in 1989–90 to supply the requisite machinery and equipment.

14. In order to reach a significantly increased volume of construction, the Azerbaidzhan SSR Council of Ministers, in conjunction with the USSR Gosstroi and USSR Gosplan, is to elaborate and approve in the first half of 1988 a concrete program to develop the material and technical base of construction organizations in the Nagorno-Karabakh Autonomous Oblast in 1989–95, with the goal of increasing the amount of construction and installation work being done in the Thirteenth Five-

year Plan period by 80–100%, including as first importance capacities of large panel housing construction and also capacities for the production of prefabricated ferroconcrete structures and local construction materials.

In 1989–90 the USSR Ministry of the Construction Materials Industry is to allocate stoneworking machine tools, machinery, and equipment to the Azerbaidzhan SSR Ministry of Construction Materials to establish a construction materials combine in Stepanakert.

The USSR Ministry of Construction, Road, and Municipal Machine Building and the USSR State Committee on Supplies are to insure the manufacture and supply to the Azerbaidzhan SSR Council of Ministers in 1989–92 of four highly mechanized brick works each capable of producing 5 million bricks a year.

The USSR Gosstroi is to ensure the creation of a branch of the Azerbaidzhan SSR Gosstroi "Azgosproekt" planning institute in Stepanakert in 1989.

The Azerbaidzhan SSR Council of Ministers and corresponding USSR ministries and departments are authorized to carry out, as an exception, in 1988–89, the construction of production and social facilities in the Nagorno-Karabakh Autonomous Oblast in accordance with working drawings and estimate before the drafts have been approved in the established manner.

15. In order to insure start of work on meeting the assignments set out by the present resolution:

the quota of the Azerbaidzhan SSR Council of Ministers for centralized state capital investments is to be increased by 12.4 million rubles, including 3.9 million rubles for construction and installation work. Financing for these capital investments is to come out of the USSR Council of Ministers reserve fund;

USSR Gossnab, USSR Gosagroprom, and USSR Ministry of Land Reclamation and Water Resources are to place additional material and technical resources at the disposal of the Azerbaidzhan SSR Council of Ministers in 1988 for the needs of the Nagorno-Karabakh Autonomous Oblast.

16. The USSR Gosplan is provide for state capital investments for the Azerbaidzhan SSR Council of Ministers from all sources of finance and material resources in 1989–90 in excess of the five-year plan targets and, in the calculations for the Thirteenth Five-year Plan, in amounts ensuring the fulfillment of the targets intended by the present resolution.

17. The USSR State Committee for People's Education, the Azerbaidzhan SSR Council of Ministers, and the Armenian SSR Council of Ministers are to provide elaboration and implementation of joint organizational, pedagogical and methodological measures to improve work in the Armenian-language schools in the Nagorno-Karabakh Autonomous Oblast and also in other parts of the Azerbaidzhan SSR.

18. Starting in 1988, the USSR State Committee for Public Education, in conjunction with the Azerbaidzhan SSR Council of Ministers and Armenian SSR Council of Ministers, is to include in its plans training of specialists on a shared basis, allotment of special places in the higher educational institutions of the Armenian SSR specifically for people living in the Nagorno-Karabakh Autonomous Oblast.

19. In order to improve the quality of training of specialists with higher educa-

tion and satisfy more fully the Nagorno-Karabakh Autonomous Oblast's need for highly skilled cadres, the USSR State Committee for Public Education and the Azerbaidzhan SSR Council of Ministers are to elaborate and implement measures to accelerate the development of the material and technical base of the Stepanakert Pedagogical Institute and to equip it with modern technical training facilities and the requisite laboratory training equipment and computers.

20. In connection with the desires of citizens living in the Nagorno-Karabakh Autonomous Oblast to see the names of institutions and organizations inscribed in Armenian, the Azerbaidzhan SSR Council of Ministers is instructed to consider and resolve this issue.

21. The Central Committee of the Communist Party of Azerbaidzhan, the Azerbaidzhan SSR Council of Ministers, the Nagorno-Karabakh Autonomous Oblast Committee of the Communist Party, and the Nagorno-Karabakh Oblast Executive Committee are to direct the organizational and political work of the Party, government, and economic bodies and trade union and Komosomol organizations to fulfill the targets intended in the present resolution and to concentrate working people's efforts primarily on the solution of economic and social tasks, making all possible use of the rights granted to local soviets in the planning and management of the oblast economy.

Every effort is to be made to develop the initiative and creative activity of working people and to actively support their desire to respond with patriotic deeds to the call of the CPSU to accelerate and deepen restructuring, improve the style of work, develop criticism and self-criticism, and guarantee extensive *glasnost'* in solving questions of economic and social development.

The mass news and propaganda media are to provide regular and multifaceted coverage of problems of the region's social and economic development, to analyze thoroughly the pace of fulfillment of plan targets, to enlarge the experience of real restructuring, and to propagandize modern methods of management and improvement of labor efficiency.

The Central Committee of the CPSU and the Council of Ministers of the USSR express firm confidence that the Communists and all the working people of the Nagorno-Karabakh Autonomous Oblast of the Azerbaidzhan SSR will display political maturity and an appreciation of the responsibility of the moment and will demonstrate solidarity and a high degree of organization. It is the duty of the oblast's labor collectives to strengthen the friendship of the Armenian, Azerbaidzhani, and other peoples of our country and to direct all efforts at eliminating the lag that has developed, by unconditionally fulfilling the plans for 1988 and for the Twelfth Five-year Plan as a whole.

M. Gorbachev, Secretary of the CPSU Central Committee
N. Ryzhkov, Chairman of the USSR Council of Ministers

The Riot in Sumgait

About the Situation in Sumgait *

As has already been announced, in Sumgait on 28 February a group of hooligan elements provoked disorder. Unsteady, immature people who had fallen under the influence of provocational rumors and inflammatory conversations about events in Nagorno-Karabakh and Armenia were drawn into unlawful actions. Taking advantage of the unleashed passions and emotions, criminal elements committed acts of banditry. There were tragic occurrences and there were victims. Party, government, and law enforcement organs took decisive steps to normalize the situation. The law enforcement organs detained people discovered in criminal acts.

A government commission has been formed, headed by the President of the Soviet of Ministers of the Azerbaidzhan SSR, G. N. Seidov, which is to decide all questions concerning the guarantee of uninterrupted functioning of the city services, the repair of homes and public buildings, and the support of social order. Necessary assistance is being given to victims. The requests and appeals of citizens are being considered, and based upon them operative measures are being taken.

The workers of the city are showing restraint, are strengthening the internationalist atmosphere in their collectives. The rhythm of labor has not been interrupted even for a minute. The institutions of industry, transportation, trade, food supply, public services, and others are working in the proper manner, and activities proceed in the schools.

Candidate member of the Politburo of the Central Committee of the CPSU and first deputy President of the Presidium of the Supreme Soviet of the USSR P. N. Demichev and the First Secretary of the Central Committee of the Communist Party of Azerbaidzhan K. M. Bagirov met with the workers of Sumgait and showed interest in the basic questions of life in the city and the guaranteeing of social order, and the measures taken to investigate antisocial phenomena.

An investigative group of the Procurator of the USSR is taking measures to investigate crimes and bring to responsibility the people who took part in them.

The Situation in Sumgait†

As has already been announced, in Sumgait on 28 February a group of hooligan elements provoked disorder. Unsteady, immature people who had fallen under the influence of false rumors about events in Nagorno-Karabakh and Armenia were drawn into unlawful actions. Criminal elements committed violent acts and robberies. Thirty-one people died at their hands. Among them were people of various nationalities, old people and women.

Bakinskii rabochii, 3 March 1988.
†*Bakinskii rabochii*, 5 March 1988.

Decisive measures were taken to normalize the situation. Those guilty of crimes were arrested and brought to criminal responsibility in strict agreement with Soviet laws.

A government commission has been formed, headed by the President of the Soviet of Ministers of the Azerbaidzhan SSR, G. N. Seidov,[a] to decide all questions concerning the guarantee of uninterrupted functioning of the city services and the support of social order. Necessary assistance is being given to victims. The requests and appeals of citizens are being considered, and based upon them operative measures are being taken.

The workers of the city are showing restraint and demonstrating feelings of internationalism. The rhythm of labor has not been interrupted. The institutions of industry, transportation, trade, food supply, civic services, and others are working in the proper manner, and activities proceed in the schools.

Editor's note

a. G. N. Seidov is Azerbaidzhani.

NOTICE

As has already been announced, since the well-known events in the city of Sumgait, families and citizens of Armenian nationality have been arriving in the [Armenian] republic.

At present 1,761 people (435 families) have come to the Armenian SSR. Some of them have been housed with relatives, and others have been temporarily housed in republic holiday houses.

A commission to examine questions pertaining to the new arrivals from Sumgait is working under the first deputy chairman of the Council of Ministers of the Armenian SSR, comrade V. M. Movsisian.

A decision of the republic's government provides the arriving families and people in need with effective material and other assistance. The requests and appeals of citizens are examined, and the corresponding measures are taken.

A special group of the Procurator of the USSR is conducting an investigation of the events in Sumgait. The Procurator of the USSR has delegated the Procurator of the Armenian SSR to form an investigative group to find victims and eyewitnesses who have left Sumgait and who are now in the republic, in order to conduct the necessary investigative acts, following the criminal investigation procedural laws for establishing the condition of commission of a crime.

(*Komsomolets*, 19 March 1988)

Sumgait City Party Committee Plenum *

There has been a plenum of the Sumgait City Committee of the Communist Party of Azerbaidzhan, which discussed an organizational issue.

The plenum released D. M. Muslim-Zade from his duties as first secretary of the Sumgait City Party Committee for gross political negligence, major shortcomings in organizational and political work, and conduct not befitting a Party member, which led to tragic consequences in the city.

Z. S. Gadzhiev, who has hitherto worked as chairman of the Nakhichevan ASSR Council of Ministers, was elected first secretary of the Sumgait City Party Committee.

K .M. Bagirov, first secretary of the Azerbaidzhan Communist Party Central Committee, took part in the plenum's work and delivered a speech.

Sumgait City Soviet Session†

A session of the Sumgait City Soviet, 18th Convocation, has discussed an organizational question. T. Ia. Mamedov was released from his duties as president of the city executive committee for serious shortcomings in the organization of work to insure proper order and discipline in the city, for political shortsightedness, and for failure to take measures in good time to prevent the negative phenomena which led to tragic consequences in the city.

R. F. Eminbeili, formerly director of the 60th Anniversary of Soviet Azerbaidzhan Aluminum Plant in Sumgait, was chosen chairman of the Sumgait City Executive Committee of the Party. K. M. Bagirov, first secretary of the Azerbaidzhan Communist Party Central Committee, took part in the session and delivered a speech.

In the Central Committee of the Communist Party of Azerbaidzhan‡

The Central Committee of the Communist Party of Azerbaidzhan has discussed the question of "Major Shortcomings in Organizational Work Among the Population and the Political Shortsightedness and Inactivity of the Bureau of the Sumgait City Committee of the Party in Preventing the Tragic Events in the City."

The resolution adopted points out that the Sumgait city committee of the Party showed political shortsightedness and irresponsibility in organization of meeting the orders of the Central Committee of the CPSU and the directives contained in M. S. Gorbachev's appeal to the working people and peoples of Azerbaidzhan and Armenia. The bureau of the city party committee and its secretaries, and the city soviet executive committee underestimated the complex situation in the republic, and did

---

Komsomolets, 19 March 1988.
†*Komsomolets*, 19 March 1988.
‡*Bakinskii rabochii*, 19 March 1988.

not take concrete measures to increase vigilance and guarantee public order in the city, taking a waiting position, which led to tragic consequences.

At the end of February of this year a group of hooligans provoked disturbances in Sumgait. Unstable, immature people influenced by provocative rumors and inflammatory talk were drawn into illegal acts. Taking advantage of this unleashing of emotions, criminal elements committed acts of banditry which entailed human casualties, among whom were people of various nationalities. These tragic events gave rise to unhealthy rumors and inflicted enormous damage on the age-old friendship between the Azerbaidzhani and Armenian peoples.

The resolution stresses that the disturbances in Sumgait were the result of major miscalculations in the work of the Sumgait city committee of the Party for ideological-political and international education of the workers, especially of young people, and also the result of the unconcern and shortsightedness of the city administrators. In this complex situation a number of Party, government, and economic leaders, Party activists, and the city's Communists showed indecision and confusion, underestimating the full danger of the consequences of the events as they unfolded. Labor collectives were not mustered to cut short the disorders and people's militia patrols in fact did nothing. Unusual extraordinary measures were needed to restore and impose order in the city. The Procurator's Office is investigating the crimes and finding the ringleaders and rabble-rousers.

A great deal of the blame for the tragic events which occurred falls personally on Comrade D. M. Muslim-Zade, first secretary of Sumgait city committee of the Party. Despite repeated warning he did not fulfill instructions regarding his immediate return from leave and ignored the decision of the republic's Party activists about immediate organization of work to fulfill the demands of the Central Committee of the CPSU.

In the critical situation Comrade Muslim-Zade was unable to mobilize Party activists to fight to normalize the situation in the city, displayed unforgivable arrogance, and proved not to be up to the demands made on a political leader. Elements of a superficial approach to resolving essential questions, lack of self-control, ostentation, and a desire to draw heightened attention to himself had been apparent earlier in Comrade Muslim-Zade's actions and deeds. Believing his actions to be without error, he reacted incorrectly to critical comments.

The resolution stresses that the following people did not display the qualities required a Party member, in acting half-heartedly, without initiative and without the necessary persistence on principle in the complex situation: Comrades M. A. Bairamova and A. Kh. Samolazov, secretaries of the Sumgait city committee of the Party; Comrade T. Ia. Mamedov, chairman of the city soviet executive committee; and other members of the bureau of the city committee of the Party.[a] Having no information about the state of affairs in the localities and having a poor knowledge of people's mood they did not take timely measures to prevent the ripening events.

The departments of the Central Committee of the Communist Party of Azerbaidzhan did not have the necessary control over the workings of the Sumgait city committee of the Party.

The city Department of Internal Affairs department (Comrade Kh. Kh. Dzhafarov)[b] proved professionally unprepared to counteract disorderly elements. The unconcern and irresponsibility of many members of the city's law enforcement bodies about execution of their official duties did not permit forestalling the disturbances in time.

Thanks to the steps taken by the republic's organs the situation in the city is now resuming its normal channel, although tension is persisting. Labor collectives are working intensively and classes are being held in educational establishments.

The Bureau of the Central Committee of the Azerbaidzhan Communist Party has removed Comrade D. M. Muslim-Zade from his post as first secretary of the Sumgait city committee of the Party and expelled him from the CPSU for the political unconcern he displayed, the major shortcomings he allowed in organizational and political work and for his non-Party behavior, which led to the tragic consequences in Sumgait, and also for his incorrect conduct at the Central Committee Bureau and his self-justifying assessment of what occurred.

It has been decided that it is pointless to permit Comrade T. Ia. Mamedov, chairman of Sumgait city soviet executive committee, to remain in his post, and he has already been strictly reprimanded, with notation on his CPSU history card, for the serious shortcomings he permitted in organizing work to insure the proper order and discipline in the city, for the political shortsightedness he displayed, and for his failure to take timely measures to prevent the negative phenomena which resulted in the tragic consequences.

Comrade M.A. Baiamova, second secretary of Sumgait city committee of the Party, and Comrade A. Kh. Samolazov, secretary of the city committee of the Party, have been given strict reprimands and had their Party cards endorsed for their complacency, uncritical approach to the assessment of the situation in the city, and their failure to take effective and timely measures to curb the illegal actions.

Comrade Kh. Kh. Dzhafarov, then acting chief of the city Department of Internal Affairs, has been expelled from the CPSU for his irresponsible attitude toward guaranteeing public order in Sumgait, which led to the disturbances and disorders with tragic consequences.

The Central Committee of the Communist Party of Azerbaidzhan has ordered the bureau of the Sumgait city committee of the Party to consider the personal responsibility of other officials, Communists who did not insure implementation of measures to prevent the tragic events.

A commission headed by Comrade V. N. Konovalov,[c] second secretary of the Central Committee of the Communist Party of Azerbaidzhan, has been established to examine and study closely the causes and circumstances which made the disturbances in Sumgait possible. The results of its work will be examined by the Central Committee of the Communist Party of Azerbaidzhan.

The fact has been noted that the Procurator of the USSR, with participation by the republic Procurator is conducting an investigation into the events which took place and that a number of those involved have been arrested and are facing criminal responsibility.

The Central Committee of the Communist Party of Azerbaidzhan demanded that the republic's Ministry of Internal Affairs [MVD] (Comrade A. I. Mamedov) take immediate measures to strengthen the personnel of the Sumgait Internal Affairs Department and increase the militia workers' professional training. The Sumgait city committees of the Party and Komsomol have been ordered to send the best Communists and Komsomol members to fill out the ranks of militia workers.

Proceeding on the basis of the CPSU Central Committee's instructions and the tasks and directives put forward by M. S. Gorbachev, the Sumgait city committee of the Party and the primary Party organizations must implement specific measures for the radical improvement of the working people's international education and all ideological and mass political work, eliminating the serious shortcomings and oversights of this job. Departments of the Central Committee of the Communist Party of Azerbaidzhan are required to give the Sumgait city committee of the Party and the primary Party organizations the necessary help in strengthening ideological and political work among the population, especially among young people, educating working people in the revolutionary, battle, work, and international traditions of the Party and the people, mobilizing their efforts to speed up restructuring.

Particular attention must be paid to a high standard of inter-nationality relations and firm internationalist convictions in working people. Processes and tendencies in national relations must be profoundly analyzed, the situation realistically assessed, taking account of the specific features of the various categories and groups of the population. Constant concern must be shown to meet their consumer and cultural requirements, to resolve emergent problems in good time, and to note and reject firmly any departures from the Leninist principles of nationality policy. True democratism must be consistently asserted in practice and Soviet laws strictly observed.

The education of leading officials in the spirit of socialist internationalism and implacability toward any negative phenomena must be intensified. Party, government, trade union, and Komsomol activists must persistently master the habits of active and assertive propaganda and political discussion and make leaders strictly accountable for the state of the moral and psychological mood in labor collectives.

The Central Committee of the Azerbaidzhan Communist Party obligates the Sumgait city committee of the Party, primary Party organizations, and economic leaders to do all that is possible to step up work to normalize the situation in the city, reinforce order, organization, and discipline, and direct the labor collectives to make up lost production in the shortest time, to insure unfailing fulfillment of this year's plans and socialist obligations.

The Sumgait city committee of the Party, and Party, trade union, and Komsomol organizations, and education bodies must boost the efficiency of their work in teaching young people the spirit of fraternity and friendship of peoples, to provide graphic and convincing examples of the age-old friendship between the Azerbaidzhani and Armenian peoples, the peoples of the Soviet Transcaucasus, and all the peoples of our multinational Motherland, to mold class consciousness in young men and women, and devote more attention to their legal education. There must be regular meetings between leading Party and government officials, economic leaders, scientists, and representatives of the creative intelligentsia, Komsomol members and young people.

Regional, city, and district committees of the Party have been shown the necessity of directing all means of political and ideological influence at promulgating Leninist nationality policy and its essence at the modern stage. There must be no yielding to the provocations of irresponsible elements but rather reason, calm, and restraint, to restrain people's unhealthy emotions and impulses and to prevent thoughtless actions and violations of discipline and public order. Everything must be done to strengthen the great achievement of socialism, the fraternal friendship of the Soviet peoples. All this work should proceed, as the Central Committee of the CPSU points out, from the premise that the national question demands intense, constant attention to national specifics and psychology, taking account of the vital interest of the working people. It must be guaranteed that all Communists are consistent and sincere bearers of the ideas of the internationalism, friendship, and fraternity of peoples and active defenders of the rights and interests of all nations.

Editor's notes

a. Bairamova and Mamedov are Azerbaidzhani surnames; Samolazov is a Russian surname.

b. Dzhafarov is an Azerbaidzhani surname.

c. Konovalov, second secretary of the Communist Party of Azerbaidzhan is a Russian, and Bagirov, then Azerbaidzhan Party first secretary, is an Azerbaidzhani.

The Strikes in the Nagorno-Karabakh AO

Coverage in the Azerbaidzhan Press

The Economy of the Mountain Region *

As are other regions of the Azerbaidzhan SSR, the NKAO (Nagorno-Karabakh Autonomous Oblast) is developing dynamically. In many economic, cultural and spiritual spheres, it noticeably exceeds the republic average. This is the result of strenuous work by people in all spheres of the economy of the NKAO and of constant attention and assistance on the part of the Party, government, and economic organs of the republic.

As has already been reported, though, a tense situation has recently came about in the NKAO because of irresponsible and thoughtless acts of certain people demanding the transfer of Nagorno-Karabakh from the Azerbaidzhan SSR to the Armenian SSR. There are attempts to base these nonsensical demands upon the purported economic backwardness of the autonomous oblast. A correspondent of AZERINFORM asked the deputy chairman of the Azerbaidzhan SSR Council of Ministers and chairman of the Azerbaidzhan SSR Gosplan, A. N. Mutalibov, about the real economic situation in Nagorno-Karabakh, realization of tasks on the agenda during the second stage of restructuring, and intended long-range development.

"Nagorno-Karabakh," he said, "is a developed industrial and agrarian oblast which plays an important role in the economy of the entire republic." Development of economy in NKAO is insured by close collaboration and cooperation with other regions of Azerbaidzhan, from which Nagorno-Karabakh receives various types of equipment, metal products, construction materials, fuel and energy resources, raw materials, and other varied goods.

Industry takes a leading position in the oblast's economy. In the past 15 years volume of industrial production has risen more than three times. The food and light industries and machine building have developed with particular intensity, now accounting for more than 80 percent of industrial production. The accelerated tempos of development of the oblast's economy are assured thanks to substantial capital investments, the volume of which has more than tripled over the past three five-year plans, as compared to the previous three five-years plans. Growth of the volume of capital investment is also planned for the current five-year plan, too, and faster than for the republic as a whole, at that.

Prospects for the further development of industry in the oblast have also been defined. The economic plan includes completion of construction of a large farm equipment factory in Stepanakert and expansion of an electrical engineering plant.

Bakinskii rabochii, 23 February 1988.

As a result of Party decisions the creation of filials of industrial enterprises is also planned.

The plan adopted in Azerbaidzhan for allocation of productive forces through the year 2005 calls for further development of the basis for light industry and the agro-industrial complex base in the NKAO in the next five-year plan. It is proposed to remodel the silk spinning production at the Karshelkokombinat and to convert a number of wineries to the production of fruit juices, marinades, and preserves. Comprehensive socioeconomic development of the Shusha and Gadrut mountain areas is also planned.

Measures are also planned to further improve farming. However, it must be said, that even today, with adequately large harvests the level of state purchases in the NKAO does not exceed the average for Azerbaidzhan and for the majority of farm crops is considerably lower than the average.

With the opening of the Agdam-Stepanakert branch railroad the oblast has gotten a direct railroad link to the industrial centers of the republic. The Fevlakh–Stepanakert gas pipeline has made it possible to start comprehensive gasification of population centers in the NKAO. Development of the oblast's productive forces and its social infrastructure has permitted a significant part of the able-bodied population to be drawn into public production. According to data from sociological investigations, the percentage of labor resources not engaged in social production today is two times lower than the figure for the republic as a whole. The long-term republic-wide "Demography" program foresees achievement of full employment by the end of the five-year plan.

A broad program of social development is planned for the oblast. For the most rapid possible solution of the housing problem a shop for the building slabs for prefabricated houses is to be built in Stepanakert. Questions of equipping a Palace of Culture and a Young Pioneers' Center in the NKAO's capital, and a House of Culture in Askeran Raion will be decided. Construction of schools, preschool institutions, and hospitals will continue.

The implementation of such a large-scale program is on a firm base. Per capita services in the NKAO are above the average for the republic. There are more hospital beds, retail trade and public food establishments per 10,000 inhabitants in the oblast. The number of children at preschool institutions is higher than the average index for the republic, and there are more movie theaters, libraries, and other cultural facilities in the NKAO.

Affirmations of a supposedly inadequate supply of consumer goods to the workers of the autonomous oblast are absolutely without reality. For example, the structure of food usage in the NKAO is completely normal. For each inhabitant of Stepanakert, for instance, there is more than 12 kg. of oil a year. For comparison, I will cite other figures—in Baku the average is 13 kg., in Ali-Bairamly 10 kg., in Mingechaur 11.5 kg., in Sumgait 10.6 kg., and in Kirovabad 10.5 kg. Per capita consumption of milk and meat in Stepanakert is also second only to the republic's capital, Baku. Of course, it may not be said that there are no problems in the NKAO. But I must say that many of them would be solved quicker if the localities made greater efforts to assimilate the resources allocated and to realize plans already made. Unfortunately here there have been no noticeable improvements for a number of years. Commissioning of a number of important projects has dragged on. Last year the oblast failed to fulfill the plan for the production of potatoes and grapes. The level of livestock breeding is low. A great deal needs to be improved in the social sphere.

At the same time, additional measures are being taken to solve questions of the oblast's socioeconomic development and a special program is being elaborated. The working people of the NKAO, just as all workers in Azerbaidzhan, and the entire Soviet people, have every basis on which to look to the future with firm faith and optimism.

A Time for Reason and for Sober Decisions *

Yesterday our correspondent met with the First Secretary of the Nagorno-Karabakh Oblast Committee[a] of the Communist Party of Azerbaidzhan, Genrikh Andreevich Pogosian[b] and requested that he answer the editorial board's questions.

How have the communists and workers of the oblast received the Appeal of the General Secretary of the Central Committee of the CPSU, to the workers and peoples of Azerbaidzhan and Armenia?

With understanding and a sense of gratitude. M. S. Gorbachev's appeal is convincing evidence of very close attention, deep concern and sincere interest in resolving the social and economic problems which have arisen in the new stage of the development of NKAO. We wholly share the thought that the solution of these questions requires a balanced and democratic approach. The Appeal clearly indicates that overcoming the difficulties of growth requires new approaches and new orientations. In order to have these, there must be a calm and businesslike atmosphere in the oblast. The main thing, as M. S. Gorbachev said in his appeal, is to demonstrate civic maturity and restraint, to return to normal life.

The situation in Nagorno-Karabakh is normalizing.

The process of normalization in Nagorno-Karabakh is complex, and does not have the same meaning in all institutions. However, people are taking part in the labor process. A number of industrial enterprises are reaching their planned tempos. The kolkhozes and sovkhozes of NKAO are beginning to complete spring field work. The tempos are growing on the livestock breeding farms. As for transport and communal enterprises, all the services of life support were working normally before. The composition of Nagorno-Karabakh is multinational. Armenians and Azerbaidzhanis, Russians and Ukrainains, Georgians and Belorussians live side by side in the oblast. Of course, there are also unresolved problems in our life. It is a mistake though to think that inflating them will allow anyone to acquire some sort of capital. It is important today not to allow some people to play on this. Democracy can not be

_____
Bakinskii rabochii, 3 March 1988.

understood one-sidedly, by tearing rights away from duties. That would harm the social and economic development of society, and the friendship of peoples.

I would like to note that through the fault of the former leadership of the oblast committee of the Party artificial difficulties concerning cultural exchange, supplies of literature and schoolbooks in the native language, and other aspects of the multifaceted and traditional links between the workers of Nagorno-Karabakh and fraternal Armenia were created. These problems can and must be solved in the order of work.

What measures are being taken for the further normalization of conditions in the Nagorno-Karabakh Autonomous Oblast?

We understand that the main thing now is ideological, propagandistic, and explanatory work in the working collectives, the sovkhozes and kolkhozes, and in the schools. It is very important that every resident of the oblast recognize fully the extreme clarity and precision of the CPSU Central Committee's position, so that each person will find it the time for reason and sober decisions, so that the preeminent thing will be a sense of civic duty, responsibility for the unity and solidarity of our multinational state.

The industrial enterprises of NKAO are bound with close economic ties to many other enterprises of the country. Under conditions of financial accountability [*khozraschet*], every lost hour causes a loss not just for each working man of the autonomous oblast, but also for our partners in the various regions of the country. The oblast committee of the Party is certain that the difficulties will be overcome, that the Party, government, trade union, economic, and Komsomol organs will do all that is necessary to fully stabilize the economic and political life of the oblast, to meet the debts incurred and fulfill their contractual obligations.

The main role we assign to Party activists, the primary Party organizations, is not only to accomplish their social and productive tasks, but also to form a sober attitude to the current situation. The readiness of the Central Committee The main role we assign to Party activists, the primary Party organizations, is not only to accomplish their social and productive tasks, but also to form a sober attitude to the current situation. The readiness of the Central Committee of the CPSU to review the entire complex of social and economic problems in the development of NKAO is one more evidence of the wisdom of Leninist nationality policy. I can say with all definitude that everyone has come to understand that today the main thing, as M. S. Gorbachev's Appeal notes, is to concentrate on solving concrete economic and social tasks in the spirit of the policy of restructuring and renewal.

Correspondent G. Pogosov in Stepanakert

Editor's notes

a. The *oblast'* [regional] committee of the Party, know as the obkom, is in this case the Party body charged with the supervision of Nagorno-Karabakh.

b. Pogosian is an Armenian surname.

Working Rhythm *

Andronik Dzhalalian's duty is to supply a metal-stamping unit with metal. His powerful tractor-trailer has brought the Stepanakert electrotechnical factory about 70 tons of the steel they must have to make lamps.

This is more than Andronik usually brought, but it had to be so. After all, the enterprise was now in great debt to consumers, because no production had occurred in the last weeks, and this is of lamps of various types, amounting to almost a million rubles.

This lag of production is serious. Everyone knows that well. Today their work is going well. The cuttings that come from the warehouse to the sector are quickly worked and then sent to the presses. Metal cutters S. Oganesian, S. Guseinov, stamper A. Beglarian and their comrades are moving expertly.[a] People are hurrying. It is not easy to get into a normal rhythm, while to give the extra-plan production which is necessary now is many times more complex. After all the workers of the sector have decided to produce 500 more armature complexes for lights than the plan demands.

Hundreds of consumers in various parts of the country are waiting for the factory's production. More than a million lamps are produced every year. The demand for them is great, in industrial enterprises, in medical institutions, and, of course, in daily life. And suddenly there is a break; they have fallen behind the plan.

A way out is found. It is decided to set up a third shift, which will put engineers and administrators into working positions. Part of the unrealized production is intended to be finished during days off. The workers have announced firmly that the program for the quarter will be met.

*   *   *

Today or tomorrow the customary stove smoke will cease to blanket the high mountain village of Turshsu, in Shushinskii Raion of Nagorno-Karabakh. A blue torch will also be ignited in the central garden of the S. Shaumian[b] Kolkhoz.

The beginning of gasification of the autonomous oblast was laid in 1976, when work began to convert Stepanakert to supplies of natural fuel. Blue gas comes without interruption into Nagorno-Karabakh along the main gas line of Evlakh–Stepanakert–Nakhichevan. In telling about this, the supervisor of the zonal gas combine of Stepanakert of the State Gas Committee of the Republic, G. Movsesian told a correspondent of *Bakinskii rabochii* that the complete gasification of Stepanakert, Martuni, Shushi, and Askeran have been achieved. Now these labors have been turned to the kolkhozes and sovkhozes of the autonomous oblast. Four enterprises of Martuni and Askeran regions are preparing to convert to the blue fuel, and soon the gas flame will burn welcomingly in the houses of kolkhozniks of the livestock breeding farms. This work is being done by construction workers of the SMU–5 sector of Azerbaidzhan Gas Construction.

---

*Bakinskii rabochii, 4 March 1988.

Conversion of the entire oblast to natural fuel will permit the preservation of a great deal of forest and other sources of nonrenewable energy, and will give city-dwellers and villagers the opportunity to do without their accustomed tanks of liquified gas.

Stepanakert, 3 March (Azerinform)
Correspondent G. Pogosov

Editor's notes

a. Oganesian and Beglarian are Armenian surnames; Guseinov is an Azerbaidzhani surname.

b. S. Shaumian, an Armenian, was one of the leaders of Soviet Azerbaidzhan at the time of its formation. He was killed during the civil war.

The Strikes in the Nagorno-Karabakh AO

Coverage in Armenia

Statement of K. S. Demirchian, First Secretary of the Central Committee of the Communist Party of Armenia, on Armenian Television, 29 February 1988 *

Dear Comrades,

First of all I would like to tell you that the situation in the republic has already been normalized for three days; in all the enterprises and educational institutions the rythm of labor has been restored.

Unanimously endorsing the ''Appeal of the General Secretary of the CPSU Central Committee, Mikhail Sergeyevich Gorbachev, to the Workers and Peoples of Azerbaidzhan and Armenia, the workers of the republic expressed their readiness to make up for what was lost, and thus worked on Saturday and Sunday.

Now I would like to draw your attention to a matter that disturbs us. The situation that has come about here, in connection with events in Nagorno Karabakh, as you already probably know has caused concern among a segment of the Azerbaidzhani population.[a] Several Azerbaidzhani families have crossed the borders of the republic. This is due to various rumors that have spread through a number of raions, as well as the lack of attention to their needs and to the questions that were disturbing them. Of course, not many people left the republic. But, not matter; this fact, cannot but be echoed with pain in our hearts and does not leave us indifferent. Thanks to measures being taken, a number of these families are already returning home to their hearths.

Komsomolets, 1 March 1988.

However, the events around Karabakh, the noted migration of population, the spread of various rumors could not fail in its turn to have an effect on the situation in Azerbaidzhan, where, according to our information, there have been clashes. In particular, in Sumgait on 28 February, a group of hooligan elements provoked disorders. There were instances of pillaging and violence.

By now, the situation there is fully under control. Measures have been taken to normalize life in the city and to ensure discipline and social order. The investigative authorities are conducting an enquiry.

All this demands from us even greater attention to relations between Armenians and Azerbaidzhanis on the territory of our republic.

The Bureau of the Central Committee of the Communist Party of Armenia has examined this question and charged district and city committees [of the Party] and the executive committees of raion, city, and rural soviets, trade unions and Komsomol organizations, and their leaders personally, with carrying out all the necessary work in every town and raion, in every village, in enterprises, households, and families with the goal of preempting similar cases, to do all that is necessary so that the Azerbaidzhani population will have no basis for concern. In the course of explanatory work, to decisively squelch any rumors, providing more detailed, truthful, and practical information. It is necessary to bring to severest accountability those who display a careless and irresponsible attitude toward the demands of our people.

The most important task is to establish everywhere an atmosphere of friendship, mutual understanding, and genuine fraternity between Armenians and Azerbaidzhanis.

I want to remind you of the emotion and caring in the moving words of Mikhail Sergeyevich Gorbachev's: "No mother would consent to her children being threatened by national feuds instead of firm bonds of friendship, equality, mutual assistance, and the truly great acquisition of socialism. The traditions of friendship between the Azerbaidzhani and Armenian people, which have formed over the years of Soviet rule, must be cherished and in every way strengthened. Only this approach corresponds to the genuine interests of all the peoples of the USSR."

The friendship of nations is the greatest spiritual wealth of Soviet society, it is the basis of our country's might, and the guarantee of the flourishing of all our nations and peoples. It is the sacred duty of all of us to safeguard, to defend, and to strengthen it through practical deeds, and to develop its rich international traditions. We cannot forget that the friendship of peoples is also a practical task; the deep mutual respect, this and the caring for each other, as well as timely help in every small detail, all of which make up the life and existence of every person.

The brotherhood of the Armenian and Azerbaidzhani peoples comes from the depths of centuries. It has been put to the test more than once at the crossroads of history, but nothing has been able to spoil and shake it. I believe that in this hour of hour of testing of our brotherhood, I think that no one Armenian nor one Azerbaidzhani will not harm that brotherhood, not cast a shadow upon it.

We have lived side by side for ages, have labored side by side getting our daily bread, and we must live and work together in the future, shoulder to shoulder along the road to a new life, forging our own happiness by working together in the united Soviet family.

Editor's notes

a. Reference is to the Azerbaidzhani population of Armenia, of whom several hundred, especially those living in Erevan and its suburbs, fled their homes.

Speech by K. S. Demirchian, First Secretary of the Central Committee of the Communist Party of Armenia, on Armenian Television, 22 March 1988 *

Esteemed comrades!

The situation which has occurred in the republic in connection with the events in Nagorno-Karabakh has basically been normalized and life in the labor collectives has resumed its normal routine.

The "Appeal of M. S. Gorbachev, General Secretary of the Central Committee of the CPSU, To The Workers and Peoples of Azerbaidzhan and Armenia" played a decisive role in this.

The workers of our republic have responded in a businesslike way to this appeal; they displayed common sense, Soviet internationalism, and unshakable faith in the ideas of the Communist Party and socialism. They greeted the statement by the leader of our party that the complex issues of inter-national relations must be resolved calmly, solely within the limits of the democratic process and the law, without permitting the slightest damage to the internationalist cohesion of the Soviet peoples with great approval and understanding. We cannot give over very serious questions of the people's fate to rule by primordial forces and emotions.

Unfortunately, this is not understood by all. They have not thoroughly understood all the complexity of the situation and their responsibility for the people's fate in this difficult hour of trial. Moreover, you must be aware that some elements are still today organizing meetings which are of a character that is incompatible with our national interests and is antithetical to the ideas of socialism. It is also noticeable that a considerable number of people are unable to display civic maturity and the patience to overcome the existing situation. You know from press reports that a March 9 conference held at the Central Committee of the CPSU examined this issue in detail.

There has been very strong condemnation of the crimes committed on 28 February in the city of Sumgait. You already know that law-enforcement organs are continuing to carry out investigations with the goal of identifying the ringleaders and participants and punishing them with the full force of the law. The results of the investigation will be published in the press. The Central Committee of the Communist Party of Armenia, the Armenian Supreme Soviet, and the republic's government are deeply saddened that as result of unprecedented excesses, alien to the nationality relations of our peoples, citizens of various nationalities have perished. We once again express our deep condolences to their relatives and dear ones. By

Komsomolets, 24 March 1988.

decision of the republic's government, the families which have come from Sumgait are being given the necessary material and other assistance, and the appropriate measures are being taken to meet their requests.

You will also be aware that, following a decision by the CPSU Central Committee Politburo, the Central Committee Secretariat has been assigned the organization of a thorough, comprehensive study of the problems which have accumulated in Nagorno-Karabakh Autonomous Oblast and the reasons for the exacerbation of interethnic relations around it, to draft the relevant proposals, and, when they are ready, to submit them for the consideration of the CPSU Central Committee and the Soviet Government.

It has recommended that the Central Committee of the Communist Party of Azerbaidzhan and the Central Committee of the Communist Party of Armenia draft a package of long-term measures for improvement of the international education of the working people and jointly resolve current problems of the socioeconomic, consumer, scientific, cultural, linguistic, and other aspects of relations between our two republics, on the basis of the Leninist principles of internationalism.

Standing ever on internationalist positions, the Armenian people, who today are seeped in the ideas of the revolutionary transformations in our society, have suffered numerous ordeals on their path through history and have always been able to find strength within them to look the truth in the eye and seek the correct ways out of complex situations.

The present situation requires every one of us to show a great sense of civic responsibility, political foresight, determination, and restraint so that ill-considered acts or rallies may not create new difficulties about this problem.

Comrade M. S. Gorbachev urges us to appreciate that none of the questions of restructuring can be solved without taking account of their impact on national relations, that progress in restructuring demands the amicable, persistent, united work of all working people and representatives of all of the Soviet Union's nationalities.

At a meeting with foreign journalists in Belgrade on 16 March, touching on the events in and around Karabakh, Comrade M. S. Gorbachev announced that no one had raised the question of Soviet power, the question of leaving the Soviet state, or of socialism! People acknowledge the role of the Party and the policy it has implemented since Lenin time in the sphere of national relations.

This is a correct assessment of the peaceful demonstrations held in February.

It must be said that certain unhealthy attitudes had a negative effect on the course of events also, because not every element of our press and ideological service was on the necessary high level. The incorrect assessments of events given in some publications, inadequate information, and the absence of a principled appraisal of the situation evoked dissatisfaction in some people.

The Central Committee of the Communist Party of Armenia is taking the necessary measures to rectify the situation, in accordance with the demands of democratizing civic life.

However, the events of the past days show that irresponsible people who do not understand the whole political situation are by unlawful actions casting a shadow on the expression of our people's international will and are trying to channel events in an undesirable direction.

Esteemed comrades! The question of nationality relations is very complex and, at the same time, very delicate, and an ill-considered approach to its solution could only damage the invaluable achievements of the Soviet peoples, their fraternity and union. Genuinely national ideas are, without doubt, genuinely internationalist ideas. Internationalism does not conflict with national ideas but, on the contrary, conditions them. This is proven by the experience of our life over the last 70 years.

Each of us knows that no one yet has been able to make the right decisions in a nervous atmosphere, in conditions of excitement and passion. The meeting which some unwise people and some who have cast aside all restraint are proposing to hold 26 March will lead, without a doubt, to new stimulation of feelings and emotions and is ripe with unpredictable, possibly tragic consequences.

That is why each one of us individually and all of us together must once again decide to make today a day of reason and sober decisions. We must recognize the full responsibility of the moment and allow no one to cast a shadow on our talented, industrious people, a people with enormous moral and creative potential, a people reborn who, in the united family of Soviet peoples, have built a new Armenia, a flourishing country, which, to use the vivid description of William Saroyan,[a] is the best argument for Soviet power.

Do we have the right, the political, moral, or human right, to ignore the danger which exists, of losing in a moment the unstained reputation of our people, which has been built up over many centuries? No, we do not have that right. Future generations would not forgive us for this. History would not forgive us.

Our civic, patriotic, international duty is to do all we can to end the tension in the republic which has lasted about a month.

Today the Armenian Communist Party Central Committee appeals to you again, urging you at this difficult time to show good sense, wisdom, restraint, and political maturity, to refrain from any unhealthy emotions and impulses, to suppress any ill-considered actions, and decisively to rebuff any actions which incite people to disorder and other unlawful acts.

Appealing to the working people of city and town, to our workers and peasants, we urge them to remain at the height of their historical missions, to show a deep understanding of events, to allow no one to upset the normal rhythm of life and labor, and to behave like active warriors for the ideas of internationalism, friendship, and fraternity between the Armenian and Azerbaidzhani peoples and all Soviet peoples.

Appealing to the mothers of Armenia, to teachers, lecturers, and to everyone nurturing the younger generation, we urge them to protect their children and our young people against ill-considered actions, not to allow them to be drawn into outbursts of unhealthy emotions stirred up by irresponsible, dullwitted people whose actions, as I have already said, may have unpredictable, tragic consequences. Appealing to our cultural and scientific figures, we ask them to use their impassioned words and their authority to help calm agitated people and persuade them of the needlessness and, what is more, the harm of attempts to solve very complex problems by "demonstration." Masters of culture, you must now show the wisdom problems by ''demonstration.'' Masters of culture, you must now show the wisdom and fearlessness of Tumanian[b] for the sake of calm and for the sake of strengthening the centuries-old fraternity of our peoples.

Appealing to party organizations and all of the republic's Communists, we urge them to consider themselves mobilized now, to consider it their primary duty to rebuff firmly all those whose actions are clearly becoming anti-national, not to let these people stirring up the masses. Communists bring the people, along behind them, must direct their efforts to solving the tasks facing the republic, must fight to strengthen the internationalist traditions of the Armenian Communist Party.

It is a matter of honor for Communists to take every measure to strengthen calm and a normal situation in the republic.

Our glorious working class, kolkhoz peasantry, remarkable intelligentsia, and fine young people will allow no one to encroach on the achievements of Soviet power, achievements won on the barricades of the Great October Revolution, in the cruel fighting of the Great Patriotic War, and in socialist and communist construction.

Editor's notes

    a. The American-born writer of Armenian descent.
    b. Ovanes Tumanian was an Armenian writer and nationalist who lived at the turn of the century.

The Strikes in the Nagorno-Karabakh AO

Coverage in Moscow

How Do Our Countrymen Live? *
More Democracy–More Socialism

RACHIIA KAPLANIAN

The events in Nagorno-Karabakh and the large demonstrations in Erevan disturbed me to the depths of my soul.

I am not a historian and would not want to go into the substance of the question here, but it lies in the area of national relations. It has long been thought that the nationalities question in our country was well resolved and people preferred to discuss it more in congratulatory tones, in the style of a toastmaster. What happened, however, showed that we have inherited a number of unsolved questions, including national ones. This was mentioned by M. S. Gorbachev in his ''Appeal to the working people of Azerbaidzhan and Armenia.'' One of the future plenums of the CPSU Central Committee will also be devoted to these problems.

It is another matter that we so neglected this illness which was contracted back in the dramatic 1930s and which with the years is never difficult to cure. Our theater is currently preparing a play based on A. Rybakov's novel *Children of the Arbat*.

Sovetskaia kul'tura, 17 March 1988. Russian text © 1988 by ''Sovetskaia kul'tura.''

People ask me, as director: "Why not take the Armenian theme?" But was the personality cult really a problem of only one national group? After all, all of us, Armenians, Russians, and other nationalities, suffered from arbitrary decisions and voluntarism. To stage the play you need to know the era apart from the novel. And when I study documents connected with those times I often have just a single thought, Please God, our children shouldn't experience anything like that. . . . Yes, it was in those years that a bureaucratic approach to solving the nationalities question was born, and the pompous image of the "elder brother"[a] who looked after everyone else migrated from book to book, from theater to theater, when responsibility for our relations—as we now understand perfectly well—must be shared equally. In a real friendship everyone is equal. And we do not choose our friends on the basis of national traits. For example, I think that every people has scoundrels and bad men, but there are also remarkable people, of whom of course, there are many more.

We got used to talking and writing about this theme only in rosy terms. Unsolved problems and oversights were often driven deep underground, with no way of

knowing where or how they would surface again. Restructuring disturbed all these deep-lying processes and caused an increase in national self-awareness. It became clear, that the feelings of peoples cannot be ignored, or even more so exploited, for their subtle structure is very easily damaged. International awareness must be taught carefully, tactfully, step by step, to form a culture of international relations which we still lack acutely.

Teach and form, only how? This, clearly, is the whole nub of things. I must admit that I was astonished at the way events in Nagorno-Karabakh were covered. Stereotyped responses, as if cut to a standard, in which author after author gave assurances of friendship for the brother people. But was that friendship which dates back centuries, ever in doubt?!

Under one such comment I suddenly discovered my own name. Who dared to disgrace me like that? Furious, I telephoned ARMENPRESS[b] and tried to find out who was the pirate who had done it. They told me over the telephone that they apologized and asked me not to make a scandal, "otherwise we'll lose our job." Then, as if to console me they told me a sad story. It turns out that I was not the only one to suffered like that. One of the news agency staff even had his engagement broken off because he put his girlfriend's name to such an article. . . .

I must be honest, that with all the respect that I have for the mass media, which sometimes work so selflessly "for *glasnost'*," I feel sorry for scum like that. Their soulless repetition of obvious truths and old pre-restructuring slogans brings to nothing all of the Party's enormous work to shape new thinking. After all, if it comes to that, I could say far more, myself about real friendship and better too, I hope.

About a year and a half ago I got sick, and then had a bad seizure. . . Within an hour Mikhail Ul'ianov was in my house (he was vacationing at the time in Dilizhan), and it was immediately decided to move me to Moscow. You would have to know the energy of our famous, beloved actor; that same day he flew to the capital, and when I arrived afterwards, Mikhail met me at the gate. Not trusting anyone, he took me to the hospital himself, to see the best surgeon.

At it turned out, they were right to hurry. "A perforation like death," the doctors later explained to me. But this was not the end of the trouble I caused. For almost two months I ate nothing, lying under an IV, and a second operation was necessary. And through it all, and believe me this isn't just a turn of phrase, I felt my friend alongside. There was a crisis, and only the actor's face told me that my business was in a bad way . . .

I owe thanks to the doctor, Academician Nikolai Malinovskii, who did something that I consider impossible. But I was also helped by my friends. I could name Kirill Lavrov and Georgii Lordkipanidze, and the staff of the Hotel Budapest in Moscow, who took charge of me after the hospital, scores of good people. . . They were my "medicine," that hard-to-find good, and charity, participation, and mutual assistance which unite all of us, people of different nationalities, into the Soviet people. Without these we are simply tribes. I speak this way because it seems to me I have the right. I was still in the hospital, while in the republic they were already debating who would replace me. . .

When demonstrators appeared on the square in front of the opera house I heard people saying, that's what democracy leads to. . . . Well, of course, it is far easier to blame democracy, but it is bureaucracy in national relations which has led to this, not democracy. After all the Karabakh problem did not tumble on our heads from the sky; the Party and government bodies were well aware of it. So what did they do to calm people?

Alas, the Party workers got moving too late. Some of them, true, tried the conventional method in such cases, to forbid, but that was no use. Now they prefer to blame the central press, saying that recent press criticism of Armenia has undermined the authority of some leading workers. Perhaps they have simply forgotten how to talk to people as human beings? Perhaps they never knew?

I say this not just to be saying it, and of course not trying to put everyone into the same box. The raion Party committee phoned recently, the caller was embarrassed, confused, asking, many collectives have set up Karabakh committees; what would you advise us to do? What advice is there to give? You have to go to where the committees are set up, know people's feelings, know how to convince them, in short, convey to people the great truth of our socialist communal life. Otherwise it is possible that there won't be democratization that restructuring has raised.

It is clear today that the people are ready to listen to wise words, the voice of reason, and balanced, sober decisions. They even ask us, cultural figures and writers to answer, to explain what is going on. We all live in one home, one family. And no matter what part of that home, what room we are in, we are constantly feel each other's presence. But this is still our common home and we have to be tactful and considerate, we have to observe the rules of communal life; we need to know how to control our own emotions. When families quarrel, life can sometimes become intolerable. But what have we done to end the quarrels, to strengthen the family of fraternal peoples?

We are used to writing hackneyed phrases: "The cultural ties between the union republics develop every year.'' But in fact, as we know, things are not like that. It is these very cultural ties which have noticeably weakened recently of late: cultural weeks and exchange visits by cultural and art figures have disappeared. Increasingly often, scientific and literary publications carry debates which do not seek scientific truth but, on the contrary, distort history.

I have in mind the national arrogance of some ''scientists'' who, in a frenzy of local patriotism, either exaggerate the antiquity of their people or crown them with fabulous exploits as though there are not enough real ones of which to be truly proud.

Not long ago we marked the glorious jubilee of the October Revolution. The very best occasion for interesting theater shows and profound journalistic reflections on the great achievement of socialism, which is the friendship of peoples. But somehow I cannot remember that any popular and respected newspaper described revolutionary brotherhood and the battling internationalism of the remarkable sons of the Russian, Azerbaidzhani, Georgian, and Armenian peoples—the 26 Baku Commissars!ᶜ

Such omissions cost dear.

About two years ago I chanced on an announcement in a local newspaper on the adoption of a joint resolution by the Central Committees of the Communist Parties of Armenia, Azerbaidzhan, and Georgia ''On Measures For the Further Development of International Ties Among the Working People of the Fraternal Republics of the Transcaucasus.'' What kind of document was this? What specific measures were indicated to develop ties between the nationalities in the Transcaucasus region? And, finally, by what forms and methods of ideological work are they to be implemented? Not a word about this. Had it been adopted for show? Or take another announcement, that in Idzhevan, a raion center, a University of the Friendship of the Peoples had opened, where scientists from the three fraternal republics delivered lectures on internationalism. And that was that? Their work was done?

Everyone knows that the great majority of the population of Nagorno-Karabakh is Armenian. How are my fellow countrymen living? How is this region developing? I would like to find regular selections of materials on this theme in the newspapers which ARMENPRESS and AZERINFORM could exchange and offer to their mass media. After all, there are also many Azerbaidzhanis living in my republic.

Here is another strange fact from this same sphere of ideological omissions, that the inhabitants of Georgia, Azerbaidzhan, and Armenia are unable to watch television broadcasts from the neighboring republics. Can it be all that difficult to arrange? After all, they can watch shows from Turkey and even Iran! But how a brother people lives and breathes, that we don't know. . . . Let's say that it's been over 10 years now that our opera has not demonstrated its art on the Moscow stage. It is also a long time since the Sundukian Drama Theater toured in the capital. Does one have to spell out how dangerous it is for creativity to retreat into a national shell?

When I put on a play in the union republics, and there have been many, in Moscow, in Tbilisi, Baku, Kishinev, I always try somehow to help the theater and the troupe to expose the possibilities of the actors, the traits of the national character. And if I hear anywhere, either of a single person or of a whole people, that they are "nationality-limited," I can't imagine or understand who measures these limits in our multinational country, and using what measure? Is there really a limit to perfection, to uniqueness?

Famous actors have asked me, an Armenian, to work in the truly Russian Malyi Theater. I will never forget how, after the premier of the play "Much Ado About Nothing" at the Pushkin Theater of Moldavia, the artists took me to the airport not having had time even to take off their costumes, or the make-up from their sad, agitated faces. . . .

From these sorts of artistic contacts friendship can only grow stronger, knowing no bounds. For example many theaters want to stage plays I put on and bring them to Erevan for the traditional Shakespeare festival.

At the CPSU Central Committee February Plenum, M. S. Gorbachev said: "The unique feature of our culture is its multinational nature. We speak about it often and matter of factly, but I think that we have not yet learned how to value it. . . . We must do everything we can to promote the further expansion of contacts between national cultures, their mutual enrichment, and their development and flowering."

Yes, we have become accustomed to applause when speaking about friendship of the fraternal peoples. But it is necessary to argue and prove, to teach and learn democracy. It is necessary to know how to judge that line beyond which the national develops into the nationalistic, the line beyond which man begins to think about his exclusive position among others like himself.

Democracy presupposes the power of authority. But when you see presumptuousness, arrogance, and haughtiness in some leaders with no sharp mind or profound knowledge to back it up, sad thoughts came to mind. We underestimated the possibility of rapid mimicry of the attitudes of beys, princes, and boyars, but they proved alive in some people and are now bearing fruit.

And when, in an attempt to hold on to his easy chair, some functionary for the arts spreads a bitter and clumsy rumor that distortions in national relations are possible because of democracy and *glasnost'*, you want to respond immediately. If there were true *glasnost'* there would be no place for the rumors which have such fertile conditions now.

"They gave us a chance to speak and we began to shout. . . ," one actor joked during a discussion on the democratization of society. Even a joke has a lot of truth. We often see democracy, the basis of all future changes, in a one-sided way, as it benefits ourselves. But we ought to think about others. We ought to listen to other people's opinions, but we have become use to respecting our own more.

And here in the Sundukian Theater where the experiment is going on, here and there voices are raised, in which impatience may be heard, that there are no results to be felt . . . Let's redo the repetoire, use the actors . . . But where are we to find the plays that will let every actor have a role? I am advised to "rid myself of the ballast" as quickly as possible. But these are first of all people for me, with whom I have worked together long years, and no vote would make me turn them out into the street . . . I am criticized of course, that I am too kind, that you can't administer like that . . . Since when did this kindness, a humane attitude to people suddenly become a grounds for criticism? In my opinion, whatever we may lack most acutely, it is humanity, at work and in politics and in relationships with people of other nationalities.

When I served in the army, I was astonished by this detail, that when I encountered strangers they greeted me politely. I remembered my native Stepananvan in the mountains—where Pushkin had once met the body of Griboedov[d]. It was the same in the village of Ger-Ger, where I was born. People said "Hello" to strangers. Human, personable ways are good everywhere, among Russians, among Armenians, and among other peoples.

They say that you can't choose your father. Recalling my own life, I nevertheless think that there are exceptions. In 1941 my father went to the front. At the time I was an under-aged 17. And at the entire Young People's Theater, where there were mostly girls and the entire repertoire depended on me, I could not act calmly. I wrote a note to my mother saying that I wanted to see my father. Soon I was in the Tbilisi Cavalry School and then, six months later, in the front lines. I didn't fight for long. I sent a letter to mam from the hospital in Tuaps. And suddenly I got a letter back that said I had the same postal box as my father, but just in a different wing. It turned out that we had lain side by side for two weeks, but I still wasn't able to see my father. Mkrtych Kaplanian died in the Battle of Kerch.

Then after the war, a number of years after, another person showed up, to announce that he was my natural father. Only I couldn't feel him as natural; the stepfather who had died in the war was closer to me. However, life is full of surprises. Thanks to the father who showed up too late, I discovered my brother Leonid Engibarov and I am boundlessly happy that I was friends with this talented artist.

Why do I say all this? I remember that in the war no one asked our nationality. Trouble joined us all into one family, and we were like real brothers. Our relations were supported by trust and deep, sincere sympathy for each other. We didn't talk about friendship; it was like bread or air, together with us. That state when a brother is strong because of his brother. Perhaps that was why we were able to withstand in heavy testing.

All of our glorious history serves as a guarantee that we shall find worthy answers to the questions disturbing my people. We must think more often of the past, in order not to repeat the mistakes in the future.

Editor's notes

a. The practice of joint nationality policy often asserted the Russians as beneficent "elder brothers."

b. ARMENPRESS is the official news agency of Soviet Armenia; AZERINFORM is its counterpart in Azerbaidzhan.

c. The 26 Baku Commissars were Bolshevik officials killed in a British siege during the civil war.

d. In 1928, when Pushkin traveled to Erzrum, then in Russia. On his way he met the cortege bringing the body of Griboedov, poet, playwright, and ambassador, which was being transported from Teheran where he had been killed in a riot.

Emotions and Reason *
On the Events in and around Nagorno-Karabakh

Right now, when heart and mind are still oppressed by the events which have riveted the entire country's attention on Azerbaidzhan and Armenia, it is difficult to fully comprehend what happened. However every hasty or unconsidered word can gener- ate—as has occurred—a new outburst of emotions, passions,or even crimes. But remaining silent is impossible; a herd of incredible rumors rampant primarily at the behest of Western "radio voices,"ª whose information is supplied by people with an interest in inflaming passions, can also lead to serious consequences.

So, just what is going on in and around Nagorno-Karabakh?

On February 20 an event without precedent in our country for the practice of international relations occurred. A majority of votes by the deputies of the oblast soviet of Azerbaijan's Nagorno-Karabakh Autonomous Oblast [NKAO] have adopt- ed an appeal which requests the Supreme Soviets of the Azerbaidzhan and Armenian SSR's to transfer the NKAO from Azerbaidzhan to Armenia, and the USSR Su- preme Soviet to examine this question.

What, it would seem, is bad or strange in this? The time would seem to be past when there can be only one opinion on any issue. And if other opinions have emerged, why not examine them and test them in frank discussion? Prove to people that in the given instance petty local interests have prevailed over state interests?

The Nagorno-Karabakh problem is not as simple as it may appear at first glance, and its roots go back many centuries. Control of the region's territory may be the most complex in the history of international relations among the Transcaucasian peoples. In the past control led to many tragic conflicts exacerbated by religious differences. In 1918–20 alone, just before the establishment of Soviet power in Azerbaidzhan and Armenia, almost one-fifth of the inhabitants of Karabakh were destroyed in a fratricidal war unleashed by members of the *Musavat*ᵇ and the *Dashnaks.*ᶜ

The question of control of the region's territory was also resolved contradictorily during the first years of Soviet power. It is enough to say that the NKAO was formed as part of the Azerbaidzhan SSR only in July 1923. That would seem to end the matter.

However, the Nagorno-Karabakh problem surfaced again many times in the future, as a rule, when Armenian leaders found it advantageous to distract the public's attention from the mass of unresolved economic and social issues and from the Party organization's unfitting working style and methods. Proposals were made then too, to transfer the autonomous oblast to the Armenian SSR, because it was claimed, the region's population is mainly Armenian and the farming conditions are similar to conditions in Armenia's mountain regions. In turn the Azerbai- dzhani leadership would make counter proposals, that the administrative borders of the Armenian SSR, as well as of Georgia and Dagestan be changed, based on the national composition of the population of a number of regions in those republics.

Experts from both republics joined in the argument. They "dove" into the depths

---

*Pravda, 21 March 1988.

of the ages, seeking to discover which of the peoples originally owned the land. Unfortunately, the scientific arguments were not marked by specifics or objectivity, and no clarification was brought to the issue; rather they further confused it. Even today, if Azerbaidzhani and Armenian historians sit down to a discussion, each side will have diametrically opposed explanations for one and the same fact. Still these people have masters' degrees and doctorates and are academicians, and quotations from their contradictory works are brandished like swords in the two republics.

In the heat of argument, which only alienates the people, one from another, principles of Leninist nationalities policy are betrayed. The point of forming the Union of Soviet Socialist Republics was precisely to put an end to national strife and attempts by one people to prove its superiority over another, by carefully preserving the language, culture, and traditions of each people and ethnic group. And when the question of the territorial affiliation of Nagorno-Karabakh was being determined, the Communists of the Russian Communist Party (Bolsheviks) Caucasian Bureau consided the point as uppermost, in which republic could the region develop most rapidly, economically and socially, so that people's lives would improve. These conditions were preferable in Azerbaidzhan, with its industrial and multinational complex. It was this which determined the choice. It was not a question of which republic to live in, but of how to live. And in order to prevent any offense to the national sentiments of the main population, Armenians, the oblast was offered autonomous status.

Unfortunately, when the style and methods of the personality cult period were condemned, for some reason the question of the further development of Leninist traditions of nationalities policy was passed by in shame. During the years of stagnation people tried not to approach the question from any angle. Thus, many of society's ills were submerged and carefully hidden. It was somehow forgotten that our union is historically young while the roots of persisting nationalism are hidden deep in the centuries, and, whether we wish it or not, they can grow up again under certain conditions. Thus every new generation needs the most serious education in a culture of national feelings, which harvested gives rise to international consciousness. In the Orient people say that blind reason is worse than blind eyes. While teaching a culture of national feelings was left to drift, shoots of a feeling of national egoism appeared. It was this feeling that ultimately brought thousands and thousands of people out onto the streets and squares of Armenia. But let's think, where and to what were they going? Into national isolation and exclusivity.

Over the last few decades the NKAO has become bound to the Republic of Azerbaidzhan in thousands of ways. So should these links be broken, should a working mechanism be broken? But that would have a negative effect on the socio-economic position not only of Nagorno-Karabakh and Azerbaidzhan, but of the whole country. And what if using the analogy other regions start satisfying their own interests at the expense of those of other peoples? What then would become of the union of fraternal peoples and the country's economy? Finally, what would be done with the non-Armenian inhabitants of Nagorno-Karabakh, what about their concerns and needs? Despise them?

Did those in Erevan's Theater Square who welcomed every speaker demanding that the NKAO be made part of Armenia ask themselves these questions? Unlikely.

Because, had they thought about these difficult questions, to which there is not clear answer, they would have understood that passions and sentiments are unnecessary here. Because, as M.S. Gorbachev said in his appeal to the workers and peoples of Azerbaidzhan and Armenia, the complex problems of international relations can only be resolved within the framework of the democratic process and legality, not permitting even the slightest damage to the international cohesion of the Soviet peoples and without leaving extremely important questions of the fate of the people to whatever random whims and emotions. This does not mean that the Party is avoiding serious problems. On the contrary, restructuring, like any revolutionary situation is, revealing such problems, and sometimes precisely because of the development of democratic initiatives and *glasnost'* brings them to the point where, as doctors say, intensive treatment results in an improvement in the condition. Thus it is now planned to hold a plenum of the Central Committee of the CPSU on the nationalities question, where it will be examined comprehensively and integratively. Incidentally, this was announced at the CPSU Central Committee's February Plenum, on many days before the events in and around Nagorno-Karabakh.

However, to judge by events, it is precisely this sober and businesslike approach to the problem which some people do not like. It is as thought they replace the true, consistent democratization of society by the democracy of the rally or the street, where emotions and passions take pride of place. This is the source of attempts to pressure the state leadership with mass rallies, demonstrations, and strikes. On some days up to 60 enterprises in Armenia were not working, while in the NKAO labor activity was virtually paralyzed.

The people who took to the streets and squares of Erevan came from various parts of the republic and were well organized and disciplined. The long planned and carefully prepared organization of "popular disturbances" played a role here. At enterprises, institutions, and schools there "suddenly" appeared leaders who knew in advance where to lead people, and what slogans to chant. What is more, if someone refused to go to rallies they were publicly shamed, called virtually traitors to the nation, and forced to go to the demonstrations.

There was an efficient system for supplying water, drinks, and food to people as they stood there for many hours. It "suddenly" emerged that there was a substantial fund of money. Speakers who by the level of their preparation were far from knowledgable about science and history "suddenly" astounded everyone with a surprising torrent of quotations, economic statistics, and digressions into the ancient past. This all sounded convincing, even if the authenticity of what was being said was highly questionable. In any event, when we talked with some of the speakers they found it hard to name the book or scientific work from which they had taken their quotations and figures. The impression was that they were only speaking with the words of others.

Incidentally, today it is already well known that all the speeches in Armenia and the NKAO were organized by people who had been insisting on the autonomous oblast's joining the Armenian SSR for many years already. And that they had recently joined the so-called "Karabakh" committee and had been working for its official recognition.

We were able to attend a session of that committee, where its action program was approved. We think that if everything which was said that day in the Writers' House, whose auditorium was obligingly placed at the complete disposal of the committee members, had been repeated on Theater Square there would have been uninterrupted ovations. For example, there were demands to dismiss enterprise and Party organization leaders and elect new ones, to recall people's deputies, to expel them all from the Party if they obstructed the creation of the founding committees of "Karabakh." But what are these for?

We received no clear answer to that question. Claims that the committees should struggle for the socioeconomic development of the NKAO and the improvement of the population's well-being were rejected at the session itself. For instance, when he began to itemize points of a program for Nagorno-Karabakh's socioeconomic development the speaker was firmly interrupted: "If the Azerbaidzhan leadership fulfills these demands, Armenia will never see Nagorno-Karabakh."

So. Thus the committee is not concerned with the needs of the Armenian population of Nagorno-Karabakh at all. However its anthem includes such unambiguous lines as "Karabakh today needs living idols," and "we shall defy death and the fear of prison to save our Karabakh." In other words, there is a need for idols which people must blindly obey and follow even to the brink, and possibly into lawlessness, or why else have "death and the fear of prison" here? The impression is that actions of the members of the newly formed committee are directly prompted, whether they wish it or not, by those transatlantic Sovietologists who announce that socialism in the USSR can only be defeated by tearing it down into national compartments.

This method, incidentally, is not new. Back in 1905 and again in 1918 and 1920 the forces of reaction fanned inter-communal conflict between Armenians and Azerbaidzhanis so as to beat down the revolutionary fervor of the proletariat in the two republics. Restructuring is in progress in the country now, a process which is revolutionary in its essence, and so to weaken it some people are again artificially fueling national discord, but this time under the cloak of democratization and glasnost'. Thus, as we can see, the "noble" idea of "reunification" has an obvious antisocialist overtone.

"The events concerning Nagorno-Karabakh," G. Kocharian,[d] an assembly worker at the "Elektron" association, believes, "resulted from shortcomings in ideological work and in international education, above all among the younger generation." If all representatives of the intelligentsia in the two republics thought that way, then passions would probably not have boiled up as they did, neither in Stepanakert nor in Erevan, not in Baku, nor Sumgait. In recent years the Central Committee of the CPSU has repeatedly drawn the attention of Party and soviet leaders in Azerbaidzhan and Armenia to serious shortcomings in forming a class approach to social phenomena in working people and to their education in the spirit of Soviet patriotism and socialist internationalism. But so far there have been no noticeable changes. Both regions still lack a self-critical approach to analysis of the situation in the ideological and moral sphere, lack political acuteness in the evaluation of negative phenomena, and the proper exactitude. Restructuring of ideological work is slowed by the atmosphere of complacency and conciliatoriness. Many shortcomings and omissions in ideological and educational work have not been overcome for many years. Party committees and many economic bodies have not thoroughly recognized the vital need to work in a new way in conditions of *glasnost'*, an open exchange of opinions, and criticism and self-criticism.

This was already discussed at the extraordinary plenum of the Central Committee of the Armenian Communist Party. The Communists critically assessed actions by the Bureau of the Central Committee of the republic Party, discussing its loss of contact with the masses, its indecisiveness, the unseemly practice of hushing up negative phenomena in Armenia, and attempts to whitewash problems between nationalities, all of which, taken altogether, led to a loss of faith among the masses.

Participants in the plenum also spoke about reasons why the explanatory work carried out in labor collectives and among students came to naught. The main one was that the agitation personnel and the Party activists were not armed with knowledge about the question under discussion. Thus generalized appeals calling for calm and patience resounded at enterprises, but no constructive solutions were proposed.

The Azerbaidzhan Party organization, particularly its leadership, also deserves severe criticism. After all, it was not just the desire for territorial affiliation to Armenia which brought tens of thousands of Armenians out onto the streets of Stepanakert. They were brought out primarily by dissatisfaction with shortcomings in the socioeconomic development of NKAO and the encroachment on national and other rights.

There is no argument that the NKAO has achieved a good deal economically as part of the Azerbaidzhan SSR during the years of Soviet power. Of course, not all questions of economic and social life have been resolved here as quickly as might be wished. Unfortunately, when the April wind of change blew, it hardly touched Nagorno-Karabakh. We were given facts showing that even now, just as in the years of stagnation, local initiative is hobbled by Azerbaidzhan's administrative bodies, that per capita capital investment is lower in the NKAO than in other regions of the republic, that in Baku the study of the history of Armenia's people had been abolished in Armenian schools by arbitrary orders from above, and that it was even necessary to get permission for a program of cultural links with Armenia in republic departments.

These questions exist. And it would seem not just in Nagorno-Karabakh. Unfortunately, the laws for each autonomous oblast, adopted ten years ago, are far from being in full force and are sometimes even ignored by republic authorities. This only shows once again that the problem needs to be resolved comprehensively, for the whole country. And such work has now started, on the threshold of the plenum of the Central Committee of the CPSU on nationality problems. The Politburo has instructed the Secretariat of the Central Committee of the CPSU to organize an in-depth and comprehensive study of the accumulated problems of the NKAO and reasons for the exacerbation of national relations around it, to elaborate appropriate proposals. B. Kevorkov, first secretary of the Nagorno-Karabakh Oblast Party Committee, who in a great deal was to blame for the negative phenomena that accumulated in the NKAO and which people are talking about today with such pain, has already been dismissed.

But let us return to events in and around Karabakh. Though at first not exceeding the bounds of democratic processes in the country, they quickly grew into nationalist phenonema. As we have already noted, the Party organizations' distance from the masses and the leaders' inability to conduct a sincere conversation with people made themselves felt. And this vacuum was instantly exploited by people attempting to make themselves "leaders" and "chiefs" of their nations, to disguise their own ambitious desires as a purported display of the people's will. They goaded their audiences with demagogic half-truths, they played free with history, they disseminated absurd rumors, and using irresponsible statements they showered sparks of national dissension. Could they imagine what all this might lead to?

Meanwhile the situation continued to get more serious. The first outburst occurred in Azerbaidzhan's Agdam District, next door to NKAO. Nationalistically inclined elements were able to herd together a crowd and lead it into the NKAO's Askeran District "to impose order." As a result of the ensuing clashes two people were killed and many injured people were hospitalized. If not for the decisive actions of the militia and sensible citizens, there could have been many more casualties.

The events in Sumgait were more terrible. Exploiting the explosive situation in order to loot, criminal elements forced their way into some apartments where Armenians were living. Lawlessness, violence, and the humiliation of people went to extremes in this multinational city. Not only Armenians suffered but also people of other nationalities as well. Most of those to blame for the disorders, in which 32 people died and over a hundred were injured, have been arrested. To this must be added that a great deal of damage was inflicted on the economy of the autonomous oblast, Azerbaidzhan and Armenia, and the country as a whole. After all, no matter which union republic, autonomous republic, or oblast you take, it constitutes an inalienable link in the integrated national economic and political complex which has formed in the years of Soviet power. Moral and political harm was also caused to the people in the fraternal republics.

Yet there is no doubt that the events which occurred will not shake the friendship of the Azerbaidzhani and Armenian peoples. It is stronger and firmer than any manifestations of nationalist egoism. This friendship has been tested by time.

In Shamshadin Rayon one of us managed to talk with A. Dzhagarian, a veteran of the revolution. He had set up a communist cell there and fought as a partisan in the mountains. The hospitality of Museib Aliev, a Bolshevik in the Azerbaidzhani settlement of Tavuz, was particularly strong in his memory.[e] When Musavitists cut the road, the Azerbaidzhani communists answered his appeal for help and supplied the beseiged Armenians with kerosene, bread, and grain. . . .

That was in the 1920s. In the 1970s a monument was erected here in honor of communards M. Aliev, M. Mamedov, S. Shakibekov, and others. Beneath the Azerbaidzhani names of the communards the chisel of an Armenian craftsman has cut the wise words: "You do not shoot people who offer hospitality!" The incomparable Saiat-Nova[f] sang of the same theme in the three Transcaucasian languages: "Do not spurn hospitality but stay faithful to your oath. . . ."

Sayat-Nova sang of the oath of friendship among peoples. This legacy of his was remembered by both Azerbaidzhanis and Armenians during the most ponderous events surrounding Nagorno-Karabakh. Such as the many Azerbaidzhani residents of Sumgait who even facing threats to their own lives, showed themselves to be genuine internationalists. They selflessly rescued Armenian families—their comrades at work, their neighbors, their relatives. They sheltered them from the raging mob in their own apartments, homes, and places of work.

"There would have been more casualties," General V. Kraiev said, "if we had not been helped by residents. For example one bus driver, an Azerbaidzhani, immediately took dozens of Armenians to the city of Sheki, his own home town. Another Azerbaidzhani family prevented some hooligans from entering a multistory apartment building. A worker was traveling on a bus with his Armenian friend. The bus was suddenly stopped by a group of people who demanded that he be handed over. The Azerbaidzhani himself sustained injuries, but he saved his friend."

Many Azerbaidzhani internationalists acted in this way. In the city legends are already forming about an elderly woman who fearlessly disregarded danger to intercept some young hooligan thugs and stopped them.

But there were also those who in the hour of trouble did not extend the hand of help to their compatriots. Shame on them. . . .

Recently a session of the Bureau of the Central Committee of the Communist Party of Azerbaidzhan considered questions of responsibility of Party, government, and administrative bodies for the mass disturbances and the disorders which occurred in Sumgait on 28 February. By a decision of the Bureau, Party city committee First Secretary Muslim-Zade was relieved of his duties and expelled from the Party. Responsible supervisor of the city Division of Internal Affairs Dzhafarov was expelled from the Party, and dismissed from the Internal Affairs body. City executive committee President Mamedov was relieved of his duties and given a severe reprimand, to be noted on his work record. Penalties were also imposed on other city Party committee secretaries.

It has still to be discovered who incited the unstable, unaware segment of the population and how, who directed it, and who stoked its nationalist hysteria. The investigation now under way in Sumgait will answer these questions. One thing is certain, that criminals will receive what they deserve, and every one of their acts will receive proper evaluation in accordance with Soviet laws. *Pravda* will describe it.

. . . Now it is difficult to understand fully and completely all that has happened in Azerbaidzhan and Armenia. That will take time. But here is an instance that contributes a great deal in understanding the events around Nagorno-Karabakh. A large family lives in Stepanakert, the Velievs. The family head, Sattar the manly, an Azerbaidzhani and war veteran, is no longer alive. But his widow is, Gegush, an Armenian, and his six sons and a daughter. The boys married Armenians, the girl married an Azerbaidzhani.[g] They have children. Where are they all to go in international disturbances?

The USSR is our common home, built by our grandfathers, and fathers, our brothers, and sisters. To protect it and care for it is the duty of each of us. This idea runs like a red line through the readers' letters now being received by the editorial office. Working people in the country are deeply concerned about what has occurred, and they urge not to give in to emotions, but to approach matters soberly and logically.

Iu. Arakelian, *Pravda* correspondent in Armenia

Z. Kadymbekov, *Pravda* correspondent in Azerbaidzhan

G. Ovcharenko, *Pravda* special correspondent

Editor's notes

a. "Radio voices" is a reference to Voice of Armenia and Radio Liberty.
b. The *Musavat* was an Azerbaidzhani nationalist party.
c. The *Dashnaks* were an Armenian nationalist party.
d. Kocharian is an Armenian surname.
e. Dzhagarian is an Armenian surname; Aliev an Azerbaidzhani one.
f. Saiat-Nova was an eighteenth-century Armenian poet and martyr.
g. According to Muslim law, the father transmits the faith automatically to his children, but the mother does not. Thus only the daughter of the Veliev family would have to marry an Azerbaidzhani in order for all the family descendants to be Azerbaidzhanis.

Who Has Violated Journalistic Ethics? *
Concerning Iu. Arakelian's Note

The editorial office of *Pravda* has received a memo from our correspondent in the Armenian SSR, Iu. Arakelian, in which he disassociates himself from the article "Emotions and Reason," published on 21 March of this year, accuses the editorial office of violating journalistic ethics, and writes that he did not see the galley proofs, and consequently, the content, of the article attributed to him. As we learned, Iu. Arakelian's memo, which was transmitted by telephone, has been photocopied and is now circulating in Erevan, and has found its way into the hands of certain Western correspondents accredited in our country.

Because of this, we consider it necessary to make the following statement. Iu. Arakelian and other comrades collected material for this article between 23 February and 11 March of this year in the Armenian SSR, which he sent to the editorial office. From 11 to 17 March he was in Moscow and prepared the article for publication with other journalists. He made a number of suggestions, which were taken into account. The editorial office has the originals of the suggestions and of the corrections made in Iu. Arakelian's own hand.

On the morning of 21 March, the editorial office had a telephone conversation with Iu. Arakelian, in which he did not disassociate himself from the article, but merely spoke of initial reactions to the publication in Erevan. The text of the memo mentioned above reached the editorial office in the evening.

"Iu. Arakelian's conduct obliges the editorial office to suspend his authority to act as *Pravda* correspondent in the Armenian SSR pending his explanation of the affair at a session of the paper's editorial board."

Editorial Board, *Pravda*

Pravda, 25 March 1988.

Meetings after the Demonstrations *
A Report from Our Correspondents in Nagorno-Karabakh

It so happened that a group of us journalists from the central newspapers, arrived in Nagorno-Karabakh when the main events in this small autonomous oblast and its center, Stepanakert, seemed to have passed. When we set off on this assignment we had no advance plan, no preconceived assessments or prescriptions; we had set ourselves a single task: to be objective, to avoid any one-sidedness or prejudice. Incidentally, there was one thing that we agreed on in advance: caution! For even harsh if objective assessment by an outsider can offend and set off an unpredictable reaction.

The first thing we heard from almost everyone whom we were able to talk to was complaints about the press: Why is coverage of events here so meager? Meager or one-sided.

''What is there to prevent you from speaking the truth?'' people demanded of us.

In theory, nothing. The truth, to put it briefly, is that over two weeks in February big demonstrations were held here in the oblast center day and night. The main slogan was to transfer the NKAO (the Nagorno-Karabakh Autonomous Oblast) from the Azerbaidzhan SSR to the neighboring Armenian SSR. A multitude of grounds for doing so were cited: socioeconomic, ethnic, cultural and historical. . . .

Demonstrations like those in Karabakh but even bigger were also held in Erevan. Special committees were set up both there and here. The committee in Erevan is called ''Karabakh,'' and the one in Stephanakert is called ''Krunk,'' which means ''crane'',—a symbol of homesickness. Both there and here along with the main slogan, about the status of the NKAO, there were slogans in support of *perestroika*, *glasnost'*, democratization, and the friendship of peoples.

In fact however, both *perestroika* and the friendship of these two neighboring peoples, Armenians and Azerbaidzhanis suffered serious trials during these days.

To begin with, in Azerbaidzhan reaction to the very posing of the question of transferring the NKAO to its neighbors was unlike that in Armenia: what are we, not a sovereign republic? And when talking, groups of Azerbaidzhanis who had listened to the rumors of provocateurs moved out of Karabakh and a number of raions of Armenia, going to Azerbaidzhan to ''seek salvation,'' word of some kind of ''Armenian threat'' arose. Then in Sumgait events took a turn that required troops be moved in. Now order has been restored there and, as the procuraton of the USSR has recently reported, the guilty are being found. These tragic events have yet to be described.

Tens of dead, many wounded and arrested, and Armenian refugees, from Sumgait now, abandoning homes, school, and jobs. Add to that the general shock felt by the population of both republics, and add too that a number of enterprises are not yet able to regain a normal work rhythm. That's what the truth is.

But for us who do the writing, the difficulty is not in telling the truth, but in that

---

Izvestiia, 24 March 1988. Russian text © 1988 by ''Izvestiia.''

not everyone likes the truth. And that the same facts are evaluated differently in Erevan and in Baku, regarded differently in Stepanakert and in the neighboring raions of Azerbaidzhan.

One of our very first meetings in Stepanakert was with a large group of Party and government workers, journalists, and teachers from a pedagogical institute. What they shared with us, passionately and with conviction, about the problems that had built up in Nagorno-Karabakh could be put in a few words: "It hurt."

On the way here, when we asked the responsible comrades in Baku at the Central Committee of the Communist Party of Azerbaidzhan what they thought had brought up the question of changing the autonomous oblast's status, they explained that the issue in principle did not exist. Or if it did exist, they said, it was created by the intrigues of subversive centers abroad that are trying to play the Armenian national card.

We are not going to argue. For some people abroad the events surrounding Karabakh are an outright gift, making easy propaganda for a while. But frankly speaking, is it someone's intriguing that schools here in the NKAO have two Armenian language textbooks for the entire class? No, it is the result of the "far-sightedness" of certain republic organs. The history of the Armenian people has been removed from the curriculum of the schools here and the question of constructing a television relay station so that Erevan programs can be received in Nagorno-Karabakh, already decided in principle, has been impossibly dragged out. Who thought to draw up the documents so that the deputies' credentials and passports of local Armenians contain not a single word in Armenian? Maybe this was done in the struggle against manifestations of nationalism?

Why, we were asked later, does every visit by a touring group from Armenia, which, let us note, is just a few kilometers from here, always have to be cleared with Baku? And why is it impossible even to hire a nurse in a polyclinic here in the autonomous oblast without approval again from Baku?

The list of economic, social, and other distortions which they cited seemed endless. It must be noted that the problems mentioned are much like those of the deep provinces everywhere, and not just national provinces. On one hand, we can see here the center's old habit of taking a free ride on the provinces, taking more from them than it provides for development; on the other hand, the rights of local, oblast organs are extremely limited. Such relations are in themselves very outdated; the local soviets have to be given more rights and more real power. On national soil, as there is in our concrete instance, proscribed rights are not merely an obstacle to development but grounds for offense. We see this as the main real aspect of the problem here.

Of course, it is a pity that the oblast and republic leaders permitted all this. What is worse, even today, they try to present matters as if the NKAO lives better than other regions in Azerbaidzhan and that, as they said, there is no problem here.

The processes permitted by the leadership of the republic and the oblast gradually found interpreters, and even directors outside the Party and government organs. Alongside them, under their noses. Visitors from Erevan frequented Nagorno-Karabakh. Letters were drafted, signatures were collected, and delegations were sent to Moscow to get support there for the idea of uniting the NKAO with Armenia. Rumors were circulated that Moscow was nearly "in favor" of it, just that the demand had to be firmer.

Then around 10 February, the process that had long been gathering strength found an outlet, on the square in front of the Party obkom. The number of people going there increased; first they came in small groups, then in entire shops, departments, and classes. The speakers and slogans succeeded one another, but the main slogan was still the same: "Karabakh."

Nevertheless, there are also questions that were not discussed there in the square. And which we understood that the people we spoke with did not much like. Such as, for instance, what would be the specific advantages if the NKAO were transferred to Armenia? Have they been calculated, and by whom? Has any account been taken of what this would mean for neighbors, for their interests, and for the country in general?

To which we heard the answer, how can this all be reduced to some kind of numbers and calculations when we are talking about something sacred!

We are aware of how easy it is to offend the people we were speaking with in this matter. Nevertheless, doesn't the new situation in society make it possible to solve the problems of the NKAO, including that of restoring links with Armenia, without the radical demand to your neighbors, "Get out of the way!"

"We are in favor of friendship with them," they tried to convince us.

True, there were slogans about friendship there in the square, eternal friendship at that. But one question: was there even one Azerbaidzhani at those demonstrations? Did any Azerbaidzhani speak? After all, the Azerbaidzhanis are still one-fourth of the population of the NKAO. They make up a similar proportion of the oblast Soviet of People's Deputies. Or does the issue so widely aired at the rallies not concern them? Or do they not care whether they, along with their homes, land, and livestock, are transferred to the neighboring republic or left as they are?

When we asked about this, we got a strange answer:

"What's that got to do with it?"

And anyway, why were we asking such questions? Because we had come via Baku, where of course they had time, you could tell!, to get us "on the Azerbaidzhani side"!

To be frank, these demands that we only listen to them, believe only them, disturbed us and jibed poorly both with their assurances of friendship with their neighbors and with our understanding of the norms of democracy and justice.

People tried to prove that it is enough merely to explain to Azerbaidzhanis that transfer of the NKAO to Armenia will leave them no worse. Just that. Not ask them, but explain to them. But how could the Azerbaidzhanis accept this explanation? Wouldn't they have their own answers, also of substance? And what then?

Another detail was missing from the accounts by participants in February's events, and no small one—how went the session of the Nagorno-Karabakh Oblast Soviet the people in the square had demanded. That is, they told us about the clumsy attempts from on high to block the session, and how the chairman of the oblast executive committee of the Party "lost" his seal, so the results of the vote remained "uncertified," which certain people now take advantage of to declare the vote illegal. All that is true. But, we repeat, there is one detail missing from the accounts, that, angered by the very fact the question had been raised, the Azerbaidzhani deputies did not even vote.

"And so?" the people we spoke with blazed. "The majority still voted yes!"

You cannot answer all questions with arithmetic. After all there is another body the USSR Constitution says must examine the question, the Supreme Soviet of Azerbaidzhan. You cannot get around it; its prerogatives, just like those of the Supreme Soviet of the Armenian SSR and the supreme soviets of all our republics, are defined by fundamental law of the Soviet Union. Law and democracy are to be respected in its form. But in response we hear something very strange indeed from our Armenian comrades:

"Then we will hand in our Party cards!" A. Lachichan, a retired lieutenant colonel and member of "Krunk," declared. A natural question: What will become of those who wish to keep their Party cards? But natural questions prompted an unnatural reaction.

"There will be no such people!"

So democracy means . . . everything is known in advance!

"Guerrilla warfare will begin!" another "Krunk" activist, G. Grigorian, senior lecturer at the Stepanakert Pedagogical Institute predicted.

Against whom?

"If there's no Karabakh, we don't want any *perestroika*," he was echoed from Erevan by S. Khanzadian. A writer. A Hero of Labor.

Yet after all this they protest the use of the word "extremism" about them in the mass media, demand that the press be boycotted as a sign of protest, and declare Tass and the State Committee for Television and Radio Broadcasting to be "criminal organizations," as "Karabakh" leader I. Muradian did, when he called for new strikes. But if that isn't extremism, what is?

There is something else that must be said. Officially the "Krunk" society has no political goals. It has announced what might be called research and educational projects, studying the history of the region, its links with Armenia, restoring ancient monuments. But in fact it leaders, operating in the name of the people, try to dictate their will to Party, government, and economic bodies in the oblast, as though the people there in the square gave them a "mandate" to do anything they wish. Some of them get so carried away that the word "Karabakh" itself is disappearing from their speeches, replaced by demands to "demote" some leaders and promote others in their place.

There is something else that is disturbing. Demonstrating, the city did not work for two weeks. The shortfall in the work of the enterprises has caused a long chain of disruptions for partners throughout the country. What does all this have in common with *perestroika* and its goals? Who benefits if all the well-known and in many respects common problems of two neighboring Transcaucasian republics simultaneously seem to vanish, reduced to a single problem of territory? A disputed problem. A dead problem. Whose hands does this play into?

We have discussed only a few of the tight "knots" tangling this region. Today they are common knowledge. And we all seem to realize that untying them requires time and common effort, patience and tolerance, wisdom and deliberation at every step, every word. People of different ages, professions, and nationalities, in Erevan, in Sumgait, and in Stepanakert talked about this with all their passions, their varying views and assessments. Today the whole country is watching here, waiting and hoping that emotions will abate and common sense will pevail, reflecting the whole experience of our multinational people. We are certain that it will.

The reader may properly ask, what specifically is proposed for solving the accumulated problems? There will be a piece about this in one of the next issues of the paper.

S. Dardykin, R. Lynev

"Reportage" *
Responsibility to the Whole Country

The windows of the dilapidated "Karabakh" Hotel, the city's largest, look out on a beautiful marble and concrete building, the House of Political Enlightenment. Despite its external glitter, it does not attract people. Various events go on there but, as I was told, not often. And any other time, there is almost nothing for an ordinary citizen to do there. Cleaners meticulously clean the dust from windows and banisters. They polish floors. That is all. . . . Why is there a building like this in a city of 50,000, where there is not even a Young Pioneers' House. Maybe this was the beginning of the suddenly exposed gap between the interest of people who have power and the interests of those who today are in conflict with power? The situation in the city remains complex. Most factory shops in Stepanakert continue to be deserted.

The Nagorno Karabakh Komsomol regional committee worked out a plan of measures designed to convince young people to return to their shopfloors. Every day regional and and city committee personnel spend most of their time at the city's enterprises. Aktiv members talk with young people in dorms, in stores, and out in the streets.

Vladimir Akopian,[a] secretary of the Karabakh silk combine Komsomol organization, has a well-annotated appointment hook on his desk. At 8 o'clock yesterday Volodya was already at the silk reeling shop. The situation there is extremely complex. Azerbaidzhanis and Armenians work at the same stations. Now it is not easy to find a common language. And Volodia has to help with this. He and Reikhan Kulieva,[b]2 the shop's Komsomol group organizer, say the same thing, that the most important thing now is to think of the dear enterprise, how to overcome the break in production, how to clear the huge debt they owe to their partners.

---

*Komsomolskaia pravda, 3 April 1988. Russian text © 1988 by "Komsomol'skaia

The circuit ends at about 10. The picture is clear—Hardly any change, unfortunately. Fewer than half the workers are in the shops; in the largest, the weaving shop, there are 34 out of 1,100.

Akopian calls the activists together: It is necessary to go to the people, to persuade them.

I conversed with Komsomol leader Karen Gulian.[c] The same problems. Some 70 percent of the enterprise's work force are Komsomol members. The enterprise maintains economic ties with scores of plants in the country. This means that not only in Karabakh the workshops are standing idle. People have started realizing this recently: about 70 percent of workers reported for the first shift yesterday.

By chance I met Margarita Sarkisian[d] twice at the silk combine. She is the full-time secretary of the Komsomol organization in one of the shops. However in the city's difficult days the girl has been putting on her work clothes and taking a machine. She set a worthy example which so far, alas, few have followed.

Margarita lives with her mother, who is a pensioner. Bluntly speaking, she needs the money. But the girl believes that this is not the main point, that something else is: the worker's conscience.

On the very first day Margarita was met just outside the gate. Later on, "accidentally," in a store. Later still, in a radio repair workshop. Everyone asked her the same question: Why was she going to work?

Who are those people? What are their goals? Why is their authority higher than that of some Komsomol, trade union, and Party workers? Margarita is a brave and honest girl. The interests of her people are no less dear to her than to those who are now idly strolling the streets of Stepanakert. She understood that the main point in today's circumstances is to be a conscientious and responsible, person, responsible to one's work, to the workers of the whole country.

S. Romanink (our special correspondent)
Stepanakert, NKAO, Azerbaidzhan SSR

Editor's notes

a. Akopian is an Armenian surname.
b. Kulieva is an Azerbaidzhani surname.
c. Gulian is an Armenian surname.
d. Sarkisian is an Armenian surname.

Continuing Ethnic Violence
in the Nagorno-Karabakh AO

"A Day Full of Events"

Shusha (Nagorno-Karabakh Autonomous Oblast)

In high-mountain Shusha, the town where the first Bolshevik organization in Nagorno-Karabakh was founded, a monument to V. I. Lenin has been opened. The bronze figure of the leader on a granite pedestal has been placed in the central square of the town. The sculptors are People's Artist of Azerbaidzhan I. Zeinalov and architect P. Guseinov.

From *Sovetskaia kul'tura*, 14 May 1988

Appeal of the Central Committee of the Communist Party of Azerbaidzhan, the Presidium of the Supreme Soviet of the Azerbaidzhan SSR, and the Council of Ministers of Azerbaidzhan *

Dear comrades!

Existing conditions make it necessary once more to appeal to you.

As is known, the Appeal of the General Secretary of the Central Committee of the CPSU, M. S. Gorbachev, to the workers and peoples of Azerbaidzhan and Armenia was received with the necessary understanding in both republics. The passions and emotions which boiled up in connection with events in Nagorno Karabakh and around it had begun gradually to yield to a sober and reasoned approach to the solution of problems which have arisen.

However, in recent days the situation has once again begun to grow tenser, rumors have become more frequent, as have various inventions, which has given rise to unhealthy attitudes and acted negatively on the process of further normalization in the republic. On May 16 in Baku there was meeting of youth, students, members of the intelligentsia, who were attentively listened to by members of the Bureau of the Central Committee of the Communist Party of Azerbaidzhan.

We understand and feel closely the natural alarm of people, their desire to know more about the situation as it is in Nagorno Karabakh, in our republic and in the Armenian SSR, and to get answers to the questions which disturb them. However, this does not have to proceed in an atmosphere of nerves and excitement, in "meet-

Bakinskii rabochii, 18 May 1988.

ing democracy,'' which are, as we are all convinced, pregnant with unforeseeable consequences. The questions posed by the participants of the meeting were examined attentively. Certain of them will be used taking immediate measures. It must be noted though that other questions were also posed, the resolution of which will require deep study and a certain amount of time.

The present alarm of a certain part of the population is caused, in part, by the events which took place in certain settlements of the Arat region of the Armenian SSR on 11 May of this year, when incidents occurred among the local residents. There were wounds, but no dead. Measures are being taken by Party and government organs to normalize the situation. The Procurator of the USSR is investigating all incidents. There may be no doubt that the guilty will be exposed and brought to responsibility, according to the full strictness of the law.

The Central Committee of the Communist Party of Azerbaidzhan, the Presidium of the Supreme Soviet, and the government of the republic will take all necessary measures to heal the situation, to return life to its normal rhythm. In this disturbed atmosphere each of us must have patience and extreme self-possession, qualities innate in the best representatives of our people. In no instance should we give opportunity for someone, through unthinking conversations or ill-considered acts, to drive a wedge into the decades-long traditions of friendship between peoples, or discredit restructuring in the country, or the first steps of democratization.

The Central Committee of the CPSU today sees the development of inter-nationality relations as of utmost importance. There will be a special Plenum of the Central Committee of the CPSU on this topic. The Party says firmly that all problems of national relations can be resolved only within the framework of legality and the democratic process, without the slightest loss of internationalist solidarity of our peoples. The Azerbaidzhani people have always shown themselves to be an example of socialist internationalism. We are rightly proud of these traditions, and it is the duty of all of us to keep them holy and increase them.

In appealing to the multinational population of Azerbaidzhan we are asking for the wisdom of *aksakals*[a] and of our mothers, and the reason of our youth. Only restraint and self-respect, a sense of profound responsibility for the fate of one's own people can bear witness to its freedom and power of soul.

We appeal to all our fellow citizens and citizens of the republic, to Azerbaidzhanis and Armenians, to Russians and people of all nationalities living in Azerbaidzhan: do not submit to emotions and rumors, give decisive rebuffs to inciters and provocateurs who are sowing international discord, exhibit calm and restraint. Remember, all of us must answer for the honor of our republic, for the honor of the Azerbaidzhani people.

Editor's note

a. *Aksakal*: literally ''white beard'' in Azerbaidzhani; a term used for an elder of the community.

In the MVD of the Republic *

In connection with the events in Nagorno-Karabakh and its environs, the organs of internal affairs,[a] together with other law enforcement establishments, have stepped up work to maintain public order and to suppress the violation of the soil of internationality relations.

At the same time, as a result of a lack of control, several workers of the militia were guilty of shortsightedness and irresponsibility when examining the complaints and statements of citizens concerning violations of rights of this type. Thus, on 20 May of this year Baku residents A. Ramazanov and E. Ismailov, motivated by hooliganism, attempted to assault and batter citizen R. Arakeluants.[b] The two were arrested and sent to the Nasiminskii ROVD.[c] However, the station duty officer, Senior Lieutenant Ia. Ibadov of the militia, behaved irresponsibly in the execution of his official duty by not taking the incident into account and by unjustifiably releasing the transgressors.

The Ministry of Internal Affairs of the republic has dismissed Ibadov from the organs of internal affairs. Acting chief of the ROVD F. Guseinov has been sternly warned. Ramazanov and Ismailov have been charged.

Editor's notes

a. MVD: the Ministry of Internal Affairs, which includes the police (the militia).
b. The victim is a female Armenian.
c. The raion department of internal affairs.

Today in Nagorno-Karabakh†

Recently the flow of letters to the editor requesting information about what is happening in Nagorno-Karabakh has increased significantly. Readers ask whether the situation there is normalizing.

It would seem that not long ago almost all the central newspapers were vying to report the events of February in Nagorno-Karabakh Autonomous Oblast of the Azerbaidzhan SSR. The events were also covered by central television. Then there was much talk and discussion, but now passions seem to have subsided and mention of the region in the press is less and less frequent. At the same time tension has not subsided in the oblast.

Today the majority of industrial enterprises, institutions, and public transport are not working in Stepanakert and the raion centers Martuni, Mardakert, and Askeran.

Almost all public food outlets and shops are closed and the sales of foodstuffs are very limited—money to buy food cannot be drawn, and economic and other links with Baku are disrupted. The strike—unusual and unexpected as this word may sound to us!—is in its third week. The Armenian population of Nagorno-Karabakh is

---

Bakinskii rabochii, 24 May 1988.

†*Pravda*, 10 June 1988.

demanding in an ultimatum consideration without delay of the question of the possibility separating from Azerbaidzhan and its uniting with Armenia.

Every morning tens of thousands of people march in columns along the streets leading to the city center carrying slogans and banners. Rallies are being held. The meaning is always the same: "Hold out to the end." At night lights burn alarmingly in specially built huts in the streets and alleys, where the so-called "self-defense posts" are set up. Small detachments watch unblinking until the morning, believing they are guaranteeing the security and tranquility of their families. From whom are they protecting themselves? The answer is unequivocal: "From the Azerbaidzhanis." And although there are no attacks, and although there already is somebody, so to say, whose duty it is to guard the tranquillity and sleep of the residents, the volunteer "watchmen" peer into the dark, suspiciously studying every chance passer-by.

These posts not only do not provide peace of mind, but on the contrary, are sources of conflict. Several clashes have already occurred here.

The present spiritual condition of the oblast's inhabitants and the oppressive moral atmosphere took several months to develop. Almost everyday something has either really happened in the oblast or people have imagined that it has. These events, surrounded by rumors and fabrications, have taken hold of people's minds and feelings, disrupting the normal rhythm of life. In March and April the psychological climate in Nagorno-Karabakh was influenced by the stories of Armenians who had left Sumgait. Truth alternated with invention. The tragedy that had occurred grew over with horrifying details that had no relation to reality.

After the May Day demonstration, became in fact a "demonstration of union" there was a demonstration of Armenians protesting the appointment of an Azerbaidzhani as oblast deputy prosecutor. Then there followed reciprocal firings in Stepanakert and Shusha, as *Pravda* has already reported. At the same time illegal acts were committed which intended to complicate the situation.

On 14–15 May, A. Mamedov and A. Gasanov, inhabitants of the oblast center, fled to Shusha after being beaten up, and consequently a rally was held in the city square. At the rally the Azerbaidzhani section of the population condemned the events in Stepanakert and categorically opposed a territorial reorganization. Similar statements were also made at rallies in Baku.

Following the Azerbaidzhan Communist Party Central Committee Plenum on 23 May, a strike began which continues to this day. Farm work is being done. Despite the appeals of certain persons for dairies and bakeries to stop work, these enterprises are operating.

The oblast party organs are not in control of the existing situation. There has been no response to the appeals of the Oblast Committee of the Communist Party of Azerbaidzhan[a] to normalize the situation and return to work. Equally unanswered was a similar request in the oblast newspaper by the well-known Armenian writer Silva Kaputikian.

Nevertheless, the rallies and demonstrations which take place are carefully organized and skillfully directed. There are grounds for asserting that the "Krunk" committee,[b] although dissolved by decree of the republic Supreme Soviet Presidium, continues to operate. Organizers of the mass actions are helping to maintain tensions by playing on the Armenians' national sentiments and their desire to live together with their fellows.

The population is tired after many months of agitation. The disturbing situation with food is making their position more difficult. Despite this, certain people still propose "raising the question even more sharply."

According to figures of the Azerbaidzhan SSR State Statistics Committee, from February through 1 June this year Nagorno-Karabakh Autonomous Oblast enterprises have underproduced by 25.4 million rubles. This figure continues to grow.

N. Demidov (special correspondent, *Pravda*) Stepanakert.

Editor's notes

a. Reference is to the Oblast Party Committee of the Nagorno-Karabakh AO, which is a constituent unit of the Communist Party of Azerbaidzhan.

b. Krunk is the name of the outlawed Armenian nationalist organization in Nagorno-Karabakh. *Krunk* is the Armenian word for crane, and the crane is a traditional symbol of homesickness.

"Special Status" Curfew Declared *

The situation in the Nagorno-Karabakh Autonomous Oblast, which has deteriorated as a result of clashes between Armenians and Azerbaidzhanians, remains tense.

Despite measures being taken to prevent interethnic incidents, cases of arson against private homes and cars as well as other illegal activities took place again last night.

Shots were fired in some places. There were no casualties. But all this still generated tension and many people in Stepanakert and in rural areas are expressing concern about their security.

Factories, building organizations, transport and schools were not working in Stepanakert.

Party bodies and local governing council together with social organizations are seek to restore economic activity and bring the situation in the Nagorno-Karabakh autonomous oblast and neighboring districts back to normal.

The representative of the CPSU Central Committee and the Presidium of the USSR Supreme Soviet in Nagorno-Karabakh, Arkadii Volskii, spoke on local television and radio in connection with the situation.

He said, inter alia: "The Party and government have adopted a number of important decisions to develop the Nagorno-Karabakh Autonomous Oblast and resolve as soon as possible various problems that have accumulated here.

"But this does not apparently suit a certain group of people. "The situation in the

---

*Moscow Tass in English, 1646 GMT, 21 September 1988.

region over recent days has been sharply aggravated. Strikes have started at factories, in building organizations and on public transport. Classes have been discontinued at schools.

"There have been unauthorized rallies and marches. An attack has been provoked on the regional public prosecutor's office. Insults have been made against organs of power. There were cases where the dignity of Interior Ministry troops and militiamen ensuring public order was denigrated."

With regard to the existing situation, a state of emergency[a] and a curfew are being introduced on the territory of Stepanakert and Agdam District as of September 21.

Every essential measure is being taken to ensure public calm and security, public order and strict respect for socialist legality.

The bureau of the Nagorno-Karabakh oblast Party committee and the executive committee of the oblast soviet of people's deputies issued an appeal to the Communists and all the working people of Nagorno-Karabakh, urging them to retain self-control and soberness, to show civic maturity and patience, and not to yield to provocations under any circumstances.

"All the arising issues and problems need to be tackled in an atmosphere of legality. The events of the past few days have been developing under a scenario written by provocateurs seeking to destabilize the situation and whip up tension, by those eager to compromise *perestroika* and democracy and push us off the right path," the appeal said.

It added: "In the situation that has come to exist any rallies, demonstrations, marches and meetings can exacerbate the situation even further. Proceeding from this, the regional party committee and (the regional governing council's) executive committee consider such activities at present inadmissible."

Editor's note

a. According to the U.S. Foreign Broadcast Information Service, TASS reportedly transmitted a "corrected version" of this item, rendering the preceding sentence as follows: "With regard to the existing situation, Stepanakert and Agdam District are being put on a special status and a curfew is being introduced on their territory as of September 21." Moscow *Pravda* in Russian on page 6 of its 22 September, second edition carries a similar report, attributed to TASS and titled "Regarding Events in Nagorno-Karabakh," also noting that "a special status" (*osoboe polozhenie*) is being introduced to the area.

Selected Bibliography

English-language Books

Alexiev, Alexander R. and Wimbush, S. Enders, *Ethnic Minorities in the Red Army* (Boulder: Westview Press, 1987).

Allworth, Edward, *The Nationality Question in Soviet Central Asia* (New York: Praeger, 1973).

Azrael, Jeremy R., ed., *Soviet Nationality Policies and Practices* (New York: Praeger, 1978).

Bennigsen, Alexandre and Broxup, Marie, *The Islamic Threat to The Soviet State* (London: Croon Helm, 1983).

Bennigsen, Alexandre and Lemercier-Quelquejay, Chantal, *Islam in the Soviet Union* (London: Pall Mall Press, 1967).

Bennigsen, Alexandre and Wimbush, S. Enders, *Muslim National Consciousness in the Soviet Union* (Chicago: University of Chicago Press, 1979).

Bennigsen, Alexandre and Wimbush, S. Enders, *Muslims of the Soviet Empire: A Guide* (Bloomington: Indiana University Press, 1986).

Bennigsen, Alexandre and Wimbush, S. Enders, *Mystics and Commissars* (Berkeley: University of California Press, 1985).

Carrere d'Encausse, Helene, *Decline of an Empire: The Soviet Socialist Republics in Revolt* (New York: Newsweek Books, 1979).

Conquest, Robert, *Soviet Nationalities Policy in Practice* (New York: Praeger, 1967).

Conquest, Robert, *The Harvest of Sorrow* (New York: Oxford University Press, 1986).

Conquest, Robert, ed., *The Last Empire* (Stanford: Hoover Institution Press, 1986).

Dunlop, John B., *The Faces of Contemporary Russian Nationalism* (Princeton, New Jersey: Princeton University Press, 1983).

Fisher, Alan, *The Crimean Tatars* (Stanford: Hoover Institution Press, 1978).

Freedman, Robert O., *Soviet Jewry in the Decisive Decade, 1971–1980* (Durham, North Carolina: Duke University Press, 1984).

Kamenetsky, Ihor, ed., *Nationalism and Human Rights* (Littleton, Colorado: Libraries Unlimited, 1977).

Karklins, Rasma, *Ethnic Relations in the USSR: The Perspective from Below* (Boston: Allen and Unwin, 1986).

Katz, Zev., ed., *Handbook of Major Soviet Nationalities* (New York: Free Press, 1975).

Lewis, Robert A. et al., *Nationality and Population Change in Russia: An Evaluation of Census Data, 1897–1900* (New York: Columbia University Press, 1976).

Lubin, Nancy, *Labour and Nationality in Soviet Central Asia* (Princeton, New Jersey: Princeton University Press, 1984).

McCagg, William O., Jr. and Silver, Brian D., *Soviet-Asian Ethnic Frontiers* (New York: Pergamon Press, 1979).

Motyl, Alexander, *Will the Non-Russians Rebel?* (Ithaca, New York: Cornell University Press, 1987).

Nekrich, Alexandr, *The Punished Peoples* (New York: Norton, 1979).

Olcott, Martha Brill, *The Kazakhs* (Stanford: Hoover Institution Press, 1987).

Roi, Yaacov, *The USSR and the Muslim World* (London: George Allen and Unwin, 1984).

Rorlich, Azade-Ayse, *The Volga Tatars* (Stanford: Hoover Institution Press, 1986).

Simmonds, George W., *Nationalism in the USSR in the Era of Brezhnev and Kosygin* (Detroit: University of Detroit Press, 1977).

Zwick, Peter, *National Communism* (Boulder: Westview Press, 1982).

Periodicals

Cahiers du Monde Russe et Sovietique
Central Asian Survey
Journal of Ukrainian Studies
Problems of Communism
Radio Liberty Research Bulletin
Religion in Communist Lands
Russian Review
Slavic Review
Soviet Anthropology & Archeology
Soviet Jewish Affairs
Soviet Law and Government
Soviet Nationality Papers
Soviet Sociology
Soviet Studies
Soviet Union
Ukrainian Review

Russian-language Books

Abramovich, A. M., *Konstitutsiia SSSR. Voploshchenie leninskoi natsional'noi politiki* (Moscow, 1986).
Aktual'nye problemy natsional'nogo i internatsional'nogo v dukhovnom mire sovetskogo cheloveka (Baku, 1984) 3 vols.
Arutiunian, Iu. V., *Etnosotsiologiia* (Moscow, 1984).
Arutiunian, Iu. V. and Drobizheva, L. M., *Mnogoobrazie kul'turnoi zhizni narodov SSSR* (Moscow, 1987).
Bromlei, Iu. V., *Ocherki teorii etnosa* (Moscow, 1983).
Bromlei, Iu. V., *Sovremennye problemy etnografii* (Moscow, 1981).
Drobizheva, L. M., *Dukhovnaia obshchnost' narodov SSSR* (Moscow, 1981).
Dzhafarov, I. B., *Russkii iazyk—iazyk druzhby i bratstva* (Moscow, 1982).
Dzhunusov, M. S., *Burzhuaznyi natsionalizm: Printsipy kritiki* (Moscow, 1981).
Etnokul'turnye protsessy: metody istoricheskogo i sinkhronnogo izucheniia (Moscow, 1982).
Guboglo, N., *Sovremennye etnoiazykovoi protsessy v SSSR* (Moscow, 1986).
Ideologicheskie problemy sovershenstvovaniia sotsialisticheskogo obraza zhizni (Baku, 1984).
Internatsionalizm mnogonatsional'nogo kollektiva (Alma-Ata, 1984).
Internatsional'noe i natsional'noe v sotsialisticheskom obraze zhizni Sovetskogo naroda (Moscow, 1985).
Karakeev, K. K., et.al., *Problemy upravleniia stroitel'stvom Sovetskogo mnogonatsional'nogo gosudarstva* (Moscow, 1982).
Kommunizm i natsii (Moscow, 1985).
Lenin, V. I., *O Bor'be s natsionalizmom* (Moscow, 1985).
Leninskaia politika internatsionalizma (Kiev, 1983).
Natsional'nye otnosheniia v SSSR v trudakh uchenykh soiuznykh respublik (Moscow, 1986).
Razvitie natsional'nykh otnoshenii v SSSR v svete reshenii XXVI s"ezda KPSS (Moscow, 1982).
Osnovy zakonodatel'stva Soiuza SSR i soiuznykh respublic (Moscow, 1987).
Razvitie natsional'nykh otnoshenii v SSSR (Moscow, 1986).
Soiuz nerushimvi respublik svobodnykh (Moscow, 1981).
Sotsial'no-kul'turnyi oblik sovetskikh natsii (Moscow, 1986).
Sovremennye etnosotsial'nye protsessy na sele (Moscow, 1986).

Tankybaev, S. D., *Dialektika dvukh tendentsii v byty sotsialisticheskikh natsii* (Alma-Ata, 1985).
Teoriia i praktika razvitiia sotsiallsticheskikh natsii (Leningrad, 1984).
Vospityvat' ubezhdennykh patriotov-internatsionalistov (Moscow, 1982).
Zimanov, S. Z., *Sovetskaia natsional'naie gosuderstvennost' i sblizhenie natsii* (Alma-Ata, 1983).

Periodicals

Istoriia SSSR
Polevye issledovaniia Institute etnografii (annual)
Rasy i narody (annual)
Russkii iazyk v natsional'noi shkole
Sotsiologicheskie issledovaniia
Sovetskaia etnografiia
Voprosy istorii
Voprosy istorii KPSS

Appendix: Nationalities of the USSR in 1979

Nationality	Population in USSR Total	%	Main geographical location	Titular Political Unit Status	% of group residing in unit	Population of unit Total	% Native	National Language Family	Claimed as native by group (%)	Main traditional religion(s)
1. Russian	137,397,089	52.42		SSR	82.6	137,409,921	82.6	IE–Slavic	99.9	Orthodox
2. Ukrainian	42,347,387	16.16	Southwest	SSR	86.2	49,609,333	73.6	IE–Slavic	82.8	Orthodox/Uniate
3. Uzbek	12,455,978	4.75	Central Asia	SSR	84.9	15,389,307	68.7	A–Turkic	98.5	Muslim (Sunni)
4. Belorussian	9,462,715	3.61	Southwest	SSR	80.0	9,532,516	79.4	IE–Slavic	74.2	Orthodox/Uniate
5. Kazakh	6,556,442	2.50	Central Asia	SSR	80.7	14,684,283	36.0	A–Turkic	97.5	Muslim (Sunni)
6. Tatar	6,317,468	2.41	Volga–Urals	ASSR	26.0	3,445,412	47.6	A–Turkic	85.9	Muslim (Sunni)
7. Azerbaidzhani	5,477,330	2.09	Transcaucasia	SSR[b]	86.0	6,026,515	78.1	A–Turkic	97.9	Muslim (Shiite)
8. Armenian	4,151,241	1.58	Transcaucasia	SSR[c]	65.6	3,037,259	89.7	IE–Armenian	90.7	Gregorian Christian
9. Georgian	3,570,504	1.36	Transcaucasia	SSR[d]	96.1	4,993,182	68.8	Caucasian–S	98.3	Orthodox/Muslim (Sunni)
10. Moldavian	2,968,224	1.13	Southwest	SSR	85.1	3,949,756	63.9	IE–Romance	93.2	Orthodox
11. Tadzhik	2,897,697	1.11	Central Asia	SSR[e]	77.2	3,806,220	58.8	IE–Iranian	97.8	Muslim (Sunni)
12. Lithuanian	2,850,905	1.09	Baltic	SSR	95.1	3,391,490	80.0	IE–Baltic	97.9	Catholic
13. Turkmen	2,027,913	0.77	Central Asia	SSR	93.3	2,764,748	68.4	A–Turkic	98.7	Muslim (Sunni)
14. German	1,936,214	0.74	Central Asia	—	—	—	—	IE–Germanic	57.0	Lutheran/Catholic
15. Kirghiz	1,906,271	0.73	Central Asia	SSR	88.5	3,522,832	47.9	A–Turkic	97.9	Muslim (Sunni)
16. Jewish	1,810,876	0.69	dispersed	AOb	0.6	188,710	5.4	various	14.2	Judaic
17. Chuvash	1,751,366	0.67	Volga–Urals	ASSR	50.7	1,298,611	68.4	A–Turkic	81.7	Orthodox/animist
18.–27. Peoples of Daghestan	(1,656,676)	(0.63)	North Caucasus	ASSR	(76.5)	1,628,159	(77.8)	—	(95.9)	Muslim (Sunni)
18. Avar	482,844	0.18			86.7		25.7	Caucasian–NE	97.7	
19. Lezghian	382,611	0.15			49.3		11.6	Caucasian–NE	90.9	
20. Darghin	287,282	0.11			85.9		15.2	Caucasian–NE	98.3	
21. Kumyk	228,418	0.09			88.6		12.4	A–Turkic	98.2	
22. Lak	100,148	0.04			83.3		5.1	Caucasian–NE	95.0	
23. Tabasaran	75,239	0.03			95.3		4.4	Caucasian–NE	97.4	
24. Nogai	59,546	0.02			41.9		1.5	A–Turkic	90.3	
25. Rutul	15,032	0.006			95.1		0.9	Caucasian–NE	99.1	
26. Tsakhur	13,478	0.005			33.8		0.3	Caucasian–NE	95.2	
27. Agul	12,078	0.005			94.9		0.7	Caucasian–NE	98.3	
28. Latvian	1,439,037	0.55	Baltic	SSR	93.4	2,502,816	53.7	IE–Baltic	95.0	Lutheran/Catholic
29. Bashkir	1,371,452	0.52	Volga–Urals	ASSR	68.2	3,844,280	24.3	A–Turkic	67.0	Muslim (Sunni)

No. & Name	Population	%	Region	Status	% in unit	Pop. of unit	% of unit	Language	% native	Religion
30. Mordvinian	1,191,765	0.45	Volga-Urals	ASSR	28.4	989,509	34.2	U-Finnic	72.6	Orthodox/animist
31. Polish	1,150,991	0.44	Southwest	—	—	—	—	IE-Slavic	29.1	Catholic
32. Estonian	1,019,851	0.39	Baltic	SSR	92.9	1,464,476	64.7	U-Finnic	95.3	Lutheran
33. Chechen	755,782	0.29	North Caucasus	ASSR	80.9	1,155,805	52.9	Caucasian-NE	98.6	Muslim (Sunni)
34. Udmurt	713,696	0.27	Volga-Urals	ASSR	67.2	1,492,172	32.1	U-Finnic	76.5	Orthodox/animist
35. Mari	621,961	0.24	Volga-Urals	ASSR	49.3	704,207	43.5	U-Finnic	86.7	Orthodox/animist
36. Ossetian	541,893	0.21	North Caucasus	1. ASSR / 2. AOb	55.2 / 12.0	592,002 / 97,988	50.5 / 66.4	IE-Iranian	88.2	Orthodox/Muslim (Sunni)
37–38. Komi and Komi-Permiak	(477,468)	(0.18)							(76.5)	
37. Komi	326,700	0.12	Volga-Urals	ASSR	85.9	1,110,361	25.3	U-Finnic	76.2	Orthodox
38. Komi-Permiak	150,768	0.06		AOk	70.0	172,039	61.4		77.1	
39. Korean	388,926	0.15	Central Asia	—	—	—	—	Korean (A?)	55.4	Buddhist/Confucian
40. Bulgarian	361,082	0.14	Southwest	—	—	—	—	IE-Slavic	68.0	Orthodox
41. Buriat	352,646	0.13	Siberia	1. ASSR / 2. AOk / 3. AOk	58.7 / 10.2 / 12.9	899,398 / 69,035 / 132,153	23.0 / 52.0 / 34.4	A-Mongolian	90.2	Buddhist
42. Greek	343,809	0.13	Southwest	—	—	—	—	IE-Hellenic	38.0	Orthodox
43. Yakut	328,018	0.13	Siberia	ASSR	95.7	851,840	36.9	A-Turkic	95.3	Orthodox/animist
44. Kabardinian	321,719	0.12	North Caucasus	ASSR	94.4	666,546	45.5	Caucasian-NW	97.9	Muslim (Sunni)
45. Karakalpak	303,324	0.12	Central Asia	ASSR	92.9	905,500	31.1	A-Turkic	95.9	Muslim (Sunni)
46. Uighur	210,612	0.08	Central Asia	—	—	—	—	A-Turkic	86.1	Muslim (Sunni)
47. Gypsy	209,159	0.08	dispersed	—	—	—	—	IE-Indic	74.1	Christian (various)
48. Ingush	186,198	0.07	North Caucasus	ASSR	72.4	1,155,805	11.7	Caucasian-NE	97.4	Muslim (Sunni)
49. Gagauz	173,179	0.07	Southwest	—	—	—	—	A-Turkic	89.3	Orthodox
50. Hungarian	170,553	0.07	Southwest	—	—	—	—	U-Ugric	95.4	Catholic
51. Tuvinian	166,082	0.06	Siberia	ASSR	97.5	267,599	60.5	A-Turkic	98.8	Buddhist
52.–74. Peoples of the North	(158,324)	(0.06)							(61.8)	animist/Orthodox
52. Nenets	29,894	0.01	Siberia	1. AOk / 2. AOk / 3. AOk	20.2 / 7.8 / 58.2	47,218 / 44,953 / 158,844	12.8 / 5.2 / 11.0	U-Samoyedic	80.4	
53. Evenki	27,531	0.01		AOk	11.8	15,968	20.3	A-Tungus	43.1	
54. Khanty	20,934	0.008		AOk	53.6	570,763	2.0	U-Ugric	67.8	
55. Chukchi	14,000	0.005		AOk	80.7	139,944	8.1	Paleo-Asiatic	78.3	
56. Eveny	12,286	0.005		—	—	—	—	A-Tungus	56.7	
57. Nanai	10,516	0.004		—	—	—	—	A-Tungus	55.8	
58. Koriak	7,879	0.003		AOk	71.8	34,851	16.2	Paleo-Asiatic	69.1	
59. Mansi	7,563	0.003		AOk	81.4	570,763	1.1	U-Ugric	49.5	
60. Dolgan	5,053	0.002		AOk	85.8	44,953	9.7	A-Turkic	90.0	
61. Nivkhi	4,397	0.002		—	—	—	—	Paleo-Asiatic	30.6	
62. Selkup	3,565	0.001		—	—	—	—	U-Samoyedic	56.6	
63. Ulchi	2,552	0.001		—	—	—	—	A-Tungus	38.8	
64. Saami (Lapp)	1,888	0.001		—	—	—	—	U-Finnic	53.0	

No.	Group	Population	%	Region	Admin	%	Number	%	Language	%	Religion
65.	Udegei	1,551	0.001	—	—	—	—	—	A–Tungus	31.0	
66.	Eskimo	1,510	0.001	—	—	—	—	—	Paleo-Asiatic	60.7	
67.	Itelmen	1,370	0.001	—	—	—	—	—	Paleo-Asiatic	24.4	
68.	Orochi	1,198	0.000	—	—	—	—	—	A–Tungus	40.6	
69.	Ket	1,122	0.000	—	—	—	—	—	Paleo-Asiatic	61.0	
70.	Nganasan	867	0.000	—	—	—	—	—	U–Samoyedic	90.2	
71.	Yukagir	835	0.000	—	—	—	—	—	Paleo-Asiatic	37.5	
72.	Tofa	763	0.000	—	—	—	—	—	A–Turkic	62.1	
73.	Aleut	546	0.000	—	—	—	—	—	Paleo-Asiatic	17.7	
74.	Negidal	504	0.000	—	—	—	—	—	A–Tungus	44.4	
75.	Kalmyk	146,631	0.06	North Caucasus	ASSR	83.3	294,527	41.5	A–Mongolian	91.3	Buddhist
76.	Karelian	138,429	0.05	Baltic	ASSR	58.7	732,193	11.1	U–Finnic	55.6	Orthodox
77.	Karachai	131,074	0.05	North Caucasus	AOb^b	83.3	367,111	29.7	A–Turkic	97.7	Muslim (Sunni)
78.	Rumanian	128,792	0.05	Southwest		—	—	—	IE–Romance	41.1	Orthodox
79.	Kurdish	115,858	0.04	Transcaucasia		—	—	—	IE–Iranian	83.6	Muslim (Sunni)
80.	Adygei	108,711	0.04	North Caucasus	AOb	79.5	404,390	21.4	Caucasian–NW	95.7	Muslim (Sunni)
81.	Turkish	92,689	0.04	Transcaucasia		—	—	—	A–Turkic	84.7	Muslim (Sunni)
82.	Abkhaz	90,915	0.03	Transcaucasia	ASSR	91.4	486,082	17.1	Caucasian–NW	94.3	Muslim (Sunni)
83.	Finnish	77,079	0.03	Baltic		—	—	—	U–Finnic	40.9	Lutheran/Orthodox
84.	Khakas	70,776	0.03	Siberia	AOb	80.9	498,384	11.5	A–Turkic	80.9	animist/Orthodox
85.	Balkar	66,334	0.03	North Caucasus	ASSR*	90.0	666,546	9.0	A–Turkic	96.9	Muslim (Sunni)
86.	Altai	60,015	0.02	Siberia	AOb	83.7	172,040	29.2	A–Turkic	86.4	animist/Orthodox
87.	Dungan	51,694	0.02	Central Asia		—	—	—	Sino-Tibetan	94.8	Muslim (Sunni)
88.	Cherkess	46,470	0.02	North Caucasus	AOb^b	74.1	367,111	9.4	Caucasian–NW	91.4	Muslim (Sunni)
89.	Persian	31,313	0.01	Central Asia		—	—	—	IE–Iranian	30.7	Muslim (Shiite)
90.	Abaza	29,497	0.01	North Caucasus		—	—	—	Caucasian–NW	95.3	Muslim (Sunni)
91.	Assyrian	25,170	0.01	Transcaucasia		—	—	—	Semitic	54.9	Nestorian Christian
92.	Tat	22,441	0.009	Transcaucasia		—	—	—	IE–Iranian	67.4	Muslim (Shiite)/ Judaic
93.	Baluchi	18,997	0.007	Central Asia		—	—	—	IE–Iranian	98.1	Muslim (Sunni)
94.	Czech	17,812	0.007	Southwest		—	—	—	IE–Slavic	32.7	Catholic
95.	Shor	16,033	0.006	Siberia		—	—	—	A–Turkic	61.2	animist/Orthodox
96.	Slovak	9,409	0.004	Southwest		—	—	—	IE–Slavic	41.7	Catholic
97.	Veps	8,094	0.003	Baltic		—	—	—	U–Finnic	38.3	Orthodox
98.	Udin	6,863	0.003	Transcaucasia		—	—	—	Caucasian–NE	89.9	Orthodox
99.	Karaim	3,341	0.001	Southwest		—	—	—	A–Turkic	16.0	Judaic (Karaite)
100.	Mongolian	3,228	0.001	Siberia		—	—	—	A–Mongolian	91.3	Buddhist
101.	Izhora	748	0.000	Baltic		—	—	—	U–Finnic	32.6	Orthodox
	Others	66,418	0.03							58.9	
	TOTAL	262,084,654								93.1	

SSR = Soviet Socialist Republic (union republic)
ASSR = Autonomous Soviet Socialist Republic (autonomous republic)
AOb = Autonomous Oblast (autonomous province)

IE = Indo-European
A = Altaic
U = Uralic

NE = North-East
NW = North-West
S = South

AOk = Autonomous Okrug (autonomous district)

a. Presumably includes ca. 400,000 Crimean Tatars, a separate nationality in political disgrace after 1944.

b. Includes Nakhichevan ASSR, a detached territory with a predominantly Azerbaidzhani population.

c. Armenians also constitute the main nationality of the Nagorno-Karabakh AOb (in Azerbaidzhani SSR).

d. Includes Adzhar ASSR for Georgian Muslim minority.

e. Includes Gorno-Badakhshan AOb for Pamir Mountain peoples (nevertheless considered as Tadzhiks by nationality).

f. Chechen-Ingush ASSR, joint unit for two nationalities.

g. North Ossetian ASSR (in RSFSR).

h. South Ossetian AOb (in Georgian SSR).

i. Agin Buriat AOk.

j. Ust'-Orda Buriat AOk.

k. Kabardinian-Balkar ASSR, joint unit for two nationalities.

l. Nenets AOk.

m. Taimyr (Dolgan-Nenets) AOk, joint unit for two nationalities.

n. Yamal Nenets AOk.

o. Khanty-Mansi AOk; joint unit for two nationalities.

p. Karachai-Cherkess AOb, joint unit for two nationalities.

Prepared by Lubomyr Hajda

About the Editors

MARTHA B.OLCOTT, professor of political science at Colgate University, is a specialist on Soviet nationalities policy. She is the author of *The Kazakhs* as well as numerous articles on Soviet politics.

ANTHONY OLCOTT is assistant professor of Russian at Colgate University, and LUBOMYR HAJDA is affiliated with the Russian Research Center.